THE
GAINESVILLE
RIPPER

THE GAINESVILLE RIPPER

A Summer's Madness, Five Young Victims—
the Investigation, the Arrest and the Trial

Mary S. Ryzuk

DONALD I. FINE, INC.
New York

Library of Congress Catalogue Card Number: 92-54466
ISBN: 1-55611-352-8

Manufactured in the United States of America

10   9   8   7   6   5   4   3   2   1

Designed by Irving Perkins Associates

This book is dedicated to my lifetime companion and love
Ony Ryzuk
for his never-ending encouragement, patience and support

Acknowledgments

Special thanks to: Donald Fine, for his brilliant editorial skills . . . to his indefatigable staff, Jason Poston, Larry Bernstein and Bob Gales . . . to my agent, Ivy Fischer Stone of Fifi Oscard, Inc., for believing in me and supporting me throughout the painful creation of this book . . . to Sarah Gallick for her help in the early stages . . .

. . . to Jenny Kanne and Amelia Marshall, both of whom requested anonymity and gave unstintingly of their time, energy and feelings . . . to Pat Berkman, without whose friendship and encouragement I would not have embarked on my first true-crime book, *Thou Shalt Not Kill,* which led to an unexpected turn in my writing career . . . to Gene Light, who was instrumental in gathering all the transcripts of Danny Rolling's trial . . . to my daughter-in-law, Pamela Ryzuk, without whose extraordinary patience and secretarial skills my task would have been overwhelming . . . to my dear friends, Diane and Richard Cappel, who spent weeks reading, proofing, suggesting and always encouraging the preliminary drafts of this work . . . to Janet Mathews, who was my eyes and ears in southern Florida . . . to Bobby Lewis, fellow inmate of Danny Rolling in Florida State Prison, who initiated a correspondence with me and filled me in on many of the details of Danny Rolling's confession, his behavior in prison, his personality as Bobby observed it on a day-to-day basis and on Rolling's relationship with Sondra London . . . to Mitch Stacy* of the Gainesville *Sun* who was helpful in the early stages of research for this book by interviewing several key people for me through his connections, and by relating his personal feelings, not only as a journalist but as someone who lived through the trauma in Gainesville at the time of the murders . . . to my sons, Regan and Mitchell, who continue to believe in and encourage their mom . . .

. . . and very particularly to my sister, Gerry Lundy, who lives in Ocala, Florida, and was profoundly instrumental in gathering research for this book. Unending in her drive and energy, for two and a half years she

---

* Mitch Stacy's work has been recognized with awards from the Associated Press, the Florida Society of Newspaper Editors, the Newspaper Guild and the New York *Times.* He was a member of the reporting team that was awarded first place for the news reporting from the Florida Society of the Newspaper Editors for coverage of the Gainesville student murders. He lives in Gainesville, Florida, with his wife Holly.

gathered material, spoke to people, taped interviews, sent me newspapers, discussed impressions, took photos and kept me immediately current and abreast of every nuance and development in the case from her particular vantage point in Florida.

Author's Note

The Gainesville Ripper is an account of a true crime. The crime has been carefully reconstructed according to all physical evidence. Every event is based on fact as taken directly from:

1) Thousands of pages of documented interviews (the investigative reports) conducted by the special agents and detectives of the Multi-Agency Task Force of the Florida Department of Law Enforcement. In addition to scanning some seven hundred pages of the investigative reports, I spent many days in the law library at the Gainesville courthouse perusing both the soft computer copies and hard copies of the remaining investigative reports that were stacked high atop two long tables next to the computers. I also spent days verbally transcribing pertinent information into a tape recorder. Hundreds upon hundreds of people were interviewed by the task force agents. With the exception of a few redacted sections that were later brought out in Rolling's trial, all of the resulting reports were public-access information.

2) Many hours of personal taped interviews and telephone conversations, correspondence and meetings with persons who were directly concerned in the tragic events: University of Florida students Amelia Marshall and Jenny Kanne, who lived in Gainesville at the time of the killings, and although they insisted upon remaining anonymous, spent days sharing much of their feelings, fears and observations with me; Lt. Sadie Darnell of the Gainesville Police Department, who began as spokesman for the GPD and ended up as support for the families of the victims; Det. Alan Baxter of the Alachua County Sheriff's Office; Sheriff Lu Hindery of the Alachua County Sheriff's Office; State Attorney Len Register, who was a key figure in the first two years of the investigation into the killings; UF law student George Humphrey, Jr.; Elna Hlavaty of Indialantic (phone conversations only); JoAnne Adelberger and Jeanette Baer, managers of Hawaiian Village Apartments; Gainesville *Sun* journalist Mitch Stacy; his wife, UF law student Holly Stacy; Kim Norman of the Alachua County Sheriff's Office; Gainesville Police Chief Wayland Clifton; Det. Sgt. Ed Polil of Morristown, New Jersey's Homicide division; Joseph Kays of the University of Florida; Rev. Michael Hudspeth of Shreveport, Louisiana; Claudia Rolling, Danny Rolling's mother (phone conversations only); Lt. Spencer Mann, spokesman for the Alachua County Sheriff's Office; his wife, Pat Mann; Patrick Sessions, father of the missing Tiffany Sessions;

Khris Pascarella (phone conversations only); Professor Slobogin of the University of Florida; Professor Radelet of the University of Florida; Randall "Randy" Wilson, manager of the Winn-Dixie Supermarket in Ocala, Florida, where Rolling was eventually captured; Bipin Patel, owner-manager of the University Inn, Gainesville, Florida, where Rolling stayed before the murders; extensive correspondence with Florida State Prison inmate Bobby Lewis, who was a fellow inmate of Danny Rolling and to whom Rolling confessed.

3) Extensive newspaper coverage and magazine articles from August 1990 to the end of the trial in March of 1994 (see Bibliography).

4) The full day-to-day transcripts of Danny Rolling's penalty-phase trial in February–March 1994, the Honorable Judge Stanley Morris presiding.

5) Researched information on serial killers and serial rapists from the Federal Bureau of Investigation in Washington, D.C.

Although my doctorate is in the area of dramatic theory and criticism, and I have an extensive background in psychology, I nevertheless turned to experts in the field of psychology in order to portray as accurately as possible the making of the killer: J. T. Francisco, Psy.D.; Vincent L. DeChiaro, Ed.D., ACSW.

I chose in certain instances to dramatize the facts of the story while re-creating the chronology of events with as much historical accuracy as possible, always allowing, particularly when dealing with personal interviews, for the possibility of errors in research through the distortion of time and memory. Even the interviews conducted by the task force special agents could be tainted by such distortions as people try to remember past events and conversations. Nevertheless, it is through the personal recollections of these hundreds of people that part of the story can be re-created at all. It has been like a gigantic puzzle to be pieced together with patience and prayer that accuracy would be the end result.

The style I have chosen to work in is, in some degree, one that was initiated in 1965 by Truman Capote with his true-crime book *In Cold Blood.* In the twenty-nine years since its publication, *In Cold Blood* has set the standard for many of the true-crime books that have followed.

I wish to make the following point very clear: no license has been taken in the re-creation of events and incidents; to the best of my knowledge and information, they are all based upon fact. It is in the re-creation of the private moments, most particularly in some of the dialogue of the public figures in this case, that the most dramatic license has been taken and in which errors of interpretation may have been made. The intent has always been to help in understanding of the characters.

Where certain sensitive areas were touched upon, I changed names. Leila Grossman, for example, is not the real name of the woman with whom Danny Rolling had an affair in Sarasota, Florida. The incidents she described in detail to the special agents were summarized graphically in the investigative reports. Although such information is in public access, I saw no need to use her real name in this narrative. Enough that the incidents are true as she reported them.

Writing *The Gainesville Ripper* has been a very painful journey for me. It is impossible to write such a story without being affected by all the sorrow and grief that surrounds such tragic events. Literally hundreds of lives were bitterly affected by the kind of disease spread by the serial killer, Danny Rolling. The graphic carnage of his crimes was difficult to describe and always difficult to comprehend. But without an attempt to understand how such things happen, there can be no hope for prevention.

—MARY S. RYZUK
May 1994

Cast of Characters

Sonja Larson	Murdered
Christina Powell	Murdered
Christa Hoyt	Murdered
Manuel Taboada	Murdered
Tracy Paules	Murdered
Edward Humphrey	Suspect
Daniel Harold Rolling	Murderer

Also murdered by Rolling in Shreveport, Louisiana

Julie Grissom
Tom Grissom, her father
Sean Grissom, her eight-year-old nephew

Eighth Circuit Court
Judge—Stanley J. Morris
State Attorney—Rodney Smith
Public Defender—C. Richard Parker
Barbara Blount-Powell—for the defense
James Nilon—for the prosecution
John Kearns—for the defense
John Fischer—for the defense
Don Royston—for the defense
Jeanne M. Singer—defense

The Jury: Gloria Lynn Bass, Leslie Geraldine Brown, Jerry Ward Coleman, Brenda Jones Diaz, John Odyssey Green, Carrie Jeanne Kerrick, Alfreda Verlinda McDaniel, Holly Paige Sajczuk, Arlie C. Staab, Daren Scott Stubbs, Anne Marie Tignor, Tonja Williams
4 Alternates: Scott Coleman, Brenda Malcolm, Robert Smith, Kathleen Wilson

Psychologists for the Defense
Dr. Harry Krop, Dr. Betty McMahon, Dr. Robert Sadoff

Alachua County Sheriff's Office
Dep. Alexander; Dep. Gail Barber; Lt. Alan Baxter; Dep. Bishop; John Carlin, Assistant to State Attorney; Nancy Carlton, Records Supervisor; Jim Eckert, Squad Supervisor; Det. Ryan Garrett; Correctional Officer Glaab; Task Force Capt. Andy Hamilton; Dep. Don Hayes; Sheriff Lu Hindery; Teesha Jackson, Records Clerk; Deputy Chuck Jempson; Lt. Jones; Dep. Mike Kittle; Dep. Jim Lydel; Lt. Spencer Mann, PIO; Correctional Officer McCullough; Dep. Steve Meary; Deputy Sheriff Tim Merrill; Dep. Al Miller; Sgt. Joe Moro; Nancy Noe, Records Clerk; Lt. John Nobles; Kim Norman, Shift Supervisor; Deputy Keith O'Hara; Danny Pascucci; Michelle Pothier, Records Clerk; Correctional Officer Rainey; Deputy Al Rawls; Michelle Romas, Records Clerk, Charlie Sanders; Lt. Lonnie Scott; Dep. Chuck Simpson; Investigator Jack Smith; Dep. Martin Snook; Investigator Greg Weeks; Deputy Pete Zeller

Federal Bureau of Investigation
Bureau Chief Robert Smith, Assistant Bureau Chief Jack Wise

FBI and Florida Dept. of Law Enforcement (Special Agents)
SA Michael Brick
SA Bigelow
SA John Burton
SA Carmichael
SA Davenport
SA Davis
SA Donaway
SA Dennis Fisher
SA Wally Gossett
Task Force Chief J. O. Jackson
SA Mercurio
SA Dan Miller
SA Domenic Pape
SA Bureau Chief Steve Platt
SA Wayne Porter
SA A. L. Strope
Sergeant Tamillo
SA Thorpe—Crime scene technician
SA Turner
SA Waller
SA Yowell

Gainesville Police Department
Officer Ray Barber
Chief Wayland Clifton
Lt. Sadie Darnell
Officer Brian Helmerson
Detective Johnson
State Attorney Investigator Parsons
Don Rogers—Investigator
Officer Lonnie Scott
Capt. Richard B. Ward
Officer Bradley West

Gainesville—State Attorney's Office
Maritza Arroy—Investigator
Ed Dix—Task force Investigator
Dr. William Hamilton—Gainesville County Medical Examiner
LeGran Hewitt—Task force investigator
Brad King—Assistant State Attorney
Steve Kramig—Task force investigator
Jim Nilon—Assistant State Attorney
Len Register—Eighth Circuit State Attorney
Charles Sauls—Investigator

Marion County and Marion County Jail
T. Beam—Trustee
Sgt. Donna Borgione—Correctional Officer
Officer Carl Durham—Correctional Officer
Sheriff Lt. W. G. Ergle
Major Hendry
Officer Sharon Moran—Correctional Officer
Willard Pape—Sheriff's Attorney
Sharon Roberts, Correctional Officer
Thomas Sawaya—Marion County Judge
Officer Charles Skipper—Correctional Officer
Dr. Thompson—Marion County Jail dentist
Sgt. K. K. Williams—Correctional Officer

Florida State Prison and Marion County Jail Inmates
Anthony Adams—MCJ
Russell "Rusty" Binstead—FSP
Paul Fuqua—FSP
Bobby Lewis—FSP

Paul LaMarche, Sr.—FSP
Osborn—MCJ
Raymond Taylor—FSP

University of Florida Security
Officer Andy Bigelow, Officer Kathy Singletary, Dept. Sgt. Melvin Smith

Rolling's Defense Team
Public Defender Rick Parker
Victoria Lisarralde—Armed robbery offense

Christa Hoyt's Family
Eric Garren—Christa's stepfather
Theresa Ann Garren—Christa's mother
Ralph and Ann Hoyt—Christa's adoptive parents
Edward Phitzenmeir—Uncle, Miami, Florida
Joy Willingham—Aunt

Sonja Larson's Family
Ada and James Larson—Sonja's parents
James Larson, Jr.—Sonja's brother
Carla Thomas—Ada's sister-in-law

Tracy Paules' Family
Ricky Paules, Tracy's mother
George Paules, Tracy's father
Laurie Leahy, Tracy's sister

Christina Powell's Family
James Cullinane—Patricia's uncle
Barbara Milcum—Christina's sister
Frank and Patricia Powell—Christina's parents

Manny Taboada's Family
Gladys Taboada, Manny's mother
Mario Taboada, Manny's brother

Ed Humphrey's Family
Aunt Ann Davis—Elna Hlavaty's sister
Elna Hlavaty—Grandmother
Daniel Humphrey—Brother
Daniel Humphrey—Uncle, Hamilton, Montana
Elna Humphrey—Mother

George Humphrey, Jr.—Brother
George Humphrey, Sr.—Father
Hannah Humphrey—Cousin, Hamilton, Montana
Susan Humphrey—Sister

Daniel Harold Rolling's family
O'Mather Ann Halko Rolling Lummis—Daniel Rolling's divorced wife, Shreveport, Louisiana
KileyAnn Lummis—Daniel Rolling's daughter—Shreveport, Louisiana
James Harold Rolling—Father, Shreveport, Louisiana
Claudia Beatrice Rolling—Mother, Shreveport, Louisiana
Kevin James Rolling—Brother, Wacom, Texas
Homer Rolling—James' father and Daniel Rolling's grandfather
Cavis Rolling—Daniel Rolling's grandmother
Aunt Jeanette Caughey—Phoenix City, Alabama
Uncle Joseph Rolling—Camarillo, California
Aunt Mira Rolling—Camarillo, California
Cousin Donald David Rolling—Camarillo, California
Mrs. Artie Strozier—Claudia Rolling's sister
Chuck Strozier—Daniel Rolling's cousin
Aunt Nadine Johnson—Claudia Rolling's sister, Birmingham, Alabama
Eric Johnson, Sr.—Birmingham, Alabama
Cousin Eric Bonell Johnson, Jr.—Birmingham, Alabama

Murder Victims with Similar MO—(FBI reports)
Sara Clark, Phoenix, Arizona
Mary Sue Cobb, Alabama
Laurie Colanni, Pinnellas, Florida
Julie Grissom, Shreveport, Louisiana
Sean Grissom, Shreveport, Louisiana
Tom Grissom, Shreveport, Louisiana
Jennifer Jenning, Rockford, Illinois
Lisa Kopanakis, Portage, Indiana
Mary Jo Peitzmeier, Lincoln, Nebraska
Sherry Perisho, Monroe County, Florida

Others (Either interviewed personally or interviewed by special agents of the Multi-Agency Task Force or quoted from newspapers)
Catherine and Tom Adams—Gatorwood Apartment residents
JoAnn Adelberger—Manager, Hawaiian Village Apartments, Gainesville, Florida
Melissa Adelberger, JoAnn Adelberger's daughter
Iysha Adell, Manny Taboada's girlfriend

Gwen Antee, Shreveport, Louisiana

Jeannette Baer—Manager, Hawaiian Village Apartments, Gainesville, Florida
Jason Beaupied—Williamsburg Village Apartments resident
Eric Bedesem—Ed Humphrey's friend, Indialantic, Florida
Tim Bentley—Frozen Food Manager of Winn-Dixie Supermarket in Ocala, Florida
Andy Bigelow—UF campus police
Adele Bos—Burglary victim, Tampa, Florida
Rick Brenner—Manager of Gainesville International House of Pancakes
Pete Brigette—Christa Hoyt's boyfriend
Pierce Brook—Los Angeles Police Detective, retired
Ron Brown—V.P. of Regency Windsor Corp. (Williamsburg Village Apartments
Laura Brown—Tracy Paules' friend, Miami, Fla.
Jeffrey and Steve Bunin—Gatorwood Apts.
Stephanie Burzenski—UF student
Lisa Buyer—Tracy Paules' best friend

John Caplan (Pseudonym)—Williamsburg Village Apartments
Valerie Cappalleri—Gainesville, Florida
Carvando (Armando) Careaga—Manny Taboada's friend
Arthur Carlisle—Attorney, Clinton, Mississippi
Debra Carroll—lived near Christa Hoyt's apartment
Donald Carroll—Rollings' neighbor, Shreveport, La.
Tom Carroll—UF student, Gatorwood Apartments resident
Steve Carson—Market Manager of Winn-Dixie Supermarket in Ocala, Florida
John A. Carter—Gainesville waiter at Skeeter's
Kellie Chesser—waitress, Shoney's, Gainesville, Florida
Rev. Ronald Chrisner—Coach, Episcopal High School, Jacksonville, Florida
Mrs. Class—Manager of Cove Apartments, Gainesville, Florida
Stephen and Louisa Biederharn Clausen—Shreveport, Louisiana
James Clore—Indialantic, Florida
Russel and Mary Cobb—neighbors of the Hlavaty/Humphrey family
Rachel Comers—Hamilton, Montana
Truman Cooley—Electrician, Shreveport, Louisiana
Junior Cornblow (Pseudonym)—Shreveport, Louisiana
Alan Cossaboom—Ed Humphrey's friend, Indialantic, Florida
Teresa Lynn Cousins—Sarasota, Florida
Jennifer Cox—Waitress at Gainesville International House of Pancakes

Bob Coyles—Shreveport, Louisiana
Steve Cross—George Humphrey, Jr.'s friend
Brian Cruickshank—Ed Humphrey's friend, Indialantic, Florida

Linda and Robert Darfus—Managers, Sunnyside Motel, Sarasota, Florida
Mr. Daniels—neighbor of the Hlavaty/Humphrey family, Indialantic, Florida
Tony Danzy—Daniel Rolling's acquaintance
Ron Davis—parent of UF student
Tommy Lynn Doll—UF student, Gatorwood Apartments resident
Anita Dupres—Williamsburg Village resident

Bruce Einchen, Jr.—Indialantic, Florida
Phyllis Elam—murder victim, Warren County, Ohio
Beth Engle—Miama, Florida
Leila Evans (Pseudonym)—Williamsburg Village resident

Sarah Fiala—UF student, Gatorwood Apartments resident
James Robert Ford—Sarasota, Florida
Forouzandeh Forghani—Waitress, Ashley's Pub, Gainesville, Florida
James A. Fox—Professor of Criminal Justice, Northwestern University
Mike Francisco—Indialantic, Florida
Bruno Frauenfeld—Deputy, Hillsborough County, Tampa, Florida
Joseph Freck—Customer at Panama Joe's Billiards, Gainesville, Florida

Christina Garcia—Miami, Florida
Shawn Gardner—partygoer at Jennifer Cox's party
Mr. Garrison—Gatorwood Apartments maintenance man
Sabrina Gimrock—UF student, Gatorwood Apartments resident
Jorge Giraldo—Gainsville, Florida
Jeanie and Julie Goforth—twin sisters, friends of George Humphrey, Jr., Gainesville, Florida
Andrew Golden—Polk County Jail inmate
Jeff Goldstein—Indialantic, Fla.
Lillian Greaves—Ely H.S. athletic coach—Deerfield Beach, Florida
Scott Greint—Doorman at Gainesville Central City Lounge
Loraine Grinnel—UF student
Leila Grossman (Pseudonym)—Sarasota, Florida
Doug Guy—Hawaiian Village Apartments maintenance man

Bernadine Holder—Rolling neighbor, Shreveport, Louisiana
Scott Hamel—UF student, Gatorwood Apartments resident

Deputy Hammock—Melbourne, Florida
Richard Hannah—X-ray technician, Indialantic, Florida
Scott Henratty—UF student, Sonja Larson's friend
Jack Heller (Pseudonym) Williamsburg Village resident
Joseph Hester (Pseudonym)—Shreveport, Louisiana Police
Susan Hester (Pseudonym)—Rolling neighbor, Shreveport, Louisiana
Dawn Hodges—Bookkeeper of Winn-Dixie Supermarket in Ocala, Florida
Elnert J. Hoover—Owner of apartment complex where Christa Hoyt was murdered
Ms. Howell—Gainesville Roy Roger countergirl
Lydia Huber—Gainesville Video Movie Time
Glenda Hudspeth—minister's wife, Shreveport, Louisiana
Rev. Michael Hudspeth—Kings Temple United Pentecostal Church, Shreveport, Louisiana
Inez Hutto—Rolling neighbor, Shreveport, Louisiana
Carol Hyde, Gatorwood Apartments Manager

Wendy Fay Jaguette—Gainesville, Florida
Sarah Jeane—Sarasota, Florida
Teresa Johnson—Deputy, Hillsborough County, Tampa, Florida
James Jones—Principal, Ely High School, Jacksonville, Florida
Ken Jones—Director of Public Relations, Department of Corrections, Mississippi
Marthe Jules—Sonja Larson's roommate at Weaver Hall, UF

Derek Kababel—Sarasota, Florida
Jenny Kanne (Pseudonym)—UF student, Gatorwood Apartments resident
Steve Kerns—LensCrafters, Sarasota, Florida
Aaf Kina—Gatorwood Apartments
Harvey Kitzman—UF student, Williamsburg Village Apartments resident

Edward Alan Laventure—Polk County Jail inmate
Larry Dole Lawrence—Tampa, Florida, burglary victim
David LeRoy—UF student, Gatorwood Apartments resident
John Lombardi—President, University of Florida
Sondra London—Danny Rolling's fiancée, freelance writer

Patrick Paul McCaffey—Forensic Expert
Ms. McCarthy—Gainesville Roy Rogers countergirl
Sydney McGrath—Countergirl at Gainesville Krispy Kreme Donuts

Roberta Marshall—UF student
Steve Matt—Jacksonville Lab Bureau Chief
Amelia Marshall (Pseudonym)—UF student, Gatorwood Apartments resident
Carlos Malave—Sarasota, Florida
Russell Marguis, Melbourne, Florida
Diane Mays, Shreveport, Louisiana
Jake Miller—Brevard Co. Sheriff
Lillian "Bunnie" Mills—Rolling's friend, Shreveport, Louisiana
Corey Minard—Manager, Shreveport, Louisiana
John Bernard Mince—Ed's friend, Melbourne, Florida
Steven Morton—Photographer for the Gainsville *Sun*
Jennifer Mulhearn—Waitress at Gainesville International House of Pancakes

Noy—Williamsburg Village Apartments resident
Beth Norman—Manager Surplus Army and Navy Store, Tallahassee, Florida

Kevin Orr—Tracy Paules' boyfriend, Miami, Florida
Christopher Osborn—UF student, burglary victim
Bryan Oulton—UF student, Sonja Larson's friend

Catherine Palmer—Juvenile Alternative Program, South Florida
Khris Pascarella—Tracy Paules' boyfriend
Bipin Patel—Owner-manager of University Inn, Gainesville, Florida
Holly Jo Paula—Tampa, Florida burglary victim
Ann Pave—UF student
William T. "Bill" Pickens—Shreveport Police Department, retired
Mr. Poffa—Gatorwood Apartments maintenance man
Richard Pollard—Christa Hoyt's friend
Mark Powell—used car salesman, Ocala, Florida
Sheriff Printz—Ravvalli County Sheriff's Office, Montana

Hosh Ranick—Counterman, Baskin-Robbins, Gainesville, Florida
Mr. Ratcliff—Gatorwood Apartments maintenance man
Steve Records—University of Florida security personnel
Det. Reslowski—Deerfield Beach Police Department
Dr. Harry M. Richter—Christa Hoyt's dentist
Reynaldo and Patricia Rio and their son Anthony—Burglary victims, Tampa, Florida
Carmen Ringer (Pseudonym)—Rolling neighbor, Shreveport, Louisiana
Godfrey Lanness Robinson—Sonja Larson's friend

Timothy Roberts—George Humphrey, Sr.'s friend
Elsa Rule—UF student, Gatorwood Apartments resident

Paula Santini (Pseudonym)—Williamsburg Village resident
Marleen Scandera—UF student, Gatorwood Apartments resident
John Thomans Schneider—Polk County Jail inmate
Paul Daniel Schwartz—Christa Hoyt's friend
Richard and Alice Schwartz—Paul Daniel Schwartz' parents
Joana Senft—Gainesville hairdresser
Patrick Sessions—Father of Tiffany Sessions
Tiffany Sessions—UF student who disappeared the year before Gainesville murders
Irene Sharp—Manager at Gainesville Central City Lounge
Paul Simon—Bartender, Superior Bar and Grill, Shreveport, Louisiana
Kathy Singletary—UF Campus Police
Pat Siracusa—Doorman at Gainesville Central City Lounge
Jill Slattery—UF student, Gatorwood Apartments resident
Shannon Slattery—Williamsburg Village Apartments resident
Christopher Smith—Maintenance man, Gatorwood Apartments
Andrew Sorensen—Provost, University of Florida
Kathy South—Manager, Royalty Inn, Melbourne, Florida
Howard and Tillie Southerland—Pat Mann's parents
Dr. Philip K. Springer—Ed Humphrey's psychologist
Holly Stacy—Mitch Stacy's wife, UF law student
Art Stevens—Principal, American High School, Hialeah, Miami, Florida
Elsa Streppe—Christina Powell and Sonja Larson's roommate, Ormond Beach, Florida
Elmo St. John (Pseudonym)—Shreveport, Louisiana Police
Dr. Edward L. St. Mary—Ed Humphrey's orthopedic surgeon
Reverend Stoile—Priest of Catholic Church, Melbourne, Florida, where the Hlavaty/Humphrey family worshipped
Elsa Streppe—Powell's and Larson's roommate
Raymond Sumpter—University of Florida security personnel
Ptl. Clifford Swank—Melbourne, Florida, Police Dept.

Raymond Taylor—Manager "Poncho's," Shreveport, Louisiana
Robert T. Temple—Hawaiian Village Apartments maintenance man
Brigette Toombs—Christa Hoyt's ex-roommate
Laura Toth—Clerk, Royalty Inn, Melbourne, Florida
Alan Tripp—Gatorwood Apartments maintenance man
Dr. Vincent Troia—Optometrist, Sarasota, Florida
Tom Trozzi (Pseudonym)—Williamsburg Village resident

Jay Walker—Manager, Poncho's, Shreveport, Louisiana
Cindy Warner—Registrar Episcopal H.S. Jacksonville, Florida
Erin Strachan Watson—UF student, Gatorwood Apartments resident
Mr. Watson—Gainesville, Florida
Evangeline Webster—Indialantic neighbor of Hlavaty/Humphrey family
Michael West—Forensic expert, Hattiesville, Mississippi
Valerie Wheeler—Miami, Florida
Adrienne White—Christina Powell's boyfriend, St. Augustine, Florida
Ben Wigham—Ed Humphrey's friend, Indialantic, Florida
Randall "Randy" Wilson—Manager of Winn-Dixie Supermarket in Ocala, Florida
Royce Wilson—Latent print examiner, Hillsborough County Sheriff's Office
Beverly Woodall—Rolling neighbor, Shreveport, Louisiana

Johanna Yarborough—Manager, Williamsburg Village Apartments
Alan Youngblood—Ocala *Star Banner* photographer

Stella Zaffarano—UF student, Gatorwood Apartments resident
Jason Zahner—Indialantic, Florida

(All reporters are listed individually in the Bibliography)

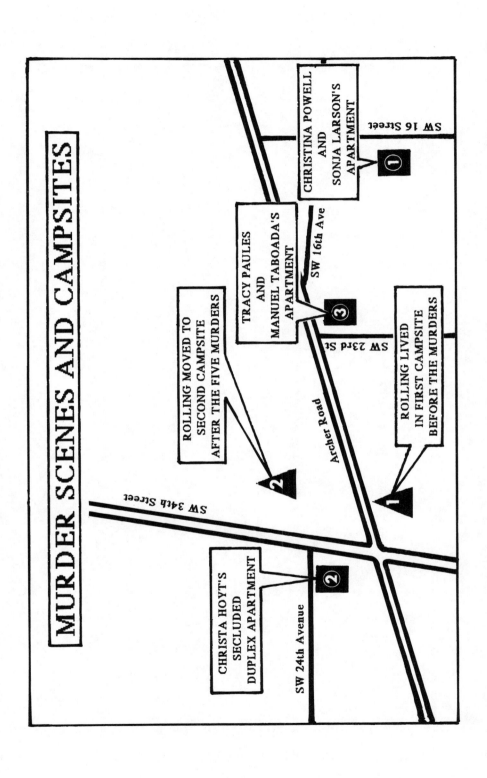

MURDER SCENES AND CAMPSITES

CHRISTINA POWELL
AND
SONJA LARSON'S
APARTMENT

SW 16 Street

SW 16th Ave

TRACY PAULES
AND
MANUEL TABOADA'S
APARTMENT

ROLLING MOVED TO
SECOND CAMPSITE
AFTER THE FIVE MURDERS

SW 23rd St

Archer Road

ROLLING LIVED
IN FIRST CAMPSITE
BEFORE THE MURDERS

SW 34th Street

CHRISTA HOYT'S
SECLUDED
DUPLEX APARTMENT

SW 24th Avenue

Contents

PART I
One Long Weekend of Murder

PART II
The Rollings

PART III
One Week Before the Murders
The Coming Together

PART IV
The Murders

PART V
The Trial

ONE LONG WEEKEND
OF MURDER

1

The Shock of the First Discovery

Gainesville, Florida

Who could have predicted the forty-eight hours of murder that would terrorize the beautiful, historic town of Gainesville?

It was a sprawling university town with many museums, state preserves, nature parks and botanical gardens. Leisure activities ran the gamut from fishing for bass and speckled perch in one of the many freshwater lakes to wildly cheering the "Fightin' Gator" football team in the 83,000–seat Florida Field directly east of the O'Connell Center with its more modest but performer-friendly 12,000 seats under an air-supported roof.

With its own historic clock tower as a distinguishing landmark, solidly built of brick with multiple arches, a high-centered bell and a four-sided block regularly tolling out the correct time, Gainesville was the home of the University of Florida and Santa Fe Community College with their modern architectural designs and excellent academic reputations. Still, despite the modernity of the prestigious academic centers, one could step back in time by touring Gainesville's sixty-three-block historic district with old Floridian architectural styles dating back to the early 1880s. Over two hundred ninety historic buildings, delicately restored and preserved, richly proclaimed the past splendor of Gainesville.

No question, it was a beautiful town with an eclectic aura of vitality, nostalgia, youth and academic fervor, even though it was often too hot during the August months to encourage an excessive expenditure of energy. The average year-round climate was mild enough to attract athletes from around the world for training in track, swimming and baseball, but the late August temperatures hovered persistently around the upper nineties.

And then there was that wonderful moment of national recognition.

During the week of August 14, 1990, Gainesville city officials happily

3

noted that Money magazine had ranked Gainesville, Florida, as the thirteenth best place to live in all of the United States.

Was that only last week?

While there were those who were superstitious about the oft-maligned, ill-omened number thirteen—"Couldn't we be twelfth?" was the presiding joke. "Or fourteenth?"—at such a shining moment of national recognition, superstition gave way to pride.

But then there were the murders, and in less than a week's time, out-of-town newspapers would be referring to it as Grisly Gainesville.

Thursday, August 23, 1990
Williamsburg Village Apartments—2000 SW 16th Street

The temperature had hit a scalding ninety-seven degrees at its daytime peak. By eleven that evening it had diminished only to the upper sixties. That was the hour seventeen-year-old Christina Powell finally got around to calling her parents in Jacksonville. She stood with the pay phone in her hand, distractedly glancing out into the parking lot of the mall as she spoke animatedly into the receiver. She hadn't had her phone installed yet and was using the public phone at the WalMart shopping mall.

Christina and her eighteen-year-old roommate, Sonja Larson, had been so busy with the final stages of moving into their new off-campus apartment at Williamsburg Village that she hadn't had the chance to call them until this hour. And there was still so much to do. Hanging curtain rods took precedence over phone calls home.

Christina and Sonja, whose family came from Deerfield Beach on the southeastern coast of Florida, were terribly excited about starting their new careers as freshmen at the University of Florida. They had spent their summer in school, living in a UF dorm. Now here they were, in their own duplex. Their parents had wanted them to remain on campus, but they hadn't been able to get permanent rooms. Still, what difference did it make? So many college students lived at the complex, it almost felt like a dormitory. A third roommate, Elsa Streppe, probably wouldn't show up until Sunday or Monday.

Patricia Powell told her daughter Christina that she and Dad would come to Gainesville to help the girls settle into their new apartment on Sunday.

"Okay," Christina said cheerfully. "Here's a list of the things we need . . ."

The Powell home in Jacksonville was near enough to keep in close physical contact. The Powells didn't like to admit it but they were not yet fully prepared emotionally to break the ties with their daughter. She was only seventeen. This was the first time she would be away from home. Even though living near the campus was only a transitional phase before the complete break between parent and child, it felt as though Christina were already moving out of their lives. They already missed her and were eager to see the new apartment.

"Want to come Saturday?" Christina asked over the phone that last Thursday night of her life.

"No, we can't on Saturday," her mother said. "We'll be there Sunday morning."

Frank and Patricia Powell would wonder for the rest of their lives if things might have turned out differently had they gone to Gainesville to visit their daughter on Saturday.

Friday, August 24

George Michael's "Faith" had been blaring from Christina and Sonja's apartment all morning. Jack Heller had just moved into the Williamsburg Village complex himself. He could hear the loud music through the walls. He also heard pounding, as though one of the girls was hammering nails into the wall between the two apartments. He had already seen his new neighbors. Nice, he'd told himself, filing a mental note to close in on a meeting as soon as he was settled in.

But then, as the day wore on, the music became so loud it was almost abnormal even for a place that had so many pre-semester parties going on.

I should go over and tell them to tone it down, he thought. All he would have to do was step outside his back door onto the white wooden common porch they shared and knock on their door. It was half glass. He could even peer inside. Yet so many students were moving into the complex to prepare for Monday's opening day at UF that the din was really spread throughout the entire building. There wasn't much point in singling them out and he didn't want to spoil his future chances with the girls. They were both knockouts. The little one in shorts with shoulder-length dark hair and straight-lined brows had deep dimples on both sides of a widely stretched smile. The other one with loose hair falling gently over her forehead as she strained under a heavy box had delicately arched brows over shiny black eyes. And that smile. Real friendly.

He would come to regret not knocking on their door.

Then again, later, when he heard it wasn't only girls who were being struck down by a killer, he found himself thinking that maybe the fact that he hadn't knocked on that door might have saved his own life.

Again and again in his mind he would go over the sounds he had heard —the loud music, the banging, every nuance he could remember. Had it been some kind of intentional coverup? Or had the natural noises of the get-reacquainted parties throughout the complex hidden the sounds of a terrified scream or a death struggle?

And Jack Heller wasn't the only one. The time would come when instead of talking about new courses, new professors, new loves and old, the conversations would relentlessly evolve into wondering how come no one heard the murders.

"It's because there were a lot of parties."

"So what! The walls between the apartments are very thin," Paula Santini said.

"Yeah," John Caplan agreed, "it's easy to hear what's going on in the next room."

"So how come?" Paula asked again.

It was possible that they had died to the blaring sounds of "Faith."

By nightfall on Friday the twenty-fourth the parties had resumed within the apartment complex with appropriate collegiate vigor. No one thought anything of the fact that Christina and Sonja's door had stayed closed throughout the fun.

Saturday, August 25, 1990

When Christina's older brother and sister came to visit the girls on Saturday to welcome them into their new home they found the apartment door locked. There was no answer to their knocks, but they thought little of it.

"Didn't she know we were coming?"

"I thought we'd surprise her."

"Some surprise. On us. They're not even here."

They finally gave up.

No one else at Williamsburg Village Apartments paid much attention to the closed door either. There were so many things to do, so many things to think about.

It was going to be a good semester.

It wasn't until later, when seemingly unimportant moments were reevaluated and forced to the forefront of memory under the painful spotlight of police questions, that it was realized the apartment shared by Christina Powell and Sonja Larson had been quiet all day Saturday. Even "Faith" had been shut off.

"Come to think of it," said Leila Evans, a neighbor, frowning under the weight of memory, "they'd been here for a while. Friendly girls, both of them. But I never saw them after I waved at them the other day when they were carrying in some stuff. Boxes, I think. Or maybe it was books. Yeah, books."

"When was that?"

"Friday, I think. I can't remember exactly. I wish I could remember. Something in their arms . . ."

"They were moving in?" the detective asked.

"Yes. That's it."

Actually, the girls had moved in earlier in the month.

"They didn't even get a chance to see if they'd like it here . . . or anything . . . not really." Tears filled Leila's eyes. "It's really not a bad place to live. At least I never thought so before . . ."

Sunday, August 26, 1990
10 A.M.

The morning sun couldn't break through the gray rain clouds that would hang heavily all day.

The Friday and Saturday night parties were over. An early Sunday morning pall had settled throughout all of the Williamsburg Village Apartments, complexes separated by individual courtyards, as partygoers slept away the numbing price of youthful excess.

By ten A.M. the thermometer had already hit eighty-nine degrees. The soft whir of air conditioners sounded throughout the complex.

Tom Trozzi had a brutal hangover. He didn't usually drink so much. This time the homemade, heavily salted margaritas he favored over the cans of beer floating around the night before had gone to his head with a vengeance.

No more, he thought as he trudged past that particular closed door. Now he was on his way to buy the Sunday newspaper, much of which he would read over coffee and sweet rolls. What the hell, he thought, resenting the price he was paying for a little fun the night before. The thought of sweet rolls, usually so appetizing on a Sunday morning, had become nauseating.

Anita Dupres smelled it too. She thought it was sour milk coming from the girls' apartment as she passed their closed door.

I hope those two aren't the kind to store garbage in their apartment, she thought as she squeezed her nostrils together on her way out of the building.

11:00 A.M.

Mr. and Mrs. Powell had brought the bits of furniture Christina wanted. A chair. A lamp. A small dresser. It was all packed in the back of the car.

They pulled in to the Williamsburg Village Apartments off SW Sixteenth Street past the main building. It was an imposing three-story white brick colonial building with a front roof overhanging seven stately white columns. Even with Spanish moss hanging off the huge oaks it looked as though it belonged in Virginia rather than Florida.

Now they stood at the door of their daughter's apartment located in one of the back buildings situated deep off the main road.

"Why don't they answer?" Patricia Powell said a bit uneasily.

As arranged, she and her husband had come from Jacksonville to help the girls settle in.

Mr. and Mrs. Powell had felt little concern when their elder daughter told them Christina hadn't been in when she and her brother visited the day before.

"We never saw her. She wasn't there when we knocked."

Nothing to worry about.

"They were probably out."

The Powells were not able to call Christina before leaving Jacksonville, since the girls had no phone yet and were not early risers anyway. They had packed up the car with all the items Christina wanted and settled in for a leisurely drive to Gainesville.

But now, late risers or not, it was a different matter. She should *be* there.

They knocked again. Louder.

The Powells had been standing outside their daughter's door for a long time with no response to their knocking. They even waited outside the building for a while, thinking the girls might have gone out for breakfast.

When the Powells came back inside and pounded on their daughter's door again, a next-door neighbor opened his door and peered out. Disheveled and unshaven, he had obviously been awakened by the noise.

"No, I didn't see them all day yesterday," he responded to Mr. Powell's questions. "Actually, I haven't seen either one of them since . . ." He thought a moment. "Friday, I think."

Mr. and Mrs. Powell looked at each other.

Something was wrong . . .

3:30 P.M.

By 3:30 P.M. the Powells could no longer contain their anxiety. It was not like Christina to take off without a word, especially when she knew they were coming all the way from Jacksonville to be with her.

"I think we should call the manager," she said.

"What about calling Sonja's parents first," Frank suggested. "They might know something."

They placed a call to the Larson home in Deerfield Beach.

"Ada, they're not here," Patricia told Sonja's mother. "We thought you might know where they've gone."

"Gone?"

"Have you heard anything from Sonja?"

"No," Ada Larson said, unable to contain the slight rise in her voice, "and Sonja was supposed to call me yesterday. She never did."

"Yesterday?"

Now all of the concerns that had subtly gnawed at Ada Larson when she had not heard from her own daughter the day before came rushing forward. It was just inconsistent with Sonja's personality not to keep her word.

"Get somebody to open that door!" Ada said to Patricia Powell. "They could be in there!"

Ada Larson's concerns had added fuel to their own. The Powells knew they had to get someone to let them inside the apartment

4:00 P.M.

He needed a haircut. His slightly receding hairline, just beginning to show signs of gray at the temples, was a little long at the nape. The best part of the day had been spent. Now that his shift was almost over, thirty-five-year-old Officer Ray Barber was beginning to look forward to the three days off he had coming to him. He had been on the force for eight and a half years and had come to look forward to the time on his small farm with his wife Gail as the most relaxing, though physical, time he spent. Gail, who was also a police officer working out of the sheriff's office in

Alachua County just over the Gainesville city line, was not on duty and would probably be home when he arrived. A comforting thought.

He was just about to sign off for the day when the car radio came to life.

"Barber here," he said as he waited for the red light on the corner to turn green.

"Ray," the communications operator said, "someone's complaining about loud music."

Nothing much, Barber thought. There was always someone who was going to take advantage of pre-semester party time and annoy the neighbors. Most of his buddies didn't like to bother too much with the kids unless it was absolutely necessary. You never knew if they were the kids of some VIP, and so there was always the chance of antagonizing someone with important connections.

"I'll check it out on my way home," Barber said, noting the address of the apartment complex where the complaint had been registered.

"By the way," the communications operator's voice added almost as an afterthought, "there's a Signal Sixty-four coming from the complex right across the street. The Williamsburg Village Apartments. Maybe you should look into that first since it's in the same area."

A Signal 64. That was a "call to assist a citizen."

Barber yawned as he disconnected. "Okay," he said aloud, hoping the well-being check wouldn't take too long.

As soon as he pulled into the Williamsburg Village Apartments courtyard he saw a maintenance man waving his arms to flag him down. The paunchy, gray-haired man looked flushed with heat and frustration.

"Look," the man said almost apologetically when the police officer pulled over to his side, "we have a couple of parents who are really uptight over here."

"What's the problem?"

"They can't get their daughter to answer her door. They want me to use my master key, but I don't know . . . I thought I'd call you guys first."

Officer Barber walked over to Mr. and Mrs. Powell, who were standing in the courtyard at the foot of the steps leading up to the building. As they started telling him their worries he knew he would have a tough time calming them down. And there was a troubling edge to their story.

"She *knew* we were coming," Mrs. Powell was saying. "Christina always keeps her appointments. They should *be* here."

"They're starting tomorrow at the University of Florida as incoming freshmen," Mr. Powell added.

"And Sonja, a very reliable girl, never called her mother yesterday in Deerfield Beach after she promised she would."

"Sonja?" Barber asked.

"One of our daughter's roommates."

Officer Barber tried to calm them down. He got dozens of calls about "missing" sons and daughters all the time; the kids usually turned up with a logical explanation of where they had been.

"They're probably out with friends," Barber said, trying to offset the fears that had built up during the hours the Powells had been waiting.

"No!" Mrs. Powell insisted. "Her car is here. In the parking lot."

"Okay. You wait here," Officer Barber told them. And now he was uneasy. He didn't like it, something didn't feel right. "You have your master key?" he said to the maintenance man.

The flushed man nodded.

Reluctantly the Powells waited downstairs while Barber and the maintenance man went upstairs to the girls' apartment. They didn't say much.

"It'll be all right," Powell told his wife. She only stared at the closed door at the top of the stairs.

Inexplicably, the master key failed to open the apartment door. Barber broke one of the glass panes with his stick and reached inside. But it was a double key deadbolt.

"We'll have to bust it," Barber said when there was no response to his bangs on the door . . . And he did not like that smell.

"I can't do that," the maintenance man protested. "I can't break down a door."

Barber looked at him. "Get the permission of the apartment manager if you have to. Do it *now.*"

The apartment was stifling. The air conditioner had not been turned on. The odor they were aware of in the hallway became more pronounced as the door crashed open under the force of two pairs of shoulders.

"As soon as the door broke, I saw a body, and it was pretty bad. I said to myself, I don't want to be here," Officer Barber would later say.

The first thing Barber and the maintenance man saw was the bloodied nude body of a young female, positioned grotesquely on the bed with her arms above her head. Barber had come across dead people before in his duties as a policeman but he had never seen anything like this. Instinctively he put up a restraining arm over the threshold to hold back the maintenance man. But they could tell, even without looking closely, that the girl had been repeatedly stabbed and mutilated, then propped up at the entrance.

"Out!" Officer Barber said, shoving the maintenance man into the hallway.

The door slammed behind him.

Alone in the apartment, Officer Barber took a long moment to pull his thoughts together and get control of himself.

You role-play how you're going to react in certain situations. He didn't realize he was in a state of shock himself.

He couldn't bring himself to look too closely. There was a great deal of blood.

But they say when you're in a bad situation you go back to how you were trained. It was true. He knew she had been dead awhile, that the perpetrator was probably nowhere to be found, but he drew his revolver anyway and moved gingerly forward. Secure the area. Look for others. The father had said there were two, maybe three girls in the apartment.

He came to the staircase that led to the lower level of the duplex. Slowly, carefully, he went down where he stumbled upon a second body. Another young female. She too had been stabbed repeatedly, mutilated and positioned for maximum shock effect.

Training, he thought. Go back to training.

Don't touch anything.

Don't contaminate the scene.

It was impossible to tell which of the girls had died first. That was up to forensics. But he *could* tell that in the searing heat both bodies had already begun to decompose.

He thought of the parents outside, waiting for news of their daughter. There was going to be need for immediate crisis intervention, and he sure wasn't the one to handle it.

Still, he had to face the parents.

Barber came out of the apartment into the blistering courtyard.

Christina's parents looked at his grim face, his evasive glance. Mrs. Powell gripped her husband's arm. They could barely ask the question.

"Christina . . . ?"

Barber paused with a deep swallow before he said, "We'll have to wait for identification."

"I want to see my daughter," the father said.

"I'm sorry, sir—"

"I want to go up there and see my daughter."

Barber looked at the entrance to the courtyard on SW Sixteenth Street, wishing that *someone* from the department or the crisis center were already there.

"I insist."

"You can't go up there and you can't see your daughter—"

They followed him closely, intensely as he went to his patrol car parked immediately outside.

"Looks like a double homicide," he heard himself whisper into the car phone so that the Powells could not hear. He didn't recognize his own voice. "Two girls. Multiple stab wounds." He was speaking in short, clipped sentences. "And . . . some other stuff. Mutilations." Mechanically, he gave Dispatch the exact address. "I'll seal off the area. And you better get in touch with the Alachua Crisis Center. I've got *parents* down here. Get them to send over a crisis team. Right away."

"You've got to tell me what's happening," Powell demanded when Barber finally stepped out of the car. "I have a right to know."

Mrs. Powell broke down, all the anxiety and fears of the day finally coming out. She wanted to know too, but of course she was terrified of what Barber was going to tell them. Her husband, though, would not let up as the afternoon sun continued to beat down on them.

"I demand that you tell me what's going on. Don't you think we have a right to know?"

"Sir . . ."

"Not knowing is worse than anything you could tell us . . ."

Barber didn't think so as he thought of the carnage he had seen upstairs.

"Please . . ."

"Sir," the young officer said, finally giving in to their need. "I have a body upstairs . . ."

Mr. Powell put his arm around his wife as she moaned aloud. Their nightmare had begun.

"Sir, I don't know if it's your daughter or not," Barber said. "I believe we have a homicide here. I've put in a call to the department." He could feel the perspiration drenching the back of his shirt. "I can't allow you to see."

Mr. Powell asked no more.

Barber recognized members of the Alachua County Crisis Center, who arrived on the scene to relieve him.

"I never thought I would encounter anything like this," Barber told one old friend among them.

"Are you okay?"

"Sure." A lie. "I have to fill out a report now." And walked away.

It had seemed an eternity but was only minutes before his call to Dispatch brought action. At least twenty law-enforcement personnel now converged on the beautiful old apartment complex, from Chief of Police Wayland Clifton to the state's attorney, and including Lt. Sadie Darnell, thirty-seven, five-foot-five, dark eyes. Feminine. A pro.

When she woke up the morning of August 26th she couldn't possibly have known how involved she was to become in the horror that had already begun to unfold at the Williamsburg Village apartment complex. As she moved almost automatically into position between the police and the assembled media representatives, she did not know that she would ultimately serve as the foil between the police and the media.

"The [first] deaths occurred sometime between eleven-thirty P.M. August twenty-third and four P.M. August twenty-sixth," she said in a light voice that belied the enormous reservoir of strength behind it. "It is believed that someone forced their way through the door of the Williamsburg Village apartment." Sadie told the reporters the investigators "believe the brutal murders are an isolated case."

"Do you have any clues as to who's responsible?"

"It's a double murder and there doesn't seem to be a motive."

"Can you give us their names? Of the girls?"

"No. Not yet."

"What kind of weapon was used?"

"That has yet to be determined. An autopsy will be performed this morning and results will be disclosed later in the week."

"Was a gun used?"

"I don't believe so."

"Did they die a violent death?"

"That appears to be the case."

"Was there a struggle?"

"That would be hard to say."

Finding the bodies marked only the beginning for Officer Ray Barber. After completing his reports and doing his best to forget the crime scene, he went home to sleep. Out of the question. Fortunately his wife Gail was home. She listened quietly to his account of the horror of the mutilated bodies, the broken mother and father. She knew he wouldn't sleep that night. She couldn't imagine—not really—what it would be like to come across such a scene and to know that another human being had created it.

Word spread quickly throughout the Williamsburg Village Apartments. Everyone was stunned by the murders. What had been going on next door on the other side of the paper-thin walls? Why hadn't anyone heard something—a scream, a thump, *any* sound of a struggle? All there had been the following morning in the lull after the slaughter was the acrid smell of what had seemed like sour milk.

"We've never had this kind of thing before," said one University of Florida female student who had lived at the complex for the past three years and was willing to disclose her feelings if not her name.

Mitch Stacy from the Gainesville *Sun* was a twenty-nine-year-old staff reporter. He wore a closely trimmed, neat beard and glasses and had a receding hairline that he usually kept under a cap. He had a ready smile, but it was his pale blue eyes that were his most prominent feature. Eyes that had seen a great deal in his short life. Like Lt. Sadie Darnell, Mitch, too, was about to begin a journey of discovery not only of the crime but of himself.

"No serious problems with crime," the girl was going on, "not even burglaries."

As though it was essential to emphasize the aberrant nature of the discovery of two murdered fellow students down the hall.

No one from the Gainesville police would release the names of the girls, but word spread along the grapevine that they had been incoming freshmen and had just moved into the complex.

"And I thought someone had forgotten to take their garbage out."

"Who were they? Anybody know?"

"I hear one of the girls had a car registered in Palm Beach County," Mike Fellows whispered to the gathered group of returning seniors standing in the back courtyard of Williamsburg Village at the foot of the wooden steps leading up to the back porch of his own apartment.

"How'd you find that out?" his girlfriend Myra asked.

"I know one of the cops," he said. "And the other girl is from Jacksonville."

"I don't know anyone from Jacksonville," Myra said, a bit relieved as she sat down on the bottom step watching a tiny gray salamander scurry away under the porch. "Or Palm Beach County either. I don't want to know them personally," she said quietly. "You know what I mean? That would be too awful."

"One thing . . ." Jack said, "I could swear I heard the shower water running in their apartment this morning . . ."

"This morning? But I heard they were dead between forty-eight and seventy-two hours," Mike Fellows said. "That's what my cop friend told me. I mean they had started to . . . you know . . . decompose."

"I could swear to it," Jack repeated.

"But if they were already dead, who was taking the shower?"

Police spent most of Sunday evening interviewing dozens of students and checking the girls' apartment for fingerprints. They had not yet determined whether the apartment had been broken into or even whether there had been a struggle before death.

With the growing official presence at the complex, the news of the murders soon spread beyond Williamsburg Village. The night before had been so full of the joy of anticipation. Now, word of the double murder exploded the campus town into a different kind of activity—telephone calls, whispered conversations, questions.

The questions, all of them unanswered, did not help to dispel the growing panic. Just the opposite. Imaginations were even outrunning rumor.

Soon word got out that one of the girls had been mutilated. Something about the girl's breasts. Which girl? Christina or Sonja? Mutilated how?

Next door, on the opposite side of the girls' apartment, Leila Evans crossed her arms over her own breasts and shuddered at the thought of what had been going on only a few feet away while she was partying before the opening moments of the new semester.

The newly arrived, somewhat heavy-set girl hadn't heard about the murders. She had been in her car traveling toward her new apartment and had not yet caught up on the local news.

Now she frowned in wonder. By the time she parked her car she saw that the complex was riddled with police activity.

Gainesville officer Brian Helmerson stood guard at the door of her building, which was cordoned off with yellow crime-scene tape.

Crime scene? What had happened? A burglary, probably.

The girl looked at the crowds. She noticed police-service technicians in white suits and masks sifting through one of the dumpsters near where she had parked her car. They looked like something out of a sci-fi movie.

More than a burglary, she thought.

The others standing about knew the authorities were looking for clues. What they did not know was that the men in white were also searching for body parts.

The newly arrived girl was carrying shoulder luggage. Casually dressed, with short-cropped blond hair, she tried to move past the policemen. It looked as though she was going to be forced to get police clearance to enter her own apartment.

"But I live here," she said. "What's going on?"

"May I ask your name, please?"

"Elsa Streppe."

Did he look at her oddly and take a beat before asking, "Who do you live with?"

"I'm rooming with a couple of friends."

"Can you tell me their names?"

"Christina Powell and Sonja Larson," she said. "We moved in early this month but I've been out of town for a few days."

The policeman motioned to a plainclothesman standing some distance away going through a small pocket-sized notebook. Elsa watched the muted exchange between them before the detective moved over to her and she suddenly found herself being photographed by a staff photographer from the Gainesville *Sun.*

"Would you come with us, please?" the detective said.

"But why?" She tried to shield herself from the photographer's lens. "What's *happened?*"

Elsa Streppe was escorted to the Alachua County Crisis Center where, in the protective presence of a crisis intervention team, she finally was told what had happened to her roommates. She nearly collapsed. Her friends were gone? *Gone.* And she, obviously, had narrowly missed an appointment with death herself.

Less than twenty-four hours after Christina and Sonja were discovered, the time had come to remove the girls from the bloody scenes of their deaths.

Many stood outside and quietly watched in the white glare of the late morning sunlight.

Across the parking lot was Jorge Giraldo. He had taken his dog for a walk when he realized he had come on the solemn moment of removal.

With three men to each girl, the two stiff bodybags with a slight angled sag in the middle of each were carried out to the waiting ambulances.

Giraldo was deeply moved. He thought of the parents. Those girls, he thought. Just freshmen.

The bodies were moved to the county morgue where autopsies would be performed on Monday morning.

Monday morning

Mitch Stacy went to see Ron Brown at his office. He knew that Brown was a vice-president of Regency Windsor Management Corp., which managed the Williamsburg Village Apartments. The man was obviously deeply upset.

"The police told me very little about the . . . killings," he said to Mitch.

Brown knew the young man was from the Gainesville *Sun* and he didn't mind talking to a reporter as long as he was from a local newspaper and not some out-of-town opportunist. "We've seen a very unfortunate situation that . . . will happen once in a lifetime," he said, looking at Mitch.

"We really haven't had an opportunity to sit and think . . . we're trying to help the parents . . . they're here. But we know very little about what's happened."

"You say the police haven't told you much?"

"Very little. And they told me not to release any information about the victims."

Mitch waited for him to go on. He didn't want to press the man too hard, but experience had taught him whenever there were silences, anxious or nervous people usually rushed to fill in the gaps.

"The murders seemed to be random," Brown added with a conviction born more of need than of certainty. "Random."

"Do you think this will prompt changes in security at the complex?"

"I don't know yet," Brown said. Security? His mind jumped. "That's a difficult question. We have very good security," he said quickly before looking off somewhere. He paused for a moment. "Everything is so new," he said quietly, "it's difficult to evaluate right now."

A young woman touched Mitch's arm. "I live here at the complex," she said, "and I work at Shands Hospital."

Shands Hospital was within walking distance of Williamsburg Apartments. Only a few blocks.

"Your name?" Mitch asked, turning to the young woman.

"No," she said, shaking her head solemnly. "I don't want to give you my name."

"Okay."

"But I will tell you that Williamsburg Village has a good reputation. It's a quiet place to live."

"How do you feel about it now?"

"Worried. My friends and I . . . the other nurses, even the ones who don't live here, we're so close to the scene of the murder, you know? Less than a mile away. And there's always the areas of the parking lots . . ." She paused a moment.

Mitch knew what she meant. The large empty parking lots where a lone nurse's vulnerability was more frightening than ever. Especially at night.

"I'll tell you the truth," the young nurse said, looking at him closely with dark worried eyes. "Since they heard about this, a lot of the girls have started talking about Richard Speck."

"The guy who—"

"—killed all those nurses back in nineteen sixty-six or sixty-seven."

Mitch had a sense that this was only the beginning. . . .

"It's usually so quiet back here," the nurse said, "but now . . ."

She gestured toward the police cars and TV vans jamming the parking lot, nearly blocking the back entrance to her own apartment. "This is a nice place to live. And I've always felt safe here. Until this."

Mitch suspected that ghosts of other infamous killers were about to be resurrected in troubled dreams.

"Now everyone's scared," she continued. "You can feel it in the air."

. . . Just the beginning . . .

"But everyone is trying to be supportive to each other too. The neighbors have been really helpful, letting everyone bunk together if we get too scared to stay alone. And we walked to the parking lot at Shands in groups tonight."

Richard Speck. He was that guy who killed eight nurses in Chicago almost twenty-five years earlier.

But why was this young woman thinking of a mass murderer? The situation at Williamsburg Village was hardly the same. At least so far.

2

Number Three: Decapitated

"Christa liked racquetball. She liked anything that she could be doing outdoors."
—KIM NORMAN, Shift Supervisor,
Alachua County Sheriff's Office

Monday, August 27
12:19 A.M.

The phone in Kimberly Norman's home in Starke, Florida, rang at 12:19 A.M. The call was from Teesha Jackson of the Alachua County Sheriff's Office in Gainesville where Kim worked as a shift supervisor. When Teesha looked over at Christa's empty desk situated around the corner from the double-glass windows that partitioned off the lobby from where the clerks worked, she had a distinct sense of unease. Since Christa ordinarily started her part-time shift at the sheriff's office promptly at midnight, Teesha decided to call her supervisor Kim Norman.

"She didn't come in," she told the sleepy Kim.

Even in her groggy state, Kim thought that was odd. Christa was always prompt.

Christa Leigh Hoyt was from Gainesville. She was eighteen, well-liked and beautiful, with long chestnut-colored hair, bright blue eyes and a dimpled smile that got her the nickname "Glowworm." In addition to her studies as a chemistry major at nearby Santa Fe Community College, she worked the midnight shift as a records clerk at the Alachua County Sheriff's Office.

"Did she call in sick?" Kim asked. She knew that Christa was on medication. She had had her wisdom teeth pulled and the penicillin and codeine that had been prescribed for infection and pain might have made her oversleep.

"No," Teesha answered. "She didn't call in."

Kim found herself thinking she was going to have to write her up, and they had become such good friends over the past two months she didn't really want to do that. Still, it was office policy that employees had to call in if they were not going to report for work. Christa's days off were Saturday and Sunday. She should have reported for work at midnight Monday.

"All right," she told Teesha. "I'll call her and see what's up."

"Okay."

Kim dialed Christa's number, vaguely thinking about the last time she had seen her. She had driven Christa home on Friday morning because she hadn't taken her own car to work. Even on Thursday night her brother brought her to work for the Friday morning shift. She hadn't wanted to drive because the penicillin and codeine made her a bit groggy. She needed a ride home and it was no problem for Kim to take her home.

The drive had taken about fifteen minutes. They talked about work, some personal things on the way. Kim made a left turn off SW Thirty-fourth Street onto the dirt lane of SW Twenty-fourth Street, past Ed's Cleaners on the right corner, down a street that looked like a small industrial park with ABC Research on the left and Nicosi's All About Nails on the right.

Kim knew Christa had recently moved into the inexpensive complex and it was the first time Kim had ever been there. Actually she didn't much like the area. "It's pretty scary-looking in there," Kim had said as she turned into the entrance to Christa's apartment complex.

"No worse than where we work," Christa answered cheerfully.

That was true. The sheriff's office was situated in a rather dangerous part of town, an industrial area next to an electrical park and a yard of huge oil holding tanks. It looked like the proverbial other side of the tracks, but Kim was used to it there. Here, where Christa lived, it seemed even more deserted and it wasn't kept clean. Kim noticed the entrance to the complex had a high flatboard fence on both sides leading to an unpaved central court with a few parked cars, a van and pickup trucks. The one-story brown apartments, surrounded by scraggly black oaks and dense overgrowth, looked like converted trailers with dark brown flat roofs.

They both knew security in the apartment complex barely existed. There weren't even any streetlights.

"I guess this place isn't as safe and secure as I'd like it to be," Christa admitted as she looked at the complex through Kim's eyes. "I'm going to move as soon as I have enough money."

"That's probably a good idea," Kim said with her gentle southern accent lifting up the ends of her words.

"It was all I could afford."

Kim nodded. "I can understand that."

And then she had left—the last time she would see Christa.

After the fourth ring, the answering machine in Christa's apartment automatically clicked into the line.

Kim hung up on the familiar sound of Christa's voice, not waiting for the usual high-pitched tone to beep. Instead of leaving a message she dialed again, hoping that the persistent ringing would wake Christa up if, indeed, she had overslept. Again, the machine was the only answer.

Just as Kim was about to call the sheriff's office, the phone rang under the palm of her hand. This time it was Michele Romas calling. Michele also worked at the Alachua County Sheriff's Office.

"She's not answering her phone," Kim told Michele.

"Want me to have Communications send someone over to check on her?" Michele asked.

"A good idea," Kim said, stifling a yawn. "Keep me on the line while you do."

While Michele punched into another line to make the arrangements, Kim remembered that she had almost stopped by Christa's apartment yesterday morning when Christa did not keep their scheduled date. They had agreed to meet at the county office gym Sunday morning to work out after Kim finished her shift at 8:00 A.M. A small workout. Nothing major. The gym was conveniently located on the premises. Quick workouts were a common practice.

But something stopped Kim as she drove by the intersection of SW Thirty-fourth Street and Archer Road. No, don't stop by her place, she had thought to herself as she passed the Shell gas station and the Gainesville State Bank where Christa kept her accounts. She's probably sleeping.

Kim had continued driving on to Starke, where she usually visited her family on Sundays. With Monday and Tuesday designated as her own days off, the arrangement made possible long pleasant weekend visits at home with her granny.

Now, while she waited on the line for Michele to contact Communications, her thoughts wandered to the Williamsburg Village apartment complex. She had also been called at home yesterday when Teesha phoned to inform her of the double homicide that had occurred there. Kim knew only too well that it was the main topic of conversation on everyone's lips in town and especially on the campus of the University of Florida. Although it was more than likely that it really was the isolated case the Gainesville police said it was, she also knew those kinds of official statements were often made in a deliberate attempt to keep the lid on a potential panic. Still, it really didn't hit anybody at the sheriff's office where she and the girls worked; they dealt with homicides of one kind or another every day. The double homicide was a bad thing, but none of the girls at the office felt particularly vulnerable because of it.

As she waited, Kim found herself wondering if Christa knew about the murders since she hadn't had a chance to speak with her about them. She knew that Christa's roommate, Brigitte Toombs, had moved out shortly after they had taken the apartment and that Christa now lived alone.

Michele's voice broke into her thoughts. "Keith O'Hara and Gail Barber are going over."

"Okay."

Kim hung up and lay down again. For some reason she found herself smiling as she remembered their midnight shift together on Friday. She and Christa had had a real good time that night. They'd talked, laughed, joked around. Kim could still see Christa in her attractive white dress. She looked like an angel, Kim thought as she closed her eyes to the pressing need of sleep. She was so pure-looking in that dress—tall, long slender neck, beautiful long legs. She remembered they intended to get together outside of work. They had talked about it on the drive to Christa's.

Kim had looked around the isolated complex as Christa swung her long legs out of the car. The astonished look on her face when she accidentally hit the mirror on the side of the car was priceless.

Kim grinned. "Don't worry about it." But she would probably tell her she had to pay for the mirror when they got back to work. A joke. The mirror wasn't broken.

"Can you come over and go to a party with me on Saturday?" Christa had asked.

"No, sorry, I can't."

"Okay," she said. "How about coming over Saturday night for Sunday?"

"I wish I could," Kim said, "but I have to work at Lilia's."

They both worked hard, holding down two jobs while going to school at the same time, so Christa knew about Kim's part-time job at Lilia's. She said, "Sure. Okay." First things first. "Want to come in for a minute?"

"I should get going. I might come over after I get off from Lilia's."

"Great."

But Kim had ended up the day feeling too tired when she finished at Lilia's, so she went home and slept instead of going over to Christa's.

On such simple decisions life and death often depended.

"If you don't come," Christa suggested, "we'll meet in the morning at the gym, okay?"

"Sure," Kim agreed, "when I get off at eight."

"Take care. I'll see you Sunday."

"See you Sunday . . ."

Kim began to doze off now.

Funny, she thought vaguely again. Christa never showed up at the county gym even though it was she who had suggested the workout . . .

12:30 A.M.

The two deputies, Keith O'Hara and Gail Barber, were working road patrol on the midnight shift. They were dispatched to the girl's apartment on SW Twenty-fourth Avenue west of SW Thirty-fourth Street just outside the Gainesville city limits. O'Hara felt a little silly, believing that the search for the girl who had not shown up for work was a bit precipitous, even with the tension from the discovery of the double murder only a short distance away. But Gail Barber didn't like the feel of it all. It was her own husband, Officer Ray Barber, who had discovered the two girls' bodies at Williamsburg Village only hours earlier. She had spent a long time with him after he had come off duty, comforting him, listening to him describe the horror.

Gail knew Christa's apartment complex was directly opposite the Pinehurst Trailer Park. "Here it is," she said to Keith.

A dirt road.

Now, as they pulled in past an outside dumpster to the right of the main entrance, their wheels momentarily sagging into a deep, muddy, water-filled hole in the middle of the cracked road at the entrance, her thoughts turned to husband Ray's grisly account of the murder scene at Williamsburg Village. Gail tried to push aside her unease as she looked around; but this place was so dark at night, unlike the brightly lit complex where Ray had discovered the two murdered girls. The few apartments surrounding the courtyard seemed like an extension of Erskine Caldwell's Tobacco Road, the kind of place for a killer.

Gail shook her head. It would be just too coincidental, and awful, for her to be present at the discovery of another murder . . . especially Christa's, whom she knew so well . . . As a Police Explorer, Christa had trained directly under her. She was an extraordinarily bright girl who had a real future with law enforcement if that was her ultimate career choice. She was also looking into forensic lab work in her courses as a chemistry major at Santa Fe.

Christa did not answer her door.

"That doesn't mean anything."

"I know. Maybe she left already."

"Isn't that her car? The one parked on an angle by the door?"

It was a small Nissan Sentra, an older model, maybe 1979, she thought, with an old purplish tint, kind of a primer red, two doors. Just a car.

"Looks like it."

Christa's apartment was the first one on the left with the letter *M* nailed high on the side. The front door faced the entrance to the court.

It was locked.

They knocked again. Louder. No response.

The deputies looked at each other. Neither wanted even to consider the possibility of what they were both thinking.

To the right of the front door a living-room window faced the unpaved courtyard. To the left, there was a high wall of flatboard fencing that served to conceal the back portion of apartment *M.*

Elbert Hoover, the manager, heard them banging on the door and came out to see what the trouble was. When they went around to the glass door at the back of the apartment, Hoover knew immediately something was wrong with the gate. And the chain-link fence was down. They stepped over it in the dark. O'Hara now asked Hoover to wait by the front of the building as a safety precaution, but in the beam of a C-cell flashlight, it was apparent no one was there. The sliding glass doors in the back of Christa's apartment were easily accessible. There did not seem to be any security.

Keith tried sliding it open. It, too, was locked from the inside.

They could see that bamboo shades covered the glass doors on the inside but did not reach the interior floor. There was a small crack at the bottom.

On hands and knees, they bent down low enough to peer in under the curtain. Beaming the C-cell into the dark bedroom, they saw what appeared to be a nude body, seated on the edge of the bed, bent over at the waist—a corpse with a small pool of blood at its feet, still clad in shoes and socks.

But something far more grotesque.

"Oh my God," from Gail. "She doesn't have a head—"

Keith yanked her away from the glass doors.

"Don't touch anything."

That couldn't be Christa. Hysteria, quickly swallowed. Hang on.

As they ran back to their car to call for backup, Gail thought of the odds on two people from the same family discovering two sadistic murder scenes inside a matter of hours.

O'Hara immediately put the station on emergency traffic. Only people connected with the call that he was on were to be on the primary channel.

Then they waited. It was one o'clock in the morning.

A mass of backup arrived quickly.

As road supervisor, Sgt. Alan Baxter was the first one Keith O'Hara called. Now Sergeant Baxter and Lt. John Nobles got out of the car in the dark courtyard in front of Christa's apartment. Sergeant Baxter quickly assessed the situation. The two deputies who had made the discovery were both very shocked.

"Do you want an ambulance?" Nobles asked.

"She's not going to need an ambulance," O'Hara answered. "Her name is Christa Hoyt."

Suddenly Gail moved away from them.

"She works in Records," O'Hara went on.

Sergeant Baxter and Lieutenant Nobles looked at each other. "We'll go in," Nobles said.

O'Hara warned: "I think I heard water running somewhere inside. In the bathroom, I think. And I saw some blood on the girl."

Baxter and Nobles looked at each other. There was always the possibility that the killer was still inside. Guns were drawn.

Baxter and Nobles placed the deputies already on the scene in various areas on the property. Others were arriving from the Alachua County Sheriff's Office. They already knew the victim had been one of their own. They were supposed to be untouchable, murderers weren't supposed to get one of *them.*

By the time they were all in place, a full half-hour had passed. Nobles unlocked the door. Sergeant Baxter and Lieutenant Nobles peered into the darkness. The air conditioner was not turned on. The air was stale. Nobles and Baxter pressed forward. One was up high and one was squatting down low as they positioned themselves at opposite sides of the door. A nod between them and they moved swiftly. Covering each other, they went in with low flashlights.

Inside the small apartment, Baxter and Nobles moved as though in a minefield.

Drip . . . drip . . . drip . . .

They pointed their beams in the bathroom.

Empty.

Nobles remained outside the bathroom as Baxter pressed the flashlight beam into the corners of the room. He wanted to reach into the shower and turn the handle to stop the dripping sound, but he did not touch anything. "Nobody here," Baxter whispered. But there were bloodstains in the shower, on the floor.

The head was propped up on a bookshelf in the bedroom, facing them. The face was an ashen mask. The grisly human fragment seemed to have been deliberately placed on the shelf for shock value. Beautiful eighteen-year-old Christa Leigh Hoyt had been decapitated. A mirror had been positioned on the shelf next to the head so that her face would be the first thing one saw upon entering the bedroom.

An unexpected movement across the room . . . hands tightened on revolvers . . . a nervous burst of relief—Christa's cat.

They moved their flashlight beams to the bed and found the rest of her. A headless corpse carefully positioned at the foot of the bed.

Christa . . .

It took a moment to realize what they were seeing on the bed next to her. Two nipples, placed alongside her.

Moments passed before they could check the closets . . . under the bed . . .

Nothing.

The two policemen finally left the stifling rooms and stepped into the cool night air. Deep breaths. Eyes momentarily closed against the sights indelibly stored in their memories. The apartment was secure.

Baxter looked past the crime-scene investigators "doing their thing." He couldn't explain it, he just had a *sense* of something. He looked into the surrounding darkness. He had been a policeman for more than sixteen years and he couldn't shake it . . . the feeling that whoever was responsible for the murder was watching them, from someplace out there . . . watching them trying to sort out what he had done.

Finally he made himself think about what he had not wanted to deal with from the moment he stepped out of the car in front of Christa Hoyt's apartment. Christa's mother, Theresa Ann Garren, was a good friend of his.

It had been only nine hours since the discovery of the first two murders at Williamsburg Village Apartments.

It was a dark night. CID had locked the scene down.

They went through the procedural motions, and then they waited, nobody feeling like talking.

The second murder scene had exploded with activity. Police personnel, who had been fine-combing the bloodied apartment at Williamsburg Village, now rushed to the second murder scene. Obviously they had to determine if there was a connection.

As they piled into cars, even without official verification, most in their hearts believed that a connection would, indeed, be found. Even without knowing the similarity of details it was difficult to imagine that such brutal murders, so closely linked together in time and space, could have been coincidence.

Gainesville Police Chief Wayland Clifton arrived on the scene with other police as well as the police photographer and reporter Mitch Stacy.

When the GPD investigators arrived the Alachua County deputies barred them from entering the crime scene. "We'll fill you in . . ." It wasn't only because of jurisdictional protocol. The tiny rooms were already packed to overflowing with CID.

The Alachua County chief investigator's quiet, controlled face seemed to be drained of color even underneath his naturally ruddy complexion. It was time to move Christa.

The body, with sneakers and socks, had been positioned very carefully. There was not much blood on the floor beneath where the head would have been.

Her bed, only a little messed, had a bit of blood on it. On second glance it was clear the apartment had not been helter-skelter ransacked. The violation of personal possessions had been methodical, carefully done. Whoever had done this knew exactly what he was doing.

"Have the photographers finished with the body in this position?" The chief's voice sounded a little gruff even to himself.

"I believe so."

She had been so young. "Okay." He swallowed. He heard she had been very pretty. "Move the body back on the bed. Straighten it out . . ." He thought of the parents. "Do it easy."

When the investigative team moved the body back onto the bed from the stooped position in which it had been found, one of the men let out what seemed like a low growl.

"Easy," the inspector said, but he understood the man's rage.

In addition to the breast mutilations, the girl had been sliced from the breastbone to the pubic bone. Seemingly, the cut had been made with care. It was not a slaughter cut but a precise one. Nothing was ripped or torn. Not the act of a disgruntled boyfriend or lover. This was calculated, ceremonious, precise. On the surface, at least. Whoever did this knew exactly what he was doing—from the placement of the head, the positioning of the body, the removal of body parts, the arrangement of the nipples. The indications of obsessive needs amplified by an intensely psychotic imagination smacked of ritualistic behavior.

At both murder scenes undergarments were missing. At both a knife with a four-to-six-inch blade had been used. At both there was clear evidence of the use of adhesive tape for restraint. How much had the three young victims been aware of before death came?

Once word got out, the inspector knew that the city would be in panic. How to prevent that? He hoped the media would help but didn't think it would. Or even could.

As he considered the similarities between the two murder scenes, he watched the photographer busy himself with the second position of the body. He had seen a good many scenes of violence, but this . . . this was different. What surrounded a series of murders like this? Yes, he was already thinking in terms of a *series* of murders. What happened to a community? What happened to individuals emotionally? He looked at the faces of all who were witness to the scene of slaughter laid out before them like a ritualistic "gift." He thought again of the families that had to be told. He thought of the aftershocks—the years of pain and grief to come. They never put that part in films or on TV. Violence for entertainment. They should come and see this. The photographer was almost finished. How many angles could there be? Some entertainment . . .

He didn't need a coroner's report or autopsy to know there were body parts missing.

She might have been caught in the shower.

Psycho.

Before the lid of secrecy was put on the investigation Sheriff Lu Hindery moved toward his car, distractedly stepping into a group of reporters that had grown considerably while he was inside the apartment.

"Sheriff, can you give us a statement?"

Hindery stood there for a moment staring at the faces in front of him. He had known Christa Hoyt personally. Beautiful, skilled, ambitious. "She was sliced from her lower abdomen to her breastbone," he said. He took a breath. "She was also decapitated," and moved to his car. He didn't hear the rush of questions thrown at him after the momentary stunned silence that followed his statement.

At the Gainesville police headquarters that afternoon, crowds were gathered. Chief Wayland Clifton continued to maintain a tight air of control and detachment as he passed quickly between his car and the front door of the GPD.

"Chief Clifton," one of the young reporters called. "Chief Clifton, over here!"

He turned to look in the direction of the voice.

"Tell us about the mutilations."

He thought he recognized Cynthia Barnett of the Gainesville *Sun*. He also thought that was Mitch Stacy standing next to her. Not sure.

"Any idea who might be responsible? Was it the same guy as at Williamsburg Village?"

The chief refused to discuss similarities between the two crime scenes. He hoped reporters wouldn't get carried away with their theories. He knew they had a job to do, that their editors wanted headlines, that the more gory the headlines, the more newspapers would be sold. But there were sensitive issues here. Not only did he want to protect the families of the victims from knowing the details of the murders, he also wanted to keep the intimate particulars solely between the department and the killer. He wasn't about to let anything interfere in getting this guy. He wasn't going to permit *anything* to compromise this investigation.

"Chief Clifton . . . were they sexually assaulted?"

No, the chief wasn't ready to talk, not yet, and he surely wasn't about to speculate on what had happened without more investigation and lab work.

There was another reason for restraint. Chief Clifton knew that the underlying panic triggered by the discovery of the first two girls had only begun. He was sure the brutality of the latest murder would fan the flame.

He was right.

"Can you give us any statement at all?" Mitch Stacy pressed.

"My first objective as police chief of the City of Gainesville is to protect the city from further crimes," he said routinely as Lt. Sadie Darnell quietly stepped to his side to run interference if necessary. Almost unconsciously, Sadie had taken her first step as liaison between the department and the press. Her own feelings were hard to control. "That's it," the chief ended.

Sadie ran her fingers through her dark hair that was beginning to show traces of gray. She kept it cropped short on the top and long at the nape of her neck. She usually wore a smile and had a sense of humor. Now they were gone. She didn't say much to the reporters, most of whom she knew personally. The mutilations had already been confirmed to them by Sheriff Hindery. They could tell that enough immediate evidence had been found to support the building theory that a serial killer of hideous proportions had descended on their once peaceful community.

The double murder at Williamsburg Village Apartments no longer appeared to be an isolated case.

Reporters from the Gainesville *Sun* as well as reporters from Tampa watched solemnly as five men from the sheriff's office assisted in removing Christa Hoyt's body from her apartment. Cameras clicked with repetitive monotony. One photograph would appear in a double-page spread in People magazine.

Reporter Mitch Stacy was excited. This was, after all, the kind of story a reporter dreamt about. He had no way of knowing that he was on the threshold of an illuminating self-discovery of compassion that in his capacity as a reporter he would never have imagined possible. Right now he had the attitude of most newspapermen—to a good reporter, a bad story was a good story.

* * *

It seemed no time had passed, as though she had just closed her eyes, when Kim Norman was awakened by the persistent ringing of the phone.

"It's Michele again. I'm sorry to bother you . . ."

The girl's voice sounded strained. Kim was immediately wide-awake. "What?"

"You have to come back in to work."

"Why? What's happened? Is it about Christa?"

"I think so. Something bad, I think. They've already called CIP and Crime Scene."

"Why?"

"I don't *know.*"

"I'm on my way."

Kim already had on her shorts. She had been so tired when she got home she hadn't showered, had just fallen into bed in her bra and shorts. Now she grabbed her shirt, her shoes and her gun and ran out the door. She got dressed in the car on the drive back to the sheriff's office on SW Depot and Fourth streets, driving fast through the dark humid night. She came to a screeching halt in front of the one-story red-brick building with the American flag unfurling in the hot breeze overhead. She rushed through the glass entrance surrounded by flowers and two marble Roman-esque benches on either side almost overgrown with masses of pink impa-tiens.

The area was well lit at night even though it was quiet and looked deserted. She paused in the lobby with the huge glass cabinet holding the department's many trophies for sharpshooting and realized she was carry-ing her gun in her hand. She stopped to look through the double glass windows partitioning the large desk-littered space that separated the office of records from the lobby. She could see that none of the girls were at their jobs; they were all in a group, talking quietly.

Teesha saw Kim through the glass and motioned her in.

Before going to the right to be buzzed inside the records office, Kim caught sight of the plaque within the cabinet just to the left of the glass partition. It was from Patrick Sessions, father of nineteen-year-old Univer-sity of Florida student Tiffany Sessions, who had disappeared without a trace on February 9, 1989, after leaving her southwest Gainesville apart-ment to go jogging. In spite of a massive search for the young woman, her disappearance remained unsolved. There was also a Missing Person poster of Tiffany with a photo of the beautiful blonde smiling girl. The plaque had been donated to the sheriff's office by Patrick Sessions to thank the department for all its help in the vain search for his daughter. Usually Kim walked by without noticing it anymore. This time, for some reason, the poster seemed to jump out at her.

As she entered the office and joined the midnight shift Kim absently thought of the fax machine Patrick Sessions had also donated to the department.

"What about Nancy?" Kim inquired about her own supervisor, Nancy Carlton, once inside the records room.

"She's already been called."

"Why? Does anybody know what's going on?"

No one spoke.

Nancy Carlton arrived at the office a little before two A.M., a few moments after Kim.

"Do *you* know what's going on?" Kim asked, hoping that, as supervisor, Nancy might have gotten more information when she had been called back to duty.

"No," Nancy told her. "But I got a feeling it's going to be a long day."

"Why?"

"I don't know why. Just a feeling."

The phone began ringing as they spoke.

Teesha answered the phone. "Nancy," Teesha said, "there's a phone call for you."

Was this the answer?

"I'll take it in there," Nancy said, disappearing into her office.

There was deep silence in the records office while the women watched Nancy's door, waiting for her to come back.

Finally Nancy appeared at her door. Her eyes were red. Kim's own eyes closed under the weight of resignation. At the moment that she saw Nancy Carlton's face, she *knew* that Christa was gone. Until this moment she had not allowed herself to consider such a possibility.

"Christa's dead," Nancy said dully. "She's been murdered, they just found her."

Kim backed up involuntarily against a file cabinet for support. She just stood there, trying to sort out her feelings. And then she realized that she had no feelings. She felt numb, anaesthetized. Long moments passed until she could feel her cheeks were wet. She had other people depending on her. "You're a supervisor," she told herself sternly. "You can't lose control." At least that's what the book said.

For Kimberly Norman the next hour was spent in a blur of phone calls, questions, speculations and her attempts to lend support to the other women. It all seemed to be happening in slow motion through a haze of automatic behavior and programmed responses.

She looked up as Nancy Carlton stopped by her desk.

"Kim."

"Yes?"

"Nancy Noe just showed up. I'm going to let her run you home."

"No, I—"

"They're going to question you."

"Me? What for?"

"It seems you might have been the last to see Christa alive."

Kim thought about that for a moment . . . how Christa had bumped into her car mirror when she got out of her car . . . how Christa had invited her in . . . the implications of it all hadn't fully hit her until now.

"Oh," she said flatly.

"Nancy Noe just came in," Nancy Carlton repeated. "She'll take you home so you can shower and change. You know, before all the questions begin. I have a feeling it's going to be a real long day."

"Okay," Kim answered numbly.

In the car, Nancy Noe was grim as she drove silently through the night with Kim beside her.

"You know what happened, don't you?" Nancy finally blurted out.

"No." Kim looked at her in the dark interior of the car illuminated only by the dull glare of widely spaced streetlights. "What do you mean? What?"

"The guy . . . whoever did this . . ." Nancy swallowed . . . "he cut Christa's head off and propped it up on a shelf . . ." That last was like a whisper.

"I lost it in the car. I just had to get it out of my system. I screamed, and screamed, and screamed . . ." Kim Norman later said.

When Kim had called Christa earlier—twice—she had not really paid attention to the sound of Christa's voice on her answering machine. *Now* she realized that while she was waiting for Christa to pick up the phone, Christa had been in the silent apartment separated from her own body, the recorded voice of the answering machine all that was left of the Christa she had known.

She wished she had listened.

Once home, she took a shower while Nancy, lost in her own thoughts, waited for her. Kim's eyes teared even as the water ran over her face.

As soon as she dressed she called her grandmother in Starke twenty-five miles away. She had to hear the reassuring sound of the old woman's voice. Now. This minute. And she had to tell her what had happened to her friend.

"I'm okay, Granny," she finally said. "No matter what you hear, I'm all right. *Okay?*"

"Yes, Kim," her granny said, not believing a word of it.

Kim's supervisor Nancy Carlton looked closely at her as she reappeared at the Alachua County sheriff's office, this time dressed in uniform. The first thing one usually noticed about Kimberly Norman was a sweet smile. Somebody said it preceded her by several seconds like the high beams of an auto. Then one noticed that she was short and a bit heavy for her height. She had a pale round face, dark eyes and almost-shoulder-length ash-blonde hair cut in a modified Afro style. Tonight her face was paler than usual, with no smile.

Kim was questioned the whole of Monday, and somewhere throughout the long hours of questioning it occurred to her, oddly, that Monday was her day off.

> I knew I might have been a victim the very first day when they were trying to pinpoint a time when she was murdered. They said she had come home from playing racquetball instead of going to the party we were going to go to. She had gotten some chicken and some donuts. They were never eaten by her. They were left on the table. I guess those pigs ate it. I guess when they got finished with the murder, they had worked up an appetite. There's a lot of anger and hate and a lot of emotions that come out at this time. I realize I could have been a victim and that I'm lucky . . .

It wasn't until 11:00 p.m. that night that Kim Norman was released to go home. Lieutenant Jones had been assigned to drive her home in his car while Sgt. Joe Moro followed behind in her car. On the silent ride they heard on the radio that the Gainesville Bank on Archer Road, just blocks away from Christa Hoyt's apartment, had been robbed during the afternoon. Enmeshed as they were in far deeper concerns, the brief news item made little impression on them.

Just another robbery. The time would come, though, when they would remember this particular bank robbery very clearly:

> "I had returned to work on Thursday," Kim stated, "because I had been off on Wednesday. The day I returned to work the state brought in a crisis team and they sat with us all night because it was really hard to deal with the press. The press had no understanding of what it was like to receive the calls from them about someone that we knew and loved. The other girls in the offices

were just as devastated. A lot of them were hurt, angry. They couldn't understand why."

Later that night, on her first day back at work when things had calmed down a bit, Sergeant Baxter stopped by Kim's desk with two cups of coffee. They were good friends and both needed to talk supportively.

Then, knowing he had been one of the people at the scene, Kim began to ask questions about what he had found. He told her about how the police had removed the drainage system under the apartment.

"Why?"

"It looks like most of the damage was done to her in the shower," he said between sips of coffee. "I think she was strangled . . . the way she died . . . and then her head was cut off . . ."

Kim stared off. "Do you think . . . I mean, did she know what was being done to her?"

He hesitated.

"Please tell me."

He looked at Kim closely, wondering whether he should go into specifics. What he saw was a seemingly calm professional looking back at him. Okay. "I believe," he said quietly, "that she was restrained with adhesive tape and raped before she was killed."

Silence. Then: "There was evidence of rape?"

"Yes."

Restrained. Adhesive tape. Christa knew what was happening to her, all right. That would always be the part that hurt the most—the thought for Kim of Christa's last terrifying moments before she died.

"And then," he said, "he cleaned up. Washed her with soap and water."

They stared at each other, each trying to absorb the reality of the act and the bizarre needs that motivated it.

"The other murders too?"

"Adhesive, restraint, rape, cleaning up. Yes."

"Destroying evidence?"

"I hear it's going to be a forensic nightmare."

Silence again for a long while.

"Are you okay, Kim?" Baxter finally asked.

She paused before she nodded. "I believe they broke into her apartment before she got home, saw the uniforms, went out of the apartment and waited for her to come back." Kim spoke quietly, with a conviction born of hours of intensely trying to reconstruct the murder of her friend, in an effort to *understand* it. "Her uniforms had a badge on them, a sheriff's office patch. That's what I believe, that they went outside and waited for her to come home. They wanted some kind of revenge on her because she worked for the sheriff's office."

"You keep saying *they.*"

"Could one person have pushed that bookcase across the room? One person alone?"

"It would be hard. But adrenalin . . ."

"Well, we'll see," she said, sticking to her convictions. "I say there was more than one."

No one would ever convince Kim that only one man could have moved that heavy bookcase across the room to the window. It was too bulky, too heavy. It had to be two, not one.

3

Panic, Rumor, Security and the Media

Newspapers emptied off the stands and out of the vending machines almost as quickly as they were in place for sale. The early stories in the local Gainesville *Sun,* mostly written by Mitch Stacy, Tom Lyons, Cynthia Barnett and Ronald Dupont, Jr., were gruesome even in their brevity:

CHRISTA HOYT WAS DECAPITATED.

HER BREASTS AND THOSE OF AT LEAST ONE OTHER VICTIM WERE MUTILATED.

Word had spread quickly throughout the college community even without benefit of headlines. What kind of madness had come into their community? The suddenness of the murders, the visions of a lurking killer with a knife, the viciousness of the crimes—all of it increased the sense of vulnerability. Many students on the campuses of the University of Florida and Santa Fe Community College, all of whom identified with the deaths of their schoolmates, whether they knew them personally or not, tried to reconstruct what had happened. Any thought that the first killings might have been the work of someone who knew Christina and Sonja was quickly dissipated with the murder of Christa Leigh Hoyt. The three didn't even attend the same colleges. Christina and Sonja had been freshmen at the University of Florida, Christa was a sophomore at Santa Fe. Deep within the veils of the mystery was a stark reality—a vicious slasher in their midst . . . "slashed from lower abdomen to breastbone . . ."

Another Ripper.

But this time it wasn't nineteenth-century England. The victims weren't common streetwalkers of London's seamy Whitechapel district. This time it was open season on beautiful, nubile college students in the thirteenth best place to live in the whole U.S. of A.

"But who's superstitious?" said one pale young sophomore in business management who always read Money magazine.

*   *   *

As they sat in her black Toyota, Jenny Kanne was annoyed that she had to loosen her belt. Short, red-haired and rather heavy, she had gained additional pounds since last week. Unlike her roommate, Amelia Marshall, who was sitting in the passenger seat, Jenny hated exercise. Weighing in at 158 pounds, Jenny found herself thinking she was probably born to be fat. Well, she had no intention of giving up eating. It was one of the few great pleasures in life.

She slammed last semester's gerontology notes in the back seat of the car as she and Amelia pulled up in front of Williamsburg Village. Gerontology was Jenny's major at the University of Florida, but she didn't feel like gerontology at this moment. All of her hidden sleuthing instincts had been aroused. Actually, she had always been a little ashamed of her morbid fascination with murder but she was a born snoop and an avid reader of mysteries. Now she found herself deeply involved in the mental process of detection and wished that she could be a fly on the wall of the Gainesville Police Department's offices.

Jenny and Amelia got out of the car now to get closer to the murder scene. They could see the heavy police presence. Investigators had not mentioned evidence of sexual assault, although the student rumor mill had rape in the picture of both murder scenes.

"Well, I for one can't stand all the rumors!" Amelia said to Jenny. A contrast to Jenny, Amelia was petite, dark and athletic, a natural tennis player and a vegetarian. A shiver ran up her spine as she scanned the sprawling complex. She remembered they had almost taken an apartment there themselves. She had always been sort of tentative about things . . . that was one of the reasons, she said, she had picked botany as her major, envisioning a future of quiet research and contemplation of nature's secrets. It was also one of the reasons she liked being with Jenny, who, being so sure of herself all the time, was her exact opposite in temperament.

"There are lots of rumors going around right now," Amelia continued with a tug at her lower lip with her forefingers. "Everyone says it was rape, but maybe not. The police didn't say it was rape."

Jenny shook her head in that way she had when she was certain about something. "Even if they weren't actually raped, these were sex crimes!" she said.

"You don't *know* that for a fact."

"They were nude, weren't they? That means the sexual part was there. No *question* about it."

"I guess . . ." And Amelia tugged again at her lip.

"Stop *doing* that!"

Amelia dropped her hand.

"Did you tell the police about that guy?" Jenny demanded.

"You mean the peeping Tom?"

"Him!"

"No."

"Well, we'll have to tell them, won't we?"

"Jenny, I don't want to get involved . . ."

Jenny took Amelia's arm and pulled her toward one of the policemen newly installed at Williamsburg Village.

Amelia had been alone in their new apartment a few days earlier when they were moving into Gatorwood Apartments on Archer Road. Gatorwood was on SW Sixteenth Street, less than a mile from Williamsburg Village. Perhaps, Jenny insisted, there was a connection between the peeping Tom incident and what happened at Williamsburg. Shortly after dark that night Jenny had gone to the laundry room, then next door to the swimming pool directly behind Gatorwood's main lobby. She had jumped into the shallow end of the pool and stood waist-deep with an open book sprawled over the damp side. It was a hot night. Great way to hide her bulk, wait for the end of the laundry cycle, get a few more chapters in and cool off all at the same time. She had left Amelia looking for an extension cord.

Amelia had been rummaging in a large corrugated box on the rug in the middle of her bedroom thinking how lucky they were to have gotten this beautiful two-bedroom apartment on the main floor. Just outside their door were the tall graceful palm trees, and from their patio they could see the well-kept grounds edged with crepe myrtle and brilliant fuchsia impatiens. Both she and Jenny liked it that they were close to the bank of mailboxes next to the jam-packed bicycle racks. The area was convenient and well lit at night. Good. There was always a lot of mail coming from their families up north.

Finally Amelia found the electrical cord at the bottom of the box. And, unaccountably, she suddenly felt uncomfortable. Chilly. She turned abruptly toward the uncurtained window and caught sight of a man staring at her. She gasped.

He did not move. He looked to be in his late thirties or early forties. He wore green fatigues or workclothes of some kind, but he didn't look like a maintenance man, and he didn't look like he belonged there either. He certainly didn't look like a student.

It was when Amelia pulled back a step toward her open closet doors that he slipped away.

She rushed through the little hallway past the bathroom she shared with Jenny to the sliding glass door at the short side of the living room. She wasn't sure if she had locked it when she came in from her late afternoon sunbath on their patio. She liked being on the main floor, but looking up to see a strange man staring at her through a bedroom window . . . that was something *else.*

She had not locked the sliding glass doors.

Unlike Amelia, Jenny had a New York City mentality when it came to keeping doors locked. She was always warning Amelia about such things. Now, as Amelia punched the latch shut, she looked to see if she could spot the man from the patio side of the apartment. He was gone.

Jenny took over. Yes, there would always be peeping Toms, but Jenny gave her another lecture on "locking up," accompanied by a verbal dissertation on the potentially psychopathic sexual component in voyeuristic impulses . . .

"How do you know so much about it?" Amelia said.

"I read!"

"Why about things like that?"

"It's *interesting.*"

After that neither Amelia nor Jenny thought much of the incident again, until now.

"I'm not telling them my *name,*" Amelia said as Jenny stopped in front of the policeman.

While people like Amelia Marshall offered personal "tips," the Gainesville Police Department was being inundated with calls from as far away as California seeking to confirm the persistent rumor that a serial killer had struck the college community of Gainesville. Knowing how the story would be sensationalized and exploited, local officials were not yet willing to admit that the three murders might be the work of a serial killer. They left speculations like that to the media.

The young uniformed policewoman with a handgun clipped to her belt was seated at the huge curved front desk in the main reception area of the Gainesville Police Station. She nodded to Lt. Sadie Darnell over the receiver clasped in her damp palm as Sadie entered the building and moved quickly through the reception area.

"Wait," she whispered to Sadie. "Wait! What do I tell all these jokers?"

"Nothing," Sadie said in her thick southern drawl. "Absolutely nothing."

Much more work had to be done on the investigation before any questions could be answered. Besides, Sadie knew they were hoping that the three homicides were the work of a spree killer who had sated his bloodlust, at least temporarily.

The policewoman sighed at Sadie's evasion and buzzed her through the thick double glass doors into the inner arteries of the station.

The young woman in Communications was flushed as she fielded the torrent of calls. A uniformed man seated next to her beside the computer felt just as overwhelmed. The questions were gory.

"Were the girls mutilated?" "Were they raped?" "Is it true that body parts were missing?" "What's being done about it?" "Is it a serial killer?" "Do you have any leads, suspects?" "How did the killer enter the apartments?"

And the most important personal question of all, this one from an unidentified young female voice: "Are we in jeopardy? I heard a noise outside my window . . ."

While the phones continued to ring off the hook, the policewoman at the front desk paused long enough to put in a call through the standing desk microphone at her right elbow, hoping to catch Chief Clifton, knowing he was back in the building. Maybe he could fill them in on what the current official word was to be. Not surprisingly, the chief wasn't answering the call.

She took another call: "Gainesville Police Department."

This one was from ABC-TV. She winced. With no preamble other than identifying himself with his network, the male voice demanded: "Tell us about the decapitation. Where was the rest of her found?"

She could almost hear the six o'clock sound bites.

While the front desk ran interference with the calls, Sadie took the steps two at a time to her second-floor office. Although at this time police did not want officially to label the homicides the work of a serial killer, the third murder prompted the immediate formation of a task force. The homicide had occurred just outside Gainesville city proper, within the Alachua County jurisdiction, and the speed with which the task force was assembled attested not only to the seriousness of the situation but to the local officials' ability to get things done. Right on target, Sadie thought.

Sheriff Lu Hindery had gone back to his office to try to give some help to his distraught young staff, but as soon as he arrived the police chief was on the line. He grabbed up the receiver in his thick palm. "Sheriff Hindery here."

"Lu? Wayland Clifton here."

"I know what you're going to say."

"It's not our homicide and your homicide. They're linked."

"I know."

"All jurisdictional lines are drawn. This is the same guy. I'd bet my life on it."

"A task force?"

"The works."

Hindery nodded. "I'll draw up the mutual-aid agreement."

The investigative task force would include top crime-scene technicians and investigators from both the Gainesville Police Department and the Alachua County Sheriff's Office as well as fifty representatives from the Florida Department of Law Enforcement, thirty from the Florida Highway Patrol and ten of the top criminal behavioral specialists from the Federal Bureau of Investigation in Quantico, Virginia, all of whom had extensive experience with the country's growing phenomenon of serial killers.

Good to get the FBI in on this! the chief thought. The Bureau was an invaluable source of information and analytical input since the Behavioral Science Unit had been formed over ten years ago. In 1977, when it was statistically determined that motiveless serial killings had reached epidemic proportions, a pilot program to study the phenomenon was begun at the Behavioral Science Unit at the FBI Academy in Quantico, Virginia. Under the supervision of Robert K. Ressler, M.S.; John E. Douglas, M.S.; Ann W. Burgess, R.N., D.N.Sc.; and Ralph B. D'Agostino, Ph.D., the program was to become highly effective in drawing up profiles of serial killers to help in apprehending the perpetrators. The profiles proved to be remarkably accurate once the killers were caught.

With Capt. R. B. Ward as task force commander, J.O. Jackson as commander of the Florida Department of Law Enforcement and Hamilton, the huge task force with three separate but united chiefs was an impressive group. Many had extensive experience on cases that had made history. Commander Jackson, for example, had been the principal agent on the Ted Bundy case.

By the end of the official formation of the task force, more than a hundred experts would be involved in the investigation of the three murders, and hundreds of support staff would commit the major portion of their time to the case as well.

Early in the investigation Lt. Sadie Darnell offered to be Chief Clifton's public information officer.

"Someone has to deal with the press. I'll be your PIO," she told him, "and we can get someone from the sheriff's office too. Kind of like an extension of both departments."

"That's out of the front line," the chief said, aware of Sadie's preferred involvement.

"I don't mind staying in that capacity," she told him.

"You could catch a lot of heat," Wayland warned her.

Sadie nodded and shrugged.

"Because some people will wonder," the chief went on, "are you saying too much? Are you saying too little? Nobody's going to be happy."

Sadie nodded. "We'll be out there. You tell us what you want the papers to know and that's what they'll get."

The chief punched absently on the stapler on top of his mahogany desk cluttered with police memorabilia and family photos. Smiling faces, children, family.

Those girls.

He shook his head imperceptibly. "I'll talk to Lu. You're right. We'll get someone from his department too."

"Spenser Mann?" she suggested.

"I'll check with the sheriff."

Young, personable, Lt. Spenser Mann would be able to handle himself, the chief thought. Sadie would be an effective spokesman for the police department and Spenser would be equally effective for the sheriff's office.

"I want to build up credibility between our PIOs and the media so that if we have some reporters covering the case and they've heard something . . . a rumor, whatever . . . they'll know they can take it to you guys and you can help them with it. Maybe not answer it directly but let them know if they've gotten themselves somewhere way off in left field."

"Left field is going to be crowded," Sadie said.

At Gatorwood Apartments on Archer Road the drapes were drawn tightly across the sliding glass doors in the living room of Jenny and Amelia's apartment.

They had some courses they wanted to change at the college. Students usually queued up by seven A.M. for the drop/add lines and they had to hurry to be early in line since University of Florida President John Lombardi was going to speak to the students at Union Reitz Hall about what had been happening and they didn't want to miss that.

Jenny watched Amelia with a frown as she slipped into a pair of short-shorts.

"What?" Amelia said.

"You're making yourself grist for the psycho mill. What are you trying to do? Everything you wear is a neon sign. *Look at me, I'm sexy . . . I'm available.*" Jenny was really upset. Amelia, after all, fitted the profile of each of the three girls who had just been murdered—college student, dark-haired, petite. "Everything you wear turns up the testosterone level in the guys."

"Come on!" But Amelia turned and flared toward the mirror and saw it was true. She did have the kind of body that turned heads. She had always been proud of it. She also knew she sort of liked to flash it around. But now . . .

Jenny's voice softened as she saw Amelia's face. "Save it for someone special, honey. Why flash it to everyone out there? And out there are sickos."

"You sound like my mother."

"I'm your *friend.*"

"What about you?"

"Me? Hey, I don't have to worry. I'm heavy. Guys turn their heads *away* from me. But you . . ."

They remembered the peeping Tom.

"Just keep it a little under wraps, there are too many creeps out there."

Suddenly Amelia was crying. "Damn it, it's all I have—"

"No, it isn't," Jenny told her gently. "There's a lot more to you than a body. Take it from me, Amelia, your friend."

Amelia reached for a long pair of loose white slacks. It was just the beginning. Lives were going to be changed forever . . .

As expected, the news had hit the campus hard. The heavy gloom was almost palpable. Talk was subdued. Reactions underlaid with genuine fear that were the groundwork for a panic to come.

Still, Jenny and Amelia learned that to their surprise some new arrivals hadn't yet read a newspaper or heard about the murders. And some of them had queued up by seven A.M. that morning for the drop/add routine.

"Well, what happened?" asked one girl.

"Where are you from?" Jenny asked.

"Manhattan."

"Hey, I'm from Long Island. By way of Westbury."

"Nice to meet you. So? Are you going to tell me what everybody's so excited about?"

Jenny told her.

But by the time they got to the Reitz Union Hall that Monday afternoon it was obvious that everyone there *had* heard about the murders. It was also clear that officials had joined forces to tear down the bureaucratic lines that usually separated them. Mr. Deeds of the task force and university administrative and academic officials had pooled ideas with leaders from the Division of Student Affairs. *Pull together* was the priority of the day.

Michael Browne, president of the student body, sharp, strong and determined, spoke to the assembled students first.

"Everybody's scared," he said. "We need to show to whoever it is out there that this is a solid community. Think about your safety and the safety of your friends. Everyone on campus and in the county can help make Gainesville safer for themselves and for each other. Females may be most at risk, but we're all at risk. If you have a car, offer rides, even if it means staying at work a little longer. Walk friends, classmates, staff members and professors to cars, dorms, sorority and fraternity houses. There's safety in numbers! Anyone going somewhere at night should plan ahead. Find others who need to go to the same place or nearby. Stick *together.*"

"Can you imagine?" Jenny whispered. "We're talking about how not to get killed."

Amelia nodded and felt shivers inside.

As President John Lombardi stepped up to the microphone, Michael Browne moved next to Myra Morgan, director of campus activities. The old lines between staff and student had been erased.

"I'm concerned by what I'm hearing from students," he whispered to her. "Some of it's understandable fear, but some of it's way past fear and that worries me."

"I know," she whispered back, remembering Provost Andrew Sorensen's memo urging each member of the faculty to devote some class time to discuss how best the university community could respond to the murders.

"The staff members," Myra Morgan whispered to Browne, "are as much a problem as the students."

Now they looked up at President Lombardi as a deep hush fell over the crowd.

"As the parent of a young daughter who starts next week at the University of Michigan," he began, "I can understand your fears as well as the fears expressed by your parents. The case is being investigated by the Gainesville Police Department. I deeply regret that we at the university cannot provide more information about the deaths. We're just not able to be much more specific. Everybody's understandably concerned, but I plead for calm and control throughout our university community. We have to consider the rights of the victims' families and the needs of effective law enforcement."

Lombardi took a deep breath. "The murders have shocked us into the realization that universities are no longer cocoons, cloistered from the rest of the world. It has made us realize that universities live in the real world. Sometimes we come to believe we live a charmed existence, but in fact we do not."

He took another deep breath, wondering whether or not he was saying any of the right things. "The senseless violence comes with no reason, and the loss has no explanations . . ."

There was a deep silence as he spoke.

"As we know, the random violence in our civilization and culture is unfortunately high. These kinds of events are so random it's hard to deal with them in any systematic way. Still, this is not a community given to hysteria. It has responded to these events with the kind of stable maturity you would expect. We will use every tool at our command to urge students, faculty and staff alike to take safety precautions. We also urge you to get counseling if your fears prey on you. Student escort services and on-campus security will be stepped up. *No one* has to walk alone, either literally or figuratively."

Good stuff, Mitch Stacy thought as he looked at the faces around him and jotted down notes. The words were strong, but the fear and resentment in the room was palpable. He had his byline.

RESENTMENT

by Mitch Stacy

Many of the residents of the SW 16th Street complex were clearly shaken Monday, and the lack of information from police on the killings seemed to fuel the fire . . .

President Lombardi's plea for calm did not take. They no longer believed that the first two murders were an isolated aberration. Now they believed that the nightmare had only begun.

The news and subsequent rumors overshadowed the usual excitement and festive chaos of the first day of fall semester. Some residents had moved into the complex just days ago, and others had returned Sunday to prepare to start another semester. Few residents had met their neighbors . . .

Dave Krupsezaki, a twenty-one-year-old student from Miami, said to a girl standing next to him, "With what happened last year with Tiffany Sessions, everybody is afraid."

"Oh God, yes . . ." she murmured. "Tiffany Sessions. I remember her. Do you suppose there's any connection?"

In Miami, Tiffany's father, Patrick Sessions, was wondering the same thing. There had never been any closure on his grief. Not knowing what had happened to Tiffany was the worst part, and now, a terrible sense of *déjà vu* overcame him as he pored over the morning papers. He, too, couldn't help wondering if there could be a link between these murders and Tiffany's disappearance from Gainesville the previous year?

Officials knew that they had serious problems. With students moving in daily and with all the related activity that goes with it, people are especially vulnerable to violent strangers who may pass as new neighbors or workers . . .

Advice was beginning to come at the students from all sides . . . "Call home!" cried public-service announcement broadcasts . . . "If you haven't spoken to your parents in the last twenty-four hours, call them to reassure them you're okay. Let them hear your voices . . ."

Campus radio stations were also broadcasting announcements to call home. It wasn't only to ease parental worries but to alleviate some of the burden on the Gainesville police and the Alachua County sheriff. They had been flooded with calls from parents who could not reach their sons and daughters, and the tied-up lines were impacting the investigation.

As Hoyt's neighbor, Glenda Williamson said, "It was really a good time to do a murder in Gainesville . . . A murderer could hide in so many ways. He could pass as a new neighbor, a student moving in, a moving man, a delivery man . . ."

Mitch was riding high on adrenalin.

At the Monday night police press conference Lt. Sadie Darnell stood behind the dais set up outdoors. The media had collected on the doorstep of the long, three-story red-brick Gainesville Police Headquarters. The podium at the crown of the crowd had been hastily set up. It was weighed down with almost two dozen microphones leading into national television stations as well as the local ABC, WCJB, WOGX, WUFT. Also represented were all the local radio stations from WRUF/AM to WYKS/FM.

Along with their fellow students, Jenny Kanne and Amelia Marshall stood on the periphery of the crowd waiting for Lieutenant Darnell to begin her press conference. As usual, Lieutenant Darnell was the picture of professional composure, but she knew the demand for information was already disintegrating into a serious problem since there was so little information to be given out.

Lt. Spenser Mann of the Alachua County Sheriff's Office moved up to the dais next to her. She nodded to Spenser and let him take the lead.

"I can offer no information," Lieutenant Mann said, "about investigators' theories on how the killer or killers entered the two apartments. All I can do at this time is to urge caution and reasonable security efforts by everyone." He looked out at the young faces. "Especially young women encountering strangers."

"Are the bizarre mutilations the major link between the killings?" someone asked suddenly.

"I can't confirm that. We don't know for sure if the victims were linked while alive in any way."

Jenny nudged Amelia. "That's how rumors get started," Jenny whispered. "Now we'll hear that the victims knew each other."

"I already heard they had partied together last night," Amelia whispered back.

But Sadie was saying, "Investigators have no reason to think they even knew each other. They were young female students who died violently in their apartments. We believe there are similarities and correlations between the homicides, but there doesn't seem to be a direct connection between the victims."

"What about the other bodies?" came a male voice from the rear. "We heard that several more have been found."

"No," Lt. Darnell answered firmly as the attention shifted to the students hovering in the rear. "There's no truth to that."

By now, mid-afternoon, there was a pervasive story that a fourth victim, a female nursing student from Shands Hospital, was missing or found dead. Although the PIOs flatly denied the existence of a fourth victim, the widespread rumor had been translated into belief.

That's all we need, Sadie thought, those kinds of stories. But she also knew that it didn't help that the department had been forced to adopt the position of silence on all details of the murders.

She could still hear Chief Clifton's words, spoken the day she had offered her services as Public Information Officer: "We're going to get this guy. Nothing is going to stop us. And when we do he's going to go to trial. I don't want *anything* to jeopardize that. Watch what you say. Even about what you've seen here today. Anything that we say—it will be easy to make inferences from what we did initially—even such things as the uniform and covert protection of the city, to trace back to something that's going to be presented in the trial . . ."

Lieutenants Darnell and Mann deliberately made little or no reference to details of the three murders, not even the method of entry into the apartments. But they knew that when hard facts were missing, speculation could take on the hard edge of fact. Sadie was also well aware that the kids were very nervous; that they felt knowing the details of what had happened might help them to avoid potentially lethal situations for themselves.

Mitch Stacy turned to see if he could put a face to the voice that came from the rear. "We have a right to know . . ."

Privately, Sadie agreed.

"In order to protect ourselves!"

Sadie braced herself. "Sorry, no details."

"And the mutilations? Were there mutilations or *not?*"

It was Lieutenant Mann who confirmed that all three bodies had been mutilated, with some body parts removed.

"So that's what they were looking for in the dumpsters!" Jenny muttered to Amelia. "God . . ."

Mitch Stacy found it interesting that students had pushed themselves into a press conference, their questions directly reflecting the growing panic inside the student community.

"I heard one of the girls had been decapitated and her breasts mutilated," another male voice called out.

A tremor ran through the crowd.

"And the girls at Williamsburg Apartments were badly cut."

"I read in the papers that one had her nipples cut off—"

"Why are they saying that kind of stuff out loud!" Jenny said angrily, aware of Amelia's growing pallor. "It just pumps up the panic."

While Sadie thought, how the hell do these things leak out?

"What about the fourth victim?" another student shouted up to Mann and Sadie.

"*No.* Again, there is no basis to that," Spenser Mann insisted. "Lots of false rumors are being spread around. To help stop them and help diminish some of the fear, we urge you to call up your parents and tell them you're okay."

"We still can't get through, the phones are jammed."

"And lots of us don't have phone hookups yet," called out a coed. "I just moved in."

"Make an effort," Sadie added firmly. "Keep trying. By this afternoon the University of Florida Foundation will have put its fundraising phone banks at the disposal of students. Take advantage of them. Also, if you have to walk at night, travel only in well-lighted areas and buddy-up!"

Amelia whispered, "Who feels like going anyplace, anyway?"

And she thought about how in 1986 Gainesville had made headlines when the Florida Department of Law Enforcement charted a more than thirty percent increase in crime, mostly in burglaries and other property crimes. According to FBI statistics the rise made Gainesville rank number one in Florida and number four in the United States in crime increase. Then, go figure, it was singled out again as a wonderful place to live. Amelia found herself badly missing her home on Long Island.

Unlike Amelia, Jenny found herself feeling a rush of excitement. Lt. Sadie Darnell was what she had always wanted to be. She was majoring in gerontology—"How can a career like that miss in a retirement state like Florida?" her mother had said—and her father wanted her to be an English teacher, but she was more interested in crime. Go figure.

"It's ghoulish," Amelia was saying.

"Someone has to think about these things," Jenny said quietly, and looked at Lieutenant Darnell. How had she ever gotten herself stuck in *gerontology* . . .

"For a while Gainesville will face a certain stigma from the murders," Lieutenant Darnell was saying. "Some things we don't have any control over. We recognize that we lost something. Not only lives. We lost a lot of innocence for Gainesville. We'll have to work to get it back . . ."

As expected, Gainesville's telephone lines would continue to be jammed with students calling home to parents and with parents calling just to hear the sound of their children's voices. Fear was an intrinsic part of the hour. By Monday night female students were asking male friends to sleep in their apartments, since only females seemed to be targeted by the murderer. All coed restrictions, real or self-imposed, were thrown out in light of the intense fears. Others who did not yet know any young men and who didn't want to take the chance of admitting strangers into their apartments even if they were students—"You never *know*"—clustered five and six to a room.

But few slept well, whatever the arrangements. Rumors would persist throughout the day that more victims had been found, and officials would continue to deny it.

And yet . . .

Later, at their Gatorwood apartment, Jenny turned up the TV news. "Listen to this." It was the governor's press release.

Through his press secretary Jon Peck, Gov. Bob Martinez contacted law enforcement officials in Gainesville on Monday. His press secretary and the governor wanted the Florida Department of Law Enforcement involved because there "are going to be concerned parents all over the state," said Jon Peck. "It's a local crime and yet it's not a local crime."

The governor pledged full support from the FDLE in a press release from his office:

> What a shocking, tragic way to start a new school year. I am determined that every possible resource is made available to help capture those responsible for these murders. Murder under any circumstances is horrible, but these killings of innocent women on the threshold of life are particularly senseless.

Despite all of the student crisis coordination, all the suggestions, all the reassurances, the bottom line was that a madman was loose and killing beautiful young coeds. Disbelief and fear hung in the air as heavily as the humidity. Students who had never met before now reached out to one another, sharing whispered conversations as they stood about in the white glare of the blistering sun.

And beneath the disbelief, the shared confidences, the common feelings of shock and grief, was the unspoken suspicion: *Could the murderer have been one of them? A student?*

That night at the Union Reitz Café the murders were the subject at every table. Shocked and uncertain, students crowded in and outside, discussing the events.

"We've lived at Williamsburg Village two years and we always thought it was safe."

Another UF student who lived alone in the same building as the girl who spoke said she was so terrified, her mother drove from Ocala to stay with her at her apartment Sunday night. "Even so, I still didn't sleep last night."

"What can you really say about it?" The girl was a tall blonde junior who had lived in the Williamsburg Village complex for two years. "It was two doors down from me. I know I'm looking for a new apartment. All the girls are."

"Not me!" said Jenny Kanne. "He's not going to make me run."

"But—"

"We'll protect ourselves."

"How?"

"I'm thinking of buying a gun!"

"You think the dorms are safe? Not on your life!" Jake Fellows said, banging his fist on his table, surrounded by students he knew from the previous semester. "I've seen people without keys getting in behind someone who unlocks the door and just lets them in. I've done it myself . . . followed someone in . . . when I've forgotten my own key. They never ask me if I belong, they just let me in."

"It seems to me the buddy system can help," Jenny Kanne said. "It has to be a sink-or-swim kind of thing."

"Well, I resent not knowing more," Jake's girlfriend Paula said. "Did the guy break in? Did the girls let him in? Did they know him? Why don't the police *tell* us some of these things? We need to know to *protect* ourselves."

"You girls have to assume the worst," Jake said, gulping a diet soda—he was so thirsty all the time, and since this had happened he couldn't get enough to drink—"and protect yourselves against every possibility."

"And whatever you do," his friend John Sandson joined in, *"don't* walk alone anymore."

But many others felt that walking together wasn't the solution either. Maybe you could feel more secure with others, but that was about all.

"It's a false sense of security," Jenny Kanne said. "Guys like the one who did these things are cowards. They never put *themselves* at any risk.

They work *indoors.* They need privacy and time to do all the dirty stuff their sick minds can think of."

People looked at each other, some privately imagining what had been done behind closed doors.

"Still . . . the Indians are attacking."

They turned to look at the young man with pale blond hair who spoke from the nearby table. "We have to circle the wagons."

He was an incoming freshman. No one knew him. And most didn't want to. A stranger.

Amelia, though, felt sorry for him. She smiled at him, ready to introduce herself until Jenny kicked her under the table, as if to say this was not the time to make new friends.

"Do you want us to come with you?" Jake asked when they were leaving the Union Reitz.

"Yes," Amelia said quickly.

"No," Jenny broke in. "We're all right."

"Jenny!"

"We've got something to do," she said to Jake.

"Be careful, then."

"Sure, thanks."

They got into the car. "What do we have to do?" Amelia protested.

"I want to go see where it happened."

"No! No *way!* You're crazy."

Jenny had already started the Toyota.

"Who do you think you are, Sherlock Holmes, for God's sake?"

"I've got to see it."

"Why?"

"I don't know. Lock your door. It's okay."

Amelia did not want to go but Jenny was insistent. They locked themselves in Jenny's little black Toyota and drove south on Thirty-fourth Street.

"This is morbid!" Amelia said, shaking her head.

"I want to get close to it."

"Why?"

"Just come on, okay?"

Amelia shut up then. When Jenny was like this it did no good to argue.

They came to SW Sixteenth Street and made the right turn at the bank. Once they had driven the couple of blocks west to NW Thirty-fourth they pulled over to the side of the road. Except for sheriff's deputies standing guard over the duplex where the murdered girl had lived and a few police cars and vans still blocking the intersection, it was actually fairly quiet at Christa Hoyt's apartment, not like Williamsburg Village, which was inundated with curiosity-seekers. The secluded cluster of old single-story buildings was almost deserted by comparison.

Mitch Stacy wrote in the *Sun:*

A few residents of the adjacent mobile home park occasionally walked over to talk to deputies, who were questioning every motorist that drove in about anything suspicious that they might have seen or heard in the past few days.

The manager of Pinehurst Park, the nearby mobile home park, said many residents were lamenting the senseless death of a young woman more than worrying about their safety in the quiet, tree-shaded park.

"It doesn't really matter how close it was," said the manager, who would not give her name. "Here's a young girl that was murdered, and for what? I've lived here nineteen years and I feel secure here because I have neighbors, and if they hear anything they'll be over here pounding on the door."

Glenda Williamson, who lived in the building behind Hoyt's, said news of the murder frightened her. "I'm just going to be careful," she said, adding that she might not even open the door at night for her cats.

Williamson said Hoyt had lived alone for a time since a roommate had moved out. Hoyt's only companion lately was a kitten.

One wondered what happened to Christa's kitten?

The flag at the Alachua County Sheriff's Office flew at half-mast.

Kim Norman lay in bed thinking about what had happened. That last weekend when Christa had died was still blurry. You block things out of your mind, Kim thought, and try to forget things that hurt too badly.

Suddenly she remembered the button.

She had lost a button off her jacket that last morning when she drove Christa home. She had asked Christa if she would hang onto it until they got to her house so she could put it in her purse. By the time they arrived at the secluded complex they had both forgotten about it. Strange to think about that button now. Kim never did get it back. The jacket was still missing a button. Kim stared up at the ceiling and wondered if she would wear it again. Somehow she doubted it.

Then she found herself wondering what would have happened if . . . Her gun was in her car . . . Kim's friend had said she couldn't get over the fact that Kim, too, might have been a victim if she had accepted Christa's invitation to "come in for a minute." At least if she had been there she might have been able to help prevent what happened. And then again, she most likely would not have taken the revolver she kept in her car. And even if she had, would that have been an equalizer against a vicious madman? But everything happens for a reason and God makes things happen the way they do for a reason, she told herself, still wondering why she had been spared. But for how long? Well, from now on she would say what was on her mind. She would let people know how she felt because she might not be here tomorrow to say it. She would voice her opinions, try to help people, not be rude, try to be nice. Because, she thought, because . . . there was no time for anger.

Then, when everything had quieted down some, when they were all talked out, when classes began again and other subjects came into conversations, when law-enforcement personnel concentrated their efforts on the three murders and the two murder scenes and special agents began to move out into the community to begin the task of seeking out the endless details of movement and behavior that would fit into the large jigsaw puzzle of the investigation—it happened.

The killer struck again.

4

Two More: The First Male

Tuesday, August 28—"The Place to Be"

Less than two miles away was the eighteen-year-old Gatorwood Apartments on Archer Road. A white-and-red-trimmed sign outside, topped with a happy cartoon alligator in a red shirt, hailed Gatorwood Apartments as "The Place to Be." It was a busy twenty-building complex that accommodated as many as five hundred residents. Most were students from the University of Florida or Santa Fe Community College. Seventy-five percent were undergraduates. It had a reputation among local law enforcement officials for being relatively free of crime.

Carol Hyde, the manager of the Gatorwood Apartments, listened to the young man's voice on the other end of the line. He sounded worried. "Who're you?" she asked.

"Khris Pascarella. I tried to get them on the phone late Sunday, all day yesterday and now this morning. I'm in Miami or I would have come myself. They haven't been answering and I'm worried. They room together. I called a friend of mine to check on them but I haven't heard yet."

"What are their names?" Mrs. Hyde asked.

"Tracy Paules and Manny Taboada," Khris said.

"Someone else just asked about them."

"Who? Tommy Carrol?"

"That's him, yes."

"I called him too. He's a friend of mine."

"Well, I got one of the maintenance men to open their door but I don't think there's anything to worry about," Mrs. Hyde said. "Security has been pretty tight here since this all started."

After the three student murders, manager Carol Hyde—tough, pragmatic, protective of the kids she considered her "charges" and quick to action—issued flyers to her residents to take extra precautionary measures.

KEEP APARTMENTS LOCKED.

ADMIT NO ONE BUT GATORWOOD PERSONNEL.

CALL 911 . . .

55

The flyer even had pictures of Gatorwood's security guard and two maintenance workers for quick and easy identification.

It was Tuesday morning at 9:52 A.M. when the call came in to the Alachua County sheriff's office. A maintenance man and a young man named Thomas Carrol had come on two more bodies at Gatorwood Apartments.

"Not again. *Two* more?"

"Two."

"College girls again?"

"One college girl. The other was a college guy."

A long beat. A male. A new twist had just darkened an already black scenario.

The bodies of two twenty-three-year-old friends, Tracy Inez Paules and Manuel R. Taboada, were found in a two-bedroom ground-floor unit at Gatorwood Apartments at 2337 SW Archer Road. The killer had forced his way in through the ground floor apartment's sliding glass door, making them the fourth and fifth victims in the bizarre killing spree that apparently no longer seemed to be targeting only women. For the first time, men in Gainesville were frightened. Though it appeared the killer had been drawn to petite brunette women, this time one of the victims was a powerful young man. Manuel (Manny) Taboada. He was a six-foot-three-inch athlete who weighed in at over two hundred muscular pounds, a former football player who already had been approached to join UF's crew team because of his known athletic abilities. So it no longer was only women who were at risk, but how was it possible to get a jump on Manny?

Although Tracy and Manny were not mutilated, as had been the case with the three other victims, their bodies comprised a grisly sight, having been subjected to repeated stabbings.

The toll had now reached five dead in forty-eight hours. And this time the murders occurred right on "Elm" Street. "Freddie" was on the loose.

Manuel had just been accepted at Santa Fe Community College with plans to study architecture. Tracy was a University of Florida pre-law senior. The two twenty-three-year-olds had graduated together in 1984 from American High School of Miami. In spite of the horror of what was happening in Gainesville, their families took comfort in the fact that they were rooming together and that Manuel was strong and powerful; few would be likely to take him on.

As the Paules and Taboada families sat in their comfortable Miami homes, fixed on television reports of the Gainesville murders, their phones rang, and they were informed that their children had become the latest victims of the Gainesville murderer. Media coverage in Gainesville was so swift and intense that Manny's widowed mother, Gayle, did not get a chance to notify her other son, Mario, of their personal tragedy before the news of his brother's murder had been transmitted over the air into his car as he drove home, related in the cool, well-modulated, perfunctory tones of the newscaster.

This time, the names of the victims were immediately known in Gainesville, despite requests of Lt. Spencer Mann and Lt. Sadie Darnell to the media not to release the names before notification of the families. While the families tried to deal with the tragedy thrust upon them, the headlines screamed: TWO MORE FOUND MURDERED.

Alachua County sheriff's spokesman, Lt. Spencer Mann, said, "I don't think it takes a rocket scientist to figure out that anybody who commits homicide using mutilation is a pretty sick individual, somebody we want to get off the streets very very badly." Every student could only wonder when and where the killer would strike next.

Five murders pushed everyone over the edge. University officials announced that academic deadlines would be moved back so students could go home if they so chose. Many went. Others took up residence at local Holiday Inns rather than stay in their apartments; still others sat tight and waited for parents to come to Gainesville.

Joe Bertolucci of Davie, Florida, drove to Gainesville even before the discovery of the last two bodies to stay with his freshman daughter, Laurie. "If they don't discover the person by the weekend I'm taking you home," he told his daughter firmly. She didn't object. When Tracy and Manuel were discovered murdered, he did not wait until the end of the week.

Micheline Jones, a nineteen-year-old junior from Satellite Beach, was not going to wait for the weekend either. She decided to go home after frantic calls back and forth with her parents. "I don't want to get dropped from classes," she told Dorothy Roden, a counselor at the Alachua Crisis Center. "I don't want to fall behind, but my life is more important." A sound perspective, understated.

Dorothy Roden remained with the other counselors from the quickly drawn together Alachua County Crisis Center stationed at the Gatorwood rental office throughout the day on Tuesday, talking with residents and staff members about how to cope.

"What we're telling people who're feeling overwhelmed," Dorothy told her husband, Dick, after she went home, "is that this is a random, tragic event. Some people will be able to cope with this but others will need additional counseling."

"But is it really random?" Dick said.

Dorothy, of course, had no good answer to that. Nor was there any comfort in the belief that the killings were random—*anybody*, after all, could be next.

Whatever, the campus town felt itself under a state of siege. And now many wanted to take action. Gatorwood Apartments already had the security provided by one of two deputies who lived at the complex, but manager Carol Hyde hired an extra armed guard to patrol the buildings from nine P.M. until six A.M. All residents, families and friends were now required to show identification before being admitted to the complex.

John Lombardi, five months as president of the University of Florida, had known one crisis after another. Now he had to worry about guns on campus. While some students left to go home, others prepared drastic defensive measures. It was understandable that stores would have a run on deadbolts and locks despite the countless number already distributed by Golden Glass & Mirror, but when stores like M&C Army Surplus also had a run on guns, mace and stun guns, Lombardi's concern grew in direct proportion to the volume of sales. M&C's salesman Steven Schwartz could barely keep up with the demand for weapons, testament to the town's understandable panic.

Lt. Sadie Darnell was not alone in the police department in fearing a proliferation of the misuse of all the newly purchased weapons. Handgun rookies caused headaches for everyone. They presented, she felt, more of a trigger-happy hazard to themselves and to their friends than to any potential killer. She knew that the odds were that most of the people who now had handguns would never encounter the killer. Yet everyone they knew who was in any way in contact with them, or any stranger who stepped on the wrong twig outside their door, could be the potential victim of an accidental shooting. She knew that many more people were now exposed to handguns than before the weekend of terror began. But Florida law on handguns permitted their purchase. The terror was still out there. Now it had a double edge.

At six P.M. Tuesday evening the majority of the nearly five hundred Gatorwood apartment residents attended an information and security meeting with counselors and law-enforcement officials. Attendance was enhanced by Police Chief Wayland Clifton's declaration to the press: "We have a serial or lust killer at large. We have every reason to believe that all five murders are connected and committed by either one or two murderers."

Jenny looked for Amelia. They were supposed to meet at the meeting. She wasn't there.

Headlines Across the Country

By Wednesday, August 29, the media, including networks and newspaper reporters, had arrived in "Grisly Gainesville" in full force. Said the New York *Post* headline: MANIAC ON THE LOOSE. Satellite link-up trucks from TV stations with call letters from all over the state had begun arriving in Gainesville Monday morning. They were in place by Wednesday. Huge white satellite dishes pointed toward the hot blue-gray sky, aimed at the appropriate satellite off in space. The murders were no longer a local story. Between one hundred twenty-five and one hundred fifty media outlets were intensely covering it. Gainesville hit television nightly newscasts and the front pages not only across the nation but across national boundaries.

Lt. Spencer Mann had been averaging four hundred calls a day since the discovery of the first bodies. The brutal deaths of five attractive young people at the beginning of their adult lives was something everyone could identify with as parent, teacher, police or potential prey. Phil Donahue interviewed participants for his national talk show. Erin Hayes, a CBS-TV reporter, said several factors made the Gainesville murders a national story, not the least of which was the similarity to the Ted Bundy murders in Tallahassee, Florida, in 1978. It was the first time Bundy's name had been prominently mentioned in connection with the Gainesville murders. Before the investigation was over, Bundy's specter would loom everywhere.

It was inevitable that throughout the campus the killings would stir memories of Bundy, the most notorious serial killer in Florida's history. It had been said that when Bundy was in search of a university town he had considered Gainesville but stayed in Tallahassee when he decided Gainesville was too far from the beach, one of his favorite trawling grounds.

Everyone knew who Ted Bundy was. But what kind of a killer was the Gainesville Ripper? And, of course, *who*? Was he a spree killer?—one violent burst of murder and the murderer was sated? Were the killings over? Or was this the first chapter in the cycle of another serial killer?

A massive dragnet was deployed. A combined task force included the FBI and the Florida Department of Law Enforcement. Stories about the method of the killings began to filter out of the closed investigation . . . Manuel had cuts on his arms; he was attacked in his sleep but had tried to fend off blows from the sharp weapon that eventually killed him. Either

Manuel had not been able to offset the element of surprise or the first blow had been too severe to give him a chance to fight. Both girls in the Williamsburg Village apartment had marks that indicated they had been restrained and gagged with adhesive tape, which would explain the silence. More mutilated bodies had been found but the police wouldn't admit it. The police had gotten phone calls from the killer warning of more murders to come. The five slain victims partied together hours before the first victims were found. The killings were linked to the recently released film *Exorcist III*, which had a series of grisly murders at the center of the plot. One of the victims survived one of the attacks and was under heavy police guard at an area hospital. The killings had earmarks of Satanic worship.

All denied by officials. Not all denials believed.

The police had to deal with the macabre jokers attracted to such high-profile cases. A letter delivered to a Tampa television station on Thursday morning described the killer as a failed medical student who "will move to another college campus in Florida to kill again."

"We haven't established a profile of the murderer yet," Lieutenant Darnell told the press. "It's too early for that. We get at least thirty letters like that a day and they're not accurate as far as we know."

Privately Sadie fumed. Hoaxes fanned the flames, and used up energy needed for the investigation.

Inside the Gatorwood office, Hyde directed her staff to beef up security. All apartments in the three-story Gatorwood buildings were already equipped with deadbolts and window locks before the murders, but workers were now directed to install additional bolts and to cut wood strips to block sliding doors shut. Non-denominational candlelit vigils by students were held throughout the city, crisis-response drop-in counseling was set up at the University of Florida's Reitz Union. C. B. Daniel, area supervisor for First Union National Bank, opened toll-free telephone lines for students. Alltel Mobile and WKTK radio set up free phone banks at Butler Plaza on Archer Road while Central Cellular had free long-distance service for students at the Oaks Mall.

At Golden Glass & Mirror on Northwest Industrial Park off State Road 121 customers were lined up for free window locks. Crowds at nearby Oaks Mall were non-existent. At Danny's, a well-frequented local eatery, the crisis had impacted the staff as well. Waitresses left town after receiving calls from worried parents. Deborah Lakey, manager of Skeeter's on NW Thirteenth street, wasn't sure how she could continue to run her business. She already had lost seven waitresses. Alachua General Hospital had stepped up security, fearful that the attacks might branch out from the campuses to include nurses, many of whom remembered Richard Speck, who had murdered eight of their own in 1966.

Late Tuesday night four Guardian Angels in their red berets, white shirts and black pants arrived from the Tampa chapter to stand guard in front of the Gatorwood complex. Their presence seemed largely symbolic, though, given the scores of police in the area. Not surprisingly, Gainesville authorities were not happy at the high-profile aspect of the well-publicized Guardian Angels, the grassroots operation that had originated in New York City to patrol subways and other high crime areas. George Moore, a spokesman for the Angels, said his contingent arrived "to be the extra eyes and ears patrolling and looking around." He said the group would patrol surrounding apartment complexes and the University of Florida campus on foot.

"Don't worry," he said. "We won't overstep our bounds. If we find a suspect we'll immediately turn him over to the local police."

Mayor-Commissioner Courtland Collier declared, "There is not rampant fear on the streets. There is a coming together." He added that the killings were "something that's completely foreign to our area. Not like New York City or Chicago where they have a number of crazy people. Gainesville," he said, "has only one."

"Small comfort," thought Leslie Reid, a University of Florida student who lived at Gatorwood, as she read an advertisement for the slasher film *Friday the 13th* in a local newspaper.

The last two murders had taken place in a ground-floor two-bedroom Gatorwood apartment identical to their own. Jenny had the same bedroom as Manny, Amelia had the same bedroom as Tracy. The night before, Jenny and Amelia let two girlfriends stay overnight with them. They camped together on the living room floor closely propped up with blankets, sheets and pillows.

"Violence as entertainment!" Leslie Reid said. "And we put up with it. Hey, we're *encouraged* to."

Leslie Reid and Joanne Rodriguez were both University of Florida students too. They remembered what fun it had always been to watch the slasher movies. Now it was as though they were shedding their innocence. They had often gone to see "Freddie" accompanied by their boyfriends, seizing the opportunity to cling to each other as the girls in the films were being chased by crazed killers through empty halls, darkened schools, wooded campsites—wherever there was enough isolation to fuel the terror. Now the fun was gone. The reality of a knife actually cutting into flesh was all too real. The pain of having schoolmates mutilated and decapitated took the fun out of being prey for the psychopaths. Thoughts began to shift to the insanity of using the images of young females being slaughtered as the subject of films to be seen by the insane as well as the sane. New parameters were being set in their thinking. New guidelines would be sought in their viewing pleasures. Jenny, particularly, began a deep search into herself. From this moment forward, she would forever question the controversial lack of responsibility on the part of the media in presenting the graphic screen gore as viewing sport.

Lives had been changed forever.

That was last night.

Now two murders so close by, and they hadn't heard a thing.

Jenny Kanne looked out her window at the Gatorwood parking lot. There were only three cars left there by nightfall. It was an exodus, even though the extraordinary police presence made Gatorwood perhaps the safest place in Gainesville. Jenny did not feel comfortable about staying in a huge complex now virtually abandoned, but she was not going to be driven out! She secured the windows, slipped a metal pin in the sliding glass doors, left a note for Amelia, who was not yet home, and drove to M&C Army Surplus at the corner of SW Seventh and W. University, which featured a wide assortment of military supplies: "Guns—Ammo—Camping." She walked into the pale blue Texas-style construction, past its four display windows decorated with dummies in fatigues, boots, helmets and camouflage military apparel, waited her turn—a long line at the counter—and bought a gun and ammunition. She proceeded to the Gainesville library, a beautiful yellow, green-trimmed building. As she crossed from the parking lot to the entrance she glanced up at the tall pole centered on the top octagonal rotunda looking like an unlit candle.

A candle for the dead, she thought, and tried to dismiss the image.

She paused for a moment before entering and grasped her shoulder-strap bag tightly under her arm. Strange, walking into this lovely building shuttered with green sunscreens angled out over balconies, topped with red Spanish roof tiles, carrying a hidden revolver in her purse.

It was late. Amelia was alone. The note said Jenny had gone to the library to do some research. For what? Classes had barely started.

While Amelia waited for Jenny to return, all she could think of was that *he* was still out there. She imagined what the victims must have felt like when they realized they had become part of *his* world.

Earlier Jenny had tried to convince her she was near panic, tried to be calm at the news that the new murders were practically *next door*, for God's sake.

"He won't come back here again . . . and now with the police all around . . ."

Amelia wasn't buying. "Remember the peeping Tom? Maybe he was looking around."

"Don't jump to conclusions."

"Which would mean he came back—"

"We don't know it's the same man," Jenny told her.

"We don't know that it's not either."

Jenny had waited until Amelia had apparently dozed off on the couch before slipping out on her errands. She should have stayed with her, she told herself, but she was obsessed with the notion of the gun. Besides, there was an army of policemen around. Amelia was safe, at least as safe as she could be, with or without her roommate.

Amelia was still not buying any reassurances. Her eyes opened at the sound of a door banging somewhere within the complex. She checked and rechecked the windows in the bedrooms, the sliding glass doors in the living room. She jammed a broom across its lower channel. She could see a police car outside in the courtyard, but it didn't make her feel safe, it only brought the terror right into her own backyard. She violently drew the drapes shut. She turned off the air conditioner, afraid that its soft *whir* might mask the sound of an intruder trying to break in.

Her breath was short. The front door had a deadbolt and a chain, but she placed a chair under the knob, propped her old TWA tote bag and her shoulder-strap handbag on its seat and tied the knob with an electric cord, then wrapped both the tote bag and handbag around the doorknob as tight as she could. She also tied the electric cord to the bottom of the chair before she finally felt secure enough even to close her eyes.

It was too damn hot. She turned on the air conditioner and lay down on the couch again. Jenny had put a soft pink sheet on the couch for her, and she covered herself with it now as though it were, irrationally, a protective shield. The air conditioner sounded strangely loud. She fanned the sheet up and down over her body, trying to get some relief from the heat.

She got up and checked the windows again, jumped at the sound of the soft knock on her door.

"Who is it?" she said, grabbing for the telephone to dial 911.

She would not open the door, the murderer had kept getting closer and closer, now he had come to Gatorwood . . .

"I have a brochure . . ." came the deep male voice on the other side of the door.

She held onto the phone with one hand and the doorknob with the other. "*I don't want it.*"

"But—"

"I don't know who you are!" She heard someone screaming—herself.

"Okay, *okay*," the male voice said, "I'll slip it under the door."

Amelia jumped away from the door and looked at the piece of paper being slipped under it as though it were a snake entering into the sanctum of her private rooms.

"Read it," the voice said quietly, "it's okay, I understand."

Finally, after long moments, Amelia picked it up as though it were contaminated and read:

ASK POLICE OFFICERS FOR PROTECTION RATHER THAN WALK ALONE.

PEOPLE SHOULD TELL ROOMMATES AND FRIENDS WHERE THEY ARE GOING AND WHAT ROUTE THEY WILL BE USING WHEN THEY ARE OUT.

DON'T OPEN DOORS TO STRANGERS AND BE CAUTIOUS ABOUT DEALINGS WITH NEW ACQUAINTANCES.

She could barely see the words.

LOOK THROUGH PEEPHOLES IN DOORS BEFORE OPENING DOORS TO CALLERS.

KEEP DORMITORY, FRATERNITY AND SORORITY HOUSE AND APARTMENT DOORS AND WINDOWS LOCKED AT ALL TIMES.

KEEP BLINDS DRAWN WHILE DRESSING.

It was at once a huge relief, and a warning. It didn't help.

Such was the state Jenny found her in when she returned from the library. She didn't tell Amelia about the gun in her purse. The girl was too close to the edge.

"Are you okay?"

"Yes!" Amelia shouted at her, and Jenny knew she wasn't.

Amelia spotted the titles of the library books Jenny had brought home: *Serial Killers*, *When a Madman Is Loose*, *What Murder Leaves Behind*, *Ted Bundy: The Deliberate Stranger*.

"Are you *crazy*?" Amelia whispered, pushing them aside as though the books themselves had been contaminated.

Jenny shook her head slowly. "I want to know. I want to know what we're dealing with—"

"What is there to *know*? It's some crazy sicko, that's all, and that's too much."

"It could be another Ted Bundy."

Amelia was close to tears. "Well, just keep those books away from me!" She flipped on the television. She was angry that Jenny had brought them home. She thought Jenny was crazy to want to read about all that stuff.

The news bulletin, of course, was about the latest murders.

"Manuel Toboada was probably attacked in his sleep," Lieutenant Darnell was saying into the mass of microphones before her. "His body was found in bed . . ."

Jenny had heard through a friend who had heard from a friend at *The*

Gainesville Sun that Manny had cuts all over his arms. Probably trying to ward off the attacker, she thought. If he'd had a gun, like she had now . . .

"A razor-sharp knife was used in the murders," came from the television. She stopped to look at Lieutenant Darnell. "Investigators don't know if the killer targeted Mr. Taboada for some unknown reason or stumbled upon him accidentally as he stalked Ms. Paules. Investigators also do not know if the murder of Mr. Taboada was part of a heated escalation in the killings—"

"Amelia?" Jenny called when she realized Amelia was staring at the screen and hadn't moved an inch since she had turned on the set.

No answer.

"Whoever killed the five students was careful, shrewd and methodical," Lieutenant Darnell was saying of the five deaths.

"A lot has been happening," Jenny began carefully to Amelia. "I've found out that the university police department has joined with the Gainesville police and the sheriff's office and they're putting out a major effort to promote security measures . . ."

Amelia still didn't answer. She was in front of the television, as though mesmerized by the broadcast. Lieutenant Darnell would not confirm rumors that the killer had cleaned up the scenes or the bodies in order to destroy evidence. "Investigators believe the victims were killed in the order in which their bodies were discovered, although they haven't yet narrowed down the times of death."

Jenny reached to turn off the TV.

"Leave it alone." Amelia's voice was low and over-controlled.

Darnell's voice continued. Though investigators believed the perpetrator spent "a considerable amount of time" in each of the victims' apartments after each murder, she refused to say whether any of the five victims was killed quickly and then mutilated or slowly tortured to death.

Jenny moved in front of the TV, blocking Amelia's view of the screen.

"They should tell us the truth," Amelia said, still looking toward the screen as though she could see through Jenny.

Jenny knelt down to Amelia and took her hands. "It's okay." Jenny tried to reassure her. "He won't come back here again. Not with all the police presence here. I could barely get through myself . . ."

"I'm leaving," Amelia said quietly.

"I don't think we should."

Amelia looked at her. "You do what you want. I'm going home."

They both jumped as the phone rang.

Jenny picked up the receiver. The sound was too jarring to allow it to ring twice. It was her mother on the line calling from Long Island. The news of the fourth and fifth victims had reached their families up north.

When Jenny hung up the phone, she turned to Amelia. "I'm coming home with you. Mom insists." She dialed 411.

Without another word, Amelia went into the other room and began to pack.

"Information?" Jenny's usual assured voice was subdued. "Delta Airlines, please. Reservations . . ."

Reservations was doing a land-office business. No surprise.

At 10 A.M. on August 30, 1990, eighteen-year-old Sonya Larson was buried after a service at the First Baptist Church on First Street in Pompano Beach. Later that same evening in Miami, visitation for twenty-three-year-old Tracy Paules was held from 6:30 to 9:30 P.M. at Van Orsdel–Coral Gables Chapel on SW 8th St. The next day, on August 31, 1990, she was laid to rest at Woodlawn Park in Miami. Not far away funeral services were held for twenty-three-year-old Manuel Taboada. The friends who had lived together and died together would rest close to each other. In Jacksonville, at 10 A.M. on August 31, seventeen-year-old Christina Powell's funeral was conducted at St. David's Episcopal Church, on Fort Caroline Road. That afternoon at 4:30 P.M. in Gainesville, services were held for eighteen-year-old Christa Leigh Hoyt in the gymnasium of Newberry High, the school from which she had recently graduated. Interment was at Arlington Memorial Park.

Sonya, Christina, Christa, Tracy, Manny. Mourners in Gainesville gathered to pay tribute to the five slain students at a memorial service on campus. There was a sharp edge of anger with the mourning . . . along with a shared sentiment that the killer had brought them together.

Mitch Stacy was covering the memorial and spotted State Attorney Len Register standing aside at the memorial service. Register, at six-foot-six, towered over the young reporter. A native Floridian, he was tanned, but up close he looked pale to Mitch.

"How's it going?" Mitch asked. "Anything happening yet?"

Len shook his head. "No, but I just saw the photographs."

"You were at the crime scenes themselves, weren't you?"

Len nodded again. Yes, he had been there. But seeing the photographs again a week later, after the initial shock of discovery had subsided, was another matter. And seeing the five pure white floral wreaths lying on the ground side by side, each representing someone's murdered child—he had his own children now, he thought, and suddenly, unexpectedly, the huge man broke down and wept uncontrollably.

His wife moved to his side, whispered. He nodded to Mitch, and the Registers moved to seats towards the back of the room.

Mitch looked at the man's silently heaving shoulders thoughtfully. Len

Register had been around a long time in his capacity as Eighth Circuit State Attorney. He had seen a lot. For him to get so overcome with grief when he mentally reviewed the photos and looked at the five floral wreaths . . . Mitch paused in his thoughts . . . those photos must have been even beyond Mitch's wildest imagination. What had that monster actually done to those kids?

He looked around.

It was obvious by the looks on their faces that these people had been brought together, not to their knees.

But despite the anger and the touch of bravado anger can instill, the fears remained. Too many whispered to each other the desperate truth, that the singular most important element about serial killers, repeatedly pointed out by the experts, was that of all killers, the serial lust killer was the one most likely to repeat his crime. He could strike again. At any moment. At any place. At any one.

PART

II

THE ROLLINGS

5

A Psychological Puzzle

The ceremonial, sadistic traits of the Gainesville Ripper bespoke a particular type of killer. The fantasy-driven murders, the ritualistic aspect of the displayed trophies of his kills, the attention to detail at the crime scenes all led authorities to conclude that Gainesville, Florida had been caught up in the grip of a near-classic lust serial killer. By day he walked unnoticed among the innocent. By night he invaded the privacy of his victims' rooms and stayed for however long it took to do the things he did to his victims.

The public was still in the dark about details, but the word was out that the Ripper was smart. No one was secure. How could this happen again? Only the year before, in 1989, the state of Florida had sent 2,000 volts through the body of one of the most charming, sociopathic, lust serial killers that had ever stalked an unsuspecting community. Two thousand cheering spectators had taken up an all-night vigil in a grassy field across the highway from Florida's death row in Starke, chanting, "Fry, Bundy, fry!" right up to the moment of his execution.

That was thirty miles away in Starke's maximum-security state prison. That evil was over, destroyed. And yet within one year Florida's students were again being singled out for death. It was as though Ted Bundy walked again.

Multiple murders have been on the increase in the United States since the 1960s. Some have called them "motiveless," but, of course, there is no such thing as motiveless murder; the motive may not be apparent but it is there and most often it is linked to so-called sex crimes. Yet sex is not the driving force behind the act of the lust killer, rather it is the part that strikes the greatest terror. By the 1980s the phenomenon of the serial killer became increasingly clear to American law-enforcement agencies that were charged with coping with a rise from 8.5 percent of all murders committed in 1960 to 22.1 percent by 1984. Although serial killing is hardly an American phenomenon, in recent years the United States has become the nation most often afflicted by this specie of predator.

The *modus operandi* of the killers may vary occasionally, but essentially, as Joel Norris points out in *Serial Killers*, "the ritual aspect of the crime . . . which is conceived of fantasy and endlessly rehearsed in the offender's mind before he kills for the first time . . . is his 'signature', his mark; and it is principally this 'signature' which enables a series of crimes to be linked through behavioral analysis." And often, as will be noted, the killer's own behavior is eventually the key to his capture.

Mysteries remain, the human psyche is still hardly an open book. But it is clear that the lust serial killer does not develop overnight. Somewhere along the developmental line, nature and nurture became scrambled in an irreversible pattern of normal need and abnormal neglect, opening the pathway for a form of sexual psychopathology. Abuse is often the fertile ground in which the lust serial killer is bred. His development usually follows a chronicle of persecution, whether psychological, emotional, physical, sexual or a combination thereof. It begins at a very young age, during the most crucial, formative years of physical and psychological growth, destroying the natural development of self-esteem, creating instead an abnormal need for self-gratification. Because of the persistence of the abuse, he becomes one who has been almost trained to suffer a poor self-image and live with a constant, debilitating feeling of inferiority. In a wild distortion of expectations, however, instead of becoming beaten down and passive, the more stubborn ones become vengeful and aggressive. In order to live through their own wounds, their aggressive impulses eventually have to be acted upon in order to achieve some form of pathological release from the constancy of pain that is the normal sum of their lives.

In order to give some meaning to the child's painful existence, pleasurable daydreams of revenge become twisted in the developing psyche and evolve to an unhealthy degree in the culminating need for power. The daydreams often turn to full-blown violent, often sadistic fantasies in which total control is exercised, not only over himself but over the people who have made his life miserable—or more aptly, the people who, in some deep demented corner of his mind, *represent* his tormentors. When fantasies no longer suffice, he progresses to the final lethal phase where violent fantasies, rehearsed over and over again in a world of make-believe, become the blueprint for his murderous acting-out. The end product is a murderously diseased human being.

For those who became caught up in his deadly pathological needs, the next stop of one particular lust serial killer was Gainesville, Florida.

6

The Unwanted

The story of the Gainesville murders goes back as far as 1954 to Shreveport, Louisiana, a river town of some two hundred thousand residents bordering along the southern coast of the wide, ambling Red River one hundred fifty miles east of Dallas. The skyline of its busy downtown rises out of the haze of Interstate 20, still called the Hart's Island Road by the locals, in the northwestern corner of Louisiana.

The young family lived in a modest home in the southwest section of the city. It was here, on May 26, 1954, that a boy named Daniel Harold Rolling was born to Claudia Beatrice and James Harold Rolling. The mother was young, inexperienced and dominated by James' strong, forceful personality that bordered on the oppressive.

At the time of Daniel Rolling's birth, Shreveport was the commercial center of northern Louisiana. Though it boasted natural gas, lumber, cotton and steel products, oil was still king in this part of the south. The economy boomed in the tri-state area known locally as the ArkLaTex. James Rolling, recently back from service in the Korean War, for which he was highly decorated, wanted nothing to do with the dominant local industry, but with a family to support and no special skills other than soldiering, he took a job that he hated on an oil rig.

Twenty-two-year-old Claudia Rolling welcomed the birth of her first son, but the father did not adjust well to fatherhood. Claudia quickly got the feeling he was jealous of the baby. He didn't want her to pick up Daniel when he cried or show him the kind of affection it was in her nature to give. She didn't understand her husband's behavior, didn't know how to deal with it. She only knew that she had to hide her show of affection to avoid her husband's anger.

She tried, but essentially Claudia was ineffective in her attempts to protect her child, even when her husband dragged a screaming six-month-old infant down the hall in their apartment by his leg because he didn't like the way the child's leg "crippled up" under him.

When she learned she was pregnant again she was terrified at what

73

James' reaction was going to be, she told her sister Agnes Mitchell. "I can't tell him about this. What can I do?"

"I don't know what to tell you except to leave that man," Agnes said. "No . . . I can't do that."

When a second son, Kevin, was born a year later, the situation was the same, only worse: James still had little knowledge of or use for the role of father. The kids cried all the time. Claudia, learning well the role of secretiveness and protectiveness early, devoted herself to the boys when he wasn't around, and especially devoted herself to Danny, who always seemed in particular to arouse her husband's resentment.

She walked on eggshells to avoid a scene. Touching, caressing was a secret, hidden thing . . .

Early patterns persisted as the years passed. James was domineering and abusive to his wife and sons. He had no use for shows of affection. He had a heavy hand that often cracked across Danny's head—underneath the boy's sweet, passive facade he was headstrong and stubborn, creating a wall of continual conflict between father and son from the time he was old enough to walk. But, of course, the father was bigger, dominant, in control.

Oddly, if following a classic clinical pattern, in his desire to get closer to the abusive parent, the boy was always following around after his father, trying to get his attention, dangling, stomping, desperate for his approval, which brought another rattling blow to the side of the head.

His mother tried to protect him against the brutalization, but was hardly effective. And psychologists have suggested that early on, *the child became resentful of the mother. For being weak. For giving in. For not protecting him. For marrying his father in the first place.*

But at the same time, setting up a deep conflict, he would also forgive her. Or try to. In spite of her being too needy and whiny with his father.

Still—conflicts and opposites were the pattern—she was pretty in the boy's eyes, small, brunette, and he did love her, he knew she tried, he even prayed for her at the same time he begged God to make his father like him.

It didn't work.

James Rolling was a hothead who believed in corporal punishment, regularly dispensing "ass whippings" to both of his sons for all rule infractions, major or minor. The younger son, Kevin, learned at an early age to go off by himself, when to make himself scarce, especially when to stay clear of Danny, who was usually at the center of the family upset. Often Kevin caught it too, the heavy hand of punishment was indiscriminate, but it was Danny who was James' particular whipping boy.

When the boys were five and four years old, James and Claudia had to move in with her sister Agnes. Although Claudia was working, James was out of a job and they had little choice but to accept Agnes' help. Agnes was eleven years older than Claudia, and her children were much older than Danny and Kevin. Claudia was happy to be with her sister and her family. Now there would be another adult around while she was away at work and she would not have to worry so much about James' treatment of the boys.

But for Agnes, it was a nightmare. The children carried bruises, they were in physical pain. At times James wanted them to sit and not talk. Aunt Agnes would insist they go into the yard to play, but he always managed to find a way to stop them—"something" they had done wrong.

The story from Agnes came out at Rolling's penalty-phase trial. One time she came home to find the boys tied up. Danny would squirm and scream and run around to get away from his father's heavy hand. James would tie Kevin up too. Agnes testified that she had seen the children tied up at least a dozen times within that six-month period of time they lived together. Claudia was incapable of stopping James, so Agnes took the line that under her roof some of the responsibility for those children was hers. She would get onto James and complain about his abuse of the children in her house. James would become furious and leave. But when he was alone with them he would do it again.

Twice they were blindfolded at the dinner table at Agnes' house. The second time her seventeen-year-old daughter Caroline became so enraged she was about ready to come to blows with her uncle James Harold unless he removed the blindfolds from her cousins' eyes.

Finally, enough was enough. The disruption of her own home was too much to bear and Agnes told James, "You have to leave!"

Claudia was devastated but she understood. She couldn't ask James to leave alone, and they moved into her parents' home four blocks away.

At approximately thirty years of age, James Rolling brought his little son Danny to visit his parents Homer and Cavis Rolling at their home in Bibb City, Columbus, Georgia.

Homer and Cavis hadn't seen either their son or grandson in a while. They weren't a very close family, not much given to phone calling or letter writing. Their daughter, Jeanette Caughey, who lived in Phoenix City, Alabama, located directly across the Chattahoochee River from Columbus, Georgia, was the only one of their daughters and two sons they saw on a regular basis. Their other son, Joe, lived on the West Coast with his wife Mira. Homer and Cavis didn't even know how to contact him by phone. Somewhere in California. Camarillo, they thought.

And now, here was James with one of his young ones, looking for a job in an effort to relocate to the Columbus, Georgia, area. Homer and Cavis didn't know what kind of job he was looking for. They didn't ask. He didn't offer. He left Daniel with them every day while he went out.

Aunt Jeanette liked Danny Boy. He was a good child, never disrespectful like some kids were.

He moved near his grandpa and stared at the gun the older man had in a leather holster.

"What're you looking at?"

Danny lowered his eyes.

"Y'like guns?"

"I'm gonna hunt when I get big."

Grandpa Rolling reached into his pocket and took out his wallet. The boy watched as he took out a silver miniature Muscogee County Deputy Sheriff's badge. "Your grandpa is a reserve deputy sheriff so I got a permit to carry a concealed weapon. Never forget that. Y'gotta have a permit if you're gonna carry around a concealed gun."

He took his holster out of the holster and showed it to the boy. "This was given t'me by the Muscogee County Sheriff himself."

The boy was duly impressed but his father gave him a warning look from across the room.

"Why don't you just shut up," he said to his son. "Leave your grandpa alone."

The older man slid the gun into its holster and pocketed his wallet. "Do like your daddy says," but he was annoyed. He liked talking about himself. The kid obviously liked it too. He listened wide-eyed. Well, James was always tough. Okay, it would make the kid tough. Need to be tough in this world to get along right. The kid always looked like he was going to cry. Claudia probably pampered him too much. Last thing they needed was a sissy in the family.

But listening to his father had given James an idea. He told his father without preamble that things weren't working out on the job hunt, and taking Danny with him, he went back to Louisiana the next day.

Once there, he began the preliminary arrangements to join the Shreveport police department, and after he was hired he knew it had been the right choice. He felt more secure in a uniform with a service revolver strapped to his side than he ever had in his life. James Rolling had found his vocation, and his refuge.

He was, on the record, a good cop. It was not long before he became Shreveport police lieutenant. But apparently because of his short stocky build his associates on the force called him "Baby Dumpling." It is not difficult to imagine how he felt about *that*.

*   *   *

West Canal Boulevard in Shreveport is a quiet middle-class neighborhood known as Sunset Acres. In 1961, when James Rolling joined the police force and his family moved to 6314 West Canal Boulevard, Daniel was seven.

One of the first things James Harold did was to set up wire traps in his backyard to trap neighborhood cats, which he would shoot with a .22 and watch die.

Inez Hutto, who had lived at 6217 West Canal Boulevard since 1954, liked the boy. He was a handsome child, she says, who for some unknown reason always seemed depressed to her. The most beautiful, saddest hazel eyes she had ever seen. They unfortunately gave him a wimplike appearance, she thought, but no matter how hard she encouraged them to get together, Danny and her own son, who went to the same school, could never quite hit it off. Too bad, she thought. He sure enough looked like he could use a friend.

Another neighbor, "Carmen Ringer," a pseudonym, tried to befriend him. "Hey, things ain't all that bad," he had said when he found the boy sitting out by his father's car quietly sulking. The boy wouldn't look at him directly, Ringer says. He wouldn't, or couldn't, pay attention to a neighbor's attempt to be friendly. Apparently brooding over punishment that seemed a constant as long as he could remember, he looked on the neighbor as meddlesome and stupid.

"Hey, lookit this," Ringer had once said, extending a hand that had a scar from a sharp cut on its palm, "ever see such a slice in your life? I cut it fishing. Still hurts like the dickens."

Ringer had the feeling that the boy didn't care. He was right.

Compassion for others was already nearly gone by the age of seven. One day it would leave an "adult" warped beyond redemption. By the time Danny was old enough to begin reacting with petty thievery, teenage alcoholic abuse and truancy he was considered "troublesome" and the cycle of punishment, begun with his father, that he incurred at the hands of widening circles of authority continued, with escalating provocation.

Daniel's mother, guilty and passive all at once, kept making excuses for his behavior. His father became even more punitive, helping to shape the dangerous sub-specie of killer it was his job to hunt down. And he was a tough cop. He was even tougher at home. A couple of times Danny actually tried to pull his father off his mother when James shoved her up against the wall by her neck. His father came at him with a frying pan for interfering, grabbed him by the hair and shoved him up against the wall in her place. Then James began hitting him in the face and beating him with a belt. Danny was nine years old.

Charles "Chuck" Strozier was a cousin. Most of Claudia's family was barred from paying visits of any kind, but for some reason Chuck was permitted to visit Danny and Kevin.

"There's no love here," he had always thought, often an unwilling and embarrassed witness to the demeaning remarks. Danny continually tried to please his father, Strozier testified.

Uncle James Harold wanted to be in control. He scared even Chuck. How many times had he heard the beatings in the bedroom? And for what? Sitting on the wrong piece of furniture. Going into those parts of the house in which they were not permitted. Making what to Uncle James Harold was too much noise. There were so many rules. Don't wear your shoes inside. Don't sit on the furniture. He could hear the stroke of that leather policeman's belt. He could hear them crying and at the same time trying to control themselves. But the crying caused more beatings. They had to hide their feelings, especially Danny.

One day when the boy was nine, he came home to find his mother lying on the bathroom floor crying uncontrollably, victim of a complete nervous breakdown. He tried to hold her, to comfort her. At least this is how she remembers it.

When the attendants came he looked to his father, who did not interfere. No doubt he wanted to punch him, to kill him. "I love you, Mom," he said as they took her away. But, in her fashion, through *his* eyes, she was also failing him.

By the time Claudia was sedated and released, Danny had been acting up in school. The principal of the grammar school looked at a weary mother. Mrs. Rolling must have been worn beyond her years.

He told her he was going to have to hold Danny back in third grade. He was sorry but Danny was not meeting the minimum academic requirements set by the school board. He was rude, inattentive, and there were even indications that he might be responsible for a series of petty thefts that had been plaguing the school in recent months. Also, he was disruptive in class, rude to the teacher. Claudia said, "It didn't sound like my Danny. He was a regular shirttail little boy, a good boy, he don't mean nothing by it . . ." She didn't like to be disloyal to her husband, but her son was in trouble again. "His father was too hard on him," she finally got out. Always had been. "Danny's just natured that way . . ."

The boy had already been evaluated by the school's psychological team as having a marked inferiority complex and aggressive tendencies which, with the right provocation, could easily erupt. But the school didn't have the facilities to deal with serious emotional problems. Theirs was an educational facility, not a psychiatric one. To the mother's teary assurance that Daniel didn't mean anything by the things he did, that he always apologized for any misdeeds, the principal pointed out the apologies didn't stop the behavior. They would have to keep him back.

But he would be in the same class as his younger brother, she protested.

He was left back. And by the time he got to junior high he hated school —and his hatreds were passionate.

Daniel, at his mother's suggestion, prayed to the Lord.

"Nearer my God to Thee," he would intone. "Nearer my God to Thee."

He learned how to play the guitar and sang his prayers, accompanying himself on the guitar. (Later, at trial, the defense would make much of this.) He had, it was said, a nice voice. He dreamed of being a singing star, a celebrity, people would know who he was. But it seems there was a part of him that could never believe anyone would care enough to want to listen. Poor self-image, the psychologists like to call it, further creasing the deep frown in his forehead over the "saddest eyes" that his neighbor, Ms. Hutto, said she had ever seen.

Daydreaming, common to most people, escalated into fantasies that he began to enrich with violent sadistic scenes. He became increasingly secretive. The violence took on sexual overtones . . . his pubescent sexuality becoming an intense part of his nighttime world of fantasy. And so a dangerous merging of impulses had begun.

His nights had become endurable. His days were not, absent of alcohol. He was resourceful. He found illegal ways of getting the alcohol that made him feel "real good" in the light of day. Sometimes he stole it, sometimes he got it from friends. The night his father caught him he had gotten a half-gallon of rotgut whiskey from his friend, the white-bearded old wino who had set up house in a shack behind the Sunset Drive-In. When he came home his father grabbed him by the scruff of the neck. Usually he kept his mouth shut, afraid of his father, but this time alcohol loosened his tongue. His father threw him to the kitchen floor, cuffed his hands behind his back.

His mother screamed and begged as she watched James drag the boy out of the house. Not to the woodshed. The thirteen-year-old son would spend two weeks in jail, on his father's charge.

The pot was boiling.

And far away in southern Florida on September 14, 1966, a boy was born to Cuban parents who had emigrated to Florida. The boy was received with all

*the joy usually reserved for the birth of a male child. The new, healthy-lunged
addition to the close-knit family was baptized Manuel Taboada. . . .*

*On October 4, less than three weeks later, fifty miles north of Manuel
Toboada's baptismal site, a baby girl was born to middle-class American parents, Ricky and George Paules, who would come to adore and dote on her.
The girl was baptized Tracy Inez Paules in Deerfield Beach, Florida. Tracy
and Manuel's paths would converge one violent day a quarter-century later.*

*While both sets of these parents built their great expectations for Manny and
Tracy and planned for their futures, including the time when they would one
day go to college—thirteen-year-old Danny Harold Rolling was being dragged
down the hallway to the local Shreveport jail by his father.*

*Elmo St. Jones (pseudonym), a police officer who worked with the father
down at the station, watched as James Rolling, a cigar clenched in his teeth,
dragged his teenage son down the hall of the jailhouse, presumably to frighten
him into better behavior.*

*That was Danny's first time in jail, a portent of a future that would fulfill
his father's worst predictions.*

*Not surprisingly, many psychological evaluations later—whether adminis-
tered by school, military or penal institutions—it was repeatedly diagnosed
that Danny Rolling's relationship with his father had helped foster his emotional instability and shape the lethal personality of the adult he was to become.*

When Danny got back to the little house in Sunset Acres after being "released from jail" by his father, his mother, in her fashion, tried to soften
the impact of his experience. She asked how he was, did they do "anythin'
awful" to him in that place?

Danny didn't answer. Not then. But one night, when the house was
asleep, he pulled out the knapsack he had already packed and secreted
under his bed and slipped out of the house. It was the first time he would
leave home.

He spent the night in a nearby woods (as years later he would do before
and after he murdered the five University of Florida students in Gainesville). This first night he was frightened of the noise-filled darkness. The
next night he slipped through that increasingly available trap-door into his
world of daydreams and fantasy, of private make-believe where he was a
power. His body was growing. He could hurt people. In his fantasies he
had control even over his life and death. He could watch people die and
they couldn't do a damn thing about it. He masturbated through the imagined scenes of death, shaping his revenge by fantasizing acts of increasing
sadistic violence against the world, but against women in particular. It was

his mother who was to blame for not fulfilling her most important function
—protecting him.

He stayed in the woods until hunger finally drove him back home. He
hadn't yet learned the military-style survival techniques in which he would
one day be extremely adept. The line between fantasy and reality had not
yet been totally crossed, but the pattern for the nascent serial killer was
taking form.

The second leave-taking occurred after an argument with his father over
whether Danny could wear jeans to church. His father demanded unchal-
lenged obedience and this time ordered the boy out of the house, over the
mother's usual tearful but useless protestations.

Later, after James had gone to bed, Claudia slipped out of the house
and searched the streets for her son, eventually finding him wandering
about through the center of town. She proceeded to bring him back to
Sunset Acres, sneaking him into the darkened house.

What was he really thinking and feeling? That his mother had rescued
him or that she had stood by while his father evicted him? Later events
would indicate the latter dominated.

Claudia and James Rolling became increasingly estranged over their differences. Since they did not communicate in depth with either side of their
respective families, most of their relatives had little idea of what life in the
Rolling household was like. Their home was often a quiet, clouded space
of noncommunication and dark hostility. The atmosphere was heavy, tense
and debilitating.

As for Danny, he was increasingly in trouble in school and with school
officials. The frowning apologetic personality that was usually in the forefront of all his social interactions was beginning to recede. Now the dark
side of him was emerging more prominently—the violent, angry side that
seemed in contrast with the passivity he often tried to project.

Claudia continued to defend him, and began the process of frequent
letter writing to school officials (who would one day be replaced by prison
officials). She openly blamed her son's antisocial behavior on his father's
abusive treatment. A family friend said that deep inside all Danny ever
wanted was communication with his dad; he wanted his dad to be proud of
him.

Who really knows? Maybe she was right. Danny, it was later said, was
often preoccupied with thoughts of how he could get closer to his father,
right up to the day when, as a grown man, he shot him.

*   *   *

Now seventeen years old and already one year behind because he had had to repeat third grade, Danny finally left Woodlawn High School in his sophomore year. He had other plans.

James Rolling looked at the piece of paper that his son asked him to sign. It would relieve him of his son's presence. Danny stood at almost six feet now. He was flexing his muscles more of late. He was becoming even more difficult to control. His signature would give parental permission for Danny to join the air force before he was of age.

The father signed the paper.

When the time for departure came, Claudia, still petite, still a deep brunette, showed deep lines in her pretty face. She blamed her husband for Danny Boy's leaving. He was only seventeen. Too young to be going off on his own.

His brother Kevin looked awkwardly the other way when Danny started to the front door. His mother told him to be sure to write. He said he would. He looked to his father, who told him to "see to it you don't screw up."

Hoping for the Wild Blue Yonder

Danny Rolling became an airman in June of 1971.

Things went well at first. Never lacking in natural intelligence, he managed to earn his high-school equivalency diploma in record time. He managed to discipline himself enough to complete the necessary coursework he had refused to take seriously at Woodlawn High School. He wrote home about it. Claudia wrote back, real proud. No word from James. He earned a stripe. Again he wrote home about it. Again his mom wrote back, even more proud. Still no word from his father.

Danny told himself he was doing fine. He liked being away from home on his own, but he also began drinking heavily. While he had started out as an occasional drunk as a young teenager, now he got down to some serious drinking. From the first time he learned about corn whiskey, his drinking sprees were high lonesomes. It was a little different now but it was still easy to be chummy in the service without getting close. Drinking buddies were the easiest to find and the least demanding to be with. He discovered other drugs as well. He used LSD and smoked marijuana. Getting high, on alcohol or drugs, was the only time he truly felt good. It was the only time the deep-seated anxieties seemed relieved.

The violence of his repetitive nocturnal fantasies while alone and undisturbed in his bunk gave another level of release. The fantasies took on sadistic qualities until the line between the sex and the violence blurred and merged, as though two aggressive impulses had become inextricably woven together. And now the multiple fantasies had dwindled down to the same one—the one with the knife and the powerless victim. The masturbatory rushes came only with the envisioning of knives penetrating into flesh, the more violent, the better the feeling.

Did his fantasies, and their release, frighten him?

"Nearer my God to Thee . . ." he sang.

Then he went peeping.

In his waking life he fell into his old patterns of antisocial behavior, and soon ran into persistent serious trouble with air force authorities.

He was stripped of his stripe for disobeying orders. He was found with marijuana in his possession and disciplined. He was caught with a stolen bicycle after he crashed into an army truck and wrecked the bicycle.

The bicycle was just standing there, he thought. Unchained. *Asking* to be taken. It was the fault of the guy who left it there for the taking.

"You may think it's a little thing, taking someone else's bike," his superior officer said.

"Oh no, sir, not at all."

He was remorseful for his behavior. He apologized. He was sorry. He was convincing.

His superior officer, however, dismissed the apology and gave him a thirty-day sentence.

Alone, whatever the fear and remorse expressed earlier metamorphosized into deep-rooted anger that could shield him, for a while, against the suppressed feelings of anxiety. Anger made possible the endurance of the unendurable. Military prison was a new low point. He learned what it felt like to be totally under the domination of others with no possibility of escape.

He was nineteen.

Someday he would get even.

With everyone.

His predictable difficulty in adjusting to life in the service and his chronic failure to obey regulations eventually led the air force to discharge him. Before his discharge, in 1973, an air force psychiatrist completed an evaluation, concluding with the unremarkable diagnosis: "A personality disorder."

"I'm a kid in a man's body," Danny said solemnly.

He would make the same self-diagnosis years later to another psychiatrist during one of the many evaluations he would have after one of the petty robberies that kept landing him in trouble with the law.

7

The Wanted

July, 1971. Edward Phitzenmeir, a Florida State Alcohol and Beverage agent, working out of the Miami office, was a caring man. His new secretary, he could tell, was pregnant and trying to hide it. He told her she didn't have to hide it from him. Embarrassed, she said she wasn't married but she didn't believe in abortion. She also said she knew she couldn't afford to keep a baby, she needed a job. Five months pregnant, she told him she would have the baby and give it up for adoption.

He told her he would try to help, went into his office and called his sister Joy Willingham. He remembered that Joy had a sister-in-law who lived in Archer, Florida, a town some twenty miles southwest of Gainesville. And he remembered Joy telling him that her sister-in-law couldn't have children but wanted to adopt.

Ralph and Ann Hoyt, it turned out, still wanted a baby, and arranged to adopt the secretary's unborn baby. Forty-five days later, on November 20, 1971, a baby girl was born to the young unwed secretary in Miami.

At about the time Ralph and Ann Hoyt proudly christened their adopted baby Christa Leigh Hoyt, eighteen-year-old Daniel Harold Rolling was stealing a bicycle at Patrick Air Force Base . . .

A few weeks later, fifty miles north of where Christa was born, in the eastern coastal town of Deerfield Beach, Florida, at approximately the same time Danny Rolling was being escorted into a military prison, a woman by the name of Ada Larson gave birth to a baby girl on the first day of 1972. It was a wonderful New Year's gift. She and her husband Jim called the dark-eyed infant Sonja. She was, and would remain, the baby of the family.

The last of the principal players in the Gainesville tragedy came into the world later that same year on November 30, 1972, a baby girl born to Frank and Patricia Powell in Jacksonville, Florida. Christina, too, was the baby of the family.

There would come a time when all these lives would brutally converge— the unloved killing the beloved—but for the next year and a half, life progressed normally for the Taboadas, the Paules, the Hoyts, the Larsons, the Powells. While the Taboadas and the Paules planned for their children's futures, and the Larsons doted on their sparkling Sonja, and Christa, an only child, was tended to with the zeal of converts, Danny Rolling was discharged from the air force, and was back on the streets of Shreveport, Louisiana, with nothing to do.

8

Home Again

1973, two years later.

Back home in Shreveport, Danny Rolling had no close relationships. While his father the cop sat at home and no longer physically bothered him much—in fact, except for berating him for not having a steady job and insisting that Claudia not wash his clothes—"Let him do it himself . . . I'm warning you . . ."—he mostly ignored his son's presence. And his son began in earnest the series of robberies that eventually would land him in jail for most of the rest of his life.

"You'll be dead or in jail by the time you're fifteen" echoed in his head, but Danny had fooled the old man. Except for the time his father dragged him behind bars and the time spent in the military prison, he had not yet set foot inside a jail by order of a judge.

Getting fired from a few menial jobs seemed to increase the anger, which in turn increased the fantasies. The sense of inferiority deepened. Once again, the songs he made up on his guitar managed to a degree to soothe the savage feelings still lying dormant. And again, trying to get away from the sadistic sexual fantasies he had entertained for years that, in his saner, more passive moments, still frightened him, Danny drank and continued the drug taking that had begun in the service. He didn't like himself much.

Often drunk and high on drugs, Danny eventually found religion.

The two young men and young woman were on their way to church when they saw the nineteen-year-old man flailing about doing karate chops at the tree in front of the Kings Temple on Kingston Road. He was big. Strong-looking. One of the men said he looked drunk, that they should steer clear of him. The other said maybe he needed help.

Although the drunken youth standing so close to the mouth of the church was hostile and unfriendly, they asked if he would like to come inside the church. He swung lamely at them, said no, but they persisted, the Lord was waiting for him. He started laughing. "Nearer my God to *me*?" he said through slurred speech.

Now the girl, who had stayed in the background, moved forward between the two men. "C'mon," she said quietly, "you've nothing to lose, now, have you? God's inside there, you know." She touched his arm.

He began attending Shreveport's Kings Temple United Pentecostal Church. Reverend Michael Hudspeth was immediately aware that the young man his youthful parishioners had just brought into the church was very "troubled." At Reverend Hudspeth's urging he joined the youth group, sang in the choir and wrote songs and played his guitar. The reverend was pleased, impressed. One of the other young parishioners was also impressed, particularly by his unusual strength. Rolling was one of the strongest guys he had ever known. When one of the cars was having engine trouble Rolling *carried* its transmission all the way across the parking lot on his shoulders as though it were weightless, and placed it gently in the back of a pickup truck.

He was a solitary person, difficult to know. But he responded to the attention he received at the church. He liked the reverend, he liked the warm sound of his soft voice, lilting with the familiar regional Louisiana accent.

The reverend knew he had been involved in drugs like marijuana. He had no knowledge of anything heavier, such as heroin or cocaine, but eventually he felt it his duty to ask. Danny emphatically said he wasn't using marijuana and had never used or trafficked in anything heavier. Me? Oh, no sir . . .

Reverend Hudspeth didn't know if he was telling the truth but decided it didn't matter. From all indications, Danny Rolling was on the way to straightening himself out . . . singing in the choir, drawing, which he said his mother taught him when the reverend commented on one of the birds he had drawn. She was an artist, he said.

He had never before received as much attention or acceptance. Some of the violent fantasies stopped. But he was still lonely, and he asked God to send him someone, someone to marry.

It did not surprise Reverend Hudspeth when Danny confided the nature of his prayers to him, and he convinced Danny to attend one of the church's socials.

It was at one of these socials that he met her. It was at the moment he was praying to God to send him someone that she walked into the room. He was *convinced* that God had heard him and sent the girl directly to him *in answer to his prayers.* She was petite, dark-haired, with a gracefully long, slender neck. The reverend didn't consider her especially attractive but it seemed to him that Danny was immediately attracted to her.

Her name was O'Mather Ann Halko.

He had never had a girlfriend before, but O'Mather encouraged him. Reverend Hudspeth could tell she liked him. After all, he was certainly handsome enough with his full head of dark hair and his ever-changing hazel eyes and his sad puppy-dog expression.

They began dating. He stopped drinking. So far as the reverend could tell. She found him the most gentlemanly date she had ever had, demanding little of her except an occasional goodnight kiss.

Eventually he even brought her home to meet his parents. O'Mather liked them, though she felt the mother was a little anxious, maybe over-protective, but accepting of her as Danny's "girl." She noted how his mother kept glancing at Danny, then at his father, as though waiting for something to happen, but the father, a policeman, treated her politely. One funny thing, though. James Harold took her aside and asked her if she was sure that being with Danny was what she wanted. She was surprised at the question but told him that it was.

Later, James demanded to know where Danny got off getting himself a girl and how the hell did he expect to take care of one.

Danny ignored him, and soon after the couple approached Reverend Hudspeth and told him they had filled out an application for a marriage license at the office of the Clerk of Court in Caddo Parish.

On September 6, 1974, they became man and wife. She was nineteen, he was twenty years old.

9

Someone of His Own

No surprise, at least in retrospect, the marriage between Danny and O'Mather was no great success. As psychologists would say, his feelings of sexual inadequacy, which increased in marriage once he was expected to perform in a steady relationship, exacerbated his emotional problems by operating as another rejection. There had always been in his world of fantasies an underlying need for power over his partner in order to perform. It sprang out of his unabated sense of inferiority and out of an unconscious resentment towards all who had ever rejected him. He did not have that kind of power over O'Mather. He could never, he felt, control someone he knew. Not face to face. But control had always been a powerful element in achieving the height of sexual performance in his masturbatory fantasies. Reality without control was not remotely as satisfying.

And then inevitably, O'Mather kept talking to him about his inability to latch onto a steady job. When she went to Reverend Hudspeth to confide in him about her disappointment in her marriage, she couldn't bring herself to talk about their sex life . . . that it had been okay at first, that he kept having difficulty with impotence, that he had started drinking again . . . She only told Reverend Hudspeth that it was Danny's irresponsible behavior and his inability to keep a job that was at the root of their troubles.

The reverend asked if there was a resurgence of drug use.

She couldn't tell. He could be so sneaky sometimes, she didn't know. And he would apologize all the time. She just didn't think she could live with it any longer.

And then . . . she hesitated . . . she was pregnant.

"Give it another try," the reverend urged. It was too soon to give up.

She left then. Reverend Hudspeth tried to follow their progress but it was difficult since they had stopped coming to church. The last he heard, Danny had gotten himself a job in a restaurant in Shreveport. And then he lost track of them.

"O'Mather had become pregnant during the summer of 1975. It was during her pregnancy that her feelings about the marriage began to change drastically.

It started that time Danny came back to the apartment late in the evening. He was evasive about where he had been, mentioning only that he had gone to a neighbor's house. "No, not a neighbor's house," he amended. "Someone I work with . . ." He told O'Mather he knocked on the door and claimed the wife came to the door with just a shirt on.

Later on that evening, after Danny had gone out again, there was a knock on the door. To her shock, there were two police officers looking for him.

"What's the trouble, officer?"

And they told her that Danny had been seen peeping in windows.

She had never been so humiliated or embarrassed in her life. Her husband peeping in windows? It didn't set very well with her at all. Still, no matter how upset she was, she felt that she had to try to understand and work it out. For the sake of the child who was coming.

He denied it.

But the marriage got really shaky. They were having trouble all the time. Danny worked for the Water Department. One early morning O'Mather called his parents in frustration. "You've got to come over because he won't get up and go to work."

James and Claudia went over to their apartment. James didn't stop to say hello to O'Mather, who was in the kitchen when they arrived. He went straight into their bedroom. He ripped the covers off his son, jumped astride him, grabbed his hair and put a knife to his throat.

Months later, Reverend Michael and his wife Glenda Hudspeth were having one of their rare nights out for dinner—he taking a break from his duties as pastor of Kings Temple, she taking a break from the affiliated responsibilities she undertook as a preacher's wife. It was at the Mexican restaurant they had chosen as their night out that they saw him waiting on tables.

"Glenda, look," he said. "It's Danny Rolling."

"So he got a job at last."

Danny recognized them and went right over to them. With hardly a preamble he pulled out his wallet and opened it to a picture of a little baby girl.

"My daughter," he said.

"Well now," said Glenda, "She's certainly a pretty little thing."

"My daughter," he said again.

Several months passed before the reverend saw either Danny or O'Mather again. He had heard they moved out of the parish and hoped they had worked out their problems. He imagined that the baby girl had cemented the relationship. If nothing else, Danny seemed devoted to the child. His hope ended the evening that Rolling showed up at the rectory of Kings Temple and told Reverend Hudspeth that O'Mather was gone. And with her his daughter.

"Now God's against me too," he said. "Now God's punishing me too."

"Why would God be punishing you?" Reverend Hudspeth remembered asking.

"For being born," Danny drawled. "So much for praying," he added.

O'Mather filed divorce papers in Grant Parish. It was 1977, they had been married less than three years. Reverend Hudspeth believed the divorce was going to be a blow for Rolling, another rejection. In retrospect, he further believed it was a major turning point for Rolling, the loss of his marriage and more, of his daughter. The rector, of course, could have no idea of the need to take mental note of every detail, that the day would come when he would wish he could remember the details of these meetings with Danny more clearly. He did remember that he tried to console Rolling and had no impact. As for his parents . . . Claudia cried, his father shrugged—he had expected no better from him.

Shortly after O'Mather left, Danny took his father's Smith & Wesson revolver and began driving, he didn't know where. The window was open. The wind rushed in, curling around his neck, brushing his hair. He finally pulled up to an isolated spot in the woods and turned off the motor.

It was getting dark. He could hear the *wicker, wicker, wicker* of the yellowhammer somewhere off in the distance and the staccato drumming of its pointed bill on a hollow limb. He sat for a long moment in the front seat of the car.

He took out the revolver and held it in his palm. His hand rested in his lap. He lifted the gun and put its long barrel into his mouth. He could taste the cold of the metal against his tongue, the tip of the barrel resting against the roof of his mouth. His hand began to shake. He could feel the perspiration drenching through his T-shirt even in the cool evening air.

His finger tensed on the trigger. Moments passed. He didn't have the courage to pull the trigger.

By the time he took the barrel out of his mouth he had made a decision. A rationalization. He would go out and get himself killed. He would rob. He would be open and brazen about it. Maybe he couldn't pull the trigger, but he could let the policeman's bullet do it for him. A nice symmetry . . . a policeman's bullet for a son of a policeman.

Resentment had finally pushed Danny to a deadly jump in "logic." He would get revenge on anyone he could overpower to pay back all the people who he believed had hurt him. At the same time, while searching for his bullet, he could exact revenge on all of society for all the ill-treatment he had received, real or imagined. With the breakup of his marriage to O'Mather, he said he took the blame, at least on a conscious level with Reverend Hudspeth, but on a deeper unconscious level he was still laying the blame for all his problems on others. With Claudia's help, blaming others for his problems was a habit he had developed early in life. It had operated relentlessly throughout adolescence and into maturity. Now deciding to act on his frustrations, and looking to punish "them," he was, it seemed, in the early stages of what Jean-Paul Sartre called "magical thinking." If he couldn't directly hurt those who had injured him, then by "magical thinking," it would be just as satisfying and effective to hurt someone else.

Now as an adult he had the physical power to lay claim to his superiority —at least behind a gun.

Resolves taken, he moved away from Shreveport. Reverend Hudspeth would not hear from him again until years later when he would receive a letter from his former parishioner postmarked from a state prison in Georgia.

10

The Turning Point

All the learned explanations notwithstanding, there was still nothing in Daniel Rolling's background that could adequately account for the sadistic lust serial killer he was to become.

Yes, he was a psychologically damaged individual.

Yes, there was an impoverished emotional upbringing resulting in all the usual psychological jargon to explain aberrant behavior—poor self-image, poor sex life, a marked inferiority complex, poor self-control, an inability to connect with people on an intimate level.

Yes, there were physical beatings that perhaps could have resulted in brain damage to the limbic region of the brain, the part that controls violent impulses, but this has never been established.

It is largely accepted in psychological circles that a child reared in love does not have to overpower. A child reared in trust need not control. *But* many children are abused and many grow up loveless and they do not grow up to become serial killers. Is it the combination of abuse from one parent and overprotective love from the other that is the most damaging? Are the messages given so contradictory as to be deeply confusing at a time of emotional development when stability is crucial for the healthy development of the normal psyche? Or is it a genetic weak link? A defective chromosome? Brain damage? If the limbic region of the brain were damaged, control over violent impulses could, conceivably, be seriously impaired. There had been many blows to the head from his father.

No one knows for sure. There are many theories. All the experts can do is follow the patterns and continue to study the malevolence that ultimately destroys not only the abused child but so many of those unfortunate enough to step into the path of his violent aggressions after he has crossed the line from which, once stepped over, he can never return.

The chronicle of petty crimes begun in Daniel Harold Rolling's teenage years was to resume in earnest now that he was once again unattached. No wife. No daughter. No responsibilities. That was okay. His rich fantasy life made up for all the deprivation. It would one day be noted in a Florida newspaper covering the front-page crime that would forever haunt the families and friends of the Gainesville victims:

> Daniel Harold Rolling was a mentally unstable high school dropout, an alcoholic and a small-time crook. He would spend much of his adult life in prisons for sloppy supermarket robberies. When cornered, he readily confessed to the robberies. Often he sincerely apologized in his slow southern drawl for causing so much trouble.

The brutal violence had not yet started. Once it did, it would become addictive. All the seeds for the monster were there, but the triggering mechanism had not yet been sprung. What were the triggering factors that made the man cross the line to the patterns that comprised the makeup of the lust serial killer?

It was May 31, 1979. Aunt Jeanette was his father's sister and Danny had always liked her. Jeanette Caughey lived in Phenix City, Alabama, located directly across the Chattahoochee River from Columbus, Georgia. That was where his grandparents, Homer and Cavis Rolling, also resided.

Drifting now from place to place, Danny wound up in Phenix City standing on his aunt's front porch shaded from the harsh morning sun by cypress trees and slim longleaf pines. He asked if he could stay awhile. Just for the night. No, there was nothing wrong at home, nothing like that.

Well sure, Danny, welcome. The day hadn't come that she didn't have room for kin for a night. Aunt Jeanette had picked up a slow Alabamian twang in her speech since she had moved from Louisiana. It wasn't all that different from home, but there was a new edge. She had always liked the boy. Now as a man, his speech soft and fluid, he sure knew how to turn the spigot and let the words come.

His uncle would be home by dinnertime, she told him. Yes, he still preferred largemouth freshwater bass to saltwater tarpons. Yes, everyone in these parts still hunted 'coons and fox and 'possum and wild turkey.

But Danny seemed restless, antsy. He watched a cropduster swinging low on the far horizon. He asked after Grandma and Grandpa and was told they were doing poorly. Grandpa could hardly drive anymore. Did Danny want to visit them while he was there? Maybe tomorrow, he said. Right then he asked her to go out with him to celebrate his birthday. Well, okay, it wasn't today but it was a few days ago. When she laughed and said that didn't count anymore he let her off the hook and said he'd go by himself. If she'd let him borrow the car.

She was sorry, she never lent her car to anybody. Insurance and all, could be a real problem.

Another rejection. Even though she had agreed to let him spend the night she wouldn't go out with him—his own aunt—on his birthday, and she wouldn't lend him her damned car. Well, he didn't need her or her car or her handouts.

By the time he had gone out and was walking toward the center of town he had worked himself up into a proper fury. He found himself a car. It was pretty easy. Folks around those parts often left their keys in the ignition.

He drove west on Interstate 85. Thirty-five miles into the center of the Yellowhammer state he hit Tuskegee. Hungry, he almost pulled off the highway but instead found himself pressing down on the accelerator. It was another thirty-five miles before he hit Montgomery.

Okay, now what? . . .

That afternoon Rolling used his father's Smith & Wesson revolver to rob a Winn-Dixie grocery store just outside the capital. James wasn't even aware that his son had taken the gun.

They gave him the money. Just like that. In brown paper bags. It was amazing, the power of a gun when it was pointing at someone's belly. He calmly walked out of the store, easy as harvesting bait worms on a wet morning.

Actually, he told himself, he had been in too much of a hurry. He had only hit two of the registers. It wasn't much of a haul. As he drove east on I–85 back toward Phenix City he dumped the contents of the brown bags onto the front seat. Just a couple of hundred dollars spread out on the seat next to him.

This time, speeding past peach groves, peanut farms and huge sprawling fields of cotton, when he got to the turnoff for Phenix City he passed it. Phenix City was situated on I–85 close to the Alabama border just southwest of Columbus, Georgia. On a whim he crossed the state line over the Chattahoochee River, endlessly churning its way south to Lake Seminole and the Gulf of Mexico, and entered into the neighboring peach state.

He hit the outskirts of Columbus.

Maybe he would visit Grandma Cavis and Grandpa Homer in Bibb City. Maybe not.

As soon as he finished what he was going to do in Columbus, he figured maybe he wouldn't even go back to Phenix City. Instead he'd continue on along Georgia's Fall Line hills to—where? To Augusta, maybe. He remembered the country well. A lot of rivers flowed through Georgia on their way down to the Gulf. The Flint, the Ocmulgee at Macon, the Oconee at Milledgeville and the Ogeechee River, past miles and miles of the indigenous tobacco fields before you got to Augusta. He could make it there by nightfall. It was only 175 miles as the crow flies and I–85 was a pretty straight run. He would have enough money to live it up big in Augusta. Go bar-hopping in style. He'd have even more once he made his next stop. Maybe he would even cross the Savannah River into South Carolina. He could go any which way he wanted . . .

He slowed the car when he saw it. Another Winn-Dixie on the outskirts of Columbus, Georgia, He parked the car at a safe distance, reached for the Smith & Wesson and hid it in his pants belt under his shirt until he entered the large grocery store.

But this time he wasn't as lucky as he had been in Montgomery.

Immediately following his second armed robbery of the day, a $956 haul this time, he was spotted by two sheriff's deputies who happened to be pulling up outside the store as he was coming out still holding the gun in his hand. They stood between him and his car.

He ran in the opposite direction. They chased him. He finally stopped running. Funny. They didn't shoot.

The moment he was captured, he hung his head in shame. "Yes sir," he said to the two arresting officers. "It's me. I did it. And I'm real sorry."

That night Aunt Jeanette sat in front of her television to catch the late night news before going to bed. To her surprise, she heard about the arrest of her nephew on the eleven o'clock news. Right there, big as life, on her own television screen! But it couldn't be, he had been here in Phenix City with her only that afternoon. What was he doing in Columbus, Georgia?

His handcuffed image flashed on-screen as he was being escorted into the county sheriff's office. It was him, all right. She looked toward the porch where she had just prepared a guest bed for him. As soon as the news brief was over she went to the phone and dialed area code 318 and then her brother's telephone number.

Claudia answered. Jeanette identified herself, started to say what she'd seen on TV.

Claudia whispered she couldn't talk.

How was James? The answer was the dial tone from Claudia's disconnect. She didn't really have to ask how James was. He was a cop and his son had just been arrested for armed robbery.

Daniel Harold Rolling was charged with two counts of armed robbery since two clerks were robbed at separate registers within the Winn-Dixie grocery store in Columbus. In August of 1979, less than two months after the offense, he was convicted of the robbery and sentenced to six years in prison.

He had turned twenty-five on May 26. Ten years overdue, but he was in jail as his dad had always said he would be.

Grandpa Homer Rolling offered no conversation about the matter as they entered the county sheriff's office in Columbus. When his son James came to Georgia he went with him to retrieve the Smith & Wesson revolver Danny had used in the armed robberies.

"We both got permits to carry concealed weapons," Homer Rolling told the clerk who was holding the official release papers that had to be signed. "I'm with the Muscogee County Deputy Sheriff's office, and my son here is with the Shreveport Police Department in Louisiana."

"Well now, y'all don't say."

"Law enforcement's a bit of a family tradition in the Rolling family."

The clerk behind the desk grinned. "Now with your grandson, so's law breaking, it looks like."

James signed for the weapon and left without saying a word. His father followed him out of the car.

"What the hell happened with Danny anyway?" Homer asked.

"He always was no damn good," the father said.

"Can't he hold down a job?"

"A job! The l'il sunova bitch couldn't organize a piss-off in a brewery."

Up in the Valley Lands of Louisiana, when the neighbors in Sunset Acres heard of his arrest, there were few who were especially surprised.

He was kinda nice, thought neighbor Beverly Woodall as she read the local newspaper, but he was always kinda odd too . . .

Susan Hester remembered that the first thing she and her husband Joey were told when they moved across the street from the Rollings was that they were all weird. The father often berated the son in public while the mother overprotected him. Susan's husband Joey worked on the police force with James Rolling. He thought James was an okay feller, always kept his corners up. It was the kid who was the one who had the problems. Getting himself locked up for armed robbery just proved it . . .

Claudia Rolling found herself hiding inside her home. She didn't have to hear them. She could sense the neighbors bone-carrying to each other about her son being in jail.

On August 20, 1979, Rolling was sent to Jackson, Georgia, a small town of twenty-five hundred north of the Georgia Fall Line. After the brief evaluative process in Jackson, he was shipped to the Georgia State Prison in Reidsville to begin his sentence. It was one hundred seventy miles east of where the first armed robbery took place.

Security on the work detail to which he was assigned was minimal. Less than three weeks after he was admitted to Georgia State Prison, Rolling simply walked away from the detail. Reidsville, however, was a small rural hamlet of twelve hundred. Easily spotted in town, he was recaptured only hours later.

"I'm sorry," he apologized, sincerely.

A year was added to his sentence.

Military prison was a picnic compared to state prison life. Put under heavier guard, he was now in a prison population with violent racial tension, knifings, killings and lorded over by guards armed with shotguns that would pump buckshot over their heads—hit or miss—whenever a fight broke out. The pattern of physical abuse in his life continued through the internal brutality of the penal institutions. He was a good-looking young man. A vicious sexual component had been added. At the same time he learned he was powerful himself and it wasn't long before he was able to turn the tables. For the first time he realized it was just as easy to give punishment as to receive it. He had never realized before how vicious his own temper was and how intimidating it could be to others. *They* became afraid of *him*. He had his first taste of real power. It was heady, invigorating. It was the *answer*.

But at the same time there were the countervailing fear and feeling of helplessness from the fresh assaults he had not been able to repel at first, which added fresh scars, deepened old wounds. And with little to do in prison and little to occupy his mind—especially nothing to nourish the neediest, most urgent part of his personality—the nocturnal fantasies exploded, becoming more graphic, more violent, more involved with sexual exploitation. Now he lingered in his fantasies over the vividness of knives cutting through flesh, a secret life that brought rushes of sexual release. It was surprising to realize that he had never felt this way with O'Mather. She was always complaining, always making him unsure of his performance with her. Whether he was satisfying her. In his fantasies that never mattered . . . the women were objects for his pleasure.

He told no one about these dreams that occupied more and more of his silent moments alone in his bunk. On the surface, he was quiet, a loner. He was also cooperative with the prison personnel, and eventually they left him alone. He was too big, too strong, even too nice. His fellow inmates never really got to know him but they tended to like him . . . except there was something about him. For example, at Reidsville he caught a huge black cat that used to hang around the prison and stoned it to death.

On May 13, 1980, he was sent to the Medical Classification Center in

Jackson, Georgia, for a week of psychological evaluation. The testing lasted a full seven days until May 19. The results were not surprising. They were typical of the kind of shorthand evaluative blurbs scribbled in the spaces of psychological reports that were reserved for "Comments and Recommendations." They were also almost monotonously familiar.

Craves power . . .
Deep self-pity . . .
Persists in blaming others for his troubles . . .
Poor self-image . . .
Marked inferiority complex . . .
Complex violent impulses . . .
Deeply ambivalent feelings towards his mother . . .
A violent love/hate relationship with his father whom he idolizes and wants desperately to impress . . .

It was decided his relationship with his father seemed to be the most determining factor in his psychological makeup and the most damaging one.

Technically diagnosed once again as a "personality disorder," the evaluation now seemed to indicate irreversible psychological damage, but until the violence projected in the MMPI and TAT evaluative tests were acted on, nothing much could be done in the way of preventive measures. Not only did the authorities not have the means or the personnel to step in with intrusive therapy, but the psychological tests were, after all, evaluative tools, not scientific prophecies. Besides, the authorities really didn't pay much attention to the old psychological evaluations anyway.

Daniel Harold Rolling, a model prisoner, after all, even self-effacing, was brought back to Reidsville with few recommendations other than to return him to the Medical Classification Center for further testing if he displayed any marked antisocial behavior.

He didn't. What he did was write a letter.

"Glenda," the reverend called out to his wife as he opened up the letter with *Georgia State Prison* stamped across the top in pale red ink. "I've received a letter from Danny Rolling."

"From prison?"

Reverend Hudspeth nodded. "It's been a long time since I've heard anything of him."

"What's he say?"

"Nothing much," he said, scanning the legal-size yellow paper quickly. "Looks to me like he's just trying to keep in touch."

"You going to write back?"

"Of course."

"I'll jot him a note too."

"Yes, he sounds depressed . . ."

They both did write back and tried to encourage him to lift his spirits. Reverend Hudspeth did not keep Danny's letter. He never explained why.

In February of 1980, while still serving time in Georgia, on advice of the public defender Danny Rolling pleaded guilty to the July, 1979, armed robbery of the Winn-Dixie store in Montgomery, Alabama, and was sentenced to an additional ten years.

Now the Alabama penal system had a claim on him once he was released from Reidsville, Georgia.

"Don't you worry," the public defender said, avoiding the fierce look in his client's eyes. "You'll never serve that much."

By now, at age twenty-six, Danny knew the prison game and played it well. He was classified a trustee and housed in a cell with approximately forty other inmates. Being a model prisoner was easy. Keep to yourself, don't tell anyone what you're thinking, bide your time. The day would come for vengeance. "Magical thinking" was always operating beneath the sad-eyed self-effacing facade.

Approved visitors listed on the card were James Harold Rolling, Claudia Beatrice Rolling and Kevin James Rolling. James rarely visited his son in prison. Why should he? The kid was no good. He had lived up to all his worst expectations. Claudia came religiously.

"I love you, son."

"I love you too, ma."

In 1981, while his firstborn was still incarcerated in a Georgia prison, James Harold Rolling, fifty-nine, retired from the Shreveport police force after twenty-three years of service.

It was June 7, 1982. After serving three years in Georgia State Prison, the state of Alabama wanted Daniel Harold Rolling for another ten. Rolling was transferred from the Georgia penal system to the Alabama Department of Corrections to serve his designated decade for the Montgomery, Alabama, armed robbery.

The hated public defender in Georgia had been right about one thing . . . he hadn't served his full sentence in Georgia and he probably wouldn't serve the full ten in Alabama. But Rolling didn't like the thought

of going to another jail; he had gotten used to Reidsville. What he wanted
was *out*. But if he couldn't get out he didn't want to change.

Once in the Alabama prison he found he didn't mind being the only white
guy on a detail of forty blacks. He picked all the cotton they wanted, he
dug their damned ditches, he planted their crops, always watching the guy
on horseback with the .357 magnum that gave him his power, he sang for
the other cons—*they* appreciated his songs, sometimes even asking him to
sing for them—until eventually he was sent to the bakehouse where he
became known for his yeast rolls. He made no trouble, they called him
Cowboy, and eventually he was permitted a one-day furlough, so long as
he didn't leave the state.

Actually he didn't know where to go, what to do. He could have called
his mother in Louisiana, she would have come to spend the day with him,
but he decided against it. Instead he remembered he had kin in Birmingham, his own born cousin, Eric Bonnel Johnson, Jr., son of his mother's
sister Aunt Nadine.

Danny and Eric Jr., who was in his forties, were of different generations,
but when Danny called him, Eric Jr. invited him to dinner. He had seen
Danny Boy last at a family reunion a while back at the Wilkersons in
Shreveport. Not knowing what he was like these days, knowing only that
he was in jail for armed robbery, taking him out to dinner was better than
having him to the house during his day out. Like the rest of the family,
they had never been close.

They had a short quiet dinner, and after Danny went back to prison they
had no further contact. Eric had let it be known that he wasn't really
interested in any further relationship.

Well, who cared, who needed him? Danny also wondered why the hell
he had returned to prison anyway.

In July such thoughts had apparently hardened and he escaped from a
work camp out of the Alabama prison.

This time, steering clear of populated areas, he headed for the woods.
Again, the woods. He wasn't, though, about to stay in those woods too
long. He didn't know them well enough to feel comfortable. He did get to
know that besides rabbit and the raccoons, which were everywhere, the
wildcat was also ubiquitous in these parts, and insects were soaring annoy-
ingly around his head in eddying droves, beating against his eyelashes.

He began to make his way back home to Louisiana. And along the way
he came on a tiny tent revival meeting in progress and found himself
standing outside listening to the spiritually uplifting sermon. He spent a

hot humid night in a pecan orchard, wakened in the morning by a small, slow-moving herd of cattle grazing in the spaces between the trees.

Two days later he was apprehended by the Alabama authorities. It was at a run-down little crossroads store euphemistically labeled a *Supermarket* in big, bold, hand-painted letters.

He had, he said, been looking for food.

This time he did not apologize. This time he *looked* as though he could kill. He would be a free man for about one year out of the next nine.

Meanwhile . . .

Tracy Inez Paules, at twelve years of age, was a petite, dark-eyed girl with long dark hair flowing over her shoulders. She was growing up to be an extremely beautiful young lady—goal-oriented, athletic and an honor student with career ambitions in law. She had been elected president of her 1984 senior class at American High School in Hialeah, Miami, and was so popular she had been named Homecoming Queen—riding an enormous, flowered float in the parade, crowned with a glittering tiara and a smile to match while her father, George, a construction worker, and her mother, Ricky, a softball coordinator for the Department of Parks, looked on with unreserved pride.

Tracy was, indeed, energetic, bright. She was sports editor for Century, *the high-school newspaper, a member of the National Honor Society, played for the girls' soccer and softball teams, and was in the Sorota and Key clubs, high-school service organizations that worked at events such as Special Olympics . . .*

Manuel Taboada, Tracy's high-school chum, was tall, handsome and was in the same 1984 graduating class. They had been friends for some five years. They frequently spoke of how she planned to get a degree in political science and then go on to law school. His goals were simpler if no less ambitious: to be an architect. They planned to apply to the University of Florida at Gainesville together.

Like Tracy, Manny was an athletic, goal-oriented honor student whose size, after his built-in grin, was the first thing one noticed about him. A guard for the American High football team, Manny stood at six-foot-two and weighed 200 pounds. Like Tracy, he had the energy and extracurricular activities that made the two young friends stand out above the crowd. He worked for the high-school principal, Art Stevens, for a year and a half in the adult education program, showing teachers how to use projectors and television equipment. He was a member of the National Honor Society, a member of Sorota, a member of the television club and president of the high-school thespians club.

When a multi-departmental group at American High School put together the musical Grease *as its spring production, it was Manny Taboada who won the coveted lead role.*

One day over lunch in the school cafeteria Tracy brought up a serious subject they had talked about before. "There's too much crime," she said, and he agreed.

The two friends put their convictions into practice by taking part in crime prevention as members of their high school's Crime Watch program.

11

Back Home

While Tracy Paules was riding the streets of Hialeah on a decorated float, and while Manuel Taboada was taking curtain calls to audiences in the school auditorium, Danny Rolling was being released from the Alabama State Prison. He had served only two years in Alabama. So his lawyer had been right about that much too. He went back home to Shreveport, on the way staring out of the bus window at the familiar tall pine forests of the Louisiana uplands, past the miles and miles of sugar cane and rice planta-tions that lined Hart's Island Road–La. I–20. The closer the bus came to the Valley Lands of northern Louisiana the more nervous he became . . . he hadn't seen his father in a long time . . . Now the skeletal oil wells sprouted like weeds on all sides as though they germinated and grew by the natural process of pollination. And finally in town . . . home . . . past the ten-story Caddo Parish courthouse, where he and O'Mather had recorded first their marriage and then their divorce. It was seven years since she had taken off.

Bitch . . . Married another guy on him . . . The other guy adopted his own little girl . . . They were all alike . . .

During his incarceration, predictably, he had become substantially more needy, less apologetic and considerably more hardened. The dark side of his personality had become more pronounced in prison. It was now the dominant force.

The bus pulled into Shreveport's Continental Trailways on the corner of Fannin and Edwards. People romanticized the magnolia blossom, the bril-liant, multi-blooming Louisiana state flower. But all Rolling caught whiff of as he stepped off the bus was the town's huge municipal incinerator. That was the way the wind was blowing for him . . . On the surface his hometown looked the same. A close look, however, revealed the skeleton left by a crippling recession that had gutted the region while he was in jail. When the crude dried up, oil companies pulled out. The economy and civic pride among its two hundred thousand residents were slow to re-cover. Grime covered empty storefronts, and many office buildings along Market, Edwards and Marshall streets stood partially empty.

So what? Not only had Shreveport changed, so had Danny Rolling.

*   *   *

At home he got the usual response from his father, who informed him that he'd better get a job, Danny wasn't living off him anymore. He was retired now and money was tight.

But, also as usual, he couldn't find a job. He spent his days in the yard working out with weights, wearing fatigues and army boots. Sometimes he ventured out of his front yard to go jogging. It became a sight to watch him jogging through the neighborhood carrying a heavy log across his shoulders. He looked intense and powerful. And he started drinking again.

The last time he had come home his mother wasn't allowed to wash his clothes. Now she wasn't allowed to cook his meals. His dad always was tight as a tick with a dollar where he was concerned; now more so, it seemed, when she told him the restrictions James put on her. But Danny didn't think the restrictions were on account of monetary reasons. It was because his father hated him, nothing had changed. And she couldn't do anything about it. Back home again didn't work. He had to get out of there.

Where to?

He remembered his born-cousin Eric's parents, his Uncle Eric, Sr., and his mother's sister, Aunt Nadine. They lived in Havana, Florida, just north of Tallahassee. As he vaguely remembered from the family reunion at the Wilkersons in Shreveport, Uncle Eric was okay. A plumber by trade. That wouldn't be bad for a while maybe, and the thought of Tallahassee appealed to him.

Uncle Eric and Aunt Nadine, God-fearing people, were quick to open up their door and welcome him into their home. But when Aunt Nadine found marijuana in his room she immediately handed over the illegal "green tobacco" to her husband. "I'm sorry, Uncle Eric," Danny apologized. But Uncle Eric informed Danny Boy he'd have to leave.

Aunt Nadine, Danny's own mother's sister, looked sad but she wasn't interfering with her husband Eric. He knew best in these matters. Just like his own mother not standing up to his father.

Danny left the home of Uncle Eric and Aunt Nadine, and the vagabond pattern of existence continued as he drifted from relative to relative. He would try another part of the country . . . he was sick of the South anyway. California. He knew he had relatives in California.

His father's brother, Uncle Joe Rolling, lived in Camarillo with his wife, Mira, and his son, Donald David. His father and Uncle Joe rarely contacted one another, but it was a relative.

When he telephoned from the bus station Aunt Mira was the one who answered the phone.

He said, in his soft-spoken drawl, that he was wondering if he could set himself down for a while with them.

It might be a little disconcerting, but how could she refuse him? He was already in town. She asked how his ma and pa were. Just great, he told her. They wanted him home but he had the itch to travel a little. See California. Sure. Well, he was certainly welcome to stay for a while, Danny Boy . . .

He had another born-cousin in her son Donald David, but again, as with Cousin Eric Bonnel Johnson, Jr., they had little to do with each other. It wasn't only because of the difference in their ages—Donald David was younger—but mostly because Danny was still a loner. While staying with them there was the obvious drinking problem, which Aunt Mira wasn't too happy about. Kin was kin, but just because Danny was her husband's brother's son didn't mean she had to put up with a drinking problem under her own roof.

When he asked to borrow $400, she gave it to him, thinking that he would probably buy himself a ticket out of Camarillo. Instead he came back to the house driving a Suzuki motorcycle.

"Where did you get *that*?"

"Bought it."

"What're you going to do with it?"

"Oh, I dunno, drive around, see some things, I guess . . ."

Well, at least he would be gone for a while. She was getting tired having him hang around with nothing to do.

He headed north for Ventura on 101. He liked the feel of the motorcycle under him, the roar of the engine enveloping him, the sense of power it gave him to be able to speed past other people.

Then a skid.

Panic. He felt the heavy cycle slide out from under him around a turn. He tried to control it but could not. The motorcycle skidded off the road and crashed against a tree, throwing him into a deep ditch. But except for a few scrapes and bruises he wasn't seriously injured—the ditch was padded with soft vegetation debris.

It was recorded as a single vehicle accident. The date was February 13, 1985. He wasn't drunk this time, just pushing too hard on something he wasn't practiced on. The motorcycle was completely wrecked. The accident report indicated that the bike was still registered to a Christopher David Herron.

Suddenly he decided he had had enough of sunny California, and nursing a series of black-and-blue bruises, he left Uncle Joe's and Aunt Mira's at the end of March. The reason he gave for his abrupt departure was that he missed his daughter and wanted to return to Shreveport. He left the area by bus, without repaying his aunt's loan.

He drifted back east . . . through Arizona, New Mexico, hitchhiking, stealing a car here and there, picking up a few dollars at small-time, out-of-the-way grocery stores or service stations, idling at the growing number of shopping malls he came across. When he called Aunt Mira from somewhere outside Sweetwater, Texas, and asked if she would write to him when he got back to Shreveport, she refused.

That saddened him but didn't surprise him. Bitch . . .

"Can you imagine the nerve, him leaving like he did never paying back the four hundred dollars he borrowed!" Aunt Mira said to Uncle Joe, who shared her indignation.

"He'll never get bowlegged from totin' his brains, I'll tell ya," he said in good Louisiana parlance. "We don't have to have anything to do with any of them anymore."

Danny could tell he was getting closer to home when a dollop of grits came with the scrambled eggs in the morning. Home, he was almost there . . . but he bypassed Louisiana and made his way north, crossing the Red River into Arkansas, and wound up in Nashville, Tennessee.

By July of 1985 he was hitchhiking through Jackson, Mississippi, from Tennessee with a "nice feller" by the name of Jake. He was an okay sort, friendly enough and talkative, with long, probably exaggerated stories about his exploits with women. They were having a gay old time when a local police car with his lights twirling got on their tail.

Danny wondered what they were onto him about now.

"You done anything?" Jake asked.

"Not much in Tennessee."

Jake reached under the driver's seat, taking his time, slowing down to the edge of the road, and pulled out a .45–caliber semiautomatic handgun from its hiding place. "Here, take it," he said, thrusting the automatic at Danny. "It's me they want."

Danny slipped it in his belt under his shirt.

Once pulled over, Jake stepped out of the car and nodded toward Danny. "Don't mind him, none," Jake told the arresting officer who was cuffing his hands behind his back. "He's just a hitchhiker I was giving a ride to from up the road a ways."

"Listen," Danny called out of the window as he slid over to the driver's seat—last thing he wanted was to get himself searched—"I'll follow you if you want. I'll drive the car to the station for you."

Danny took the car to the police station, following close behind the officer's vehicle. He delivered the car, but kept the gun.

He then took off by bus and eventually arrived in Clinton, Mississippi, a few miles west of Jackson, where he decided he was hungry. He felt the hard edge of the gun against his belly, warm now with his own sweat, as he entered the Kroger grocery store. It was broad daylight, about two in the afternoon.

He walked about the store easily filling up the small cart he was pushing. Not too much. He didn't want to carry a large bag or anything like that. The girl at the counter, with thick eyeglasses and a long black ponytail that started at the crown of her head, glanced in his direction at the far end of the aisle facing her. The squeaky wheels pinpointed his position in the store. Once he had done his shopping, he waited at the back of the store while the girl bagged another patron's groceries. She was slower than molasses but it didn't matter. The store was almost empty.

When the checkout counter was empty he abandoned his squeaky cart, pulled on the ski mask he had purchased for just such a purpose and walked directly up to the counter. He pulled out the gun. "Give me your money," he said.

The girl looked up startled, thinking for a moment it was a joke. He shook the barrel directly at her stomach with a gentle flick of his wrist. She looked down at the barrel, then up at his covered face. She pushed the cash button on the register. The drawer rang open. Just as slowly as she had done the bagging, she pulled out the twenties, the tens, the fives and the singles.

"Keep the change," he said.

He got $290, ran from the store and hid in a wooded area across the interstate. He needed wheels. He was almost sorry now that he had returned the car. Well, he'd had little choice at the time with the cops on Jake's tail.

Now he spotted a nearby house and noted that one of the glass panes on the door was broken. Getting into the house was easy. Good, it was empty. He searched the house, taking whatever he needed, whatever suited his fancy. In the kitchen he opened the refrigerator and helped himself to some bananas and yogurt. He left the empty yogurt cup in the middle of the kitchen table with the spoon he had used delicately balanced across the top of it, and the banana peel on the table next to it carefully positioned like a tent.

He was signing his signature.

As he was to do later in a more horrible, gruesome fashion. He wanted the owners of the burglarized house to find a message from him when they returned. Leaving the yogurt cup and the banana peel on display like that for them to discover when they returned was his subconscious way of showing them that it might be their house but *he* was the one who was in control. He could violate their home, rob them of their possessions, eat their yogurt and fruit, and leave the remnants displayed on their table for them to see the moment they entered the kitchen. Not just as an indignity, but more importantly, as the ultimate display of power. *His* power over them.

They had left their car keys lying on a table by the front door and the car parked right outside. Now that was right nice of them. He wondered briefly where they were. It didn't matter. He took the car.

The next day, while driving through the neighborhood, a policeman saw the car moving erratically and stopped him.

He always was a lousy driver.

Looking inside the vehicle, the policeman spotted a ski mask on the seat next to the driver. That's what the man who had robbed the grocery store had used; he had heard about the Kroger robbery on the car radio. He reached for his revolver and took Danny Rolling to jail. The prisoner was soft-spoken, even apologetic when the policeman searched the car and found the gun used in the Kroger holdup.

The charge was grand larceny and armed robbery.

Clinton, Mississippi, attorney Arthur Carlisle was appointed to defend Rolling on the charges, and found himself liking his new client. Thirty-one years old, Rolling stood at six feet two inches. He was a large man, but there was something that seemed vulnerable, needy about him. He was like a big kid. The minute Carlisle smiled at him, Rolling seemed to lean into him as though lapping up his friendliness, wanting more. Carlisle could tell that his new client "liked him a bunch." He was always so happy to see him when he came to visit him at the jail, and so eager to please.

Carlisle would sneak candy bars to the prisoners, and his client Rolling was partial to Snickers bars. That small surreptitious kindness cinched the relationship between attorney and client. To thank him, the next time Carlisle came Rolling slipped him a drawing he had made especially for him.

"That's pretty good," Carlisle said. The guy seemed to be a gifted artist, he thought. "I'm right impressed."

Rolling beamed. He had given him a drawing of a vine with crisscrossed tendrils. At the top was a dove in different stages of flight.

Carlisle thought the drawing was really good. "Are you an artist?"

"Not really. I'm a musician."

"Is that right?"

"But my ma teaches art sometimes. To older folk. I guess that's where I get it from. My ma. What I really want . . ."

"What?" the attorney urged. "You can tell me."

"I have a dream. I want t'be in a musical band."

And then Rolling softly performed for him, simulating a harmonica by humming through his cupped hands.

"Harmonica, huh?"

"Guitar, really. I play it pretty good. Taught m'self most of it." He grinned, apparently embarrassed. "I had plenty of time."

Carlisle looked at the drawing again. On the side of the drawing was a twelve-line poem. "Did you write this?"

Danny nodded.

Carlisle began to read it to himself, then looked up. "It says here something about how you must die alone and try to live your life to the fullest for excellence."

"That's right," Danny said. "We have to live, love and die."

"Out of the twelve lines," Carlisle said, looking at his client, "at least four or five of 'em talk about death."

"Yeah, I know."

"Now all that strikes me as strange."

"Why?"

"Why all this stuff about dying?"

"Oh, it's nothing."

"After all, you're only in here for robbery."

"That's just my dad."

It was a slip. Arthur Carlisle was no psychiatrist but he was sure he knew what his client meant. He had already been in touch with the father. What a difference between the two. For an armed robber, Danny Rolling was pretty nice on the whole. He seemed to be one of those guys who goes along fine and then the fuse goes and he just flips. But the old man . . .

As though able to read his thoughts, Danny suddenly asked, "Did you call my dad?"

"Yep."

"What'd he say?"

"We'd better leave him out of it."

"Sure, I know. I get it." There was a long moment of silence before he added, "Man, I sure wish I could please the old man."

Carlisle didn't want to tell him the truth of the conversation he had had with the father. What good would it do? He had to keep his client together and able to handle himself in front of the judge when the time came to stand before him. This man definitely had problems, and his attorney had an idea where some of them came from. When he had called Shreveport he got the mother on the phone, and she warned him to keep their conversation "hush-hush" because of his father. Then he could hear a smothered argument on the other end of the line before a man's voice came on.

"Who is this?"

"My name's Arthur Carlisle. I'm an attorney in Clinton, Mississippi—"

"Are you out to defend my son?"

"Yes, I . . ."

"You don't call this house anymore, y'heah?"

"Mr. Rolling—"

"You don't need to help that son of a bitch," the father shouted into the receiver. "And don't call me for help." And he hung up.

"I'm real sorry for what I done," Danny Rolling was telling him quietly now. ("I regret with all my heart what my hands have done," Rolling would say years later at his confession for the students' murders. He was getting the words to his deadly music early on.) "But I don't want to go back to prison."

"I'll do the best I can for you," Carlisle said.

Rolling was like a bird that, once let out of its cage, went wild, out of control until he was captured and returned. And in a sense it was almost as though, on an unconscious level, he would do anything, regardless of what he said about prison, to get back into the controlled environment of prison, where there was the safety of routine. It was his home.

Rolling looked to be close to tears. "I know I did wrong, and like I said, I'm sorry . . ."

Like a big kid, Carlisle thought again.

Rolling hesitated before looking his lawyer in the eye. "But instead of going back to jail," he continued seriously, "couldn't I just have my hands cut off?"

Carlisle stared. He wasn't joking. "I don't think that's possible."

"Don't you see," Rolling said, "then I wouldn't be able to do any more bad things . . ."

Now that was just plain crazy. "I don't think the judge'd go for it."

Carlisle was also amazed that Rolling was so willing to plead guilty to the charges.

"What's your hurry?"

"Might as well. I just want to get it over with."

Something was definitely off the mark here, but he felt that Rolling knew right from wrong, though he had an inner world he protected from others. Still, as soon as he left his client, Carlisle asked the court to have him psychiatrically evaluated. The lawyer was dedicated enough to his profession and to his client to have that done, not depend on his own feelings.

Carlisle was interested in the quality of his client's psychological thought processes, thinking them perhaps bizarre enough to make him less culpable in the eyes of the law. The tests were geared more toward the ability to distinguish between right and wrong. The McNaghten rules which were used to determine whether one was capable of such a distinction had come to American jurisprudence from England in the 1800s and were the cornerstone of the concept of legal insanity. There is little in this evaluation process, though, to probe through the facade that can hide the dark side or to reveal the sadistic fantasies that persist in a private make-believe world.

The prisoner apparently understood the charges against him and even though he was, once again, diagnosed on paper as having a "Personality Disorder—internal emotional scars . . . perhaps inflicted by abusive parents when a child . . . talks of desire for freedom but seems to be 'at home' in a prison environment"—it was a routine case, legally and clinically. He was not legally insane.

Carlisle had gotten very busy with other clients shortly after his request to the court for an evaluation on Rolling, and his dealings with him dwindled to waiting for the psychiatric reports and meeting him in court the day of sentencing.

Two court officers brought Daniel Harold Rolling into the room to stand before the judge.

Arthur Carlisle hardly recognized his client. While awaiting his sentence Rolling had shaved off all of his hair and eyebrows.

"Why'd you do that?" he whispered. This was not the way to present himself to the court for sentencing. He looked bizarre, maniacal.

"I want to change," Danny said stiffly. "That's why. I'm cleaning up."

Grim, frowning, he faced the judge. He was sentenced to fifteen years in a Mississippi prison for armed robbery, burglary and grand auto theft. Carlisle tried to convince the judge that his client should serve only three years in prison followed by five years of probation.

As Rolling was led out of the courtroom, Carlisle saw him mouth the words "I love you" to a little woman seated at the back of the room with dark hair that was beginning to turn gray across the top.

This was a client attorney Arthur Carlisle was not likely to forget. Many months later Rolling wrote him a letter to thank him and to tell him he was doing fine. After that, Carlisle lost contact with him until years later when he would read about him in the headlines.

Daniel Harold Rolling began his formal sentence at Mississippi's Parchmont State Penitentiary on July 25, 1985. He was put in solitary on a regular basis. His cell was cold, damp, sewage leaking through the cracks in the crumbling walls. His companions were spiders and an occasional rat.

Three months later, in October, he was taken out of his cell and attached to a chain-gang. The work assignment was fields of cane grass that had to be cut and pounded down. Then cotton fields. "Asses and elbows up, girls!" "Get that cotton!" Shotguns and loaded holsters, vicious in the abuse piled on the weak, the respect paid to the ruthless. But Danny was getting stronger. No one messed with him anymore. They had seen him fight his way through his "problems" with other inmates. He was a wildman, and they had nicknamed him "Psycho."

His mother visited him on a regular basis. His father never came.

He was thirty-one now with an enormous craving for power and an abiding resentment at the world. He didn't care about the fact that he was a thief and an armed robber. The laws of an unjust society that had refused to give him a chance deserved to be broken. People who lived behind doors that were always locked up tight to him deserved to be stolen from. "Magical thinking." If he couldn't hurt people who had hurt him he would hurt someone else. The self-justification of his attitude was based on deep self-pity. He didn't realize that, by now, he was always looking for someone on whom he could lay the blame for his misfortunes. By blaming others, his criminal violence was, in his warped mentality, justified. The son of a father who had consciously sworn to uphold the law had unconsciously sworn to break it.

Nothing here or elsewhere in this work should be interpreted as excusing or condoning violent antisocial behavior. Some experts, however, do claim that so-called human monsters can be created. A child, they say, who is abused, beaten, sexually assaulted and emotionally starved is a candidate to be turned into a monster. Other violently antisocial "monsters," such as, for example, Charles Manson, have said if they couldn't hurt those who had hurt them they would get even by hurting someone else. Danny Rolling said it and he, as he admitted, did it. The countervailing argument, of course, is that the vast majority of children who have suffered abuse and deprivation, often extreme, do not turn into Charles Mansons or Danny Harold Rollings.

12

Free Again

Ken Jones, director of Public Relations for the Mississippi Department of Corrections, noted that inmate Daniel Harold Rolling was discharged from Parchmont State Penitentiary on July 29, 1988.

His attorney Arthur Carlisle had been correct. Danny had served only three years and four days of his sentence, after all. After his release he was placed on a five-year probation term that he could serve in his home state of Louisiana. So he had to go back home, no place else to go. And he wanted to see his father anyway, maybe this time . . .

No one, of course, knew he had spent most of the three years of his Mississippi prison sentence fantasizing about killing.

A free man, he headed home once again to Shreveport, Louisiana.

Well into his thirties now and with no marketable skills, he moved back in with his parents. His brother Kevin was gone by now, he had moved across the state line to Wascom, Texas, rarely communicating with his parents. His father, retired, was older, more dour and even less accepting of Danny than before. His mother, always feeling a little sick and a little depressed, was heavier, duller, sadder . . . You be a good boy, now, won't you, Danny? . . . Sure, Ma . . .

His mother still was not permitted by his father to wash Danny's clothes or cook his meals. He still had to take off his shoes when he left the kitchen. Nothing had changed.

He had left prison muscular and strong and with a penchant for camouflage fatigues and combat boots, as though a return to military-style fatigues and olive drab T-shirts somehow erased the years spent in prison.

A neighbor, Inez Hutto, observed him from her window. The strangest thing, she said, was seeing him home from prison with his head shaved smooth wearing a bandanna and jogging through the neighborhood with a big log over his shoulder. She could still remember when her own son and Danny had attended school together. They had never been friends. Danny didn't seem to have any long-time friends. An odd one. One thing, dressed as he was, he attracted the neighborhood children. He set up a weight bench in his front yard and the kids would come over and Danny would

115

spot for them. She saw him playing his guitar and singing songs to them. From across the street she could hear and thought he had a nice singing voice. The neighborhood children, though, called him Rambo behind his back. They also said he was a nice guy. The adults thought he was strange and were wary of him.

His father's old police buddy Joey Hester noted that Danny never came out of the yard except to jog with that log across the back of his shoulders. And another neighbor, Beverly Woodall, remarked to her family, "He's really a weird one." But aside from that cursory observation she never gave him any more thought. After all, he didn't bother anybody . . .

Rolling finally landed a steady job in a small convenience store in Shreveport. He liked convenience stores. His relationship with his father, however, didn't improve. James Rolling constantly reminded his son that he was a "big zero."

"I see your son's back," Bernadine Holder said to her neighbor James Rolling. She had lived across the street from them for the last twenty-four years and had watched the Rolling family go through more ups and downs than a roller coaster. Especially Danny. Now he was back. She was about to congratulate the father and wish them all well when his expression stopped her.

"That sunova bitch's back here freeloadin' again."

She knew the two had never gotten along too well. You couldn't live across the street from them all the years she had without knowing that much. Poor Claudia. But she was sure James was just loudin' off again. "Well, maybe if you gave him a chance to—"

"To what? T'screw up again? I wish that sunova bitch would just drop dead and be outta here f'good an' all."

His own son. Poor Danny, she thought. "Now, you know he wants nothing more'n t'please y'all," she tried. " 'Specially you."

The angry father leaned toward her as they stood on the macadam driveway already beginning to blister under the noonday sun. "He's narrow between the eyes," he told her. "Always was. Always will be. I wish the little bastard would die."

"You don't *mean* that . . ."

"Don't I, though! He ain't nothing but a no-good, good-f'nothin' thief!"

Actually it wasn't the first time he had told Bernadine he wished his son dead. Now Danny had come home a full-grown man, big and strong, a good six inches taller than his father. Bernadine Holder found herself fearing for the whole family.

* * *

Danny had started his job at Western Sizzler Steak House on October 3, 1988. On November 21 he was fired. He had managed to keep the job for only seven weeks. He didn't want to tell his parents he had been fired. One night he just didn't go home.

Falling into his old pattern of drifting, he again began wandering from relative to relative. He couldn't go to visit Uncle Joe and Aunt Mira. She had refused to write to him. He couldn't go back to Aunt Jeanette in Alabama. He'd never forgiven her for not lending him her car. Instead he went across the entire state of Alabama, crossed the state line into Georgia, and went to see his grandparents in Bibb City just outside of Columbus.

"You out now?"

"Yes, Grandpa."

"You learn anything in there?" Grandma Cavis asked quietly.

"Yes'm. I was wonderin'—"

"What?"

"I thought maybe I could get a job around here. Stay with y'all for a while." He never mentioned that his parole stated that he had to remain in Louisiana.

Grandma Cavis said sure. He looked to Grandpa Homer. "Well, okay, if she don't mind, I don't mind." Every time he thought about it he still smarted from the snickering aimed in their direction when he and James had gone to pick up the Smith & Wesson at the police station. "One thing though . . . I ain't gonna leave a door to the house unlocked and let you come and go from this residence as you please. If you ain't home by the time your grandma and I go to bed you won't be able t'git in."

Danny hemmed and hawed. He couldn't be restricted that tightly in his movements. A familiar level of resentment was rising in his gorge. "I guess I won't be stayin'," he finally murmured with a smile, not showing the rage that was inside him.

"Suit yourself."

"I was wonderin' . . . Could I borrow some money for bus fare back home?"

Homer Rolling grimaced. He might have known. He gave Danny a few dollars but not enough to purchase a bus ticket to Shreveport. He hitchhiked the rest of the way.

So once again Danny drifted his way back home to Shreveport.

No place else to go.

13

Poor Danny Rolling

No matter what he did it was never good enough for any of them! Danny Rolling was having a tough time holding onto a job. Everybody had to die sooner or later. Why not all of them? Sure, sometimes he was late for work but so what. What did they mean "too emotional"? "Too irrational"? He was trying real hard, wasn't he? What did they all want out of him anyway?

God, God, God. Nearer my God to Thee. Damn. He'd give it another go. Another try. If he couldn't find anything, he wasn't responsible for what happened anymore. It was their fault. Where was that bullet anyway? It was still out there somewhere. Waiting for him but it was sure taking its time finding him!

Everybody had to die sooner or later.

Sooner, later, what difference did it make?

He managed to get himself another job, this time working at Western Sizzler in Shreveport's South Park Mall, where he kept pretty much to himself.

Dying, death, dead. That's what the poems and the songs were always about. He didn't think it was so goddamned special.

He saw her one day after work when he had wandered into Dillard's department store in the South Park Mall near Western Sizzler. She was small, dark-haired and pretty enough to model at the mall. She looked familiar. He felt a flood of resentment, so strong it made him want to throw up. From a distant aisle near the main entrance of the department store he squinted at her across one of the cosmetics counters where she was smiling at a customer. Smiling! He was miserable and she was smiling! Hadn't he seen her at Kings Temple church during those days when he used to go there with O'Mather? Probably not. She would have been too young back then and would have changed a lot by now.

But in fact he had been right. He *had* seen her. She was twenty-three years old now. Her family used to attend the same church that he and O'Mather went to in the days when he had a wife and daughter.

Her name was Julie Grissom.

*   *   *

While Danny cooked steaks at Western Sizzler and often dawdled outside Dillard's just to stare at dark-haired Julie Grissom who brought back so many bad memories, sixteen-year-old Christa Leigh Hoyt took another step toward her career goal.

After her junior year in Newberry High School, she had the opportunity to work as a part-time summer apprentice with the United States Department of Agriculture Entomology Lab in Gainesville. She took the opportunity. She knew that working in a lab would help her toward one of her ambitions—to become a chemist and work in criminal forensics. The chemistry-lab job was in line with her career goal.

By February of her final high-school year she joined the Alachua County Sheriff's Explorer Post #983 and became an active Explorer in both the Florida Sheriff's Explorer Association and the Alachua County Sheriff's Office. She loved it . . . "exploring" gave her a taste of the law-enforcement experience she craved. And it was here that she met Kim Norman, her supervisor, who became her good friend.

Always willing to do more than was expected of her, she soon earned the rank of senior sergeant and as such took on the duties of post secretary. She also rode patrol with Alachua County Deputy Gail Barber.

Tracy Paules, twenty-one, was more stunning than ever.

In the fall, she would be heading for her sophomore year at the University of Florida to continue her pre-law studies. In order to begin practical experience, at the close of her freshman year at UF she went to work at a law firm in Miami as an apprentice.

It was at this point that life began to get more complicated for her. She was immediately attracted to Kevin Orr, a handsome young black man. And within a month, they were dating steadily, beginning in July of 1988. When they met, Kevin was seeing another white girl by the name of Cindy, but when his and Tracy's dating became steady he told Tracy that he had broken off his relationship with Cindy.

Kevin Orr was probably one of the most exciting men Tracy had ever met. Not only was there the added attraction of dating someone secretly— she couldn't tell her parents about Kevin, they would never understand, she felt—but there was the lure of the forbidden. He was worldly, well-known in the establishments they frequented in Miami—the Club New, the Firehouse Bar, the Sports Rock Cafe. When he started taking her to his Key Biscayne condominium, she was attracted to the point of wondering whether she was in love with him. By late September, after much soul-searching, they became intimate.

Tracy Paules was in love.

In December she had left the law firm job to go back to school. But she was uneasy about her relationship. Cindy had not disappeared from Kevin's life, it seemed. Tracy had arrived at Kevin's Key Biscayne condominium unannounced and found Cindy there. And Cindy was just as upset as Tracy . . . rather obviously Kevin told her that he was no longer dating Tracy. The two women were not only angry at Kevin but confrontational with each other. At one point during all the ensuing scenes the two young women had agreed not to date him again. But Tracy had seen him every day on the job, and it wasn't long before the romance rekindled, perhaps heated by its very adversity—breaking up and making up could be very seductive.

Meanwhile, Danny was fired from Western Sizzler, quit a clerking job at a Circle K convenience store, and took a temporary part-time job as Christmas help at a Wal-Mart store.

He kept almost exclusively to himself.

The days were black.

The nights were full of familiar sexual fantasies.

By January of 1989 when Tracy Paules left Miami to attend school in Gainesville, her relationship with Kevin was more solid than ever. Throughout the spring semester she flew to Miami almost weekly to spend the weekend with him in Key Biscayne. Her parents were still not aware of this relationship nor did they know how often she was in the Miami area without coming home. Tracy felt terribly guilty about the deception, the behavior was very unlike her, but she was deeply involved and she knew her parents would not approve of Kevin. Perhaps it would end on its own, but she felt she could not give him up, not yet. It was best to keep it a secret.

It was June of 1989. Christa Hoyt was applying for the FSEA State secretarial post at the State Delegates Meeting in Tallahassee. Where it indicated on the application that she should describe herself, she wrote one word: "Perfectionist."

And she was. She worked very hard at everything she did.

Once again the long litany of accomplishments established another one of the Ripper's victims as a living embodiment of spectacular achievements.

When Christa Hoyt graduated from Newberry High School, it was no surprise to anyone who knew her that she was an honor student. In her senior year she received the award for Most Outstanding Humanities Student. She was also awarded the Most Outstanding American Government Student. On graduation she won a scholarship to Santa Fe Community College. Her parents had divorced by now, Teresa Ann marrying a man named Garren and her father Ralph had also remarried. At first it was difficult when her parents divorced, but ever the pragmatist, and viewer of the silver lining, Christa came to the point where she decided she was lucky to have two sets of parents. She actually was very fond of her stepmother Diana, but felt her stepfather was "something else again." Mom had her hands full with him.

Always interested in the law, especially criminal forensic science, Christa now took a full-time job with the Alachua County Sheriff's Office in the records department. All her activities were bringing her a step closer to her career goal.

Danny Rolling often turned to Bunny Mills for support. His good old friend. Bunny. That's who he should have stuck with. They dated sometimes, but more than a date, she was a friend who liked him and was always there when he needed her. Bunny didn't mind that he turned to her whenever he was in a real bind. She recognized what she thought of as his built-in panic button, which she believed made it more difficult for him to deal with stressful situations. He was so nervous sometimes.

"Nothing has ever gone right in my life," he said to her. "Nothing! And now look, I'm out of a job again!"

He was thirty-five.

Suddenly he was on his knees.

"Danny . . ." She was shocked at his emotional display.

"Why don't my father love me? I'd do anything to get that ol' man to love me some. I mean, we all gotta die someday, right? He's gonna die, I'm gonna die, you're gonna die . . ."

"Danny . . ." She knew all about his abusive father. Once she had seen Danny take off and put on his shoes seven or eight times in less than an hour's time to abide by his father's rule. "Danny . . . Come on, Danny, get up." She hated it when he talked so much about dying. And he did it a lot.

"I ache," he said. "Ache all over 'cause I can't hold my own daughter and let her know her own daddy isn't really such a horrible man."

"You're not horrible."

"In here," he said, pointing to his temple. "If you could see in here."

The escalating violence of the bizarre sexual acts he envisioned disturbed even him. That's *not* the way he was! He had a good heart. He had idealistic dreams. He believed in love and family and God. He wanted to compose and play music and sing and draw pictures. He didn't understand why, lately, those fantasies seemed to be the only way he could feel sexual arousal. He remembered it had never been good with O'Mather. He didn't know why. Even drugs didn't help. That's why she left. Bitch. Took his daughter away from him. Sex-starved bitch. Running around with another guy. I'll bet she had more'n one mule in the stable. She lit off quick enough.

"If I could just hold my li'l girl," he said. "You know, she's got t'be close to thirteen by now . . ."

Her life had passed him by, and self-pity gave way to sudden rage again. Then: "Never you mind! I know what I'll do. I wrote me a song."

"A song?" Bunny asked, wondering where his mind was taking him now. He was flitting from one thing to another.

"I call it, 'I Need a Job.' "

"You'll have to play it for me sometime . . ."

"Now! I'm going to play it now! I'm going to the office of that damned oil company in town and I'm gonna sing it for them. 'I Need a Job.' "

That was just plain childish, Bunny thought. She had to talk him out of it. He'd make a damn fool of himself and for sure nobody at the local oil company would give him a job just because he came in singing for one.

"Danny, listen . . ."

"It's a good song!"

"I'm sure it is." She looked for the right words and then the thought struck her. Of course! Maybe Truman could help. "Look, you stop by my house tonight," she said to him. "I want you to meet someone."

"Who?" he demanded.

"A friend of mine. Someone who might be able to give you a job."

Danny made a face. Another crap job. He hadn't been able to hold onto any kind of job for more than a couple of months since his release. He thought it a much better idea to go sing his song.

"Will you come?"

That night at her apartment she introduced him to her good friend, Truman Cooley, an electrical engineer, an elderly, fatherly kind of guy who was in need of some help around his shop.

"Ever do any electrical stuff?" Cooley asked him.

"Some."

"Bunny over here recommends you highly."

"She does?" Unexpectedly the sullen look slipped off his face like a strip of gauze as he turned and beamed at Bunny.

She nodded to him encouragingly. "He's a friend of mine, and he needs a job," Bunny said to Cooley. "He's a good guy, and if you treat him right he'll work hard for you."

"Sure," Cooley said, "I could use some good help for a while."

Bunny looked at Danny. "I told Truman all about you—"

"All?" Danny turned and looked squarely at Truman Cooley. "I been in jail," he said before she could answer. "I'm gonna be up-front about my record, like it as not."

"Hey, that don't bother me none," Cooley said to him. "You do your work by me and we'll get along just fine. Besides . . ." He bent forward slowly to light a cigarette, and looked up at Danny over the flame cupped in his hands. "Bunny already told me."

Minimum wage again, but at least it was a job.

Manny Taboada thought it was a great job. The Moose Lodge. With his energy, if he worked it right he could make a pretty good dollar, even part-time, with tips. He had never tended bar before but he was sure it would be no problem.

The twenty-two-year-old young man had been in Gainesville since August of 1989 when he had taken an apartment at one of the nicer apartment complexes in town with his good friend Careaga, another bruiser of a guy. Together, they moved directly into apartment #1203 at Gatorwood Apartments on Archer Road. It was convenient, attractive and well kept, complete with swimming pool, tennis courts, laundry room.

And now with his being hired at the Moose Lodge as a bartender, Manny felt things were going really well. Just as planned. The future was rosy.

While Danny Rolling worked with Truman Cooley as an apprentice electrician, Manny tended bar at the Moose Lodge, and Christa Leigh Hoyt worked at the endless walls of floor-to-ceiling multicolored filing cabinets in the sheriff's office.

As for Tracy Paules, by this time her parents were aware of her relationship with Kevin Orr. She had left the law firm the previous December when she went back to school, but she and Kevin had continued seeing each other every available possible moment. And knowing about Tracy's relationship with Orr raised a considerable storm within the usually placid, almost Ozzie and Harriet kind of relationship she and her parents had always enjoyed at home. That was what most people thought when they saw the Paules family together, an all-American family, tight, warm, loving. Even with the extra emotional burden of thinking their daughter was making a mistake in her choice of boyfriends, now was no different for Tracy's mother Ricky Paules.

"I'm trying to understand, Tracy," Ricky told her.

"Mom . . ."

"But, Tracy, listen, is it really necessary to go out with a black man? He may be all that you say—"

"He is."

"I'm sure, but do you have any idea of the kind of trouble the two of you are asking for?"

"He's just a friend, Mom."

"Then let him *be* just a friend," her father said.

"We're not getting married or anything like that . . ."

Even the word frightened her parents.

"Tracy, it wouldn't be fair to you or to him," Ricky said when she saw her husband's face turn sour. "Marriage is hard enough without asking for that kind of grief from both sides—"

"He's just a date," Tracy insisted.

"You shouldn't date someone you work with anyway!" her father said.

"We don't work together anymore . . ."

George Paules was furious. In his eyes he had never been prejudiced against blacks, he resented being placed in the position of seeming like a bigot. He felt he was being put to an unfair test. He tried to control the unwanted feelings surging through him, feelings that he never wanted to have. He told himself he simply could not understand why his beautiful daughter couldn't go out with one of her own kind. She was so lovely she could have her pick of the field. Why ask for all this trouble? Why go looking for it?

"All we're doing is going out a couple of times," Tracy said. She couldn't bring herself to tell them the truth.

"Stop dating him!" her father said. "I mean it, Tracy. If you don't . . ."

Both Tracy and Ricky looked at him, waiting for him to go on, afraid of what he was going to say.

He looked directly at his wife, challenging her to disagree or intercede. "I will disown her from the family if she continues with him," he warned Ricky.

His threat shook Tracy. She had never been at such odds with her parents.

All her mother Ricky could think of was, Thank God she's going to Europe for the rest of the summer.

Her parents had helped her plan the trip to Poland. At least it would mean a complete separation from Orr, which, in turn, would give her time to think and them a blessed respite from the unexpected breach that had sprung up between them and their beautiful daughter.

Danny Rolling's job with Truman Cooley, the electrician, actually went smoothly; his boss had taken a liking to him. Cooley got to know Rolling and his parents. What a pair. Rolling told him about them from his point-of-view, complaining about how abusive his father was and, since Cooley was of his father's generation, sometimes asking for advice on how to please him. Cooley could see it for himself when sometimes Rolling's parents stopped by the shop . . . "I'd watch him hard if I was you," James Rolling told Cooley in front of his son. "Don't trust him." And his mother, Claudia, seemed the overprotective mom . . . "Never mind what he says, Danny's a good boy."

A good *boy*? Cooley thought. Rolling was thirty-five and an ex-con. You'd hardly call him a *boy*, good or otherwise. At times Cooley found him irrational and emotional but a hard worker, as Bunny said he'd be.

But soon business slackened off and Cooley was forced to let Rolling go. It had lasted only six weeks. He was out of a job again.

He heard that a new restaurant was opening up on Mansfield Road. Poncho's Mexican Restaurant. He went to apply for a job and to his surprise was included with the first group of employees hired. His duties consisted of being a seating host and a food line server.

There was also a woman there to whom he took an immediate liking. For the first time in a long time he started thinking about the possibilities of renewing relationships with women. He began to hope that they all couldn't be like his ex-wife.

"Aw, Danny," Diane Mays said gently. "I'm not ready for a new relationship in my life just now."

He looked down at his plate. He had such puppy-dog eyes, she thought. Like a basset hound. "Don't feel bad, it's not you, it's just that I've been through so much. I can't think about getting involved with anyone just yet."

Diane Mays lived on Maple Leaf Road in Shreveport. In July of 1989 she, too, began a new job at Poncho's Mexican Restaurant, which had opened only the month before. Poncho's was turning out to be a very popular lunch-and-dinner establishment, and shortly after Diane was taken on the payroll, Danny Rolling began paying her a great deal of attention.

She knew that Danny wanted to develop their relationship but decided she wasn't up to it. Now they were in a booth at Shoney's, where he had taken her for lunch in his yellow Chevrolet Malibu.

"I just thought maybe we could be friends," he said.

"Sure."

He looked at her intently. Why had she rejected him? "What do you mean, what you've been through?"

She told him she was going through a very trying time, not sensing the cold fury in his eyes. A messy divorce . . .

He immediately thought of O'Mather.

"There are even pending criminal charges leveled against my ex-husband," she said in the silence that had gathered between them. He said what for. She looked at the intense frown. Could she trust him? She thought she could. He was always nice to her and had seemed pleasant enough. Even sort of, well, tender. She leaned forward. For sexual abuse of their oldest daughter, she whispered.

Danny seemed genuinely shocked. "Shouldn't do that with your own daughter," he said as nighttime visions flashed into his head.

He really was sweet, she thought. A little passive, maybe. He had never tried anything with her. Nothing sexual. Nothing even the least bit physical. He had accepted her decline of a personal relationship between them with no apparent difficulty. He seemed to understand. Still, there was something a little strange about him. That time when his father came into the restaurant was upsetting. She heard them arguing. So did everyone else.

From what she could make out, Danny's father was upset with him, and making a big stink about it because he had spent his paycheck on a pair of boots. She found herself losing some respect for Danny when she saw his father berating him, "like he was just a kid or something."

Poncho's manager Jay Walker had missed the scene and still found Rolling to be energetic, punctual, neat and clean. He even asked him if he wanted to be a cook-trainee.

"Sure," Danny said. A promotion! He used to do some cooking. He didn't say where. In fact, they used to call him Cowboy at the Alabama prison, where he got the job of baker. He liked the guys saying they looked forward to Cowboy's yeast rolls. Cooking. It was something he could do. It was something he could be sure of.

Then the time came when one of the waitresses pulled Diane Mays aside. "Listen, Diane, I don't want to butt in, I don't know what all is going on, but I have to tell you something . . . I know Danny's a little sweet on you but . . ."

"What is it?"

"Oh, I don't know, it's really none of my business . . ."

Diane insisted her friend tell her.

"Did you know he's been in jail?"

Diane was genuinely upset. No, she didn't know that.

"Maybe that's why his old man is on top of him like he is."

"What was he in for?"

"I hear it was for armed robbery. Cook told me."

Diane looked over at Danny standing near the register. Robbing some-one with a gun!

"I hear he was in prison for years."

Danny caught her looking at him and smiled shyly. She averted her eyes quickly and moved away.

He never knew that that was the precise moment their friendship ended. She didn't need anything like that in her life. Especially considering what she'd endured with her own husband.

Danny never knew why she kept away after that, but he felt the freeze. Well, he didn't care. The bitch. Just like all the others. He should have known.

A customer named Gwen Antee stopped him in the parking lot as he was leaving the restaurant. She had pulled into the lot at Poncho's to meet a friend for dinner when she spotted him.

"Why, if it isn't Danny Rolling! Well, how are you?"

He didn't recognize her at first. A middle-aged lady with a dimly famil-iar face . . .

"It's me, Gwen Antee. We used to attend the same church. Kings Tem-ple."

Oh yes . . . he only vaguely remembered her. The hooting of an owl flashed in his head. It was a haunting sound from that night outside the rectory, the night he told Reverend Hudspeth about O'Mather leaving him.

"I haven't seen you in years."

"No."

"So how are you?"

"Fine, ma'am," he said, trying to continue on to his parked car. He didn't feel like reminiscing about Kings Temple. It held memories of the worst letdown of his life.

"Well now, I always thought you to be a very nice and people-oriented young man," she was going on.

"Thanky, ma'am."

"So how's your wife? What was her name again?" She laughed. "A strange name as I recall. Oh yes. O'Mather, isn't it?"

Mary S. Ryzuk

"Yes, ma'am."

"Such a nice girl. How is she?"

"I don't know, ma'am. She's gone. Took my daughter."

He left her standing in the parking lot looking after him.

14

A Triple Murder

The morning of November 4, 1989.

It was hot and sticky, the kind of dog-day left behind in the lazy days of a Louisiana summer. Danny Rolling came in to Poncho's wearing jeans, a T-shirt and tennis shoes.

Diane Mays realized she hadn't seen him at work in a few days. She knew he was often late these days and always looked tired, sort of depressed, but it wasn't her business. She hardly spoke to him anymore.

Suddenly she heard him yelling. Except for that weird argument with his father over the pair of boots, she had never seen shy, passive Danny Rolling act like that before. Yelling at the top of his voice. It was a little frightening.

Until she realized he was upset because he had been fired.

Becoming indifferent to the needs of his job and its routine, he failed to report for work as scheduled on November 2 and 3 without calling in. When he did come in on the fourth, manager Jay Walker fired him on the spot.

Diane moved away but she could hear the loud disagreement with the manager over the amount of his last paycheck.

"Today's November fourth!" Danny shouted.

"Maybe so," Walker insisted, "but your last workday was the first of November. So you only get paid through the first."

What a fuss, Diane thought. Since he was receiving only $3.50 an hour, the dispute was about only a few dollars, but Danny was "loudin' off" all over the place about the unfairness of it.

She couldn't know, of course, that one day she would be trying to remember the details of these very days during questioning by a special agent from Florida's Alachua County.

Once again, out of a job.

The humid heat—Louisiana in November—was like an onslaught as he left Poncho's with his final paycheck in his pocket.

129

He was right, he thought, bristling with rage. *Nothing* ever worked out for him. Suddenly it didn't matter, he didn't care. Something inside his head had gone off. He no longer tried to brace himself against the suppressed anger that had mounted now to explosive proportions, and looking for channels through which to vent, ready for an irreversible split in personality between normal and abnormal.

His hatred was vibrating at his very core, a nascent serial killer let loose. Over and over again, he hummed to himself the new song he had written, then he wandered into Dillard's department store in Oaks Mall, apparently aimlessly, actually with unconscious deadly purpose.

Savagely intent, and volatile, the sinister mystery of his fantasies was set free the moment he saw her. Pretty. Dark. Brunette. At the cosmetic counter.

He didn't know her.

For her part, she was never aware of his presence.

But, as psychiatrists say is often the case with so-called "motiveless" crimes, down deep in his own warped imaginings, Danny Rolling was certain she *knew* why he had singled her out.

November 7, 1989. Claudia Rolling opened up the Shreveport *Times*, spreading it out across the kitchen table. The newspaper headlines were all about the triple murder.

Good Lord! A triple murder right here in Shreveport.

She sipped her coffee as she read.

Late on the night of November 6, 1989, the Shreveport police discovered three mutilated bodies of the Grissom family in their Shreveport home. Believed to have been dead since November 4, the bodies of Tom Grissom, his daughter Julie Grissom, twenty-four, and his grandson Sean Grissom, eight, were found repeatedly stabbed to death by an intruder wielding a large knife. The shocking carnage was discovered by a neighbor, Bob Coyles, in Tom Grissom's brown brick home at 2011 Beth Lane.

Claudia knew where Beth Lane was. Lordy, the Southern Hills section, that was a pleasant family neighborhood in southern Shreveport. Looked like people just weren't safe even in their own homes anymore.

Due to the explicit sexual overtones of the crime, the police believed that it was the lovely Julie Grissom, a petite brunette, who was the primary target of the killer. They further believed Tom Grissom and the child inadvertently happened to come upon the scene of the murder while the killer was still present. After much crime-scene analysis, they theorized the killer heard them approaching, lay in wait, and overcame first the father—an adult male being the greater threat to the killer—and then the terrified little boy who had watched his grandfather taking the deadly knife blows.

The conspicuous viciousness of the mutilating stab wounds on both their bodies attested to the fury of the attack upon them.

However, it was the very bizarre nature of Julie Grissom's murder that made the police believe a very sick individual had been responsible and was still somewhere "out there." Not only had her wrists been taped during the attack, and now the adhesive was missing, but the killer had purposely posed the young woman's body for shock value. As soon as the police entered the bedroom where she was found, they could see her nude body had been placed with her spread legs bent at the knees, her feet touching the floor at the foot of the bed, her stabbed and mutilated body back on the bed with obvious bite marks on her breasts, and her dark hair carefully fanned out on the bedcover behind her. But the most startling point in the investigation was that while he did not wipe his saliva off her breasts, the killer meticulously cleaned the genital area of the girl's body with a blue-green liquid soap to remove all traces of evidence. The intentional positioning of the body was the kind of thing done by someone with an urgent need to be recognized.

The killer had, it seemed, signed and left his personal signature.

Immediately psychiatrists were actively engaged in psychological profiles and projections. They were certain the girl's murder was not committed out of sexual need or sexual frustration. This murder was committed out of a frustrated, twisted craving for recognition and consequent self-esteem. It was, they said, meant to satisfy a desperate vacuum left by the starvation of a brutalized ego. It demonstrated "frustration-displacement" activity. The very brutality led to the conclusion that, more than likely, the murderer was suffering from some kind of deep-seated paranoid resentment.

The Shreveport police weren't all that interested in the psychological motivations of the killer. Leave that stuff to the psychiatrists. They had not seen what he had orchestrated and left behind for them to find and for the family to grieve over. They swore to "catch the bastard" who could do such vile things. Julie Grissom would have graduated from Louisiana State University a month later, and the kid, little Sean, he was only eight.

And that poor man Tom Grissom might have been able to protect his family if he hadn't been overwhelmed by surprise. *No.* Law-enforcement personnel were not interested in the psychological makeup of the killer or "why" he had committed the murders. Many would have liked to get the killer alone in a dark alley for just a few moments.

Seated at her kitchen table, Claudia Rolling shook her head and poured herself another cup of coffee. Terrible, she thought.

No one knew, certainly not Claudia Rolling, that for the murderer the line between fantasy and action had clearly been crossed. He could never retrace his steps and go back. The recidivist nature of the classical lust killer indicated that this triple murder was just the beginning. So saying, it must be said that Daniel Harold Rolling was never indicted for these murders. By the time the connection was made between him and the Grissoms, he was under indictment for the five student murders in Gainesville, Florida. It appears that Louisiana will never formally be able to close the books on this case unless someone other than Rolling is indicted. However, it is my *legally unproven belief* that Rolling was involved in these murders prior to the five in Florida.

At another home in Shreveport, Gwen Antee read the same newspaper story. Not only did she find the story of the murders terribly shocking, but even more so since the triple murders hit close to home. She remembered the Grissom family well. They attended the same church she did. They were a lovely family. What a terrible tragedy, she thought. Who in the world could do such a terrible, ugly thing?

15

Heading for Gainesville

Hundreds of miles away from Shreveport, Louisiana, in Archer, Florida, Christa Leigh Hoyt celebrated her eighteenth birthday. It was November 20, 1989. Taking stock of her options, on her own for the first time in a new apartment, starting the next exciting phase of her life at Santa Fe Community College in Gainesville, she informed her father she had decided to move out of his home in Archer. She wanted to move out right after her birthday, the very moment she hit her majority.

Why? her father Gary asked. She told him she just wanted to be able to come and go as she pleased, and besides, with her mother living in Gainesville, it wouldn't be so bad.

A dispatcher for Southern Bell, Gary Hoyt was a good man with conventional ideas. True, Gainesville was only twelve miles northeast of Archer, and Christa's mother, Teresa Ann Garren, was there, working at the International House of Pancakes on US 441 in Gainesville, so Christa would have family nearby. Still, he wasn't happy about it. "She's too young," he told his present wife, Diana.

Christa's stepmother, Diana, understood. She was just a normal teenager, she told Gary. And she was moving in with Brigitte, so she wouldn't be living alone. Brigitte Toombs was an old chum from Newberry High School who also was moving to Gainesville to attend Santa Fe.

When the time came to leave Archer, Christa tossed everything she was taking with her into her black Chevette and moved on, eager to leave her childhood behind. The car was black because she liked everything in black, including most of her wardrobe. As she pulled away, her stepmother Diana remembered she had asked for black roses on her birthday cake. She had even been determined to wear a black dress to her junior prom in Newberry, until Diana sewed her a royal-blue prom frock. She looked so stunning in it, at the edge of womanhood, that Christa withdrew her objections over the color.

A strong-willed young adult who knew what she wanted out of life, Christa nonetheless was not quite ready to give up all of the securities of home and childhood, such as the collection of teddy bears she took along with her when she left home. She liked sleeping right in the middle of all of them. In the new Gainesville apartment she shared with Brigitte her habits did not change. Even her nightshirts had teddy bear designs on them.

She was on her way to Gainesville, like the other players continuing on to their fatal point of convergence.

After a few odd jobs to help her work her way through Santa Fe, Christa called home to her parents to say she had landed a job as an overnight clerk at the Alachua County Sheriff's Office.

The sheriff's office! Her father was pleased and reassured. What, after all, could be safer than that for his headstrong young daughter? And it suited her interests so well. She was majoring in chemistry, to become a crime-lab technician. Stamp out crime with a microscope.

There is an old saying in Louisiana: "The fox walks on moonlight nights."

Like the fox who still walked on moonlit nights, Danny Rolling became more solitary, more nervous, more secretive. At the same time, he made an extreme effort to appear normal.

He began hanging out at the Superior Bar and Grill in Shreveport, the kind of place in which he apparently thought he could disappear. Located on busy Line Avenue in one of the city's upscale neighborhoods, the Superior attracted professionals who crowded the bar every evening for after-work margaritas and a free Mexican buffet. Although in some ways Rolling's external guise of normalcy worked well to cover the inner turmoil, there was always the unabated, perhaps contradictory, perhaps complementary, need in his shredded ego to stand out and be noticed. The Superior Bar and Grill was one of the places in Shreveport to see and be seen.

He wanted to play the guitar at the Superior but the manager wouldn't let him. Paul Simon, one of the bartenders at the Superior, shook his head as Rolling talked about his "big break." About how someday he was going to make a "big score."

"In music," Rolling said. "That's where I'll make a name for myself. Music."

"Sure, okay, sure," Simon said.

"I want to make a name for myself."

"Hey, who knows, maybe someday you will."

The guy wasn't a kid anymore, Simon thought. Looked to be somewhere in his late thirties but he sure talked like a kid, always making predictions about how the "big score" was going to show his father what he could do.

Strange bird. Not a bad-looking sort, but hard to figure out. One day he would try to be the center of attention, the next he would hide in a corner, watching the others at the bar as they mingled with one another in their tightly knit little cliques. He seemed to be trying to project a macho, ladies' man image, but Rolling also had a lazy, shuffling walk that diminished such an impression, although he had quite a physique—he had been able to build up his body in prison, though, of course, Simon didn't know that. Actually, Rolling looked out of place as he wandered around listening to the conversations of the others, and he could never quite make it into a conversation with a woman . . . "My name is Rolling, I'm a musician," he would say to a pretty woman at the bar who would usually nod pleasantly and wait an appropriate moment before shutting him out and turning back to her own concerns.

Simon watched him through the corner of his eye as he tried to hit on the girls. The Superior actually had a clientele that was just not the sort this guy might be able to attract, though he did once pick up a girl named Kathy. "Who *is* that guy?" the question went. "Oh, just a guy who likes to play the guitar."

He also kept his hair cut so short that some people suspected he must be a neo-Nazi skinhead. He always charged his heavy bar bill and eventually paid it—but he surely was not popular, seemed insincere, a real turnoff who tended to come across as pretentious and a fake.

The guy never has any money, Simon thought as he hustled to serve customers pressed two-deep against the bar. Rolling was always asking for free drinks and trying to get someone to lend him money to buy drinks, borrowing five dollars here, ten there. Although he always repaid the debt, those whom he hit on found it annoying. Some customers complained but Simon didn't want to antagonize the man. Besides, that little-boy-lost look he often wore, there was something about him sometimes—"like a Jekyll and Hyde thing"—that urged care and caution. He couldn't know that other acquaintances also had used the Jekyll-and-Hyde label to describe Danny Rolling.

Rolling finally got the nerve to ask bartender Paul Simon if he could bring in his guitar and perform. Sorry, Simon told him. Boss' policy. No live music.

"That's okay," Danny said. "Don't worry about it. It's not your fault. You're the nicest guy in the world."

Simon, in a way, sort of felt sorry for him. If it had been up to him, he would have liked to help him out even though he wasn't sure if he was any good on the guitar he talked so much about.

"Can you lend me some money?" Rolling whispered to Simon across the bar during a brief lull.

"Hey, come on, I don't lend money."

Rolling looked at him. "I'll remember that," he said angrily. So much for the "nicest guy in the world," Simon thought as Rolling strode off.

*   *   *

The birds were always there, hovering overhead, following him around. Even the brown thrasher with its hissing sound and clicking call seemed to be making fun of him as it sat up there on its tree-top perch. Well, screw Paul Simon and the rest of 'em all. Messin' around with all their "chinchy dollars" and "high 'coon ways," maybe they all would have the edge enough to spit on his gravestone, but he could *fill* theirs. *Him!* One of these days he might put it all out on the front porch. Let everyone know for sure. Then they'd know who he was for certain. Why not? It was a poor dog who couldn't wag its own tail.

Someday.

Rolling wandered into another bar. Leaving the Superior Bar and Grill lengths behind on another plane, Willy's Way wasn't in the "best" of neighborhoods; it was more down to earth, full of country boys bound and determined to drink each other under the table on a Friday night.

It was at Willy's Way that he ran into Junior Cornblow, an old acquaintance from the other side of Shreveport.

"Well, see heah, now," Junior said. "It's almost Christmas. Every man oughta have a job at Christmas time. There may be an openin' for you where I'm workin' these days."

Rolling wanted to get away from him. Junior was drunk. He couldn't even sit up straight and he was telling *him* about a job. What a howl. Couldn't trust him. Nothing falls off an empty wagon, anyway. Get away from him.

But Junior hung onto him. He had been talking up a wild storm all night. Now here he was, insistent on telling him about "this job . . . I mean it," Junior persisted, starting to get ticked off at Rolling's lack of enthusiasm. "Listen, I always go by my own name. If I'm sittin' here tellin' you there's work where I'm at, then there's work where I'm at!"

Empty barrels make the loudest noises, Rolling thought, moving a bit away from the whiskey smell. He didn't feel like listening but what the hell. "Doin' what all?"

"Easy," Junior said, easily prompted into a good mood again by what he perceived as Rolling's interest. "Telephone work. Solicitin'. Sales. It's easy. You just have to be able to talk, like me, that's all, and as long as you put on a few airs and don't go roun' soundin' like an ol' country boy on a pissin'-drunk Friday night, y'all can't miss."

Rolling got the job. The company was called the GFHL Group, a professional telephone-solicitation business in Shreveport. Using his best articulation, Rolling spoke to manager Corey Minard, the man Junior had told him to see. After filling out the initial employment papers in which he omitted most of his personal history, Rolling began working for the GFHL Group on December 8, 1989. He was assigned the dinner-hour shift, from five P.M. to nine P.M., Monday to Friday and the nine A.M. to one P.M. shift on Saturdays.

The very next day Minard began to experience a deep sense of reservation about having hired Rolling. The employee dress code required a shirt and tie. Rolling didn't comply. Sometimes he came to work wearing tight blue jeans and white tennis shoes. If he was good at his job, though, Minard rationalized, he might be able to overlook the man's unwillingness to follow the simple dress code of the job. But it made him uneasy when Rolling appeared in a pullover type shirt, green army fatigues, black combat-type boots and sporting a large hunting knife placed in a pants sheath on the outside of his right leg. He never unsheathed the knife but Minard could see that the dark-handled knife sported a blade that was approximately six or seven inches long.

The office was no place to look as though he were going hunting.

Rolling continued to be a loner. He did not have any friends and hardly interacted much with other employees, not even Junior Cornblow. In a sober state, Junior did not push the relationship himself. It was a little embarrassing; Rolling and his hunting knife in the office made him sorry he had suggested the job to Rolling. If he had been sober that time they met at the bar he might have caught the now discernible hard twist in the man that had become apparent in the sober light of day. Rolling's car had broken down. He had no transportation and always walked to and from home to work. Except for asking if he needed a ride home, which he always refused, Junior decided to take Rolling's cue and leave him alone. Corey Minard also offered him rides but Rolling turned them down too, saying he liked to walk. And, in fact, the offices of the GFHL Group located at 2701 Meadow Avenue were only about ten blocks from where Rolling lived.

A week after Rolling started on the job one of the office secretaries came to Minard. He was standing by within earshot of Rolling, actually monitoring Rolling's sales pitch on the phone.

"The police are here," she told Minard. "Looking for someone . . ."

Rolling immediately ended the phone call when he heard her words. "Why are they here?" he demanded nervously. "What do they want?"

Minard thought the man's overreaction to the presence of the Shreveport police was surprising.

"They're looking for someone," the girl repeated to the manager, dismissing the nervous Rolling.

Minard watched as Rolling again got into the situation. *"Who?"* he demanded again.

"It doesn't have anything to do with you," the secretary said. She turned her back on him. Listening intensely, Rolling heard her tell Minard: "They're here to serve domestic papers on Chester. You know, for all that trouble he's having at home."

Rolling relaxed. It took some moments before he picked up the telephone again and began a slow-drawled lazy sales pitch to the woman on the other end of the line.

A week later, three days before Christmas, Rolling was terminated.

"You tellin' me I ain't good enough for this crap outfit? Talking to dumb-ass housewives sittin' at home all day! Is that what you're tellin' me?"

The entire office stopped what they were doing.

"It has to do with performance—"

"All this bullshit stuff. What d'ya mean, performance?"

"A normal worker generates approximately two hundred fifty dollars—"

"Normal. What do you mean, *normal?*"

"Listen, Rolling, you've been generating only about thirty dollars a shift. Normal is two hundred fifty. That's poor performance around here and I'm letting you go. I have to."

Rolling stormed out, cursing employers in general at the top of his voice.

A few days later he returned to GFHL to pick up his final check. "Mr. Minard . . ." he said quietly. "I want to sincerely apologize to you and to this outfit for the things I said here the other day and for my previous actions."

"That's okay, Rolling."

"I'm truly sorry."

Minard nodded. As with most people who came into contact with Danny, he too would remember Danny Rolling for a long time to come.

16

The Year of 1990

Gainesville, Florida

"Let's not go in that direction."

"Why?"

"I've heard there's a devil cult that lives at the end of Twenty-fourth Avenue," she told him.

Christa Hoyt was taking a walk with Christopher Hayes near her apartment. She didn't mind walking as long as she wasn't alone. The handsome young man was excellent insurance against any potential problems. It was a comfortable cool evening. A perfectly hued twilight tone hovered over their hand-holding walk. Christa and Christopher had known each other since early March when he took a job at the Oaks Mall as a security guard. He became so immediately attracted to her that he never told her he was living with a girl by the name of Gina at the time they met and began dating.

"You don't believe in that stuff, do you?" he asked. "Devil cults?"

"No, but . . ."

Despite her denials, he could tell she was concerned about the rumor of the cult.

"Anyway, I've been looking for a new apartment."

"Because of the devil cult?"

"No, because Brigitte moved out. It's a little too isolated out here."

He knew that she was very security-conscious and always made sure to lock her door. She had been looking for a new apartment ever since he met her back in March.

"No luck?"

"Not yet."

Shreveport, Louisiana

It was at the Superior Bar and Grill that Rolling met Stephen and Louisa Biedenharn Clausen. In their forties, the Clausens were well-regarded early retirees who had sold off most of their business interests except for a limousine service they continued to operate.

"I don't have a job," he told them. "I sure could use one."

"How are you with electricity?" Stephen asked.

"I'll probably fry in one of those chairs."

"No, seriously, can you fix electric lights and things?"

"Sure. I used to work for an electrician. Truman Cooley. Y'might know him?"

"No. We have some electrical work that has to be done over by where we live . . ."

The Clausens befriended Rolling when he offered to come out to their lakefront estate on Wildwood Drive to fix the outdoor floodlights. After that he continued to drop in on the couple, unexpected but welcome. The Clausens were hospitable and accommodating to the deep need they felt they saw in him. He in turn was impressed with their apparent affluence, the way they decorated their home, the easy, friendly lifestyle they projected. In particular he liked the thick white rug that covered their living-room floor. He had never thought of white for a floor. And they didn't even ask him to take off his shoes.

By now Rolling was beginning to show his age. His hair, once thick and bushy, had thinned out considerably; the hairline had receded high onto his forehead. His face had fleshed out and his skin was a bit mottled. He still always looked a bit sad and in need of emotional support. Although he was approaching his late thirties, there was something almost childlike in the way he latched onto the Clausens. His visits were so frequent they began to look on him more as a friend than a hired man; so much so that in April, they even invited him to Louisa's birthday party. It was going to be a pretty big affair with more than one hundred guests. One more or less didn't matter. They even let Rolling talk them into letting him play his guitar and sing for the party.

The party was held outdoors by the lakefront. It was a mild cloudless April evening. Rolling showed up at the party dressed all in white. He looked just as he did when he went to Sunday church meetings. The floodlights he had fixed removed the shadows from the surrounding trees and shrubs and cast a brilliant sheen across the surface of the lake. The aroma of the showily blooming hibiscus was delicate and fragrant. The guests were well-dressed in casual attire. To his eye they looked affluent, professional, like those who frequented the Superior, the ones who always snubbed him.

He took a seat out back close to the lake and placed his guitar across his knees. To Stephen's and Louisa's surprise, he was a good musician; he played the guitar well even though they thought what he sang was on the depressing side. It impressed them that he wrote his own music. They had no idea how important his performance was to him or how much singing and music were the means by which he believed he would get recognition.

But the Clausens' guests mostly ignored him and his music. It was the children who gathered around him, listening to him play, watching his Adam's apple bobbing up and down, studying the crooked arrangement of his teeth as the sad words poured forth. Though his lyrics were secular, he performed them almost reverently. Sometimes he closed his eyes as he sang, frowning intently through a weeping musical phrase. The children didn't notice that he mostly sang of death.

Although Rolling wasn't aware that some of the guests were whispering about him behind their drinks, he was offended that the children were the only ones paying attention. Everyone should have been quiet. Everyone should have paid attention to his performance.

A friend of Stephen's came up to him and pulled him aside as Rolling began another song. "Steve, who is that guy?"

"A friend," Clausen responded. "He does odd jobs around here for us. Stops by every so often."

"Well, there's something wrong with him."

"He's a good enough guy."

"I'm telling you, my wife and I were talking and we both think there's something wrong with him."

Clausen rejected his friend's critical assessment of the man dressed in white, singing softly, his face lifted upward and his eyes shut tight. "Louisa and I like him," Clausen said.

Deerfield Beach, Florida

As manager of the Ely High School girls' basketball team, seventeen-year-old Sonja Larson knew well what an important game this one was for the team. She didn't want to lose one of her best players, but the girl who had been dominating the play throughout the third period looked all in after making a near-impossible basket from close to center court. As soon as the period ended Sonja rushed over to her with a cup of Gatorade. "Great shot," Sonja said. "Are you going to be able to go on?"

"Oh sure," the girl said, gulping the drink.

"Don't drink so fast."

Sonja turned to another one of her players sitting on the edge of the bench rubbing the underside of her knee joint. "How's the knee?"

"Fair."

She, too, would be a loss to the team if she sat out, but the girl's knee was more important than her game. When she insisted on staying in, Sonja proceeded to tape the girl's knee expertly. As manager of the team she took it on herself to see to the needs of her teammates.

Lillian Greaves, the girls' athletics coach at Ely High, watched the sideline interaction between team manager and her teammates.

She liked that Sonja Larson. The kid was always there when someone needed her. After the game Sonja ran up to the coach's side, face flushed.

"Good work," Greaves said.

"Thanks. Guess what," Sonja said excitedly. "I've been accepted at the University of Florida."

"Congratulations," Lillian Greaves said, not the least bit surprised. As a senior at Ely, Sonja was a member of the National Honor Society, the Mu Alpha Theta Mathematical Society and the Key Club, a service organization that named her Most Dedicated. Sonja seemed to have always known who she was and what she wanted out of life. From the time she had first started talking about it with her coach, her future plans invariably included a college education at the University of Florida.

"I'm going to where I can major in early childhood care."

"I knew you'd make it," the coach told her.

"UF, here I come," Sonja said happily.

Jacksonville, Florida

Sonja's future roommate, Christina Powell, was also planning her future.

You had to like her the moment she walked into the room, Cindy Warner thought. Her smile almost seemed to precede her. Warner was the registrar at Episcopal High. She got to know Christina well while helping her update her transcripts to send to her college choices. "What's your first choice?" she asked.

"The University of Florida," Christina said immediately.

Cindy Warner was not surprised. Most of the bright ones wanted to go to the flagship college of the sunshine state.

"I want to study architecture. I want to build things."

She was a bright, vivacious, fun-loving person.

Like Sonja Larson, when Christina was accepted to the University of Florida she felt as though her future had been mapped out for her. Positive by nature, there was little doubt in her mind that one day she would, indeed, be an architect.

Gainesville, Florida

"You should have told me," Christa Hoyt said. "It wasn't fair not to tell me."

By April, Christa had found out that her boyfriend, the security guard Christopher Hayes, was living with another girl and had been from the time they began dating a month before. The moment she became aware of Gina Spivey's existence in his life Christa broke off their relationship. She agreed to stay friends but dating was over.

Deception was cross-grained to her nature. What kind of future could there be if she went along with that . . .

Tracy Paules was going to move in with her old school chum Manny Taboada. He had been living in a two-bedroom apartment in Gatorwood Apartments on Archer Road in Gainesville with his buddy Armando Careaga. Now Armando was leaving to move in with a girlfriend, and Tracy and Manny had been discussing sharing the apartment for their last year at UF. It was a move they both felt would work out well. They had never been sweethearts but they had always been very good friends. They hadn't worked out the details yet but the basic arrangements were agreed on.

Tracy liked Gatorwood. She had frequently visited Manny and Armando during spring term, often riding over on her bicycle from her apartment near Oaks Mall, and found it a pleasant "place to be"—just as the sign outside said.

The white-trimmed pale blue arrow led to the rental office and lobby that included the manager's desk. With orange block letters on a musty brown-colored sign, Gatorwood was a brownish green, three-story complex with attractive rail-fence and deep brown balconies, but the first thing one saw on entering the courtyard from Archer Road was a series of air-conditioning units set on the ground between the walls of the complex. There were electric meters and air-conditioning units everywhere interspersed between the flowing canopy umbrellas of palm trees. The grounds were well-maintained with crepe myrtle and clusters of brilliant fuchsia impatiens.

Pineapple palm trees, neatly trimmed bushes. The bank of mailboxes situated next to jam-packed bicycle racks was under a black roof that was well-lit at night. Gatorwood housed mostly college students in their late teens and twenties—a thirty-one-year-old married couple who lived there was considered on the "old" side.

Tracy was planning to move in by the end of August just before the fall semester began but had already transferred some of her personal belongings into Manny's apartment.

Now in the early evening hours of a warm May night toward the end of the spring term, Tracy was cooling off in the Gatorwood pool behind the manager's office.

"Let me tell you about Manny," his friend Armando Careaga was saying when Tracy swam her last lap and paused at the edge of the pool. She loved swimming. She and her friend Valerie Wheeler were going to enroll in a diving class at the Flamingo Dive Center in Miami Lakes when she returned home in a few weeks.

Armando sat at the edge of the Gatorwood pool, his feet dangling in the water. Manny sat to one side, listening as Armando teased Tracy about the upcoming living arrangement. "Manny has the rear east bedroom and your bedroom's the rear west one, which used to be mine."

"I know."

"Manny's a heavy sleeper," he said.

"*That* I didn't know."

"You will," Armando told her. "He usually sleeps facedown in underwear and a T-shirt."

"Come on," Manny put in.

"I know this because he always sleeps with his bedroom door open about six inches so that Sasha can come in and out. I'm sure he'll still leave the door open with you living in the apartment. And you might as well get used to it right now, you'll always come after Sasha."

Tracy was well aware of Manny's attachment to his furry white Persian.

"You'll have to be very careful not to leave any doors open," Armando went on, "because Sasha might run away. I mean, there's a lot of rules because of that cat. The sliding glass doors have to be kept closed and secured. Manny usually keeps the curtains pulled. You'll have to make sure the air conditioner is set right so that Sasha doesn't overheat. You'll also have to be careful not to leave any windows open so that Sasha doesn't sneak out. The one time she did get out, Manny went nuts looking for her, so now he forbids anyone to monkey with any of the windows. They have to be locked at all times."

Manny splashed him with water but that didn't stop Armando. "If he works late and is tired he may come straight into the apartment and go right to bed. Those are your *lucky* nights. If he's not tired he may eat a snack or watch TV for a few minutes before he and Sasha retire for the night."

"I'm not so sure I want to play second fiddle to a cat," Tracy said.

"You'll have no choice."

"What are you going to do after term?" Tracy asked, turning to Manny.

"I'm going back home to spend about ten days with my folks before coming back in August to get ready for the final semester. You?"

"I'm leaving on May sixth to go home for the summer. I have a lot of plans."

"Me too."

Both would be going back home to their parents' homes in Miami for the last time.

Armando Careaga often wondered what would have happened if he had not moved out. Would the killer have come into their apartment anyway? Was he stalking Tracy? If the killer had entered and he had been present along with Manny, would they have been able to overcome him? Questions that would haunt Careaga for the rest of his life.

Tracy Paules would move back to Gainesville and into the apartment with Manny Taboada in the week prior to their deaths.

17

The Shooting

Shreveport, Louisiana—The Sunday Before . . .

The last time Artie May Strozier, Rolling's aunt, saw Danny Boy was the Sunday before he shot his father. She thought he was so handsome, Danny Boy going to church dressed all in white.

"You know," Auntie Artie told police, after her nephew left town, "no matter what he's done he was always a happy and good person." She paused. "I have to admit, though, in recent years he's shown some depression."

"Tell us about him," the investigator urged.

"Well, he usually dresses in jeans and he's always real neat. But on that Sunday when he shot James so bad, he looked like a choirboy all dressed in white like that. Now, you know, of course, he has a very close relationship with his mother. That's my sister. The problem is his father."

"In what way?"

"You see, James was always too hard on him."

"Did his father abuse him?"

"Now I'm not saying that. I'm not going to speak of abuse. It's just that James was too hard on him."

"Could you be more specific?"

"Well, it seems to me, ever since I can remember, the punishment was always too harsh for the crime. Y'all get what I mean? James never showed affection or anything like that. Sometimes I used to think where Danny Boy was concerned, James was so crippled even a walkin' stick wouldn't've helped."

"Have you ever met any of Danny's male friends or female friends?"

"None, except for Bunny Mills," she responded. "Did y'all know Danny Boy liked to lift weights and play guitar? He played real nice," she said, and then she leaned forward as though ready to impart a confidence. "I have to admit, there was some change in Danny Boy since he was in prison. He told me he never wanted to go back to prison. I asked him was it bad and he told me, 'There's a lot of abuse in those places.' I asked him what he meant and he said, "I mean just what I say. While I was in there I was abused in a way no man should have t'be." Of course I never asked him what he meant. Some things shouldn't be spoken about, but I assumed Danny Boy meant . . . abuse from the other inmates in there."

"Did he tell you anything else about it?"

"He told me he took care've it. 'They left me alone right quick once they got t'know who they were dealing with,' that's what he said."

She told them about how after one particularly brutal fight in which he threw himself at them—fists, feet, teeth—they started calling him Psycho.

"Go on," the investigator urged.

"I don't like to talk about some things. Family matters . . ."

"It's a police matter now, ma'am."

"Y'all ought t'talk to my sister Claudia."

"We will, ma'am. Please go on."

"Well," she said, "it's always been my understanding that Danny's former wife was running around on him. I don't know for sure. Who knows? But the rumors didn't help his mood none, I can tell you. And then she left Shreveport with the child, the daughter, and her new boyfriend she eventually married, so I hear. I remember that Sunday I asked him—"

"What Sunday?"

"The Sunday before he shot James. I asked him, 'Danny Boy, d'you ever hear anything from O'Mather?' And he shook his head."

"Do you know what started the argument?"

"You mean the one that led to the shooting?"

"Yes, ma'am."

"Oh yes," she said. "My sister Claudia told me. She was there, y'know. Saw the whole thing. Awful for her. It began with an argument over whether or not Danny Boy should roll up the car windows . . ."

May 17, 1990—The Shooting

Bartender Paul Simon noticed that Rolling came into the Superior Bar and Grill nearly every Friday for about a year. This particular Friday, a dreary rainy night, was no different. He didn't talk much. Just sat on the side and quietly watched everyone socializing at the bar. The room was smoke-filled, noisy, and he was not a part of it. With every passing moment, he became more withdrawn and sullen.

It was after leaving the Superior and arriving home that a screaming argument erupted between Rolling and his father over whether car windows should be rolled up in the rain! In the middle of the argument a gun was drawn by James. Whether James Rolling intended to shoot his son that stormy Friday night in May is not clear.

"Roll 'em up!"

"What for?"

"It's raining, that's what for."

"It's under the carport!"

Suddenly the Smith & Wesson appeared in James' hand. "You ain't got sense enough to keep out've a fire."

"It's not getting wet!" his son insisted . . .

Claudia Rolling would tell the police that her husband had been waving a handgun and had fired first.

Danny stormed out of the house followed by his father, carrying the pistol.

Three or four shots were fired into the air outside the house before James Rolling returned indoors.

"He's mean and sorry as the devil!"

"Who's fault is that?" Claudia retorted, but he was fuming too hard to pay her any mind. Claudia had put on a little weight with age but she was still small and petitely built. The gun in her husband's hand terrified her. "Don't," she begged him. "Please . . ." But she had never been a match for the full force of her husband's dominance when he was on one of his rampages.

"That'll show him," James said after firing the last of the shots into the night sky through the open door. "He's gone!" The door slammed behind him after the last shot. He locked Danny out of the house . . .

Thirty-two-year-old Donald Carroll, a neighbor, heard what sounded like firecrackers coming from the direction of the Rolling house.

James didn't know his son had gone to the backyard to get a .38 pistol that he kept stashed in the corner of the back shed.

Danny rummaged wildly to find it. His usual non-confrontational facade, avenging himself in his dreams, covering his inner life by the appearance of a God-loving hymnal man, fell apart with the sound of his father's gunshots. Submerged feelings exploded, feelings he had held down since that time with the girl and her family. They had ended up dead, although nobody ever claimed that he was in any way responsible. Now his father was in there with his mom and a loaded pistol.

Claudia watched apprehensively as her husband, still waving his gun around, shouted, "I'm gonna kill the whole damn family, once and for all," loudly commenting on his son's lack of employment to his wife. "How many jobs has he been fired from, tell me that!"

The door was locked.

James was standing in the middle of the kitchen when his son kicked in the back door, forcing the sultry night air into the room. James turned to see the white face of his enraged son framed in the doorway. In all his years on the Shreveport police force, James had never seen such rage, the years of hatred now ending in a gun confrontation between father and son.

"Old man!" his son yelled. "You want to shoot it out?"

Claudia ran from the room screaming as shots were fired in her kitchen. Indoors, within the walls of her little room, the shots sounded monstrously loud, reverberating again and again in her head. She held both hands over her mouth to keep the sounds locked in the back of her throat although she wanted to scream. She heard yelling. The thud of a body falling. Another shot. Then silence.

Until she heard her son rummaging in his bedroom. Banging. Drawers opening and closing. Closet doors slamming. Should she go talk to him? What had happened? Should she look inside the kitchen? She remembered the look on Danny Boy's face.

Then she heard the back door slam shut, leaving behind an ominous silence. It had been a hushed night before the shots were fired. Now she thought she heard a siren in the distance.

It never occurred to Daniel Harold Rolling as he got into the car with the rolled-down window that this was the last time he would ever pass the threshold of his parents' home. All he could think of was that he had shot his father, more than once, and when he was lying on the kitchen floor, bleeding and helpless—"Lord God forgive me"—he had kicked his prone body.

After a very long moment of inertia, Claudia Rolling came back to peek into her kitchen. She saw him. The blood spread around her husband's body. He was on the floor with bullet holes in his head and stomach.

And now the screams came as she looked around for her Danny.

But her son was gone.

So was her husband's revolver.

"He was just trying to protect me," Claudia Rolling told the police investigator. She didn't tell him that somewhere deep inside, she had the feeling that if she hadn't run out of the kitchen when she did, she might have been shot too. Accidentally.

It was the neighbors who had called the authorities, and it seemed only moments after the last shots were fired in the modest little house in the quiet middle-class neighborhood known as Sunset Acres before the area was crowded with police and emergency personnel.

The man on the kitchen floor looked dead. He had been one of their own, and was recognized by the policemen who responded to a neighbor's frantic call that "they're shootin' over there, y'all better hurry on over here . . ."

James Harold Rolling was taken to the hospital in critical condition.

A desperate Rolling drove out to the lakefront home of his friends, Steve and Louisa Clausen. Dressed in the Rambo outfit he had hurriedly put on in his bedroom—fatigues, a camouflage bandanna tied around his forehead and combat boots with a six-inch hunting knife stuck in the side of his right boot—he broke in through the French doors downstairs, tracking mud on the thick white living-room carpet he admired so much.

He followed the sound of the television and burst into the upstairs bedroom, where Steve and Louisa were sprawled on their bed watching television. He pointed a large handgun at them.

"This is no joke," he said. "I'm in big trouble. I just shot my father and I want all your money."

The Clausens were stunned, discovering with a vengeance that things were not always what they seemed. Where was the Danny Rolling they had come to know and like?

"Danny," Steve said carefully, aware of the wild look behind the tears in Rolling's eyes. His face had always been masked in normalcy, now it had the tense wild-eyed look of a desperate fugitive. "I thought we were friends."

"Yeah, I know, I know . . ."

Louisa got out of bed and approached him. "Danny, don't point that. Tell us what happened."

"I told you, I shot my father. I think I killed him."

"Was it an accident?"

"No. I meant to kill him. But not now . . ." He began to cry. "I don't want him dead now. I'm sorry . . ."

"Come on, Danny. Let's go downstairs," she urged. "Let's talk. I'll make us something to drink . . ."

And for the next two hours Rolling gave them a terrifying performance of a man going in and out of violent moods so swiftly they could only wonder what would happen to them. It was an astonishing Jekyll-and-Hyde presentation.

"We're friends, aren't we?" Steve said again, sitting at the kitchen table, appealing to the friendship he sensed was still important to Rolling. In some odd way, it was that very friendship that had brought him bursting into their home in such a threatening manner. "Aren't we? Friends?"

Rolling nodded.

"Then give me the gun. You don't want to hurt anybody, do you?"

"No," he said gently and laid the gun down on the table. "I love you guys. I don't know why I'm doing this."

Steve looked at the gun but didn't touch it.

They watched as he kept going in and out of his aggressive side. They had never before seen the violence. "I shot him!" he shouted. "No one's gonna shoot at me like he did and get away with it."

Little by little the story of what happened in the kitchen in Sunset Acres came out. In the telling, one minute Rolling was meanly aggressive . . . "I meant to kill him, that bastard should be dead! I should've done him in a long time ago!" And the next minute he would come out of it and cry like a little kid . . . "I really love that old man, I wonder if he's dead, I don't know, y'know? I don't even know if he's alive or dead . . ." It was awesome to observe him switching between two different, apparently conflicting, personalities.

Louisa continued to try to calm him down . . . a cup of coffee . . . a comforting word.

"We heard you were in some kind of auto accident and we called your house to see if you were all right."

"You guys care enough to ask how I was?" he asked, surprised, his "sweet" side coming out.

"Yes, of course . . ."

"I'm gonna have t'be on the run for the rest've my life now that I killed him," Rolling said. "See what he's done to me? That bastard!"

"Maybe you didn't kill him," Louisa said. "Why don't we find out? Why don't I call the hospital?"

"Would you? 'Cause I'm afraid I hurt him real bad. Would you do that?"

"Where do you think he's been taken?"

"Try the Willis-Knighton Medical Center," Steve said to his wife.

She picked up the phone.

"Can I have the gun, Danny?"

Danny picked the gun up from the table and handed it to Steve while Louisa dialed.

Steve emptied the gun of its bullets. At least now Danny was disarmed.

It was Danny's mother who finally got on the line. Louisa thought it was strange . . . there her husband was in the emergency room, bleeding, seriously injured, and the woman was siding with her son. A mother's instinct, she thought before she replaced the receiver and turned to Rolling. "You didn't kill him, Danny. He's still alive."

Rolling jumped up. "Well, he should be dead! That sonovabitch should be dead, all right!" And he pulled out a second gun and pointed it at Steve. "Give me back my gun!" he demanded. "And my bullets!"

Steve immediately placed them on the kitchen table, and Danny grabbed the gun and stuck it in his belt.

"I've gotta get out've heah!" he yelled, waving the gun angrily. "I'm gonna need some money!"

"I have about thirty dollars on me," Steve said.

"Really?" Danny put the gun down on the table again and wiped his eyes. "You guys are good to me. You're my friends, I don't want your money."

"No, go ahead, take it. You can have it."

"Where are you going to go, Danny?" Louisa asked.

"I have to get to Dallas."

"Listen," she said, understandably anxious to help him leave, "I can pack you some food."

"D'you have any cookies? Or some fruit?"

"Cookies, sure. And I have an apple here. I don't have much else in the way of fruit."

"I can survive for weeks in the woods," he told them, "with just a knife and a pack of matches. But it can get pretty cold out there."

"I've got an old jacket I can give you," Steve said quickly. It was a jacket someone had left behind at the birthday party. "It's good and warm."

Rolling placed the cookies and the apple in the pocket of the old jacket and stuck both guns in his belt.

It had been more than two hours since he first burst into their bedroom. As he walked toward the front door, finally, to leave, he looked down at the mud he had tracked onto the white living-room carpet. "Gee," he said softly, "I'm sorry for doing that." Then he started crying again. After a moment he opened the front door. He was almost gone, framed in the doorway for a moment before turning his back to them.

"God bless y'all," Dr. Jekyll said, and walked out the door.

The Clausens were the last people to see him in Shreveport, Louisiana.

Now began his long escape.

At first he wandered aimlessly, hiding from the police, knowing only that he had to get out of Louisiana.

Last seen getting into a truck headed west on I–20, he changed his direction and headed north. He camped in Superior National Forest Park in Minnesota. Just like a reconnaissance mission . . . a pack of matches, some cigarettes, some grub. What more did he need? Whom else did he need? He had just almost killed his father in the long-building confrontation. He was breaking his parole. He was a wanted man, unable ever to return home. The incubation period was over. The wanted man was a living virulent disease that was about to spread. It had been set free to do its work on the human environment. Rolling had joined a sub-species of killers, the sheer brutality of whose sexually sadistic crimes make them the most feared of all sex killers. The so-called lust killer who tortures and mutilates his victims cannot stop once he has started, especially when the last of all external restraints has been stripped away.

T. William "Bill" Pickens, fifty-nine, a retired major in the Shreveport police department, heard about the shooting of his former colleague, James Rolling, and had to stop down at the station to find out what the hell happened.

"I don't believe the stories going around now about James being an abusive father," Bill said. "I policed with that man for twenty-two years and I never saw that side of him." Yet in looking over the shooting with his former associates he did concede, "I always had the feeling Jim preferred the company of the fellers down heah to being at home with his family."

"Even so, you gotta admit, James was less than congenial most times."

"It wasn't his fault," Bill insisted. "It's just his way."

"Well, *something* must've been goin' on between 'em for his own son to try to do 'im in like he done."

Pickens nodded. He heard the younger Rolling had even stomped his father before firing another round into his stomach.

James Rolling had been seriously wounded, obliged to undergo extensive surgery for the removal of the bullets in his head and stomach.

Claudia sat in the waiting room surrounded by a few family members as she waited for the result of the surgery . . . they weren't even sure if James was going to survive.

"He was only trying to protect me," Claudia murmured to herself, as she had earlier.

And now her son was a fugitive.

When he heard about it, Rolling's previous employer Truman Cooley did not believe Rolling robbed that couple at gunpoint the night he fled from Shreveport.

"No way," he said to Bunny over the phone. "Why, he doesn't have it in him to do something like that. I think they made it up."

Bunny wasn't so sure.

"I liked Danny," Cooley told her. "I still like him. If the economy had held up I guess Danny'd still be working for me today."

"I always liked Danny, too."

"Too bad he ran off," Truman went on. "Things here were starting to pick up and I was even thinking of taking him on again. I would have if he hadn't left town."

"Truman," Bunny said slowly. "He shot his father."

"Yeah, I know. Now why do you suppose he did a thing like that?"

Bunny didn't feel like going into it.

Jacksonville, Florida

Christina Powell was, among a lot of other things, a good infielder. Today she was filling in as catcher. She was smiling now behind her catcher's mask as the "strike-two" call came from behind her.

The next pitch came in fast. The batter reached for it, swung and missed, but she lost her balance and the bat hit Christina hard in the head. She fell over, momentarily stunned.

Reverend Ronald Chrisner, the softball coach, came running over. He had known Christina for some four years.

"I'm okay," she murmured to him. "It's nothing . . ."

Reverend Chrisner looked at the blood coming from the cut on her head and told her he was taking her out of the game.

"No, I'm okay, we're close to winning—"

"No, that cut looks like it needs stitches."

She hated to be taken out of the game, but suddenly she smiled at him. "Oh, okay, *okay*."

Smiling. This girl was almost too much, he thought. But that was the way Christina always was, laughing, having a good time and doing the same for others. He knew firsthand. She spent time around the building where his office was, and the corridors always sounded with laughter. Good feelings seemed to follow her wherever she went.

Gainesville, Florida

Sonja Larson and her mother had been in Gainesville for the University of Florida orientation on May 21 and 22. They roomed together at UF's Broward Hall during their stay, and by the time they left Gainesville for Deerfield Beach, Sonja was even more excited by the prospects of her new life . . . she loved Gainesville, its atmosphere, its energy, and she welcomed the idea of being on her own for the summer in Weaver Hall.

Marthe Jules was Sonja's roommate at Weaver Hall during the summer term, and besides attending classes they did the usual things . . . watched

movies on television on Sunday nights, congregated at the Hub after selecting their library books, or at the Reitz Union for lunch, or went to
Skeeter's on 34th for dinner. Sonja always returned to the dorm after class
or called Marthe to tell her where she was going to be if she wasn't coming
straight back. Most of the time, if she didn't return to Weaver Hall right
after classes it was because she went over to Christina Powell's room.

Sonja and Christina had become friends almost from the moment they
met. It was hardly surprising, since they had so much in common in terms
of goals, personality, even to the kind of young men they preferred.

One afternoon, Marthe became worried when she didn't hear from
Sonja after class as usual. She later learned that Sonja and Christina Powell had gone to St. Augustine to visit Christina's boyfriend, a handsome
young black man by the name of Adrienne White. Sonja's regular boyfriend Miguel was also a young black man, although she was not seeing
him during the summer term. She was dating an old friend, Godfrey Lanness Robinson, whom she knew from the time they both attended Ely
High School. Their romance lasted from June to July of that last summer,
until she and Miguel decided to see each other again. Even so, never able
to easily say goodbye to an old friend, Sonja and Godfrey continued to
correspond with letters and phone calls—until the day she could no longer
call or write.

The girls also met Elsa Streppe from Ormond Beach, Florida, during
the summer term at the university and another friendship was formed.
They had only known each other for about three months, but the three of
them got along so well they decided to move in together for the fall term.
They even had their eye on a perfect duplex apartment at Williamsburg
Village . . .

Miami Lakes, Florida

They hung around after the evening class to watch the moon rise over the
ocean. It was luminous, incandescent, truly splendid. As they had promised to themselves, Tracy Paules and Valerie Wheeler enrolled in an evening dive class at the Flamingo Dive Center in Miami Lakes.

Tracy's sun-filtered hair blew in the breeze as they headed for the spot
in the Biscayne Bay area. Even with her first dive, Tracy hit the water
cleanly, an almost sure prospect for a diving certificate.

Tracy Paules, especially, exemplified all that was different between the
existence of her eventual killer and that of his victims. It was another
world, free of anxiety, full of certainty, fun and love. Like the others whose

lives were to end, at age twenty-three, Tracy's future was bright, her prospects for a meaningful life apparently unlimited.

Kansas City, Kansas

They were going to be looking for him everywhere, he was sure. He had
violated his probation after his father was shot. They would probably
check all of his relatives. He couldn't go from relative to relative anymore
. . . He no longer thought about a job. They had all been crap anyway.
That was the reason he couldn't hang onto any of them. But he was on the
run and he needed money. Lots of it. If there was a bullet out there
waiting for him, like he always thought, now was the time . . .

The store's security camera made a video of the robbery. It occurred on
June 12, 1990 at ten P.M. at the Westwood United Super Store at 4701
Mission Road in Kansas City, Kansas. The robber was described as a white
male, six-foot, slender build, wearing a brown knit ski mask and cloth
gloves. He was armed with a large-caliber revolver-type handgun with at
least a four-inch barrel. The clerks of Westwood United found themselves
enduring the fictitious benevolence of his politeness. "Thank you. God
bless," he had said to the clerks at Westwood United after robbing them at
gunpoint. "Please pray for me, I need it."

He left the store with approximately sixteen hundred dollars in cash.

Camarillo, California

In June of 1990 Aunt Mira Rolling suffered the indignities of having her
home in Camarillo, California, searched by the police. They were trying to
locate the Shreveport fugitive after the shooting of his father.

"He left here a long time ago," she told the authorities. "He never came
back. He left me without so much as a thank-you and owing me four
hundred dollars besides."

In describing the relationship between Danny's father and his brother,
her husband Joe Donald Rolling, Mira Rolling told them the two had had
very little contact over the years. She assured them she and her husband
had absolutely no information about the Shreveport shooting, with the
exception of some sketchy facts by Kevin Rolling, Danny's brother.

They wanted no involvement nor any contact with Danny Rolling, she
said emphatically.

18

The Summer of 1990

During the early part of 1990 Kevin Orr traveled to Gainesville to spend the weekends with Tracy Paules. Then when she was back in the Miami area for the summer working temporarily for the law firm of Terry Connor, he wanted to continue seeing her. It was difficult to break up with him even though he was now dating another girl known to Tracy only as Karen. Because of Karen's presence in Kevin's life, Tracy could spend only several weekday nights a week with him at his condo at Biscayne Bay. She hated to keep the truth from her parents, it made her feel guilty, but during her visits with Kevin she told her parents she was staying at a girlfriend's house for the night. Tracy did try to distance herself from the relationship toward the middle of the summer, not only because of all her parents' objections but because of this Karen whom he spent his weekends with.

Besides, now there was Khris.

Her parents were happy with Khris Pascarella. Tracy had met him in Miami at a May barbecue given by Tracy's best friend, Lisa Buyer. He was tall, intelligent, sensitive, good-looking and had a bright future that had been encouraged by Patrick Sessions, his old boss at the Weston Project, where he was an intern, and his beautiful daughter Tiffany, who, tragically, had been missing since one early morning in February of 1988 when she'd gone jogging and never was heard from again. Tracy's parents thought Khris Pascarella was perfect for their daughter, even as a potential son-in-law. They no longer had to deal with the ambivalence of their feelings about her previous boyfriend. Family friction was over.

Now it was the beginning of summer.

It was to be one of the happiest summers for all the eventual victims. They were high on being young and newly on their own. The future would always be there to be drawn on like a bank account.

Christina Powell and Sonja Larson were starting fresh with their summer terms. In between classes and studying, they spent hours on shopping trips at the Oaks Mall in shops like Victoria's Secret.

Manny Taboada went home to Miami to spend part of the summer, happily dating a girl who worked at Blockbuster Video. He had been accepted to the University of Florida department of architecture after attending Santa Fe Community College, and had already been approached by the UF rowing coach, Jon Grant, to be a member of the crew team.

The summer was mostly a time for parties, summer romances, even weddings. Tracy Paules attended the one of Laura Brown and William Rose at the Fort Lauderdale Country Club. Christa Hoyt went to Michelle Pothier's graduation party and became involved in a serious new romance with Pete Brigette, a deputy from the Alachua County sheriff's office.

On one weekend Tracy left Miami with a group of high-school and college friends for a day trip to Holiday Isle Resort in Islamorada, Florida. Her friend Lisa Buyer was part of the group as were Christi Hoyo, Judy Brock, Paul Brock, Derick Schwartz, Jimmy Hall, Tony Miller and Brian Maranuchi. They stayed at the Tropical Reef resort, spending afternoons at the Tiki Bar, then on to dinner at Perri's Restaurant, later for drinks at the Firehouse Bar or Woody's Bar.

It was all almost so headily unrestricted, always looking for "new songs to sing," and finding them . . .

Kansas City, Kansas

The $1,660 from the robbery of the Westwood United Super Store was almost gone.

It was 10:40 P.M. on June 30 when Rolling entered the same store. Some of the clerks recognized the man holding the gun on them as the same man who had robbed them some three weeks earlier on June 12. However, he seemed to have gained in stature since the last robbery. Now he was described as being six foot to six-three and 180 to 200 lbs. He was wearing the same ski mask and gloves. He was again armed with the same style and size handgun. This time there was hardly any cash in the store, the manager having left earlier for the bank with most of the receipts.

He drove across the state line to Westport, Missouri. The Sunfresh Grocery Store at 1000 Westport Road was only about one mile from the United Super Store in Kansas City. Here he was described to the police as being a white male, six-two to six-three, 190 pounds. Again he was wearing a brown ski mask and was armed with a large caliber revolver. And this time he hit a jackpot and walked away with $8,902 dollars.

At the Sunfresh Grocery Store, before exiting he stopped and mockingly called back to the clerks standing mutely with their hands in the air, "Life's a bitch. Sorry, guys."

On June 30, shortly after the last robbery, Rolling called Bunny Mills from a pay phone.

"Where are you, Danny?"

He wasn't saying, he just called to tell her . . .

Why didn't he come back? she said.

And go back to prison again? No thanks. Had she heard anything about his dad?

"He's still in the hospital." She didn't have the heart to tell him his father would be blind in one eye and deaf in one ear.

"So I didn't kill him after all."

"So maybe if you come back . . ."

All he ever wanted to do was please that man.

There was a long pause. She couldn't tell for sure if he was crying or not. He always did get very emotional whenever he talked about his father. "How are you getting on? Do you have money?"

"Oh yes, ma'am," he said firmly, his voice taking on a hard edge. "I got me a bundle full."

"Where'd you get it, Danny?"

"Never you mind. I finally got me a job. A good paying job . . . I just called to tell you . . ."

"What?"

Goodbye, he guessed. And he was sorry for everything. "You've always been a real good friend t'me."

Lillian Bunny Mills heard the click on the other end of the line.

Rolling got into his car and headed east across one state line after another.

Going where?

He had no idea. He had kin in Florida although he knew he could never stop in to see any of them again. That was a sure way back to the slammer again.

What the hell. He headed for Florida anyway.

Gainesville, Florida

Ten days later, on his way to Sarasota, he stopped briefly in Gainesville, just long enough to make a phone call. It took him all that time before he could bring himself to call home. During the entire drive to Florida he had been thinking about what Bunny had said.

On July 9, he finally stepped into a pay phone on Route 441 and dialed 318–635–7328. As he listened to the low electronic ringing he looked around—a nice town—waiting for what seemed like an eternity before he heard the tired, familiar voice on the other end.

"Hello, Ma? How's Dad?"

19

Differences

For some a summer of great expectations . . .

Sonja Larson was the baby in her family.

"I hate it that she's not going to be on campus," thought her mother, Ada.

The eighteen-year-old freshman had lived at one of the University of Florida dormitories for the summer season but she was not able to get a dorm room for her freshman semester as an elementary-education student. Ada would always be aware that if Sonja had been able to stay on campus, things might have turned out very differently for her and for Christina Powell, who had decided to move in with Sonja no matter where she lived.

Now working as an accountant, Ada knew she would have to take time out to help Sonja, Christina and their third roommate, Elsa, find a new place, one that was safe, secure and close to campus. So she drove north to Gainesville to help the girls hunt for one. It was the season to look. Every rental office at the off-campus apartment complexes was crowded either with students who were returning or those on a first-time search for accommodations. It was easy to tell the first-timers; they were the ones whose eyes showed that extra anticipation as they moved onto the next plateau of their lives. Ada enjoyed being with the girls, charged as they were with the energy of their youth. They lunched, they shopped and they went to different apartment complexes on their quest—Oxford Manor, Gatorwood Apartments, Country Gardens—before they finally settled on the lovely duplex unit at the Williamsburg Village Apartments on SW Sixteenth Street. It was just four blocks from the university. Except for one fleeting moment of concern over the isolation of the back courtyard, Ada felt Williamsburg could not have been more desirable.

Mission accomplished.

Elsa would move into the apartment at the end of August. Sonja and Christina would move in earlier in mid-August, just two weeks before their murders.

At 3:30 P.M. on July 31, Ada Larson left Gainesville for the drive back to

160

Deerfield Beach. She felt pretty good about it, even envying the girls just a little for what she knew was the excitement of starting out on the first day of a future that beckoned to them with such hope and promise.

It was at approximately the same time that Ada Larson left her daughter to return to Deerfield Beach that Godfrey Robinson arrived in Gainesville from his home in Broward County to visit her daughter Sonja. He knew that Sonja was leaning toward seeing her old boyfriend Mik again. They had already talked about it and about the future of their own relationship. He felt deeply attached to Sonja and sorry that she had decided to go back to Mik. And not one to give up friends easily, Sonja still felt a strong attachment to Godfrey as well. However, in a special way she could not define to him or even to herself, it was Mik who was especially attracting her.

Before Godfrey left her they went to DisneyWorld for one last day together surrounded by a world of fantasy, blue-green waters, warm sand and a bright yellow sun, then returned to her dorm in Gainesville to make love for the last time. It was lovely, quiet and unsafe sex, since they had used no birth control. Later Sonja would write to Godfrey telling him that she thought she might be pregnant; as it turned out, she was not. She felt lucky, but then she had always been lucky. When Godfrey left Gainesville to return to Broward County, his voice was low when they said goodbye. He knew that they would continue to be friends, that they would continue talking to each other and corresponding. Even though he would not be seeing much of her anymore, she would always be special to him.

He could have no idea when they parted that it was the last time he would see her alive.

For another, a summer of deceit . . .

Rolling spent the five days between July 17 and July 22, 1990, in Tallahassee, Florida. He had been driving on a southeasterly course, drifting from one place to another until he crossed the most southwestern tip of the Georgia state line into Florida's panhandle.

He pulled into the Travel Lodge Motel in Tallahassee. Using identification he had stolen in Kansas City, it was the first time Rolling introduced himself as Michael J. Kennedy with an address of 2030 Seventh and Rainbow, Kansas City, Kansas.

He massaged his nose with slow small caresses as he watched the motel clerk fill in his name.

"Kennedy," the clerk repeated as he wrote in the register. "Room One twenty-four."

Rolling nodded. It was a common enough name. He knew it would not arouse any undue suspicions. It had been easy to assume the identity.

"Thirty-six dollars a day."

He nodded again. He could afford it.

The motel room was old with faded wallpaper, especially over the headboards where innumerable transient heads had been propped up against the wall to watch TV. The air conditioning that whirred loudly was largely ineffectual but it didn't matter; he was exhausted. At first he slept like a dead man. But before dawn, consciousness began to come over him as he tossed in bed. Unwanted thoughts interrupted his sleep. Again he thought of his dad. He thought of how he had looked as he stood over him in the kitchen. He could still see the red puddle expanding around his head on the kitchen floor. He thought of the power he had felt as he continued to pump bullets into his father's body, his own rigid with fury. He thought of how it had felt when he kicked him. He thought of God. He thought of soft flesh. He thought of his soul. Nearer my God to Thee . . .

He got up and groped his way toward the bathroom to douse his face with cold water. The small white room was pretty clean except for the deepest corners that still had accumulations of dust clods, but it had thick layers of paint and a rusty drain in the small white porcelain sink beneath a leaky faucet that even his large hand could not shut tightly enough to stop the dripping.

In the full light of morning he ate a breakfast of steak and eggs at the Kitchen on West Tennessee Street, a likely spot for anyone staying at the Travel Lodge Motel. He tried to strike up a conversation with the waitress, who edged away. Something about the chill in his eyes kept her at a busy distance at the other end of the counter. He shrugged it off.

On July 18 he bought a USMC Ka-Bar knife in an army and navy surplus store. As soon as he walked into the store he could see the series of military-style knives stretched before him in a display case. He looked at the Ka-Bar knife. Heavy, easy-grip wood handle, thick, eight-inch long blade with a jagged edge, a bloodline running the full length of the blade for easy "in and out" and a tilted point capable of cutting through live flesh and bone. It was the only one of its kind in the case. A good silent weapon.

The manager, Beth Norman, moved over to the display case and stood before him. She had a round, pleasant, pretty face framed by long, straight black hair that was parted in the middle and hanging well past her shoulders.

"How much?" he asked her, pointing to the Ka-Bar.

"Thirty-four dollars."

"With the case?"

She nodded.

He smiled at her. "I'll take it."

He paid cash.

By the fifth rudderless day, Tallahassee had become increasingly vapid for him. He paid the motel bill of $195 and left the city. Not only was he on the run, he was becoming increasingly bored, restless and edgy, all of which made him a fragile notch above lethal.

Where now?

He drove south, a private reclusive nature that appeared friendly and sad on the surface but continued to be fueled by sadistic fantasies at its core.

Drifting.

The cruel July Florida sun was starting to beat down in the direct rays of high noon. His left elbow, leaning on the sill of the open car window, was deeply bronzed.

Past the forest of tall scrub pines spaced enough to be able to see through them to long, flat clearings beyond. Driving. Until he saw the sign —*Jacksonville.*

But once there, tired of drifting and suddenly made anxious by the car that pinpointed him back to Louisiana by its identifying license plate, he decided to leave Jacksonville immediately.

He got on a bus that was heading for . . . where? Sarasota. Why not? He was getting closer.

Sarasota—July 22, 1990

It was a beachside city full of nighttime activities. This place might work out okay.

The registration card at the time of his check-in at the Cabana Inn on Tamiami Trail read, Michael J. Kennedy, from Rainbow, Kansas City.

Sarasota wasn't a bad place. The Cabana Inn lounge even had a coin-operated crane machine he played for hours at a time. He was pretty good at it, and soon had an accumulation of soft stuffed animals he had managed to pick up with the crane.

Eye size—51. Bridge size—20. Temple length—CC.

At eleven A.M., on July 25, Michael Kennedy was examined by Dr. Vincent Troia at the LensCrafters located in Southgate Plaza in Sarasota.

The frames were MFG-31 Renaissance, Owen C, color, demi amber.

The bill came to $89.95 for the frames, $54.95 for the lenses, $15.95 for a service agreement and $1.12 for sales tax. That included Dr. Troia's examination.

"How much total?"

"You said you're from Kansas City?" Steve Kerns, general manager of LensCrafters, asked as he made the calculation.

"Yes."

It came to $161.97 total. "You're a long way from home," Kerns said, writing.

"I'm always a long way from home."

Kerns glanced up.

Kennedy pulled a roll of bills out of his pocket and peeled off $165 in cash.

Kerns handed him a receipt and $3.03 in change.

Kennedy nodded.

Kerns watched him walk away, his new glasses covering the cold blue of his eyes.

He went to eat at Shoney's.

He went to the movies at the South Trail Cinema.

He went to Tilden Ross Jewelers, where he bought a gold chain for $417.30 and a violet amethyst ring for $616.16. A bit extravagant but he still had plenty of money from his robberies, so why the hell not—an internal growl of self-justification and rationalization. He was entitled to some of life's better things, wasn't he? About time.

But he was always alone. Isolation was necessary until he was sure the police trail behind him had cooled off, but it was almost two months since he had shot his father. Keeping a low profile, he had trusted no one during this time. But now, the hollow emptiness, added to the old sense of impotence for any kind of significant intimacy, had created a dangerously lonely man.

On July 26, Rolling walked into the Brown Derby Lounge, where Teresa Lynn Cousins was tending bar.

He introduced himself as "Kennedy, Mike Kennedy," and said he was from Kansas.

"What'll you have?"

"A bloody mary. What's your name?"

"Terry."

He watched her closely as she prepared his drink. She was a very pretty if somewhat heavy-set brunette woman of about five-foot-six. "Would you like to have breakfast after you get off work?" he asked when she placed the bloody mary in front of him.

He seemed nice enough but she told him, no thanks, sorry, she was real tired.

"Suit yourself," he said quickly. "No problem," but of course he was seething inside. They were all alike. He downed his drink and took off.

James Robert Ford worked in the men's department of Burdine's Department Store located in the Southgate Plaza mall in Sarasota.

"I'm from Kansas."

Ford looked up toward the voice with the lazy southern drawl, physically sizing up the man standing before him in a glance. He was about six-foot-four, two hundred pounds, with huge hands, brown hair, skin on his face incongruously fair.

"I'm new in town," the man said pleasantly. "Don't know anybody."

Although Rolling used a duffel-type bag for the bulk of his personal possessions, he often carried a tote bag around with him, which he now placed on the counter in front of the salesman.

"Can I help you with something?" Ford asked.

"Polo shirts?"

"Sure . . ."

"My name's Kennedy, Mike Kennedy."

"Okay," Ford said.

It was hardly usual for a customer to offer such personal information about himself. Ford took a closer look. He couldn't see the color of Kennedy's eyes behind what looked to him like expensive Ralph Lauren-style gold wire-rimmed sunglasses. His hair, combed straight back past a receding hairline, was slightly longer at the nape of the neck.

Mike Kennedy purchased a white polo-type Marite François Girbaud shirt and a pair of multicolored beach pants. He paid for the hundred-dollar purchase with cash. The ease with which he pulled out a large roll of money held together with a thick rubber band made Ford take notice.

"Thanks," Kennedy said, all smiles and friendly before leaving the store.

Ford did not see him again until the end of his workday. When he was ready to leave the Southgate mall he encountered Kennedy once more near the front entrance of Burdine's department store. Ford got the impression that Kennedy had been waiting for him. He was extremely friendly, insisting on shaking hands like a long-lost friend. Ford noticed the strength of the man's hands in the very firm handshake.

He was wearing the Marite François Girbaud shirt, the wire-rimmed glasses, a gold neckchain, a couple of brightly gemmed rings and new sneakers.

"Listen, like I said before," Kennedy said with a smile topped by a deep frown, "I'm all alone in town and I was wondering if you'd like to have dinner with me."

Ford heard himself agreeing. The guy did appear straight, not drunk or on drugs. He just seemed lonely and he made it clear he would pick up the tab. Already having labeled him a big spender, Ford thought, hey, why not?

"Is your car here?" Ford asked.

"I don't have a car. It broke down in Jacksonville. I came to Sarasota by bus."

"Well, there's always Beasley's Restaurant."

"Where's that?"

"Right here in the mall."

"Great."

They started to walk in the direction of the restaurant.

"It's hard to get around in Sarasota without a car," Ford said.

"I use taxis."

"That can get pretty tough on the pocket, can't it?"

"That's okay," Kennedy said. "I recently got ten thousand for selling a song I wrote."

"No kidding."

"Yeah. To a major record company."

"That's pretty impressive, Kennedy."

"Call me Mike."

After ordering dinner at Beasley's, Mike suddenly stuck a huge foot out from under the table and pointed to his sneakers.

"See these?"

He was wearing new Reebok high-top tennis shoes. For some reason Mike made a point of telling him they had been manufactured in Kansas.

"Kansas, huh? I'm originally from Muncie, Indiana, myself," Ford said. "I only moved to Florida about three years ago."

"How'd y'all wind up here?"

"I like it," Ford said. "I used to be a garage-door installer until I got hurt on the job and had to go on workmen's compensation for about a year. I went back to Muncie to recuperate. Then I came back to Sarasota and got this job with Burdine's."

"You like it?"

"It's better than garage doors. What do you do in Kansas City?"

"Me? Besides my music, I'm in trucking."

By the end of the dinner Rolling had manufactured an entire new life. Keeping the conversation impersonal, with no talk of marriages or girlfriends or prison, he used "on vacation" as a reason for his presence in Sarasota. Starting with the identity of Michael J. Kennedy, who in actuality was a Vietnam War veteran who had passed away in 1975, he told Ford about the Ace Trucking Company, the red Firebird, and the Harley-Davidson motorcycle he claimed to own back home in Kansas City.

It sounded pretty good to Ford.

It sounded even better to Rolling.

Two days later, as Mike Kennedy, he returned to Burdine's and asked Ford about local nightclubs. And with Ford and Ford's roommate, Derek Kabobel, leading the way, a round of restaurants, bars and strip joints followed, all blending into one another like a movie montage, sometimes in a taxi, sometimes in Ford's car, always with Mike's money cutting through any resistance. Mike insisted on paying for everything. Ford and Kabobel didn't mind. The big spender and big tipper sometimes left as much as a three-dollar tip for one drink, the guy had to be loaded . . .

Wearing a red bandanna around his head and adopting an air of joviality, Mike demanded that the taxicab driver take them to a nude dancing establishment. "Babes," he said. "We gotta get us some babes."

The driver, a man in his mid-thirties with dark scraggly hair and a moustache, looked in the rearview mirror, running through his mental list of local exotic dance establishments and suggested Club Mary. Ford seconded it.

But they found it closed, which didn't faze Kennedy. Keep going. There were other places, other bars, other eateries. The Cabana Inn bar, the Brown Derby Lounge—she was still there at the Brown Derby, Terry, the one who had rebuffed him—the Club Bandstand, the Five-O Club . . .

Actually, although Mike had talked about meeting some "babes," it seemed more a forced air to live up to macho expectations rather than a genuine desire for female companionship. He did not seem preoccupied with sex and had never inquired about the availability of prostitutes in the Sarasota area. In fact, he indicated that paying for sex was a turnoff. Watching the hand-in-his-pocket manner in which he operated, Ford and Kabobel felt that Kennedy's main interest was in putting out a freewheeling, high-living, lusty image having a buddy-buddy friendship, even if he had to buy it.

"Why don't we get something to eat first?" Ford suggested on another night out. "We can go to the Chop House Restaurant and then to Club Bandstand. They're both in the Sarasota Quay entertainment complex."

This time they drove over to the Quay in Ford's car, and shortly after arrival Ford and Kabobel left Kennedy alone when they saw him hovering over a young woman at the bar. Ford looked her over. About five-foot-three or -four, slightly plump with black shoulder-length hair. Pretty, except for too much makeup. The interesting thing was the goofy manner in which Kennedy began to behave the moment he was with her. Grinning, slapping his thighs, talking loud one minute, making telltale observations about himself and his background in order to impress her, pulling way back the next, leaning on her every word, listening intently as he let her take the conversational lead. He took off the gold necklace he had bought at Tilden Ross Jewelers for $417.30 and draped it around her neck.

Ford and Kabobel finally left him to his own devices with his newly adorned acquaintance and departed the club.

"Don't worry 'bout me," he called to them as they waved a good-luck, thumbs-up so-long at him. "I'll grab a taxi . . ."

Shortly after they left Club Bandstand, Kennedy would get himself into a wild scrap with a huge male patron at the bar over a perceived slight to the woman he was with. First words, then fists—his striking the first unexpected blows—then kicks, wrestling on the floor punctuated with grunts and obscenities. The fight was so serious and disruptive, and so thoroughly perceived as his fault, that he was removed from the premises and thrown out onto the street.

The woman he had fought over had disappeared.

The next night, when Fred visited Mike in his room at the Cabana Inn, Mike was playing his Ovation guitar. Mike called to him from his bed to "come in" and continued to play and sing. To Ford's surprise he seemed a fairly talented rhythm-and-blues guitar player even though the ring finger of his left hand had been amputated above the first joint.

"Is that the song you sold to the record company?" he asked.

Mike nodded. Dreaming the lie. "It should be coming out in the spring," he said. Lying the dream.

He continued playing and singing.

"We ought to go to the Irish Pub where you could play your guitar," Ford said.

Mike said no.

"A lot of guitar players go there . . ."

No.

Then Ford noticed the gold chain Kennedy had given to the woman at the Club Bandstand bar the night before. It was on top of a handwritten letter on the bed next to him. Ford couldn't make out what was in the letter but the envelope next to it had no postmark, indicating it had been hand-delivered to his room.

Mike saw him looking at it. "She didn't want it. She sent it back." But there was something chilling in the way the corners of his mouth lowered as his blue eyes lingered on the rejected gift.

Terry Cousins saw him as he walked into the Brown Derby Lounge accompanied for the second time by a guy somewhere in his mid-forties with dark hair and glasses. She had often seen him around although he was known to her only as a guitar player named Mike.

The moment she saw them enter, she went over to them. The last time they had been in they had left the lounge before paying their bar tab.

"I know, I know," Mike said. "We forgot."

She watched as he placed a large bill on the bartop.

"Okay," she smiled. "Anyone can make a mistake."

"Keep the change," he said quietly.

"Thanks," she said. She watched as they left the bar and entered the lounge. Through the door, she could see him at the crane machine.

He won again. He was feeling better about himself. He returned to the bar and tried again with the barmaid. This time Terry agreed when he invited her to have dinner with him that evening.

On their first date he told her about the song he had sold to a major record company. He talked about being in the Vietnam War. He told about the trucking outfit he owned, Ace Trucking. He looked at her closely as he added he had a potential buyer for this trucking company "back home" and was considering moving to Sarasota.

Maybe he could fit in here. But her "that's nice" was not what he was looking for.

"Are those Kansas patches on your jeans?" she asked, changing the subject.

He nodded. "That's where my trucking company is."

She nodded. She was finding it difficult to believe what he was telling her.

Afterward they went to his room.

She saw a small nylon duffel bag full of the stuffed animals apparently obtained from the crane machine in the Cabana Inn lounge. Strange, she thought. What's he going to do with them all?

On top of his television she noted a gold herringbone neckchain, turquoise-and-silver rings and a gold ring with a crosslike design.

"You like it?" he asked quickly, and put the gold ring on her finger. "Wear it."

She wasn't sure if he was giving it to her or just letting her wear it.

He tried, tentatively, to initiate sex, but nothing happened. He dropped it.

Shortly afterward she left, realizing that although he had tried he had not really made an effective pass. He was a little strange, she thought, but he was nice enough. Not pushy or anything like that. In fact, he was turning out to be a gentleman.

It was not long before she was to see another side of him. One night after she finished work she met him in the Cabana Inn lounge and watched him at the crane machine. While he was intent on the game she caught sight of a male friend walking by the lounge. Not having seen him in a while, she left the room to talk to him.

Within moments, Kennedy came storming out of the lounge, looking for her. The veins on his neck were protruding as he yelled, "If you need to talk to someone, talk to *me*."

"Hey, what is this—?"

"You *heard* me. Talk to *me*."

Intimidated, she didn't feel like challenging him and went back to the Cabana Inn lounge with him.

Later, several of the patrons in the lounge told her that Kennedy had behaved like a crazy man while he was looking for her.

"Who *is* this guy, anyway?" Terry wondered.

Kennedy reacted in the same irrational fashion later that evening when she went to the restroom and did not come back quickly enough to suit him.

"What are you so *touchy* about?" she asked. After all, he didn't own her. They were just casual friends, if that.

Kennedy launched into tales of Vietnam, apologetic for his behavior. Vietnam, she thought. Maybe that's why. She almost bought it.

The University Inn. Danny Rolling stayed here before moving into the woods and beginning his weekend murder spree. (*Courtesy of Mary Ryzuk*)

The Gatorwood Apartment complex. (*Courtesy of Mary Ryzuk*)

Rear of the Williamsburg
Apartments.
(*Courtesy of Mary Ryzuk*)

The courtyard of the
Williamsburg Apartments.
(*Courtesy of Mary Ryzuk*)

Shands Hospital.
(*Courtesy of Mary Ryzuk*)

Flags all over
Gainesville flew at
half-mast just after the
student murders.
(*Courtesy of Mary Ryzuk*)

Mitch Stacy (*Courtesy of Mary Ryzuk*)

Tiffany Sessions (*Courtesy of Mary Ryzuk*)

Patrick Sessions (*Courtesy of Mary Ryzuk*)

Danny Harold Rolling (*Courtesy of the Gainesville* Sun)

Christina Powell
(*Courtesy of the Gainesville* Sun)

Tracy Paules
(*Courtesy of the Gainesville* Sun)

Manuel Taboada
(*Courtesy of the Gainesville* Sun)

Christa Leigh Hoyt
(*Courtesy of the Gainesville* Sun)

Sonja Larson
(*Courtesy of the Gainesville* Sun)

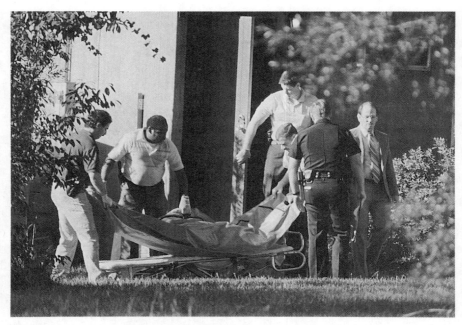

Members fo the Alachua County Sheriff's office and the medical examiner's office remove the body of Santa Fe Community College student Christa Hoyt from her apartment. (*Courtesy of the Gainesville* Sun)

Steve Platt, center, Director of the Florida Department of Law Enforcement with Alachua County Sheriff's spokesman Spenser Mann, right, and Gainesville Police spokeswoman Sadie Darnell at a news conference about the student murders. (*Courtesy of the Gainesville* Sun)

George Paules (left), Jim Larson, Ann Garren, Ricky Paules and Laurie Lahey, all relatives of the five murder victims, look at the SW 34th Street memorial wall in Gainesville. (*Courtesy of the Gainesville* Sun)

Florida State Prison near Starke where Danny Rolling is incarcerated, has housed the state's most dangerous criminals, including serial killer Ted Bundy. (*Courtesy of the Independent Florida* Alligator)

On the night of Christy Hoyts murder... I, DANNY Rolling broke into her apartment by using a screw driver to pry open the double glass doors to... and entered her bedroom. The time was approachimently 10:00 p.m. ...

I waited until Ms Hoyt returned... she had apperently been playing tennis. She was dressed in athletic T-shirt and shorts... and tennis shoes..

I watched her approach across the green lawn. She opened the door to her apartment and entered closing the door behind her.

It was dark and I had moved a Book cAse to her bedroom earlier to have a place to hide in the corner by the front door.

She place the tennis balls and racket on the kitchen table... Her back was to me.. but she heard me moving towards her.

She turned just as I grabbed her. _ There was a brief struggle and we went to the floor.

I then duck-taped her mouth closed and taped her hands behind her back. Then ... I moved her to the bedroom...

She was placed on her wAter bed and her clothing was removed...

I discovered she was on her period and so ... I removed her tompax. Then I raped

Danny Rolling's handwritten confession. It was written in prison to a fellow inmate.

her...

afterwards... I turned her on her back
and stabbed her once over the heart through
the back on the right side.

She died quickly... 8 to 10 seconds and
it was over...

I then turned her over on her back

...and left...

The knife I used was a Military issue
K-Bar...

after I had left... I discovered I had
lost my wallet... so... I returned to Ms.
Hoyts apartment to look for it...

It was no where to be found... as I
was leaving...

Then... I sat up Ms. Hoyts
body so it was sitting up on the edge of the
water-bed with its arms resting on its knees
a stream of blood poured
and pooled at its feet...
Then... I left it that way... sitting up

Gemini

The moan... the groan...
    the Silver moon shown...
The whisper... the cry...
    dead leaves fly...
Though the haze it smells your fears...
    Then... it appears...
Your nightmare come to life...
    A maniac with a knife...
The moan... the groan...
    the Silver moon shown...
The whisper... the cry...
    dead leaves fly...
Tonight... in the arms of Gemini...
    A captured butterfly will die...
Burned red with fever...
    Then turned gold forever...
    forever my dear...
    no more pain... no more fear.
    Close your eyes my dear...
    And sleep...
The moan... the groan...
    the Silver moon shown...
The whisper... the cry...
    into the night comes Gemini...
    And tonight... you die...

      by Danny Rolling

Gemini is one of Rolling's handwritten poems.

20

Collision Course

August 5

It was a perfectly weathered Sunday morning. Tracy Paules and Khris Pascarella went to Six Flags resort in Atlanta, Georgia, with her friends Malynn and Laurie. They spent most of their time riding the roller coaster, screaming, laughing, waiting for their stomachs to lurch at the sudden drops and turns.

At approximately three P.M., Laurie took Tracy and Khris directly to the Atlanta airport for a return flight to Miami. She would never see her friend Tracy's smile again.

August 7

Shands Hospital in Gainesville, with its radio tower soaring high above its roof, looked like a red brick fortress. It was a welcome sight to Christina Powell as she pulled up to the emergency room entrance. She could no longer tolerate the severe lower back and abdominal pains that had kept her awake all night and continued to afflict her once morning had come. At precisely 1:56 P.M. Christina finally went to Shands emergency room to find out what was wrong. She remained until 6:50 P.M. for treatment of what were subsequently determined to be kidney stones.

August 9

Mr. and Mrs. Larson arrived in Gainesville and contacted Sonja at her dorm.

They met for breakfast at the University of Florida's Reitz Union before Sonja went to her nine A.M. class. When she got out at eleven-thirty, Sonja, her parents, James Sr. and Ada; her brother James Jr.; Carla Thomas, Ada's sister-in-law; and Sonja's girlfriend Marthe spent the rest of the morning and afternoon going to three different places to pick up furniture and pictures that Ada had purchased for her daughter. They also moved into Sonja's rooms the furniture Carla was giving her from Carla's own apartment. Ada was aware that Christina's parents and Elsa Streppe's parents also had been in the apartment earlier to help them move in. At seven P.M. Elsa showed up at Williamsburg Village, moving in some of her own furnishings and personal belongings.

Although moving was hard work, particularly in Florida's August heat, and they didn't get finished until eight P.M., the mood throughout the day and evening was gay and bright with anticipation. Marthe and Carla could never have imagined that when they left, it was the last time they would ever see Sonja alive.

By nine P.M., Mr. and Mrs. Larson had left Gainesville to return to Deerfield Beach knowing that Sonja was going to come back home for one final visit before her fall freshman semester began.

"See you soon," Sonja called as they left.

"Drive carefully on your way back."

"I will."

The next day, one line for each name, Sonja, Christina and Elsa signed the Williamsburg Village Apartments rental lease on apartment #113 in which Sonja and Christine would die. Afterward, Elsa returned to her home in Ormond Beach.

Tuesday, August 12

Christa Leigh Hoyt's roommate, Brigitte Toombs, moved out of Apartment M, the duplex they shared on Archer Road. It was an amicable parting . . . "I'll call next week," Brigitte said on leaving . . . "Take your time. I'll give you a few days to settle in."

Brigitte Toombs' decision to leave had put her out of harm's way. Christa, on the other hand, lived alone now for the first time in her life. She loved the freedom and the independence. Her life was her own now. Still, she wasn't used to it. Being a cautious sort, she was sure never to open the door to a stranger.

August 12

Manny Taboada spent the night with his good friend Armando, bar-hopping throughout the Miami area, both trying to cram in as much fun as they could before they would have to settle down again to their studies.

The next night, keeping up the same pace, they met Iysha Adell and Valerie Cappalleri at the Charcoal Lounge and Restaurant in Miami Lakes. They did not begin to wind down until the early hours of the morning. After taking Armando home at approximately 3:15 A.M., Manny and Iysha still were not through for the night. They stopped by his mother's house to let Iysha see his beautiful Persian cat Sasha—snowy white, clean, pampered and loved, just home from a visit to the veterinarian. Iysha knew Manny was a real sucker for the cat. An endearing quality.

Finally, after watching Sasha purr herself to sleep under hypnotic fingertip caresses, they returned to the Charcoal for a nightcap before bidding each other farewell and parting company at approximately four-thirty in the morning.

He was staying at the Cabana Inn. They met in the lounge at the crane machine.

She pretended not to notice him watching her as she tried and failed to win a stuffed animal from the coin-operated crane machine.

Could he help?

No, thanks.

She kept trying, but no matter how she manipulated the crane she couldn't seem to snare one of the prizes. Rolling excused himself and soon returned from his room with an armful of the stuffed animals he had won from the machine.

She thought that was pretty funny. Seeing her reaction, he told her his name was Mike, Mike Kennedy. Hers was Leila Grossman.

She lived in Sarasota and, in jeans and a loose-fitting shirt, often rode her bicycle to the Cabana Inn lounge for evening cocktails. She was a forty-year-old, very attractive six-foot-tall blonde woman, not the sort that usually attracted him, but she seemed friendly enough once he had broken the ice by giving her the stuffed animals.

He offered to buy her a drink at the bar, and before long they were quite drunk on bloody marys and screwdrivers. She liked him. He certainly seemed harmless, and although he did nothing to force himself on her she was sure that they were going to wind up in bed in his motel room. They even set down ground rules for their relationship as they ordered more drinks and talked about sex. He brought up the subject of anal intercourse as they sat at the bar. She said she didn't go in for that and he didn't press it.

His room was only a hop away from where they sat. The first thing he did when they were in his room was show her a great deal of cash that he produced from a box under his bed.

Where did that all come from? He told her he had brought $10,000 to

$15,000 dollars with him from Kansas to spend here on vacation in Sara-sota vacationing for a month or so.

Not bad, she thought, smiling at him. A good time could be had by all for that kind of money.

"I just broke up with my girlfriend and I'm getting away while she moves out of my home."

She didn't really care. They stripped off each other's clothes and got into the shower together. Then Kennedy performed oral sex on her. He asked her to do the same. She didn't like that, she wasn't in the mood. He didn't insist. He also didn't make penetration. The whole business turned out to be less than satisfying.

On their next date they went to the movies at the Sarasota Square Mall, after which they went back to the Cabana Inn and had drinks. Then, as both anticipated, they went to Kennedy's room a second time. This time, since he didn't seem to be much for penetration, Leila had brought a vibrator with her. She knew she could be pushy sometimes but she also realized she had to take the lead in their sexual relationship. He had no particularly bizarre sexual preferences, and although he was never force-ful, in fact rather reserved, he was open-minded about the vibrator. He never did anything that she didn't want him to do and this time it was a little better for her. And he ejaculated twice that night, once into her and once on the bedsheets.

She still thought it odd that Kennedy never made penile penetration. Something was wrong, she thought. It didn't seem to matter to the guy whether he was inside her or not. As though touching himself and mastur-bating were the most he could do or wanted to do. She saw how he liked to stroke himself. Trying to help out, she reached to touch his testicles but he flinched and pulled away.

"Tender," he said.

"What happened?"

"I got kicked in the groin in a fight over at Club Bandstand."

PART

|||

ONE WEEK BEFORE THE MURDERS: THE COMING TOGETHER

21

A.K.A.

Sarasota, Florida

He sat in his hotel room with his cassette recorder on his lap. He listened to the *whir* of the recorder for a moment before he began to speak, slowly, quietly. He didn't *sound* like a monster.

Well, contrary to popular belief, I suppose, I don't know, I don't know what people think anymore. All I know is I'm just one man alone in this world, facing the whole world by himself, and I'm sending this to the three people I love the most and I'll always love. I love my mother, I love my father, and I love my brother, and no matter anybody thinks about this man, Danny Harold Rollings, I want these three people that I'm talking to right now to know, that this is not the road I really wanted, but it is the road that is before me now, and I will walk it like a man, and you know Dad, you know I love you Pop, and I'm so sorry, Dad. It rips my heart out by the roots to think what happened between you and I. I'm sorry Pop, if it means anything, I'm so very sorry, and I suffer a lot behind this. I hurt, I hurt in my heart and it never goes away, Pop. I wish it was me instead of you. I wish it had happened to me instead of you. This isn't easy. Nothing ever been easy for me. Well, I always wanted to make you proud of me, Dad, but it's somehow or another I always fell short, but I promise you this much. No matter what happens on the road ahead of me, at least, I'll walk it as a man. I will do that.

Mom, you're such a precious soul. There ain't a woman on the face of this earth that can cook like you, sugar. You hear me? You got to be the best cook in the whole wide world and believe me, I miss it. I love you, Mom, and I want you to know your boy is okay. I'm gonna be alright. There's something I want you to know and I want you to understand this. The last time I saw you, I saw how much it hurt you to say goodbye to me and you know something, Mom? I'm not gonna put you through that again. I love you too much for that, but I want you to purpose it in your mind and in your heart and in your soul, that I'm a man now, and God only knows, even God himself said that being a man wasn't easy, and, oh, how well I know (*Sniffling*) that it isn't easy. Especially a man that's, huh, shoot! like myself. (*Sniffling*) Can't trust anyone, can't be totally true. I have to always live (*Pause*) live this lie that I'm

177

living. Mom, don't blame yourself for anything that's happened. None of it is your fault. I don't really believe it's anybody's fault. It's just the way things happen sometimes. Sometimes we want so much for things to be right, especially with the ones we love. But it doesn't always happen that way, does it, Mom? So we have to go on as long as there is breath in our body. We gotta go on, Mom. You gotta go on. You know you're a very special woman, and oh, how well I know that I was raised by one of the sweetest women on the face of this earth, and you know I know Dad is so glad to have you. He picked him a gem alright. Yeah, Pop you got a good one and she got her a good one too. (*Sniffling*) And you're a good man, Pop. Oh (*Pause*) Mom, I want you to go on. What I'm trying to say is after this tape, you're not going to hear anything else from me. Just . . . just forget about me. Well, I won't say that, 'cause you can't forget your own. I'm just saying, I want you to go on and live your life. I don't want you to have sleepless nights because of me. Do this for me, Mom. You deserved a hell of a lot more than . . . that the pain that I've brought you, and I regret with all my heart, but you know, if you will make things easier on me, Mom, please, I'm asking you . . . go on. I love you. Go on and live your life, and enjoy your life, for your life is your own. No one can take that from you. I love you, Mom.

On this tape, I'm gonna . . . I'm . . . gonna sing every song I ever wrote. I'm gonna sing it to you, Mom, and I'm gonna sing it to you, Dad. I know you wanted me to write them songs down, and you know, I was going to (*Pause*) But, instead, I'll sing 'em to you, Pop, if you wanna listen. You probably hate me now, and I don't blame you for that, Dad. But maybe, in the hereafter, when it's all said and done, all the ships are in, and all the chips are in, and . . . and everything's sorted out, perhaps we'll understand this one day. I don't. I don't even understand myself half the time, but I know that there was once some good in me and, perhaps, there is still a little, 'cause my heart can still be touched. Perhaps there's some hope in that.

Kevin . . . Kevin, I love you. You know, you said something to me that . . . that hurt me. Made me wonder. Maybe you didn't know me as well as you thought you did. Maybe I didn't know you as well as I thought I did. Last time I saw you, you said that I enjoyed this. You're wrong, Kevin. I hate this. I hate what's happened. I hate the way I have to live. I'd trade it all. I'd trade both my arms if I could go back and do it all over. Please believe me that I don't enjoy this. (*Sniffling*) You're . . . I'm not going to say you're a good man, because you can't handle that. Why? I don't know. When your loved ones tell you how much they think of you, why can't you accept that, brother? You are good, as good men go. I know that we're all basically evil, but there is some good in you, Kevin. You said that you didn't care anymore. Don't say that, brother, please, I beg you. As your brother speaking to you now, I know not what the future holds for me or for anyone, but I know that you care, Kevin, and you care a lot. Don't bottle up your feelings, brother. I know that it's easy to get hurt when you wear your heart on your sleeve, 'cause it's easy for people to reach up there and grab it . . . squeeze it.

Kevin, you got a lot of good in you. Don't let what happened between Dad and me . . . I know it's got the family tore up, but hey, Mom and Dad need you right now. They need you now more than they ever have, and between the two of us, you were the strongest. I love you Kevin. I love you, brother, more than . . . than . . . than even words can justify.

I wish it could have been different. I wanted so much for you and I to strike out together and make a dent in this world, and make something out of our lives. But it doesn't always happen that way, does it? No, I guess it doesn't, but I love you, brother. (*Sniffling*) And I . . . I want you to go on. I want you to have a good life. My life, as it is, is not easy, but I will walk it until the Lord decides to take me home. I will walk the road before me the best I can. And I prayed, and I've asked God . . . I've asked him . . . I said, "Dear Lord, God of Heaven and earth, I would rather be judged of you that judged of men, because I know that judgments of men and how it stinks." Man does not judge rightfully and justly. No, this world is corrupt, and so is the system that rose it up, and that system is the system of the Devil. (*Sniffling*) Civilization, it's not of the Lord. It's of the Devil, brother. So, I've asked God that if I am to be judged, not to be judged of men but let me fall into the hands of my maker, who I still love and believe in. I'll always believe in my Lord and my savior, Jesus Christ. Oh Kevin, try to bring the family together, what's left of it. And I don't know why people, nowadays, are so hard on the church. I know there are people there that are hypocrites but there are really true Christians, God fearing people to go to church, brother, and there's no excuse that a man can give under God's blue sky that justifies not going to church and worshipping Him. Surely, if you give tithes and it goes in a man's pocket, that's not your fault, and the judgment does not lie upon you but upon the man that took the money for wrongful purpose. (*Sniffling*) Seek you out a church, brother, and take Mom and Dad because we both know time is so short and let's not be hypocritical. We can't come to God on our terms. We can't have God the way we want him to be. We've got to humble ourself and come before God as he said, humble and meek like a child. And does a child think how the Father should, should, should be? No, a little child loves his maker, loves his Father, and looks to Him for everything, and no matter what, he loves Him.

(*Sniffling*) Try to get Mom and Dad to go to church with you, Kevin, and maybe, hopefully, y'all pray for me. I need your prayers. Y'all don't know how difficult it is. I haven't done without. No, I'm doing well. I'm well fed. I'm well clothed, and I have a place to stay. Please look after Mom and Dad, and look after yourself, brother, and maybe, maybe your prayers, maybe you can touch the thorn of God and His Mercy and wisdom. He'll look down on me with compassion and see a way out for me. I don't know anymore. I really don't, brother. This is very hard for me. You said I love this. I think you only said that out of your hurt. I don't think you meant it. I think if you ever really knew me, you knew that, really, all I ever wanted to do was serve God. I love him so much. How could I have went so far astray? I don't know. I regret it all, but I can't change it, and I'm not going to deliver myself into the hands of men to be tormented by them, by men that are even lesser than myself. No. I'll go to my grave first. (*Sniffs*) I love you, brother. Take care.

And now I'm gonna sing every song I ever wrote for my family and for the three people that I love the most in this world, and the ones that probably I hurt the most . . . (*Sniff*) . . . and then get this, get myself together.

There was a long pause on the recorder, and then he sang song after song, accompanying himself on the guitar. "When the sun won't shine, the rain keeps pouring down on you . . ." "I got the blues on a moody night . . ." A song about Jesse James, who "Chose a life of crime . . ." Another about rotting in a smoky jailhouse cell. A song called "Boggy Bayou." The song he wrote out in his front yard one summer, "I Need a Job . . ." The one about the "mystery rider gone insane. You're a killer, a drifter, gone insane . . ." The songs were all in the same key, using similar chord progressions, the usual style of the self-taught guitarist with a limited singing range.

"Somebody's knocking at my door," he said. "Who's that knocking at my door?"

It was Leila Grossman. She had come over to Mike's room on her bicycle. "Why is your key in the door?" she called as she entered.

"Is it?"

"Yes."

"Boy, that's pretty stupid. Did I leave my key in the door?"

"Well, sweetie . . ."

"I guess I did."

"Somebody did."

"Let me turn this off." And then into the cassette, "We are signing off for the minute. I got a visitor here. Boop. Say hello."

"It's hot in here."

He turned the recorder off.

Tonight Kennedy didn't seem to be in the mood for sex. It didn't matter to Leila. Sometimes he played his black acoustic guitar with the round back for her. Not bad, even the songs he claimed to have written, but they were all "message" songs.

When she arrived, pulling out the keys he had accidentally left in the lock—pretty careless with all that cash lying around—he was sitting in an armchair, watching television. She didn't mind. She had a magazine.

As she sat propped up on the bed, reading, she suddenly realized that the sobbing sound she heard was not coming from the television set but from him.

"Is that you?"

"I'm depressed about life."

"Yeah? What about?"

"A former girlfriend of mine . . ."

That again, she thought, getting bored.

"And my Vietnam war experiences," he added.

"Hey," she said, "things are tough all over."

"Well, I don't like the way Vietnam veterans are being treated."

Leila's eyes drifted back to her magazine. She did not feel like listening to his hard-luck story.

The next night, knowing that it was after hours at Burdine's department store, he went to James Robert Ford's home in a taxi. It was then that he saw Ford's Taurus 9mm semi-automatic pistol.

He picked it up.

"Hey, I'll buy this from you."

"Well . . ."

"For my gun collection. I'll give you five hundred dollars for it."

He said he planned to put his new acquisition on the wall with the others but the way he handled the pistol indicated to Ford that he was hardly an expert on the workings of 9mm semi-automatic pistols. Ford thought it strange that the guy didn't know how to work the gun. After all, not only had he boasted about a gun collection but he had claimed he'd been in the Vietnam War. Well, not his business, Ford thought. All he really wanted to see was the color of the guy's money. He seemed to have plenty of it. For Ford it was a quick $200 profit, he'd paid only $300 for the gun. He agreed to sell the pistol, which was contained in a hard black plastic Dokosil gun case with a foam interior. Two clips, one of which contained Remington silver-tip hollow-point ammunition, were included.

Back at his room at the Cabana Inn, Mike removed a large amount of U.S. currency from the box under the bed. Although Ford could not see the denominations the bills were held together by a thick rubber band. After the gun transaction Mike told Ford that he had not had any pot in a long time. Not since he had been in Jacksonville. He asked Ford if he could get some. He'd sure appreciate it, he could use a hit.

Ford said okay, he'd stop by Mike's place later.

Mike fondled the pistol after Ford left.

As promised, Ford delivered approximately one-quarter of an ounce of marijuana. Mike then produced a stone pipe and the two smoked.

Ford suggested Mike play his guitar.

"I pawned it," Mike said, pointing in the direction of northbound US 41.

Ford wondered why Mike had pawned his guitar.

Leila was surprised when Kennedy became very angry at the Cabana Inn after he came back from the men's room and she was talking to another man. When she complained he told her he often lost his temper over stupid little things.

Well, not with her, he didn't. She was getting tired of him anyway. Bad sex, depressions, rages, childish behavior. Like when they went to the Sarasota Square Mall and she could barely pull him away from the video arcade. He liked the war games. She also knew he was preoccupied by things that he could do to people with his karate skills. Like she could care less. It was a little sick anyway.

Apparently sensing her waning interest, Kennedy wanted to buy her expensive jewelry at the mall.

No, she said, not wanting to feel obligated to him. She didn't want any.

Maybe I'll move down here, he tried. To Sarasota. Permanent.

Suit yourself, she told him.

It wouldn't change her life. She had already decided that there was something weird about him and she wanted to break away from him. Even sexually he was too unassertive. She didn't mind taking the lead sometimes, but she didn't appreciate having to take the initiative all the time.

That night, when she ignored him in the Cabana Inn bar, she had no idea of the explosive chain of emotional reactions her rejection was unleashing in him, reactions that had their roots in events long since lost to his own consciousness.

Later, she felt sorry, or guilty, about rejecting him so out of hand. She looked around for him in the bar that night, but he had disappeared. She called him up in his room and tried to smooth things over. Never mind, he told her. Don't even think about it.

"Can I come over?" she asked.

"You left your bicycle here."

Not actually an invitation but she went to his room anyway, handing him a little make-up note she had written for him at the bar.

Somehow, although he appeared friendly, the way he looked at her, those odd blue eyes, without feeling, made her decide again she was well out of it.

In a flat voice he told her he planned to take a bus back to Kansas City.

When curiosity led her to call the Cabana Inn the next day, he had checked out.

That was the last she would see of Mike Kennedy.

But he had lied to her.

When he checked out of the Cabana Inn he did not buy a bus ticket to Kansas City. Instead he moved next door to the Sunnyside Motel. Linda and Robert Darfus, the resident managers of the motel on the Tamiami Trail, thought he seemed a pleasant enough fellow. They pegged him as an "accountant type." Over six foot tall with blue eyes and light collar-length brown hair combed straight back, he wasn't bad-looking, they thought. The motel rate was $25 per day, $27.25 with tax.

"Fine."

"How long will you be staying?"

"I don't know. I'll pay on a daily basis," he said and paid cash for his first day.

"Room number fourteen."

But apparently the fun had gone out of it. He wasn't down to $200, as he had told Leila, but his money was dwindling fast, and, no surprise, he began to get the feeling that he was being used. That night he wandered into the Brown Derby Lounge. It was quiet, dull. Even the crane machine held no allure for him this night.

Terry Cousins was surprised to see him. "I heard you moved out."

"I moved next door to the Sunnyside Motel."

"Next door? What for?"

"Allergies."

"What are you allergic to?"

"People," he said quietly.

She felt a chill.

"I'll wait for you," he said, not taking his eyes off her.

"Sure . . ."

He stayed until she completed her shift, then they walked to the Maison Blanche department store at the south end of the mall, where he purchased a shirt and a pair of shorts for her.

"That's real nice of you," she said.

"It's nothing."

"Steve told me you're a pretty good musician."

"Doesn't matter. I sold my guitar."

"Why?"

"I don't know. I wish I hadn't."

This time, he didn't ask her to go back to his room with him.

*   *   *

He remained a guest at Sunnyside only until Saturday, August 18, 1990, just five days before the first Gainesville murder. He made no long-distance calls. He didn't want to talk to anyone. Not even his mother. He was feeling edgy, restless again. He had gone through thousands of dollars and still nothing ever went his way.

He thought of Terry. That bitch had accepted his jewelry and all the dinners he had bought for her and her friends but she never came through for him, not really, not in any way that counted. How often had they gone to the Sarasota Quay and he footed the bill for dinner—for her, for her family, for her friends. There was that time at Ripple's Restaurant, taken there by her friends Carlos Malave and Sarah Jeane. At least that time he didn't have to pay cab fare. He even gave one of his gold star earrings to Carlos Malave. Why did he do *that*? And that other time at the Down Under . . . he had paid for all the food and drink. Sure, he was the one who insisted but they didn't make even a phony attempt to stick their hands in their wallets. Not even for one round. "I'll get it!" he always said, and they always let him. Then to the Cabana Inn lounge, where he kept on buying the drinks until they took him back to the Sunnyside Inn at the end of the evening in Carlos' car.

Or what about that time he took Terry to dinner at the Outback Steak House on US 41 along with her sister Donna, Donna's son and her sister's friend Joann. Again he paid for all the food and drink. Before going to the Outback Steak House he had given Terry an expensive gift. Did she really appreciate the surprise he had for her when he presented her with a twisted gold rope chain bracelet wrapped in a Tilden Ross Jewelers box? All she said was, "That ain't cheap."

"No, it ain't," he said, adding that he had to return to Tilden Ross Jewelers to make a final payment on the bracelet.

"I don't get it," she said admiring the bracelet on her wrist. "Where do you get all your money?"

She hadn't noticed his eyes narrow at the question.

"It's wired to me from my business in Kansas City." His resentment was building. They were all alike, she didn't really care about him. Only what he could do and buy for her and her friends. Even a bitch like Leila, who always had to do it her own way or not at all, she didn't care whether he was around or not. The moment he indicated his funds were running low, he thought he sensed a decided drop in their interest in him.

After the fact, it seems clear it was his own need to control that made him insist he be the one to pay for everything. Big bills. Big tips. He felt a rush even in tossing a three-dollar tip on the bartop for one drink. People looked at him with what he interpreted as respect when he played big spender.

The more he thought on it, the angrier he became. The angrier he became, the greater the reality of his endlessly rehearsed nightly fantasies . . . *But he would never be able to do it face-to-face to someone he actually knew. They might say something. It had to be strangers* . . .

He asked Terry to return the gold ring with the crosslike design, saying he wanted it back "for sentimental reasons."

He didn't say goodbye to anyone when he hoisted his duffel bag and boarded a bus out of Sarasota. Not to Ford or Steve or those two bitches.

He left Sarasota and headed northwest for the town of Gainesville.

He had already been there. It was a college town full of all those wealthy kids who "had it made" all their lives. He didn't have anything specific in mind. It was chance that was taking him back to Gainesville. It didn't matter where he went anyway. Nothing ever went right. As he headed in the direction of the innocent young people who would happen to get in his way, to be there, a frightful serendipity, he was consumed with what had become an uncontrollably lethal rage. The moment he boarded the bus to Gainesville, the collision course was set in high gear.

It was only five days before the first murders.

22

The Other World

Miami Beach, Florida

Manny Taboada slept late into the morning and afternoon hours. When he finally forced himself to get up he telephoned Iysha Adell to tell her he was going to go to the Escapades Disco Bar in downtown Miami with Armando. His final year was going to be tough; he knew he would have to buckle down as he had always done before, but he would get in as much fun as possible before looking for the part-time job that would see him through to graduation. He had, he figured, earned it.

"That's the first thing I'm going to do when I get back to Gainesville. Look for a job."

But right now it was the Escapades Disco Bar.

Manny was still Manny, even when having a good time at Fascade's in Miami Beach or at the Charcoal Lounge or Joseph's Bar on Oakland Park Boulevard or window-shopping at the Ocean Mall or stopping at one of the game rooms in the mall area. One particular evening he broke up a fight between two overheated young men. It wasn't a major incident but it was typical of Manny to intervene. He hated violence and was often quick to interject his own large body between two swinging opponents.

"Why do you do that?" Iysha asked later as they spent the night at her apartment on NE 172nd St.

"I don't know." He shrugged.

"Someday you'll get hurt."

"Who me? Naw." He grinned. "I'm too big."

Fort Lauderdale, Florida

It was Khris Pascarella's birthday and he was celebrating it with Tracy Paules, Lisa and Paul at the Ski Watch Restaurant. He knew that Tracy wasn't sure how she felt about him yet but he knew he had fallen head over heels in love with her. Being there at Ski Watch with her, he felt it was the best birthday of his life.

Tracy and Khris would attend the wedding of one of his friends at the Tower Club in Fort Lauderdale. Not surprisingly, the wedding introduced its own touch of romance—the smell of flowers mingled with saltwater, white lace and perfume, dancing on a highly polished floor, twirling pastel dresses, brilliant sunshine fading into a moonlit sky.

Tracy spent the night with Khris. She told her mother she was staying at Lisa's, not wanting to tell Ricky Paules yet about the depth of her mounting feelings for Khris. Not until she was sure.

That night they talked about his job, her law studies, the past, the future.

"Will you come with me?" he asked.

"To Merritt Island?"

"To visit my parents."

She agreed. She wanted to spend the weekend with him on Merritt Island, visit his parents, explore each other, and most importantly, perhaps complete the transition from friendship to love.

During the weekend she finally told him she loved him, and when she did, as they made love, he felt what he had never felt before. He was sure this was special, this was forever.

And while Tracy and Khris exchanged their vows of love for each other on what would be their only weekend together, a bus was arriving in Gainesville in the middle of the night.

He got off with his duffel bag hoisted high on his shoulder. Lightly packed with the meager stuff of his life, it felt nearly weightless. He heard the bus door grind shut behind him. As he stood for a long moment looking around, the corners of his mouth turned down and the deep frown accentuated the natural droop to his brows. It was a hot, sticky, uncomfortable night. He began to walk. Actually he didn't mind the heat. He minded the people. He knew who they were. They were everything he was not.

Using the same alias he had assumed in Sarasota—Mike Kennedy—Rolling checked into the University Inn on Route 441. From a distance it didn't look too bad with its two-story wrought-iron balconies and its huge maroon-colored sunburst logo stretching across its entrance. Close up, however, the motel looked old and run-down.

It was managed by an Indian named Bipin Patel. A single room? Why not. A couple of nights? Of course. Inexpensive? Very reasonable.

And it was only about a mile from the center of the University of Florida campus.

It was a good place to be.

He had to get to know his way around.

He could take his time in planning. Sometimes, he thought, that was the best part of the fantasy. The planning. But his money was running out.

In the solitude of his motel room, the 9mm Taurus pistol disappeared in the hugeness of the palm of his hand. He knew that, pretty soon, he was going to have to make another strike somewhere to replenish pockets that had been drained by all the high-living bitches in Sarasota.

Late that same night, he stared up at the stained, lightly cracked ceiling of his motel room waiting for the endlessly rehearsed fantasies of sexual power to begin. They were, as they had always been, his only *true* source of pleasure. He closed his eyes. He began at the beginning. Step by step. The collision course had been set. Only a few nights remained before the first Gainesville murder—before the endlessly rehearsed fantasy became reality once again. Through the misty darkness of a morning trying to break through the night, angry and yet melancholy thoughts engulfed him. He would take his time in reconnoitering the locale. That's one thing he had plenty of. Time.

He tugged lightly at the earring in his left ear and started again at the beginning until, ejaculations later, he was too spent to go on.

He tried to buy a car in Gainesville on 3580 North Main Street from Mark Powell, but Powell didn't seem interested in him as a customer. He only stayed for about ten minutes. It didn't matter, he'd get even.

He ate at Ashley's Pub, a Mexican-American restaurant in the Butler Plaza, usually sitting alone at the bar. Farouzandeh Forghani served him. He was soft-spoken with a southern-type accent. He seemed like a nice guy, she tried to be friendly—he had such "sad puppy-dog eyes"—but he wasn't responsive.

He spent time at the bar of Panama Joe's Billiards on Archer Road. Another customer, Joseph Freck, tried to be friendly with him when he saw him at the bar a few times. Nothing doing. He was having no part of such friends anymore.

He walked through the plaza at the University of Florida, deeply shaded against the burning Florida sun. There were many outdoor areas with concrete picnic tables and attached benches. Red brick buildings, palm trees, cut grass, maintenance crews, clean, scraped, manicured.

So this was what college was like.

He squinted at the beautifully trimmed lawns of the university, at the romantic mossy oak trees dotting the rolling landscape. He could see groups of students pocketed here and there, heads together, holding hands, moving, going somewhere, with a purpose.

Passing a huge yellow object at the Marston Science Library, he over-heard one of the students call it "French Fries from Hell." The odd-shaped sculpture overlooked the pond with shooting showers of water reaching halfway across the water. He saw the well-dressed and probably well-heeled students gathering on the lawn outside the Hub, hanging off the curved metal stairs that sculpted the rise to the second story of the bookstore. Not one of them seemed to notice him—an older guy—as he passed them.

He watched a black-and-white dog sitting in the center of one of the circular plazas near a long row of bicycles strapped to a bank, waiting for someone to come and fetch him. He whistled quietly to the dog. It did not move.

Cars, bikes and scooters lined the periphery of the campus; they were everywhere. He had had a motorcycle once—he tried to remember—but this was a walking campus. Once a parking spot was found, no one gave it up until the end of the day. All moves after that were by shoe leather.

He passed Constans Theater across the open arcade from Reitz Union, wondering what the inside of the theater looked like. Then there was the wide-open series of tennis courts—sixteen, he counted. He had never had the chance to learn how to play tennis. Situated near the swimming pool, the sixteen courts were lit at night with huge floodlights on three-story-high posts. Great. A game and a dip. What a life.

A black student, balanced on a skateboard, skidded past him, almost sideswiping him. "Sorry," he threw over his shoulder as he sped away . . . Even black kids had more breaks than he did, he thought. But they weren't the ones . . . the kind of victims he wanted had been subcon-sciously selected a long time ago. Staking out the college locale to trawl for them, though a subconscious process, was no accident. He was follow-ing a classic behavior pattern of a serial killer.

College girls were easy targets.

Hunger took him to Union 76 on SW Sixteenth Street. BEER WORLD in bold letters spread across a long canopy that stretched across the lot. De-spite its offers of everything from golden fried chicken to ice cream to hot dogs (with the letter *D* missing in the word *dogs),* Union 76 was dreary and gray-looking. The window ad for "49–Cent Money Orders" gave it a transient look. But it was on the same side as the University Inn. He could walk there from the room he had taken, passing under the maroon starburst sign of the motel on 441 North.

Sgt. Alan Baxter stopped at the International House of Pancakes. As he waited for his order, he glanced up at the vaulted ceilings with international flags hanging overhead and waving in the rising heat on the one side and the gentle air flow coming out of the air-conditioning units in the ceiling. The only identifying Floridian feature were the Gator pennants lining both walls over the windows. He found the familiarity comforting, especially late at night, coming off duty.

He spotted Theresa Ann Garren waiting on a table on the other side of the room. They had a casual, friendly relationship going.

She came over. "Hi, Alan," she said. "Coffee?"

He nodded.

"How're you doing tonight?"

"Beat."

"Yeah," she said softly, "I know what you mean."

The Alachua County detective smiled at her. He liked Theresa Ann Garren. Nice lady. Christa Hoyt's mother.

When Sgt. Alan Baxter said goodnight and moved to leave after a pleasant twenty-minute respite from a busy night, he brushed close to the man who was to become an ugly presence in his life.

Theresa Ann Garren noticed the man sitting at Table F in the isolated corner reserved for the die-hards who still smoked in spite of all the years of advertised precautions. Well, she couldn't criticize even though he was bumming a light from another customer; after all, she still smoked herself. Wearing jeans and a T-shirt, he looked sloppy but she could see he was muscular and tall; his sneakered feet stuck out from under the table . . .

Rolling watched her as she came over to him in her blue uniform with the light blue blouse and apron. The national franchise uniform reminded him of prison garb.

"Coffee," he murmured.

She looked like a hundred other waitresses who had stood in front of him. He couldn't tell if the damn place he was sitting in was located in Florida or in any one of the other forty-nine states. *Y'seen one've these places, you've seen 'em all* . . . the usual rust-brown leather seats in the usual booths with the usual Formica tables with the usual simulated wood-grain patterns. He looked up at the yellow lighting fixtures. At the hanging imitation plants, no one had to water *them*. Foam cups, plastic containers, disposable this, disposable that, disposable people. Why not?

The girl came into IHOP while he was still at Table F. His eyes immediately went to her. Something inside him clicked. She looked vaguely familiar. (In fact, *seemingly* random-choice victims were never chosen at random.) The long dark hair. The slender figure. The age. A little tall perhaps but with all the attributes that tormented his nights . . . she was perfect. She had always rejected him. His fantasies were wrapped around her. Maybe he didn't know her but he felt something deeper, a special relationship. He believed she would "know" why she was being chosen.

She was talking to the waitress who had brought him coffee. He watched them at the counter. He heard her say, "I'll wait for you, Mom."

He got up, paid his check and went outside. He waited too.

Everything died. People. Animals. Grass. Trees. His father. His mother. Let it end. So what? On to a new world. Eternity.

He knew he was a dead man.

He saw her.

He followed.

Palm trees and pansies welcomed shoppers at the entrance of Butler Plaza on Archer Road. Christa Hoyt and her mother Ann often shopped at the Publix in the plaza. Not only was it within walking distance of her apartment, but Christa liked browsing through the widely spaced tiled aisles of Publix, "Where shopping is a pleasure" and where everything seemed to gleam with chromelike cleanliness.

Once finished, they walked past Mr. Data and Bageland, and Cinema 'N Cafe and the U.S. Armed Forces Recruiting Center. She glanced opposite at the canary-yellow stucco topped with the red Spanish-tiled roof of the WalMart shopping complex of stores, now looking cool after baking all day in the Florida sun.

She did not notice that there was someone watching her every move . . .

He saw that she lived in a deserted kind of place. Well, he was so clever and powerful, he could do whatever he wanted to do in broad daylight and no one would know.

She was still with the older woman, though.

There was time.

"Why do you want to move?" Nancy Noe, Christa's co-worker at the Alachua County Sheriff's Office, asked her the next day.

"I just don't feel comfortable where I am anymore," Christa told her.

They had been talking about the possibility of Christa's moving into Nancy's back bedroom.

"I just feel a little edgy lately."

Come to think of it, Nancy did notice that Christa had been sort of jumpy around work and, for some reason, seemed to be easily frightened. Maybe it was where she was living . . .

During the morning hours Manny and Iysha went to the beach at Sunny Isles. Bronzed—a bit burned, hair colored by the sun. They met other couples there who were friends of Manny. No unusual incidents took place. Between four and five P.M. they left the beach for home, stopping at Taco Bell several blocks from the beach location. Manny arrived home at approximately six P.M. after taking Iysha to her apartment.

He had dinner with his family—his grandmother, his brother, his mother.

It was to be their last dinner with Manny.

Monday, August 20—Gainesville

Shoney's was a little further from the University Inn.

He stopped in front of the aqua-white-and-red awning that distinguished the generic style of all Shoney restaurant franchises. He knew what the inside looked like even before he stepped foot inside; deep red booths, tan Formica tables, imitation plants hanging down, twirling fans, tile floors, dark green walls. Here the waitresses wore lightly striped white blouses with neck bows over black skirts covered with maroon aprons. But to him they all looked alike no matter which fast-food joint he happened to be in.

There was something depressing about the fast-food emporiums he frequented in his rambling, drifting lifestyle. When these places became the confining parameters of his daily life, well, it was no vacation and back home. This wasn't a vacation. Since when did he ever have a vacation . . . this was his life.

He had even seen a Western Sizzler Steak House—the same kind he had been fired from in Louisiana for . . . what was the reason that time? . . . For losing his temper, wasn't it? Couldn't remember.

Even though there was the familiarity of it all, state after state, city after city, all of these places crowding to the edges of highways, it left him feeling bitter, lonely. Even the smiles were the same. Standing at the edge of the table with the order pad pressed against a waistband—"What'll it be?"—*pretending* to be friendly, to care. All they wanted was a good tip. Not one of them, he was sure, cared even whether he lived or died.

He often studied people, listened to their conversation. Sometimes he smiled. Mostly he hated them. He tried to listen in on their worlds. But their backs were always turned, figuratively and literally.

Order, eat, pay, get out.

He got out.

He went trawling.

He saw the dark-haired girl come out of the bagel shop as it was closing. She was all alone. Her arms were loaded with packages. A surge of recognition . . . he followed her as she headed into the semi-darkness toward her parked car, weaving in and out of dark lanes of cars. She was wearing sneakers. He was wearing sneakers too. They were both almost noiseless. It was eerie the way the two of them moved silently through the parking lot. He reeling with anticipation, she oblivious that she was being stalked by a lethal disease.

Two aisles over, he saw her pause at a car. He quickened his pace, beginning to breathe heavily.

As soon as she opened the car door, he heard human voices.

"What took you so long?"

He could see a man get out of the car to help her with the packages as a baby started crying and an argument erupted between two small boys in the back seat.

He turned away.

Lucky bitch.

"What are you doing?" Iysha asked Manny over the telephone.

"Spraying for fleas. With Joh."

"Who's that?"

"Just an acquaintance."

"Did Tracy get there yet?"

"No. She's not due for a couple of days, I think."

Iysha wasn't jealous that Manny and Tracy Paules were going to be roommates at Gatorwood. She knew they were good friends from high school, and she felt sure of Manny's affections. He was that kind of guy.

Manny Taboada had left his home in Miami for the drive to Gainesville during the morning hours and arrived at his apartment at approximately 8:30 P.M. that evening, at which point Iysha telephoned him.

Only gone half a day and she missed him already.

*   *   *

By eleven-thirty the next morning Manny was on the phone with Iysha again, this time utilizing her office WATS line number.

He had a job, he told her. It was the hiring season in Gainesville, time to set it up for the busy times when school reopened full schedule in the fall. Iysha could tell how pleased he was to have gotten the job, not only because it was at Bennigan's—a great place to work—but because he had gotten it so quickly.

"I told them that I worked at the Moose Lodge last semester as a bartender," he said. "That probably cinched it."

How typical of Manny, she thought, not to realize what a strong impression he made on people. It was no surprise to her that when the manager of Bennigan's saw the tall good-looking youth with the ready smile and experience besides, he had hired him on the spot.

Wednesday, August 22—Miami

Now back from Merritt Island and home for the last time before school, Tracy Paules, the ex-beauty queen, was happily in love. This time her parents approved. Khris Pascarella was special even to them. Tracy and Khris, Lisa Buyer, Beth Engle and Christina Garcia had a farewell lunch at Kokomo's Rest because Tracy was returning to Gainesville. Summer fun over. Time to buckle down for her senior semester.

After a doctor's appointment for a school vaccination, she dined with Khris for what would be the last time.

At 8:00 P.M., Tracy's mother Ricky stood in the carport watching her youngest child climb into her charcoal-gray Toyota.

"Neither one of us is going to cry, right?" Tracy said to her mother when she saw her moist eyes in the shadow of the carport.

"Right," Ricky agreed. "Now get out of here."

"Okay, dude."

Tracy pulled the Toyota out of the driveway into the street, suddenly looked back at her mother, stopped at the curb and motioned her mother over. As Ricky approached, Tracy got out of the car and grabbed her. They hugged through a few tears and kissed each other.

"I love you, Mom," she said.

Ricky Paules would never see her daughter again.

*   *   *

Another farewell scene was enacted as Sonja Larson drove away from her parents' home in Deerfield Beach, north of Miami, in the Honda they had given her in 1988.

"We'll be there on Sunday."

"Okay."

"Drive carefully."

"I will."

"Call the minute you arrive."

"I promise . . ."

And still another farewell in Jacksonville as Christina Powell said her goodbyes to her family and returned to Gainesville.

"Your brother and sister will be there . . ."

"Yes, yes."

"On Saturday."

"I know."

"If you think of anything else you need . . ."

"I'll call . . ."

Not having too far to drive, seventeen-year-old Christina arrived in Gainesville that same evening.

One at a time, bit by bit, like a mosaic, the principal players were coming back to Gainesville primed for the fall after a happy, uneventful summer.

PART

IV

THE MURDERS

23

When Different Worlds Collide

Thursday, August 23

Harvey Kitzman had lived at Williamsburg Village in Apartment 111 for about two years. On August 23 he got up at his usual time, approximately 6:00 A.M. showered, dressed and went to the biochemistry lab at the University of Florida, where he would work until about 6 P.M. Apartment 111 was located directly below Apartment 113, where Sonja Larson and Christina Powell would die.

Rolling went to Wal-Mart.

He knew what he was going to do. His malevolent intent, already settled into his subconscious for some time, was now mobilized into the active planning stage. At Wal-Mart he bought himself a pup tent and a mattress. More importantly, in preparation he stole a Stanley screwdriver, a roll of duct tape and two pairs of tight-fitting gloves. He already had the knife. As he stood at the checkout counter, several aisles over, Christina Powell and Sonja Larson were waiting in line to pay for the items they had bought for their new apartment at Williamsburg Village.

Rolling checked out of the University Inn.

The pressure was building. He was tingling with the anticipation of venting a lifetime of rage.

He moved into the woods off the northeast corner of Archer Road and SW 34th Street, building himself a campsite. He didn't have much, he didn't need much. His duffel bag. His cassette recorder. He remembered telling the Clausens when he left Louisiana the night he shot his father that all he needed was "a knife and a book of matches" to survive in the

199

woods. A far cry from the frightened fourteen-year-old runaway who had camped out in the woods so many years earlier.

Memories. Feeling left out and isolated while trying to decide what to do next, he was the proverbial walking time bomb.

The trawling process continued in earnest.

He eyed the girls, barelegged, hiking, jogging, with bouncing breasts through thin shirts. Getting ready for a new semester. Leading lives of luxury and ease. No doubt paid for by the old man. Who paid for him? "You'll be in jail by the time you're fifteen!" His father's legacy.

He didn't know any of them but he knew what they were like, who they were. He knew how they looked down on someone like him. He was at least twenty years older than they were, and when he was their age he was rotting away in prison. His life was already gone. They were just starting out with breaks he never had. They were probably having parties left and right. It was "rush" week, wasn't it? Look at them strolling across the greens looking as though they owned it. Nobody noticed him. He was invisible in their world. He didn't even matter in his own.

But if he was invisible . . . well . . . it was something how invisible he could be. He'd always been pretty good at that—being invisible when he wanted to be. Not being him.

In a brief sane moment—even the sickest have them—he tried to figure it out. He couldn't understand his anger. It came up in his throat. His daughter. How old was she now? What did she look like? She was a teenager herself. Almost as old as some of those girls he had been watching. He didn't realize that behind his sightseeing he was thinking of his father. His mother. His wife. The relatives he had tried to cozy up to. Those bitches in Sarasota. The most difficult confrontation of all was turning out to be the one he was having with himself. The ache was so deep it created a schism right down the middle of him. And everything inside was about to explode out.

Sonja arrived back in Gainesville at 4:30 P.M. The drive was easy and uneventful. Separated for only a brief period, it was, nonetheless, a happy reunion between Sonja and Christina. They were on their way to their new life.

Scott called to Sonja from his open car window as he and Bryan drove into the Williamsburg complex parking lot to find her. Luckily they spotted her with Christina just as they were about to drive out. They pulled up next to Sonja and Christina—nineteen-year-old Bryan Oulton and eighteen-year-old Scott Henratty had gone to Ely High School with Sonja. Both UF students now, they roomed together not too far away from Williamsburg on SE Sixteenth Street.

Small world. They agreed to have dinner together.

From a pay phone at the restaurant Christina called home at five P.M. and told her folks she and Sonja were having dinner with a couple of Sonja's high-school friends who were also attending UF and they probably would not stay out too late since she and Sonja planned to get up early the next morning to make some changes in their schedules at the university.

"Talk to you soon," Christina said as she hung up.

It was the last time the Powells would hear their seventeen-year-old daughter's voice.

That night, dinner with Bryan Oulton and Scott Henratty over, a little last-minute shopping done, Sonja called her mother at 10:55 P.M. as promised from a pay phone at a gas station located near their apartment—her own phone still had not yet been connected—to let her family know she had nicely survived their imagined hazards of a long car trip. She told them she and Christina had been shopping at Wal-Mart and were now on their way back to their apartment.

He had seen them.

He followed them.

He saw one of them go into the phone booth to make a call.

He waited.

"Call me tomorrow," Ada Larson said.

"Okay, Mom. I promise."

When Ada hung up she dismissed her moment of anxiety about her daughter's new life away from home, reminding herself she was a worrier at heart.

It was the last time Ada would speak with her daughter.

Danny Rolling's Farewell

Alone at the campsite, Danny took out his cassette recorder. He had never sent home the long, rambling tape he had recorded for his family in Sarasota. So now he would add to the original tape.

He turned on the recorder and began to speak. This time, there was a hard edge to his words. And then the most chilling part of all, how he had to sign off, because he had "something" he had to go do:

Can ya hear myself? I can hear myself. Wow! Well, I'm in a different place than the last time I recorded. Now I got the sky for a blanket, the earth for a bed and some rumpled up clothes for a pillow, but it's okay. It's just the way it is. You take the good with the bad. And you know, at the first part of this recording that I did . . . ummm . . . I, you know, I don't know . . . I just . . . My heart was real heavy and I was toting a cold and was trying to get over that. And so you know, the guitar playing wasn't all that good, but at any rate, I just wanted y'all to have something to remember me by . . . and listen to those crickets! Man! Well, I don't know, y'know. I'm just here making do, but kinda lost for words. I really am. I don't . . . you know . . . I'm just sitting here thinking about what to say. (*A long pause*) I really don't know what to say. I just know how much I love you and I know we can't ever be together. But at least, it's one consolation . . . at least I'm free. At least I'm healthy. I know I have to run the rest of my life, but I'm getting pretty good at it, if that means anything. Shoot! I've been stopped by the police I don't know how many times, checking IDs and stuff. So I guess I make do. I hope I do.

Mom, I love you and listen, I know you are a lot stronger than you know, than you make out to be. You'll get along okay without me. I wish that it wasn't so. I'd love to be there by your side. But you know, it's just like the little lion cubs. They grow up one day and go off on their own. Yeah, well, it's just the way it is. I don't want you feeling sorry for me. I don't want you worrying about me. I'm a big boy. I can take care of myself. So, I don't want you to worry about me, okay? I'll be alright. We're all down here for just a breath anyway.

Kevin . . . (*Laughing*) you better get a daggum deer for me with that bow I got ya now. Yeaaah. Just go a couple of times. See if you don't get lucky with it. Take it out in the backyard and practice with it when y'ain't got nuttin' else to do before deer season come up this October, and give it a shot. Just make sure that you put on some camouflage. Good camouflage, 'cause, y'know, when you go bow hunting, you got to have camouflage. And I tell you something else, too. Aim for the lungs, straight through the rib cage. Either there or the heart. But best thing to do is hit the lungs. It's the best shot for a deer, straight through the lungs. He don't go far. Don't chase after him when you stick him . . . when . . . when that arrow hits him. What you gotta do is, you got to just watch which way he goes, and when he goes, and when he goes outta sight, listen. You hear him banging into trees and stuff. And then, finally, you'll hear him either fall down, or you hear him stop running. He'll stay right there until he bleeds to death if you don't go and chase him. So, what you need to do after you stick 'em, is just sit right down there for about thirty minutes to an hour. That just depend on how you feel about it. That is, if you ever gonna do any deer hunting. I never could get you interested in it when you and I was able to go. You just . . . I don't know . . . that just didn't interest ya. Well, brother, I'm hangin' in there. Yeah. I'm hangin' in there. I'll say that much for myself for the moment. Plan on going the distance. I give it my best shot.

Well, Dad, I hope you're doing better. Y'know, it's probably . . . [you] don't even wanna hear from me. Well, y'know, Pop, I don't think you was ever really concerned about the way I felt anyway. Nope. I really don't. You never would take time to listen to me. Never cared about what I thought or felt. I never had a daddy that I could go to and confide in with my problems. Or, you just pushed me away at a young age, Pop. I guess you and I, we both missed out on a lot. I wanted to make you proud of me. I let you down. I'm sorry for that.

Well, I'm gonna sign off for a little bit. I got something I gotta do. I love ya. Bye.

He had something he had to do . . .

24

That Night

Thursday, August 23

He cast long, angry shadows, but shadows are lost in the dark; he moved about stealthily, unnoticed. He had been trolling for his victims since he had been in Gainesville, peeking into windows, following girls home, having already made up his mind that he had to "do in" eight—one for every rotten year he had spent in prison. He already had three down, only five more to go.

It was too early.

He went to see *The Exorcist III*. His high level of suggestibility was working overtime as he sat in the dark theatre and watched the deliberately graphic horror film. He could never imagine a more horrific death than to be killed in the night, in the dark with a knife. He, too, would terrorize by the way he dressed; dark clothes for a dark night for a dark purpose. The girl in the film was decapitated. He had never thought of that. The "possessed" killer in the film called himself "Gemini." That's what he was! He was born under the sign of Gemini. Magical thinking was in effect. It was all a sign. At the end of *Exorcist III*, Gemini died. Maybe that was a sign too.

If it was, so be it. What was life anyway but a short breath. "We're all down here for just a breath . . ."

He stood on top of a garbage can outside one of the apartment complexes common to the college town. He could see two young women within. Before he could make a decision whether or not to enter, a night watchman spotted him.

"You there! What are you doing?"

Rolling immediately jumped off the can and took off, thinking how he had let that guy live.

* * *

Later that night, he climbed up to the second floor of a balconied apartment and peered within. He could see a young woman at the kitchen sink washing dishes. She had her back turned to him.

This was the one.

Not wanting to get blood on his clothes, he decided to strip himself naked. When he had stripped down to only the fanny pack pouch that contained the duct tape, the 9mm. gun and the Ka-Bar killing knife, he was suddenly interrupted again.

"Hey!" cried the drunk on the ground beneath him "What're y'doin' there! Hey!"

. . . Damn! . . .

He gathered the clothes he had piled up in a corner of the balcony, yanked on his pants and jumped to the ground, leaving the drunk calling after him loudly. "Hey . . . !"

Several girls had had extremely lucky breaks that night.

Once again, it was time. This time it was 3 A.M. This time there was no one around.

He had previously prowled around the Williamsburg apartment complex as he had many others in the reconnoitering stages of his predations. He knew it fairly well by now. Many of the apartments had wooden stairs that led down to the courtyard thickly edged with parked cars.

Stay away from the front of the buildings. Too much activity, even at night.

The pool was behind the main building in front of the car washing area. There was a small lot to the side of the building that housed apartments 102 to 106. Several steps went down next to a cyclone fence that had a handrail that looked as though it was constructed of an assortment of plumbing pipe. It was next to an old rusting bicycle rack. When it rained, poor drainage forced water to gather in the lot in deep black puddles.

That was not the way to go. Wet shoes leave too many footprints.

He knew it was easier to escape detection by going around the other way to the back of the buildings. He stopped next door in the L. H. Rogers Rotary Scholarship Foundation House parking lot. The Foundation House was opposite another apartment complex that housed a good many senior citizens.

They usually went to bed early.

After waiting long, patient moments to see if anyone was going to question his presence in the Foundation House parking lot, he stealthily made his way past the red brick building to the deepest part of the complex behind the fence where the white brick buildings were. There was an enormous oak tree dripping romantically with Spanish moss. During the day it shaded the building against the onslaught of the Florida summer sun. At night it was the perfect setup for cover.

Good spot. Easy to hide.

He looked around noticing the four electric meters, the half-glass doors in the back of each individual townhouse.

The shack in the Foundation's parking lot acted as a cover and helped in his selection of that particular building—110, 111, 112, and 113—rather than one of the others. The end of the back steps of the upstairs townhouse—Apartment 113—butted up almost to the fence. It was very dark at night with an isolated feeling that could be mistaken for privacy. Fate was spinning its terrible wheel of indifference at the moment of selection.

Upstairs was the duplex where the girls lived. The windows were dark. Now he put on the black ski mask; the killing outfit was complete—black ninja outfit, black ski mask and tight athletic gloves. He had both the revolver and the knife with him.

He went to the back door off the back stairs, expertly placing the stolen Stanley screwdriver at the very bottom of the wooden door. He knew they would find the pry marks. It didn't matter; he knew prymarks on wooden doors were harder to match than those on metal doors since wood contracts and expands with heat and moisture, thereby often changing the indentation of the tool used for the break in.

Bad for evidence. Good for breaking and entering.

Then he realized that the back door at the top of the stairs was unlocked! With his own brand of magical thinking, he took that as a sign that he was right to do what he was about to do. It had been made accessible to him for a *reason.*

Once within, he silently waited until his eyes became accustomed to the dark. There was something very exhilarating about breaking into the privacy of someone else's home. It demonstrated the supremacy of true power and control over the lives of others. He could violate the privacy of total strangers in this way and they were helpless to do anything about it.

The point of no return had been reached a long time ago. The stunned hiatus after the murders in Louisiana was a direct result of the shock of shooting his father. Now that seemed so long ago. Now the killing machine was coiled, primed and ready to spring once again.

He saw her. Christina Powell was fast asleep on the couch. He stood over the sleeping seventeen-year-old for almost ten full minutes. He could have changed his mind during that time. He didn't. She was clad only in a sleeveless ochre-colored tank top, a bra and multicolored panties. Excitement was beginning to well up in him. But first he had to check out the other one. He knew there were two in the apartment. He didn't know which one he wanted. He crept upstairs where he saw Sonja Larson asleep in one of the bedrooms.

He paused to consider. Which one? He struggled awhile, trying to make up his mind what to do. He stood over Sonja for another five to ten minutes before he finally made his decision. He decided to kill this one first. Get her out of the way, then take his time raping the other one. He pulled out the duct tape and the knife.

The knife was quieter than the gun.

He had come well prepared. The double duct tape was to muffle her cries should she try to scream. He plunged the knife into the upper part of her chest near the collarbone and at the same moment he used his left hand to cover the sleeping girl's mouth with the tape.

Startled at the tape over her mouth, feeling as though she was suffocating, the girl's eyes darted open. She couldn't breathe. She didn't understand the sudden excruciating pain in her chest . . . She was terror-stricken by the huge black form standing over her, stabbing at her. Not knowing what was happening, she nevertheless fought her assailant. He continued to strike at the struggling girl with the knife, slicing her hands, her arms, her thigh as she tried to kick at him, stabbing her wherever he could through the futile defenses she threw up. She actually put up a pretty good struggle, but she was a small girl. The assault ultimately was too much for her. She stopped struggling. The attack lasted maybe thirty, forty-five seconds. Actually, he thought, she took a fairly long time to die. It had been a life-and-death struggle. Death won. He stood over her, waited, and watched her die.

Then he went down the stairs.

Christina was still asleep.

He could wait no longer. The killing had raised an enormous erection. He overpowered the startled girl quickly. This one put up little resistance but he made her completely helpless by taping her hands behind her back. She was terrified. She tried to protest. He warned her not to scream. Then he took the lethal-looking knife, still red with Sonja's blood, and cut Christina's T-shirt up the middle. She began to cry. She begged. He cut the bra she was wearing up the middle and ripped off her multicolored panties. With her wrists taped behind her, he played with her sexually for a long period of time. Then he exposed himself and forced the girl to perform oral sex on him. She was so terrified, he thought contemptuously, she'd do anything to stay alive. When he forced himself into her, she cried out in pain.

"Take the pain, bitch!" he snarled viciously. "Take the pain!"

Penetration had been physically a little difficult, but psychologically easier than it had ever been in his life. He was at the height of his powers, at the pit of his humanity. But in his diseased mind, he was finally a total man. Still, at the moment of ejaculation, he spilled most of himself onto her panties.

When he had finally finished with her and he was limp, he taped her mouth and he deliberately told her exactly what he was going to do next; he was going to kill her, and then he was going to cut off her nipples. Christina was in such shock, she would not have been able to plead for her life even had her mouth not been taped shut. He let her wait. Give her time to think about what he had said while he dumped the contents of their purses onto the living-room floor, took what he wanted and then, proceeded to burgle the apartment.

To his surprise, he had worked up an appetite. He went into the kitchen, opened the refrigerator, where he found an apple and a banana. He took his time eating them and left the remains of the fruit to be found.

Then he went back to Christina. He had told her he was going to kill her but the poor girl still had hope that he might let her live. It was a vain hope. He turned the brutalized girl over onto her stomach, took in hand the deadly knife, raised it high above her body, and plunged it into her back up to its hilt. In the heart. Christina's blood splattered across the face of her hand calculator situated on the nearby dresser. He raised the knife and plunged it into the soft flesh again and again and again and again . . . easily . . . in and out like butter because of the long, deeply etched bloodline in the blade . . . into her lungs, until all the life had drained out of her and she lay dead beneath the overwhelming power and efficacy of his knife.

The orange towel, now soaked with red, fell to the floor.

He paused.

By this time he was totally caught up in the corruption of his own deviant sexuality. He was breathing hard with the exultation of the enormous power he felt.

He paused for a while in his nocturnal work to catch his breath.

He was almost through for the night, but not quite.

As he looked down at the bloody remains of the petite girl on the floor, with her dark hair lying askew about her head, he didn't realize he was no longer human.

He heard some noise outside in the hallway. The old resentments surged as he sensed the excitement of people moving into a new life, the remnants of a party, the camaraderie, a burst of laughter. All he knew was that he was being left out again. But it no longer mattered. They were all paying now.

He looked down again at the girl. He sensed the power of total control. What else could he do that would recreate the same rush? Then slowly, carefully, with the precision of a mad surgeon, he cut off the girl's breasts. He would take them with him wrapped in a plastic bag from her kitchen. It worked. Only through the mutilation was he able to achieve immense sexual gratification such as he had never before experienced.

He looked around in a glazed euphoria of sensuous pleasure and power. The cane chair and the couch cushion were smeared with the girl's blood. In the brief intense struggle for her life, she had dropped the wine-colored towel; it had slipped under the dining table. A nearby clothes basket waiting for the wash also had blood splatters from the stabbing.

But he had to clean himself first. He went into the bathroom and carefully wiped his limp penis on a paper towel, which he left on the side of the sink. In the bathroom, he found birth control pills. "Bitch!" That's what happens to girls who have premarital sex. He left the pills on display.

It was a long night for the murderer. But it wasn't over.

Remembering hearing from his father how the police always tried to link blood and semen evidence to a rapist or killer, he went into the kitchen where he found a bottle of Dawn liquid detergent. Now for a very thorough clean-up of the girl, including a careful removal of all of his own body fluids with the delicately tinted blue-green liquid. He poured it on, lathering up the pubic area. It had worked that other time. No one ever found any evidence of himself on her. Certainly no evidence that could link him to her. He had been too thorough. She had had her chance when he tried to talk to her at Dillard's Department Store. He liked her. He would have been nice to her. She reminded him of someone. He couldn't remember who. But she snubbed him.

At least, that had been his perception. Actually, the girl never even noticed him.

He had followed her.

It had been a beginning.

But it had also frightened him. When the man and the boy came in unexpectedly, he had had to confront them head-on. That wasn't part of the plan. He had to fight for his own life.

It had frightened him enough to make him stop. At least for a while.

Now, here, with these two, inside a closed apartment, with no chance of anyone interrupting, he could no longer control the beast once it had been let out of the cage. The excitement was too keen, his anger too overwhelming.

He took his time.

He left the bottle of detergent on the floor next to the dead girl.

Then the final touch. He decided to pose each of their lifeless bodies in such a way that whoever found them would be shocked and would come to realize that they had met their match in him. He posed Christina lewdly and slid one of her school notebooks under her head. He went back upstairs to Sonja and removed the tape. She had on her panties. He cut them off but had no sex with her. She was a bloody mess and he didn't want to get dirtied. Besides, by now he was spent. He placed Sonja on top of the comforter on her bed. The bed was covered at the head with blue and blue-plaid pillows.

He pulled her down to the end of the bed, placing her at the foot of the mattress. He left her spread out, lying on her back with her legs bent at the knees and her feet on the floor hanging over the side at a ninety-degree angle. He had a flash of the way he had left Julie Grisson back in Shreveport.

He left them carefully positioned for maximum shock effect when discovered—one on the bed upstairs, one spread out on the living-room floor, face up with her breasts removed—inwardly gloating at the thought of their shock. The police. He could outwit them any old day. He knew enough about police matters through his father to know what to do to avoid detection. Mad though he might be, he had given a great deal of careful thought and planning to avoid detection. He took particular pleasure at his own cleverness not realizing that, in his personal exultation, he was leaving behind his own personal killer's "signature" in the manner in which he left the bodies.

It was the beginning of a weekend of frenzied murderous activities. Having begun again, he was like an out-of-control power mower, running rampant through a field of flowers, cutting down and mutilating everything in its path.

He was tired.

He dozed.

He showered.

It was bright sunlight when he slipped out of the apartment and went back to the outdoor campsite, trying to decide what to do next.

The pathetic abused little boy he had been had long ago given way to the runaway teenager, who in turn had disappeared into the self-pitying, violently angry adult. The pitiable little boy had metamorphosed into a monster.

"Nearer my God to Thee," he sang quietly.

He stopped singing and thought of the next time.

By the time Kim Norman dropped Christa Leigh Hoyt off at her apartment after work at the Alachua County sheriff's office it was 12:19 A.M. Thursday had turned into Friday morning, August 24.

25

The Day After

6:30 A.M.

At Williamsburg Village Apartments, Anita Dupres heard the shower running in Apartment 113. She, of course, could not imagine that the person showering on the other side of the wall was a person washing away the evidence of a bloody night.

8:00 A.M.

Christa Hoyt was still on codeine and penicillin after having two wisdom teeth extracted by Dr. Harry M. Richter. Since she had not taken her own car to work, Kim Norman, shift supervisor at the Alachua County sheriff's office, drove her home after their shift. They parted at the door of Apartment M on Archer Avenue, planning to meet in the public gym on Sunday morning.

Kim agreed, when she got off at eight.

Take care, see you Sunday, said Christa.

10:00 A.M.

When Jason Beaupied woke up he heard music playing. ("Faith," by George Michael.) He didn't really notice the music until he went downstairs and realized it was coming directly from the apartment next to his, 113. He also heard banging on the common wall that separated the two living rooms of the apartments. It sounded as if someone was hammering nails into the wall. It never occurred to him it could be someone banging to loosen up a jammed back door.

The bodies of Christina Powell and Sonja Larson, viciously mutilated, lay displayed in the rooms in which they had been slaughtered. Jason Beaupied passed their door and continued out into the glaring morning brightness of the parking lot.

212

* * *

Christa Hoyt's aunt, Joy Willingham, who along with her brother Edward Phitzenmeir had been instrumental in Christa's adoption eighteen years earlier, had come from Miami to visit her. When she arrived at her apartment that Friday morning, Christa was wearing the white strapless dress that made Kim Norman think that she "looked like an angel." But Christa's conservative side made her self-conscious. Her Aunt Joy told her not to worry about it, she looked lovely. "Show me your apartment," she said.

Christa had obviously cleaned the apartment for Joy's visit. Everything was in place. The bookshelf, positioned under the air-conditioning unit in the living room, had been neatly arranged. The bed in the small bedroom with three pillows was covered with a pale blue quilted coverlet sprinkled with orange flowers. A clock was at the foot of the bed. Her photographs, jewelry box and a new brown teddy bear were on top of the tall dresser. Her bicycle was located in the space between the bed and the sliding glass doors.

She opened the blinds over the glass doors to give her aunt a view of the backyard. Joy didn't much like the area. She thought the yard, overgrown as it was with trees and shrubbery, was awfully secluded.

She asked her niece if she ever got nervous living there alone.

Sometimes, Christa told her, and added that she was looking for a new place. But she could take care of herself.

Her aunt knew that was true. Christa worked for the sheriff's office and was considering a career in law enforcement. She could be aggressive in some ways and wasn't easily frightened by a confrontation with anyone.

11:05 A.M.

Shannon Slattery saw a man hanging around the dumpster on the inside of the fence at the Williamsburg Village Apartments. She had been working community service hours at a counseling center for cancer patients at the Winn-Dixie Hope Lodge on Sixteenth Street when she came home and saw what she thought was a suspicious-looking white man standing on the right side of the dumpster. He did not seem to be trying to hide but he did seem to be lingering behind the dumpster. Shannon did not see a car parked next to the dumpster as she drove by and couldn't help wondering what he was doing there. He didn't look as though he lived at the complex.

It happened that the man was standing a short distance from the rear entrance of the apartment where the bodies of Christina and Sonja had been left by their killer.

*   *   *

Before they left her apartment, Christa put a black jacket over the strapless white dress and told her aunt she felt more comfortable with the jacket.

Aunt Joy had not seen her sister-in-law, Ann Garren, in a while and willingly accompanied Christa to the International House of Pancakes, where Ann worked as a waitress.

Christa said her aunt chatted with Ann and a young waitress, Jennifer Cox, and Jennifer invited Christa to a party to be held that night at the Gatorwood Apartments. Christa hesitated, said she didn't know anybody there. Most of the people who were coming didn't know each other either, Jennifer told her. While Christa and her aunt shared a banana split, Jennifer continued to try to convince Christa that she should come to the party. "It's at my place. Gatorwood Apartments, Fourteen-oh-six."

Well, maybe, Christa told her.

The manager of IHOP, Rick Brenner, had seen him a couple of times before. Each time he sat in the smoking section at Table F ordering only coffee, and each time Brenner saw him asking other customers for cigarettes. Wearing blue jeans and a T-shirt, long hair pushed back over his ears into angel wings, the man appeared to be a transient. If he kept on bothering the other customers for cigarettes, Brenner decided he might have to say something to him.

Neither Christa nor her Aunt Joy noticed the cold blue eyes of the man at Table F looking at Christa over the rim of his coffee cup.

That night Tracy Paules called her suburban Miami home and talked to her father, George. He was proud of his daughter. Only twenty-three, an honor student in her major of political science, a University of Florida senior. Soon she would start on the next chapter in her life, probably with Khris Pascarella. Which was a good thought after all his worries about her boyfriend. So many opportunities, professional and personal. Her whole life in front of her.

They joked around some over the phone. "Boy, am I glad you're out of here. Now I can get my parking space back and I don't have to walk through a bunch of junk in the bedroom."

He heard her laughter over the phone.

Then: "I love you, Tracy."

"I love you, Daddy."

He liked it when she called him that.

They hung up soon after that. He would come to wish he had said more.

7:30 P.M.

"We had a fight," Ann Garren told her daughter Christa over the phone from her home in Newberry.

"Bad?"

"Well, you know."

"Has he been drinking?"

"Yes."

"I'll come get you," Christa offered, though her jaw was beginning to ache again from the extractions. She would have to renew her prescription at the Phar-Mor store in Newberry Square anyway.

"You don't mind?"

"I'm on my way."

Christa knew what it was like when her stepfather Eric Garren was drinking. That and other behavior that she considered inappropriate led her as a young teenager to move in with her father and his new wife, Diana.

"Maybe I'll stay with you until he cools off," Ann said.

The domestic dispute would be responsible for what turned out to be the last evening Ann would spend with her daughter.

8:00 P.M.

Debra Carroll lived in a one-bedroom apartment directly behind Christa's Apartment M.

She saw him from her window.

He was leaning up against the wire fence inside the apartment complex perimeter at the rear of Christa's apartment.

Debra squinted in an attempt to see better. Nearsighted, she couldn't see him too well, standing as he was some forty feet from her, but she was sure she had never seen him before and that he did not live in the complex. She could make out, even with her eyesight, that he was wearing high-top tennis shoes, loose-fitting sweatpants and a cut-off T-shirt.

He wasn't doing anything. Just standing there holding a cigarette in his right hand, occasionally bringing it up to his mouth.

For some reason Debra Carroll found his presence frightening. There was something about him.

Still, he wasn't doing anything.

8:30 P.M.

Not being prepared for her mother's overnight stay, Christa was short on groceries, so they walked from her apartment to the Publix store in Butler Plaza to shop. Then on to Dunkin' Donuts, also in Butler Plaza, where they bought donuts with their favorite fillings. Afterward they ran into a high-school acquaintance of Christa, chatted briefly and moved on.

They walked by the theaters in Butler Plaza and cut through the rear of the apartment complex abutting the plaza to Christa's apartment.

By nine o'clock they had prepared dinner while talking about everything from Ann's problems with Eric to how Christa found out she was anemic when she went to use the services of Planned Parenthood.

As they ate dinner and watched television, Christa's pet cat, Emily, kept playing with a string under the table.

While Ann washed the dishes Christa bathed, still debating about going to the party at Gatorwood.

Why don't you go, Ann called to her through the bathroom door. Ann was tired and talked-out, she'd probably go straight to bed.

Okay. Christa finally made up her mind to go.

Ann knew that Christa was security-minded. She had often expressed her concern about the crime rate in her neighborhood and knew her daughter planned to move from the apartment after the first of the year now that Brigitte was gone. So it did not surprise Ann when Christa told her to make sure the doors were locked after she left for the party.

"I usually leave the lights on if I know I'm coming back after dark, but you don't have to do that. They'll keep you awake. And don't open the front door without first asking who's there."

Ann smiled at her parental admonitions.

Ann stepped outside to smoke while Christa got dressed. She had gone out the front door of the apartment rather than out to the back-yard because of the position of Christa's bicycle between the sliding glass door and the foot of the bed; she was tired and felt it would be too much trouble to move.

She smoked a couple of Vantage cigarettes while she again mulled over her earlier dispute with Eric.

He moved so that he could watch.

Too early. Too much light. Wait. Too many people around. The woman was too close in age to his mother. Made him feel uncomfortable. The trigger was nevertheless squeezed again. *She* should have stopped the fight, the shooting, the pain.

He waited, sweating in the heat of anticipation as well as the mugginess of the night. Fantasizing. Then remembering the two he had just taken care of . . . *that* wasn't fantasy, that was real, better than fantasies. Feeling an erection at the mere thought of it again.

10:19 P.M.

At 10:19 that night, dressed in black jogging shorts, a white tank top with a white design, flat black shoes and carrying a small brown leather purse with a long strap, Christa Hoyt left her mother at home to attend Jennifer Cox's party at Gatorwood.

Ann fell asleep almost immediately on the narrow little bed made up in the living room.

The party turned out to be pretty much what Christa expected—noisy and crowded but fun. She was talking to Jennifer Mulhearn, another waitress from the International House of Pancakes, when an unknown young man kept breaking into their conversation.

"Where do you work?" he asked Christa.

"I work on the computers at the sheriff's office."

"I knew a girl who worked on computers but the computer exploded and blew her head off. I was upset at her."

"Really? Why?"

"Because she got some blood on me."

"Oh," she said. What else could you say?

He was having a party the next week and all were invited. He edged closer. "I know I'm a little gross but I'm practicing."

Jennifer figured he was maybe practicing to be a writer. He'd been talking about Stephen King novels.

"I had a girlfriend once but she fell into a pond and was eaten by piranhas."

That did it. Christa and Jennifer Mulhearn moved onto the balcony, where they spent the rest of the evening until Christa decided to go home.

"But it's early," Jennifer said.

"I'm expecting a phone call from my boyfriend."

26

Stalking and Murder

Saturday, August 25—Midnight

The phone call Christa had been expecting from Pete Brigette had come while she was at the party. By 12:30 she left the apartment and drove to Pete's. A few miles away at Williamsburg Village Apartments, Noy, the young man from Apartment 112, first noticed the unusual smell of garbage in the stairwell of the apartments.

6:30 A.M.

Christa had spent the night with Pete and returned to the apartment shortly before 6:30 in the morning in time to drive her mother to her job at the IHOP.

"I'll call you around five tonight," Ann told her. "I may come back and stay the night with you again. It all depends on Eric."

Ann then went to work. It was the first time she had spent any time in Christa's apartment, it had been a pleasure.

At 11:30 that morning Bryan Oulton and Scott Henratty went to Sonja's apartment. There was no answer to their knocks on her door. Apparently they paid no attention to the odor in the stairwell. But by 1:00 P.M. Jason Beaupied also noticed it in the stairwell that adjoined the front entrances of all the apartments. He knew he had never smelled such an odor before. What Bryan and Scott thought was the natural odor of this particular apartment began to bother Beaupied. Why were people leaving their rotting garbage around?

3:00 P.M.

Bryan Oulton and Scott Henratty tried knocking on Sonja's door again. Still no answer. Should they try the back? What for? If the girls were home they'd answer . . .

If they had gone to the back door, which was unlocked but jammed shut, and given it a strong push they could have been inside one of the murder rooms. They didn't, and so spared themselves some future nightmares.

They were not the only ones trying to reach the girls. Christina's brother and sister went to her rooms to visit her. No one answered their knocks either. Her sister, Barbara Milcum, had come all the way from Jacksonville to deliver some furniture. Over the next three to four hours she checked several times, but when no one answered the door she too left. They were out, that's all. None of them could have imagined what was on the other side of that locked front door.

They were still checking the door at 5:30 P.M. when Ann Garren telephoned Christa as promised.

"Are you going to stay over again?" Christa asked her mother.

"I planned to but . . . I changed my mind."

Christa sighed. "You're going back to Newberry, aren't you?"

"I guess I better."

Ann Garren would not be there when the killer came calling for her daughter. They did not know that the killer had already singled Christa out. Rolling the voyeur had hidden outside Christa's apartment and watched her through her sliding glass back door several days before he broke into her apartment. Not only did he find Christa very attractive, he was overwhelmed by how much she looked like O'Mather. Silently, he had watched as she came out of her bathroom after a shower and went into her bedroom. She toweled herself off in front of his hidden eyes. For some reason, he wasn't ready to make his move yet, but he would not forget her. He knew he had to come back for her.

That evening, even with the ache left by her extracted teeth still nagging her, Christa called her friend, Paul Daniel Schwartz, to ask him if he wanted to play racquetball. Not getting an answer, she left a phone message and went to the courts near the UF law school to find another partner.

Paul had traveled to Orlando to pick up his mother, then returned to Gainesville at about 6:30 P.M. A check of the answering machine revealed

Christa's message telling him she was off to the courts and asking him if he was up to a game. He dialed her back.

"Hey, I'm sorry I missed you," he said. "How'd you like to play racquetball again?"

She said she would, and she'd come by and pick him up as soon as she put her tennis clothes back on.

She changed into black shorts, a white T-shirt with a design on the left breast and on the back, and athletic socks rolled down to the tops of her low white tennis shoes.

They went to a park off Thirty-fourth Street near the FHP station, arriving about 7:45 P.M.. There were other people at the park but they easily managed to get a court.

Before the game she took off her black-banded wristwatch and rings and placed them in the ball can. Paul noticed she was wearing a gold necklace that she did not remove.

Christa and Paul played for the next hour until the sky turned a deep royal blue with the coming of night.

Christa was feeling great, she'd never played better . . . While she played, the shadowy figure inserted a Stanley screwdriver into the slim crack between the door and frame and forced open the sliding glass door. It had no crossbar to seal it shut. Forcing it open was easy. He had been concealed by darkness and by the solitude of the yard at the back of her apartment. He entered, and waited.

The apartment was small. It consisted of a bedroom and a living room. Each of the rooms was no more than twelve by sixteen feet, with a small bathroom and a kitchen area separating the two. There was a free-standing bookcase set in a small recessed area to the side of the front door. If he moved the bookcase out of the way, he could create a place for himself to hide. He moved the bookcase without too much effort down the hall, past the bathroom and into the bedroom. Now he could hide where the bookcase had been and not be seen by his victim when she entered the apartment. He would have the advantage of total surprise added to the obvious advantage of his greater strength in the coming encounter. From his position he could look out of the window while he waited to see when she was approaching. In this way he would be ready to pounce on his unsuspecting victim. The trap was set.

"Let me drive," Paul said after they had completed their game. "I want to see if I can still drive a standard shift."

"Sure," she said as she put her racquetball equipment in the trunk of her sun-faded reddish Nissan Sentra and Paul threw his in the back seat under the tinted windows.

They left the courts at the park, heading for his home, where she had picked him up earlier.

"Want to come in for a drink?"

His parents, Richard and Alice Schwartz, and their other son Russell were at home when they arrived. Christa stayed for about forty-five minutes. They sat in Paul's room and talked about the difficulties of juggling work and school schedules. She also told him Michelle Pothier might move in with her and about how she and Michelle had gotten themselves badly sunburned when they went to the beach the month before. She gave him directions to her apartment and had him write down the address so he could pick her up next time they wanted to play.

Richard and Alice Schwartz spoke briefly to her as she left at 9:45 P.M. They liked her.

After she had left, Paul confirmed their positive reaction—she was a positive, outgoing person who tended to be a perfectionist. "She's also a pretty good racquetball player."

At the same time that Christa was on her way back from the Schwartzes to her apartment on Archer Road, Bryan Oulton and Scott Henratty were finally giving up and leaving a note for Sonja and Christina that they had been looking for them all day.

By Saturday night, with still no word from Sonja, Ada Larson was beginning to get concerned.

Christa came home through the front door of her apartment and switched on the air-conditioning unit, which as usual she had turned off when she left. Looking forward to a cool shower, she headed for the bathroom.

He was there.

She saw the cold blue metal in his eyes, the deeply furrowed frown. He pulled her into the bathroom and this time there was a violent life-and-death struggle. Christa put up a strong fight. But he had surprise and size on his side, plus the strength shaped by hours of bench presses in his front yard while neighborhood children watched.

Toiletries were spilled. Towels were ripped off the rack. Blood was splattered. She had no chance against his fists. When the knife was drawn, it was all over for her. He had all the time he needed to orchestrate his scenario of mutilation and ritualistic placing of body parts. He had much to do. First the adhesive. Then the rituals. The mutilations were necessary to insure the sexual gratification that in his impotence he was incapable of achieving any other way. He had become energized by the flood of stimuli he had already set in motion . . . the stalking, the first confrontation provided the foreplay that vitalized and led to the erection, and then, at the moment of death, that brought the temporary release of ejaculation spilled onto her body.

He slit her open, easy as field-gutting a deer, a clean incision from her pubic bone straight up to her breasts. He was adept. He had not touched or damaged a single organ. Caught up in the carnage, he cut off her nipples and placed them on the bed next to her, then sliced off her breasts, wrapped them in her toweling and placed them on the other side of the bed. He intended to take them with him.

He was erect again. He positioned himself to ejaculate into her mouth. Suddenly he pulled back. Her mouth. Get rid of that mouth gaping at him. Accusing him.

He pulled up her body from its prone position, bent her over the foot of the bed. Using his hunting knife, he cut off her head. As he did so her gold necklace fell into the palm of his hand.

He could leave her head for the cops to find. He went to the living room, looked around and made his decision. The bookcase under the air-conditioning unit, which was loudly whirring, was heavy, but in his energized state he had the strength. Slowly he pushed the bookcase across the floor and positioned it next to the window.

He went back to the bedroom. He left her in a bent-over position at the foot of the bed and carried her head into the living room and set it up on the bookcase.

He did not consider himself a "lust murderer." He did not think of himself as perverted or a carrier of an evil disease. He did not think of the girls as innocent victims of the disease, fatally infected by his poison. At most he thought of them as objects meant for him to use to satisfy his needs.

A last touch. He placed a mirror on the bookshelf, tilting it in such a way that the head would be the first item someone had to see when looking into the window. Very clever. What a challenge he was leaving for them. Let them try to figure *this* one out.

Ritualistic mutilation, repetitive, sadistic crimes, targeting a particular type of victim, selecting a trawling ground—a college town in his case— where those who represented everything the killer was not could be found . . . Once again Rolling was signing his highly personal signature to the crimes, a signature that in its basic components included classic patterns of the so-called serial lust killer.

The telephone attached to Christa's answering machine rang. It was just inside the front door next to the shelf upon which he had displayed her decapitated head.

He stared at the answering machine as a female voice penetrated into the room.

Beep . . .

"Your beep is too long," the voice said cheerfully. "I know you're home. You're probably sleeping and you refuse to talk to me right now. I'm upset because I'm dying to talk to you right now. So I'm going to keep on calling you until you finally pick up the phone and answer it. Okay? I'll call back in five minutes. Bye."

Beep . . .

It was unnerving to hear the sound of a voice, as though the voice had eyes to see. Get out.

When he left he turned off the air conditioner but neglected to take her breasts wrapped in toweling beside her on the bed.

Debra Carroll, who had seen a white male standing at the rear of the Hoyt residence earlier in the evening, was asleep in her bedroom located behind Christa's apartment. At 4:00 A.M. that morning she was awakened by the sound of someone running past her apartment. She could hear the runner clearly because she was sleeping on the floor and the wall air-conditioning unit was off. She heard no vehicle leaving.

Later that day Rolling had the audacity to call the police station to ask if a wallet with the Kennedy I. D. had been found. What bravura. Nice touch. He reported it stolen.

That Sunday night he was on the prowl again. He walked around Gatorwood Apartments, about a mile from his campsite across SW Archer Road. To all outward appearances he did not look vile or depraved.

Then he spotted Tracy Paules.

27

Discovering the First Two Bodies

Sunday, August 26

While Kim Norman wondered why Christa had not shown up at the Alachua County gym for their planned workout, and neighbors Noy and Kitzman wondered whom they could complain to about the growing stench at Williamsburg Village Apartments, Frank and Patricia Powell left Jacksonville for the trip to their daughter's new apartment in Gainesville.

3:30 P.M.

Once at Williamsburg Village, with no response to their repeated knocking, Christina Powell's parents finally called the Larsons in Deerfield Beach to ask if they had heard from Sonja. It was at this point that Ada said, "Get somebody to open the door. They could be in there!"

When Gainesville police department Officer Ray Barber finally got in, snapping the door frame out of the wall as he broke through, the bodies of Christina Powell and Sonja Larson, lying dead in a hot airless room, were discovered at last.

Charles Sauls was the investigator on duty at the state attorney's office. Maritza Arroyo, one of the new assistant state attorneys, had been working with the department less than a year; it was her weekend on-call with Sauls.

When the call from GPD came into the state attorney's office, Charlie Sauls immediately called Len Register, the Eighth Circuit State Attorney, at his home in Gainesville.

"Looks like we've got a double homicide here at the Williamsburg Apartments," Charlie told him. "You might want to come over."

224

"Meet you there." Len Register said in his deep voice flavored with a native-born Floridian accent; he had grown up in adjacent Brevard County and had gone to high school in Brevard County and to the University of Florida Law School.

When Register arrived at the apartments he saw that along with a full complement of Gainesville police personnel, students were beginning to mill around. He saw GPD Officer Brian Helmerson, with mirrored sunglasses, standing guard outside the complex in front of the yellow crime-scene tape.

There was a subdued greeting when Len arrived. He was asked if he wanted to go inside to take a look.

"In a minute."

He first went to Sauls and Arroyo, since they were on duty from his department and they could bring him up to date.

"There are two dead girls inside," Charlie told him. "Students. One upstairs, one downstairs."

"You been in yet?"

Headshakes.

"Let's do it," he said.

They were accompanied by two GPD detectives as they walked through the broken door, then went to the upstairs bedroom, where Sonja Larson was on the bed.

They stopped short. Maritza almost turned white. As a new prosecutor she had never been subjected to such a sight. Few had. But she held her own.

Len and Charlie had to take deep breaths when they saw the body pulled down to the end of the bed at the foot of the mattress. She was lying on her back, her legs were bent at the knees, her foot on the floor at a ninety-degree angle, hanging over the side. She was wearing something on top . . . a rolled-up T-shirt. No bottoms.

He looked closely. Tough as it was, he wanted to remember this, every detail. She had stab wounds in her chest around her left breast, her chest had a gaping hole. He thought the wound had probably been smaller than it appeared now because it was apparent that the girl had been dead for some time; the tissue had begun to shrink and pull away, which made the wound look bigger than it had originally been. Len could see leg injuries on the inner and outer portions of the girl's left thigh. Some flesh was missing; maybe that unidentified mass on the floor.

This was the first homicide scene State Attorney Len Register had witnessed since becoming a parent of a one-year-old and two-year-old. How would he feel if . . . he couldn't help thinking. Many of the mutilations appeared to be post mortem; there was no significant bleeding from those areas. Small comfort in that. But there was evidence of restraint with adhesive tape, now missing. What did that mean?

They didn't touch anything. They simply walked through the room and looked. They stayed no more than five minutes, five of the longest minutes of Len's life. Then he, Charlie, Maritza and the detectives went downstairs to the nude body of Christina Powell on the floor. Len's immediate impression was that she had been laid out on display, a pair of panties nearby. Her breasts had been cut off.

He glanced at Maritza, whose jaw was clamped shut. "You okay?"

She nodded. Quickly.

They were told she had been stabbed in the back.

He could only imagine what the parents would be going through.

Something real odd. There was a bottle of some kind of dishwashing liquid near her. Blue-green. Dawn. At first it wasn't obvious that she had been soaped in the pubic area; later they would learn that there was residue of blue liquid detergent on pubic hairs.

They found themselves moving around, numbed, quietly speculating on how the double murder might have happened. Talking was better than silence. Had the killer burst in with them or was he waiting for them? It wasn't clear if he gained entry after they were inside and getting ready for bed and jumped them or was waiting in, say, a closet. Len said he felt that the Larson girl must have been killed first, and then the killer went upstairs and did the Powell girl.

They did not go upstairs to examine the back door for pry marks. They stayed out of the way. Everybody was being very careful not to contaminate or disturb any trace evidence so that the best possible professional job of processing the murder scene could be done by the Gainesville Police Department.

State Attorney Len Register and his crew left the murder scene as the process of gathering evidence continued. Everything was carefully itemized, labeled and bagged:

clothes baskets with possible blood splatters
cane chair
cushion with possible hair and blood
wine-colored towel from under the dining-room table
orange towel, pair of panties, blood swabbing from door frame of Apt. 110
couch cushion with possible blood smear
sheet used to wrap body of Powell during transportation
empty beer can found outside Apt. 113
paper bags from the hands of Sonja

paper bags from the hands of Christina
sheet used to wrap body of Sonja during transportation
plastic bottle of contact lens wash
trapped contents from upstairs sink
trapped contents from downstairs sink
trapped contents from kitchen sink
small blood-soaked piece of paper found under Christina's body
calculator with blood splatters
blue pillow case from Sonja's bed
white pillow case from Sonja's bed
blue plaid pillow case from Sonja's bed
light blue pillow from Sonja's bed
2 other blue pillow cases
11 latent prints from her car
61 latent prints from interior of apartment
panty liner
women's panties
14 latent prints from her car
20 latent prints from interior of apartment
the bed comforter from Sonja's bed with bloodstains
9 latent print cards from interior of apartment
18 print cards
plastic bag from ground area at rear of Apt. 113
card and photo case from kitchen counter.

Len, Charlie and Maritza went outside, where the air was thickly hot and humid but to them incredibly fresh and sweet-smelling. They were told that the family of one of the victims was on hand. The staff from Crime Victim Associates was also at the scene. Students kept crowding the area, as though magnetically drawn to the tragedy.

Then Elsa Streppe arrived. Fortune had intervened to save her. It was past 3:30 when she appeared with her luggage at Williamsburg Village, so crowded with onlookers and police that she was unable to get in.

"I was delayed . . ." Questioning her at this time would be neither productive nor humane. In a state of shock, she was escorted to the Alachua County Crisis Center, where a team of experts would do their best to help her deal with the inevitable trauma.

Len sent Charlie and Maritza home and stayed around for nearly an hour in the parking lot. There was not, though, much more that he could do. There appeared to be no need for a search or arrest warrant, which would have been within his area of responsibility. But it was difficult to leave with so much anxiety hanging in the air.

*   *   *

At this time in his career Mitch Stacy was covering the courts for the *Gainesville Sun*. Tom Lyons and Susan Dewey were the crime reporters, but it was Ron Dupont, one of the *Sun*'s younger reporters, who was doing night cops on the weekend when the bodies were discovered.

Mitch's wife, Holly Stacy, was at the *Sun* at a desk across from Ron writing obituaries on her usual four-to-six part-time shift, to supplement her law studies. Ron didn't hear anything on the scanner to tip him off, but Holly looked up briefly as he received a phone call from Lt. Sadie Darnell. Mitch had told her that Ron was tight with Sadie. He had worked murders before.

Ron hung up the receiver, looked at Holly. "We've got a murder, maybe two, and they might be students. That was Sadie from her car phone. She's on her way out there. I'm going."

He got up and left, and never got back to his desk that night.

Holly continued writing an obituary.

When she left the office at six and went home she didn't mention the incident to Mitch.

Ron Dupont arrived at Williamsburg and immediately ran into his old friend Lt. Sadie Darnell. On seeing her he started to say something light-hearted about what had happened and quickly realized that Sadie was dead serious about this one. No wise-guy humor, forced or otherwise. She moved away, not able yet to fill him in on what was going on.

He moved closer to the apartments to get a better look. State Prosecutor Len Register was there, and GPD Chief Wayland Clifton along with considerable GPD presence. There was even a group of GPD's senior detectives on the scene. They're really out in force, Ron thought. He turned his head in time to see a police officer come out of the apartment and go off to the side of the building to throw up.

He watched officers come out with black body bags that were placed in a small unmarked van, then removed to the county medical examiner where Dr. Hamilton, the county coroner, would perform the autopsies.

Len Register went home and told his wife what he had seen. This was the town they had grown up in. Homicides, he'd seen them, but this . . .

"Who would do something like that?" his wife asked.

"I don't know," he told her. "But he has got to be real sick."

She had seen him come home other times after being called out on homicides, but this one affected him in a very different way.

The pressure was already beginning to build. Ultimately it would be his department's case in the courtroom. He hoped it would be resolved quickly and with a level of conclusiveness that would insure justice being done. Nobody ever wanted a marginal case. Especially not with this one.

Meanwhile, inside Christa's Apartment M, the answering machine on the little table next to Christa's decapitated body was activated.

Beep . . .

"This is Pete. Call me in about twenty minutes."

Beep . . .

"Hey, it's me. It's a little after four. Call me when you get in," the male caller said.

6:30 P.M.

Tracy Paules now arrived in Gainesville. Tomorrow she was to begin attending classes at the university. Less than three hours had elapsed since the first two bodies were found at Williamsburg Apartments. When she returned to the Gatorwood Apartments that Sunday evening, she dutifully called her mother Ricky, who had already heard about the murders.

"I heard too," Tracy said, stunned at the news.

Ricky was glad that her daughter's roommate was a burly six-foot-two, 200–pounder. "You stay close to Manny," she ordered.

"You know Manny's steady girlfriend is his cat Sasha," Tracy said, trying to relieve her mother's anxiety, and her own.

"You know what I mean," her mother said, knowing the two were not romantically involved. "About what's happened up there . . ."

Tracy knew.

8 P.M.

Paul Daniel Schwartz picked up his friend Richard Pollard and they went to the Reitz Union to shoot pool until ten. Like a replay of Oulton and Henratty trying to contact Sonja, Paul decided to see if he could locate Christa Hoyt's apartment.

At approximately 10:15 Paul and Richard arrived in the area of Christa's apartment and parked Paul's 1982 Dodge station wagon behind her Nissan Sentra, which he spotted next to a large tree. He got out and asked a tall young girl whose apartment door was wide open if she knew where Christa Hoyt lived.

"Sorry," she said. "I just moved in. I don't know any of my neighbors yet."

Paul and Richard did not walk around. It was dark in the complex area where Christa's vehicle was parked.

"Well, she's gotta be here somewhere. Her car's here."

They finally gave up and left.

10:15 P.M.

At Gatorwood Building 10, Apartment 1002, Sarah Fiala was alone. Her roommate, Sabrina Gimrock, was at work at the University Health Center when Sarah heard someone try to open the door. It was locked. She could hear the person move down the hall. Sarah was about to open the door to look outside, but suddenly nervous, she slipped the chain in place instead.

A few minutes later Jenny Kanne saw the doorknob of her apartment door turn. She went to the door, listened with her ear to the door, then banged on the door with her fist as hard as she could, over and over again. Amelia Marshall came running in.

"What is it!"

"Shh."

Jenny looked at the front doorknob. It did not turn again. It was probably nothing, she thought. Someone had the wrong apartment. Probably had one too many.

10:30 P.M.

Although GPD Officer Ray Barber had entered Apartment 113 shortly after being summoned by the Powells, some seven hours passed before a Brevard County sheriff arrived at the Larsons' home in Deerfield Beach and asked them to call Detective Johnson at the Gainesville Police Department.

Ada had the sick feeling the moment the sheriff told them to call Gainesville that her daughter was dead. James Larson, a quiet-spoken retired boatyard owner, could barely calm her down enough to make the call. He, too, had a sinking premonition.

An accident? An injury? The automobile?

But when he called, Detective Johnson was at a meeting and not summoned to the phone.

Spencer Mann, the public information officer for the Alachua County sheriff's office, was thirty-six years old with dark brown hair and a moustache. A bit portly at 5 feet 10 inches and 240 pounds, he was a former journalist who wanted to write a manual on how to handle the media during crises such as oil-tanker spillages, crash scenes and murders.

He was lying on the couch in his living room listening to the eleven o'clock news with his wife Pat when he heard that two students had been found murdered in Gainesville. No details. He was, of course, sorry about it. He didn't think he'd be involved, though. He was wrong. He would soon be called on to handle the media as public information officer for the Alachua County sheriff's office.

In another house on NW Eighth Street, Mitch and Holly Stacy also heard the news report on TV 20: "Two roommates, UF students, found murdered in their apartment . . ."

And then it hit Holly. That's where Ron was going when he left the office. A double-murder. Mitch had covered dozens of murders as a reporter. Still, maybe they'd need help on this one. He decided to go in early.

TV 20 was also on in Elsa Rule's Gatorwood apartment as her two dogs began a chorus of excited barking. They ran to the door, growling, snarling, howling—until the person who had opened the unlocked door closed it shut and his alien scent disappeared down the hall beyond the range of their quivering nostrils. Elsa looked from the newscast about the murders at Williamsburg to the dogs, to the door, and back to the screen. She quietly moved to the door, locked it and patted the excited animals.

11:45 P.M.

It wasn't until 11:45 that Detective Johnson was notified the Larsons had returned his call. He went to the detective bureau and called the Larson home.

Ada answered the phone.

"May I please speak to your husband?"

"I'll talk to you . . ."

"Could your husband get on the line also, ma'am?"

"No. I don't want him to be on the phone. Talk to me."

He took a deep breath. "It's my duty to tell you, ma'am, that the Gainesville Police Department is working on the death of two young ladies in apartment One-one-three at Williamsburg—"

He could hear Mrs. Larson become hysterical. He stared at the floor and waited, the woman's cries muffled by distance and a dropped phone.

Mr. Larson got on the phone. Detective Johnson could still hear Mrs. Larson screaming in the background as her husband tried to speak.

"This is James Larson. What happened?"

Detective Johnson told the father as quickly as possible.

Silence.

"Would you like me to call you back?" Having been through this part before, Detective Johnson wanted to give them some room to react.

"Yes," James finally whispered.

At 11:59 P.M. Detective Johnson called the Larsons again.

"We'll leave right away," the father said. "We're coming to Gainesville."

"Please," the detective said quietly. "This is not the time. There's nothing you can do here right now—"

"But—"

"It would be better if you wait until tomorrow . . ."

"Tomorrow . . ."

"And . . . please contact Sonja's dentist and if possible bring her dental records with you . . ."

"We'll wait until tomorrow," the father said, shaking his head, feeling numb.

Later, when Ada Larson was told that a neighbor heard someone taking a shower in the girls' apartment at 6:30 A.M. Friday, she was convinced that the person taking the shower was the killer. "Those girls were not early risers," she said. At ten A.M. next-door neighbor Jason Beaupied had heard George Michael's "Faith" blaring from the apartment and a banging on the wall, "like they were putting in a nail." Ada thought her daughter's murderer may have been trying to mask the noise as he pounded on a back door, which often was stuck, in order to get out of the apartment.

Inside the cedar hope chest in Sonja's bedroom was her tattered blue-and-pink baby blanket. Her childhood security blanket. Next to the blanket there was a Bible engraved with her name. A marker remained where Sonja had last read the Bible. She had highlighted one of the passages in yellow:

In Thee O Lord I have taken refuge
Incline Thine ear to me, rescue me quickly
Be Thou to me a rock of strength
A strong hold to save me.

28

And Then There Were Three

Monday, August 27—12:30 A.M.

Shortly past midnight when Tracy Paules' friend Lisa Buyer called she could tell that Tracy was deeply upset about the murders. The campus was already in the early stages of panic. It was difficult not to get caught up in it. "Be careful," Lisa said to her.

"Don't worry, I will," Tracy said. "Everybody's just crazy right now. I've never seen anything like it."

After she hung up, Tracy called her sister Laurie. She couldn't stop talking about the murders, until her sister asked her about her weekend on Merritt Island with Khris. It at least diverted her enough to say how she felt about Khris, that she had fallen in love, and they had made love for the first time.

When she hung up the fear came back. She felt much better when Manny Taboada came home.

12:30 A.M.

While Tracy was confiding to her sister that she had fallen in love, Teesha Jackson of the Alachua County Sheriff's Office looked over at Christa Hoyt's empty desk and, belatedly, realized that she had not come to work as usual. It was not like Christa to be late.

She decided to call the shift supervisor, Kim Norman.

Kim glanced up at the clock when the phone rang next to her bed: 12:30.

Apartment M

Beep . . .

"Hi, Christa, it's Michelle. It's five after one and we haven't heard anything. We're wondering what happened. We're just worried about you. Talk to you later. Bye."

Beep . . .

"Christa, if you're there pick up the telephone. This is Gail in CDC. Hello—hello, Christa. It's one-thirty-six in the morning and you need to be at work. Hello."

Beep . . .

"Chris. This is the sheriff's office. Answer the door. Answer the phone or the door. It's one-twenty-three on Monday. Chris, if you're home, answer the phone."

Christa Hoyt never answered.

It was 1:30 A.M. Monday morning when the discovery of Christa Hoyt's decapitated body was made by Deputies Keith O'Hara and Gail Barber shortly after the last call on her answering machine.

Road supervisor Lt. Alan Baxter was the first to arrive at the scene after O'Hara had put in his emergency call. Within minutes, Investigator Greg Weeks and Lt. John Nobles arrived. It was Baxter and Nobles who entered the death scene.

In checking the area they found that the murder had not happened in the last few hours. They could feel the oppressive stench of death the moment they entered the dark, airless rooms. As Rolling intended, the first thing they came on was the head. Teeth gritting. Low flashlights. Hand signals. Room by room. The blood-smeared bathroom. The bent-over headless body on the bed. Little blood on the bedroom floor underneath where her head should have been. The pale blue quilted coverlet sprinkled with orange flowers was only slightly mussed; it had a little blood on it. It appeared that the girl had tried to fight her assailant—hence, the beating in the bathroom, the restraints, the excessive mutilation.

The first responsibility of responding officers was to check for signs of life. No life here. They did not want to touch anything. They could only stare at the head on the bookshelf.

There was a heavy Gainesville Police Department presence, although they were not permitted entry into the apartment; the crime had been committed outside of city limits and therefore out of GPD's jurisdiction, but almost immediately it was felt that Christa Hoyt's murder was connected to those of Christina Powell and Sonja Larson.

The Criminal Investigation Division captain was in charge. It was obvious that the entire bookcase had been moved. The apartment was in some disarray. There was a little blood, thin streaks, almost wiped clean. Not a mess. It looked as though the killer had rummaged through the girl's things and, perhaps, had taken some personal belongings. Difficult to tell what at this point, but one of the men said, "Looks like the girl's undergarments are missing."

The captain nodded. Then he walked into the bathroom. "She may have been caught up in here at some point," he muttered, looking at the blood smears. "Or maybe he cleaned himself off. . . . I want the entire drainage system taken out," he ordered quietly. "In one piece."

Next he moved into the bedroom. The clicking camera shutter was the only sound in the room as the forensic photographer worked the scene. An official from the Alachua County Sheriff's Office was standing by the side of the bed. His face seemed drained of color underneath an ordinarily ruddy complexion.

Only the medical examiner was permitted to touch the body, and he had not yet arrived. They waited in the silence of the room, standing guard over the body, until the medical examiner, Dr. Hamilton, arrived in an unmarked black station wagon, similar to a funeral director's car with a collapsible gurney.

"Have you finished with the body in this position?" the medical examiner asked.

"In a minute . . ."

Dr. Hamilton waited. A crime scene like this took dozens of rolls of film. Nothing could be touched, moved, dusted until the photographer finished. When he was done the medical examiner confirmed for the world that the headless body was dead. By the book. The cause of death—probably not the decapitation. It would be determined at the autopsy. He was told she had been only eighteen. He heard she had been very pretty. "I'm going to move her back on the bed now to straighten her out."

The captain thought of the parents. "Do it easy."

When the medical examiner moved her body back onto the bed from the position in which she had been left, a subdued guttural sound came from a witness. It was a sound of rage.

It was at this point that they became aware that, in addition to the mutilations, the girl had been cut open, from the breastbone to the pubic bone. This was not the act of a disgruntled boyfriend or lover. This was cold, calculated, ceremonious and methodical. On the surface, the medical examiner thought, whoever did this knew what he was doing—from the placement of the head, the positioning of the body, the removal of the breasts, the arrangement of the nipples.

And to a man, they now realized they had all become unwilling participants in the acts of a sadistic sex criminal. At both scenes undergarments were missing. At both scenes a knife with a four-to-six-inch blade had been used. At both scenes there was evidence of the use of adhesive tape for restraint.

More photos were taken. Every angle. Full color. The prosecutor's office at the scene coordinated the procedural investigations of the units. Forensics could have it now. Physical evidence was needed to prosecute the crime. Something concrete for the DNA genetic fingerprinting, vacuuming for hairs, fibers, collecting blood, body fluids, fingerprints, footprints, tool marks, tire tracks.

They vacuumed their way to the body from the sliding door in the back, the obvious point of entry of the killer, and then the entire apartment, every square inch of the floor, because of "the theory of transfer"; everyone loses hairs and fibers from his clothing.

The vacuum head was skimming an inch above the floor to pick up only the most recent hairs that were lying on the surface. As soon as the collection kit filled up, the head was changed and the contents were dated, marked and numbered before the vacuum was purged and the next square foot of floor was slowly vacuumed.

Then they did the bookcase.

Lt. Alan Baxter stood outside Apartment M as the units moved in, everyone with a specialized job to do. It wasn't a wild scene, it was more like pervasive shock; he's killed one of our own people . . . Alan knew there was often a deceptively insular feeling among law people, that as part of a private family of police officers they were somehow immune to this kind of victimization. Bad people stay back from law enforcement. So it was a shock to realize "he got one of us."

Baxter glanced at Gail Barber and thought of her husband, GPD Officer Ray Barber, not easily shocked. Gail had told Alan how hard Ray had taken the discovery of the bodies of Christina and Sonja, and now here she was in the same situation he had been in only ten hours earlier.

As Alan looked into the deep, thicketed darkness of the area surrounding Christa's apartment, waiting for his eyes to become accustomed to the dark of the night, he had the feeling *he* was out there, close. Alan Baxter had been a policeman for over sixteen years and he felt it in his gut . . . that whoever was responsible was watching them. It would not have been surprising or even unusual if he had been. Alan searched the perimeter of the area. Somewhere, out there, maybe close by, maybe not, was a calm killer, spent and drained for now.

But this guy, he believed, wasn't finished.

He was right. Of all killers, the serial lust killer was the one most likely to repeat his crime. It became easier and easier. He dehumanized his victims, viewing them as objects for his sexual pleasure. First he established control, then left the "message" behind—the ritual signature mutilation. Ordinarily there was a cooling-off period, then the inner impulse would build up again, like the craving for an addictive drug, until he had to seek out another victim to achieve his release. And, somewhere deep inside, looking for that bullet.

The professionals were at work trying to figure out *what* he was, in order to find out *who* he was, leading to where he was.

Plastic does not breathe; if moisture forms, condensation destroys hair or fiber evidence. The hands were bagged, each finger separately. New brown bags taped shut. S.O.P, standard operating procedure in a stabbing where there were defensive wounds and there was a chance there could be flesh under the fingernails if the victim had scratched her assailant. Standard 8½-by-11-inch paper folded into quarters, evidence in the center, paper folded over and over, put in an envelope, stamped. The body was placed in one bag. The head in another.

It seemed as though she had just closed her eyes when Kim Norman was awakened by the persistent ringing of the phone.

It was Michelle again, sorry to bother Kim. The girl's voice sounded strained. "You have to come back in to work," Michelle said.

"Why? What's happened?"

"I don't know."

"Is it about Christa?"

"I think so. Something bad, I think. They've already called CID and Crime Scene."

"I'm on my way."

Kim drove back to the Alachua County Sheriff's Office on SW Depot and Fourth streets.

"Does *anybody* know what's going on?" Kim asked when she arrived.

No one spoke up.

Spencer Mann got the call at home in the middle of the night, from a male dispatcher who informed him that Christa Hoyt had been found murdered. He remembered the others. This one *was* in his jurisdiction. Christa? Christa Hoyt? He didn't know her well but recalled she was a tall pretty girl with a bright personality. He used to say hello to her walking down the hallway at the county sheriff's office. Christa Hoyt . . .

As Spencer Mann walked about the complex there was an atmosphere to the scene he had never seen, or felt, before. The M.O. was too systematic. Go ahead, try and figure this one out, I got you beat, the killer seemed to be saying.

Sheriff Lu Hindery of Alachua County lived twenty miles away. When he got to the crime scene he could tell the level of anxiety was even more significant than at the first scene.

The investigators on the scene invited the sheriff in to see. No, he didn't want to be a witness. He was going to retire soon, perhaps he didn't want to get involved in such an investigation at this late stage of his career. Who could blame him?

"Did you know Christa?"

Very attractive young woman, worked hard to make something of herself . . .

Nancy Carlton arrived at the sheriff's office a little before two A.M., a few moments after Kim Norman.

Did she know what was going on? Kim asked her supervisor.

The phone began ringing. Nancy took it in her office. When she came out her eyes were wet. "Christa's dead, murdered. They just found her."

Kim looked up as Nancy Carlton stopped by her desk. "Kim, Nancy Noe just showed up, I'm going to let her run you home. They're going to question you. It seems that you might have been the last one to see Christa alive."

Kim thought about that for a moment . . . how Christa had bumped into her car mirror when she jumped out of her car . . . how she had invited her in . . . The implications of possibilities if she had accepted began to hit home.

Nancy Noe was grim-faced as she drove through the night with Kim sitting beside her.

"You do know what happened, don't you?" Nancy Noe finally blurted out.

"No. What do you mean?"

When Nancy Noe told her the grotesque details, Kim began to scream.

*   *   *

When Kim had called Christa earlier—twice—she hadn't really paid attention to the sound of Christa's voice on her answering machine. Now she realized that while she was waiting on the line for Christa to pick up the phone, Christa had been separated from herself in the silent apartment, the answering machine talking mechanically, the voice all that was left of Christa Hoyt.

Once home, Kim called her grandmother in Starke twenty-five miles away to tell her she was okay. Starke, Florida, where another serial killer was put to death in the electric chair—Ted Bundy.

The night Christa Hoyt was killed Manny Taboada's former roommate, Armando Careaga, called to find out what he was up to for the weekend.

"I'll be working at Bennigan's."

"Did Tracy move in yet?"

Manny said she had and, lightheartedly, added that she didn't keep her side of the apartment as clean as Armando used to keep his.

"You're not sorry she's there, are you?"

"Not at all," Manny said. "We'll work it out. She's a good kid. Just trying to make you feel good, that's all. Like I miss you."

29

A Scream at Gatorwood

Blood dries dark on black clothing. He knew when he put on the black clothes that he was going to have blood on them before the night was over.

At 10:30 P.M. that fatal Sunday, August 26th, Manuel Taboada's mother, Gladys Taboada called his apartment from her home in Hialeah. Tracy Paules, his roommate, answered and took the message.

"Have him call me when he gets in, no matter how late," his mother said.

Tracy was worried that Manny wasn't home yet, that she was alone.

1:30 A.M., shortly after Christa Hoyt's mutilated body was found, the killer stalked Tracy. Ever the voyeur, now turned killer, he peeped into her window; she was going to be his next victim. But, even at this hour, there were still people about. He had to duck down into the bushes when they came by. It wasn't safe. He decided to return later when he was sure the complex would be silent for the night.

When Manny finally got in at two A.M. from his new job at *Bennigan's,* he thought it was too late to return his mother's call. He would call her the next morning. He never did.

Once again, the first two murders—the only ones they knew about—became the main topic of Tracy's conversation, but Manny reassured her that they were safe together.

They said goodnight and went to their separate rooms.

He fell asleep immediately leaving his door open a crack for Sasha.

Tracy was restless. She lay in bed staring at the ceiling for a while before falling asleep.

When the silent predator returned, it was approximately three A.M.

He jimmied the pin out of the sliding glass door with the point of his

Stanley screwdriver. It made a loud popping sound. He paused . . . listened . . . it had not been heard.

As he entered the living room, he waited until his eyes became accustomed to the dark. In a reversal of the customary police procedure of "securing" a location, he had to clear the area to suit his own needs. He pushed in the partially open door and slipped quietly into the dark room where the young man slept in a red Bacardi Rum T-shirt and shorts.

A man.

Rolling looked at the large figure in the bed. He hesitated. He hadn't expected to find a man; he hadn't been present when he had peeked into the apartment earlier. Now he knew if he wanted to get to the girl—and he did—he had to eliminate the man first. The guy was asleep. He had him beat.

Manny stirred, sensing a malevolent presence even in his sleep.

Too late. The killer raised the knife, which extended his arm by eight inches of steel. He plunged the blade into the sleeping man with such force that it ripped all the way through to the solar plexis region of the 6 foot 3, former football player, and penetrated through to his thoracic vertebrae.

But Manny surprised him. Even with such a lethal knife blow, he fought back. Awake now, Manny instinctively knew he was in a life-and-death struggle, a fight for his life. "Bastard!" he cried.

Rolling suddenly became terrified. The guy was big and more powerful than he had realized. Manny actually got in a couple of blows that almost knocked him out. Fighting now to keep from losing consciousness, he continued to strike at Manny as hard and as fast as he could. The knife sliced at his face, cutting a gaping wound along his chin. Still, Manny managed to grab his silent attacker, cursed him, held him close in a bear hug. His own strength was so great that he almost had the murderous intruder. "Son of a bitch!" he cried, trying even in the middle of his own life-and-death struggle to warn Tracy. To give her a chance to get away.

Manny struggled for a full minute before it was over. Rolling couldn't believe it. Even with all the stab wounds, the guy was putting up one hell of a fight. But the life blood was quickly draining out of the two hundred-pound young man, weakening him; he was no longer a match for his equally strong assailant who had the advantage of a deadly knife on his side. The killer finally managed to pull back enough to plunge the knife into him and pull hard and up. It was the lethal blow, opening up his chest with a jagged diagonal incision from left to right.

The powerful athlete, in the prime of young manhood, finally fell back and lay still. It had taken an unbelievable thirty-one stab wounds to his chest, face, arms, hands and legs before the killer could subdue him.

When he died, he had a piece of Rolling's black ninja shirt clutched in his hand.

Tracy finally heard the commotion and opened her door. Holding a hair-curling iron in her hand, she emerged from her room at the very last moment of the life-and-death battle. The moment she saw Rolling, in black ninja outfit and ski mask still hovering over Manny, she put it all together. She screamed and dashed for her bedroom. Rolling came after her. She locked her door. He kicked it open. She backed up as he came at her, his black clothes drenched in Manny's blood.

"You're the one, aren't you?" she asked terrified.

"Yeah," he answered. "I'm the one."

Jenny jumped at the sound, got out of bed and went to Amelia's room. Amelia was sitting up in her bed.

"Did you hear that?"

She had. What did Jenny think it was?

"It sounded like a scream."

They were both thinking the same thing. They were still reeling from the discovery of the two girls at Williamsburg. That wasn't so far away. They did not yet know about Christa Hoyt.

Jenny looked around and then listened at the door.

"Don't put the lights on."

"I'm not."

"Is everything locked?"

"Yes."

They went back to bed, only to be startled by an inexplicable banging on their sliding glass door.

Jenny and Amelia were not the only ones who heard the scream.

Scott Hamel in Apartment 1305 heard it too. He couldn't tell which direction the sound came from. He thought someone was having a party and dismissed it at that. He went back to sleep . . .

Marleen Scandera, who roomed with Stella Zaffarano and Tammy Lynn Doll in Apartment 1207 located directly above that of Manny and Tracy, also heard the scream but thought she may have been dreaming . . .

In the next room Stella, who had been so frightened by the murders she had asked her boyfriend David LeRoy to spend the night, was awakened by him.

"What's the matter?"

"I heard a scream. Loud. And a crash."

"Who?"

"I don't know. It was a girl."

Stella looked at the digital clock on the nightstand next to the bed. Three A.M.

Stella, Marleen and Tammy watched as David checked the hallway. He didn't see anything.

He slid open the glass door onto the balcony and looked outside. Nothing. He stepped out onto the balcony to look around. Parked nearby he could see two golf carts that belonged to the maintenance staff and a Service Master carpet and furniture cleaning truck. Suspended over the empty lounge chairs on many of the adjoining balconies were all sizes and shapes of hanging plants swinging gently in the breeze of a seventy-one-degree night.

He shook his head as he reentered the apartment and slid the door closed.

One of the girls dismissed the noise as the sound of partying. She asked though, "Did you lock the door?"

He locked it and slipped in the pin and they all went back to bed.

As he taped her hands behind her back, Tracy said to him, "You're gonna get caught." Her last words.

He taped her mouth shut.

She was wearing only a T-shirt. Tracy's shirt was cut vertically up the front and horizontally left to right through both sleeves, in order to cut off the arms of the T-shirt. Tauntingly, he told her what he was going to do to her. Over her muffled protests, he played with her sexually for a protracted period of time . . . turned her over . . . raped her anally. Still unable to look at them face to face when he killed, he stabbed her again and again in the back.

Then he dragged her body into the hallway between the bathroom and living room, where he posed her in a lewd, spread-out position. He removed the tape. She wasn't dead yet. He went into the bathroom, got a washcloth, wiped the blood from her face and raped her again. He took a towel out of the bathroom, hoisted her up and put it underneath her hips. Now came the cleanup. He washed her body off, noticing with contemptuous interest the way she shaved herself . . . because of those bathing suits that showed just about everything, he thought. He douched her vagina with a liquid detergent he found in the apartment and wiped her with a white muscle shirt from Manny's dresser.

This one took a long time to die.

He waited and watched.

*   *   *

When he burglarized the apartment he took a black muscle T-shirt of Manny's that was on the dresser. He left the apartment in the early dawn. But he had a problem: blood covered his clothes. He jumped in the Gatorwood pool to wash off the evidence of a bloody night's work. No one heard the splash.

The Gatorwood entrance, always well-lit at night with ball lights, was deserted. The blue-and-orange pennant hung listlessly on the twenty-foot flagpole.

7:00 A.M.

Lt. Alan Baxter stayed at the scene of Christa's murder even after his responsibilities had ended. He couldn't seem to pull himself away, as though leaving would somehow detract from the gravity of what had happened. He met with the second shift at seven A.M. and gave them a review of what had happened.

An hour later, one of the men came over to him. "Do you remember that waitress at IHOP, Ann? The friendly one? I think her full name's Theresa Ann Garren."

"Yeah, sure."

"She's Christa Hoyt's mother."

Alan Baxter swallowed. "Oh." That was a tough one, he hadn't expected that. The last names were different. Only last week Ann had casually touched him on his shoulder as he sat at IHOP when she passed by him.

He finally left to go home. He had a desperate need to see his wife and two small children.

9:00 A.M.

Mitch Stacy went to Williamsburg Village Apartments with photographer Steven Morton, who took the Gainesville *Sun*'s front-page photo of GPD Officer Brian Helmerson standing with his sunglasses in front of Apartment 113 with the taut yellow tape stretched in front of the townhouse.

There were a great many people standing around, several news trucks and a couple of TV satellite trucks that had come in. Stacy interviewed as many of the Williamsburg residents as would talk to him.

"Looks like everyone who lives here is scared to death," he said to Steven.

*   *   *

Mitch Stacy was already back at his desk at the Gainesville *Sun* when Holly Stacy arrived at her regular classes at the UF Law School, not knowing as yet that there had been a third murder. *Sun* reporter Tom Lyons had worked all night and was now back in the Gainesville *Sun* offices. Having been on press alert, Tom was called out on Christa Hoyt's murder and had gone to the scene shortly after discovery. He now briefed Mitch that there were three. As for Holly, when she first heard it she didn't believe any of it. Gossip already had it that there was a fourth murder and even a fifth. Since she was an obituary writer for the Gainesville *Sun*, she knew she would find out what was really going on when she arrived at work at four A.M. Until then she dismissed it all as irresponsible rumormongering.

By this time all of the *Sun* reporters were called in—Susan Dewey, Cindy Barnett, Ron Dupont—they realized for the first time the true magnitude of the story, and the fact that there were no suspects.

Monday, August 27—Late Morning

Rolling was now at his campsite. He had to eat too, just like the rest of them. Nobody was giving him any work. Not that he had been looking; he had given up looking for a job a long time ago. But here he was in that same predicament again, a predicament that he felt had been forced on him by people who certainly didn't care a hoot in hell about him. He had no choice. He was out of money and he knew he was going to have to move out of the area soon.

Late that Monday morning, he robbed the First Union National Bank on SW Archer Road at gunpoint. The bank was located less than a mile from Christa Hoyt's apartment. The five hundred dollars he had given Ford for the gun in Sarasota was finally paying off.

When he got back to his campsite and opened the parcels of money handed over by the cashiers, the money pack exploded with a blast of pink dye. Pink dye all over everything. Grocery stores and supermarkets were easier. At least they didn't have marked money that exploded on you. He couldn't use this stuff!

Kim Norman's supervisor Nancy Carlton had looked at her closely as she reappeared at the Alachua County sheriff's office, this time dressed in uniform for the long day ahead. She seemed in control.

Questioned the whole day of Monday, Kim knew they believed she might have been a victim herself when she realized they were trying to pinpoint the time that Christa was murdered. They told her Christa had come home from playing racquetball. ". . . Instead of going to the party . . ." she thought out loud. She had picked up some chicken and some donuts. They were never eaten. They were left on the table.

"I guess those pigs ate it," she said in a brief lull. "I guess when they got finished they had worked up an appetite." At this point it seemed such horror had to have been the work of more than one.

Pat Mann did not hear from her husband, Spencer, until late that afternoon when she was busy with her Monday cleaning. He called to tell her he would not be home.

"Bad case?"

"Really bad," he said sorrowfully. "And I have to tell the parents."

Difficult though it was, she thought he was the right person to perform that somber duty. It had often fallen to him to console family and friends of homicide victims. He was a very professional, very caring person. He cared about what he did and about the people around him. Pat always felt that Spencer had been given a special grace. He had the right sensitivity for grieving people in times like these and always seemed to know the right words. Some have more of a gift of mercy than others. She didn't know if she could do it with as much compassion as he.

When Spencer Mann told Ann Garren at her place of employment, her first reaction was, "I want to see my daughter."

Not now, Spencer Mann told her quietly. He had not told her all of what had happened to Christa. He wanted to wait for the father to be on hand.

He told the whole story to Mr. Hoyt at his place of employment, Bell Labs. It was the most difficult thing he had ever done in his life.

Sonja Larson's dental records were of poor quality and could not be faxed to Gainesville. Detective Reslowski in Deerfield Beach said he would send them via Delta Airlines; the x-rays and dental records would arrive in Gainesville at 15:15 hrs on Monday, August 27, 1993. They could be picked up at the Delta service counter.

8:00 P.M.

The press conference was held in one of the small rooms at the Gaines-ville Police Department. Mitch Stacy spoke: "We heard that this guy is getting in by sliding glass doors so you better let us know so that other people can protect themselves."

At the *Sun*, the phones were ringing. Mitch called a close friend who was in law enforcement. It was very late Monday night when his friend told him that he had been in Christa's apartment and had seen her head on the shelf. "When you walked in the front door it was right in front of you." It was propped up. There was a mirror next to it so that anyone who looked in the window would be able to see the reflection of the head. "It was the worst thing I've ever seen in my life," the friend said. Mitch went to Lyons. "I got a confirmation on the decapitation."

8:30 P.M.

Lydia Huber worked at Movie Time Video at the northeast corner of 16th Avenue and 43rd Street. The man was wearing dark-rimmed glasses, lime-green shorts, a T-shirt and Reeboks. He walked into the store just before closing. He was between thirty and thirty-five years old, six feet tall, one hundred ninety to two hundred pounds, receding hairline and long dark curly hair hanging just below the shoulders.

"Do y'all have to be a member to rent a video?"

"No."

There was some discussion about the subject but he did not really seem interested and left.

When the store closed at nine that night and she left to go home, Lydia became aware that the same man was silently following her toward her car. As she picked up her pace, so did the man. When she slowed down, so did he. It was like a bad slasher film. Two men passing by in a truck noticed that she was being followed and slowed down in the parking lot near her. The man stopped and pretended to look for something in his pockets.

Lydia ran in front of the truck until she reached her car, got into it and locked the doors. The truck slowly pulled away.

In her rearview mirror she watched the man standing in the parking lot looking in her direction.

As she started up her car she decided to color her hair reddish brown.

* * *

That evening Khris Pascarella called Tracy Paules again and again from Miami with increasing urgency; by then the news about Christa's murder was all over the Miami TV.

But neither Tracy nor Manny answered the phone. Perhaps they had gone out. Somewhere.

Shock was setting in. Parents were besieging the universities with calls. Students were beginning to leave. The pressure was greater than after the first two deaths, since there was a conviction that the three murders were related. The same person was involved. Except no one knew the details or the extent of mutilations involved. Whispers of a "Ripper" were beginning to make the rounds.

30

The Third Day

Tuesday, August 28
7:00 A.M.

After daylight had broken through the night and there was still no answer at Manny Taboada's and Tracy Paules' apartment, Khris Pascarella put in his phone call to manager Carol Hyde at Gatorwood. He also called a friend of Manny's, Tom Carroll, who lived in Gainesville, and asked him to check up on them.

Tom arrived at the Gatorwood complex before seven A.M. and was waiting outside the apartment when Christopher Smith, a maintenance man, showed up at manager Carol Hyde's request.

"I knocked, but there's no answer," Tom told him, "and the door's locked."

"No problem, I have a key."

As soon as Christopher Smith unlocked and opened the door he saw Tracy's body lying in the hallway between the two bedrooms. With a sharp intake of breath he grasped the door. In spite of all the talk and rumors about the other three brutal murders he had not expected to find this. Other people found things like this. Tom Carroll saw her over the maintenance man's shoulder. She had been left in the hall. She was on her back, spread-eagled, nude. She appeared to have been repeatedly stabbed in the chest and to have bled profusely. No clean-up attempts this time.

Before slamming the door shut on the scene Smith noticed a dark-colored bag lying on the floor above her head.

Smith locked the door behind him to keep people from entering the apartment before the police came. Tom followed Smith as he hurried out of the building. He waited outside for him in shock, not believing what he had seen, wondering how he was going to tell Khris. And the family. And what about Manny? Where was he?

In no more than five minutes Smith returned with the police and found the door to the apartment unlocked. They opened the door slowly. There she was. It was true. But the dark-colored bag on the floor above Tracy's head was gone. Smith could not understand it. Unless . . . the killer was still there.

Tracy and Manny were not mutilated but it looked as though it had been a frenzied, violent scene. Maybe the killer didn't get a chance to complete the sadistic ritual he had practiced on the others. Christina and Sonja were bad enough. Christa's mutilation went a step further. What had he in store for Tracy and Manny if he had not been interrupted? Sprawled on her back, Tracy had been found with a towel placed under her hips. What had he done between the hours when the first scream was heard and Smith unlocked the door? Had they interrupted him? Was the killer actually still in the apartment when he unlocked the door? Then again, Smith thought, maybe he was mistaken about the locked door and the dark bag. He was in a state of shock. Anything was possible.

By nine A.M. the news about Christa Hoyt was spread over the front pages of the newspapers. The public did not know yet about Tracy Paules and Manny Taboada. Only the police knew and those who had the misfortune to find them.

State Attorney Len Register was coming in to work when he heard the news. Ordinarily, following the chain of command, the prosecutor's investigators would call the chief investigator and he in turn would notify Register. This time someone blurted it to him in the hallway. *Two more. Five.* A young man too. He turned and went straight to Gatorwood.

When he got to the parking lot not far from the apartment where it happened he could see that, once again, all the senior detectives from the sheriff's office were present. The look on people's faces was beyond grief, beyond disbelief, surely beyond understanding. Somebody was going around killing these kids at random. This menace had to be stopped.

Manny Taboada was stabbed while in bed. A man his size, he had to have been surprised. Tracy Paules' hair was wet when she was found. Had she just gotten out of the shower? There was a towel under Tracy's hips. It seemed she had been raped anally. The lab would report a rectal swabbing that turned out to have semen in it. There would be enough sperm to do at least one DNA test. The blood on her stab wounds indicated that she lived for about twenty minutes after being stabbed. Apparently not as quick as the others. She had also been left on display.

Sgt. Alan Baxter and other investigators from the Alachua County sheriff's office worked the crime scene at Gatorwood as they had Christa Hoyt's. In a prodigious understatement, it was clear, with the discovery of the fourth and fifth bodies, that Gainesville had one very big problem.

"I've never been associated with a crime scene that had so many violent attacks and so little evidence behind," said Michael West, a forensic expert from Hattiesville, Mississippi, who was called in to go over the apartments with a high-tech, light-sensitive device that would detect previously unnoticed fingerprints.

The only physical evidence—semen and five pubic hairs—would require time-consuming, state-of-the-art scientific inquiry before it could be used to identify or eliminate potential suspects.

The body count in the killing spree had reached five. A killing pattern had been developing with the violent deaths of young girls. Vicious sexual attacks. Now there was a new component—a male. Authorities said evidence suggested that all had died at the hands of the same killer, or killers.

It was not long before the terrified Florida community was thrust into the glare of a national spotlight:

Roger Smith, assistant national editor for the Los Angeles *Times*, pointed out:

> People are fascinated by serial killers and the fact that the victims were all young college students makes the slayings even more sensational.

Newsweek played up the killer's similarity with his nineteenth-century counterpart:

> The mutilations, the skilled use of a razor-sharp blade and the macabre display of the severed head—all this was eerily reminiscent of the most infamous serial killer of all, Jack the Ripper. The Ripper, who terrorized Victorian London in the fall of 1888, eviscerated four of his five women victims. In one case, he used body parts to decorate the crime scene. Jack the Ripper was never caught.

"Never caught." Words to haunt police.

Capt. Richard B. Ward stated: "We're going to solve this case. You can take that to the bank!" His wife barricaded their door and kept a pistol on the kitchen counter . . . Lt. Spencer Mann insisted his wife Pat and their children move in with her parents, Howard and Tillie Southerland. He was working long hours with little sleep and did not want to have to worry about their safety. Their own home was out of town on quite a bit of acreage . . . Len Register sent his wife and children to his wife's mother in Orlando. It was a long shot—but his wife was a brunette, the same size as Christa. Their dog remained inside the house at all times and she toted

Len's off-duty gun around. She knew how to handle it, she was ex-military police.

People were turning each other in at alarming rates. It was a perfect time to indulge gripes against past lovers, friends, husbands, neighbors. Anyone who acted strangely was likely to be reported to the police. Jail inmates accused each other. Hundreds were questioned, shown photo packs, anyone who came into possible contact with the victims, including students who lived in or near the apartment complexes where the murders had occurred. One person who was seen in a restaurant reading a book entitled *Killing the Spirit* was turned in to the police and attacked as a suspect. A check with the county library and a local bookstore revealed that the subject matter of the book was higher education.

When the police began canvassing the neighborhoods for information, multiple fingers began to point in the direction of a young man who had repeatedly attracted attention to himself during the past summer with his erratic behavior. His name was Edward Lewis Humphrey.

31

Profile of a Red Herring

If this were a classic mystery novel—which, of course, it is not—at the time in this story it was definitely a "whodunit" so far as the authorities and public were concerned. And Ed Humphrey would have been the classic red herring of the piece, the character to divert attention from the true culprit by his *seemingly* plausible guilt, whether from behavior or history or words or a combination of all three.

Born October 5, 1971, to Elna and George Humphrey in Boston, Massachusetts, his paternity might seem incongruous with his later life— George Humphrey was attending the prestigious Harvard School of Business Administration at the time of Edward Lewis' birth. But a curriculum vitae rarely provides the whole story. In fact, the Humphrey family was divided by marital dissension; it was said that George became disenchanted and wanted out of the marriage while Elna, a Catholic, did not. There were tales of an abusive husband, a drinking wife, a small boy frightened to the point of not being able to sleep, suffering bed-wetting, nightmares, not to mention sleepwalking. His grandma was his protection. A fifth-generation Floridian, she did not like to see her grandson behaving so frightened. She and her family were strong stock, and she wanted him to be in that tradition. Nonetheless, she drew closer and closer to him, and their relationship would evolve into a close and highly emotional one.

At fifteen, Ed Humphrey seemed to be developing well. He was an A student at Melbourne High School in Indialantic, Florida, a hundred miles north of Miami. Tall for his age, with a headful of floppy golden hair and a winning smile, he still suffered from occasional bouts of sleepwalking and enuresis, but there seemed no other manifest emotional problems. By most standards, his boyhood spent with his sister Susan and his older brothers George and Dan seemed normal. Ed especially admired his brother George, and apparently worked hard to live up to his image of George. He told his family that his ambition was to do well in high school and go to a first-rate medical school. His relationship with his protective grandmother was strong, especially with his father gone and his mother having her problems with alcohol.

And then Ed Humphrey began to change. It started slowly. He felt tired most of the time, even falling asleep at the dinner table. He fell behind in his schoolwork. Finally he was diagnosed as having mononucleosis. He had to stay home from school. A tutor was provided but his illness persisted and with it a sense of depression. He began to show early signs of extreme mood swings—from being bright and overly energetic to depressed and suicidal. At first it was thought his symptoms were the result of the mononucleosis, but blood tests showed he was free of the disease and yet the mood swings persisted. Suddenly Ed was acting in an uncharacteristically cocky fashion—"I'm right on top," he told his older brother George. He felt great, he didn't have to sleep, he said. George had to wonder if he was perhaps taking some drugs, and Ed countered that he didn't need such stuff. Everything was terrific, until he crashed and became despondent. At this point even his grandma was of little help; she didn't know what to do with him. And the family situation didn't help. George and Elna had gotten a divorce, people were living under one roof with all their various tensions and pressures. Ed's behavior now included bouts of irritability and anger, even directed at his grandmother. Finally the boy was diagnosed as a manic-depressive and committed to a hospital. He was treated with lithium carbonate, which tended to control the mood swings. Brother George, however, thought the home atmosphere had also contributed to Ed's problems, and when Ed was released from the hospital in early 1988, having dropped out of high school, George suggested he come with him to Gainesville, where George was entering the University of Florida Law School. He liked the idea, and though Grandma only reluctantly agreed, Ed moved to Gainesville with his brother George.

The acting-out increased. One day George came across a new chain saw on the floor beside the closet where Ed kept his clothes. When he asked Ed why he had bought it, he said to cut down some trees. Except there weren't any trees in the area. On an outing to Crescent Beach with George and his girlfriend Jeannie, Ed suddenly opened the back door of the car and pitched himself out onto the pavement. George was shocked by his brother's act, and even Ed seemed to be, because when he was released from Sands psychiatric ward he was noticeably more subdued, and when he went back to Melbourne to his mother and grandmother he also went back to Melbourne High School and made up enough courses to graduate. Throughout this time, he took his medicine regularly to combat the manic-depressive bouts.

The situation did not hold. Ed became seriously argumentative with his grandma and mother. He began to skip his medicine. He thought that Satan was after him, that Satan was everywhere. His sister Susan, bewildered by his behavior, felt that it was in Sands hospital that Ed had gotten the crazy stuff in his head about a ninja and developed a sudden interest in knives and Rambo-type characters and began embarrassing public displays of militaristic behavior . . . "recon," "lock and load," he would blurt out. He was picked up and detained for trespassing at Patrick Air Force Base, telling the people there that he had been a first-aid counselor for Cub Scout week at the base in 1982. They confiscated two hunting knives and told him not to come back.

Ed would try suicide again, this time by crashing a Mercury Marquis into a utility pole. He sustained extensive facial cuts. Later to his friend Brian Cruickshank he said that he purposely jumped from the car in Gainesville and drove his own car intentionally into the utility pole. Why? His life was miserable, he said, worse than anybody's. And suddenly Ed assumed a kung-fu stance and began doing a series of karate kicks. He also told Brian that he had gotten into a fight with some guy who took his skateboard on the Indialantic boardwalk. Nobody had better mess with him, he showed the guy a thing or two. Jeff Goldstein, who with friends was minding his business on the boardwalk, was attacked by Ed. His friends called the police. When Catherine Palmer of the Juvenile Alternative Service tried to have Ed brought in for an intake meeting, Ed's mother Elna refused and told Ms. Palmer he was in the hospital on account of head injuries he had sustained in some fights. She said he was a manic-depressive and didn't take his medicine. He would be stabilized at the hospital and that would be that. But there was a hearing at the Juvenile Alternative Service, at which Ed appeared to be remorseful and apologized. His mother said he didn't need to do that but Ed insisted. It was to be a familiar pattern.

He now returned to Gainesville and finished a summer session at the University of Florida on June 23, but when he was back in Melbourne his behavior became more violent and irrational. His mother and grandmother believed it was because he didn't take his medicine. He angrily denied that. During a party in his room he railed against his grandmother —who throughout his life was the protective one—not his mother, calling his grandmother a bitch to one of the girls at the party.

He was compiling a history, a damaging one. He would complain to one of the waiters at Skeeter's in Gainesville that he couldn't get a girl because of the scars he had and the weight he'd gained. To an auto mechanic fixing his car he said he was going to join the army and go to Iraq. He had to recon the area . . .

Ed's bizarre behavior was also becoming well-known among residents of the Gatorwood Apartments. For a time he lived in a building across the parking lot from Manny Taboada and often went across to Gatorwood, apparently in an attempt to make friends with those he saw around the pool; he'd had little social success in the complex where he lived. Indeed, he tried very hard to make friends with people who lived in his own complex . . . walking in and out of their apartments, at times uninvited. When they locked him out he would try to look beyond the drapes of their rooms. A few of the girls became frightened of him and avoided him whenever they saw him coming.

At Gatorwood Apartments rental office, manager Carol Hyde did not know when she rented Apartment 1104 to Aaf Kira, Jeffrey and Steve Bunin on June 22, 1990, that the troublesome young man was also going to move into the apartment with them a couple of days after they signed their lease. Had she known he was going to be invited to join them at Gatorwood to help defray expenses she might have objected. The first she heard of his presence in the complex was when tenant complaints from Catherine and Tom Adams came into the management office in the early evening hours about the fight that had erupted on the basketball court between him and his new roommates on July 4. By the time the police were called the altercation had moved to their apartment. Neighbors could hear the fighting and arguing through the walls; it sounded as though it was becoming physical. They could hear the crashes as some furniture was thrown into the hallway outside Apartment 1104 during the fight.

Finally Ed was thrown out of the apartment and told he was weird, he walked in his sleep and they didn't want him around anymore. He yelled at them that his father was a colonel in the army, that he was a marine and the marines had jurisdiction over the sheriff . . . this when they threatened to call the police. Later at the Gatorwood pool, dried blood across his mouth and nose, he was told by the maintenance man that he would have to leave, to which he replied that they were all sinners and God was going to kill them. When told he might have to leave Gatorwood, he picked up a chair and charged at them. The chair crashed into the fence behind them. A police officer who lived at the complex came onto the scene and later would describe Ed as "acting mental." His roommates told management they were afraid of Humphrey . . . "a goddamned weirdo." The next day Mrs. Hyde had a telephone conversation with Ed's mother and they agreed he should move out of the apartment, which he did . . .

The noose was tightening around Ed Humphrey's neck as the most likely suspect for the murders committed by Danny Rolling. His profile as best red herring was being convincingly built. The visible trail of irrational confrontations he was leaving behind would set him up, and, indeed, would never cease to haunt him.

*   *   *

On August 7, some two weeks before the Gainesville murders, Bruce Einchen, Jr., was hitchhiking in the area of the Beeline Expressway in Orlando, Florida, when Ed, en route to Montana to see his uncle and a girl he'd become obsessed with when he was there previously, picked him up in a white Cadillac. Ed said he had to stop over at his girlfriend's place in Gainesville. That was okay with Einchen. Ed and Einchen went to the apartment of Jeannie and Julie Goforth, the former of whom was his brother George's girlfriend, and they allowed him to take a shower.

After some three hours Ed and Einchen were on the road again, and arrived in the Pensacola area during the early morning hours of August 8. While there they picked up a third hitchhiker, Rick, and made their way north, catching I–65 and eventually reaching Birmingham, Alabama, where they pulled off the road to eat. Ed would never make it to Montana. He was arrested in Ordway, Colorado, for disorderly conduct and not having money to pay for a tank of gas. He claimed hitchhikers had stolen it, but the gas-station attendant was having none of it and called the police. He split up then with the hitchhikers and was in custody some twenty-four hours for banging on the walls and swearing as well as for not paying the attendant. The police also impounded his 1979 Cadillac with the Florida license plates.

Grandma and her sister Ann Davies would fly to Colorado and rescue Ed, who was hardly grateful. His grandmother and great-aunt, rather than put up with him at home, brought him to Gainesville and enrolled him in the summer session. His grandmother also bought him another Cadillac.

It was now Wednesday, August 16, in Gainesville.

Kellie Chesser was waiting on tables at Shoney's when Ed came in and ordered breakfast for himself and coffee for his grandmother, who joined him a few minutes later.

From her station Kellie could hear them arguing. His grandmother told him to calm down. He went to the restroom three or four times. Finally his grandma said she couldn't handle it, paid the check and left. When Kellie went to check on Ed to see if he wanted something else, he called his grandmother a fucking bitch and left shortly afterward.

She was waiting for him in her room at the Holiday Inn, and setting aside the last of their arguments, they set out in her car to see apartments, during which time Ed got into a wrangle with his grandmother, was told by the manager of the Cov Homes Apartments, Mrs. Class, that he should respect his grandmother, told her to mind her own business, bitch, and was told by a man who happened to be in the lobby to settle down.

Grandma had gone out to the parking lot when Ed began to use profanity. He followed her out. Mrs. Class and Watson watched them from the door as the boy continued his verbal assaults on the old woman. He yelled at her to open the trunk, he wanted to get his gun. Frightened, Mrs. Class called the police for assistance, but Grandma managed to get her grandson into the car before the police arrived.

His grandmother got him an apartment at Hawaiian Village Apartments, where Ed told Garrison, a maintenance man, how he liked camping out military style, how he had just come back from a trip out west and had just broken up with his girlfriend. He told Garrison about the hitchhiker he had picked up and dumped because "the guy was getting on my nerves." Without elaborating he said that the hitchhiker was driving the car and got them into an accident. He also told Garrison about being arrested for stealing gasoline and how the police had kept his car. He ended up with: "I'm mad at my grandmother because she wouldn't help me to get my car back and she's making me go back to school."

JoAnn Adelberger, manager of Hawaiian Village, held his signed lease in her hand. At the end of the lease there was enough space for five separate individual tenant signatures. Ed had signed every line, "Edward Lewis Humphrey," one after the other.

JoAnn thought back to the moment the family walked into the office. Even that was a bit odd. He had followed his grandmother and his aunt into the office like a little boy. Ordinarily young prospective tenants came in by themselves and picked out their own apartments. But it was the grandmother and the aunt who had picked it out for him. When JoAnn showed the lease to Jeanette Baer, her co-manager, she too noted he had signed his name five times. No one had ever done that before. Jeanette wondered if he was slow mentally.

No, but he didn't seem to have any common sense, JoAnn said. No matter what he did in Gainesville, Ed couldn't avoid calling attention to himself.

Early morning in his new apartment in the Hawaiian Village apartment complex, Ed went to the security office in Tolbert Hall, where Raymond Sumpter and Steve Records were on duty. Ed did not seem to have come to security for any specific reason; instead he began talking about joining the Rangers and about the problems in the Middle East. He hoped the fighting held off until he could join up, he said, so he could go kill people. It was a bizarre, though very memorable, forty-five minutes with the strange young man.

* * *

That same day, around 6:30 P.M., Wendy Fay Jaguette took a dinner break from her job at Friedman Jewelers at Oaks Mall. She ate at Deli I, then walked to Barney's for coffee. Immediately after she sat down an unkempt-looking young man approached her. He was wearing a cut-off sweatshirt, and his stomach was protruding over old green fatigue pants that had a tear in one thigh. He said his name was Ed and asked her if she went to UF. She said she did not. He insisted she was in one of his classes during Session A. She wasn't sure how to respond to his insistence. She took a closer look. His hair was blondish brown and messy. Through a one- or two-day beard she could see a thin red scar running vertically down the left side of his face. He had another scar on the other cheek and one on his forehead.

He said he'd had to drop calculus because he was joining the Eighty-second Airborne and going to Kuwait. What followed was a most peculiar dialogue that went like this: "I really believe in God. Do you?" He didn't wait for an answer but continued on with a solid shake of his head. "I think God's mad at me. He must be. Suicide is a sin. Even if you don't make it. I pray a lot. Are you married?" "No." "Will you go out with me before I go to Kuwait?" "I have a boyfriend." He became angry. "I don't know why you won't go out with me. A friend of mine in the military was recently killed."

He appeared depressed about his friend, then his mood switched and he began talking about bombs and missiles. "Do you know what a banana clip is? An M-Fourteen, M-Sixteen? Would you shoot someone?" It went like that until she said she had to leave and got up to walk away. He walked after her. "My name's Ed," he said, stopping her. "Edward Lewis Humphrey."

9:30 P.M.

He finally went back to Hawaiian Village and learned his grandmother was waiting for him at Best Western. He went to meet the old bitch. Actually, although he would never admit it to himself, he was glad to see her. The symbiotic attachment was just as strong from him to her as it was from her to him even though on a conscious level he resisted it vehemently.

At 9:37 P.M. and 10:48 P.M. they tried to call George at home, but it was too soon.

The other men in his family, George L. Humphrey, Daniel H. Humphrey and their father, George E. Humphrey, landed in Newark, New Jersey, on a Continental flight from London, England.

George Sr. took his leave and continued west while George Jr. and Daniel flew to Miami, arriving at 9:30 P.M. before continuing on the last lap of their flight to Melbourne.

32

High Visibility

It was Ed Humphrey's worst period of acting out; so close to the murders, the timing could not have been more inopportune for him. He was still struggling with his identity and the perverse effects of his illness. Once again, he inexplicably neglected to take his medication. Once again, he stood out wherever he went. Once again, he became argumentative and hostile at the slightest provocation. And each of his actions would eventually become part of intensive investigative reports.

Unable to sleep, he usually was up all night. When he walked into Roy Rogers and approached the counter where Ms. Howell and Ms. McCarthy were on duty, he smelled of gasoline. A dark baseball hat over dirty blond hair, he appeared disheveled in his dark pants and army jacket. Had he been stealing gasoline? Ms. McCarthy wondered. She moved away as he ordered biscuits and gravy from Ms. Howell. When told they didn't have gravy he became irate.

"Roy Rogers said you sell biscuits and gravy!"

"We only have biscuits, if you want one."

"I'll take the biscuit."

"Forty-nine cents."

Humphrey handed her thirty-five cents.

"You owe fourteen cents more."

He became verbally abusive, causing heads to turn in his direction. He slammed his baseball cap on the counter, and she let the fourteen-cents issue drop.

"Are you tired?" he asked.

"Yes."

"I'm tired too. I've been up for five days."

She watched him as he walked out of the plaza through the northbound doors. As he exited, part of the biscuit dropped on the floor.

He had forgotten his baseball hat on the counter.

An hour later, he returned; he had another baseball cap on his head and three or four more stuffed in his pants pocket. He apologized for his earlier behavior and announced he'd be leaving the next week for the Eighty-second Airborne.

Ed could not help making himself known every place he went. Flashing his presence like a blinking neon sign, he was impossible to forget. He left a trail that was highly visible and memorable enough to be reported at length when a murderer was being sought.

At 4:15 P.M. Ed tried to retrieve his bicycle. He had lost the key and it was still shackled to the bicycle rack at Gatorwood. He approached the maintenance man, Chris Smith.

"I would appreciate it if you could cut the lock for me," Ed said.

But Chris didn't trust the young man. Remembering the altercation caused by Ed not long ago at the Gatorwood poolside when he charged at him and Carol Hyde with a lawn chair, Chris refused. "I can only do that if your former roommates confirm that it's your bike," he said. "If they tell me the bike is yours, I'll unchain it for you."

"They aren't home."

Chris provided Ed with paper from the Gatorwood office, and Ed left a note on the door of Apartment 1104 to ask his roommates to confirm his ownership of the bike to the office.

This incident placed Ed at Gatorwood Apartments between 4:00 and 4:30 P.M.

Not too far away, at nine P.M., Ed created still another memorable disturbance at the Central City Lounge at 201 West University Avenue when the doorman, Pat Siracusa, refused him entry. Ed was dressed in a dirty-looking sleeveless T-shirt and cotton shorts, and had what appeared to be a portable radio on his side connected to a set of earphones that hung down around his neck. Siracusa thought he was acting nervous, sweating even in the pouring rain that had turned the muggy night rather cool.

"I have to see your I.D.," Siracusa told him.

"I don't have it with me but I'm eighteen years old."

"Sorry," Siracusa said, pointing to manager Irene Sharp who was behind him in a glass enclosure. "The manager won't allow anyone in without identification."

Ed turned to look at her. "The bitch," he exploded. "I'm eighteen!"

Irene Sharp, who could hear him behind the glass enclosure, stepped from the booth. Even if he had a proper I.D., he looked like a trouble-maker. "I think you'd better leave," she said.

At that point Scott Greint, a second doorman, arrived, caught on to the situation and advised Ed to leave. "Right now."

Ed pointed his finger at the three of them. "You're all dead," he said.

"Bingo, bango, bongo! You're all dead!" He made slashing finger-across-his-throat gestures. "My people are going to come back and get you."

"What people?"

"I'm middleman for some drug dealer. I could cut your throat and you wouldn't even know it."

He began walking away but stopped frequently, turning back and saying, "You're all dead," before finally walking off eastbound on West University Avenue.

"I'm on recon!" he shouted to five male UF students he saw standing outside Manny's Lounge. "Don't mess with me!" When he thought one of them was eyeing his facial scars, he ran across the street and shouted, "Don't look at me!"

"I've seen this guy around before," one of the young men said. "Ignore him. He's total nuts."

But it was difficult to ignore Ed when he walked back across the street. "I could kill you guys! You ain't shit!"

Now it was their turn to cross the street away from him, leaving him standing in front of Manny's Lounge, but one of them started yelling at Ed from across the street.

Ed ran across to the men and took a karate stance, shouting, "I'm on recon! I'll cut your throat," and kicked one of the men in the left leg.

Once again Ed ran back across the street, and this time the five men started to go after him, then stopped dead in their tracks when they saw him reach into his black Cadillac. Maybe for a weapon. They decided to leave, confronting him wasn't worth it.

But they too would remember him.

So would the group of pledgers on fraternity row who had to deal with him later that night at SW 13th. They had to remove Ed forcibly when he insisted on joining them in their fraternity house.

He produced a penknife, which they mistook for a straight-edged razor. "I'll kill you, all of you!" he screamed, waving it around threateningly. "I'll get a gun too and then I'll shoot you."

The hole he kept digging for himself kept getting deeper and deeper.

Sitting at a table in Krispy Kreme Donuts, chewing an unlit cigar, reading a knife brochure, he had several days' growth of beard and clothes that looked like they had been slept in.

A girl he knew from the university, Ann Pave, walked in.

"Hi!" he called in a loud voice. "Are you still cutting up bodies?"

She laughed, knowing he was referring to the anatomy class she had been enrolled in. He insisted on sitting down with her.

"I've always wondered," he said, "how does the class get rid of the cadavers and body parts you use?"

She told him the body parts were put in plastic bags and incinerated.

"Does it bother you? Cutting people up?"

She shook her head. "No. There must be a little Ted Bundy in me."

"I have a friend who acts very much like Bundy," he said. "His name is John. He likes to stalk women and he likes knives."

They talked about Ted Bundy until she got up to leave.

"You take care now," she said. "You've got to watch out for the crazies out there."

"I'm the craziest of all."

She smiled. "I'll see you around, Ed."

She went out of the shop, and he followed her into the parking lot. "My name is John."

She watched him carefully as she continued to her car. Suddenly he began to rave about how he would act if one of the crazies were to pull a gun on him. "First I'd get these people by using a knife. Then I'd have them cut in little pieces! Gainesville's full of bastards and bitches who think they're too good and look down on people," he said. "You need to get to them before they get to you. John knows these people need to be taught a lesson." She looked at him with an almost clinical interest, as he began to refer to himself in the third person. "*He* knows they'd only be getting what they deserve."

"Come on, Ed."

"John," he insisted, pointing to himself. "John would cut these people up in little pieces and cut off their heads to make sure they didn't come back. People can be decapitated, you know, and it doesn't matter because they can grow two new heads. And he can gut them too."

"You shouldn't go around saying things like that," she said. "People might take you seriously."

"I want them to."

"Do you even have a knife?"

"Sure," he said, patting his leg to indicate he could be carrying one.

"I'm leaving now and I'm telling you, Ed, you shouldn't go around saying things like that."

It was almost six A.M. when JoAnn Adelberger, manager of Hawaiian Village Apartments, saw him. She had seen Ed earlier at three or four in the morning walking down University Avenue. The hours he kept were more than a little peculiar. Now he really frightened her as he suddenly appeared in the doorway of the laundry room. It was still dark out and she hadn't expected to see anyone. Her daughter had to be in high school that

Monday morning by seven o'clock. She had gotten her up at 5:30 and then
started doing laundry as she often did early in the morning when the
complex was mostly asleep.

"I just got in," he said.

At first she didn't know who he was, then she recognized him. This
morning he seemed melancholy, sort of detached.

"Are you all right?"

He nodded.

She watched him go to his rooms.

"I lost my car," he screamed into the receiver to his grandma. "It's not
where I parked it!"

"Call the university police. Maybe they towed it away."

"And some guy's killing people in Gainesville!"

"Did you hear what I said?" she said even louder.

"There's a guy here in Gainesville who's going around killing people!"
he shouted back.

"What?" What in the world was he talking about? "Call the police!"

Grandma Elna took the initiative and called the campus police herself to
report that his car was missing.

Dept. Sgt. Melvin Smith received the call at about two P.M. She wanted
to know if the police had towed away her grandson's car.

"Is the car registered in his name?"

"Yes, but I bought the car. It's a black nineteen seventy-five Cadillac."

"Do you know the license-plate number?"

"No," she said impatiently.

"We don't have a record of having impounded any black Cadillac."

"He said he was going to drop out of school. Someone has to go and
check on him," she insisted.

Shortly after two P.M. Officers Kathy Singletary and Andy Bigelow were
instructed by Sergeant Smith to go to Apartment 131 at Hawaiian Village
Apartments to check on Ed Humphrey.

When they arrived they noticed two legal-size notes on his door that
were addressed to the Gainesville *Sun*. When Ed finally responded to their
repeated knocks he appeared to have been sleeping.

"We're here to talk to you about the car . . ." Officer Singletary began.

He didn't seem to care about the car now. He was upset that he couldn't
go to Panama to fight in the war against Manuel Noriega.

"About the car . . ."

"I parked it near Tigert Hall at the university campus on Friday night . . . when I decided to leave the campus I couldn't find it. I got tired of walking around looking for it so I just walked home."

"Are you okay?" Bigelow asked.

"I'm upset over the Persian Gulf crisis," he said, shaking his head. "I have a friend who's in the military who was just sent to Saudi Arabia. I'm going to join the military and go where my friend is. Then the Gainesville *Sun* would really have something to write about!"

As they filed their report he interrupted with: "Don't you think it's awful?"

"What?"

"That anyone could torture and cut up these people in Gainesville," he said, beginning to move around the living room nervously.

Singletary and Bigelow glanced at each other when he mentioned the massive injuries sustained by the three victims—the extent of their injuries had not been reported in the press.

"How do you know all that?"

"Everyone's talking about it," he said, his voice changing to a higher pitch.

Singletary noticed a fresh unscabbed wound on the knuckle area of his left hand. It was not deep but appeared as if the skin was pushed up, as if, perhaps, he had hit the side of a door. She also noticed a three-inch scratch on his left arm between the elbow and the wrist and a red circular scratch on his left knee. The scratch appeared to be the size of a quarter. It might be a carpet burn, she thought.

Ed called his grandma Elna from the Turnpike at approximately nine P.M. to tell her that he was coming home.

"What time is my appointment tomorrow?" She had made one for him at the clinic in Melbourne, and was surprised he remembered.

"It's not until the late morning. Don't you think you should get some rest before you drive back?"

"Get off my back!" he muttered and hung up the phone. Always on him, no matter what he did!

He got back into his car, turned around and went back to Gainesville.

Lonnie Scott was a Gainesville police officer who lived in the Hawaiian Village Apartment complex directly above Ed Humphrey. He had become good friends with JoAnn and Jeanette and he was worried. JoAnn's daughter was medium size, dark hair and athletic. At eleven on Monday night after the murders he went to JoAnn's house. "I'm telling you," he said, standing at her door, "that Melissa fits the profile of the girls that were murdered. Just keep her in."

"Lonnie, have you seen the guy that lives underneath you?"

"No."

She almost felt guilty pointing him out, but when he mentioned Melissa . . . "He keeps strange hours . . ."

It wasn't only that he had frightened her that morning in the laundry room, but everybody was looking at everybody else with a new vision, one colored by fears.

JoAnn and Lonnie stood and talked a few minutes, sharing their thoughts, when suddenly Ed came out of his apartment across the lawn.

She nudged Lonnie, nodding in Ed's direction.

"Is that him?" he asked.

She nodded.

"Well, I think I'll follow him tonight."

They watched as Ed got into his big black Cadillac.

"When he came here he had no car," she whispered, even though Ed was too far away to hear. "Then all of a sudden, a car appeared . . ."

Lonnie followed him but lost him inside the university area.

At 2:30 on the morning of August 28 Ed went to the information desk in the lobby of the Veterans Administration Hospital in Gainesville looking for his friend. "A buddy of mine from Vietnam. I'm a vet myself. What room is he in?"

While waiting for the attendant to look up his friend he chanted a verse:

> Dealing with the devil,
> With no help from above,
> Stronger than day, stronger than night,
> Stay out of my life.

When he was told his friend was not a patient there he went up to Ward C on the third floor anyway.

Security was called.

Two young women on duty at the nurses' station thought he had an intimidating "look." He was insistent but vague in describing the person he was looking for.

By the time security arrived on the floor, Ed was gone.

He walked out of the hospital, and glanced back at the Veterans Administration Hospital. It was a pinkish-white building with a long series of round rowed windows. No wonder they couldn't find his friend. A guy from the Eighty-second Airborne wouldn't be in a place like that; it looked like a giant computer.

Tuesday, August 28

By now the Gainesville Police Department had heard a great deal about the young man, enough so that Officer Lonnie Scott went back to JoAnn Adelberger's house at Hawaiian Village Apartments and told her they wanted to "set up a surveillance in the rec room on the Humphrey kid."

She hesitated. "Do you really think it's possible," JoAnn asked, "that it could be him?"

"Well, we're taking all leads now because the city is panicking and you're not the only one who's pointed him out."

The police began to watch him.

It was nighttime. The killer was still roaming in the midst of a vulnerable population.

Joanna Senft was a Gainesville hairdresser. She was leaving the Elite Hair Salon in the Westgate Plaza Publix when a large man walked past her. The man stopped and stared at her with an intense, angry expression. She became extremely frightened; nothing as intimidating as this silent confrontation had ever happened to her before. Instead of going into the dark mini-canyons of parked cars, she hurried back to the hair salon and locked herself in.

It was a long time before she could get up the nerve to leave again. This time she had her car key ready in her hand and ran to her car in the parking lot, ready to scream bloody murder if she saw him again. The moment she jumped in her car, she locked all the car doors.

Breathing heavily, she looked around.

He was gone.

A police car moved silently by, patrolling the area.

She would not see the angry face of the man again until she was presented with a photo line-up that contained a two-hundred-pound suspect in the murders. She would pick number eight—Daniel Harold Rolling—as the man who had confronted her in the Publix parking lot.

When the police saw two men lurking about the woods near Archer Road, where Christa Hoyt had been found murdered, they naturally became suspicious. Rolling and Tony Danzy, a man who had supplied him earlier with drugs, were on their way to Rolling's campsite when the policemen ordered them to stop. Danzy did so and was detained. Rolling ran. The police chased him but he disappeared into the thick, protective darkness of the woods.

When his campsite was discovered by Alachua County deputies they found the pink-dyed money. A cassette recorder was on top of the money, but they paid little attention to the recorder. It was the pink money that interested them.

"This ol' boy has been pretty busy . . ."

Evidence and cash recovered at the campsite connected the unidentified occupant to the robbery of the First Union National Bank on August 27, the day before. Other evidence also connected the occupant of the campsite to a subject identified as Daniel H. Rolling.

It would be a very long time before a connection was made between the bank robber and the Gainesville Ripper. They had his voice on tape, but it would be months before anyone even listened to the tape in the cassette and heard the voice of the killer. "This is Danny Rolling under the stars . . ."

While Rolling was feeling sorry for himself over having lost all his campsite possessions in the confiscation of the unexpected raid, the families and friends of his victims, left to deal with their anguish, tried to comprehend the incomprehensible.

Ada Larson thought that if there had been room in the campus dorm, this would not have happened to the girls. "I'm grieving," said Ada Larson, "I think I'm going to grieve for a long time. Right now I'm mostly angry. I want the killer to die."

So did Ricky Paules: "Tracy had a bright future," she said, "and he took it all away. I'll pull the switch. I'll slit the throat. Whatever. I'm ready! No mother should have to outlive her children."

With the memory of his last conversation with his daughter Tracy, George Paules wrung his roughened stonemason's hands and began to cry. He remembered how he had said to Tracy, "Boy, am I glad you're out of here . . ."

Manny Taboada's brother Mario, a Miami radio advertising executive who wanted to become involved in advocacy groups for children and heard about Manny's murder on his car radio driving home from work, took a different view. "At first I thought if I had the guy in front of me and I could make him suffer, I would," he said. "Now I don't think I would do it. I started thinking, Why would someone do this? And then I thought, Somewhere down the line they weren't loved. We have a lot of work to do in this world. I'm not a religious person, and people don't understand me.

They don't understand how I can make it through this without some faith. But my faith is in the human race."

". . . Somewhere down the line they weren't loved . . ."

An extraordinary statement for the brother of a slain young man to make.

33

Ghost Town

After Christina and Sonja there was fear.

After Christa there was panic.

After Manny and Tracy there was an exodus.

In one weekend the once easygoing college town had changed dramatically. Even the quality and degree of fear had changed. With the presumed safety of numbers crowding ten and twenty students in a single room at night, taking turns staying awake and sometimes with someone designated to ride shotgun, the small apartments became fortresses. After the first murders deadbolt locks proliferated and wooden bars in the lower tracks attempted to minimize the vulnerability of sliding glass doors. The students had been galvanized by a combination of terror and compassion into reaching out to one another and coming closer together. But now the panic was epidemic. Apartments emptied out, everybody seemed to be leaving.

There was no more pre-school partying, no more bouncing on JoAnn Adelberger's trampoline in the backyard of Hawaiian Village Apartments. Hardly anyone was on the streets during the day, jogging or riding a bike. Nobody was out at night; the bars and restaurants were virtually empty. After Manny and Tracy there was hardly anyone left. There were only three cars in the Gatorwood parking lot by nightfall of the third day, even though the extraordinary police presence made Gatorwood arguably the safest place to be in Gainesville. Even those who were willing to tough it out, like Jenny Kanne, did not feel comfortable about staying in a huge complex that was virtually abandoned. It would take months before the number of cars in the parking lot would return to normal.

There was also a great deal of parental pressure to close the universities, as well as a similar feeling among faculty members. But President Lombardi never considered closing the University of Florida. His belief was that if the universities closed, all the support networks would stop. The people who did not have any other place to go would be totally on their own.

* * *

Mitch and Holly Stacy found themselves grieving for the town of Gainesville itself. This was like no other story. This is our town, Mitch thought, and this horror is going on in our town. They loved Gainesville and they were sad for the university because it was a wonderful school that had worked hard to build a reputation for itself, and now the students were going home.

It seemed everybody had a different theory, bolstered by rumors.

One killer or two?

He cleaned up with some kind of surgical fluid.

He probably knew a lot about human anatomy if he was hacking these people up.

Maybe he was a medical student, or an intern, or a resident.

Mitch preferred talking about how the story was being covered rather than speculating on who might have committed the murders. What did the Gainesville *Sun* have? What did the other papers have? Who had the best story? The most information? For him, the late-night meetings at Snuffy's on University Avenue were reporter-oriented.

At the *Sun* they worked on the story from dawn to dusk. The nightmare was also a journalist's dream.

Then came the night. There was something dramatic about nightfall in a murder town. During the day Mitch would not think about it. But at night . . . this guy was still in town . . .

Mitch and Holly did not live far from where the murders had occurred. Not wanting to frighten Holly unduly, he kept to himself thoughts that now they were in their house and now they were just like everybody else, just as vulnerable to this guy as anybody else in town.

Holly wouldn't even get up to go to the bathroom in the middle of the night unless Mitch went with her. She was terrified. They had two dogs, Annie and Jesse. Annie was a great watchdog; she would bark if a twig snapped outside. It made a difference. They knew some people kept golf clubs next to their beds. Tom Lyons admitted he walked around with a baseball bat to check the closets every time he went home late at night and walked into a dark house.

So in spite of the cloak of work that could protect against one's thoughts, it was inevitable that all the submerged feelings would eventually rise. After running around all day fueled by adrenaline, the reality of it would hit Mitch when he collapsed into bed. How the parents of these kids must feel. These young lives with so much potential. All lost. He tried to remember what he had been like at eighteen in Ohio. And lay in bed struggling to go to sleep while the story insisted on creeping up on him from the human angle rather than the professional one.

He was not the only one. They all grieved in the silence of the night.

34

Suspect #1

A tall pole was centered on the top rotunda of the library looking like an unlit candle. Typically, as with so many of the other students, Jenny's and Amelia's parents insisted they fly back home to Long Island, New York, and this time Jenny had to agree. No more arguments, but she stopped at the Gainesville Library first, walking with quick purpose under the double octagonal rotundas. She loved the yellow building trimmed with deep green, the red Spanish roof tiles, the balconies and shuttered green sunscreens angled out over the many windows, giving the library a sunny, tropical look.

Today, though, she barely noticed the building in which she spent so much of her spare time. Once inside, she took out every book on serial killers that she could carry with her on the plane—*Serial Killers* by Colin Wilson; *Sex, Murder and the Potential Sex Murderer*, by Eugene Revitch; *The Sadistic Murderer*, by Brittain.

Knowing that Amelia didn't like her "morbid" interest in serial murderers, Jenny would wait until flight time to begin her reading. Now, as they waited for their flight home at a table in the cafeteria overlooking the runway, they watched the extra traffic both in the cafeteria and out on the runway. And then they saw their 737 land and taxi under a small umbrella of charcoal-colored clouds hanging low over the southern end of the field in an otherwise brilliant blue sky.

As Jenny read almost feverishly, taking notes, Amelia looked out the little oval window of the plane, trying to control her annoyance at Jenny's apparently growing obsession.

Jenny read that there were three distinguishable types of serial killers: the paranoid schizophrenics who were delusional and often heard voices telling them to kill; the mass murderers who wanted to get even after harboring a serious though often irrational grievance against society; and then the sexual sadists. "An extreme form of deviation, characterized by torture and/or killing and mutilation of other persons in order to achieve sexual gratification."

274

That's the one. That's the Gainesville Ripper, she thought.

She read on, "Treatment of the sexual sadist is usually ineffective. He is the most likely of all mass murderers to be a recidivist."

The Gainesville Ripper would be in the high-profile category of killers, Jenny thought. Like Ted Bundy, the sexually sadistic serial murderer recently executed in Starke, Florida; and Richard Speck, the nurse killer; and Edmund Emil Kemper, a vicious sexual killer. They were all written up in the books on her lap. Albert De Salvo—the Boston Strangler. William George Heirens—the "Stop-me-before-I-kill-more" Lipstick Murderer. Jack the Ripper—the nineteenth century's infamous killer. Henry Lee Lucas, who claimed to have tortured and killed at least three hundred women. Charles Starkweather—the sexual mutilator whose ego went so far as to write an autobiography for posterity: "Millions will read about me and talk about me."

They knew it was a serial killer and that to apprehend and identify him the different law-enforcement agencies were going to have to work together. The task force was located in the Gainesville Police Department, where there was enough room to accommodate the extra personnel. They met at a GPD conference room—Chief Wayland Clifton, State Attorney Len Register and Sheriff Lu Hindery—where they began to discuss the formation of a task force.

Wayland recognized the need to bring them all together from "moment one," in fact, from the very first scene. The investigation was obviously going to require a tremendous pooling of resources greater than the capabilities of any one agency. Wayland's major contribution to the investigation came in setting up the task force. No small accomplishment. It quickly would develop into a formidable investigative force headed by three chiefs.

Chief Clifton assigned Lieutenant R. B. Ward to represent the GPD, and he became the commander of the task force. Not only had Ward been involved in the Appledorf case—about the fellow who had been smothered by young gay boys—but Ward had also been with the state attorney's office in Tallahassee when it successfully prosecuted Ted Bundy.

The Alachua County Sheriff's Office had its own detective division. Andy Hamilton, a captain with the sheriff's office, was assigned by Sheriff Hindery to represent the ACSO. Andy Hamilton was a very intelligent person with phenomenal recall and was importantly helpful. Shortly after his assignment R. B. Ward was promoted to captain, and Len Register couldn't help thinking that the GPD wanted to have someone of equal rank calling the shots. Even so, he knew R. B. deserved the promotion; he was a sharp investigator with a keen mind.

It amazed Len how well they all worked together. There was no sense of the traditional turf-guarding ordinarily present during joint investigations. Instead, there was the sense of urgency in "stopping this" and resolving the five homicides as quickly as possible.

At the same time the task force was set up there was a meeting in Gainesville with a contingent from the FBI in Gainesville. Bureau Chief Robert Smith, along with Assistant Bureau Chief Jack Wise, Special Agent A. L. Strope, Special Agent John Burton and Special Agent J. O. Jackson attended a briefing at the Gainesville Police Department, where it was decided that the Gainesville Police Department and Alachua County Sheriff's Office would be assisted in the investigation by agents of the Florida Department of Law Enforcement.

Special Agent J. O. Jackson, representing the FDLE, became the third chief. Everyone was aware that J. O. Jackson had worked some major, high-profile cases, including the Ted Bundy case. He won an FDLE award and recently had been designated Law Enforcement Officer of the Year. The five homicides had generated a huge amount of police reports—or "leads"—that had to be followed up by hundreds of special agents. J. O. was an expert in handling the collection and logging of the voluminous data generated by the various agencies and investigators.

The three chiefs worked well together, not only in the investigation but on the coordination of the resources that poured into town. Calls came from almost every law-enforcement agency in Florida, including calls from other state attorney offices offering their support and offering to send their best investigative staffs to Gainesville. It was in this context that a computerized leads system was set up with its comprehensive Relationship Systems, Leads Files and list of Priorities 1, 2, and 3, priorities that shifted as the investigation progressed. While the task force did the meat of the day-to-day work, Len Register and his prosecution staff worked along with them. Len felt they would have one chance to "do this thing right" and he didn't want to rush to judgment and take a chance of making a mistake that would hurt the presecution in the courtroom.

It was clear that the man who had committed the murders was responsible for setting in motion a mega-machinery apparatus of legal, journalistic and law-enforcement personnel, all hell-bent on identifying him, capturing him, convicting him and getting him into the electric chair.

Tony Danzy saw Rolling hanging around a mobile-home park where they had once gone to get drugs.

"Hey! What'd you run off for?" Tony asked, annoyed. "You left me holding the bag with those guys."

"I had to," Rolling said.

"What the hell for? All they wanted was to know about some murders. You ain't involved in anything like that, are you?"

"Aw no," he said.

"So why run? It makes you look awful suspicious."

"Well, you see, they're after me for something else."

"Like what?"

"I robbed a bank."

"You what?"

"I robbed the First Union Bank yesterday."

Tony had no intention of getting himself involved with a guy who was wanted for armed robbery. That was way out of his league.

Rolling hurried off when Danzy went to call the cops.

Even a friend was turning against him, running to turn him in. There was nobody he could trust. There wasn't one trustworthy person around. From his mother to his wife to his old man to his friends to the girls in Sarasota. All alike . . .

The investigation was concentrating on Ed Humphrey, who in his pathetic illness and ravings was now proceeding to bring himself to the worst possible conclusion with the concatenation of events—the murders, the urgent desire for an arrest on the part of the families and the authorities, and his latest and most extreme piece of acting out. Even before that event, there were those within the task force who sincerely believed he was their man, though there was no clear consensus about that. One of the first reports about Humphrey had come in from two girls who said they had watched a porno film during which, among other things, he had said, so they reported, that he would like to cut off the nipples of the girl in the picture. Add to that such statements as wanting to go to Saudi Arabia and cut some people up . . . It was not surprising that when Ed left Gainesville to go home, having told his grandma he couldn't stand it in Gainesville anymore, he was too afraid, the police followed his black Cadillac all the way south to Indialantic in Brevard County, hovering above him in a helicopter.

And then came the climactic event of August 30. While at home he finally had a violent argument with his grandmother, something building for a long time between them, in which Ed actually struck his grandmother, she said, over a tiff about picking up one of his contact lenses after she had accidentally struck him and knocked it loose. Ed's mother called the police. Grandma was seventy-nine, she told the police, and after at first resisting, at police insistence she signed a complaint charging aggravated assault. Ed admitted hitting his grandmother, but he hadn't meant to. He himself called 911 when he realized she was bleeding. He applied a cold compress. He was so deeply sorry. He loved his grandma—needed her. He tried to help her. Why was he being arrested? and consented to the officers taking his knives.

As Ed was being taken to the Regional Medical Center for treatment, agents from the Florida Department of Law Enforcement were on their way to question him. Only then did Ed begin to understand the full implications of what was happening to him, that the arrival of the agents had to do with the Gainesville murders. He protested he couldn't have killed anybody, that he had been out driving when the murders happened. As he was having his right index finger printed he blamed the cut on it on the "bitch" biting him. He also volunteered to help the police with the fingerprinting, he'd learned all about it in the Boy Scouts. He also asked Agent Donaway if he'd been fishing, and said that "John" had his fishing poles. John his friend, not John the Ripper . . .

While family members usually turned to Grandma in times of crisis, she often turned to the older brother George. He was in his apartment in Gainesville when the call came from her. He had been trying to deal with the fears permeating Gainesville and in particular with the fact that he had known one of the victims—Tracy Paules. They had been members of the same fraternity, and at one point he had even lost a fraternity election to her. "Ed's been arrested," came the jolting news from his grandmother. She said it was only over a family spat but that some of the reporters seemed to think Ed might be involved in the murders up in Gainesville. George could not believe that Ed was capable of the horrible things done to the murdered students, but he also was aware of Ed's emotional problems, his mysterious nocturnal wanderings, his not taking the prescribed medication that could stabilize him. The phones started ringing. He did not answer them.

The night Ed was arrested, the police questioned him without benefit of an attorney being present. The public defender told him not to say anything, but he was sent away by the investigator, who said he wasn't necessary since they weren't making any charges on account of "lack of evidence." He was told Ed was merely there on an assault complaint, but the grandmother wanted to drop all charges. And, in fact, her charges were dropped against him that night.

So without formal charges restricting their activity to "talk" informally to Ed without the benefit of an attorney's presence, he was interrogated for more than twenty-four hours, during which interrogation he was hyper, susceptible to suggestions, slipping in and out of passive-aggressive modes, making statements about "John" and "mutilations" and "knifings" and "cutting people up" and "killing Arabs in Saudi Arabia . . ."

The following morning, after the questioning about his behavior in Gainesville during the weeks before the murders, charges against him were reinstated. George, who had had a tremendous respect for the law and the authorities his entire life, would always believe that on the night Ed was arrested his constitutional rights were violated, and that their actions had "poisoned" the case. Fruit from the so-called poisoned tree was not supposed to be admissible in court. He would write a bylined article for the *Alligator* in which he stated that "our own law enforcement officials don't follow the law."

In the Brevard County jail at Sharpes, George had to ask Ed if he did it, and Ed, after a pause, asked him how he could even ask. And then he began to cry. Ed felt abandoned by his family, and George could do little to make him feel differently, although he was certain Ed would quickly be exonerated.

But a media blitz followed, and George was beside himself when his brother's mug shot appeared in the press and magazines. He would write to this author:

> His appearance fit in perfectly with everyone's imagination of what the man who could commit such atrocities would look like. Instantly the formless, evil image of the monster who killed five college students had taken shape—it materialized into the figure of my brother. With that photo, Ed looked the part.
>
> It was all too perfect. Within a week the multi-agency task force had its suspect . . . Ed served as a godsend to the community and to the investigators . . . When my brother's name was proffered it was as if everything magically was restored to normal . . . What could be better than to find the murderer in seven short days? . . .
>
> There was much to be gained by hinting that Ed was the possible killer—a horrified community could be relieved, the press could have their headline stories, and the task force could show that the investigation was moving along. They were heroes.

Bail for aggravated assault against a person over sixty-five years of age was set at one million dollars, even though Ed Humphrey was a first-time offender. Ed's subsequent trial on the charge brought him a sentence of twenty-two months in the Chattahoochie State Hospital, where most of the inmates were murderers. This sentence happened in spite of his grandma's subsequent insistence that she had accidentally fallen into the fireplace.

Now they had Ed where they wanted him while the investigation continued and they tried to find the evidence necessary to fit him to the student murders. Most people who read newspapers and watched televised reports were convinced that Ed was, indeed, the Gainesville Ripper. After all, once he was incarcerated the murders stopped.

Sgt. Alan Baxter had tried not to think about the girl herself while he was doing his job. At a deposition at the state attorney's office he had to review the evidentiary photos and reports that had been taken during the initial investigation. There were 52 color transparencies and autopsy reports of Manuel Taboada; 34 color transparencies and autopsy reports of Tracy Paules; 44 color transparencies and autopsy reports of Christa Hoyt; 30 color transparencies and autopsy reports of Christina Powell; 28 color transparencies and autopsy reports of Sonja Larson.

Alan had finished with the reality of the daytime nightmares. Another was about to begin; that night he suffered through an extremely frightening dream. He forced himself to wake up in order to block out the vivid photos of the victims. They were bad enough during the day, but at night, without the safety net of consciousness as protection, the photos violently broke into the serenity of sleep.

He had been avoiding Christa's mother, his old friend Ann Garren, even though he had received notes from her asking to see him. She had also let it be known by word of mouth—"Please have Alan come by and see me," "Please have Alan call me."

And Alan would say, "Okay, okay." But he kept putting it off. He dreaded facing her grief. He felt as though, somehow, it was his fault. He was trying to let it go, but she kept pressing.

Ann Garren was back at work at the International House of Pancakes.

How many times had she leaned over the counter writing out checks while Christa was alive? How many more times now that Christa was gone? The man in the tall white pleated chef's hat behind the high serving counter was almost barricaded behind a wall of counters and food warmers and coffee urns. He adjusted the navy blue kerchief around his neck as he saw Ann for the first time after the murders. He wanted to say something to show her he cared. He hesitated. It seemed to him that her eyes weren't really focusing on anything. He couldn't think of anything to say.

Finally, when she reached for one of her orders, he touched her fingers. He wasn't sure she was even aware of it.

*   *   *

Sgt. Alan Baxter finally stopped by during one of his coffee breaks. She seemed pale but in control. Still, he dreaded talking to her.

When they went out to the parking lot she said, "I've been wanting to thank you for the way you treated Christa's crime scene. I'd heard from everybody how good it was."

"I appreciate you saying that," he told her, "and I wish I could have done more. I wish that we could have prevented it. I still feel that. But I guess we couldn't have done anything to prevent it—"

"I know."

"If I could have," he said, "I would have taken that knife for Christa."

They hugged then, as they both started crying. It was a release and a relief for both of them.

"I just want to let you know," she said, "in my own way, that it wasn't your fault. Don't ever feel that."

That was important to her. She had been trying to do that with all the officers involved. Knowing how traumatized everyone was at finding her daughter the way they did, it was a remarkable gesture on the mother's part.

Leaving Ann to her own private nightmares, Alan thought he would like to see the killer die in the electric chair. He believed the killer deserved it.

Ann was thinking about the letter as she drove home—a letter that Christa wrote to her adopted mother before her graduation:

> I now understand why you pushed so hard for me to make good grades. You taught me to always do the best I can and nothing less. I may not have realized it then, but you knew what you were doing. You were always there to encourage me, console me, and push me on when I tried to give up. You made me a leader, a fighter, and a winner. You gave me all the determination I ever needed.

35

Other Suspects—Matching the Matchless

Of all the suspects investigators said they were focusing on by the week's end, part-time University of Florida student Edward Humphrey drew the most public attention, even though the six-foot, two-hundred-pound Humphrey's psychological profile did not match the cool, calculated, ingratiating serial-killer mold the police said they were looking for. Some believed they'd got him. Others were troubled. His worst recorded behavior, when he did not take his lithium, was that he became prone to sudden bursts of violence. But unfortunately for him, he always stood out.

He made what Brevard County Sheriff Jake Miller described as "erratic, unintelligible statements, grunts and animal sounds" as he was led in cuffs and leg-irons to his arraignment on the assault charges. Once there, he grinned at the TV cameras and blurted out, "Innocent until proven guilty!" Camera lenses clicked.

Although there was considerable debate within the task force over his innocence or guilt, Ed Humphrey went from Sadie's assessment to the press as "a very good suspect," to "Suspect Number One" in the headlines.

"We're on the side of caution," Spencer Mann said. "We're covering all the bases."

"We're very optimistic in a lot of areas," Sadie Darnell said, "but we certainly don't want to give the impression that an arrest is imminent." Police cautioned that Ed Humphrey was one of a dozen suspects, and although they declined to release the names of the others they did release Ed's name. His bleary-eyed, scarred face was all over the front page of every newspaper and TV screen covering the student murders.

The search for clues took investigators to nine other states—Montana, California, New York, Oregon, Alabama, Louisiana, Mississippi, Tennessee and Nevada. The inside scoop had it that there were three main suspects and five lesser ones. Soon, however, while the Indian River County Sheriff's Office issued new arrest warrants for Humphrey for sexual battery and armed burglary against two women in nearby Vero Beach in October of 1988. One was certain she recognized him as her assailant after seeing his photo in the newspapers even though her assailant had been in his twenties with a huge moustache and sixteen-year-old Ed did not even have a beard at the time. The list of other suspects began to trickle out to the public, although only two were under any kind of serious consideration, one a "charmer with the ladies," sought by the FBI in a multiple stabbing death in Middletown, Ohio, another, a man held on assault and battery charges whose home yielded a book on Jack the Ripper, a hangman's noose, pornography, satanic writings and two pairs of women's panties. He was also charged with breaking into an apartment near his own and threatening a teenage girl and her mother with a knife.

But Ed Humphrey was still prime. At the Hawaiian Village manager's office, when JoAnn Adelberger and Jeanette Barr heard Ed Humphrey had been arrested, Jeanette tried to assuage JoAnn's surge of guilt by telling her that she had to report him. But, said JoAnn, if he didn't have anything to do with the murders . . . what a tragedy for him.

"Even though I was pregnant," Jeannette told her, "and I thought there was no way the killer would want to come at me, I wouldn't walk into my apartment if my husband wasn't there. I'd wait for him at the door. We had a gun in our drawer. Each of us. Our maintenance man came and gave us a gun and we kept it in our drawer. I'd go to pick up my daughter and she'd sit in my office until I got off."

Lonnie Scott, who had come into the office, told JoAnn she'd done the right thing. "We got a killer off the streets, you were right in pointing him out to me."

"But you don't know," JoAnn said. "Not for sure. And because in my heart I don't believe it was Ed Humphrey . . ." She had said it. "All I can think is the real killer is still out there."

With Ed Humphrey's arrest, the students began to return to school. Jenny and Amelia flew back to Gainesville from Long Island. Jenny, the strong one, finally caved in to her own fears the moment she returned to Gainesville. Terror was an organic part of her every day. It kept growing, reinforced by her readings in the serial-killer literature. Amelia, presumably the weaker of the two, was able to turn it off.

Jenny installed a Radio Shack motion detector in the living room of their apartment and a security lock on the rear door.

It was Amelia who noticed pry marks on the bottom of the rear door. She looked at the security pin they usually slipped in the door.

She decided not to tell Jenny about the pry marks. She was already too upset.

*   *   *

Investigators combed through details of the victims' lives for points at which they might have crossed paths with the killer—or killers. They had to know everything about each of them—whom they knew, loved, slept with, fought with. Boyfriends. Girlfriends. Past. Present. Privacy had to be stripped away, sacrificed to the cause of discovering the truth behind the murders.

It was at this point that some of the astonishing similarities emerged: All the young women were slim, attractive brunettes who had enjoyed social and academic success. Christina, Sonja and Tracy had been excellent high-school softball players. Christina, the feminist, had insisted that her high-school coach call her a "third basewoman." All were strong, independent. Sonja liked to tube through rapids. Tracy often went skydiving and tried to talk Khris into it—even if it were the last four minutes of his life "it would be the best four minutes." Christa, headstrong, athletic, ambitious, shared these qualities with the others.

Still, as pointed out in a newspaper report, if authorities had found a Rosetta stone to unravel the mystery they were not revealing it—or much of anything else. Intent on keeping what knowledge they had from the killer, they released only the most guarded statements. A week after the killings, Gainesville Police Captain Richard B. Ward said that the murderer would not be satisfied with five victims. "He won't be satisfied until he's successful." Ward did not say what he meant by "successful."

Spokeswoman Lt. Sadie Darnell said that the killer had left messages at the crime scenes but "they were not messages as you would think of as messages. That is, they were not written out but presented somehow. It's subtle. It's not a taunt. It's not very flamboyant. It's consistent with a serial killer."

Experts were called on to give expert opinions. A serial killer, they said, could pass as almost anyone. "Most don't fit the Hollywood stereotype of a glassy-eyed lunatic," said James A. Fox, professor of criminal justice at Northeastern University in Boston and co-author of *Mass Murder—America's Growing Menace*. "Most of them are people you would not suspect. That is why, when they knock on the door and they claim they are the guy down the end of the hall, you trust them."

Now the experts tried to create a personalized profile of the Gainesville Ripper. If the murders stopped, it could be the work of a spree killer, the kind who killed with no cooling-off period in between and then stopped when he had had enough. On the other hand, the publicity might have driven the killer to another area away from Gainesville. They found the killer's "signature" at each of the killing scenes, something the killer seemed compelled to do. The FBI surmised that the killer might be a security guard or a hospital orderly. The Gainesville Ripper fell into the third category of multiple murderers with the psychiatric pattern of the sexual sadist.

> When apprehended it will be found that he is white, male, between the ages of twenty-five and thirty-five.
> He will be a person who has had a poor childhood background. He will not come from a loving home. He will have been abused either physically, sexually or psychologically during his most important formative years.
> As an adult he will perceive himself to have failed on the job and as a man. He will feel "left out" socially.
> He will be a man who needs to take his revenge on those whom he perceives to have rejected him or those who have succeeded where he has failed.
> He is a man who needs to "tell" about his mission or task through the "messages" left at the scene. Eventually, when apprehended, he will enjoy his "celebrity status."
> The games he plays with the police indicate that he is a cunning man who likes to match his wits with the authorities whom he hates. He is a man who will kill again either until caught and achieves the only kind of celebrity status he could ever have, or until he finally completes his "task" and loses the need to kill.

"Now the police are accusing the media of trying and convicting Ed Humphrey in the papers," Holly Stacy said to Mitch one night at home.

Mitch acknowledged that in some measure they were right. It was the press that proclaimed Ed Humphrey to the public as suspect number one, not the police.

Didn't it make him mad? Holly asked, that they were blaming the press?

Hindsight was twenty/twenty, he said. All he knew was the facts that they were getting: manic-depressive kid who talked about killing people and going into the woods and wearing fatigues. Three or four days after the murders he left town, drove to Indialantic, FDLE followed him, tracked him in an airplane, he beat up his grandmother, they arrested him, held him on a million bond. Plus they had sources . . . "this is the guy, he did it" . . . It never struck Stacy that Ed Humphrey didn't fit the serial-killer profile. He was the perfect suspect. He still didn't have an alibi. He thought Len Register believed Ed Humphrey was at least involved in it. But he didn't know. From what he knew, what he'd read about Humphrey's behavior, he didn't think Humphrey could have kept his act together and not leave any evidence. The police were blaming the media for victimizing Ed Humphrey, and George Humphrey was blaming the police.

Mitch and Holly had attended a panel discussion in which George demanded an apology from Sadie for his brother and she had refused to give him one. "This investigation is not completed," she had said, and George shouted, "I don't blame the media, Sadie, I blame you."

Now the help of VICAP was enlisted.

One of the difficulties in the apprehension of serial killers was that they often moved from state to state to avoid apprehension. There had never been a central point of identification method. All too often, before homicide investigators even realized they were dealing with a serial killer, the killer had already moved out of the local jurisdiction.

By 1984 random sex killing was a growing problem, a spreading disease. At that time a retired Los Angeles police detective, Pierce Brook, who often had been frustrated by the problem of losing the random sex killer to flight to another state, believed the answer to the problem of apprehension lay in computers, in devising a program that could link up all the individual computers throughout the states to one central computer into which all information could be input and assimilated. In this manner every violent crime committed within the states could be analyzed, categorized and linked through their methodological similarities. The computer program, the Violent Criminal Apprehension Program, was born. And the FBI Academy in Quantico, Virginia, was chosen as the center for the crime-fighting team.

On October 16, 1990, on one of the FBI VICAP searches, a report of similar murders came in to the task force, received by Special Agent Porter. One killing was noted in a triple November 6, 1989, killing in Shreveport, Louisiana. Here the victims were Julie Grissom, her father Tom Grissom and her eight-year-old nephew Sean Grissom. All of the information would need to be added to the six thousand individual leads that had to be followed up.

The Gainesville Ripper was linked to one of the cases cited in the VICAP report.

36

Bungling and Burgling

While the families and friends reacted bitterly and Ed Humphrey was jailed and abnormal strain promoted arguments among friends and the massive investigation continued under stress and the media continued its demands for news . . . Rolling's chronicle of lawlessness continued.

He had to get away. He had no money.

He read everything he could about the murders. He didn't know why he had done those things. At first it was exciting. Now it made him sick. He preferred thinking about God. "Nearer, my God, to Thee," he sang. And while he told himself that Jesus loved him, he broke into the home of University of Florida engineering student Christopher Osborne at a student complex in northwest Gainesville.

Still showing them who was in control, he ate oatmeal and left the dish in front of the television set, which he had turned on and did not bother to turn off.

Then he stole the keys to Osborne's tan 1978 Buick Regal and headed for Tampa. He was gone. Out of Gainesville.

In Tampa he drank heavily and for the first time in his life smoked crack cocaine. It made him feel good, made him forget. At least temporarily. He wanted to forget. All those things they were writing about. He didn't do any of it . . .

On Saturday, September 1, 1990, at approximately six A.M., Larry Dale Lawrence and Holli Jo Paula left their home at 2619 E. 113th Avenue in Tampa for a weekend camping trip. When they returned at four o'clock in the evening on September 3 they found their home had been burglarized . . .

He could tell no one was home. He got in a rear kitchen window by ripping the Miami-style window from its frame. As he entered he knocked over potted plants on the kitchen counter, spilling dirt and water. He listened . . . he had been right. No one was home. He searched every closet, every drawer, every corner where money might be kept. There was a glass mug on the desk in the master bedroom that contained approximately ten dollars in small change. He needed more than ten dollars. He ransacked the desk in the master bedroom, throwing around files and papers until he found a black leather wallet containing a few credit cards and two AMC movie passes. In another drawer he found two birth certificate cards bearing the name Anthony James Lawrence. Maybe they could come in handy. A new name. He went through the master bedroom closet and found a Nikon 35mm camera—model 8008, serial 82-87043—in a camera bag containing associated equipment and film. Must be worth something. Going through the living room he knocked over several trophies as he continued what was basically a fruitless search. The door leading from the kitchen to the garage was deadbolted. He kicked it open, damaging both the door and the lock. He searched an old desk in the garage. Not much. Just a sharpening stone that could be useful.

He finally left through a kitchen door. He had netted only a camera and a few dollars in coin. Enough to buy a ski mask. He didn't have one anymore, the cops had stolen all of his stuff from the campsite he had been forced to abandon in Gainesville.

This time, in the Lawrence/Paula house, he had not cleaned up. This time he left fingerprints.

Early that same afternoon he drove the Osborne stolen Buick Regal to a Save and Pack food store at 11612 North Nebraska Avenue on the corner of Fowler Avenue. He pulled on a ski mask and robbed cashiers at gunpoint.

Hillsborough County Sheriff's Deputies Teresa Johnson and Bruno Frauenfeld happened to be eating lunch at a restaurant next door. They heard the commotion when the robber ran out of the Save and Pack and the cashiers began calling for help. The two deputies rushed out into the street and confronted the robber in his Buick as he tried to drive away.

They had their guns drawn on him. He put the car in gear and drove directly at the two officers, narrowly missing Deputy Frauenfeld by inches. Deputy Johnson crouched down and started firing at the fleeing car. Frauenfeld also fired. People who had gathered around ducked as the sounds of the pistol shots popped through the air. By the time the deputies got to their patrol car the Buick had disappeared . . .

Rolling finally screeched to a halt and bailed out of the Buick, then ran into a thickly wooded area full of underbrush—running, jumping, accustomed to the woods at home. They could not catch him.

Later, the car with the stolen money was found by the Tampa police abandoned a short distance away. Seventeen bullets had hit Osborne's tan Buick Regal. The car was impounded by the Hillsborough County Sheriff's Office and taken to the impound lot at 3310 South Seventy-eighth Street.

It was not long before it was determined that the car used in the robbery was a vehicle that had been reported stolen by Christopher Osborne of Gainesville, Florida. Inside the trunk the police discovered several items that had been stolen from the reported Lawrence burglary that morning. Recovered were the Nikon 35mm camera and camera bag, the sharpening stone, the black leather wallet still containing credit cards and movie passes, and two birth certificate cards. The stolen coins from the glass jar were not found . . .

He stopped running. He had lost them. He sat down to collect his breath, feeling hot, sweaty and thirsty. He was in excellent physical shape, capable of covering a great deal of ground, but the run through the woods had temporarily winded him. When he collected himself he was in a rage. Now he had no car and no money. He also knew he had to get out of the woods. It wouldn't be long before they would be out trying to hunt him down with dogs.

That Sunday afternoon, September 2, in broad daylight, the home of Janet Adele Bos located on Orleans Street in Tampa was burgled. She had gone to Pine Island to visit friends. When she returned the next afternoon at about four o'clock, she discovered the break-in . . .

He had to be careful. People were usually hanging around their homes on Sundays. He chose a backyard that was isolated and quiet.

He removed the aluminum screen covering the rear bedroom window of the Bos home, and dropped it in the backyard.

He looked around for something to break open the locked window and spotted a bag of azalea fertilizer inside the locked screened porch at the rear of the residence. As he broke the latch on the screened porch he noticed the red Rally ten-speed woman's bicycle stored in a corner.

He picked up the bag of azalea fertilizer and returned to the rear window. Holding it high above his head, he crashed it into the window. He dropped the bag of fertilizer in the backyard and entered the rear guest bedroom, careful not to cut himself on the shards of broken glass covering the windowsill and the chair beneath it.

The first thing he went for was the refrigerator. He grabbed a large bottle of Ocean Spray CranApple juice from the top shelf and drank most of it in one long gulp. Now he began the ransacking search through all the closets and drawers, the hallway, the bedrooms, the medicine chest—looking for anything he could use.

He spread the contents of the blue metal lockbox he found in the front master bedroom closet onto the bed. Nothing. Personal papers, banking records, warranty information. He left the opened box on the bed. He pushed clothes around in the closet and found a red workout-type carrying bag in the closet, but in his impatience he failed to notice the .22 caliber revolver hidden in the back of the closet. He dumped the contents of the red bag onto the bed. At least he could use the bag.

He went into the bathroom next to the master bedroom, washed, used the toilet, removed the yellow rubber band he had been using to hold back his long hair, combed his hair, forgot the rubber band containing strands of his hair on the side of the sink and went into the living room.

He needed to take something to eat, and in the kitchen packed a brown Publix shopping bag with a couple of apples and took a pink plastic flashlight.

He spotted the telephone on the table in the living room, sat down and dialed his home in Shreveport, Louisiana.

"Hello, Ma . . . how's Dad?"

It was a painful twenty-minute conversation. His father, blind in one eye and deaf in one ear from the shooting the previous May, was getting better but nothing had changed. She was the same. It would never be different.

"I love you, son."

"I love you, Ma."

"Jesus loves you."

"I know, Ma."

Then he dialed his old friend, Bunny Mills. Once, twice, three times.

It was after 10:00 P.M. when he removed a security pin from the kitchen sliding glass door and left Janet Bos' house, leaving the door partially open. He forgot the Publix shopping bag on the kitchen counter between the microwave oven and stove.

He took the red Rally ten-speed bike out of the screened porch and pedaled away.

A bicycle wouldn't get him very far.

Later that week, when Janet Bos' GTE telephone bill came in she was able to provide the police with the exact times the intruder had called Louisiana. One call was at 9:32 P.M. for twenty minutes and then there were three in quick succession at 9:52, 9:54 and 9:57 P.M.

37

A Continuing Frenzy in Gainesville

Reports denied the involvement of Satanic Ritual Abuse (SRA) yet it was rumored that authorities were searching for body parts, "souvenirs," a black hood, black clothing, bondage equipment, pornography, sexual devices. Thoughts of live torture blackened an already grim scene. The search for photographs of the victims and audio or video tapes highlighted suspicions that the killer might have photographed or taped his killings. There were rumors that the success of the investigation might hang on the thread of a single pubic hair. Seventeen lab technicians worked full time on the case. Over five hundred items and pieces of possible evidence had been taken from the scenes of the crimes.

Since crimes scenes were the windows to the killer, they presumably could tell much about him, and the task-force investigators had a long list of items they were still looking for:

Women's undergarments
Photographs of the victims
A knife with a blade four inches or longer or a surgical-type instrument
A screwdriver or other type of pry tool
Black clothing, black hood, all shoes
Pornographic photos, bondage paraphernalia, adhesive tape
Bible with contents accented or containing handwritten annotations
Detective or military magazines containing handwritten annotations, and magazines displaying nude women or sexual devices
Driver's licenses or other identifications of persons other than Edward Humphrey
Gloves (cloth, latex, rubber or plastic)
Used plastic bags or wrappings
Writings, drawings, photographs, audio tapes or visual tapes depicting the murders
Greenish-blue liquid soap

Human flesh, nipples, blood, hair and/or fibers
Receipts from Publix and/or Pier One Imports and/or WalMart or other
   receipts dated 8/23/90; a Scotty's Hardware receipt
A Mexican serape
Any identifiable property of victims and any container used for trans-
   porting the aforementioned items away from the homicide scenes

Most items were not found.

With frustration following upon frustration, by mid-September everything was moving at an accelerated pace.

On Saturday, September 1, Gainesville Police Lt. Sadie Darnell publicly
called Ed Humphrey a "very good suspect for the moment." Not only
were Ed's activities, past and present, put under scrutiny, but his entire
family and Indialantic home were subjected to intense surveillance. Even
his big brother George, Jr., became a suspect in the murders because of
his relationship to Ed. To the idealistic George's dismay, not only was he
subjected to the frightening indignities of elimination fingerprint and
blood tests himself, he was suffering from the reaction of his friends . . .
"You don't really want to pal around with this guy, do you? What if he's
the one who turns out to be the killer instead of his kid brother? What if
they did it together?" Television crews actually followed and filmed him in
his law classes at the university. Since he had always respected journalists
and had once considered journalism as a career, he was doubly disillusioned now.

Grandma fought with the press, argued with the police and desperately
tried to protect the family's shattered privacy. But it was George who
became the family spokesman, continuing his strong defense of his brother
and giving interviews expressing his belief in his brother's innocence. His
protests did little to eliminate the halogen-bright spotlight focused on his
family. There was what George referred to as the media "hippie camp"
stationed around the block outside Grandma Elna's Indialantic home. The
house itself became a tourist attraction as the inquisitive drove by.

Searches were systematically conducted throughout the wooded areas
next to where the murders occurred. At various times, skin divers were
used to scour murky underwaters of nearby ponds and streams. ROTC
units were called in. A coordinated foot "grid search" was planned. Heli-
copters appeared, roaring overhead, to determine the type of terrain to be
covered on foot in field searches. The helicopter search covered ten miles
of woods where it was believed Humphrey might have roamed on his
"fantasy reconnaissance missions." More than two hundred navy and army
reservists were called in for the search, creating instant headlines and
photo coverage. It was rumored they were searching for human tissue as
well as metal objects.

But fields and ponds yielded nothing. No clues.

On September 3 a search of the wooded area west of Gatorwood Apartments behind the complex was conducted. The search encompassed the area south three hundred feet, east to the dirt road next to Gatorwood, and west two hundred feet past the Gatorwood fence line. The western fence line and drainage ditch were also searched. Eight officials from the GPD, ACSO, FDLE and the Department of Corrections were involved in the search of the wooded area.

The search did not produce any evidence.

On September 4 Room 197 in the Best Western motel at 1900 SW Thirteenth Street was searched for clues. The guest registrar indicated that Grandma Elna Hlavaty had stayed there sometime in late August. Investigators believed Ed might have visited or stayed in the room with her. Therefore the search.

Nothing was found.

On September 5 JoAnn Adelberger and Jeanette Baer quietly watched as nine members of the FDLE with metal detectors, dogs and an army of volunteers, searched the canal area behind the Hawaiian Village apartment Ed had occupied for nine days. The search encompassed one hundred yards south of the apartment and north to the Second Avenue bridge. It extended west through the canal and into the woods approximately thirty yards.

Nothing.

At the same time the canal was being searched in Gainesville, six scuba divers from the Brevard County Sheriff's water-rescue and search team entered the water in the rear of Grandma Elna's house in Indialantic to search an area that bordered on the Indian River.

Grandma came out of the residence and confronted the divers.

"I don't know why you're wasting your time like this," she said to Special Agent Turner. "He didn't do it. The reason he came home from school was because there were killings going on in Gainesville and he was scared because he had a sliding glass door himself."

Shortly, she was joined by Ed's mother.

"I'm Ed Humphrey's mother," she told the special agents.

"Go inside," Grandma Elna tried. She was sorry her daughter had come out. Grandma could tell she was "not well," but her daughter would not retreat.

"Who are you?" Ed's mother asked the agent.

"Special Agent Turner."

"Well, I have to tell you because you should know this. Many of Ed's friends are bad boys and Ed is in a good place now where he can be disciplined—"

Grandma tried to interrupt.

". . . and if he commits suicide, well, that's life."

Special Agent Turner assured them that the police would work just as hard to prove that Ed was innocent of any crime.

The water team searched an area from the bank out to two hundred yards. It also entered and searched approximately one hundred feet into a nearby canal and a nearby storm drain.

Nothing in the way of evidence was uncovered.

The atmosphere at the Hawaiian Village Apartments had taken on the aspects of a three-ring circus. Media coverage was intense. Police were everywhere, patrolling, walking, sitting, questioning. Patrol dogs went up and down the creek and stood guard at the entrance with their handlers.

JoAnn and Jeannette were appalled. While policemen sat in an adjacent empty Hawaiian Village apartment keeping a vigil over Ed's Apartment 131 until they could get the court order to search, reporters tried to sneak into the complex. There was unexpected difficulty in getting the search warrant. The task force could not seem to convince a judge there was enough reason to believe Ed was the murderer. Four days of work and a seventy-five-page statement were needed finally to convince the judge that there was "probable cause" to warrant a search of Ed's apartment, his grandmother's home, his car and his person.

The warrant was finally granted on Thursday, September 6, 1990.

Patrick Sessions was also on hand at Hawaiian Village the day the apartment was searched. The Miami businessman had become involved because of Tracy Paules. Tracy had been dating Khris Pascarella, who on his daughter Tiffany's recommendation used to work for him. When Khris first told Sessions about the Gainesville murders, Sessions' mind immediately jumped to his daughter Tiffany's disappearance. Could there be a connection? There had been no breakthrough in his daughter's case. It had been some two years, and Tiffany's case was winding down as far as the authorities were concerned. His only hope—a thin one, of course—of discovering what had happened to Tiffany was that with the huge investigation going on in Gainesville, now intensified by a fourth and fifth murder, the investigators might inadvertently stumble onto something to do with his daughter Tiffany.

As soon as Khris called him, Sessions called the Alachua County Sheriff's Office to talk to Lt. Spencer Mann, whom he knew from the lieutenant's earlier association with Tiffany's case. Spencer was surprised that Sessions already knew about Tracy and Manny since they themselves did not even know who Manny was at that point. Spencer could tell Sessions nothing.

Sessions and Khris decided to locate Tracy's parents, who had gone to work. Because of the connection between Khris and Tracy and Khris and Sessions, Sessions had become close to the Paules family, who also lived in Miami. Who should know better than he what Khris and Tracy's parents were going through? At least he could reach out to help some very desperate people.

Sessions went to the Paules house the afternoon Khris called. They had never been involved in the public eye before; the media was intrusive, and Sessions tried to help out since he had had experience in dealing with the media after Tiffany's disappearance. The Paules family was grateful. They had no idea how to deal with the situation. For a week Sessions acted as their family representative and was able to help them through an impossible time by doing what, for him, because of his own tragedy, had become almost second nature.

Now here he was at the Hawaiian Village Apartments watching along with hundreds of others as the search went on behind the closed door of Apartment 131.

This was getting close. Gatorwood Apartments, where Tracy and Manny had been murdered, was very close to the Casablanca Apartments off Wooleston Road where his Tiffany had been living at the time of her disappearance. If you looked at where the student murders happened, he thought, for instance, at Gatorwood, where Tracy was murdered . . . then drove to Tiffany's apartment, it was three-quarters of a mile away. But if you walked it—Tiffany had been jogging when she disappeared—it was across an open field, probably less than a quarter of a mile away.

Perhaps this really was all connected in some way. Perhaps whoever was responsible for whatever had happened to Tiffany had come back, less cautious this time, more overt in his craziness. Perhaps Sessions would finally find out what had happened to Tiffany.

Then again . . . if the kid were innocent he had every right to be angry, Sessions thought as he stood outside the Hawaiian Village and reviewed the quasi-indictments against Ed Humphrey that had dominated the headlines in recent days. If it turned out that he wasn't involved in these murders, then the kid was being railroaded.

"They didn't find anything," JoAnn Adelberger told a friend after the search. "They were there for hours, from nine 'til sometime after lunch. They came out with this little bag, like a Publix market bag. And you could tell there was hardly anything in the bag. His apartment didn't have much in it."

When the search team left the apartment Jeannette locked the apartment door. As far as she was concerned, it still belonged to Ed Humphrey.

Items taken by investigators during search of Ed Humphrey's apartment:

A Stanley brand screwdriver
Biology textbooks
Underwear
Misc. paper
Books entitled *The Prophesies of Love, A New Dawn, Looking Out for #1, The Good Life, Man's Search for Himself Can Be Happy, Touch the Devil, Lonesome, God's Feeling Good, Ideas in Civilization*
Various magazines
Newspaper clippings
Hardcover yearbook
White Holy Bible
Green Holy Bible
Medical files
Briefcases
Manila folder labeled "Ed's College Stuff"
Correspondence
Telephone memo books
Address books
An anatomy book
A silver-colored stainless-steel trident-shaped sword
Camouflage pants
Gloves
Video cassettes
Hunting style, camouflage hat
Army pamphlets
A *Dungeons and Dragons* game
A pair of rubber gloves

Items taken in a second body search of Humphrey at Brevard Jail:

Saliva samples
50 head hairs
50 pubic hairs
2 vials of blood
Photographs of all apparent injuries to his body

At the same time Ed's door was officially unlocked at Hawaiian Village Apartments, several hundred miles south in Indialantic, Special Agent Michael Brick knocked on the door of Six Shore View Circle.

There was no answer at Grandma Elna's home. At 9:35 in the morning Grandma's front door was opened by a locksmith. Special Agent Brick and the other FDLE agents entered and secured the residence. Special Agent Pape read the complete search warrant to the empty house, the reading witnessed by FDLE Special Agent Gossett.

As the warrant was being read, the twenty-four-hour shifts that had been arranged between Special Agents Mercurio and Carmichael to maintain surveillance of Ed's Cadillac ended. Once a warrant was secured, the car was carted away on a flatbed tow truck. (When it was eventually returned months later the paint job was destroyed, the upholstery cut up and the engine would no longer start.)

Shortly after the search began, Grandma Elna and Ed's mother returned home. Grandma, in particular, was deeply offended by the search and told them so.

"We have a search warrant—"

"How dare you enter my home when I'm not here! Get out!" she screamed. Her daughter thought she looked as though she was going to have a heart attack and an ambulance was called. Grandma refused to budge.

George Humphrey would write to the author:

> They ransacked our house literally. A team of some fifteen FDLE officers, both men and women, ran through our house. They had an ambulance parked outside for my grandmother who was hysterical and having problems breathing. They went into her room, where she hadn't touched anything since her husband died. They just threw everything around as if deriving pleasure from tearing things apart. They made an unbelievable mess. Scuba divers scoured the river bottom in the back of our house. Our neighbor next door threw things at them, telling them they didn't have a search warrant for his river property.

The FDLE team was there all day. At 6:49 P.M. Gossett and Pape gave Grandma a list of the items taken from the residence:

Items taken by investigators during search of Hlavaty house:

Six knives, including one with an eight-inch blade, a butcher knife and one found in a plastic milk jug in a recycling bin in the garage

A short-handled hooked fishing tool known as a gaff

Two screwdrivers in a drawer to the right of the stove

Paper bag with posters and hair from a garbage can

A briefcase and assorted papers with Gainesville and University of Florida phone numbers, student names, maps, notes and the "W" section of a telephone book

Miscellaneous papers and a telephone index including psychiatric records

A suitcase with clothing
Motel receipts, credit card receipts and maps
An advanced version of *Dungeons and Dragons* game taken from a box
  identified by his mother as one he brought back from Gainesville
Two drawing books
A parking citation
A vehicle title and registration listed in the name of Edward L. Hum-
  phrey
A desk calendar from December 1989 to October 1990 with the month
  of January missing
A camouflage wallet
Two bibles

Most of these items were never returned.

They had a crime. They had a suspect. There was a desperate attempt to
link the two. With one dead end after another, all the police could do at
this point was increase its patrols and seize Ed Humphrey's psychiatric
records from Gainesville psychologist Philip K. Springer.

Earlier, on the morning of September 7, sometime between midnight and
seven A.M., the same Friday that Ed's psychiatric records were confiscated,
Danny Rolling was in the midst of yet another burglary in Tampa, Florida.
He forcibly entered the residence of Reynaldo and Patricia Rio at 2208
Lee Court, #106, through a rear sliding glass door.

This time the house was not empty. This time the owners were asleep,
unaware that a killer had entered their home. Reynaldo and Patricia had
gone to dinner at Nick's Restaurant on Columbus Avenue, then returned
home at 9:00 P.M. Their sixteen-year-old son Anthony had not gone out
during the evening. By midnight all three had gone to bed, closing their
bedroom doors.

The first thing Rolling saw when his eyes became accustomed to the
dark were Rio's jacket hanging off the side of a chair and his car keys
tossed on the hall table. He realized the house was occupied.

He moved down the carpeted hall, leaned his ear against the master
bedroom door. He cracked open another bedroom door. In the darkness
he dimly could see the body of the sleeping boy. He wondered whether he
should "waken" them. He closed the door and looked down at the keys he
was holding. This was really all he wanted right now; he had the means to
escape the area in the palm of his hand and three people all at once were
dangerous, even with the element of surprise on his side.

Still, he wasn't through playing his games.

He went into the kitchen and had a snack while Reynaldo, Patricia and

Anthony Rio slept down the hall. He would wait to see if they woke up on their own and caught him in their kitchen helping himself to their breadbox. He would be ready for them. There was a rush of excitement as he ate a banana. Wondering if he would be caught.

He finished the banana and left the peel lying on the seat of the chair on the west side of the dining room. He placed it in a tentlike position in the center of the chair, once again demonstrating who was in control; they could be asleep in their own beds, but he was in the next room violating their privacy, eating their food, setting up a display for them, allowing them to live.

He took two Timex quartz watches with black plastic bands he found in the kitchen and left through the rear sliding glass door, leaving it open, a night breeze lifting the edges of the drapes.

The car wasn't bad. It was a 1983 Ford Mustang, Florida plates #1BH35E.

He headed for Ocala in central Florida.

38

Whistling Winn-Dixie at the End of the Road

Rolling followed Route 441 to 301 to State Road 200 West, past the homogenous mobile-home parks and used car and trailer dealers baking in the Florida sun, until he reached the western outskirts of Ocala.

Beautiful town. Horse country. Home of the New York Yankees owner George Steinbrenner III's horse farm. Money.

To the locals the west side of Ocala was looked upon as the "bad" side of town, the other side of the tracks. To Rolling it looked like a good place for a score.

It was just past high noon, only twelve hours after the Rio burglary and car theft in Tampa, when Rolling pulled into the parking lot of the WalMart Shopping Center on SW College Road off Route 200. It was a huge shopping district with a blue motif running throughout the shopping area. Dominating the center was an enormous Winn-Dixie supermarket.

Having done this before, little preplanning was necessary. He studied the supermarket. Burglarizing homes was penny-ante stuff. He needed a big hit, one that could not only tide him over throughout his flight but that also could give him enough pocket money to be able to play the big man again. He needed that feeling badly enough to risk going for a big hit.

White shirt and tie, dark blue pants, blue vest with "Location Manager" on the chest pocket and a nametag—this was the uniform Randy Wilson wore as manager of the Winn-Dixie supermarket. In his forties, Wilson was a good-looking man, blond hair, dark blue eyes. A strong six-foot-two, he had always been capable of taking care of himself.

It was about one o'clock on a very busy Friday afternoon. The market was crowded with shoppers waiting in deep lines at the checkout counters. Wilson was standing behind the service counter next to a cash register when he heard a man's voice behind him: "Do you know what this is?" The accent was more bayou than Floridian.

Wilson turned around to see a large, muscular man pointing the barrel of a .38 directly at his head. The man was wearing sunglasses, a fishing hat, shorts and a T-shirt. For a moment Wilson thought it was a joke. Friday was one of the store's busiest days; he couldn't imagine someone robbing the store on such a busy afternoon.

But just like in so many bad movies, the man said, "This is a holdup."

Wilson still did not say anything. He wasn't afraid. Somehow, it simply was not sinking in that this guy could actually be doing this. He had been with the company for twenty-five years, eighteen of which he had spent as a manager, and he had never been robbed before. Finally it sank in that the weapon pointed at him was real and, no doubt, loaded. This *was* happening, and this guy had the look of someone who had done this sort of thing before. He was all business, didn't appear to be too nervous, although Wilson thought he detected a subtle anxiety that was worth watching.

The man lowered the gun pointed at Wilson's head. Now it was less than three feet away from the center of his body. "Give me all the money in that drawer."

Wilson proceeded to open the register. There was a plastic bag in a rack that he opened and began to fill with money. He was busy enough not to take particular notice of the rest of the store until the man suddenly moved the gun away from him and waved it across the front of the store.

"All you girls out there," he called in a loud voice, "empty your registers."

Incredible, Wilson thought. Robbing a store like this in broad daylight . . . took guts or stupidity or both.

The average age of the cashiers at each of the seven registers stretched in a neat row before them was only eighteen. After initial disbelief there was a quiet panic. One woman who had been standing on line next to a counter dropped down on her hands and knees out of view under the register.

Some of the girls were in the middle of checking out orders. "I can't get the drawer open," one whispered in a panic. "I'm in the middle of an order—"

"Close it out," said the cashier next to her. "*Close it out*."

"I can't—"

"Total the order and hit Cash Tendered."

It was a simple operation but the girl was frightened. It took several attempts before she could do it.

Toward the rear of the store Randy Wilson's market manager, Steve Carson, and frozen food manager, Tim Bentley, were made aware of the situation by customers who had managed to back down the aisles out of view of the holdup man. Carson and Bentley quickly evacuated as many people as they could, heading out the back door of the store into the sun-drenched rear parking lot. They stood, stunned, next to the rear loading docks of the store.

Rolling had not moved from his spot next to Wilson and the cash register. After he waved to all the cashiers to open their drawers and empty the contents into brown paper bags, he looked back to Wilson, who had finished getting the money out of the cash register in front of him.

"Where's the safe?"

"Upstairs. In my office."

Keeping an eye on the young cashiers, now staring at him in frozen silence, Rolling glanced where Wilson had pointed. The manager's office was up two steps behind them in a small walled area without a ceiling.

"Let's go get the money out of the safe," he said.

Wilson turned, walked in front of Rolling, noting that although the robber was hurrying him along he didn't touch him with the gun as they made the two-step ascent to his office. As they went in, the spring-loaded door locked behind them.

From their positions they could still see the full length of the cashier stalls over the top of the wall that provided the manager's office with some degree of privacy, but the safe, which was exposed, could not be seen from where the frozen customers and cashiers remained standing.

Randy Wilson's bookkeeper, Dawn Hodges, had gone to the mailbox just before the holdup. As Wilson bent down to open the safe he was out of view of everyone in the store. One customer, who took the opportunity of Rolling's momentarily being out of sight, turned to slip out the front door and ran into Dawn Hodges. "You're being robbed . . ."

"What?"

"You're being robbed!"

Dawn Hodges stood cautiously at the doorway, ready to run if necessary, and saw a man she didn't recognize in Wilson's office. The moment she saw him she backed out of the doorway and ran to the dry-cleaning store next door.

"Can I use your phone, we're being robbed!"

She called 911.

Meanwhile, Wilson had opened the safe and was in the process of getting the money out.

"Hurry up," the robber said. "No change! Just bills!"

Now Wilson was deliberately taking his time, moving slowly, methodically. He didn't want to scare the man hovering over him. He was trying to keep him as calm as possible.

"Hurry up!"

"You don't have to use that gun," Wilson said. "I'll give you what you want."

As he packed the cash Wilson wondered briefly why the cashiers and the

customers didn't run out while he and the robber were in the office and
the gun was no longer in view. He guessed maybe they were afraid the
robber would shoot him if they moved.

"That's enough," Rolling said, even though there was still some money
left in the safe. Wilson gave him the bag. Rolling edged back to the low
swinging door that had locked behind them when they entered the manager's office. The only way out was with the key.

"Open the door."

"I'm trying." Wilson always carried the key on a ring. "I have to find the
key—"

Rolling swore in impatience, then jumped on top of the desk-counter
and over the top of the office wall six feet down to the service area below.

Wilson was still in his office trying to get the door unlocked as Rolling
went out from behind the service counter and moved across the front of
the store. The cashiers had gotten money out of their registers and the
paper bags filled with cash were set on their counters. He picked up four
of the bags, one by one, and he left by the same door the bookkeeper had
used moments before.

As soon as he left, everyone started talking at once with a rush of released tension.

Wilson moved past them, he badly wanted to follow the robber.

Outside, he saw the robber walking quickly away from Winn-Dixie's
entrance. And he saw his bookkeeper Dawn Hodges at the entrance of the
dry cleaners looking out the door and talking on the phone. He saw her
duck back in as the robber walked by, and realized that his bookkeeper
was giving the police a close-up description of the man as he walked by—
sunglasses, a fishing hat, shorts, a T-shirt.

Already he heard sirens. But the robber stayed cool. He did not run.

Wilson kept following him.

Rolling walked out facing the granite columns of the shopping center, the
gun held close against his stomach, still ready but trying to hide it. He did
not run but walked quickly past the cleaners—not noticing the girl at the
door on a long extension phone who pulled back inside as he approached.
He passed Dockside Imports with windows full of wicker furniture. It was
a good distance from the Winn-Dixie door to the breezeway where the
shopping center split next to the back. He turned right at the breezeway to
the back lot behind the stores.

Wilson lost sight of him as he broke into a run, racing over the red brick
tiles the moment he entered the breezeway.

It was a short distance to the back parking lot. As Rolling broke through
into the open, he glanced to the right and saw the group of people who

had slipped out during the robbery, gathered around the loading docks of the Winn-Dixie.

The gun in his hand was flailing about now.

He heard a woman scream.

But before the crowd could disperse he turned left, away from them, and charged around the side of the building.

At this point Wilson peered out from the protective covering of the breezeway approximately a hundred feet behind him.

But Rolling had already disappeared around the side of the building that led back up to the front of the shopping mall and now was running toward the car he had parked by Palm Chevrolet on SW College Road. He slipped the gun into his pocket, tore off his cap and pulled off his shirt as he ran—to change his appearance. He charged past Scotty's Building Supplies and finally got to his car.

As Wilson reached the lot at the back of the store, he, as Rolling had done, looked to his right at the crowd of shoppers who had gone out the back door.

"He went that way!" they shouted, pointing, just as a police car pulled into the back lot, passing them and screeching to a stop at the curb in front of Wilson.

"That way," Wilson called out, pointing to his left.

The policeman sped off, speaking into his car phone.

There was nothing more Wilson could do. As soon as he returned to the store the staff crowded around him. One of the cashiers especially shaken could not stop crying. He told her to go home.

Wilson didn't remember being scared, although he figured he must have been. And when someone asked why he risked chasing a man with a gun he had no special reason, except that he just felt he had to.

By the time Rolling reached the car he had parked at Palm Chevrolet, the police were right behind him, sirens blazing.

After a high-speed chase down State Road 200 almost to Route 441, Rolling finally wrecked his car at Route 200 and Southwest Fifth Avenue. Shirtless, he ran to nearby Bridge Street Station and into a business called Dial America Marketing, past the startled personnel who watched in amazement as the bare-chested man charged through their office toward the rear door next to the overflowing dumpster, then into the rear parking lot—where the police were waiting for him.

"Freeze!"

Rolling instinctively knew they wouldn't want to use guns in an area teeming with curious bystanders, so he dodged them and ran and they chased him on foot.

Finally they brought him down with a hard tackle.

Once he was under control and inside the confines of a squad car, his desperado demeanor vanished, melted into a passive acceptance of his capture.

To Randy Wilson it seemed no time at all had passed before the police brought an armed robber back to Winn-Dixie for identification. He had been busy reassuring his personnel and assessing the extent of the robbery when the arresting policemen asked him to come out to the squad car in front of the store. He was asked if he could identify the man inside the police car as the man who had robbed his store.

Wilson peered through the window. For a moment he actually hesitated. All of a sudden he wasn't sure, it had all happened so fast and the man in the car didn't seem like the self-assured robber who had held a loaded gun to his head. There was no hat, no T-shirt. He looked so different, meek, mild . . . almost friendly.

Wilson hesitated.

But then Danny Rolling said, "Yeah, it's me, and I'm sorry."

Wilson nodded to the policeman.

Rolling never got a chance to count his take. He had left it in the wrecked car. It was $4,700.

The robbery, the chase, the crash, the capture, the arrest, the identification—all had taken no more than twenty minutes from start to finish.

It was a major arrest.

But no one was especially thrilled by it. No one knew at the time that the Gainesville Ripper's days of terror were over.

39

The Sixth "Victim"

No one was really sure what kind of multiple killer they were dealing with. The murders had stopped, so it could be the work of a spree killer—the kind who killed in clustered surges of violence and then stopped when he was spent in his crazed need. Or, on the other hand, the publicity might have driven the killer to another area away from Gainesville, where the "serial" aspect of his mania could continue.

Most University of Florida students had returned to the campus after the long Labor Day weekend, rationalizing that since suspect number one was incarcerated they could feel safe again. Besides, all the precautionary measures that had been beefed up after the murders had been kept in place. And the police had other suspects in custody as well as Humphrey.

But Lt. Sadie Darnell reminded students returning to class that no one had been charged with the murders. Warnings continued to go out to students, not only from her but from UF Provost Andrew Sorensen and UF President John Lombardi.

There were many who were beginning to be convinced that Humphrey was not the murderer and suspected the police were not close to a solution. Still, students were letting their guards down. Feeling a sense of security because the killer had not struck again, many had stopped travelling in pairs. It was obvious the police did not know if the killer was still in the Gainesville area, but there was relief among Gainesville residents when a halt was put to the stops and searches and fingerprinting that had been going on from the first in the zealous attempts to catch the killer.

No links had been established to similar crimes in other places, even though it was there in black and white on one of the FBI VICAP reports from Quantico, Virginia.

And with no other good suspects in hand, Ed Humphrey had not been eliminated as a suspect. He was still being "looked at."

On September 10, the task force announced DNA tests were planned on semen found at the murder scenes and they were cautiously optimistic that the results would pinpoint their murderer.

Grandma was sure the tests would vindicate Ed despite the implication that charges against Ed were imminent.

Jenny Kanne was worried. She, too, couldn't believe the killer was Ed Humphrey. She realized she was just an amateur studying what most experts really knew little about themselves, and already she was making deductions, but she was worried. What if the real murderer had not been caught? If the Ripper decided to lie low because of the media scrutiny, local and national, it was obvious that the pressure was finally off. Now the articles written about the case were brief, repetitive and full of bravado and hollow optimism.

By September 12, while a multi-million-dollar Lotto frenzy suddenly gripped a community in deep need of diversion from the tragic story that had held it hostage for so long, the Gainesville student murders quietly slipped off the front pages. It was the first time the story was not on the front page of the Gainesville *Sun*.

Jenny felt like shouting a warning against what she perceived as the sudden lack of vigilance in Gainesville which could be an invitation to disaster. It was right there in the books she had been studying. And it was scary.

Of all multiple murderers it had been clearly established through extensive studies that the serial killer was the most likely to kill again. The recidivist nature of his vicious acts was well documented and corroborated in the annals of police investigative research. And he was usually out to achieve something—often subconsciously—that propelled the obsessive behavior. Not only did the killings usually fall into a pattern of some sort of warped "task" or "mission" that had to be completed, but once apprehended, serial killers achieved instant celebrity status. In many cases it was the only way they could achieve the often-craved-for immortality that was denied them as ordinary men. As Charles Starkweather, killer of ten, wrote in his autobiography: "Now millions of people will read about me and talk about me." Eventually a serial killer wanted his deeds known since he could not become a celebrity unless he was caught. So it was reasonable to suspect the Gainesville Ripper would kill again until he was caught, and immortalized.

Jenny was overwhelmed by the possibilities of slackening protective vigilance. She often spoke of it. But no one paid much attention to Jenny.

Summer ended. The sun was starting to lose some of its intensity. A cool breeze began to waft through the open campus grounds. As time passed and victim number six did not materialize, most students moved back to their own apartments. A difficult time of transformation and reflection finally led to a general calming. The precautionary measures taken earlier slowly eroded under a loose mantle of apathy. The common illusion that "it always happens to someone else anyway" helped.

With most of the preliminary investigations completed, managers of apartment complexes where the murders took place now had the painful task of cleaning up the apartments, removing blood from walls and floors, straightening up, hiding, covering, before relatives of the five victims were finally permitted to enter the apartments for the even more painful task of retrieving the personal items of their murdered children.

Johanna Yarborough, manager of Williamsburg Village Apartments, said she would turn the site of the murders into storage areas, aware of the families' suffering through personal moments of discovery as they walked through the empty rooms full of memories too agonized to record.

On September 25, 1990, it was finally announced that semen samples found at two of the scenes came from the same man. Although unofficial reports leaked that the DNA test results conducted by the FDLE did not link Ed Humphrey to the crime—his DNA did *not* match—no official word clearing Ed of the murders was ever forthcoming from the task force.

His family was devastated. George became even more embittered. The police continued to concentrate on Ed Humphrey.

Even without an indicted suspect, within a month the universities were back to the business of teaching, even though it took the students until the first exams to focus on their studies. They went home for Christmas and got back into regular courses of study when they returned. The university's football season lifted spirits. The first home football game had been a release for everybody. Optimism about a great football season was high, especially since Steve Spurrier, who had played quarterback so brilliantly for Florida that he won the Heisman Trophy in 1966, was the new football coach.

Life went on.

Jenny Kanne was one of those for whom life could not continue as usual until there was some kind of closure to the events.

She told Amelia she was still studying the subject. She was convinced, she said, according to her research, that Ed Humphrey could not possibly be the killer.

Amelia wished she would stop.

"The killer's going to be a white male in his mid- to late thirties who came from a bad family environment and who probably, as perceived by the standards of our society, is a total failure in his personal as well as his business life," Jenny stated.

Amelia badly wanted to shake away all thoughts of the murders, unwilling to join in on the discussions and theorizing that continued to permeate campus life in spite of the slackening vigilance. Jenny, on the other hand, persisted in her fascination with the serial killer, researching the subject as though she were doing a thesis. It was her way to deal with the trauma of her reaction to what had happened.

"Ed Humphrey might not be the one," she persisted. And if that was so, then Ed's story of harassment by police, media and neighbors was a truly tragic one.

Amelia said defensively that "they couldn't take a chance, they *had* to arrest him." She knew, though, what Jenny meant. The word was already getting out that Humphrey was being victimized. While under arrest he said he knew about the murders and even blamed them on his "alter egos," "John" or "Henry." He was suspected of having multiple personalities. The press continued to highlight every item of Humphrey's personal life.

Jenny was not the only one reading up on serial killers. Heated debates spread through small and large groups in cafeterias, classrooms, study halls, restrooms and campus lounges. One theory was that the police had more information on Humphrey but the information was tainted and therefore unusable because it had been obtained illegally. Another theory was that the police believed Humphrey was guilty but could not find enough evidence that would stand up in court. But with no proof other than hearsay, anecdotal evidence about his bizarre behavior, public sympathy began to turn in his favor. There was something moving about the forlorn photos of the scarred young man restrained in handcuffs and foot chains. Many students were theorizing that Humphrey was innocent.

"If Ed Humphrey is innocent," Jenny said to Amelia, "then he could be considered the Gainesville Ripper's sixth victim."

"On the other hand," Amelia said, "if Humphrey turns out to be the murderer, or in any way connected with the murders—"

"Then," Jenny insisted, "he'll be setting a new precedent in the profiles of sadistic serial killers. Did you read the FBI profile of the killer? In yesterday's paper?"

Amelia was unwilling to admit that she had. She knew that psychological profiling had been used for a long time and that now the experts were trying to create a profile of the Gainesville Ripper. It pretty well matched the description Jenny had just given—white male, mid- to late thirties, bad family environment, a failure . . .

"He's still out there."

Amelia did not want to hear it.

"Why do we have so many serial killers?" Jenny asked rhetorically.

Amelia was developing a headache. "Because there are a lot of crazy people out there!"

"If the killers are just crazy, why do they hardly ever show those symptoms?"

"I wouldn't know."

"There are a lot of easily identifiable clinical symptoms that indicate mental illness. All psychiatrists agree to that. Including disorders of thought and affect."

"I said I don't know," Amelia told her. "And you're beginning to sound like a textbook!"

"Well, think about it," Jenny said, shaking the open pages of *Compulsive Killers* at her.

"Can't we just drop it?"

"No! If Humphrey is innocent, then the real killer is still out there somewhere. And knowledge is power. Listen. It says here in Peter J. Wilson's *Study of Schizophrenia*, 'Madness is the individual's response to the obliteration of his identity by others.' But it says *here*," she said, turning to a marked page in another book, "that the sexual sadist is not mad."

She quickly scanned the page in Leyton's book for the passage she wanted to read to Amelia. Finding it, she read aloud, emphasizing the points she wanted to make. " '. . . They are not freaks. Rather they are the logical extension of many of the central themes of their culture—of worldly ambition, of success and failure, and of manly avenging violence. Although they take several forms—the serial killer whose murders provide both revenge and a *lifelong celebrity career*, and the mass killer, who no longer wishes to live, and whose murders constitute his *suicide note*—they can only be accurately and objectively perceived as'—and here's the important part," she said, glancing up. " 'They can only be accurately and objectively perceived as prime embodiment of their civilization, not twisted derangement. A person's leave-taking from conventional reality (called psychosis) *takes the form that his culture prescribes*. This is where the media responsibility is the greatest. It helps to create a culture that is eminently mimicable and repeatable. Thus madness is both a creative, self-protecting act, and a program of the culture. South American "primitives," the *Yanomano*, do not experience Arctic Hysteria and Americans do not encounter "Windigo Psychosis." ' "

"What the *hell* are you talking about?" Amelia said.

Jenny pushed on. "This has to do with all the things we've always talked about . . . the violence on television and the movies, using women as bait for the psychos. This corroborates what we've always said. Arctic Hysteria is a kind of craziness that happens only in Eskimo life. It's a madness that takes on a special form where the guy who is suffering from it rips off his clothes and races out onto the ice floes—oblivious to the danger. You won't find somebody doing that in New York, for instance, because it's not part of New York culture. And then there's . . ." she paused, scanning the book further, "there's something called Windigo Psychosis. Now, that only happens in the Ojibwa traditional culture. The Ojibwa tribe taught that people could be possessed by spirits that would give them an uncontrollable desire for human flesh. Believing what they were taught, the victims would kill humans, often their own families, and devour their flesh."

"How fascinating," Amelia said. "Just what I've always wanted to know about. People who eat their own families."

"Don't you get it? A lot of the freaks in our own culture are imitating what they see and hear all around them. In the movies. On television. That kind of thing."

She turned back to the book.

"A person taking leave from contemporary reality could very likely fall into a special category that is created by a society studded with violence and, in particular, full of graphic media violence against women. In our society, an increasing number of people kill for the pleasure it appears to give them. Are they mad, or are they acting out some analogous social message? The lesson here is that the psychiatric analogy is a false one: madness is not like cancer or any other physical ailment. Rather, it is a culturally programmed dialogue. It should not be, therefore, surprising that, except for the paranoid schizophrenic, mass murderers, no matter how hard our psychiatrists search, they are unable to discover much mental disease among our captured multiple murderers (except in the nature of their acts). Therein lies the special horror, for the killers are as 'normal' as you or me, yet they kill without mercy, and they kill to make a statement."[1]

Now she was reading more to herself than to Amelia, although despite her denials Amelia was listening intently.

"A sophisticated quantitative debate currently rages in social science over whether the ultimate cause of homicide lies in absolute poverty, relative inequality, or in regional subculture; but clearly all three embrace their share of truth, for *all* deprivation (be it absolute or relative) *provokes frustration*, and culture is ever the programmed maze instructing individuals how best to display their emotions. In any case, the multiple murderer is quite a different person: most often on the margins of the upper-working or lower-middle class, he is usually a profoundly conservative figure who comes to feel excluded from the class he so devoutly wishes to join. In an extended *campaign*

[1] Elliot Leyton, *Compulsive Killers: The Story of Modern Multiple Murder* (New York: New York University Press, 1986), pp. 21–22.

of vengeance, he murders people unknown to him, but who represent to him (in their behavior, their appearance, or their location) the class that has *rejected him* . . ."[1]

Jenny looked up to find that Amelia was staring at her coldly.
"All that stuff just excuses the killers."
"No, it doesn't. It's just a way of trying to understand, not excuse."
"Have you been listening to yourself?"
"What do you mean?"
"What is this obsession you have about all these crazy freaks?"
"It's not an obsession—"
"It's becoming one, Jenny."

Later that night, in spite of her earlier protests, Amelia did not object when Jenny installed the Radio Shack motion detector in the living room of the apartment. It was while Jenny was installing an extra security lock in the back of their apartment that they noticed pry marks on their rear door.
     This time it was Amelia who became furious.
     This time it was Jenny who began to shake.

And as Amelia and Jenny reversed roles, or more accurately, shared similar fears and anxieties, the fingers continued to be pointed at Ed Humphrey.
     One Edward Alan Laventure of the Polk County jail told the Gainesville task force that while in the isolation block he occupied a cell across from a fellow inmate, Stephen Michael Bates, who told him that he and Ed Humphrey had killed the students. He said he was Jack the Ripper and that he had met Humphrey in Ocala, and they had gone together to the apartment of a girl who had spurned Humphrey. They waited for the occupants to come home and Humphrey had slashed the throat of some big guy while he was sleeping on the couch. Bates apparently forgot that he'd said nobody was home when they broke in. When this was pointed out to Laventure he said he was just telling them what Bates had told him, including an embellishment that Humphrey and Bates killed the girl too and decapitated her. There was more, Satanism, and on and on. Much of what Laventure was telling didn't match known facts. When this was put to him, he admitted he was hoping to get some help with the authorities over his sentence. The results of a polygraph showed that Laventure had lied about Bates' alleged meeting with Humphrey in Ocala. Other items might have

[1] Leyton, p. 23.

been what Bates told Laventure, but, as the authorities pointed out, Bates could well have been lying. Manny Taboada was the only male victim, and he was not killed on a couch and Tracy Paules was not decapitated.

There was a similar interview with one John Thomas Schneider, who had also been a fellow inmate of Bates. Schneider said that Bates told him that Humphrey was into "Satanic stuff," that he didn't like brunettes because they reminded him of his mother, and it wasn't just Bates and Humphrey who did the killings, there was another man. Who? He didn't say, but after the three of them committed the murders they put a knife and some of the victims' personal property and a new pair of sneakers in a backpack, carried it into the woods by a power plant in the Gainesville area and burned it, then dug a hole and buried the pack.

Now the interrogators' interest was piqued. They remembered that during a previous session with Humphrey in August he claimed to have burned and buried items that he took from the murder scene, including the knife his "alter egos" used to stab the victims. Though unproven and made at a time when Humphrey had been under continuous interrogation without benefit of his medication, Schneider's statement seemed the most corroborative allegation made against Humphrey. When asked if anyone else had heard any of this talk from Bates, Schneider said another guy, a Calvin Calhoun, heard Bates talking about the Gainesville murders a couple of times. There was no record of a Calvin Calhoun in the jail.

And then there was an Andrew Golden, awaiting trial on a first-degree murder charge of killing his wife, who said he believed that Bates was telling him the straight dope when he claimed to have killed the students. The agents had already talked to him, as they had talked to numerous others. Bates wanted to confess, according to Golden. Why had he and Humphrey done the killings? Booze and Satanism was the reply.

Stephen Bates had apparently boasted to many of his fellow inmates about the killings, seemingly pleased to wrap himself in the celebrity mantle of the high-profile murders. At times he had enough facts correct to require attention . . . never enough to make him a prime suspect but enough to continue to pique the interest of the authorities by his re-creations involving Ed Humphrey by name.

When Ed Humphrey, on October 10, 1990, was found guilty of battery in the beating of his grandmother, in spite of the fact that Grandma Elna Hlavaty testified for her grandson and said he never struck her, and then was sentenced to twenty-two months in the state hospital at Chattahoochee, the Gainesville judge declared that the murders had played no role in his decision. Humphrey's family, among others, questioned that, inas-

40

1991—The Big Link

It was New Year's Day, 1991, a worldwide holiday, when the Mr. Hyde side of Rolling's personality made itself known to the Marion County prison authorities.

While most were celebrating the beginning of a new year, inmate Daniel Harold Rolling ripped a prison-cell toilet from its mounting with strength from years of weight lifting, and heaved it against a dayroom window. Repeatedly he picked it up and threw it against the window, trying to break through, trying to escape or, as a fellow cellmate suggested, practicing acting crazy.

His defense attorney, Victoria Lisarralde, asked for psychological tests. Under the circumstances of his bizarre behavior, she also moved for a withdrawal of the guilty plea on the armed-robbery charge he was facing.

Meanwhile, authorities in Shreveport, Louisiana, had noted striking similarities in the Gainesville student murders to the Grissom triple-murder in Shreveport in November of 1989.

One of the Shreveport detectives called the Gainesville task force and suggested they had a fellow from his area in jail down there in Ocala. Danny Rolling. He might be somebody they might want to take a look at. Why, in particular? Well, he was from Shreveport, somebody they all thought was a bad actor. Shot his father in the eye in a violent argument. He was wanted around Shreveport for attempted murder of his father.

It didn't sound connected.

"Also," the detective continued, "we had a triple murder out here with some similarities, a dark-haired, pretty girl, Julie Grissom, along with her father and nephew."

"It doesn't really sound too much alike."

Well, the caller acknowledged, Rolling wasn't what one might call a significant suspect in the Grissom murders. It was just that it was very much unsolved there, and they didn't want to ignore the coincidence.

What coincidence?

And then the detective cited what he considered a startling similarity between the murders—the killer cleaned the private parts with a blue-green liquid soap to remove all traces of evidence. And "most particularly, it was the way he positioned the body." For maximum shock effect. It was all there in the FBI VICAP reports.

The task force reexamined the FBI VICAP reports that had been received at the office of the Combined Homicide Task Force by Special Agent Porter on October 16, 1990. Item number four mentioned the Grissom case in Shreveport.

1) A similar murder had occurred in Monroe County, Florida. The Monroe County Sheriff's Office submitted the victim's name as Sherry Perisho, PX#402-471-7660/7207

2) Date 8/20/86—Victim, Mary Jo Peitzmeier, came from Lincoln, Nebraska, PX#815-987-5878

3) Date 12/30/88—Victim, Jennifer Jenning, came from Rockford P.D. Illinois

4) A similar method of killing was noted in a triple murder November 6, 1989, killing in Shreveport, Louisiana. Here the victims were Julie Grissom, her father, Tom Grissom and her eight-year-old nephew, Sean Grissom, PX#219-762-3122

5) Victim, Lisa Kopanakis

6) Date, 8/4/89, from Portage P.D., Indiana, PX#813-587-6224—Victim, Laurie Colanni

7) Date, January 1990, from Pinnellas S.O., Florida, PX#602-262-489:2, Victim, Sara Clark

8) Date, 5/18/88, Phoenix, Arizona, Cocoa P.D.—Victim, Mary Sue Dobb—Date, 1982. Adalusia Dept. Public Safety, Alabama—Victim, Julie Ann McCroy

Upon closer inspection of the Grissom case similarities began to emerge. The Gainesville Ripper showed technical proficiency and knowledge of police procedures in the manner in which he cleaned up the murder scenes. Solvents were used to clean bodies and eliminate clues. The Shreveport killer showed the same technical proficiency and knowledge of police procedures in the manner in which he cleaned up the murder scenes. He also used solvents to clean bodies and eliminate clues. Both killers used duct tape to bind their victims and then removed the tape and took it away—a knowledgeable move, since tape easily shows fingerprints.

Both used the same kind of forced entry into the apartments. Both used the same kind of knife. Both raped and mutilated their victims. As with Christa Hoyt, Julie Grissom's wounds were relatively blood-free, indicating that most of the mutilations were post mortem. Perhaps most striking, both left behind the same "messages" to taunt the police by the manner in which they placed the bodies in poses evidently designed to shock.

Okay. But careful now. Don't get too excited. But it did seem like a good deal of coincidence—if that's what it was—was at play.

Let's look at this guy for real, they decided.

It was five P.M. on January 11 when Special Agent Dennis Fisher contacted the Marion County jail to inquire about the inmate Daniel Harold Rolling. Correctional Officer Sharon Roberts responded to his call.

"Can you tell me, what are the specific charges this fellow Rolling's being held on?" Fisher asked her. "And what the current status is on them?"

When she returned to the line she had Rolling's file in front of her. "The original charges are," she said, reading them off, "one for Armed Robbery, one for Grand Theft Auto, and one for Fleeing and Eluding." She scanned the file. "Wait a minute. It seems that on November eighth, nineteen ninety, the Grand Theft Auto charge was dropped by the State Attorney's office in Ocala. Doesn't say why."

"What about the other two charges?"

"They're pending a psychological evaluation of Rolling. A twenty-five-thousand-dollar bond's been set on the armed robbery and five hundred dollars on the fleeing. There are also two Holds on Rolling filed by other law-enforcement agencies. One of them by Shreveport, Louisiana, on an attempted second-degree murder charge."

"And the other?"

"From Hillsborough County, Florida, on a Grand Theft Auto charge."

"Put a notice in Rolling's file," Special Agent Fisher requested, "to notify the Combined Homicide Task Force in Gainesville in the event Rolling is to leave the Marion County jail."

In the interim the task force decided to reexamine every crime that had taken place in the Gainesville area during the time of the murders, hoping to find a connection—somebody who might have made good their escape through burglary, robbery, a car theft. Anything.

They looked again at the First Union National Bank robbery on Archer and Thirty-fourth Avenue, a short distance from Christa Hoyt's apartment. The holdup had occurred on August 27, 1990, the morning Christa was discovered, but it was only now, in January of 1991, that the task force took a close look at the person who had run away from the nearby campsite and managed to elude the police. They had no idea who he was. Only that when his campsite was discovered by Alachua County deputies on August 28, evidence and cash recovered connected the unidentified occupant of the site to the bank robbery the day before. In the process of making his escape the robber had abandoned personal belongings at the campsite—bedding, a gun, a ski mask, a cassette tape deck, a screwdriver, all of which had been lumped together at the time of discovery and stored away.

State Attorney Len Register remembered that the FDLE lab had been able to project the type of instrument that had left the pry marks at the entry points of the murder scenes; because of the extensive record of pry-mark impressions the lab had of various kinds of tools, the technicians could tell what the tool was. What it was made of, what its model number was, as well as the dimensions of the ladling on the screwdriver. Len remembered carefully that they could predict lines that ran perpendicular to the shaft of the blade of the screwdriver for extra gripping power.

"Let's get some impressions of that screwdriver found at the campsite," Len said.

And things began to move.

The reports coming in from the lab on the screwdriver were encouraging: "The pry marks look great." "We've never seen any better." "We have seventeen separate matches from the screwdriver."

Seventeen! Len Register was almost afraid to allow himself a surge of what could be premature optimism. The screwdriver that was found at the bank robber's campsite could actually be placed at the scenes of the murders, but no one on the task force got excited until they received another lab report: DNA testing showed that a single pubic hair that had been found in the vacuum sweep of the campsite belonged to Christa Hoyt.

"Are you sure?"

"Positive."

"No short cuts on this," Len Register said. "Give it highest priority."

Now it was becoming very difficult to contain the growing euphoria. These were the first solid pieces of evidence—a screwdriver that perfectly matched the entry pry marks at the murder scenes and a pubic hair that physically connected one of the murder victims to the unknown occupant of the abandoned campsite.

"Go through everything that was found in that bag!" Register ordered.

And one of the items they found stored away was a cassette recorder with a cassette tape inside.

It had *never* been listened to.

It was LeGran Hewitt who pulled out the cassette and listened to the tape, then came running up the stairs to the task force commanders. "Listen to this!"

When he turned it on they heard:

This is Danny Harold Rolling out under the stars tonight.

They listened to him sing some songs. It was the same guy. The guy from Shreveport.

Incredible. With all of the prodigious combined efforts to track down the killer being made by the Gainesville Police Department, the Alachua County Sheriff's Office, the Florida Department of Law Enforcement, the Federal Bureau of Investigation and all the computerized resources of VICAP, the task force had him on tape from the day Tracy Paules and Manny Taboada were discovered, in his own voice, singing under the stars.

This is Danny Harold Rolling out under the stars tonight.

The screwdriver with the seventeen matching pry marks was found underneath the tape deck with the recording in which Rolling identified himself. On the one hand, Register was thrilled at what appeared to be the first serious breakthrough in the case. On the other hand, there was an element of embarrassment. They had had the tape in their custody all along, not connecting the campsite to the killings; once they found the pink-dyed money from the robbery, they knew they had found the campsite of the escaped bank robber but had not made a connection between the robber and the Gainesville Ripper.

Word of a new prime suspect spread quickly. In spite of all attempts to maintain the customary cool professionalism within the department, the excitement in the air was electric. The tape, the screwdriver and the hair triggered the matter from their point of view, creating the task force's initial focus on Rolling.

It was beginning to add up.

Register said: "We can't say Rolling is our man yet. Not until we get some DNA confirmation. We need body-fluid samples from him to do a DNA comparison on the body fluids that were recovered at the crime scene."

In a private moment Register thought about Humphrey. In his mind the hunt for the killer had always persisted even after the arrest of Humphrey. With no one else to take his place as the number-one suspect they could not let Humphrey off the hook. But no one on the task force was ever

completely satisfied with the convenient suspect. Certainly not Len Register. It was the media that insisted on plastering him all over the front
pages. Now with Rolling emerging as a distinct possibility, most of Humphrey's incomplete leads, which had been previously filed in "one,"
dropped off to the lowest priority.

The Humphrey family was not informed of the change in his status.

When Corrections Officer Sergeant Donna Borgione reported to work at
the Marion County jail at 6:00 A.M. on January 23 to begin her shift she
learned that at 5:15 that morning Sgt. K. K. Williams, with Officer Carl
Durham, had moved inmate Daniel Harold Rolling from cell 238 to 240.

"What for?" she asked.

"We've been contacted by a special agent from the FDLE Gainesville
homicide task force. John Burton."

"Why?"

"They're looking at Rolling regarding the homicides in Gainesville. He
may be connected to them in some way. Just checking out his stuff.
They've requested that we remove all items of clothing," Williams said.
"Bedsheets and trash from his cell and retain all of his personal possessions until we can turn them over to Burton."

In the privacy of an office in the jail and in the presence of Special
Agent Burton, Sergeant Williams placed the items taken from Rolling's
cell into two paper bags, which he stapled closed. The exteriors of the bags
were marked DHR–1 and DHR–2, with an inventory of the contents written by Sergeant Williams on the outside of each paper bag. Sergeant Williams also provided Burton with a written report, which he documented:

> 2 pairs of Hanes briefs
> 1 T-shirt
> 1 pair of socks
> 1 Hanes gray sweatshirt
> 1 uniform pants
> 1 uniform shirt
> 2 paper towels
> 1 piece of torn T-shirt
> 14 gauze pads, small
> 2 sheets
> 1 pillowcase
> 1 blanket

At 6:10 A.M. on January 23, 1991, Sergeant Williams turned the bags
over to Special Agent John Burton. Burton retained possession of the

items and personally sealed them with red evidence tape before returning to the FDLE Ocala field office.

At 8:35 A.M. that same morning, Burton was contacted by phone at the Ocala field office by Special Agent Bigelow of the Gainesville task force. Bigelow advised that Marion Corrections Officer Sgt. Donna Borgione had missed him at the jail. She called to report that Rolling had had a tooth extracted the day before. Burton hurried back to the Marion County jail. Sergeant Borgione had the tooth in her possession.

Rolling had been having some problems with his teeth and had been scheduled to see the dentist, Dr. Thompson, the day before. As a high-security-status prisoner, Rolling was in a red suit. All red suits had to be accompanied by a minimum of two corrections officers whenever they were outside their assigned cell block. Sgt. Donna Borgione and Officer Charles Skipper accompanied him to the dentist at the jail infirmary and were responsible for his security while he was being treated by Dr. Thompson. Both Borgione and Skipper witnessed Dr. Thompson extract a tooth from Rolling's mouth and pack the open wound with gauze. The dentist checked that there was no abnormal bleeding or other medical complications, and Sergeant Borgione watched the doctor remove the gauze packing, wrap the extracted tooth inside it, wrap both items inside the folds of a paper towel and place the package in a red medical bio-plastic bag. Borgione saw him then toss the bag into a bin of medical waste material. Officer Skipper and Sergeant Borgione then returned the slightly pale inmate to his cell block.

Now, after talking to Sgt. K. K. Williams and realizing that Rolling was being investigated in a case that had dominated the news throughout Florida late last summer and fall, Sergeant Borgione remembered Rolling's tooth extraction. She went to the jail infirmary and located the bin of medical waste that contained numerous red plastic bags not yet disposed of. Borgione removed and opened the top bag, in which she found the disposable face mask she associated with Dr. Thompson. She also found pieces of aluminum foil. From her previous experiences in the infirmary she knew that only Dr. Thompson discarded this type of waste.

She located the extracted tooth. She put the tooth, the bloodied gauze and paper towel in which it had been wrapped in a paper bag that she stapled shut. Before Sergeant Borgione called the Gainesville task force she decided to check out further the medical records on file in the jail infirmary. Once she had determined that inmate Daniel Harold Rolling was the only person to have a tooth extracted on January 22, she placed her telephone call to Gainesville. Sergeant Borgione kept the confiscated items in her personal possession until 9:10 that morning when FDLE Special Agent John Burton returned and she could personally hand over the sealed bag to him.

A few days later, when Rolling indicated in a grievance request form that he wanted to get a haircut, Sgt. Donna Borgione, once again assigned as one of his security guards, told the trustee, T. Beam, who was to cut his hair, to use a clean towel around Rolling's neck.

Beam found Rolling to be friendly—he even insisted on shaking Beam's hand—and when he got into the chair immediately began to talk about religion.

After the haircut Sergeant Borgione gathered the newly clipped hair and put it in an envelope for the investigators.

But Len Register was nervous.

It was the beginning of almost three thousand leads collected on Rolling, adding to the immense file of leads already accumulated in the computerized Leads System, and it was the first body-tissue or body-fluid sample of Rolling the FDLE had to work with. But Len knew the defense could ask to have the evidence thrown out because the manner in which it had been obtained could be construed as having gathered fruit from the poisonous tree. If something had been collected improperly and had served as the foundation for everything collected afterward, all the subsequent evidence could be thrown out. The case could fall like a house of cards if the initial foundation evidence was determined to be inadmissible. Len knew it could be difficult to get the items admitted as evidence in a trial except, perhaps, since Rolling had essentially "abandoned" them a judge might rule for the prosecution and allow the items to be admitted.

But why take chances? No poisonous-tree rulings on this one.

The prosecution team went back to the Marion County jail with a search warrant to get a blood sample and head-hair standards from the suspect. They wanted to double- and triple-cover themselves. In the warrant they made no reference to the original samples retrieved by Sergeant Borgione or to any of the results from the initial tests, so that in requesting the search warrant the results from these samples could not be tied to the poisonous-tree doctrines.

"You know what the rules are," Register reminded everyone. "We need to make sure that everything is real squeaky clean."

A search warrant was executed on all of Rolling's personal property. Special Agent Dennis Fisher, Bureau Chief Platt and Crime-scene Technician Thorpe then drove to the Ocala City Police Department to serve the warrant, and these items were confiscated and turned over to the bureau chief of the FDLE in Jacksonville to be taken directly to the lab:

    1 Walkman FM stereo, yellow
    1 hand-drawn map
    1 yellow-handled regular screwdriver
    1 blue backpack
    1 blue fanny pack
    a handwritten note-reference emergency notification
    1 light blue pocket comb
    1 gold pierced earring
    1 pair of racquetball gloves
    1 beige T-shirt
    1 black T-shirt

Once inquiries began about Rolling, it was learned that *he* had made some interesting statements to other cellmates. As usual, unlike the touted criminal code-of-silence or honor-among-thieves themes glamorized in fictional crime films, TV stories and books, most inmates were more than willing to cooperate with authorities if they sensed some potential benefit to their own situations.

"We got a report from an inmate in Ocala," one of the investigators told Register, "some guy named Johnny. An early cellmate of Rolling's. It seems Rolling had been talking to him about the interior of one of the crime-scene apartments as though he had been there, and he made a comment that one of the girls was a cat freak."

Check it out, Len told him.

The investigators pulled the crime-scene photos and saw that Christa's apartment had been decorated with cats: a poster of Garfield the Cat. A little cat magnet. Cats on the shower curtain. A cat's picture on the wall.

It was a small but pertinent detail that had *never* been published, and unless one were a participant in the murder or had been at the scene it would have been impossible to know about all the feline decorations. It had even passed over the heads of the investigators; no one recalled any cat paraphernalia, but when they went back and looked at the photos of the crime scene, there they were. Len realized that Johnny would not be the best witness in the world. He had a psychiatric history that could put his credibility factor at risk, but the cat motif was something that could not have been guessed.

Circumstantial though it might be, it significantly added to their growing conviction that Daniel Harold Rolling was their man.

The momentum of inquiry and discovery was building.

* * *

Jim Eckert of the Alachua County Sheriff's Office was the squad supervisor of the Gainesville Homicide Task Force. On January 23, at approximately nine P.M., he put in a call to Special Agent John Burton at his home. "It's about this Marion County inmate, Daniel Rolling."

"Yes?"

"Detective Ryan Garrett and a latent-print examiner from Hillsborough County Sheriff's Department, a guy by the name of Royce Wilson, are scheduled to serve a search warrant on Rolling tomorrow at the Marion County jail."

"What's the warrant for?"

"To obtain known standards of Rolling's head hair and major case prints."

"Regarding the Gainesville homicides?"

"No. In connection with an armed-robbery investigation."

"Okay." Burton nodded to himself. To start off with, anyway.

"Make direct contact with Detective Garrett," Eckert added, "and arrange to meet him in Ocala and to receipt for and submit Rolling's hair standards to the FDLE Orlando Crime Lab. Dennis Fisher will be going with you. At three-thirty P.M."

The moment Burton hung up he called Detective Garrett. "I'll be coming tomorrow, Thursday, the twenty-fourth, at three-thirty with Special Agent Fisher."

"We've already made arrangements with Royce Wilson from Hillsborough County to meet us all here at the Marion County jail."

Burton and Fisher met with Garrett and the latent-print examiner the next afternoon at 3:30 P.M. They knew they were on to something big but maintained a calculated, all-business approach. They stood silently observing Rolling being major-case printed by Royce Wilson—finger by finger by finger—as Rolling, standing out in his maximum-security red prison suit, maintained a passive, pained, frowning silence throughout the procedure. He was then taken to a room by Detective Garrett to obtain the head-hair standards that were called for in the search warrant. If Rolling suspected the warrant had been issued in connection with the Gainesville murders, he never let on. Special Agents Burton and Fisher went with Detective Garrett to the Marion County courthouse, where Garrett made a return on the search warrant.

Mitch Stacy had become nearly obsessed with the Gainesville-murders story, which was essentially being covered by his colleagues from the Gainesville *Sun* and the Ocala *Star Banner*, Tom Lyons, Cathy Crownover and Kelly Turner. Although Mitch had been involved in the story from the beginning, he had had to take time out to cover his regular Thursday night spot as court reporter at the Gainesville courthouse. While there he ran into Tom Lyons, who told him about the hot new suspect.

The guy was from Shreveport, Louisiana. Daniel Harold Rolling, Tom told him in confidence. It was the first time Mitch had heard the name. How did you know? Inside confirmation, was the answer.

And Mitch realized that his friend Tom, an excellent investigative reporter, had flushed out the identity of the suspect. Not only would Lyons write the first comprehensive articles about Rolling, linking him to the five Gainesville as well as to the three Shreveport murders, but he also managed to flush out one of the first published photographs of the suspect—a faded, smiling picture of Rolling taken in the early 1980s. There was even a dim photo taken off a videotape of Rolling in an Ocala courtroom as he pleaded guilty to reckless driving when eluding the police after the Winn-Dixie robbery.

Now the Marion County Sheriff's Office was again under siege by the news media to provide photos of the new suspect. Marion County's Major Hendry was informed that threats of court action had already been made by the media and would be aggressively pursued if photos of Rolling were not released. Major Hendry was aware of communications between Gainesville State Attorney Brad King and Marion County Sheriff's Attorney Willard Pope about the release of Rolling's photos and was momentarily caught in the middle. Hendry told Burton that the best way for them to be out of the situation was for the task force to seize all of the Rolling photos they had on file and hold them as evidence. It was a smart move. Now all requests for Rolling photos by the media would have to be referred directly to the Gainesville Combined Homicide Task Force.

At five that same evening when Detective Ryan Garrett provided Special Agent Burton with a sealed envelope containing Rolling's head-hair standards, he also gave him two Polaroid photos that he had taken, one before and one after he had pulled the head hairs from Rolling. In addition he had the major-case prints that had been retained by Royce Wilson. By 9:38 P.M. Burton talked by phone to Capt. J. O. Jackson. "I have them," he told him before passing on Major Hendry's request about Rolling's photos. Jackson said he'd contact State Attorney Register and he would tell Burton what action to take. Thirty-five minutes later Captain Jackson recontacted Burton and told him to get in touch with Major Hendry again and make arrangements to take custody of all the Rolling photos in question. "Tell him a subpoena *duces tecum* for the photos will be issued by

State Attorney Register on Friday, January twenty-fifth, nineteen ninety-one."

At 10:20 Burton recontacted Major Hendry to give him Jackson's directions. "I'll meet with you at the Marion County jail tomorrow morning and personally take custody of the photos. At eight A.M."

They would be kept under lock and key until then, Hendry told him.

When Mitch Stacy got back to the office that night he learned the paper wanted to send him on assignment to Shreveport. Tom Lyons was in the middle of a major story and could not be spared. Mitch and Holly had tickets for a Jimmy Buffett concert that night. Buffett would have to go on without him. He could not even get Holly on the phone to tell her he was going out of town. They had arranged to meet at a local bar after work. Instead, as Holly waited for him, another Gainesville *Sun* reporter showed up in his place and told Holly her husband was on his way to Shreveport. Looks like a breakthrough, he told her.

As scheduled, at eight A.M. on January 25 Major Hendry turned the Rolling photos over to Burton and Fisher at the Marion County office. At 8:45 Burton submitted Rolling's head-hair standards to the Orlando FDLE crime lab. At three P.M. Burton and Fisher met with Jim Eckert from the Alachua County Sheriff's Office at the Gainesville Homicide Task Force. Burton briefed Eckert about the laboratory submission and provided him with the affidavit, search warrant and photo of Rolling.

Steve Platt, bureau chief of the FDLE Crime Lab, went to the task force offices with orders from the commissioner to tell State Attorney Len Register first of the convincing new developments in the case. Len ordered an immediate full-staff meeting.

"We have a match on the first probe," Chief Platt announced quietly.

Preliminary DNA tests on semen left at the scenes showed that it carried Rolling's unique genetic "fingerprint." The link had been irrefutably established. Everyone knew it was a great break in the case, but nobody broke out into loud cheers. Instead, there was a subdued murmur, but Len could see the signs of relief beneath the subdued reactions.

Chief Platt was asked, "How good is that?"

"When you have a match on the first probe," he answered, "it's highly unlikely that you'd get some dissimilarity or not get a match on the second or third probe."

There was no shortage of body fluids from the murder scenes. They had more than enough of the murderer's semen needed to run multiple DNA probes from scene one alone.

When the tests continued to match with results from semen taken from the second crime scene and then the third, they were considered a "multiplier" of the first crime scene. The odds that it could have been somebody else that committed all three crimes were so long as not to count. In fact, the FDLE lab had been running tests on anyone who could possibly have committed the murders—suspects, neighbors, families, prisoners—so that they had created a far-reaching DNA data bank. Now the lab was so confident of the DNA testing on Rolling that the technicians stopped running elimination tests on anyone else's blood.

When matching multiple probes came back, there was no doubt in anyone's mind on the task force that they had the right person. They had their "big break," somebody to really focus on.

They began referring to Rolling as "the DNA guy."

While detectives from the Combined Task Force descended on James and Claudia Rolling's home at 6314 West Canal Boulevard in Shreveport the media began its detailed account of all of their older son's felony convictions, his violent outbursts and of what was perceived and analyzed in the press as his abused childhood.

Meanwhile, back in Gainesville, George Humphrey, Jr., found his answering machine full of urgent messages from his family as well as from countless reporters all wanting to know his reaction to the new suspect. He ignored the media and contacted his family. His father called from Montana wanting to know what was going on and if there was something he could do to help. What did it mean? his mother in Indialantic asked over the telephone, talking to him in his room in Gainesville. "Don't worry," he told her without believing it. He had little confidence left in a system he believed had victimized his brother. Remembering the two-killer theory that had been floating around for a while, he was even worried that they might try to connect Ed to this new fellow, Rolling. His law-school entrance exam was coming up soon. He wanted to study for it but he couldn't concentrate, he couldn't sleep.

While the Humphrey-Hlavaty family continued to worry, to the rest of those involved with the case it appeared the search was over. The families of the victims, though pleased at the news, still, of course, had their pain. Reaction on campus was heartfelt but subdued.

Shreveport, Louisiana, however, was a madhouse. By the time Mitch arrived, it seemed to him that reporters from all over the country, knowing he was from the Gainesville *Sun*, were on his tail. It was hectic, but he managed to be where he had to be one step ahead of the pack. He was surprised that the *Sun* sent one of the Ocala *Star Banner*'s photographers to go with him instead of sending one of their own photographers from Gainesville, but he liked Alan Youngblood, young, personable, with a golden head of hair and beard. He was a good photographer, a PADI-certified diver, well-known for his underwater photography and a graduate of the University of Florida.

Early in the morning they went to the Rolling house on West Canal Boulevard in Sunset Acres. They caught his mother Claudia coming out of the house on her way to work—a small, slightly plump middle-aged woman with dark hair now streaked with gray and a round face that seemed pressed into a perennial expression of grief.

Mitch was the first reporter to show up at her door. There would be others.

She became very emotional when she saw the two bearded young men and learned who they were and what they wanted . . . for her to tell them about Danny. She told them to get away from her, tears in her eyes.

"I'd like to tell your side of it," Mitch told her. "The truth, before it gets distorted."

Claudia Rolling did not want to hear any of it. She got in her car quickly and locked the car door, stepped heavily on the accelerator, backed out of the driveway and took off.

Then James Rolling came out of the house—a small, round, angry man. He stood his ground in the middle of his front lawn, pointed a finger at them and chased them away with threats to have them arrested.

Mitch persisted. He went to the neighbors. "I knew he was a strange personality," said Beverly Woodall, remembering how Danny would work out with weights in his yard or go jogging through the neighborhood carrying a heavy log across the back of his shoulders. "But I never would have expected him to do something like that."

He went to the Superior Bar and Grill to talk to Paul Simon, the bartender, who shook his head as he recalled how Rolling talked about his "big break" and how someday he was going to make a "big score."

Mitch sought out old acquaintances, old girlfriends like Bunny Mills, who tried to help him when he needed a job; ex-employers like electrician Truman Cooley, who "always liked the guy."

The next day a straight-on, round-faced mug shot from one of Rolling's earlier arrests was on the front page, along with an article by Mitch Stacy in which a preliminary picture emerged of the boy who had become the man who may have become a killer.

There were the usual reactions from people who had in one way or another been associated with Rolling, unable to believe that someone they had known personally could be as monstrous as the man depicted in the crimes: James Robert Ford, who met him in the men's department of

Burdine's department store in Sarasota; Leila Grossman, who shared inti-
macies with him after meeting him at the coin-operated crane machine of
The Cabana Bar; Theresa Lynn Cousins from the Brown Derby Lounge,
for whom he bought presents; and in particular his old minister Reverend
Hudspeth, who was stunned at the revelations coming out of Florida about
Danny. True, he had never had a very close relationship with the troubled
young man nor had taken extra special notice, and it was almost twenty
years since he had seen him, but now he wished he had paid more attention to what might have been developing. Danny did stand out as a troubled youth. Everyone knew he had problems. The minister remembered
the man in their congregation who had a genuine desire to help the boy
and had given him a job, but Danny Rolling did not follow through.

Reverend Hudspeth also remembered how devastated Rolling seemed
when he lost his wife and daughter. But now he stood accused of the worst
crimes imaginable.

To Reverend and Glenda Hudspeth's surprise, Rolling called them from
prison in Gainesville immediately after he was named a prime suspect in
the student killings. Sounding almost convincing, he told them he wanted
to "keep in contact" even though they hadn't heard from him in years.
When Glenda spoke to him she said, "Now you know what they're accusing you of."

"Yes. Don't believe everything you hear," he told her.

He didn't deny the murders or admit to them.

"The reason I called . . . I'm asking y'all to pray for me. I really need
your prayers."

Afterward Glenda asked her husband if he thought Danny Rolling
could have done all the things they were accusing him of.

"If it were based on my knowledge of those two years we knew him
twenty years ago, I would say impossible." He paused. "But," he added,
"my experience with human nature and the human family, with the drastic
changes that can occur . . . Glenda," he said, "I've had a great many
surprises in my life. Did he do it? I don't know, but I can't rule it out. You
know, I'm open-minded, I have to be. But I also have to say, if it were
based strictly on my knowledge of him when he was with us, I'd have to
say no."

Yes, he would pray for Danny. The reverend thought of saving his soul.

The Combined Homicide Task Force thought of getting his hide into the
electric chair.

Christa Hoyt's mother, Theresa Ann Garren, examined the Rolling photo
when it appeared on one of the front pages of the Gainesville *Sun*. There
was no doubt in her mind. She specifically recalled serving him as a cus-

tomer, and more than once. Probably one time while Christa was present at one of the tables, visiting her. She called the authorities to tell them she remembered him at IHOP. She added that Rolling was generally sloppy-looking, dressed in sneakers, jeans and a T-shirt. She could not remember the specific number of times he came in, sat in the smoking section and ordered coffee, but she knew it was several times before the homicides.

On February 10, 1991, came a connection between the Gainesville Ripper and the Shreveport killer of Julie Grissom, her father and nephew through DNA genetic "fingerprinting."

George Humphrey immediately demanded an apology for the way his brother's case had been handled.

None was forthcoming.

When Rolling's paternal grandmother, Cavis Rolling, and her daughter, Jeanette Caughey, returned from a doctor's appointment on February 27 they found Rolling's grandfather, Homer, being interviewed on the front porch of their home in Bibb City, Georgia.

"I'll help you any way I can in the investigation of my grandson," Homer said to Special Agent Tom Yowell. "But you know women. They get emotional."

"Just ask him," Aunt Jeanette interrupted. "He'll tell you the truth."

"Who?" Yowell asked.

"Danny. You just ask Danny what the questions are and I'm sure he'll provide a truthful answer."

Yowell said he couldn't do that, he was prevented from talking to her nephew by his defense counsel.

In his report Yowell noted that she made no statement to assert Rolling's innocence or indicate that he was not capable of committing the murders under investigation. He found her to be congenial and coopera-tive during the interview and agreed to meet with him at a later time.

Yowell asked Homer about his children.

"They won't be much help," he said. "I've got five children, three daughters and two sons, one of them is Danny's father. The other son lives someplace in California. I don't know what city or the telephone number. My other two daughters live over in Columbus, Georgia, and to my knowl-edge have had no contact with Danny in the past four or five years."

Jeanette Caughey nodded. Homer went on to say he hadn't spoken with or seen Danny during the last three years.

While Special Agent Yowell was interviewing them on the front porch, Cavis came to the screen door. They sensed her presence and turned to look at her silhouette beyond the screen that separated them. "Danny Rolling is a good boy," she said to them quietly. "He's just like the clouds in the sky. Some days it's sunny and some days it's stormy and raining, Danny changed just like the clouds and nobody knows why. Danny's a good boy," she assured them again and disappeared into the house.

Assistant State Attorney Jim Nilon had been assigned to prepare the murder case against Danny Rolling for the grand jury. While waiting for the indictment to be served, Rolling had to answer to a series of other criminal charges.

In July, while prosecutors quietly dropped the assault and burglary charges against Ed Humphrey that had resulted from the dispute between him and fraternity members prior to the discovery of the first body, Rolling was indicted by a Tallahassee federal grand jury for the First Union National Bank robbery. Marion County Judge Thomas Sawaya ruled he was mentally competent to plead guilty in the Ocala Winn-Dixie robbery, and by August he stood trial for the alleged offense.

Claudia Rolling and two of her sisters attended the trial in Tampa. Representing the Gainesville *Sun*, Mitch Stacy sat immediately behind them throughout the court proceedings. They were all no more than four feet away from where Danny Rolling was sitting with his defense attorney. From his vantage point behind them, Mitch could watch Rolling interacting with his mother and his aunts. Goofy, smiling, joking, he would look over and mouth the words "I love you, Mom," and she would say "I love you too, son." One time he wrote on a piece of paper, "Jesus loves me." He got up and showed his mother and she nodded.

When Mitch tried to interview Rolling's mother, she quietly told him she did not want to talk about the killings.

Mitch Stacy had been a reporter a long time and had always felt he could separate his feelings from his work. The first day of the murders he had started a diary but after a while got so busy he could no longer continue it. It was pure adrenaline that drove him, and putting his feelings aside, he attacked the story as a once-in-a-lifetime journalistic opportunity. Now he was wondering if his feelings weren't catching up with him after all. He did feel sorry for Claudia Rolling. What must it be like to have a son who could do such things? How did she sleep nights? He looked closely into her moist brown eyes. Denial, he thought. She didn't believe the charges against her son. That was her way of dealing with it.

On August 29, 1991, while his mother lowered her eyes to the folds of her dress, Rolling was convicted of the supermarket robbery.

Ed Humphrey's parole from prison was now imminent. The governor himself had been concerned about his release and had asked State Attorney Register if anything could be done to prevent it. But with substantial expenditures for genuine legal representation and tireless family support, particularly from Grandma Elna and George, Jr., Ed Humphrey was finally released on September 18, 1991. The one good thing about his experience in jail was that the prison doctors had managed to stabilize his medication and, providing he monitored himself carefully, he was finally free from the roller coaster of his manic-depressive behavior.

On his release, he went to live with his brother George in Orlando. George, who had graduated with honors from the University of Florida in May, was working at a public-relations firm. At first George looked after his brother with great protectiveness, afraid that the many people who came up to him to shake his hand or to ask him for his autograph or to stand at a cautious distance and stare would prevent him from getting on his feet. But Ed, sober, rational and subdued, finally seemed to be holding his own emotionally. Getting a job was another matter. Nobody would hire him and he knew why. They were afraid of him. He had never been cleared of the murders. The Gainesville Combined Task Force would be presenting the grand jury with all the accumulated evidence and be calling for an indictment against Rolling for the murders. Many expected Ed to be named in the indictment along with Rolling. So many unexpected and terrible things had happened to him over the last year, he no longer thought such an occurrence was impossible. His potential indictment on the Gainesville murders was still hanging over his head like an ax ready to fall and cut off his lifeline to sanity.

Eventually he retreated to Indialantic to wait at home for the grand jury decision.

The day Ed was released, Rolling received a life sentence for the Ocala Winn-Dixie robbery as an habitual violent felony offender.

This time, he turned to the court and said soulfully, "God bless the people of Florida, and Lord help me."

Now the judicial process moved quickly. One week later, on September 25, 1991, Rolling was convicted in the Rio burglary. What difference did it make? He had already been sentenced to life in prison. On October 4 he was convicted in the Bos burglary. On the tenth he was acquitted of burglary but convicted of stealing a camera, knife-sharpening stone and other items from the Lawrence home in Tampa. On October 18 he was sentenced to three life terms plus 170 years for the Tampa burglaries and robbery.

"This time," the judge told him, "you won't be given the opportunity to see the light of day again."

On November 1, Rolling was arraigned on the First Union National Bank robbery charges. Four days later the grand jury began hearing evidence in the case of the Gainesville student murders. The only difference between this and all the other arraignments, indictments, convictions and sentences was that this time Rolling, if convicted, would be facing a potential death penalty.

For the Humphreys and the Hlavatys, everything built up to the announced week of the indictment. Ed's family barricaded themselves in their home to wait. The media was on hand en masse. The family asked the media to respect their privacy and not to call until the grand jury had handed down its decision. But the tide was unstoppable. One persistent journalist kept banging on the front door repeatedly, demanding an interview.

Finally, fed up with the harassment, Grandma Elna swung open the door and in a rage confronted him, her long white hair askew. In the midst of the heated argument that followed, she suddenly turned ashen and began gasping for breath. She died moments later of a massive coronary.

Two days later, on November 15, the day of Grandma's wake, while the media filmed her funeral, the grand jury decision on Rolling was reached.

A broadcast reporter came into the funeral home during the wake to inform Ed Humphrey that the grand jury had returned an indictment against Rolling on five counts of murder, three counts of sexual battery and three counts of armed burglary. He, Ed Humphrey, had not been named in the indictment.

Ed turned to look at his grandmother lying in a darkened room surrounded by grieving mourners. George turned away, unforgiving.

The police blamed the media. They said it was the press that presumed Ed Humphrey was the murderer and printed erroneous, sordid stories about him. The media blamed the police, saying it was the police who leaked the rumors about Ed, from "multiple personalities" to "cautious optimism" about his guilt. The million-dollar bond was in itself a kind of indictment. Danny Harold Rolling, who had had running gun battles with the police and was considered an habitual offender, had warranted only a $25,000 bond.

George Humphrey tried to exorcise his bitterness in an angry article written for the college newspaper, the *Alligator*:

> Not once has State Attorney Len Register ever come out and said even one thing on Ed's behalf. Countless insinuations of guilt have come from his task force, but not one thing to even mention that perhaps the investigation wasn't done in the best possible way. I can't forgive him. There has never even been the slightest hint of human compassion for my brother.

As for the Combined Homicide Task Force:

> They made some mistakes. They placed all their hopes on Ed and didn't know what to do when they realized they were mistaken. So why can't they come out and apologize? Why can't they just say, "We had our men working around the clock every day, and we made some mistakes"?

About his grandma, he wrote to the author:

> I cried because it had been my grandmother and I who had worked so tirelessly to save Ed. She had been a great inspiration to me. My grandma was a character. Believing in protecting the family at all costs, she unabashedly fought for my brother's life. And even when it was my brother who had hurt her, she lied in court for him and made a mockery of the prosecution. She had a quick humor and gift for humiliating the prosecutor. However, everybody was the enemy in her mind and this made her unable to find those who would be able to help Ed. That was my job. Her death was a great loss to me.

41

The Next Step

After his indictment, Rolling's aunt, Mrs. Artie M. Strozier, wrote on his behalf to the judge in Ocala, where Danny was incarcerated:

> [James] would blame Danny boy with everything that happened and would call him "stupid" and "crazy." After Danny grew up to be a teenager, his dad became more abusive toward Danny, then I noticed Danny began to change. His personality was different. He seemed real depressed and very quiet. Everyone who knows Danny boy loves him and thinks he needs help because of the treatment he got from his dad while growing up.

James and Claudia Rolling did not believe their son was the Gainesville Ripper. James, who had spent his life fighting crime, could not believe his son capable of the monstrous things they were saying he had done. The father had said the son would come to no good. But this went beyond the pale. For the first time in his life, he was unwilling to believe the worst of Danny.

Rolling's brother, Kevin, now thirty-six, lived in Wacom, Texas, just west of Shreveport, and had no comment.

After Rolling was indicted the public defender and the judicial circuit asked for an additional million to a million and a half dollars to be able to hire additional personnel and to acquire the necessary computer software to go through the mountains of gathered materials. His attorneys insisted that Rolling's defense had to go through every single lead in order to prepare an adequate defense for the accused murderer. It would take time. There were almost seven thousand investigative reports to peruse.

All one could do now was wait for the trial to begin. Since Rolling was already incarcerated for five life sentences there was hardly any need to rush. His attorneys knew that this time Rolling would be challenging the electric chair.

Meantime, while others were left to argue about the pervasive influence of the media or the injustice of serial killers becoming "larger-than-life," or the multipurpose rubric of "bad upbringing," or society's growing vulnerability to violence, and while still others participated in endless pedantic TV talk shows about inadequate protection on the streets, adrenaline-rushed killers, justice in the courts and demands for vengeance and retribution, Daniel Harold Rolling, caught and caged, repeatedly attempted suicide—once with a razor, another time with nineteen Thorazine tablets he had hoarded, and once by wrapping a bedsheet around his neck to make a noose with which to hang himself. After the last attempt he was moved to Chattahoochie State Hospital.

Now came the long wait.

The murders occurred in August of 1990. Unlike Ed Humphrey, whom many had presumed guilty from the beginning, Daniel Rolling was by law "innocent until proven guilty." It would be three and a half years later, on February 15, 1994, that the first juror would be selected in the capital trial of *The State of Florida* v. *Daniel Harold Rolling.*

Lt. Sadie Darnell moved on in her career. She left for Quantico, Virginia, to study at the FBI academy.

Lieutenant Spencer Mann became more of a recluse after the murders. An outgoing person by nature, he found that the experience had made him pull back in distrust of the society "out there" that could spawn such evil. "There are a lot of people on the streets who shouldn't be there," he told his wife, Pat. More than ever, he appreciated the quiet solitude of his farm on the outskirts of the county.

Jenny closed her books on serial killers. All arguments with Amelia ended as she put them away. She read the published profile carefully and was satisfied that the true killer had finally been captured.

Two weeks after Rolling was indicted, JoAnn Adelberger was lying in her bed at the Hawaiian Village Apartments. It was near midnight. She heard kids bouncing on the trampoline outside her window and laughing.

That sounds so good, she said to herself.

It had been a long time.

PART

V

THE TRIAL

42

Prison

Florida State Prison—V Wing, 2nd floor

Rolling arrived at Florida State Prison in May 1992.

Florida State Prison near Starke, which houses Florida's most dangerous criminals, has a long series of four-story cinder-block barracks surrounded by twelve-foot fences with wicked-looking accordion-type barbed wire on ground level plus long rows of barbed wire strung across the fence top. Tall poles with floodlights are spaced along the grounds, hovering over the grassy grounds crisscrossed with cement walks. It is a desolate, forbidding-looking place.

Rolling's prison job was to clean the showers on the second floor of V Wing. He preferred other activity. "Life is so short," he wrote in a May 8, 1993, letter to an aspiring journalist on the staff of the University of Florida student paper, the *Independent Florida Alligator,* "and even though I am a prisoner I can enjoy running laps on the Big Yard." Not with a tree trunk across the shoulders, perhaps, like the old days in his front yard, but still running. "I feel the warmth of a beaming Florida Sun on the iron pile, pump some iron and be thankful for a healthy body."

Except for when he could be outdoors, going to the gym was the part of the day he liked best, pummeling on the heavy bag or playing basketball with other inmates. Usually he preferred to stay alone. He drew pictures with themes of demons and death that he signed in his childlike scrawl: "by Danny Rolling." He wrote songs; he wrote letters . . . "[Prison] is not very elaborate," he wrote to the journalist. "I know it sounds like a picknick [sic] Believe me it's not . . . It's prison . . . and nothing can put a pretty face on the beast."

He cut photos of the five murdered students out of the newspapers and pinned them up in his cell. Bizarre trophies? A heavy-handed reminder of guilt? As time passed he had to talk about what he had done and intimated to Bobby Lewis, a fellow inmate, that he was involved in the five Gainesville student murders. And then he recanted.

*   *   *

He would go to the music room to play the guitar and sing for a couple of hours and write songs. " 'The Grayway' is one helluva song," he bragged after he had a dream about life in prison that prompted the song. "Ah . . . but it's kind of a spooky and sad one. Prison is like that . . . spooky and sad."

"I really hold freedom of movement precious," he wrote to the *Independent Florida Alligator* journalist. "There may come a time when I will not be able to move about as freely as I do now. The state is trying to put me on DEATH ROW." He rarely thought about the precious freedom of movement he had stolen from all the people he had murdered. He was going to stand trial for five; only he knew about the others.

His mother had always stood up for him. At home she hadn't been able to stand up against his father, but she was the only one who was there at his side in court. Ill with cancer, she could not make the trip from Shreveport to visit him in Florida State Prison. Even when she could not appear for him in court during his last sentencing in Ocala she wrote a letter to the judge.

"His self-esteem was destroyed by his father's constant belittling. Danny could never please his dad, and he tried so hard to win just one small sign from his dad that he approved of him, but it never happened." Another time, she wrote the now-famous quote: "Danny was told from the time he could understand that he would be dead or in jail by the time he was fifteen years of age."

He made it to jail.

Others died.

In one of the more bizarre aspects of his frightening story, while incarcerated, Rolling allegedly fell in love with a woman by the name of Sondra London. As the self-proclaimed "media queen" of inmate literature—especially inmates on death row—London's livelihood was made mostly by publishing the art and writings of killers. Now she wanted to write Rolling's life story and coax the "artist" out of him. The relationship between Rolling and London started out as a business deal, but the correspondence, which began in June of 1992, soon escalated. The prosecution team in the case of *Florida* v. *Rolling* caught up to and confiscated the letters covered with red lipstick prints.

London was outraged when the letters were quoted in the Gainesville *Sun* of December 19, 1993. "Oh Danny . . . my darling. Hold me close to your powerful body. Bring your lips close to mine." Not only did she send him photos of herself and of loving couples, but supposedly to inspire his "art," she mailed him illustrations of murdered women drawn by some of the murderers she had previously worked with. She began calling him her "Maximum Man" and her "Dangerous Pussycat." In her letters she urged him to talk of death, killing and, in particular, about the Gainesville student murders. She made direct references to the victims. On February 17, 1993, as printed in the Gainesville *Sun* of December 29, 1993, she wrote: "I'd like you to return to the question of Sonja Larson . . . and ask yourself how you'd feel . . . and where you'd be today spiritually if I had been the little college girl—in fact, I've seen her picture and she even bears a certain resemblance to me—especially as I looked at that age." And . . . "I want to know about weapons, knives and guns," she wrote in another of her letters printed in the *Sun*.

> I wonder about the difference between a knife and a gun. Does it make you feel different to be holding one or the other? . . . You my own Danny Rolling—are MAXIMUM. Everyone compares you to Bundy. Because of Florida —college girls—good looks—big investigation—but they don't know! Bundy was a nothing . . . I know that the Danny I met—that I love—really does love me, but . . . what about the lady killer? Is he going to find a way to do me in? As much as to hurt Danny as to hurt me?

She knew he would never be released to "do her in." It was all fantasy, unrequited, impossible love, with hopes of making a killing, so to speak, of her own, no matter her denials. She has copyrighted every word and every drawing Rolling has sent her. She has prodded him into writing and drawing more—all of which immediately became copyrighted. She was able to have him sign an exclusive with her. When this author telephoned London for an interview and asked if she would share some of her personal knowledge of him, she declined.

"Are you looking to sell it?" I asked.

"You got it!" she replied. "I have financial problems and I'm looking to get as much out of this as I can."

London has appeared on television to give accounts of their love story, including the "Geraldo" television show. For Danny Rolling, a man who had always had difficulty in selecting and maintaining relationships, this one ranked as perhaps the most grotesque of all.

"I don't care if you did commit these murders and a hundred more," she wrote to him. "If [Defense Attorney] Rick Parker can prevent your execution . . . I'm all for it."

Claudia Rolling, the "best mom in the world," made it clear that she didn't think too highly of Sondra London. "She's using my son for her own advantage." James Harold Rolling felt London was taking advantage of him and the family. He felt London was trying to blame him for Danny's homicides.

Said Rolling: "I love her and it cuts me deeply to know there are people out there who have caused her pain because she finds something in Danny Rolling to love," he wrote in a February 23rd letter. "Even some of my worst critics could find something in Danny Rolling worth while. If they could only meet me in person," he wrote in a March 3rd letter. And in an interview for television's "A Current Affair," he said, "I'm madly in love with her." He even became engaged to London, including the exchange of engagement rings.

At one of Rolling's pre-trial hearings, London was standing in the court-room when Rolling walked in. He asked to address the court. Given per-mission, he turned to London. "Sondra, they might keep me from you. But I want you to know that they cannot stamp out the love and affection I have in my heart." And suddenly, to everyone's astonishment, he began to sing a song in his thin baritone country-style crooning:

> I recall the day I first saw you.
> I reached out to say I love you
> But it was hard to say
> I couldn't touch you
> Tell me baby,
> What were my words or my tears run together.
> What were my words or my tears run together.
> What were my words or my tears run together, baby
> Just just rain.

Sondra London smiled at him tenderly.

At 'one point, she had sent him a garter.

In prison, Rolling could not keep his mouth shut. He continued to have an irresistible penchant for apology and confession, as though they could somehow absolve him of what he had done.

His boasting spawned a cottage industry of jailhouse informers quick to report to the authorities his tales. One called Rolling a "maggot." Another said he'd like to see Rolling go to the electric chair. Many were ready to swear that he had confessed to the student murders as well as to a series of rapes during his days of drifting that spanned thousands of miles from as far north as Kansas City, Kansas, to Alabama in the south, to as far west as Colorado and as far southeast as Sarasota, Florida. Inmates called him "Psycho," "Psych Man," "The Ripper."

Inmate Paul Fuqua told the task force investigators that Rolling had told him: "The reason I sliced them up is because they were too pretty for anybody and I can't stand that. I made it so that they weren't so pretty anymore." Fuqua, doing five years for armed robbery, reported to investigators that Rolling told him he "cut this woman's head off" and "put it in front of a mirror so the head could see the body." And then Rolling asked him, "Well, what do you think about that? Would your God forgive me?"

At first Fuqua discounted Rolling's stories. But they spread as Rolling kept talking.

Another inmate, Paul LaMarche, Sr., told the task force that Rolling said he robbed the Winn-Dixie store in Ocala so that he would not be a suspect in the student murders—crimes that warranted the death penalty in a state that had the highest rate of executions in the country. "I'm the one that killed the broads," he bragged confidentially, "but they'll never find me here in jail. They'll never suspect me. The worst they can do is give me ten, seven years. I'll be out in five." He hadn't expected the five consecutive life sentences he was given as an habitual offender.

(In March 1986, Mississippi Circuit Judge William F. Coleman sentenced Rolling to twenty years in prison, with twelve years suspended. The sentence had been reduced after the judge conferred with both Rolling's public defender and the district attorney and came to the conclusion that the sentence was too harsh. Misinformed that Rolling was a first-time offender when, in fact, he had already spent nearly three years in a Georgia prison for a prior armed robbery, the judge trimmed his sentence to fifteen years, with twelve suspended. Rolling served his mandatory three years and was released in July of 1989. Thirteen months later, in August of 1990, he murdered the students in Gainesville. Under his original sentence he would have been required to stay in prison until 1994.)

He had even been in the confession mode back at the Marion County jail. Inmate Anthony Adams said that Rolling, calling two of his female victims "young and beautiful," confessed to him during a one-on-one bible study session in the Marion County jail in October, 1990. "Please forgive me," he said to Adams. "I need to share this with someone. I confess my sins. I shouldn't have been prowling, that's what got me into this trouble." And then, Adams told authorities, Rolling sobbed. "I murdered some people. I killed some . . . college kids. Twenty-, twenty-three years old, up in Gainesville."

"Why'd you do that?"

"A demon from hell forced me to kill these people to purge myself of all prior sins."

It made little sense, Adam thought. He committed murder to purge himself of prior sins?

Another inmate, Osborn, said Rolling went as far as asking prisoners who had been to the state mental hospital in Chattahoochee how he should act in order to look crazy.

In September of 1990 inmate Raymond Taylor wrote to Len Register, who was still state attorney. Taylor, a former criminal attorney, wrote to Register that Rolling had spent a good deal of time picking Taylor's brains to learn the legal difference between "incompetence to stand trial" and "insanity at the time of a crime." He suggested that mental health investigators should "probe deeper" before concluding Rolling was insane.

On July 25, 1991, in Marion County jail, Rolling went into a rage. He didn't know why. Something had hit him the wrong way. He ripped two thick paperback books in half with his bare hands. Marion County Sheriff Lt. W. G. Ergle, who had witnessed the feat, wrote a memo suggesting that three guards be on hand every time Rolling left his cell. "I consider him more dangerous than ever before," he wrote.

Now at Florida State Prison, in the psycho ward, Rolling on the one hand seemed to enjoy the special attention he received as a "celebrity" killer, and on the other apparently resented the negatives his status gave him. Jail guards taunted him as "animal" and "mutilator" and told him he would go to the electric chair.

Was he proud of what he had done or was he penitent? He kept switching from remorse to bragging—even about the mutilations, especially in Christa Hoyt's apartment, and her severed head. "I left it there so that anyone who came into that apartment . . . well . . . that would be the first thing they'd see."

In a statement inmate Russell Binstead would long remember, Rolling said he wanted to invoke terror.

Rolling made friends with convicted murderer Bobby Lewis, known throughout the prison system for being the only person to escape from Florida's death row. A good person to know. After a few weeks Rolling began confiding in Bobby about his involvement in the Gainesville murders. They were cellmates and they spent many hours talking about the murders. Rolling needed an ear. In one instance he complained that the choice he had made at the first murder scene had been disappointing. Sonja had a "better body" than Christina. He had chosen the "wrong" girl to rape.

He told Lewis it was while he was in prison in the eighties, long before he came to Gainesville, that he decided to kill. "I got a bad side to me, but it ain't all my fault." He blamed parental abuse and neglect at home and sexual abuse in prison. And bad times with his father, and a failed relationship with his ex-wife. "I knew what I was doing, but I couldn't control the desire at the time, y'know? It gets to me and I can't help it."

Eventually Binstead and Lewis advised him on how to fake a suicide in the psycho ward in order to stay there. The feigned mental illness was part of a plan to escape; the mental ward of FSP was easier to negotiate than the lockups. He had, one could argue, completed his mission, one life for every year he had been in prison (if you included the Grissom family). But here he was in jail again. The rage began to surge past the fears of what they could do to him. Even if he were acquitted on all eleven charges against him, Rolling knew that with the five life sentences he was already serving, he would probably never again step foot outside the prison gates unless he was successful in his plan. He had already escaped prison three times—never a maximum security prison, but still, he had beaten them. "Prison for me is the same as clipping the wings and tail on a beautiful bird meant to fly," Rolling wrote to Sondra London in a letter dated March 16, 1993. ". . . to glide the wind sweep [sic] shores of the heavens . . . but now, caged. You can see the beauty out there but you can never be a part of it." Sad stuff.

He was furious. His cell had been ransacked by the correction officers. They "trashed," he said, everything, including his Valentine's Day card for Sondra London.

Now he had something to say. On January 31, 1993, he requested the men investigating the 1990 Gainesville student murders come to Florida State Prison. Investigators LeGran Hewitt, Ed Dix and Steve Kramig had already spent almost three years investigating the murders when they were called to the prison. Rolling was insistent on playing his controlling games; his manipulative side became very evident. He wanted to confess but he was going to do it his own way and on his own terms. He told LeGran Hewitt he would tell the authorities about the Gainesville student murders only through his fellow inmate, Bobby Lewis. Why?

"Bobby's a worthy soul and he deserves a chance to make his life good," Rolling told them piously, "and out of all this I'm trying to do something good for someone. And, well, my life will more or less cease after the trial to an extent that . . . well, you know what I mean. I can't really call it living, but Bobby can." The implied reason had to do with Rolling insuring Bobby's benefit rather than his own, that maybe Bobby's role as an intermediary in his confession might one day help Bobby's own case in front of a parole board. "He's got a family," Rolling said. "He's got a life . . . and I'm trying to give him a chance." More likely he didn't want to say the things he had done. At least not then.

In the end the investigators relented. What they wanted was Rolling to tell them what happened; never mind how he wanted to do it. Lewis was permitted to join them as they gathered for Rolling's confession in the same small green prison courtroom where Rolling had been arraigned six months earlier. Bobby Lewis was middle-aged, heavy-set, with thick graying hair. Rolling called him "a library of information. Bobby is my mouthpiece. I have said he is my confessor."

Through the agreed-upon ground rules of their meeting, they would ask Lewis a question. He would answer. Then they could confirm his answer with Rolling. Occasionally Rolling would correct a point, lean over, whisper in Lewis' ear. During the next three hours, over styrofoam cups of coffee, crying jags complete with a box of tissues, the ugly story came out.

Hewitt began the inquiry with the first crime scene, the Williamsburg Village apartment where Christina Powell and Sonja Larson were killed. The process continued in this manner for each of the three scenes.

"Was Danny Rolling responsible for these homicides?" Hewitt asked.

"Yes, he was," Lewis replied.

"Is that correct, Danny?" Hewitt asked Rolling, wanting to get his response on tape out of his own mouth.

"Yes."

Throughout the interrogation, the three investigators continued to prod Rolling to speak for himself, but in the end he had Lewis speaking for him, telling the details with Rolling confirming with a single word, "Yes," or a nod of his head.

By the time the confession was over Rolling had confirmed he had killed five students. Through his mouthpiece-confessor he told how he not only planned the five killings but how they had been part of a deliberate plan to kill a total of eight people. Lewis said Rolling came to Gainesville, camped in the woods and wore black ninja clothing for the murderous rampage. But although he claimed to have been forgiven by God, he absolved himself of direct responsibility by blaming the killings on an evil side of his personality that he called "Gemini."

The reason Gemini killed, Lewis said, was that Rolling wanted to strike back at a society that had locked him up during what should have been the best years of his life. Through Lewis, Hewitt, Kramig and Dix traced Rolling's murderous weekend spree to what Rolling considered was a particularly rough term at the prison in Mississippi. "During this period of time," Lewis said, "under the conditions he was in, and the way he was being treated, he just snapped and made up his mind he was going to search out and take one victim for every year that he had been punished. That was what he did." Until he finally reached the end of his evil mission. "He was through, he decided to quit what he was doing. That was to be the last victim. He was finished." It was at that point that he buried the killing knife and the athletic gloves somewhere on the grounds of the University of Florida.

Lewis said eight victims . . . ?

"Danny is willing to clear up the Shreveport homicides," Lewis told investigators. "After the Gainesville murders [trial], he will tell everything in detail, including where to go to find the weapons. Until then, he does not want to deal with the Shreveport homicides."

The videotaped statement was drawing to a close when Danny Rolling began to talk. "I never wanted to come this way, believe me," he said in his thick Louisiana drawl. "As God is my judge, I never wanted to come this way. But I'm here, and now I've got to live with this. I ain't got nobody to blame but myself. But I want to understand as much as anybody because it's all so bad. You gentlemen are honorable people. I wish I could be you, but I wouldn't want you to be me. I wouldn't want anybody to be me."

"Why the mutilations?" Hewitt asked.

Rolling became silent again.

"He don't even in no way understand why he done these things," Lewis said. And then he went on: "Danny breaks his self down into different personalities that are behind what Danny does. There's Danny, there's a Jesse James sort of side to Danny, there is a force that comes out of Danny known as Ynnad . . . [Danny spelled backwards—the good guy] and there's a force that comes out of Danny known as Gemini. Gemini is the guy you would have found at the five murder scenes."

There was skepticism amongst the investigators. Rolling, they knew, had seen the movie *Exorcist Part III* the very week of the killings; its plot involved a prisoner who became possessed by a demonic killer who decapitated and disemboweled a female victim. The killer was named Gemini.

"People say Danny has no remorse," Rolling said aloud at one point in his videotaped confession. "They don't know Danny. I don't know how I live with myself. If it wasn't for the good Lord, Jesus Christ, I wouldn't be able to live with this man. But He gives me strength and courage. I'm not proud of myself and my life—"

"If you had something to say to these victims' families," LeGran Hewitt interrupted, "what would it be?"

"I would say to them that I don't ask them to have pity on me . . . But I would say, I would ask them if they could find it in their hearts to forgive so that, so that the bitterness and the hatred about all of this won't destroy what is left of their lives. I pray for them that God would give them strength and counsel to face every day. I believe, somehow, through all of this that the Lord will give them strength. I can't do anything for them. If I could, I would." He looked to Hewitt. "What can I do for them? Tell me."

"I have no idea," Hewitt told him.

Rolling covered his eyes.

(Over a year later, when the families saw the videotape in open court, they were outraged at what they considered his sanctimonious grief. For-giveness, no. Justice was what they wanted.)

In return for his cooperation, Rolling got his "trashed" Valentine's Day card back, which was mailed to Sondra London. It read:

You can run but you cannot hide.
You're in for one hell of a ride.

The January 31st meeting ended with investigators heading off to search for the murder weapon. It was never found.

Rolling and Bobby Lewis then had a falling-out. Rolling felt that Lewis betrayed him by leaving the ward without telling him he was going. Lewis had had enough. He knew too much about Rolling and about Sondra London. Eventually Lewis, who had been on death row for almost six years, would fear for his own life; he knew that one day he would have to turn state's evidence against Rolling.

In one of his letters to this author, he wrote:

. . . Then by the end of this month I am gone to be transferred to Utah State Prison. The reason is there is no where in the Fla. system they can put me so I am not killed. This is not my ideal but theirs. It will be just as dangerous there as hear but I knew this when it started. You ask what does the truth mean to me—I try to explain. . . . I come from the old school of criminals that dont like people who kill for no reason, especially women, kids or old people. Danny had done all three. As he told me what he done, any why, and what his future plans were, I had to stop him. I had two choices. Kill him myself, or be a witness against him. To do so I knew would send me from the top of prison society to the bottom and put my life in danger. It make the years I have in prison missarable as I be a total out cast. Danny killed 8 people in 2 states—raped and assaulted over 20 women and a lot more crimes, and I had all the details of. Myself, Im in prison for killing a man that been paid to kill me. I probably could of made some kind of deal—even got my freedom. At first I thought of this and even the money that could be made of the story. The victums were "absrack to me." Ive lived with killers 18 years. But as he told me what he did any why and this man is no where near crazy. But he put oun a lot of acts. . . . as he explain how much pleasure and enjoyment he got, the victims became so real to me that they are a part of me—that I decide I do what eaver I can to stop him—but I not make a deal to help myself. I don't beleave in that . . . also I watch Sondra and Danny and they told me how much money we all make Books, Movie, Records, T-shirt, Art work—so oun—that made me sick—and I could not help them do that—so I had to go against them eaver way I could—all this make he want to kill me—so again I was places oun Death watch 10 ft. from the chair. They execuuted 3 people scence Ive been down hear . . .

When Lewis left, Rolling felt betrayed. They had had intense conversations and now Lewis was gone. Rolling turned to Rusty Binstead. Once again, he spent weeks and weeks telling his new confidante what he had done. When Binstead was told he was going to be moved to another ward he warned Rolling of his impending move in advance. Rolling wanted to tell Rusty about the second crime scene—the one in which he wreaked such postmortem havoc with the body of the young women he had raped and killed. This time, for some incalculable reason, he wrote it down in a letter. All the grisly details. He then gave the letter to Binstead. "Copy it down in your own hand," Rolling told him. "It's valuable information to have. I'd rather you have it than Bobby. Then give it back to me so I can destroy it."

Binstead agreed. But once he returned to his cell he put up the curtain that gave him some privacy and asked a fellow inmate to give him five minutes and then yell "Shakedown."

Five minutes later the cry of "Shakedown" reverberated through the cells. Rusty immediately flushed his commode to make Rolling think he had destroyed the handwritten confession, when in fact he kept it. He wasn't sure why he did that, but information was information, and this stuff could be valuable information to have. One never could tell when it might come in handy.

Rolling was now thirty-nine years old. In May of 1994 he would turn forty.

There had been two and a half years of investigative time. The amount of information compiled in the years since that terrible weekend in August of 1990 was truly voluminous. Almost seven thousand leads had been meticulously followed. Interviews that comprised the bulk of the investigative reports on view at the Gainesville law library in the Gainesville courthouse took place from Sarasota to California in an attempt to link Rolling to the murder scenes. The trial had been postponed repeatedly, from September 1992, to September 1993, to January 1994, to—finally—a definite unpostponable date. Jury selection would begin on February 15, 1994, and was expected to take two to three weeks. The trial would begin immediately following and was expected to last eight or nine weeks.

Time was closing in on him. On January 26, 1994, three weeks before the scheduled trial was to begin, Rolling called a conference with his attorney, Public Defender Parker. C. Richard Parker, forty-six, had attended the University of Florida's law school. He now had a well-trimmed, sharply pointed graying beard. Although he had been the public defender for the

Eighth Judicial Circuit since 1984, he had not tried a case since the late 1980s.

Now, sitting opposite his client, he had to disagree with Rolling's plans to throw in the towel, even though they both knew the primary evidence against Rolling was overwhelming. A great deal of legal damage-control was necessary because of the January 1993 videotaped confession alone. It had been given without benefit of counsel and although the defense team now insisted it had been a "statement," not a confession, it was nevertheless very damaging to the defense.

How bad was it? Rolling asked. It was bad. Would he get the chair? That was what the prosecution wanted.

In a July 1993 letter to the reporter for the *Independent Florida Alligator*, Rolling wrote about the death penalty:

> I am a man who has 5 life sentences and 170 years to serve in the grand ole state of Florida . . . So either someday I will be old and gray in the prison and my heart gives out . . . or I'll be young and strong and ELECTRO-CUTED . . . Kinda speaks for its' self, doesn't it kiddo?

Now, with time getting short, it was finally getting through to him. They actually wanted to kill him.

In the book *Knockin' on Joe*, written by Sondra London, Rolling talked about how he identified with the actor James Cagney in the last moments of the film *Angels with Dirty Faces*, as he walked to his execution.

Some time earlier, when Len Register was still Alachua County State Attorney, Parker had approached him about the possibility of a plea agreement on the murder charges in exchange for a life sentence with no possibility of parole. But Register rejected a plea bargain out of hand. As one of those who had personally witnessed the carnage left behind in the silence of those rooms, he had no intention of cutting a deal, of giving Rolling any kind of legal break.

When Rod Smith defeated Register in the November 1993 election, Parker tried once again to arrange a plea bargain with the newly elected prosecutor. But Smith also refused a deal. This was one case he passionately wanted to win.

Now, three weeks before the trial was to begin, Rolling instructed Rick Parker that it was time to change his plea to Guilty.

Parker insisted he did not think it was a good move. He had personally taken an active part in the scientific aspects of evidence in Rolling's case. Although the primary evidence against him was strong—the matched screwdriver marks, the fibers from clothing left at the scenes, the video-taped confession made through Bobby Lewis and, in particular, the genetic DNA blueprints left behind by blood and semen identified as coming from Rolling—Parker still felt the defense team could make a fairly strong case for mitigating factors against a death sentence by presenting to the jury first the story of Rolling's life with all of its apparent abuses; and second, a battery of psychological and psychiatric evaluations establishing his client's mental illness.

But while in jail, Rolling claimed he had found religion. Again. "I want to confess my sins to God and man."

"You understand that by pleading guilty," Parker told him, "you face the very strong possibility of a death sentence by electrocution."

"I'm aware of that," Rolling told his attorney. "I want to stop running."

Parker told him to think about it and to search his soul.

"I'll think about it and pray on it," Rolling said. But as usual, once he made up his mind about something, he rarely wavered.

"Most capital convictions are overturned on appeal." Parker felt obligated to press his warning. Without a trial there would be no avenues for appeals if convicted other than an appeal against a death sentence. Did Rolling still want to plead guilty?

"I know we all have to die . . ."

When he appeared on the program "A Current Affair" in the fall of 1993 he had said plaintively: "They're trying to kill me." Then he leaned forward toward the interviewer and a hard edge crept into his voice. "We're all going t'die. I'm going t'die. You're going t'die. Your cameraman is going t'die."

Now, the hard edge was carefully gone as he spoke to the man who was trying to save his life. "I know they want to kill me . . ."

Parker felt obligated to repeat, "Are you sure you want to plead guilty?"

"I want to do the right thing," Rolling said in his meekest mode. And then he revealed part of the underlying reason of his overtly meek but adamant decision: "I don't want to show those pictures to anyone."

Parker knew he was referring to photographs of the crimes scenes. With all the gory details unfolded in the courtroom—the rapes, the sodomy, the sexual mutilation, the decapitation—there was little chance he could escape with his life. Better to keep the details quiet. Best to admit guilt and not take the jury step by step through the horror and brutality of the murders.

Alachua County Public Defender Richard Parker, in trying to persuade him to change his mind, decided to give his client a three-week cooling-off period before making any formal statements.

The cooling-off period did not change Rolling's decision.

43

Florida vs. Rolling

At forty-six years of age Judge Stanley R. Morris was only seven years older than the man whose fate would ultimately lie in his hands. Standing an imposing, lean six feet four inches tall, the judge had a rich deep baritone voice. His hair, reddish brown in color, was parted on the left, with white tufts beginning to show through at the temples. Known for his quick temper, he also had a warm smile. Educated at the University of Florida, Morris graduated from its law school in 1971. After a career in both civil and criminal law, by 1986 he was appointed circuit judge for the Eighth Circuit by Gov. Robert Graham and was reelected twice without opposition.

Since Rolling's indictment in November of 1991, Judge Morris was the only judge who presided over judicial matters pertaining to the student-murder case. It was his first capital case since being appointed to the bench, and he was determined it would proceed smoothly. Repeatedly, he made it clear that his goal was to make certain the case would be tried just once, without mistakes, and with no legal cause for appeal.

On February 10, the Thursday before the jury selection for the scheduled trial was to begin, Rolling signed a three-page plea-form at the Florida State Prison. His guilty pleas were now official. Even at this point, however, Defense Attorney Parker reminded him, nothing was final until he stood before the judge and admitted guilt in open court.

Pleas signed, Parker met with the judge to inform him that Rolling had decided to plead guilty to all eleven counts and had already signed the plea form. In the event Rolling changed his mind, however, Parker did not want to reveal the confession until Tuesday the fifteenth, when the case finally did come to trial.

Judge Morris ordered that no one was to be told of the pleas until the moment in court when it was announced publicly. He, too, wanted to give Rolling every opportunity to change his mind at the very last moment if he so chose.

That night Judge Morris called in the state prosecutor, Rod Smith. Youthful looking at forty-four, with bushy dark hair and horn-rimmed glasses worn for reading, Smith was excited about leading the prosecution in his first major criminal case. At one time on the other side of the table as a defense attorney, he was prepared, he was sure, he was raring to go.

When Judge Morris revealed Rolling's intentions to change his plea to guilty, Smith was disappointed. The prosecution team members had been champing at the bit to get into court with a case they were positive they would win. The forensic documentation alone was powerful. But here it was—all over before it had begun. The families would be relieved of some of the pain of revelations, but there was frustration.

Still, the prosecution would have the penalty phase of the trial, which would determine whether Rolling would get the electric chair.

With the judge's gag order regarding the latest development, Prosecutor Smith had to keep the news to himself. He could not tell the victims' families. He could not even tell his staff of clerical assistants. In order to process the necessary paperwork brought about by the new development, he had his assistant attorneys type them in absolute secrecy.

Then he called the victim advocate. "I want to make sure the victims' families are present in the courtroom on Tuesday."

"For jury selection?"

If Rolling kept his word and did plead guilty, Smith wanted them there to hear it firsthand. He would apologize later for the small ruse. "Tell them," he said, "that the judge wants to instruct them on proper court-room decorum."

He disliked not telling them the truth, but apart from not disobeying a court order, what if Rolling *did* change his mind? He did not want the families traumatized. A plea was not a plea until it happened. He was still stunned by the move but cautious. Nothing was certain. Rolling could change his mind before Tuesday.

February 15, 1994, was the first day of jury selection for the trial of *Florida v. Rolling.*

Gathered in a specially set-aside portion of the spectators' gallery, sixteen family members of the five student victims were present. Some had planned to attend all along. Some did not want to go through the trial: Frank and Patricia Powell, for example, had not intended to come. A few months earlier, Patricia had told her brother, James Cullinane, that she and Frank had finally let go and had decided to "let Christina be with God." Whatever their plans, when each of the families was called, not only by the victim advocate but by Public Defender Parker to request their attendance in order to receive directions from the judge on courtroom protocol during the run of the trial, they all came.

The talk in the courthouse was that the prosecution was ready. The case was top-heavy with evidence gilded with forensic documentation of the killer's presence at the scenes of the murders. There were dozens of indisputable pieces of evidence that the defense team would try to tear down bit by bit, putting forensic science itself on trial in an effort to throw a monkey wrench into what seemed a solid case against their client.

Tension was palpable as the family members saw for the first time, in person, the man who stood accused of murdering their children. Being led into the courtroom, he looked normal. Like an accountant.

Rolling, with neatly trimmed hair, was conservatively dressed in a tan sports jacket, white shirt and striped navy blue tie, all of which had been donated for this courtroom appearance. Beyond the look of a successful, somewhat handsome young executive whose hairline had begun to recede, however, there was the heavily furrowed brow and the rapidly blinking eyes that betrayed his nervousness. He had put on weight in prison, filling out his tall, broad frame.

The proceedings began.

When the eleven counts in the indictment against Daniel Harold Rolling were read aloud by chief prosecutor State Attorney Rod Smith, and the grisly details of the five murder charges, three sexual battery charges and three armed robbery charges were heard in open court, several family members already began to show the signs of strain. Tears flowed. Muffled cries of pain were heard as some of the particulars began to be revealed. They embraced one another. They were going to have to go through it all, relive it again, and in so doing, learn the heretofore unknown intimate details of death. In listening, they could only imagine the terrifying final moments of their loved ones, aided—for the eyes of the jury—by graphic descriptions and photographic documentation that they would not be permitted to see but would be able to imagine in all its horror.

Rolling demonstrated no reaction to the detailed account.

Aside from the families, only a smattering of media and court personnel were in the courtroom. Just ten of the fifty-four seats that had been set aside for the public were occupied. Nobody from Rolling's family was there, but Sondra London was, presumably covering the trial for "A Current Affair" and the magazine American Detective.

Public Defender Parker stood up. Barbara Blount-Powell, a member of the defense team, stood beside him. Dressed in a soft plaid jacket, she was an attractive blonde woman with a French twist reaching from the crown of her head to the nape of her neck.

Rolling bit his lower lip, stared ahead and twirled the seven-dollar gold ring Sondra London had given him and that he wore on his right middle finger.

A series of soft clicks were heard as reporters turned on their tape recorders.

With their client between them, Parker and Blount-Powell moved to the podium placed in the center of the room in front of the court stenographer. The court television camera was facing the judge. Its lens caught Rolling over his left shoulder from behind. Television stations across Florida interrupted regularly scheduled broadcasts to bring live coverage of what was to be the opening of the trial.

Rolling stood in front of the Honorable Stanley J. Morris, his sloping, frowning eyebrows following the downward curved outline of his mouth, giving him the appearance of someone about to cry. His eyes continued to blink repeatedly. How many times before had he stood in front of a judge? From the moment he shot his father in May of 1990 he had been a fugitive on the run. He was wanted for the shooting. He was wanted for breaking parole. He went on a closely spaced burglary and armed robbery spree. He killed again, and again, and again, and again, and again, and robbed a bank and a huge supermarket at gunpoint in broad daylight. He had claimed he had been looking for the bullet out there that was meant for him.

"Mr. Rolling," Judge Morris began, "do you understand that what we're going to do is proceed based upon the schedule set forth by your counsel and by the state?"

Rolling nodded.

Now came the bombshell.

"How do you plead?"

Parker leaned forward. "My client has an announcement to make."

Family members began to cry. They were going to hear his voice.

Rolling cleared his throat. His words were barely heard in the now attentive hushed courtroom. "Guilty, Your Honor."

There was a moment of stunned silence in Courtroom 4A as those present needed a moment to absorb the implications of what the defendant had said. But before they could react, Rolling continued: "Your Honor, I've been running from one thing and then another all my life," said in a quiet voice accentuated with his soft Louisiana twang. "Whether from problems at home or with the law or . . ." a brief hesitation ". . . from myself. But there are certain things that you just can't run from, this being one of those."

"Do you understand that this plea could put you on death row?" Judge Morris asked.

"Yes sir. I understand."

For each of the five murders, Rolling faced the death penalty. For each of the three rapes, he faced a forty-year sentence. For each of the three burglaries he faced an additional sentence of life in prison added on to the five life sentences he already was serving.

It was a stunning reversal.

Now that it was done, Rolling complimented the bailiff as he was being fingerprinted and turned to smile at his fiancée Sondra London before being ordered to a holding cell. She blew him a kiss.

Behavior inside Judge Morris' courtroom remained calm and decorous, but outside there was an explosive reaction. The word spread quickly throughout the Alachua County Sheriff's Office, where Christa Hoyt once worked. "He confessed! He confessed!" As soon as the words were heard, the staff crowded into the conference room to watch the drama unfold on television. Shock reverberated throughout the department. No one had any indication that the proceedings were going to take such an unexpected, dramatic turn.

"Until now it's been a real whodunit," said Major Jim Eckert, a police detective for twenty years who had been one of the lead investigators in the early days of the case.

Even Gainesville Police Chief Wayland Clifton, who had been so instrumental in putting together the multi-agency task force, didn't know a confession was in the offing. It was not until moments before he entered the room as court was about to convene that Rod Smith pulled him aside. Clifton, who had vowed the week of the slayings, "We'll get this killer," was then filled in by the state attorney about what was going to take place.

Outside, immediately after the session, Sondra London was surrounded by an army of news media pointing their microphones in her face. She said she was surprised at Rolling's plea of guilt even though she now claimed to have encouraged him to plead guilty. "But the decision was his own," she told the media, "and he made it unafraid . . . Danny has observed," London continued solemnly, "that we're all going to die and we're all going to the same place . . . What fate holds for him, holds for you. I hope he gets visitation. That's all I care about."

The moment they left the court, family members were besieged by the press for their reactions. Sadie Darnell, who had been so prominent in the early days of the investigation as spokesperson for the Gainesville Police Department and who now worked as an advocate for family members, asked the media to respect the families' privacy. Over the years she had become very close to them. "They need this time to process the information," she said. "Please show compassion for their needs." She made it clear that she strongly disagreed with the decision to keep secret the guilty plea that so surprised everyone in court. Rod Smith apologized, and although Sadie knew the state attorney could not violate a court order, she nevertheless stated: "I think it speaks of the inadequacies of the legal system. For the family members, today had to have been a real strong, bittersweet situation. It was very difficult." A bit teary herself, she ended her statement to the media with: "They are experiencing probably every emotion there is to experience. When we leave today, our lives will start getting together and back to normal. Theirs never will."

One family member, however, who wore on his jacket a green button that read "Victory over Violence," decided to speak up for the families. Mario Taboada did not accept the assertion that his brother's killer was mentally ill. "That is a cop-out," he said angrily. "It's a poor excuse. I've been imagining what took place that day over and over," he said after listening to the prosecutor's description of the last desperate moments of his brother's life. "It angers me that it ever took place. I don't choose to focus my energy, my anger and my sorrow on this individual. I have no pity for him. This is a life form gone bad." At the time of the killings his reaction was one of trying to understand. "There is not enough love in the world," he had said. "Something has to be done about it . . ." But now, after years of trying to re-create the moment of his brother's death, after years of nightmares and of watching sorrow deepen the lines of his widowed mother's face, the initial search for understanding was gone. "I didn't go out and shoot somebody and stab somebody. It's not an excuse," he said, enraged that Rolling would plead for mercy on the basis of an abused childhood. "I don't care what kind of childhood he had. I still miss my brother . . . I'm in Gainesville," he said. "This was my brother's home and I miss him dearly."

Touching his "Victory over Violence" button, he spoke of his mission to "make the streets safe for my son." He urged the reporters to focus their energies on helping the victims of crime rather than focusing on the killers, and to use their forums to expose the growing problem of violence. "This is a serious nationwide problem that needs to be addressed and needs to be resolved."

John Lombardi, president of the University of Florida, was attending a meeting in Tallahassee when the news reached him. He said the time of the murders was "very much alive in my heart and soul and will be until the day I die . . . The memory of the murders is unlikely to fade soon. The pain and memories of these heinous acts inflicted on our community will never go away. The loss of these five wonderful young people will always be a part of our institution and individual memories. It will remain a constant reminder of the fragility of life."

*   *   *

Jenny Kanne remembered too well. The streets were jammed with cars and rented U-Hauls full of furniture and luggage. It was difficult to forget how a new academic year, which had begun with the sound of the Century Tower's bells accompanying all the excited movements, had ended in an unexpected season of terror. She called Amelia Marshall.

In the time since graduating from UF, Jenny had married a successful landscape artist in Long Island, New York, and settled down to a quiet life of suburban comfort. She held her eighteen-month-old son propped against her hip as she dialed New York to call her former roommate Amelia, who at the time had suffered such trauma after the murders. But now Amelia commuted daily from Westbury, Long Island, to New York City to her job at a publishing house. She had become sure of herself and had converted her botany studies into an indoor garden in her house, where she chose to live alone. When she picked up the phone and heard Jenny's voice carrying the familiar edge of fear, she said, "Yes, I just saw it on ABC."

"It never ceases to amaze me," Jenny added after they relived some of their past moments of fear together . . . "he looks so normal." She told Amelia to be careful.

"I'm fine," Amelia told her.

It was Jenny who had insisted on multiple locks on all doors and windows when she and her husband moved into their new home together.

When Bobby Lewis heard about Rolling's plea in court and that he was saying things about how he "wanted to do the right thing," he had to laugh. He had been in correspondence with this author but had stopped writing. He had said he could not write well and was embarrassed by his penmanship and spelling. Now, however, he decided to write again:

Dear Marry,
    Hi! I have keep your address I spoke to Rod Smith Sat—Im free to talk about any thing—Danny cell is 10 ft from mine has been for months—and will be till he sentences—what he doing know in court a act. it to keep most the story for Sondra and then to sell—and it's his best chance at a life sentence—that mean population—also that mean escape! I just want Danny and Sondra not to make money—and for the truth to be told.
    If you want my help—I don't want no money, I don't want no credit. I got a lot of art work and stuff he done—that part of the trial I get back you can use—& there's no part in his life I don't know—&

what he and Sondra plan to do—I want good to come out of this—if you are in the area they may let you visit as a Media person—or we can write—or in about 30 days I be where I can call—if you don't start in Shreveport then 90% of all reason and motive a major part of his story lost.

If you don't want my help, ok, I wish you well & that you show Sondra and Danny for what they are—

Your
Robt

Rolling's confession was of great interest to the Shreveport Police Department in Louisiana. "He's still the prime suspect," said Caddo Parish District Attorney Paul Carmouche. "But we still don't have enough to ask a judge for the arrest warrant." There was nothing but the similarity between the crimes, and evidence that Rolling was in Shreveport when Julie, Sean and Thomas Grissom were stabbed to death in November 1989. "If he's in a confession mode and wants to talk about Shreveport, the Shreveport police are on call, and they'll certainly send somebody to Gainesville very quickly to talk to him," Carmouche said. "Right now we haven't gotten any word that he intends to discuss the Shreveport case."

A call to the J. H. Rolling residence in Shreveport was answered by a woman who said, "I'm sorry. I don't have anything to say."

One of the most important revelations Rolling made was in admitting he committed the crimes alone. It was not a point that was elaborated on at great length. One family—the Humphreys—began to think that maybe the end of their own nightmare was finally in sight. But the fact that Ed Humphrey was totally exonerated of the murders by Rolling's confession did not get much attention in the media.

44

Penalty Phase

The unexpected guilty plea meant that all that was left was to decide what to do with Rolling. Immediately following his plea Defense Attorney Parker went to the waiting press conference, giving a clear indication of what the defense's main strategy would be. "Danny Harold Rolling is, and has been since before these crimes, mentally ill." There was a significant amount of psychiatric evidence to suggest that his client was "blatantly delusional." Mental illness would be helpful "in understanding how the same person can rape and murder, then later regret these acts and feel compassion for the victims' loved ones surviving his violence."

State Attorney Rodney Smith, on the other hand, said Rolling knew exactly what he was doing at all times. All Smith wanted to do was place the jury in those death rooms so that they could see for themselves the horror he left in his wake. "I've heard this before," he said at the press conference. "Trust me. This one didn't regret what he did when he did it and he doesn't regret it now. He's just trying to gain sympathy from the court, from a jury."

Rolling did not want to be present during jury selection. He asked Judge Morris' permission to stay in his prison cell during the proceedings. "I have complete confidence that everything will go as it should," he said.

He had the right not to be present and was escorted back to Florida State Prison surrounded by corrections officers and a small army of news reporters and media cameras.

Prospective jurors were questioned at length on their views of the death penalty and whether they could view grisly photographs of the murder scenes. Three hundred eighty prospective jurors had been whittled down from a pool of fifteen hundred. Most knew about the case through the media. While State Attorney Rodney Smith asked if they could set aside any personal objections and recommend death if Rolling met the legal

360

criteria for such a sentence, Public Defender Parker tried to penetrate their religious and moral beliefs, particularly relating to how they felt about recommending the ultimate penalty.

Some felt killing even a murderer was against their religious beliefs. They were excused.

Some felt the act of murder demanded the death penalty no matter what the surrounding circumstances. Also excused.

Some felt the particular brutality of these crimes made mercy for the killer impossible. Excused.

Some admitted to having made up their minds before hearing any of the aggravating or mitigating factors to be presented at the trial. Excused.

Some felt graphic photographs of the victims would be emotionally devastating to them. Excused.

Some were unwavering that Rolling should get the death penalty. Excused.

While one said, "It is so unsettling to see someone who looks like a puppy dog, when he's really a dragon," there were those who said that although they believed in the death penalty and could recommend it if the evidence warranted, they were equally willing to listen to the case with open minds and take into account all of the mitigating factors presented by the defense before reaching a decision.

Twelve jurors were ultimately selected by the ninth day. The panel consisted of nine women and three men:

Gloria Lynn Bass, 32—an elementary school custodian
Leslie Geraldine Brown, 40—a clerical worker in an elementary school
Jerry Ward Coleman, 62—retired
Brenda Jones Diaz, 49—an assistant director of risk management
John Odyssey Green, 35—a power plant mechanic
Carrie Jeanne Kerrick, 62—retired
Alfreda Verlinda McDaniel, 35—a community services specialist
Holly Paige Sajczuk, 23—a delicatessen worker
Arlie C. Staab, 43—a registered nurse
Daren Scott Stubbs, 26—a financial representative
Anne Marie Tignor, 27—a bank teller
Tonja Williams, 28—a grill cook

On the tenth day, four alternates were picked:

Scott Coleman, 42—a medical clerk in a VA hospital
Brenda Malcolm, 23—a self-employed day-care operator
Robert Smith, 48—unemployed
Kathleen Wilson, 53—homemaker, wife of a police officer

Judge Morris had considered sequestering the jury but decided against it.

In the penalty phase of a capital case all that is required when innocence or guilt is not the issue is to determine the sentence to be imposed on the offender. In Florida, the impaneled jury is an advisory one. Its duty is to recommend to the judge either death by electrocution or a life sentence with no possibility of parole. Its recommendation in *Florida* v. *Rolling* was to be based on whether the state had proved sufficient aggravating circumstances to make Rolling eligible for death, or whether the defense had proved there were sufficient mitigating factors to warrant the relative leniency of a life sentence. Therefore, the prosecution would concentrate on *how*—and demand the ultimate punishment. The defense would concentrate on *why*—and plead for mercy.

Legally, while restricted by statutes, the state was required to prove only one of the eleven listed statutory aggravating factors, while the defense had greater leeway in its presentation of reasons to save Rolling's life. The mitigating factors were then to be weighed against the aggravating ones. If the mitigating outweighed the aggravating, then the jurors were to recommend life imprisonment.

Aggravating factors were:

The crimes were cold-blooded and premeditated.
The crimes were committed during sexual battery.
The crimes were particularly heinous, atrocious and cruel.
The offender had a prior history of felony convictions.
The crimes were committed for the purpose of escaping detection or avoiding arrests (particularly in the cases of Larson and Taboada, in which they were killed to avoid leaving witnesses).

Mitigating factors (a catchall category in which the defense could introduce anything pertinent to what was in essence a mini-insanity defense upon which the defense had pinned its hopes) were:

The perpetrator suffered mental illness at the time of the crimes.
The crimes were committed under extreme stress.
The perpetrator grew up in an abusive household.
There was a history of drug and alcohol abuse.
The perpetrator showed remorse.

Only seven of the twelve jurors were needed to recommend a sentence. Florida law required the judge to assign great weight to the jury's recommendation but also stated that he was not obligated to accept it. However, Judge Morris made it clear that the jury's recommendation would be a major factor in his final judgment prior to sentencing the defendant.

Tuesday, March 7, 1994—opening arguments were to begin.

Courtroom 4A was almost drab-looking, with wall-to-wall gray carpeting. The judge's bench was set against a simple wood-paneled wall flanked by the American flag on one side, Florida's state flag on the other and a Florida state seal centered over the judge's bench, which was located behind a long low wall. Microphones were placed around the room.

State Attorney Rod Smith was determined that the penalty phase proceed in the same manner as the guilt phase would have, except in an abbreviated version, as though it were a VCR on which he had pressed the fast forward button. Smith intended to leave out nothing. He wanted the jury to hear every bit of the gruesome details of the murders. With a methodical evidentiary presentation, he intended to lay out a painstaking, elaborate death-penalty case. Although there was a great deal of public and political pressure to win, he passionately believed that if ever there was a case that warranted the death penalty, this was it. He fully intended to pull out all the stops to prove the aggravating factors that would ensure the death penalty, as though there were not already a guilty plea on record. But there was always the danger that the strategy would backfire: too many gory details might convince the jury that only a severely mentally ill person was capable of such barbaric acts.

Rolling wore donated suits and horn-rimmed glasses into court. It was frightening to many that he looked so normal, clean-cut, neat, even handsome. He didn't look like a scruffy, down-and-out person who lived at a campsite. As he sat up straight in his chair with his hands folded on the table in front of him like an obedient, attentive student, he appeared the meek, remorseful, pitiful Danny, not at all like the violent murderer he had confessed to being. This Jekyll-and-Hyde aspect of Rolling's personality had been confirmed by psychological evaluations as well as fellow inmates. It remained to be seen which one of these two Dannys the jury would sentence.

Family tensions were stretched thin again as the families sat in a section of the courtroom that had been set aside for them. Lt. Sadie Darnell sat with the families. Chief Wayland Clifton, in full uniform, sat in the front row just behind the prosecution team.

Also in the front row sat Mrs. Grissom, the woman from Shreveport, Louisiana, who had lost her daughter Julie, her husband Tom, and her eight-year-old grandson Sean to a killer still unidentified.

*   *   *

The prosecution team consisted of State Attorney Rodney Smith, Assistant State Attorneys James Nilon, Jeanne M. Singer and Don Royston. Like Judge Stanley Morris, they were all in their forties, all graduates of the University of Florida's law school. Although Smith would share the questioning of witnesses with James Nilon and Jeanne Singer, it was he who presented the opening statement to the jury.

> There is no question who did it. We will never know why. But we will know *how*! And all the aggravating facts that can be brought to the penalty phase. It is for you to weight the balance. His abused childhood against the cold, cruel, calculated, premeditated, well-planned acts that he perpetrated against those innocent victims.

For the first time, Smith set forth the state's evidence against Rolling, focusing on several key areas. DNA: the defendant's genetic fingerprint matched semen collected from swabbings taken from three of the victims and from their apartments. Evidence found at Rolling's campsite: screwdriver, duct tape, ski mask, a pair of black pants stained with blood consistent with Manuel Taboada's blood (even though Rolling had jumped into the Gatorwood pool to wash off the bloody aftermath of the double murder). Analysis of the pry marks showed that a screwdriver recovered from Rolling's campsite was the same one used to pry the sliding glass doors at the residences of Christa Hoyt, Manuel Taboada and Tracy Paules. Fibers found on duct tape matched fibers of the ski mask found in a bag abandoned at the campsite. A note found at one of the scenes matched Rolling's handwriting. Statements attributed to Rolling detailed each aspect of the crimes, including details never released by investigators, such as the decor of the students' apartments and their apparel at the time of the assault. Records that established the time and place of the purchase of a certain Ka-Bar knife, which matched up with the knife Danny Rolling used in each of the murders. (One of the aggravating factors: "The crime was cold-blooded, calculated and premeditated.") A handwritten confession of one scene signed by the defendant. And finally, the videotape recording of Rolling's confession made to investigators through Bobby Lewis.

Smith presented a litany of violent crimes attributed to Rolling which, under Florida statutes, constituted another of the aggravating factors, "a prior history of felony convictions, two counts of armed robbery in Muscogee County, Georgia. One count of armed robbery in Salem, Alabama. One count of armed robbery in Hines County, Mississippi. Four counts of robbery in Hillsborough County, Florida. Attempted robbery with a firearm in Hillsborough County, Florida. Aggravated assault of law officer in Hillsborough County, Florida. Aggravated assault of an officer with a firearm in Hillsborough County, Florida. Armed bank robbery in Gainesville, Florida.

Next, Smith spoke passionately and at length of how Rolling tortured his victims, another one of the aggravating circumstances. "The crimes were committed during sexual battery and were particularly heinous, atrocious and cruel.

"He talked to them," Smith said. "He taunted three of the young women he killed by specifically telling them what he was going to do to them before he did it." Their final moments were tortured with anticipation as well as with the dehumanization and the pain of what he ultimately did. The terrible fear he imposed made his crimes even worse.

Walking slowly up and down before the jury box, Smith held up the black ski mask so that the jurors could have the full impact of the terrifying image the victims saw of their murderer. It was chilling to watch.

In an even more dramatic gesture he gripped the handle of a replica of the Ka-Bar military knife and held it above his head in a position the killer must have adopted just before he thrust the thick seven-and-a-half-inch blade into his victims.

Ann Garren, Christa Hoyt's mother, gasped audibly and looked toward the ceiling. Christa's stepmother, Diana Hoyt, welled up with tears. Tracy Paules' sister, Laurie Paules Leahy, grasped her father's hand. For even though lawyers and victim advocates had relayed to the parents and siblings of the victims the basic facts of how the students had died, hearing the full details in public and, once again, imagining the terror of their final moments was an excruciating experience.

SMITH: The foregoing evidence supports a finding that this plea of guilty is supported by sufficient facts to establish that the defendant, Danny Harold Rolling, is, in fact, guilty of each and every crime alleged in the indictment beyond and to the exclusion of every reasonable doubt.

And he intended to present every aggravating factor he could to convince the jury that only a death sentence could respond, in some small measure, to the horror Rolling had created.

In addition to Public Defender C. Richard Parker, the defense team included John J. Kearns, Barbara Blount-Powell, John Fischer, and Don Royston. Like the judge and the prosecution team, they were all in their forties, all graduates of the University of Florida law school. They, too, were an impressive group.

Recognized in 1986 as the state's outstanding public defender, John J. Kearns would handle the bulk of the case for the defense while Parker remained seated with Rolling, never leaving his side—a calculated attempt to humanize him for the jury.

Wearing a dark tan sports jacket, balding slightly, Kearns was compassionate and almost grandfatherly in manner as opposed to the hot, passionate style of Rod Smith. Now Kearns stood and approached the podium. After Smith's impressive opening and the state's abundance of concrete evidence that burdened the case for the defense, Kearns knew he had his work cut out for him.

In his opening statement Kearns spent several hours telling the twelve jurors and four alternates why Danny Rolling should not be executed. Mental illness was the excuse. Child abuse was the excuse. Immaturity was the excuse. In his low-keyed approach, he minimized the incident in which Danny shot his father, stomped him and shot him again after he had fallen. He quietly blamed the father, whose physical and emotional abuse, he claimed, had destroyed the self-esteem in his young son. "As the tree grows the bitter fruit . . ." Kearns told how he planned to bring mental-health records and expert psychiatric testimony, which, gathered after more than fifty evaluative hours with Rolling, would prove he was mentally ill. He told the jurors that Danny had been diagnosed as having a severe "borderline personality disorder which causes significant distress and impairment, severely affects how he thinks and acts and significantly inhibits functioning as a normal human being." There were no identifiable psychotic episodes, but, he said, this type of personality disorder relentlessly caused drastic alterations in conduct, creating the Jekyll-and-Hyde syndrome that was often mentioned in describing Rolling. There was a history of inappropriate behavior and reactions, from intense anger to intense laughter, from huge uncontrollable feelings of rage to feelings of total joy and even an intense belief in the supernatural. For example, while Danny was in the midst of praying for a wife, O'Mather Ann Halko happened to walk by—Danny took it as a direct sign from God that she had been sent to him to be his wife.

Kearns presented a long, generic psychiatric evaluation of nearly every textbook problem a growing boy could suffer: he was insincere, immature socially and sexually, impulsive, unpredictable, unstable, anti-social, obsessive-compulsive; he lacked empathy—the ability to feel and understand other people's feelings; he suffered from maladaptive coping skills, he had "poor to no" socialization skills; his personal relationships were poor, they had never been learned; he had no control over his obsessive voyeurism which began at age fifteen and nurtured a very severe psychosexual disorder. In addition, he suffered from an associative disorder in which a person's self-identity is forgotten or feelings of reality tended to be lost.

KEARNS: Rolling believes he is possessed by spirits or demons that unconsciously make him behave in a certain way . . . the devil made him do
it . . . It is a maladaptive coping mechanism. His concept of the devil
influences what he does—but he remembers what he does. The spirits
represent a coping mechanism.

Kearns had tried to disassociate Rolling from all responsibility for his
acts, strongly suggesting that although there was no doubt of his guilt,
there was a great deal of doubt regarding his accountability. Abusive behavior essentially takes a child and destroys him. The mitigating factors
were extreme and powerful. It was obvious the defense was aware that
while there were opinions on why some can overcome abuse and others
cannot, there were no hard scientific facts. (The "abuse excuse" was common in the light of the contemporary mania surrounding such cases as
those of the Menendez brothers and the Bobbitts.)

Kearns then warned the jury about the graphic nature of the bloody
photographs they were going to be shown by the prosecution. "They are
gut-wrenching," he admitted. "But tell yourself, I'm looking at it but I
want to know *why!*"

The defense spoke as though only the *why* was to matter. The prosecution spoke as though only the *what* and *how* were to matter. While the
state presented facts of Rolling's deeds, the defense was concentrating on
his unmet needs. Did the facts of Rolling's background, no matter how
powerful, justify his vicious behavior? The scale that would weigh the balance was in the hands of the jury.

During Kearns' statement, Rolling sat quietly, hands crossed in front of
him on the table, corners of the mouth turned down, looking sad, eyes
blinking.

45

For the Prosecution

There was a montage of witnesses and crime scene details—for example, the condition of the refrigerator at Larson and Powell . . . both doors were shut, air conditioner was running between seventy-two and seventy-eight degrees, no lights were on—to ground the prosecution's case that the guilty plea aside, Rolling deserved the extreme penalty. Rolling's strategy to keep hidden the goriest details had not worked. They were all going to be fully aired in open court. The prosecution had to make *sure* the aggravating factors were clearly introduced to the jury. Only by making the jury live through the entire horrific weekend death spree could the jury be made to see and feel the depth of rage felt by the public, and an appropriate closure to the Gainesville student murders with the death of a killer. The prosecution plodded through witness by witness and item by item of the mountain of detailed evidence it had accumulated in two and a half years of intense investigation.

Gainesville Police Department Officer Bradley West appeared on the stand testifying about what he found at the first murder scene—blood splattered on the calculator . . . Forensic expert Paul Patrick McCaffry testified to DNA fingerprinting . . . Gainesville Police Officer Ray Barber's testimony was controlled and professional, but when his eyes glanced at the photos it was obvious that the memories were painful and the photos difficult to look at . . . Sheriff's Deputy Keith O'Hara testified to finding the second scene, re-creating it for the jury—the landlord went with him to check up on Christa, things looked normal except that the back gate was open, blinds up off the ground about a foot, when they looked under the blinds the officer told the landlord, "Sir, you need to go back to your house and wait for further contact by law-enforcement officers."

Smith was ultra-careful not to introduce the condition of the bodies after the postmortem mutilations into the testimony. Judge Morris had ruled that postmortem mutilations were not relevant; their inflammatory nature could be cause for an appeal, a point the judge was intent on

368

avoiding. When speaking to Keith O'Hara about when he first entered Christa Hoyt's apartment, Smith phrased his questions carefully:

SMITH: Did you see a dead body?

O'HARA: Yes, sir, I did.

SMITH: Was it apparent to you—without telling me how—was it apparent to you that that body of that person was already dead?

O'HARA: Yes, sir. It was very clear.

SMITH: Was the body—without speaking to any of the features of the body —was the body in a sitting position?

O'HARA: Yes, sir. It was.

While the jury was being shown the floor plans of the murder scenes mounted on a tripod, Judge Morris left his seat and sat on top of the wall separating the judicial bench from the court. He propped himself up against the side wall so that he also could see the evidence being presented. He jotted notes as he looked.

Dr. William Hamilton, medical examiner of the Eighth District of Florida who performed autopsies of the five victims, took the stand.

Jeanne M. Singer, who was known for her dogged persistence with witnesses on cross-examination, took her place at the podium to begin the questioning.

SINGER: Let's start first with Sonja Larson . . . Did you perform the autopsy?

HAMILTON: The body of Sonja Larson had multiple sharp-force injuries.

SINGER: How many and where?

HAMILTON: There were eleven stab-wound injuries to the right arm. Four thrusts which went completely through the arm—four entry and four exit wounds. Three puncture wounds where the knife entered the arm but did not exit from the opposite side. Eleven separate deflects. In addition there were five stab wounds closely grouped on the right breast. Internally some of those wound tracks went through the breast, through the front of the chest wall into the right side of the chest, into the right lung, both upper and lower lobes of the lung, and into the right atrium of the heart. Associated with that pattern of wounds was a collection of about two quarts of blood in the right pleural space. The deepest wound tracks from the skin surface on the breast to the end of the wound track was five to six inches.

SINGER: What does that tell you, doctor, about the type of weapon that was used?

HAMILTON: The dimensions of the wounds and the characteristics of the entry wounds as well as the internal wounds are helpful in determining the kind of weapon that was used. In this particular case, most of the wounds were of variable length, which is normal in this situation, but the overall estimate was that we had a fairly large knife. It was sharpened on one edge. Probably at least an inch thick, probably at least six inches in length. It was suggested at that autopsy, and later we had no reason to change our opinion, that it was a fairly large knife of the type that might be found in military combat units and suggests that the ideal candidate would be the marine Ka-Bar.

SINGER: Are you able to say, based upon your expertise, whether or not Sonja Larson was awakened or in any way defended herself during the stabbing?

HAMILTON: The wound patterns in the right arm and the closely spaced wounds on the breast were a little peculiar until we looked at it and realized that that would be exactly the wound pattern that was expected to be found if her arm had been brought up over her chest perhaps in a flex mode. When one is asleep the natural response might be to throw your arm up in this fashion. It is believed that at least some of the wounds in the breast, initially, went completely through the arm and went into the breast. There were other wounds on the body as well.

Further on in the testimony, after the wounds were corroborated for the court by carefully prepared diagrams:

SINGER: Would you be able to determine how long Ms. Larson would have lived from the moment she was initially stabbed?

HAMILTON: I think the whole group of injuries could have occurred in a very short period of time in the blitz style of assault. Certainly less than half a minute.

SINGER: Did you say a blitz style?

HAMILTON: That means a rapid succession of thrusts into the body and that she probably would have lost consciousness very rapidly considering all the punctures of vital organs, heart, and both lungs. She couldn't have remained conscious for more than a minute, if that long.

SINGER: Let's go ahead then and talk about the next victim in the Williamsburg Apartments. And that would have been Christina Powell.

HAMILTON: The significant findings in the autopsy of Christina were stab wounds in the back with perforation of right lung, ligature marks and adhesive material on both wrists and adhesive material on the top of the left foot. There were small bruises on right and left legs. A rather superficial cut on the right wrist.

SINGER: Were you able to make any determination as to the type of weapon that would make these wounds?

HAMILTON: Similar to the weapon previously described . . . the same type of weapon was used in both cases. (*Referring to diagram*) The significant wounds . . . a cluster of five stab wounds in the middle of the back . . . they are located directly over the spine and over the left and right lungs.

SINGER: Are you able to tell how long Christina survived from the infliction of the first wound?

HAMILTON: I can render an estimate. The first two wounds did not penetrate into the body cavity. Wound number three did go over the spine in the right lung as well as number four . . . one of the wound tracks was about seven and a half inches . . . number five does not actually injure the lung . . . It would take a while for the blood to be pumped out of those wounds. She did not die as quickly as Sonja Larson. I think she might have had a few minutes of consciousness.

SINGER: Did you have an opportunity to examine her vaginal area?

HAMILTON: Yes.

SINGER: Do you recall seeing anything unusual around the vaginal area?

HAMILTON: There was a towel and a bottle of Dawn liquid dishwashing detergent. And a sticky fluid on the pubic hair in the entire pubic region . . . It suggested an effort was made to clean up bodily fluids.

SINGER: Was the vaginal area filled with sperm cells.

HAMILTON: I took two sets of slides from the vagina, rectum and oral cavities . . . standard tissue stain. I did not see any sperm cells in that slide. . . . There can be seminal fluid without sperm if there is a low sperm count . . .

Regarding the autopsy of Christa Hoyt:

SINGER: Would you tell the jury what was the cause of death?

HAMILTON: In my opinion the cause of death was the stab wound to the back. (*Referring to diagram*) On the left side of the chest very near the spine there is a large stab wound. Internally, it goes through the aorta and into the left breast. Following the wound track, the blade was seven and a half inches . . . It was consistent with the wounds suffered by Sonja Larson and Christina Powell.

SINGER: . . . Is there anything about the coloration of the body that tells about the length of time it was in a particular position?

HAMILTON: There is a well-established pattern of lividity and a purplish discoloration at the back of the body. Lividity is a discoloration that forms on a body after death. Circulation has ceased. The blood that is in the body settles and purplish discoloration forms on fair-skinned people. This pattern of lividity tells me that the body has been lying on its back for a while.

SINGER: Were you able to say with any certainty how long the body would have been lying on its back?

HAMILTON: Lividity takes a while to form. It can become apparent in light-skinned people in a short period of time. To become fully established, it takes anywhere from four to twelve hours.

SINGER: At the crime scene when you found her, she was apparently not on her back. What does this tell you in respect to the photograph?

HAMILTON: There is still lividity on the back and in this particular photograph the back is the highest part of the body. This is inappropriate. Blood does not flow upward in dead bodies. It goes downward. That tells me that lividity had formed on the body while it was on its back and then moved and rearranged.

SINGER: Is it your testimony that the body was moved from a lying position to a sitting position?

HAMILTON: Yes. After she had been dead for a few hours.

SINGER: Was the vaginal area of Christa Hoyt examined by you, doctor?

HAMILTON: Yes.

SINGER: What did you find?

HAMILTON: I took smears from the usual body orifices and found sperm cells in the vaginal area.

Regarding the autopsy of Manny Taboada:

HAMILTON: The body of Manuel Taboada had thirty-one cuts and stabs in the face, trunk, on the arms and on the right leg. This included a slash of the chin, stab wound of the neck, a grouping of stabs and cuts on the upper mid-chest, a large stab wound measuring two to two and a quarter inches on the skin surface of the upper abdomen—the gastro region —a slash on the lower right thigh, two cuts on the lower right leg below the knee, as well as cuts and stabs of the left wrist and hand, and lower right wrist.

SINGER: From the way that Mr. Taboada was positioned on the bed when you found him, can you draw any conclusion as to the position before he was stabbed?

HAMILTON: From the pattern of wounds it would be most likely that he was sleeping on his back. This would leave the area that was presented to opportunity.

SINGER: Were you able to determine which of these number of wounds caused the death of Mr. Taboada?

HAMILTON: In my opinion the cause of death is multiple stab wounds and cuts.

SINGER: In your opinion, how long would Mr. Taboada have lived from the time of the first stab wound?

HAMILTON: We do not know the entire duration of the assault that ended Mr. Taboada's life, but it could have occurred in a very short period of time. It doesn't take long to stab, withdraw, stab, withdraw, stab, withdraw, especially when a person is determined to accomplish the deed at hand. He would not necessarily immediately collapse. In fact, the evidence is there that he put up a struggle. These wounds on his hands are certainly consistent with that; grabbing at his assailant and then beaten away with the knife. I don't think he could have sustained a very lengthy defense because he had punctures of his internal organs and lost a great deal of blood in a short period of time . . . There were multiple wounds in both lungs. Puncture of the aorta. Stab wound in the armpit. A great deal of blood internal and external. A number of wounds to the legs. The wounds suggest that during the short battle, the killer stabbed at his hands and arms to relieve grabbing.

Regarding the autopsy of Tracy Paules:

HAMILTON: This diagram shows three stab wounds on the back of Tracy Paules, of the same size as those discussed in previous cases and could have been produced by the same weapon. There are a number into the back left lung. A fairly large wound producing a deep slice. There was an accumulation of several quarts of clotting.

SINGER: What does that indicate?

HAMILTON: It indicates that a large portion of her blood volume poured into her chest and was the cause of death. Blood loss.

SINGER: Can you give an estimation of the length of time she lived after the first wound?

HAMILTON: Wound number one would not have been expected to be fatal. Nothing internal, no large vessels were injured. Wound number two, by itself, would have been fatal. It probably would have taken a few minutes for her to lose a sufficient amount of blood to go into irreversible shock. This includes at least one third of your blood volume in a short period of time. Cause of death was acute blood loss. Time varies. One person might not go into a coma for two minutes, another might take five . . . The third wound was also potentially fatal. It punctured the lung but the lung was already collapsed.

Rolling appeared miserable listening to the results of his deeds. Only when testimony returned to less graphic items did he return to his familiar courtroom pose—hands folded on the table in front of him, hardly moving, back ramrod-straight. But the proceeding couldn't finish fast enough to suit him. He wanted it to be over, he wanted out of this place.

It would not happen. The procession of witnesses continued:

Deputy Alexander and Deputy Bishop were called to the third murder scene . . . Alexander stepped over Tracy's body to get to the rest of the apartment . . . primary duty was to secure the scene and render aid . . . to the right there was a bedroom covered with blood, to the left there was another bedroom with Manny. Rendering first aid was not necessary . . . searched rooms . . . turned over the crime scene to investigators ACSO Officer Greg Weeks, ACSO Officer Steve Meary, and ACSO Officer Al Miller . . .

Deputy Sheriff Tim Merril—heavy-set, round face, receding hairline, round glasses—was the officer who pursued two men into the woods in the early morning hours of August 28, 1990. He was in the south parking lot of Picadilly apartments on routine patrol and had just cleared a call when he observed one white and one black man walking northbound on the east side of SW Thirty-fourth Street. They walked into a fenced area that had a gate into a wooded area that he knew had no houses . . . suspicions aroused . . . events of the time, bank robberies involving a black and white man . . . also the homicides . . . also the time of day. The property belonged to the University of Florida. "Why are they going in there at one o'clock in the morning?" . . . a call for backup . . . ACSO Deputy Sheriff Jim Lydell, on routine night-shift patrol, responded they went into the woods following the foot trail that had been taken by the two men. They got close enough to see them. They called to them, identified themselves, ordered them to stop. Tony Danzy stopped. The other man ran . . . Lydell gave close chase . . . Danzy told Merril he knew the other man only as "Mike" . . . followed power-line trail up through the woods . . . left easement area . . . the man took off into the dark woods . . . could not see him anymore . . . requested Canine Unit . . . Dep. Sheriff Chuck Simpson with a dog . . . Chuck put the dog in the exact spot where the suspect was last seen fleeing into the woods . . . tracked him approximately two hundred to three hundred yards farther back into the woods . . . illuminating area with flashlights . . . they found the two-person pup tent . . . the raincoat sitting by a tree with a large sum of money underneath it . . . released dog into tent to make sure it was empty . . . Canine Unit continued its track . . . dyed pack money that had exploded, identifying it as stolen money from the bank robbery . . . A bag was sitting just inside the tent . . . searching the bag . . . gun box . . . Taurus semi-automatic pistol . . . it was a "hot" weapon . . . the magazines were fully loaded . . . took live round out of chamber . . . secured scene and did not go any further . . .

Investigator Jack Smith, a crime scene investigator, came onto the scene for the collection and preservation of evidence . . . found the Stanley screwdriver in a black-and-beige bag found at the campsite . . . the small AM-FM cassette recorder was in the bag and loaded with a cassette tape

. . . they found black clothing—pants, sleeveless T-shirt . . . an almost consumed roll of gray duct tape in bag.

(A bit surprising that their instinct buttons were not pushed to high alert.) When they processed the tape recorder for fingerprints, they found the prints belonged to Danny Rolling.

In combing the area again on the fifth of September, a blue bag with dye-stained money was found approximately seventy-five yards west of the campsite. Black-and-white athletic gloves were found in the bag along with a black ski mask with the eyes and mouth apertures outlined in white looking like something right out of the film *Jagged Edge*.

None of this evidence was challenged by defense. There were few objections. They had decided to pick their fights carefully and save their objections for the points they believed they had a chance to win.

There was then the testimony of two of Rolling's fellow inmates, Russell "Rusty" Binstead and Bobby Lewis. Earlier, during Binstead's deposition, he had been asked a throwaway question—"Do you have any writings of Danny?" It was a common question.

"Yes, I do."

"You do? What?"

"I have a letter from him describing one of the murders."

"Where is it?"

"Back in my cell. If you have a minute, I'll go get it."

Binstead returned to his cell with two correctional officers and produced the letter from Rolling. There were things in the letter that absolutely no one could have known except the person who committed the crime. They had it in his own handwriting.

Bobby Lewis' testimony was equally devastating. Lewis had a serious falling out with Rolling, presumably regarding which one was the more honorable of the two. In reality it was because Rolling felt he had been abandoned. After Lewis testified for the prosecution, not only about Rolling's confession to the Gainesville murders, but also the many additional assaults and rapes Danny had told him about. Lewis was placed on death-watch ten feet from the electric chair.

In a letter to this author after his testimony, Lewis said:

> But let me say this, I like myself. Im proud of myself in court Monday, when I was testifying. I looked up and Tracy Paules sister was crying and looking at me—and she kept saying to me "thank you" over and over so she be sure I could read her lips! Well I could and it tore me up! Those two words from her made all I have gone threw and may go threw more than worth it . . .
>
> I have no interest in money or fame. I wamnt to do some good in life—Ive did plenty wrong—That simply all I want.

Also, if Danny dont get executed he will escape and kill again—if
he goes to Death Row he will probably kill some one else there—if he
get near the chair he kill himself—I know him inside and out—what
he thinks, how he think, why he think that way. I hope we are able to
work together.

Your
Robt Lewis.

Next, the prosecution introduced the hour-long videotape that had been
made at Rolling's request. The jurors watched the bizarre interview between Rolling, investigators Hewitt, Dix and Kramig, and convicted murderer Bobby Lewis, the inmate handpicked as his confessor. "I don't have
a life, I have an existence," Rolling told them. "I have a life hereafter, but
you know my life here is less than what you would call living . . . There
are some things that are too difficult for me to speak myself," he said.
"Bobby will speak for me."

In the interview, he made the claim he suffered from multiple personalities. His alter ego, "Gemini," was the bad one. Rolling was doing all this
because he "wants to help Bobby Lewis." The prosecution told the jury it
had the opportunity to see what kind of person he was, what kind of flavor
he had. In trying to set the ground rules, he was manipulating to control
the situation. The prosecution would argue that his behavior demonstrated he knew what he was doing and that he was not suffering from
mental disease or defect.

Although Rolling claimed minor memory lapses . . . "I can't remember everything" . . . through Bobby he nevertheless gave graphic, detailed testimony of what he had done to each of his victims. Except that he
did not like talking about the sodomy or the forced oral sex. He broke
down and cried. He lied about the sodomy and only said "maybe" regarding the oral sex.

When he finally spoke for himself on the tape, expressing his remorse
and asking forgiveness from the families of his victims, the family members who were in the courtroom were outraged at what they perceived as
his sanctimonious grief.

The defense objected to the introduction of the death photographs of the
five victims.

"Overruled," said the judge.

Rolling became visibly upset. He did not want anyone to look at those
pictures.

The jurors were grim. Some looked revolted. Many cried at the sight of
the gruesome photos, heads in hands. One man appeared to be fighting

tears for the rest of the day. The silence in the room was overwhelming as they passed photo after photo from one juror to the next.

Across the courtroom, Rolling agitatedly tapped his fingers on the table in front of him and fidgeted in his chair.

A few of the jurors studied the glossy full-color eight-by-ten photos at length. Some took notes. Others dutifully glanced at them and quickly turned their eyes away. One man removed his glasses and rubbed his eyes. The photos went straight to the heart. Smith murmured, "Tough day, very tough day," as he left the courtroom at the end of the day. But at least the jury had finally seen the handiwork of the killer.

Having the jury see the photos was hard on them, but when seeking the death penalty the law obliges the prosecution to prove that the ultimate penalty is warranted. They *had* to see what he had done.

The next day they would hear it.

First, at the defense's insistence they would play the entire audio tape, the one he made at the motel room in which he professed love for his family and played his songs. And then, unable to avoid it, the recording he made at the campsite when he said farewell to them. The defense hoped it would humanize him for the jury. As Rolling listened to his music, at one point he asked to have the sound turned up. He looked back at Sondra London and patted his heart. While his music was being played she shook her head as though to say what a shame that such a talent had been reduced to this.

Meanwhile, the hushed courtroom was listening to the wailing country-and-western sounds of a man who, if he hadn't been a serial killer, would have found no one interested in him or his music. But he finally had his audience. Some of them would determine whether he was to live or die.

The prosecution believed the end of the tape, which he had recorded at the campsite just before his forty-hour murder spree, showed clear pre-meditation. Listening to himself talking to his parents, essentially saying goodbye, Rolling appeared upset, teary. "I love you, pop [the battered child still looking for the rejecting parent?] We never had it together. You never had time for me. We both lost out a lot." And finally the chilling words as he said his goodbyes and signed off. *"There's something I gotta go do . . ."*

The concert was over.

The court broke for lunch.

Rolling had followed the classic pattern of the serial killer and had finally achieved the attention he craved. As the lead character in one of the most frightening murder cases in Florida history, equalling the Ted Bundy case in notoriety, surpassing it in brutality, Rolling had finally made the impression he had never been able to achieve as an ordinary man. He was a Celebrity. People *knew* about him. He wasn't a nothing. He was *famous*. Every word he uttered was written down. The media followed him in a frenzy of pointed microphones and shouted questions, noting his every eye-twitch. He even had to wear a bulletproof vest when he moved about. They looked at his art and listened to his music! It was played in open court and heard around the nation. Maybe somebody would realize and make his music famous. Maybe Dad would appreciate him now. Maybe.

Mitch Stacy called the Rolling home in Shreveport shortly after Rolling pleaded guilty. He was hoping to catch Claudia Rolling on the phone. She had spoken to him that last time in court. Perhaps she would speak to him again. But it was James Rolling who answered the phone.

"Mr. Rolling?"

"Yes."

"This is Mitch Stacy calling, from the Gainesville *Sun*."

James Rolling cut him off. "We have nothing to say," came the angry voice. And then Mitch heard the receiver slammed down with a clang in his ear. He waited what he considered a decent interval and tried again. This time Claudia Rolling did answer the phone.

"Yes, I remember you," she said. "No, I'm sorry, Mr. Stacy, but we have nothing to say."

Mitch could understand their reluctance to talk to reporters. Beyond telephone calls, journalists and TV personnel had converged on the Rolling home after he pleaded guilty to the murders. The man who had been blamed for at least helping to create the warped personality in his son that led convolutedly to the brutal slayings was not pleased about the attention. Deaf in one ear, blind in one eye and with fragments of a bullet still lodged in his head, courtesy of his son, he sat grimly in a lawn chair on his front lawn. Across his lap he held a double-barreled shotgun.

46

For the Defense

Rolling was dressed in a white shirt and his horn-rimmed glasses.

As the defense began its case to try to save his life it became obvious that this was a story about losers. There were five murder victims who had been publically accounted for. There were three murder victims in Shreveport, Louisiana, who had not. There were family members whose lives had been shattered and would never be the same.

And then there was the Rolling family. Its history demonstrated a cycle of pain and abuse, without any intervention that could have prevented the cyclical patterns. Such behavior, even in its depicted excess, certainly does not often result in such an insane, vicious culmination as in the case of Danny Rolling. Still, once in a while a child warped during the crucial years of development grows up to seek horrific revenge, all out of proportion to his own real—and/or imagined—afflictions. The result, whatever the real cause, can be a tragedy such as the Gainesville student murders.

There was one such child with such a story . . . according to the defense account.

Preceded by other defense witnesses, longtime neighbor Bernadine Holder, Mississippi attorney Arthur Carlisle, Aunt Agnes Mitchell and Cousin Chuck Strozier, who laid down the preliminary foundations, it was Danny's mother, Claudia, whose words proved the most wrenching (see Appendix A).

Her testimony had been taped in Shreveport, Louisiana, one and a half years prior to the beginning of the trial of *Florida* v. *Rolling.* Having been diagnosed with terminal cancer of the liver, she was unable to make the trip to Florida to testify in person. At the time she spoke to John Kearns for the defense, and to Jim Nilon for the prosecution, her son was still publicly maintaining his innocence, and his mother was sure of it. Nevertheless, she was anxious to tell the story of her son's life in a sense, after the state's case, which had been presented by Rod Smith and his team in all of its graphic details, the mother's testimony, which was shown to the jury on a color videotape, was the beginning of a separate trial.

The heart of the defense's case was here. In presenting the so-called mitigating circumstances behind the murders, a much different scenario emerged from that of the heartless killer that had been presented by the prosecution.

During the mother's testimony the long history of the unhappy home life was revealed in all its pathetic misery. She told the story of her boys and their dad hesitantly, in pain, sometimes having difficulty breathing, sometimes holding her hands to her bosom. She was a sad-looking woman with full cheeks sagging almost to her jawline, huge brown pupils under high pointed eyebrows, a down-turned mouth immediately evocative of the down-turned edges of her son's mouth as he sat at the table for the defense, watching and listening to his mother speak for him, as she had done so many times in the past. And now one last time.

Her testimony laid the groundwork for the defense. It dealt with a story of paternal abuse, a childhood head injury, possible demonic possession, a history of family mental illness and institutionalization, and the constant emotional and physical abuse at home. During her testimony, Rolling seemed to become humanized, even pathetic, in having presumably been forced to lead the life she described.

The underlying question—should this man be executed?

Claudia Rolling was terminally ill. The state attorney had to be careful not to arouse undue sympathy for her. In going over her direct testimony to try to shake it, he was careful, if firm. Claudia, however, was consistent in her answers—slow, deliberate, thoughtful and pained. It was obvious that she was uncomfortable in her chair, often pressing her long-fingered hand to her bosom, trying to gulp short breaths. She spoke of Danny's wife, O'Mather, how she had had a tough life, how O'Mather's mother was killed in a car-train wreck when she was five, how she was shuttled from one person to another. She told how O'Mather's dad had different women who lived in the house and how the children had to live around them. "All of the things a little five-year-old girl had to live with. No mother."

Even on cross-examination, Claudia's painful testimony seemed to help the defense. By the time it was over it seemed established that the father controlled things; what they did, what courses they could take in school, how they could breathe at the table, even how they could chew. And the mother throughout assumed a very passive role. It was almost as though Claudia were describing a home she was not involved in, the home of someone else, that everything had happened to some other people. She spoke about how protective she was with her boys, even though she kept bringing them back into the home she described. She described a very bad situation of apparent child abuse from a very young age.

There was some question about how the jury was responding. Was the defense conjuring up enough sympathy for the abusive life Danny had allegedly endured to show him mercy? The prosecution tried to show that the beatings never sent anyone to the hospital, that the boys never missed school because of them.

Then Lillian "Bunny" Mills got on the stand. Her testimony (see Appendix B) mostly backed up the mother's. At one point she told of Danny's heightened resistance when she tried to take him to get professional counseling. This was a man in his late twenties speaking:

"I'm not going. If my dad finds out what I've said he'll kill me."

"But, Danny, the psychiatrist is not supposed to reveal what you say to him. It may come to where you may have to have the family there with you. If you can get that in your therapy . . ."

"My dad would never go."

"Well, we'll just go to your dad and find out."

"I'm not going. If my dad finds out that I've talked about . . . Oh God, I don't want to say nothing else about my dad."

"Well, Danny, we made the appointment and you're gonna go. We're gonna go over to your house right now and we're gonna talk to your mother and dad."

Eventually, she convinced him and they went to his house to talk to his parents.

"I've talked Danny into going in the Shreveport mental institute," she said to James. "If it comes to the point where Danny goes into this therapy, will you support him? If you have to go, would you go?"

"Yes, I would," he answered. "Maybe it's me that needs to go."

"Well, I don't know about that, but I'm going to take Danny."

"I'll support Danny all the way," Claudia said.

"Well, there you are, Danny. So we're going."

Then Ms. Mills described a scene of fluctuating anxieties. Danny said yes and then he said no. He ran. She literally chased him around her apartment building. "Danny, you have to go. You have to get well."

They circled her apartment complex four times in this wild chase before she managed to stop him. "No," he said. "I'm afraid of what Dad will do to me if he finds out I talked about him in therapy."

Such was her testimony.

The cross-examination produced little in the way of new facts. The record showed that Rolling was brought to LSU Medical Center on March 10, 1989, as a family referral. Ms. Mills told Mr. Nilon she had contacted Danny about publishing his music while he was in a Florida jail, but the prosecution was more interested in establishing the extent of her personal rather than her business relationship to the defendant, a move she obviously resented. After the judge's intervention, however, she eventually admitted on the stand that she and Danny had been sexually intimate.

When viewing the photos of the victims, some of the jurors, as mentioned, had cried. Now, with the testimony of Claudia and Bunny Mills, they were sitting up, looking interested, obviously trying to grasp the implications of what was being said. Maybe they could get some insight into why Rolling did what he did. The two women—Claudia and Bunny—had created a vivid picture. Added to the testimony of other relatives, neighbors and friends, there seemed no denying years of physical and emotional abuse.

Then the prosecution called a rebuttal witness to cast a deep shadow of doubt on the troubling defense testimony—another one of the important women in Rolling's life.

Pretty, dark-haired, petite, with a long neck Modigliani might have painted, from the moment she entered the court, crossing the entire room in front of him in order to take her place on the stand, Danny never took his eyes off her. He stared with tightly drawn lips, his large hands clasped in front of him, resting on the table. They had not seen each other for more than a decade. Rolling's ex-wife, O'Mather Halko Rolling Lummis, had remarried twelve years ago. Perhaps ironically, to a police officer. Their daughter, who was aware of Rolling's crimes, considered Lummis her father. It was impossible not to notice the distinct similarities between O'Mather and the girls who had been selected for murder, in particular, the startling resemblance to Christa Hoyt, the girl with the long, slender neck, the girl he had decapitated.

O'Mather would not look at her former husband where he sat at the defense table, except for a brief glance when she was asked to identify him. Sitting on the stand, dressed in a flowered dress buttoned down the middle and speaking with a thick Southern drawl, her testimony was very damaging to the defense. According to her recollections, the relationship between Danny and his father was "normal" and "caring." James Harold often helped the young couple by buying furniture and groceries for them. She saw no evidence of abuse, nor did Danny ever confide to her of any in his past. She testified that she became disillusioned about their marriage not only because of his "inconsistency" and the fact that he could not seem to hold a job, but even more so because he had been caught by the police "peeping" in windows during the time of her pregnancy. At one point he had hit her, blackening her eye, and at another he had even threatened her with a shotgun.

Rodney Smith later said he found O'Mather to be "an amazingly kind person. She literally does not have bad feelings toward Danny Rolling. She's gone on to have a happy marriage and a happy house."

The defense, on the other hand, found her to be totally unaware of anything that was going on around her. Her testimony was all on one level and very passive. According to her recollection, the family did not tell her anything, Danny did not open himself up. She did not see any signs of abuse. She never got involved. She never asked him what was wrong. She saw only a caring relationship between father and son.

Her testimony considerably weakened the abuse defense. (See Appendix C.)

47

The Psychologists

The defense hoped to put up a stream of expert witnesses with long lists of degrees and specializations in psychology, child psychology, and psychiatry. The reason: to show that damage allegedly done to Rolling as a child led to sexual dysfunction, voyeurism, low self-esteem, anger, rage, uncontrollable impulses and ultimately murder.

Once accused of the murders in January 1991, six months after the killings, Rolling spoke in detail to clinical psychologist, Dr. Harry Krop, about the Gainesville killings. By the time these evaluations were over Rolling was diagnosed as suffering from atypical psychosis.

Agitated. Difficulty concentrating. Scabs all over body. Picking at himself. Anxious. Difficulty sitting still. Very agitated. Stood up. Wandered off. Had difficulty at grasping reality. Very poor attention. [Although not psychotic] he was put on medication that was used for psychotic behavior.

Dr. Krop saw Rolling eight times. He felt that although there had been a tendency toward histrionics, Danny never tried to look mentally ill or exhibit signs of psychosis to avoid responsibility or affect insanity.

At one point Dr. Krop called the Rolling home in Shreveport. He told James Harold that he had been appointed by the court to evaluate his son. After several telephone calls, it was obvious to Krop that James Harold needed to talk about himself and at his own pace. James controlled the interview, often responding, according to Krop, with an answer that did not respond to Krop's question. He apparently had his own agenda. He needed to tell Dr. Krop things in his own order—about himself, his military experience . . . He wanted to talk about his wife, describing her as "once a schizo always a schizo." He said his wife and her family had a conspiracy against him and that they were liars with regard to him. He said he had never been abusive in his life. He did feel that his son had psychological problems for a long time but it was not because of anything he did. He had always tried to provide for Danny monetarily and to give him a home. He told Dr. Krop it was primarily his wife and her family's doing that Danny turned out the way he did.

Dr. Krop seemed to feel that many of James Harold's responses were edged with denial. He went on to speak at length about the effects of abuse:

Certainly we cannot, in the mental health field, say with one hundred percent accuracy that this kind of event, or series of events, caused this kind of behavior or this kind of personality makeup. Research, however, is pretty clear that when a child is abused either physically, mentally or sexually, depending on the kind of treatment and depending on the kind, if any, of intervention the child may have at some point later in life, there is a greater likelihood of that individual becoming dysfunctional later on in life. There is also literature that clearly indicates that an individual who is abused as a child will have a higher likelihood of being an abuser himself or herself . . .

Particularly in physical or emotional abuse, we see individuals who develop low self-esteem, who become less trusting . . . Our mothers and fathers are our primary models. If those individuals are inappropriate or ineffective, or abusive, or weak, again there is a higher likelihood that the individual is going to model that kind of behavior.

We are pretty certain that the individual who grows up in that environment in which there is abuse tends to learn various coping mechanisms to try to avoid the abuse . . . For example, one way of dealing with abuse, particularly physical and sexual abuse, is the child-victim tends to learn to accommodate or adapt the best that he can to the abuse. Some learn to avoid it as much as possible and some learn to take it, feeling that they can't escape. And they distance themselves. Become unemotional. They become individuals who have little empathy, little concern, show little affect in terms of concern for other people . . .

All of those are potential factors that develop out of abusive family backgrounds.

He also spoke about how functional families created for the child a sense of security, intimacy, responsibility, caring for each other, loving each other, which in turn created an environment in which the child could develop its potential.

And he spoke of the reverse:

When parents develop a dysfunctional unit, the children as a product of that dysfunction and they themselves develop into dysfunctional individuals . . .

There was a lot of berating, a lot of criticism, tension in the home. Fear, secrecy. Walking on eggshells all the time. There is a tendency to be nontrusting; to learn to be manipulative. To develop very poor self-esteem. Lack of confidence. Bottom line: you become more vulnerable and more sensitive to rejection. More vulnerable to stresses later on in life . . .

Danny to this day would still like to think he could get his father to love him. There's always a need to have this kind of family development wholeness. Abused children still love and go back to their parents. Constantly searching for this love and attention.

Dr. Krop found Danny to be fairly bright but very immature emotionally.

I would say Danny functions at a level of an immature teenager. Someone who tends in relationships to see what he can get from them . . . [He has a] love-hate relationship with his father. On the one hand, Danny talks about abuse, on the other, he still wants to gain his father's love and respect and affection. He talked about his mother in a very positive way. Yet I got a sense that, at the same time, there was this feeling of betrayal because [she] was weak and ineffective in terms of not being able to protect him from his father . . . The first type of diagnosis I gave him is what we call a "borderline personality disorder." The second . . . is what we call "anti-social personality disorder." The third is what we call a "personality disorder not otherwise specified." By that I mean there are a number of maladaptive personality traits that exist within Danny Rolling but they can't be categorized; they don't meet all the criteria to reach a diagnosis. We know they're maladaptive and they create problems for the individual, but they cannot be categorized into one particular category that is an acceptable diagnosis . . . [In this case] it consists of narcissism, obsessive-compulsive. Histrionic, a person who is excessively dramatic. All of these pretty much have overlapping features.

A second diagnosis beyond the personality disorders is alcohol and substance abuse . . . basically an individual who maladaptively uses alcohol or illicit drugs to create maladaptive environmental interactions.

And then the final diagnosis that we have is paraphilia, a sexual disorder, and this would be, in my opinion, the primary diagnosis for this individual: a sexual disorder which consists of . . . let me read the definition: "A paraphilia is a sexual disorder in which there are recurrent intense sexual urges and/or sexually arousing fantasies generally involving other individuals." In this case the paraphilia or sexual disorder, what we call voyeurism, is of a severe nature.

Whether Dr. Krop's diagnosis was strong enough to mitigate in a meaningful way the defendant's acts was not clear. But in cross-examination Rod Smith, not taking a chance on having a favorable impression left with the jury, delivered an attack on the psychologist's testimony.

"I give the results of my evaluations," Krop responded at one point. "It is up to the jury to determine whether they were mitigating of not."

SMITH: He understood the criminality of everything he did those nights, didn't he?
KROP: Yes.
SMITH: He understood the difference between right and wrong, didn't he?

KROP: Yes.

SMITH: When there are external controls, Danny can conform his conduct, can't he?

KROP: Yes.

SMITH: Every time he stood over the person [with the knife in hand] he knew the difference between right and wrong, and every time he chose to do wrong, didn't he?

KROP: Yes.

SMITH: No further questions.

Also testifying for the defense after psychological evaluations of Rolling was Dr. Betty McMahon. With short-cropped gray hair and a quick smile, she was unflappable on the stand. A clinical psychologist and expert witness in forensic psychology and neuropsychology, Dr. McMahon always seemed in control.

He is in the here and now . . . his clarity of perception may become a little clouded or loose at times in the presence of high anxiety, but would not reach a psychotic proportion. In other words, he knows what he's doing.

He is an individual who is likely to hold a number of mistaken beliefs. By that I mean there are times when he is likely to misperceive what is going on around him and then hold that misperception and it becomes a belief for him. He is highly anxious with a great deal of insecurity and a great deal of apprehension as to what lies ahead of him. There was a good deal of tension, stress and anxiety indicated throughout the entire testing. All the patterns that emerged from the testing were quite integrated. His perception is that there are ego-threatening forces in his environment which threaten the very organizations of his personality. He's not sure where this comes from. He has virtually no insight into his own dynamics. So he feels anxious and it is overwhelming for him . . .

His personality is extremely impoverished. By that I mean he has virtually no internal resources. Danny runs on maximum most of the time. That means he is using everything he has to keep moving all the time . . . he is using everything he has to face every day. Most of us have a reservoir of internal resources to draw on. Something happens, some crisis, some trauma, we can kind of back up, regroup, reach down and draw on strengths with a resiliency and determination; it's a problem-solving ability. Danny doesn't have that. He's running on maximum, using everything he's got just to get through.

Lots of impoverishment in terms of emotional experiences in his life. He keeps a tight rein on his way of dealing with his emotions. He keeps them very superficial, but they are not his genuine emotions. He's playing a role, not intentionally, and displays whatever emotions he feels are appropriate at the time. They are simply what he has learned to do in a social situation.

His defense mechanisms, when he gets highly anxious, are repressive and restrictive. He just shuts it down. Stifle it. Step on it. He doesn't deal with it. Constricts. He becomes virtually inflexible. He's likely to do the same thing over and over again even though he knows it is wrong. He has very poor emotional controls so that although these emotions are repressed and stuffed down, and they do get expressed periodically, but they are highly likely to be expressed in an uncontrolled way. With most of us, when we express any emotion, it is modulated by our cognitive processes. There is some thought that is going on at the same time. We're thinking, "Is this appropriate? Is the intensity appropriate? Is the target of my emotion appropriate?" With Danny, there is little of that. It's just, "There it is," and there's very little cognitive modulated.

He is extremely immature . . . There is a great impairment of empathy. That is something that tends to come with maturity. Empathy, in the sense that he does not know how to put himself in another person's shoes and appreciate what they're feeling . . .

A lot of unmet needs of dependency and affection. These are needs that start in childhood and when we don't get them in childhood, and particularly what we tend to do if we don't read a lot of self-help books or get ourselves to a therapist, is that we tend to run around as adults trying to get these needs met in childlike ways. And this he does. They are still at the level of childhood unmet needs for dependency and affection.

He tends to be suspicious He has a lot of repressed hostility and anger to the point of rage. There's a lot of underlying dynamic aggression that is simply within his internal system. He is, in large part, depressed. Fairly sad, fairly remote, fairly distant from people. He can interact in a superficial way but he perceives himself as being different from and outside the mainstream and unable to relate well. These are long-standing traits.

A log of feelings of inadequacy, hopelessness, insecurity . . . tends to be somewhat unrealistic, grandiose in his own appraisal of himself. That's sort of a flip side of someone whose needs have never been met. When one has to meet them himself, he sort of goes overboard.

Those are the main patterns that evolve over the tests.

There is no sign of malingering. At no time was he other than cooperative. He tended to do his very best. I got no sense that he was trying to run a wrap on me. I gave him plenty of attempts to try to fool me. He was distractible in the way a child is. Other than that, he was as open and honest as he could be.

Dr. McMahon came up with pretty much the same diagnosis as Harry Krop. She diagnosed Rolling as a borderline personality disorder with antisocial disorder features [secondly], features of an histrionic personality, narcissistic personality, a dependent personality.

McMahon: Nature does not satisfy man's needs to have everything in nice little neat compartments. It is difficult fitting a man of his complexity into a nice neat box. Somewhere along the line of development this person was stunted, stopped, dwarfed . . . He was abandoned as a child emotionally

. . . and he sees abandonment in most relationships . . . "If I confess directly, that's the same as committing suicide, I might get the death penalty. But if I confess through Bobby and he tells you, then that's okay." This is an exquisite example of a borderline personality. There is a slippage in the logic . . . Overwhelming majority of borderline personality disturbances are found in people who have a history of severe abuse.

She told of her meeting with Danny's brother, Kevin:

His brother, Kevin, had large memory gaps. "I tried to get out of there. I tried not to remember." He is married. He spoke about leaving home as soon as he could, wanting to be away. "I don't remember much except I know it wasn't good." It was very difficult to go back after being in the service. It was like "living on the edge of a volcano." Even used the term, when asked what occurred in the household in reaction to what Danny had done, "I disassociated and got out of there." His message was . . . "I don't remember this. I was told this, but I don't remember." He remembers Danny was taken in the patrol car but couldn't remember why. Remembers Danny was caught with voyeurism but doesn't remember what happened. He didn't want any more grief. He didn't want to know.

She spoke of how James Harold denied all and portrayed himself in a favorable light, blaming everything on Danny's ex-wife O'Mather. In another conversation, he blamed his wife and her family. Somebody else's fault.

McMAHON: Emotional abuse has the greatest destruction in the very core of a child, especially if given by the primary caretaker upon whom you rely for life. It develops paranoia, suspicions, distrust. He's angry at his father but he's *absolutely enraged* at his mother, despite all his love for her. That is the one thing he is not in touch with at all. He begged her not to go back— repeatedly. She always went back. Yet he defended her.

Dr. Robert Sadoff was the last psychiatrist for the defense. He was a Philadelphia psychiatrist specializing in forensic psychology. He, too, diagnosed Rolling as a borderline personality disorder, adding that it was a "severe" case. All three doctors, whether psychologist or psychiatrist, had independently arrived at the same conclusion.

He had strong qualities of the borderline, having all eight of the characteristics listed for clinical diagnosis of the illness. Only five of the listed qualities are needed to make a diagnosis.

Dr. Sadoff said that the abused person sees the world differently from one who is nurtured and loved. He sees it as a very dangerous place. He also stated that emotional abuse has the greater impact on a person's growth and development than physical abuse.

> He has this excessive need for his father to love him. [He also has the] perception that he has let his father down.

Rolling told the doctor his father was the most decorated veteran of the Korean War, demonstrating a case of intense overidealization. "Made Audie Murphy look like Mr. Magoo," Danny said, when in fact James Harold had only received awards for length of service, a recommendation for commendation and an honorable discharge from the U.S. Navy.

During Rod Smith's cross-examination of Dr. Sadoff it was made clear to the jury that all the experts agreed that Danny did not have multiple personalities. This was not *The Three Faces of Eve*. There was no organic brain disorder.

No psychosis.

48

Closing Arguments

Rodney Smith for the prosecution approached the podium to begin his closing statement. This was the last time he would have the opportunity to speak to this jury, to convince them that Daniel Harold Rolling deserved to die for what he had done. The prosecution had been required to prove only one of the eleven statutory aggravating factors. It believed it had proven beyond a reasonable doubt at least four. Now, the summation.

After thanking the jury for their attention and devotion to duty Smith spoke of his sworn duty to prosecute, the public defender's sworn duty to defend, the judge's sworn duty to rule on the law and the jury's sworn duty to weigh the evidence.

He said this was not a particularly difficult case to decide.

. . . One of the ironies of these proceedings is that the focus was put on Danny Harold Rolling. But the focus should be on whether or not the State of Florida has proved beyond a reasonable doubt certain aggravators that are set forth under the statutes. And . . . whether or not the defense has brought out mitigation that outweighs the aggravators. That's the focus that we have to deal with . . .

He reminded them that Danny Rolling came forward and confessed to all five murders, that he, indeed, was the murderer.

Aggravator number one—*Proven*: He committed the murders while in the commission of armed burglaries and sexual battery. If you rape someone before you kill them, if you come into someone's home, into his safe harbor, and you kill him, it is an aggravator for which the scales are balanced in favor of the death penalty.

Aggravator number two—Whether or not a person has a conviction of capital murder or felony involving the use or threat of violence. *Proven*: Judgments entered in record state Danny Rolling of having been convicted time and time again for crimes of violence. A sum total of violent criminal judgments in fifteen years over four states in five or six jurisdictions. This aggravator alone tilts the balance in favor of a recommendation of the death penalty. I find it amazing that . . . Mr. Kearns stood up and said to you he just wants you to "lock the door of the jail and throw away the key. We need him to go to prison." He's *been* to prison. This is what prison was about. You want to talk about time, I refer you to . . . judgments: two sexual batteries, three armed burglaries with the battery, three armed robberies, one robbery, four robberies with firearms, one armed bank robbery, one attempted robbery with firearm, two aggravated assaults on a law enforcement officer. That is an adult lifetime of crime. That is an aggravator and it's not one that should be difficult for you to determine. It's a matter of record. Check the kind of time. He's got three hundred months in the United States district court. He's got a life sentence that he's facing in Ocala. He's got life sentences that he's facing in Hillsborough County.

This case is about what he ought to pay for *these* crimes, because as bad as that life of violence is, as bad as those judgments are, for what he's done before he ever got here, they *pale* in comparison to what he did in Gainesville, to what he did to Sonja, to what he did to Christina, and Christa and Tracy and Manuel.

Prison's simply not enough . . .

Two statutory aggravators had already been established. The balance was weighing down.

SMITH: The third aggravating factor is that the capital murder was committed in a "cold, calculated and premeditated manner" and the court is going to give you instruction on the concept that is normally called "heightened premeditation."

To be an aggravator under the law you have to show that there was more planning, a certain amount of premeditation, more than just the amount of time to think about what you were doing. That there was a design, a plan, a commitment even . . . to kill.

Now the coldness and calculation of this case is astounding. The coolness and premeditation are chilling and is sometimes difficult for us to fathom.

He spoke of how far in advance and how carefully Rolling planned the murders.

On July eighteenth [over a month before the murders] when he went into an army-navy store to buy the Ka-Bar knife because it was "exceptional for killing." It went "in and out like butter." It had a bloodline to facilitate "in and out." He bought it in Tallahassee under a false name. He even prepared in Sarasota. He bought the gun. He carried each one into every one of the crime scenes.

In Sarasota he sings all the songs he's written, says farewell to his mom, his dad, his brother because he is now preparing for his great event. Now he came to Gainesville, the predator who was stalking out the ground in which he was going to prey. He peeks into windows. It now becomes a matter of victim identification.

He spoke of how Rolling moved into the woods, and although he bought a tent and a mattress it was the things he stole that told the true story—the screwdriver, the tight-fitting athletic gloves and the duct tape.

SMITH: You don't buy air-conditioning duct tape to move into the woods.
Danny is now prepared. We are talking about an amazing plan. A commitment. Now that circumstantial evidence alone would show you the level of commitment that he made to this case, I believe, in and of itself. But we have something more in this case. We've got a tape in his own words, in which Danny Rolling, and you remember it, at the end of the tape when he talks to his brother in what now seems almost prophetic. "You know if you're gonna kill a deer, kill him with a lung shot. Go for the heart or a vital organ . . . " Then he said, "I'm signing off now. *There's something I've got to go do.*"

Smith spoke angrily about one aspect of premeditation: how Rolling stood for so long over each girl to determine which he should kill and which he should rape.

Five to ten minutes! Now that's *cold*. You want to talk about planning. You want to talk about time to change your mind?

In reference to the third scene, Christa's murder:

He even rearranged the furniture. He moved the bookshelf! Talk about premeditation! He waits. He sets a trap. She's walking into a death trap. She cannot escape. She will not escape and she did not escape! But not because he didn't have plenty of time to change his mind. No. He was *committed* to do what he was going to do!
He is like a tiger. I think of this sometimes. Whenever someone walks by, he falls back into the grass. When they leave, he's back in his position. He goes in and he kills her. But even then he's planning everything out. He realizes that if he could peek in the window, well, then somebody else might peek in and see what he's doing. He tapes the drapes shut so no one could peek in like he did.
We've got a man who planned for months, weeks, days, hours, everything he did was completely designed for being successful at killing and raping. He was not a person that did not understand what he was doing. [It was not] a spur-of-the-moment thing. This was the cold, calculated design of a man who was committed to . . . kill. It's a horrible aggravator because of the consciencelessness of what he did. Everything he did was designed to carry out one thing. Rape and murder.

As he listened to Rod Smith's damning words Rolling sank lower into his chair, stooped over, grimacing, closing his eyes, staring down, rarely looking up at the prosecutor.

SMITH: There's a fourth statutory aggravator. "Was it capital murder especially heinous, atrocious and cruel?"

Now Smith had to talk about the murders themselves. Going over each of the last moments of each of the victims, how they were cruelly terrorized before they died. Each of them knew what was happening. How two struggled and fought for their lives. How Christina was so terrorized she would have "done anything to stay alive." How Rolling admitted to Tracy that, yeah, he was the one. How he kept Christa alive for an hour, taped up, how he sexually played with her, raped her. How he sent a message to Gainesville because he wanted "to terrorize this community."

At one point Rolling got up and attempted to leave the courtroom. The bailiff straightened up and firmly motioned to him to sit down again, while Parker turned to him and whispered, "No. You have to stay throughout this."

The jury members could barely look as, once again, Smith held up the colored photographs of Danny's grisly handiwork.

[Manny] fights for his life and his roommate's life, but thirty-one stab wounds and you lose. He fought, cursed, he fought hard, he almost overcame, but he died. There's no doubt he knew what was happening. He was gonna fight for his life. Remember Rusty's testimony? And Bobby's? "Man, he knew he was in the fight of his life!" Danny said that Manny *knew* he was fighting to stay alive. That's what we know about Manny Taboada. That he came out of his sleep with a knife *here*, but he fought for his life and he fought for his roommate's life and he died. Yeah. But in terms of thirty-one stab wounds, in terms of knowing what was gonna happen to him, being aware that his life was ebbing away in this fight. No question about it.

He shook Manny's death photo at the jury. Some members lowered their heads. Some cried. They didn't want to look anymore, but Smith persisted.

SMITH: Look at that! That's only *part* of the thirty-one wounds. How committed do you have to be to kill someone to stab him thirty-one times! That's Manuel Taboada as Danny Rolling rewarded him for having the misfortune of simply living somewhere where Danny Rolling wanted to rape someone.

Smith paused a minute before he spoke of the atrocity of Tracy Paules' murder and how she knew, without a doubt, what was going to happen to her. Rolling had on his mask and he was covered with Manny's blood. She knew, Smith said, that the only way it would end was when he killed her.

The best evidence in this case is the horror of it as it all comes out.

(*Pointing at Rolling*) Here's the man!

In speaking to his psychiatrist, he said, "If somebody shoots you, that's not so bad. But if somebody comes into your house at night and you know you're going to die, that's a really horrifying thing. I know. *I've seen it.*" Trust Danny Rolling's recollection of the horror of it. *That's* what heinous, atrocious and cruel is. It's not the quick gunshot in the daylight. It's when you make people suffer. It's when you torture people. It's when you make the last moments of their lives the worst moments of their lives and that's how every one of these students died.

Considering everything that happened to her, I can't help thinking, for Tracy, death was a respite from Danny Rolling.

(*Passionately*)

He wanted to send out a message, a symbolic gesture to the community about, This is what I am. I want you to remember what Bobby said. He wanted to be the superstar of crime. He's committed five murders, and I guarantee you, nobody committed worse murders than these. These are legendary murders. These aren't just murders you hear about or read about. These are murders you never forget about. But Danny got his wish. He *is* the superstar of crime when it comes to what he did to these people. . . . Danny said he wanted to extract a vengeance for what he perceived as mistreatment in prison. He wanted someone to suffer because he got the short end of the stick in life. Maybe not. Maybe he just wanted to be the superstar. But whatever, it doesn't matter. There isn't an excuse, there isn't a reason, there isn't a justification. Five humans tortured to death, premeditated, planned by a man with a history of crime. *Nothing* could outweigh that.

I believe that there can be no question that the state has proved beyond a reasonable doubt four of the statutory aggravators: convicted of prior felonies; committed while he was in the act of rape; murder was especially heinous, atrocious and cruel; and that the murders were committed in a cold, calculated and premeditated manner.

I cannot imagine or think of a way that we could show you more evidence. You've seen it and heard it all, even in his own words.

So we go back to the focus of the case. If we've proven not one, not two, not three, but four aggravators beyond a reasonable doubt, and we have, [the defense] has to come forth with mitigation that outweighs those statutory aggravators.

Let's talk a little bit about the mitigation. In this case you're going to get a single instruction on mitigation. You can consider anything in his background life that you think is appropriate . . . dysfunctional family. Anything.

They haven't come up with *one* person that said there's something about coming from a dysfunctional family that mitigates or even *explains* the horror of what he did here to these people. This isn't about Danny Rolling. Let's not be misled on this case. This isn't about having a fight at home, or shooting his dad or having a fight with his parents or something like that. This is about Danny Rolling, a man of average intelligence with a certain amount of gifts who, at thirty-six years of age, after most of his adult life in prison and simply because he wants to kill them and rape them, they die.

That's how simple this is.

This isn't I-shot-my-dad-cause-he-was-abusing-me. And they can't make it into that, much as they may try. He may have come from an imperfect home. *A lot of people do.* You know, if all of us, if anyone, if any expert wants to recall only the worst days of their lives, it's been a very dreary existence, a terrible home. And vice-versa. The truth is, life is filled between those lines . . . There's lots of people [with problems]. They don't wind up like this.

(*Pointing to the photos*) They don't do *that!*

Next, Smith set about to disarm the defense by projecting what its strategy would be:

This isn't about what happened to little Danny. It's about what big Danny did. It wasn't as one-sided as they're going to try to make you believe. It wasn't as bad as all that. And even if it was, *so what?* You want to know what a bad house is?

(*Holding up the photos again*) It's a house after Danny Rolling has visited it.

They're going to ask for mercy, but where was mercy when he put duct tape over their mouths before he killed then. The defense would speak for him; they couldn't speak for themselves with tape over their mouths before they were killed. If these crimes do not demand the death penalty it defies what kind of crimes would they have to *be* to require the death penalty.

Weigh on the scales of justice what they suffered against his background. Today you have to submit the appropriate and, I submit to you, the only recommendation that is commensurate with these crimes. I am confident that each of you will do your duty and you will follow the instructions of the law. I know that you know the correct recommendation for this case. I also know there will be a time when you will realize that your duty was thrust upon you. You met it. You performed it with distinction, courage and honesty. You've been true to yourself and your oath as a juror.

After recess Rolling now sat in the courtroom without a jacket. He seemed more in control. He looked clean and neat in his white shirt and tie and his horn-rimmed glasses.

John Kearns for the defense approached the podium to face the jury. He knew he had his work cut out for him. Smith had been powerfully passionate. He had a great deal of highly dramatic material to present and he had done it with great effectiveness. Kearns began talking—softly, slowly—about anger, hate and vengeance and about the profoundly negative ramifications of such bitter emotional reprisals.

This was probably the most difficult case of his career. There was no schizophrenia, no multiple personalities, no manic-depression, no clear and obvious sign of mental illness except in the very nature of Rolling's acts. Kearns cautions the jurors about the principle of the biblical eye-for-an-eye, and about the very concept of vengeance itself, quoting Martin Luther King's statement that the trouble with "an eye-for-an-eye is that it eventually leaves everybody blind."

> KEARNS: The reason I bring it up, the point being that these negative emotions never serve any purpose, not that any of you would succumb to that, but that certainly this is an emotional situation and when emotions become very high, very intense, they can cloud reasoning processes. And that's what concerns us. Certainly this is the kind of situation that generates a lot of emotional feelings.

He, too, spoke of certain aspects of the law in capital cases, this time in reference to the limitation of considering aggravating circumstances and about how mitigating circumstances were not as limited by law. The burden of standards of proof was much higher for aggravating than for mitigating factors. There was a wide range of mitigating aspects that could be considered through the pathetic record of Rolling's entire background.

> It is only the *un*mitigated homicides that warrant the death penalty. This sentence would be life without hope. No parole. Mr. Rolling is going to die in a small room behind a brick wall covered with concertina wire, with a life sentence. That's going to happen. He is going to die in that prison.

First Kearns spoke about physical abuse in the defendant's background. He went into a long review of beatings from the time *in utero* when his mother was thrown down a flight of stairs . . . the whippings with a police belt . . . the handcuffing . . . about the job at Dairy Queen his father would not let him keep . . . "I tried but I just can't make it" . . . The incident with Bernadine Holder calling Claudia to tell her James was beating Danny so hard she thought he was going to kill the boy . . . the consistency of the pattern of abuse . . . Chuck Strozier's description of the father insisting the brothers box each other in the backyard . . . About the two occasions when Mrs. Strozier, their aunt, went to Shreveport Police Lieutenant Dartoit to report the abuse and how, not surprisingly, nothing was done . . . How Agnes Mitchell, another aunt, wanted to call the Department of Welfare for the children but her sister Claudia stopped her . . . The incident when the father was chasing the sixteen-year-old boy with a revolver . . . The time the father put his son in jail for two weeks and forbade a visit from his mother . . .

> KEARNS: Abuse creates long-term repercussions. Danny spent a total of nine thousand two hundred and five days in that home.

Then Kearns spent a great deal of time on the litany of emotional abuse; the belittling . . . the put-downs . . . the fear . . . the anticipation of punishment . . . the certain terror of report card day. Leaving and coming back, fifteen to twenty times returning to turmoil and insecurity. The uncertainty of never knowing what was going to happen, when or why, was, Kearns claimed, particularly erosive to formulating personality. Kearns spoke about how psychiatrists and psychologists had found, perhaps surprising to some, that it was emotional abuse that caused the greatest destruction of the core of a person rather than the physical.

> Being told by a parent, "I hate you. I wish you'd never been born. You're not mine. You're stupid. You're no good. You'll never amount to anything"; these things destroy the very core of a child. And then ask, what effect does this kind of abuse have on a child? What is going to happen to a person as a result of it? They become paranoid. They have a sense of distrust, because the people that they turn to for help are the ones who hurt in terms of their problems. They grow up lacking social skills. They oftentimes themselves become abusive having learned the conduct of abuse. They are oftentimes depressed. Mr. Rolling has had a long history of depression all leading to poor self-esteem.

Despite Kearns' efforts, the difference in emotional intensity between prosecution and defense was beginning to be apparent. Kearns was intellectual and clinically accurate, but there was little if any passion in his summation. No sympathy was aroused for Rolling. No begging for mercy for the little boy who had never known any. Kearns reiterated, step by step, everything that the jury had already heard. But his rhetoric did not become fired up. His arguments, though clear-cut, were dry. He might have been giving a lecture on psychology. It was a clinical casebook history. Rolling was a "case." He was a cardboard character who sat at the defense table with folded hands and a persistent frown.

The part about the disproportionate mental health problems in the family were clinically accurate and interesting but did not seem to arouse sympathy. And an enormous amount of sympathy had to be aroused for the jurors to be able to say, very well, let us show him the compassion he himself could not show because he had never had any himself. He did horrible things, but he had been so desperately abused and full of pain and grief that somewhere along the line it was necessary to say, Let the cycle end here. Show him mercy.

This did not happen.

But Kearns never gave up.

He tried very hard to explain that for every strong action there was an equally strong reaction. A person of monstrous behavior like Danny Rolling did not emerge from nowhere. There were *reasons* for him to have turned out the way he did. It was a broad appeal to pay attention to child abuse. The psychological defense was strong, erudite and thorough in its assessment. Rod Smith had not seriously attempted to challenge the experts who diagnosed Rolling as having a severe borderline personality disorder. What he did was minimize the importance of their conclusions.

> KEARNS: If you're convinced that the death penalty serves society best, not out of vengeance, not to serve the families of the victims, but by deterring others, that's an honest position. Probably more today in society [than ever before] is the position that it's good for society, that it would make life in this civilization better. That's what needs to be argued here.

Some might suggest Kearns should perhaps have challenged more and put the death penalty itself on trial; admit to all the aggravating circumstances and then argue the reasons why there was a crucial need to rise above our executing each other—it creates more crime, perpetuates violence. The society that executes people like this perpetuates a continuation of the violent society and abuse that began the cycle in the first place. Rise above the base emotions of vengeance and reprisals. An argument.

And couldn't premeditation itself—the ability to think up such a twisted crime—be one of the very mitigating circumstances? It begs the issue of mental illness. Understanding the reasons for the acts does not mean excusing them. Do we execute sick people? Do we show them pity?

Some people found insulting the very notion of defending Rolling and portraying his victimization. But Kearns' final plea was to let God determine when Danny Rolling would die. Show him for the first time in his life the mercy that had always been denied him. Have pity on the abused child who became parent of the violent adult.

It was all up to the jury.

49

The Verdict

It was impossible to talk to Rod Smith while the jury was deliberating. Even his staff left him alone.

What was taking them so long?

It was an open-and-shut case.

But one and a half days passed and still the jury did not return. What had he done wrong? Had he missed something? He had surely proved more than the one aggravating factor the state required; he had proven four. Was it possible that John Kearns' arguments had struck home? That the jurors felt sorry for the monster?

Finally, after what seemed like an interminable wait, word came on the second day of deliberation that the jury had reached a verdict. The courtroom was filled to capacity.

Members of the victims' families who had been present throughout the trial were, once again, in attendance. Nearby, lending them support, was Gainesville Police Lt. Sadie Darnell. Sitting in the back, avoided by all except the media, was Sondra London. In the front row was Gainesville Chief of Police Wayland Clifton in full dress uniform. Near him were several members of the Shreveport Police Department as well as Mrs. Grissom, the mother, wife and grandmother of the murdered Grissom family in Shreveport.

As the jurors filed into the courtroom to return to the jury box, Danny watched them. Parker, Kearns and Blount-Powell tried to read their faces. Danny bit his lower lip. None of the jurors looked their way as they solemnly took the seats they had occupied throughout the trial.

There was a tense silence in the room as the jury foreman, sixty-two-year-old Jerry Ward Coleman, stood up to read the verdict.

"As to Count number one," Coleman said in a firm voice, "in the first-degree murder of Christina Powell, the majority of the jury by a vote of twelve to zero advise and recommend to the court that it impose the death penalty on Danny Harold Rolling."

There was an immediate, though subdued, reaction from the family members. Tears began to appear. Danny tightened his mouth and looked down into his folded hands, twelve to zero. All of them. That was it. It was all over but the formalities.

"As to Count number two, in the first-degree murder of Sonja Larson," Coleman continued, "the majority of the jury by a vote of twelve to zero advise and recommend to the court that it impose the death penalty on Danny Harold Rolling.

"As to Count number three, in the first-degree murder of Christa Hoyt, the majority of the jury by a vote of twelve to zero advise and recommend to the court that it impose the death penalty on Danny Harold Rolling."

Danny now nodded his head, as though in agreement.

"As to Count number four, in the first-degree murder of Manny Taboada, the majority of the jury by a vote of twelve to zero advise and recommend to the court that it impose the death penalty on Danny Harold Rolling.

"As to Count number five, in the first-degree murder of Tracy Paules, the majority of the jury by a vote of twelve to zero advise and recommend to the court that it impose the death penalty on Danny Harold Rolling. Dated the twenty-fourth day of March, nineteen ninety-four—Jerry Ward Coleman, Chairperson."

Each member of the jury was polled and a statutory line was administered to each member. "Do you agree and confirm that a majority of the jury join in the advisory sentence that you have just heard read by the clerk?"

Rolling sat and listened, his head nodding up and down with each answer of yes by the polled jury. What, one wonders, was going on in his mind as the judge spoke to the jury following the verdict? "The court will review the aggravating and mitigating factors," Judge Morris was saying, "and make an independent judgment."

Did his life flash through his mind as the kind of psychological help and support he had never had was offered to the jury members in the event the graphic gore of the case they had just reviewed gave them a problem? Did he think of the murders? Did he feel victimized by the recommended verdict? Treated fairly? Had he idealized the penalty phase of the trial as he had idealized and exaggerated most of the other important expectations of his life? He would have his opportunity to speak to the judge on his own behalf, but essentially the mind of the murderer was closed to speculation.

On March 29, 1994, Rolling did have his opportunity to speak to the judge.

"There is much I'd like to say, Your Honor, about our worlds and my beliefs. However, I feel whatever I might have to say is overshadowed by the suffering I've caused." Bearing in mind the diagnosed histrionic aspects of his personality, it was not surprising that he sounded melodramatic as he slowly drawled his brief message to the judge. "I regret with all my heart what my hand has done. I have taken what I cannot return. If only I could bend back the hands of that ageless clock and change the past. Ah, but alas, I am not the keeper of time, only a small part of history and the legacy of mankind's fall from grace." And then, the serial lust killer, who had left behind such a terrible trail of human wreckage, said: "I'm sorry, Your Honor," and shuffled back to his seat.

The families and others related to the victims had a right to speak to the judge about how their lives had been affected since the murders, but "victim impact" statements can at times be so painful that instead of helping the prosecution achieve its goal of the death penalty they can create ammunition for appeals. So Prosecutor Rod Smith contented himself with submitting to the judge only written statements from the families, which Judge Morris would read after he had already arrived at a final sentence. Even on paper, they were heartwrenching. (All were quoted in the Gainesville *Sun*.)

RICKY PAULES: I yearn to tell [Tracy] how much I love her, how much I cry for her, how much I miss her and most of all to hear her say I love you, Mom.

ROD SMITH: I don't think there was much question which way this case was going to go unless we tripped and fell. After about four hours [of deliberation] I wondered where we had fallen.

ANN GARREN: Danny Harold Rolling is a robber of life, an author of pain, a corruptor of justice and innocence, a begetter of death and a sworn enemy of the human race.

WAYLAND CLIFTON: I'm pleased. I felt like if the death penalty is ever applied, it should be applied to this case. I'm glad it was unanimous.

ADA LARSON: The anger I feel scares me sometimes. I had always been a mild-mannered person. I have given up on society. Sure, I know there are a few good people, but each time I hear of an injustice, a crime, and especially another murder, I fall to pieces. Now I trust no one.

RICK PARKER: I would not be truthful if I told you that I realistically expected to get a life sentence. I said even before we had a jury that we were staring straight in the face of a twelve-to-zero recommendation for death.

FRANK AND PATRICIA POWELL: We installed more secure locks in our home. Every night before going to bed we check the locked doors several times. We leave lights on all over the house. When we go out we leave the radios blasting in the house in the hopes that would scare away an intruder. We carry tear-gas spray on our key chains. We have an emptiness that cannot be filled.

ARMANDO CAREAGA: It was very hard to deal with the fact that if I would have remained his roommate, Manny would be alive today. I now have a four-month-old son which I named after him. Manny's mother is my son's godmother. I look forward to telling my son about who he was named after, and the crazy times him and his father used to share. As long as I live, Manny's memory will never die. Nobody will ever be able to kill that.

SADIE DARNELL: Murder should not happen in this society. When it does, it deserves the death penalty. [Rolling] is a useless nothing. He needs to be recognized as a total nothing in our society and be eliminated.

Judge Morris did listen to videotaped pleas from seven members of Rolling's family and friends as they asked him to spare Danny's life:

Kevin Rolling, who had remained in the background throughout the trial, finally made a statement. On video he appeared as a bearded, slightly heavier version of Danny. Even his voice sounded exactly like his older brother's as he spoke.

We could all beg for mercy, but I'm not sure that would help. I do hope this —that what you can hear when you make this judgment is not the law or the crowds but I hope you hear the voice of God.

The most affecting of all the pleas was that of Claudia as she asked for mercy in behalf of her son.

Thirty-nine years ago, almost forty now, the Lord gave me a miracle. I named him Danny. When I felt this little baby in my arms I had no idea, no thought he would be anything except a doctor, a lawyer, a president, anything big and wonderful . . . and at a very young age I saw changes in my son that I ignored. Changes that ultimately brought about the horror that we've gone through in the last two or three years . . . And I know that there are people that would say he deserves . . . [to die]. That could very well be true, but I'm a mother, and I love him, and I don't want him to hurt anymore. Because he's hurt all his life. I felt his pain from day one.
    (*Crying into a tissue*)
    It would be so deep in his eyes, you could swim in it. And he tried to carry it and bear it on his own. I've heard for a long time that children are a product of their environment, and if this is the case, and I believe it is, then

take me, because I would be the responsible one. I'm the one that was with him, that raised him. I'm the one that failed him somewhere.

(*She paused as she tried to control her crying.*)

Excuse me. I hate to be a crybaby. If I could take the penalty on myself I would beg you to do that. Because I feel that I did fail him. I'm the one that had to have failed him somewhere.

James Harold Rolling never spoke on behalf of his son. He never made any public statements.

On March 30, 1994, he was given a citation by the Shreveport Police for "simple battery" of his terminally ill wife, Claudia. The police had been summoned to the Rolling home in response to a neighbor's call about a violent domestic dispute.

On the same day his father was cited for beating his mother, Danny Rolling confessed to the murders of the Grissom family in Shreveport. He had always indicated that he would speak of that triple murder only after the Gainesville student murders had been tried. The day had finally come. There was, at last, a form of closure for the woman who had been seated in the front row throughout the trial. Mrs. Grissom could return home now.

April 20, 1994. The day for sentencing had come, three and a half years after the murders.

The courtroom was filled.

Judge Morris was thorough in his recitation of the aggravating and mitigating circumstances that dealt with the testimony in the long proceedings. He gave a long, sober account of the reasons for arriving at the judgments he was about to impose. He had written it in a way to demonstrate that he had given his conclusions very serious consideration, being fully aware that the sure-to-come appeals might very well be based, in large measure, on what he said this day.

One by one, he reviewed the aggravating and mitigating circumstances that had been brought up in the trial. He agreed to all the physical and emotional abuse and all the mental aberrations that, in essence, controlled Rolling's behavior, and that emotional retardation was a severe factor despite the conflicting expert testimony regarding his mental abilities. The court was not made up of social scientists, psychologists and behaviorists, and although judgments in court were restricted to the law, Judge Morris reviewed the entire history of Rolling's mental illnesses as described by the experts. He disputed none of their findings. He agreed that the defendant's immaturity, arrested at an emotional age of fifteen years, made it difficult for him to comform to the law. Judge Morris accepted all of the diagnosed chronic illnesses brought forth by the doctors. He recognized that the symptoms varied in severity and effect from time to time. He recognized that Rolling's ability to control his actions and conform them to the requirements of the law was seriously impaired by his illness.

But then he also stated that the impairment did not rise to the level envisioned by the law as substantial.

"Conforming his actions to the requirements of society is, for this defendant, more difficult than for a person not affected by the illness," he said, "but it is not impossible. He suffers from no psychosis. He is in touch with reality. He knows the difference between right and wrong. He can appreciate the criminality of his actions. He does know the difference. He does have the ability, impaired though it may be, to choose between right and wrong and to adhere to it.

"The court therefore finds that the impairment of the defendant's ability to conform his conduct to the requirements of law because of his mental disorder is a non-statutory mitigating factor. The court has considered it as such and affords it moderate weight.

"The court has very carefully considered and weighed the aggravating and mitigating circumstances as they relate to each conviction of first-degree murder as set forth in counts one through five of the indictment, being ever mindful that a human life is at stake in the balance.

"The court finds, as did the jury, that the aggravating circumstances outweigh the mitigating circumstances as they relate to each conviction of first-degree murder as set forth in counts one through five of the indictment, being ever mindful that a human life is at stake in the balance.

"The court finds, as did the jury, that the aggravating circumstances outweigh the mitigating circumstances as to each of the first-degree murders in this case. Accordingly I will impose sentence."

"Mr. Rolling, if you and your counsel will rise."

There was a total silence in the room as Danny Rolling and John Kearns stood. Rolling pulled up his pants before standing awkwardly and looking through rapidly blinking wide eyes at the judge.

"Accordingly," Judge Morris said in a clear voice, "it is ordered and adjudged that the defendant, Danny Harold Rolling, is hereby sentenced to death for the murder of the victim Sonja—"

"*Yes!*" Ricky Paules exploded under her breath, but loud enough to be heard in the courtroom.

Judge Morris looked up. "I do not want any more outbursts."

There was immediate quiet and a long moment of silence before the judge continued.

". . . Ordered and adjudged that the defendant, Danny Harold Rolling, is hereby sentenced to death for the murder of the victim, Sonja Larson, as charged in count one of the indictment.

"It is further ordered and adjudged that the defendant, Danny Harold Rolling, is hereby sentenced to death for the murder of the victim, Christina Powell, as charged in count two of the indictment.

"It is further ordered and adjudged," he continued, "that the defendant, Danny Harold Rolling, is hereby sentenced to death for the murder of Christa Hoyt as charged in count three of the indictment.

"It is further ordered and adjudged that the defendant, Danny Harold Rolling, is hereby sentenced to death for the murder of Manuel Taboada as charged in count four of the indictment.

And lastly, "It is further ordered and adjudged that the defendant, Danny Harold Rolling, is hereby sentenced to death for the murder of Tracy Paules as charged in count five of the indictment."

While Rolling had demonstrated suicidal intentions in the past, when the sentence of death was finally imposed upon him he was obviously shaken and sobered. Indeed, he appeared in shock. Rolling had started nodding his head on count two. By count three he seemed to be nodding his head in agreement. By count four, he lowered his head. After the fifth death sentence was imposed he swallowed hard and stared down at the table in front of him.

Judge Morris continued. "The defendant is hereby committed to the Department of Corrections in the state of Florida for execution of this sentence as provided by law. And may God have mercy on his soul. Done and ordered on this twentieth day of April, nineteen ninety-four."

Still a tense silence.

"Having been so sentenced," the judge continued to Rolling, "I remand you to the custody of the Division of Corrections and order that no one is to move in the courtroom until Mr. Rolling has been removed by the Division of Corrections."

He was to be sent to state prison in Starke, where he would be on death row within feet of the electric chair until the customary appeal process had been exhausted.

Rolling turned toward the bailiff, toward Kearns, toward Sondra London, looking wide-eyed, his eyebrows lifting and lowering rapidly as he turned to see which way he was to go.

Still a silence in the courtroom.

And then an emotional, unpredictable culmination to the four-week-old penalty phase of Rolling's trial—Mario Taboada could no longer restrain himself. "Five years," he shouted to the accompaniment of a short burst of applause. "You're going down in five!" he said, holding up the outstretched palm of his hand to the man who had murdered his brother. "Understand that? In less than five years!"

Although Judge Morris immediately called out to one of the bailiffs,

"Mr. Smith, remove Mr. Taboada from the courtroom," his voice was relatively subdued and understanding.

The bailiff came down the aisle from the back of the room and motioned to Mario to come toward him where he stood in the aisle.

Mario stood up and turned to point at Sondra London, who was seated in the left section of the courtroom. *"You!"*

"Mr. Taboada," the judge said a little louder, "please remove yourself from the courtroom, sir. Please."

"Justice will prevail," Mario called as he made his way unescorted to the back of the courtroom. Once begun, he couldn't seem to contain himself. He had been complaining about the long period of time it takes to carry out an execution after sentencing, and had already vowed to do everything he could to expedite the process for Rolling. "Justice is beyond these walls. We will have the last say," he shouted as he stepped out of the room. "We will prevail. Our children's names will be remembered over *him*."

It had been a startling outburst, but not one that the judge wished to cite for contempt.

"Ladies and gentlemen," he said to the court once Mario Taboada was out of the room, "I'm sorry for that. Other than that, the proceedings have been done, I think, appropriately. With that I thank you for your conduct and this court is adjourned."

The gavel smacked down hard.

Everybody stood up.

Epilogue

All the frenzied activity. The thousands upon thousand of man-hours. Almost seven thousand investigative leads that required investigation by hundreds of special agents. The millions of dollars spent for the prosecution. The millions of dollars spent for the defense. All the fearfully closed restaurants and shops at night, the sleepless nights, nightmares, terror, grief, pain and outrage. The wasted young lives, the deaths, the lingering, haunting fears left by desperate images of mutilation and carnage—all because of the violent acts of one man.

What would have happened if Danny Rolling had been a loved child? How simplistic to think that none of this might have happened had one little boy been less abused, had been given a little more encouragement in the direction the child's spirit seemed to want to go, had been a little less punished and a lot more loved. Every person has a dark side. When combined with a possible genetic defect coming dangerously close to the edges of mental aberration, the combination is often lethal enough to alter and affect the unsuspecting lives of many innocent people.

When Rolling's dark side won, humanity lost.

Feeling the pain and grasping the ramifications of the irreversible trauma is an important step in evaluating the effects that serial murderers, particularly serial lust murderers, leave in their wakes. Patterns of parental neglect, abuse and violence, undetected childhood cognitive disabilities, and alcohol and drug abuse are virtually identical in serial killers.

Joel Norris, author of *Serial Killers: The Growing Menace*, contends it is a generational disease "passed on through child abuse, negative parenting and genetic damage." Much of the extensive FBI studies supports Norris' theories. While the killers may become genetically dysfunctional in a variety of ways, the FBI studies maintain that if sexual, physical and psychological child abuse were stopped, *most serial killers would not have the environment in which to develop* (author's italics).

Of all known multiple murderers: 70 percent had family members with severe alcohol abuse problems; 50 percent had been severely beaten as children; 50 percent had family members with criminal histories; many had been sexually abused.

In most cases, early evidence of their resulting bizarre behavior was

408

ignored, supporting the development of distortions in thinking. It turned out, Joel Norris wrote: "Not only were they unwanted as children, but they were punished for being born."

In their 1980 survey FBI agents Hazelwood and Douglas conclude: "Seldom does the lust killer come from an environment of love and understanding. It is more likely that he was an abused or neglected child who experienced a great deal of conflict in his early life and was unable to develop and use adequate coping devices. Had he been able to do so, he would have withstood the stresses placed upon him and developed normally in childhood . . . These stresses, frustrations and subsequent anxieties, along with the inability to cope with them, may lead the individual to withdraw from society which he perceives as hostile and threatening."

Another expert, Donald T. Lunde, states in *Murder and Madness*: "The serial killer is a disease that is running rampant in society and threatens to overwhelm our juvenile justice, criminal justice and correctional institutions . . ." He wrote that the Surgeon General of the United States has called domestic and social violence one of the newest public health risks to the future of society. "It is something to ponder with great seriousness . . . Victims of apparently motiveless killers, whose methods and activities make them almost undetectable." Serial lust killing is not a traditional form of murder, as most police and criminologists understand it. "The crime," says Lunde, "is actually a form of disease. Its carriers are serial killers who suffer from a variety of crippling and eventually fatal symptoms, and its victims are the people struck down, seemingly at random, by the *disease carriers* (author's italics). It is the disease of serial murder that is the pattern of violence that the office of the United States Surgeon General had called one of the top-priority issues of public health.

(The author again wishes to make very clear that she in no way has intended to whitewash Danny Rolling. He became an architect of evil of such proportions as to defy all sense of humanity. However, looking at "his side" of it is imperative if there is ever to be any hope for *prevention*. It is also a moral and human responsibility. In telling this tragic story she has attempted to show the portrait of a killer in the making.)

Although, by the end of the trial, after he had heard the details of all the violence that had been done to his brother and the others, Mario Taboada understandably sought vengeance and punishment for the killer, his earlier words continue to haunt: ". . . Somewhere down the line, they weren't loved . . ."

And then . . . there was Ed Humphrey . . .

ED HUMPHREY: Thank God it's over with. I'm glad that it came to an end, finally, for me. It's great, great news, and I'm really happy about it. And I'm

APPENDIX A

Testifying for the defense—Mrs. Claudia Rolling, Danny Rolling's
mother
(Partial testimony)
JOHN KEARNS for the defense. JIM NILON for the state.

KEARNS: State your name.

CLAUDIA: Claudia Rolling.

KEARNS: Have you ever been employed?

CLAUDIA: I worked for Shreveport Housing Authority. I can't work any longer.

KEARNS: Do you have any disease?

CLAUDIA: I have cancer of the liver.

The prosecution objected to introducing her terminal illness, knowing that the fact she was dying would lend sympathy to her testimony. The judge overruled the objection.

KEARNS: What type of treatment are you receiving?

CLAUDIA: Radiation.

KEARNS: What is the extent of your education?

CLAUDIA: High school. Some nursing school.

KEARNS: How long have you lived in Shreveport?

CLAUDIA: All my life.

KEARNS: Are you currently married?

CLAUDIA: Yes.

KEARNS: To whom?

CLAUDIA: James Harold Rolling.

KEARNS: And how long have you been married?

CLAUDIA: Thirty-seven years.

KEARNS: Do you have any children?

CLAUDIA: Yes.

KEARNS: And what are their names?

CLAUDIA: Danny. He was born on May twenty-sixth, nineteen fifty-four.

411

And Kevin James Rolling. He was born . . . (*She hesitated, putting her hand to her eyes*). I can't think . . . August fifteenth, nineteen fifty-five.

KEARNS: Danny Rolling has been named as the accused. Is he the same person as your son?

CLAUDIA: Yes.

KEARNS: Where were you and James Rolling married?

CLAUDIA: Georgia. I was nineteen. It was . . . I can't remember. Oh, sometime in nineteen fifty-three.

KEARNS: How long after your marriage did you become pregnant with Danny?

CLAUDIA: A couple of weeks.

KEARNS: How did your husband feel about it?

CLAUDIA: He wasn't too happy about it. I had a friend that had just had a baby. And he told me that I did this just because she had one. He told my mother, "This is not my fault, don't blame me."

KEARNS: Where were you living at the time?

CLAUDIA: Columbus, Georgia. I don't remember the address. It was a little garage apartment.

KEARNS: At the time were there any other relatives living in Columbus, Georgia?

CLAUDIA: Yes. A sister. Nancy Johnson and her husband, Ed Johnson.

KEARNS: When you were pregnant with Danny, did your husband ever strike you?

CLAUDIA: Not exactly strike. This is very hard for me to remember. He choked me one time.

KEARNS: How bad did he choke you?

CLAUDIA: It left a red mark on my throat that disappeared within a day.

KEARNS: Did you pass out?

CLAUDIA: Almost.

KEARNS: Did he ever physically strike you?

CLAUDIA: Yes. He had a habit of making a fist. He'd hold me down. It was almost as if he were afraid I'd disappear.

KEARNS: Did he leave any impressions on you when he was holding you down?

CLAUDIA: Yes.

KEARNS: What impressions?

CLAUDIA: On my arms or wherever he would have a hold. And the marks were very easy to come by because I bruise easy.

KEARNS: How would you characterize his behavior when you were pregnant?

CLAUDIA: I sometimes felt he was ashamed of me because we never went out anymore. One time we did go downtown to a movie, but I felt like he was ashamed of me. That might have been me, but that's the way I felt.

KEARNS: During the time that you were pregnant with Danny, did you ever leave your husband?

CLAUDIA: Yes.

KEARNS: What was the reason?

CLAUDIA: He was very demanding. He had started sleeping with a knife under his pillow.

KEARNS: Is that the same bed you were sleeping in?

CLAUDIA: Yes.

KEARNS: What was the reason?

CLAUDIA: I never asked. But he played pool a lot. My mother and dad came down to visit. It just got to a point where I couldn't stay anymore. I left and went to Shreveport.

KEARNS: After you left him did you see him?

CLAUDIA: Yes, he came to Shreveport at my mother and dad's. He stayed there too. We more or less mended our differences.

KEARNS: Were there any complications with Danny's birth?

CLAUDIA: Yes, he was forceps and it broke the veins on the top of his head. It made each side of his head poke out. It terrified me but his pediatrician told me it would go away and it did.

KEARNS: How long?

CLAUDIA: About a year. It was there a long time. They would not go away like I thought they should.

KEARNS: After Danny's birth, where did you live?

CLAUDIA: We stayed in Shreveport. We moved to a garage apartment. Not with anybody.

KEARNS: After Danny was born, did his father ever handle him in a strange or abusive manner?

CLAUDIA: James always acted that even though he was a baby, he should have all the answers and know exactly how to act. He would be very verbally abusive to him. I don't recall that he ever really hit him until Danny was a crawler. And he never really crawled. He sat on his little backside and put his leg underneath, and James didn't like that. He thought it was crippling or something, and with my husband, everything has to be perfect. So he took his foot. Danny was in the hallway. We had moved to another apartment. It had a long hallway, and he took his foot and he kind of shoved him down the hall. He was on his little heinie, and he kinda bounced, and it scared him, and I just went and got him.

KEARNS: How soon after you had Danny did you become pregnant with your second child?

CLAUDIA: There's thirteen months difference in their ages, so that would be, what? About three months? Something like that?

KEARNS: How did he feel about your second pregnancy?

CLAUDIA: He never reacted one way or the other. It was almost as if he was resigned to it. Kevin was sort of an afterthought.

KEARNS: While Danny was still a young child, did you ever leave the Shreveport area?

CLAUDIA: Yes. To Columbus, Georgia, but this was after Kevin was born.

KEARNS: And why was it that you moved away?

CLAUDIA: Because James and I separated. I don't know if you want this long story . . . We had gone fishing and I had deep burns on my legs and I was sitting in the living room and he asked me for a cup of coffee, and he had been really demanding all that morning. I had turned the TV on and he kept turning it off. Well, anyway, to make a long story short, in my mind I thought I'll just throw this coffee on you. That'll stop you. I changed my mind before I ever got to the table. I put the coffee on the table. He shoved it aside and he hit me and busted my lip.

It should be pointed out that all of this testimony was being given in a melancholy, passive manner, even when she spoke of an attempted suicide on her part.

KEARNS: How old were the boys at this time?

CLAUDIA: Pre-school. About three and four. And as soon as he left, I went to my mother's with the boys . . . We stayed separated about five or six months that time. He kept begging. He kept saying this won't happen again. We'll buy us a home. We'll do all this good stuff. And I thought, well maybe in Columbus it will be really better. So that's why we moved there.

KEARNS: At any time did you consider getting a divorce?

CLAUDIA: Yes. At that time.

KEARNS: Did you ever follow through?

CLAUDIA: I never followed through.

KEARNS: Why?

CLAUDIA: I always thought that marriage was forever. I wasn't the kind of person . . . I still think, if there's a problem, there has to be a solution somewhere. But I just never found it . . . with him.

KEARNS: How long did you stay in Columbus?

CLAUDIA: Four years.

KEARNS: And while you were there, did you ever return to Shreveport?

CLAUDIA: Yes.

KEARNS: Why?

CLAUDIA: I was working for a division of Macy's and we were getting ready . . . I may get off track here. We were getting ready for a storewide sale. I had been working late hours. I rarely got a half a day off. I went to sign my leave slip. I was talking to the manager, a very sweet old man. James got off the elevator. He saw the manager take my hand. James dragged me to the elevator and took me home. There was a gun in the house.

KEARNS: Did he physically strike you?

CLAUDIA: He was shoving. He kept saying he wasn't going to have a red light hanging at his front door. Accusing me. Having anything to do with that old man was *ridiculous*. He shoved and pushed. He didn't hit. But I went into the house and he stayed outside, and the thought came to me, I don't want to do this anymore. I just don't want to do this anymore and I got the gun. I thought I was firing it at me, but when I heard the gunshot I passed out. I don't think my sisters ever knew about this. When I came to, of course, the bullet hadn't hit me. It hit the floor. Something I guess pointed my hand in the other way.

KEARNS: How old were the boys at this point?

CLAUDIA: Four and five. And they were outside. They did not see that.

KEARNS: Did you leave Columbus after that?

CLAUDIA: Shortly after. I went back to Shreveport.

KEARNS: And where did you stay?

CLAUDIA: I stayed with my mother and daddy like a good little girl.

KEARNS: Did anyone assist you in leaving Columbus?

CLAUDIA: Yes. My sister Nancy Johnson.

KEARNS: And how long did you stay in Shreveport that time?

CLAUDIA: I can't remember.

KEARNS: Where did the boys stay?

CLAUDIA: They stayed with me. Always. Wherever I went, they were with me.

KEARNS: Did you at any time go back?

CLAUDIA: I'm so confused, I can't remember now. I think we went back. Because when we left permanently, I had been fired from my job and James had been fired from his job about a week later. They rehired me for a couple of weeks.

KEARNS: So at some point you did go back?

CLAUDIA: Yes. But for a short period of time.

KEARNS: But then you, along with your family, went to Shreveport?

CLAUDIA: I may get confused on some of these dates but I'll be close.

KEARNS: What was it like when your husband came home for supper?

CLAUDIA: I always fed the boys first.

KEARNS: Was there a reason for that?

CLAUDIA: Yes, because he made them so nervous that they would invariably drop something. Knock something over. It would give him an excuse to get down on them.

KEARNS: How would he make them nervous?

CLAUDIA: For one thing we were all at the table. He would tell the boys don't breathe out. I knew what he meant. And I assumed they knew too. Then I looked at them and their faces were turning blue. They were holding their breath. I told them, please, you can breathe at the table. Danny didn't hold his utensils to suit him. James would take it out on him. He had Danny so nervous that he could hardly hold a fork to eat. He'd question about what went on during the day. And if they said anything at all that would give him an opening, then he would begin to tell him, "That's bad. You've done a bad thing," and just generally verbal abuse.

KEARNS: How long did these dinner arrangements go on, when they would eat first?

CLAUDIA: Until they left home.

KEARNS: How was discipline administered in the house?

CLAUDIA: By whom?

KEARNS: Both.

CLAUDIA: I disciplined the boys because it was just me and them. And he would discipline when he came home. Sometimes with a belt. He had a way of making a fist and in the top of their heads he would *(demonstrating how he would rub the knuckle of his fist into the tops of their heads)* real hard. And you could just see them try to hold themselves down.

KEARNS: Did he ever strike the boys excessively?

CLAUDIA: Yes.

KEARNS: Can you give an account of that?

CLAUDIA: I don't remember what it was about. They were in the hallway. Kevin was about fourteen years old. And he whipped him with a belt until Kevin wet his pants. And that's gotta be pretty hard for a fourteen year old boy to wet his pants with just a whipping. *(She started to cry at the memory.)* I have to stop for a minute. Is it okay if I stop for a minute?

KEARNS: Yes.

KEARNS: We were talking about discipline. How frequently was Danny whipped? How frequently would the boys, particularly Danny, receive a whipping?

CLAUDIA: If it was a verbal whipping we were talking about, every day.

KEARNS: How about physical?

CLAUDIA: Often. Probably about twice a week. To Danny and Kevin. Kevin never got a whole lot, though. Danny always carried the brunt of the whipping. There was a lot of shoving and holding by the throat and shoving against the wall. By the throat. He did that a lot with all of us. He holds us like that, so you can't move.

KEARNS: Did James ever strike you?

CLAUDIA: Yes.

KEARNS: Did he ever strike you in front of the boys?

CLAUDIA: I'm sure they saw it. Our house is very small. We still live in the same house. Four people couldn't live in the same house and never see. I'm sure. Well, I know they saw him push me down a lot.

KEARNS: How did the boys react to that?

CLAUDIA: As they got older they did try to help me. But you have to understand they were terrified of their dad. But they used to beg me to leave and stay away. Don't ever come back.

KEARNS: How did you manage to cope with all this?

CLAUDIA: I don't know. I think I did a lot of hiding. It was sort of like I was . . . don't look and it's not real and it will go away, and stop and disappear. Just like an ostrich that puts its head in the sand.

KEARNS: Did the boys ever have any birthday parties at your home? *(She shakes her head)*

KEARNS: Where did most of your family live?

CLAUDIA: Here in Shreveport. I have a brother that lives in Texas.

KEARNS: Did your family members visit you often at your home?

CLAUDIA: Well, as often as they could. There was always some member of my family that was not allowed in the house. Always.

KEARNS: Why?

CLAUDIA: I have no idea.

KEARNS: By whom?

CLAUDIA: James.

KEARNS: How about friends? Did you have close friends?

CLAUDIA: Not like couples. I have friends and he had friends on the police force, I'm pretty sure. But we did not have friends like you'd go eat or something.

KEARNS: Where was your husband employed?

CLAUDIA: Shreveport Police Department.

KEARNS: What was Christmas like in your house?

CLAUDIA: It was always just like another day. He always made some start at an argument. Find something wrong and just blow the whole day away.

KEARNS: Did Danny ever comment to you about Christmas?

CLAUDIA: Yes. He asked me why did he always spoil holidays and special occasions.

KEARNS: Was there any time during Christmas when you had another separation?

CLAUDIA: Yes.

KEARNS: When?

CLAUDIA: It's sort of funny. I don't remember what happened. We just had one of those big knock-down, drag-out fights and I packed a fully decorated Christmas tree in the back of the car. It was a small one. And I packed the boys and we left.

CLAUDIA: Danny was sick almost that whole year with his tonsils in the third grade. I wish I had those pictures to show. He was like a skeleton. He had gotten so thin. And the doctor said we can't take his tonsils out until we build him up. And he was out a lot that year. And he had a very special teacher. She would come by the house in the morning and leave his work and pick it up so he wouldn't miss out so much. But he did. And she called me in for a consultation. And she said we could pass Danny on the grades he has, but it would not be good for him because he really hadn't accomplished much that year. So she convinced me holding him back would be good. She suggested counseling because of Danny's personality and the talents he had. He had difficulty in just regular school things like math, reading. She suggested that we get counseling for him and also to channel his talents where they needed to be so that when he was full grown he could have some sort of livelihood.

KEARNS: Was there ever anything mentioned of some type of nervous condition?

CLAUDIA: Yes. She did mention that he was nervous but I always knew that.

KEARNS: How did your husband react to Danny staying back in the third grade?

CLAUDIA: Just as he suspected. This "no-account" kid of his failed again.

KEARNS: Did he ever express that?

CLAUDIA: Yes. "You failed, you'll have to do the third grade again. You'll be in the same grade as your baby brother. You didn't study. You didn't do your work. You're a failure." . . . You know, that kind of thing.

KEARNS: While Danny was in his pre-teens, did his father ever praise him?

CLAUDIA: The kind of praise James gave . . . this was ever since they were able to understand. They would do some special project and bring it to this man that they just loved to death. He'd look at it, whatever it was, and he'd say, "Well, it's okay, but . . . " and he'd list all the things. "You didn't do this . . . this . . . this. You left this out. It's messy. You should have done this." So the only praise they got was, "It's all right, but . . ."

KEARNS: Did the boys react differently to their father?

CLAUDIA: Yes. It almost seemed that Danny did everything to draw attention to himself. I was trying to go over in my mind last night and remember what they were really like as little boys, because I worked a lot —that means you missed a lot. But he would do things to draw attention to himself in front of his dad. It was almost as if, You won't hug me, so hit me. Something to recognize me in some way. And Kevin didn't.

Kevin learned early what Dad was like and so he would go wherever his daddy wasn't.

KEARNS: Did either of the boys ever exhibit any physical signs of nervousness?

CLAUDIA: Yes. Kevin always rubs his hands together. He still does it when he gets upset. He did it whenever his daddy walked in the door . . . Kevin always hid his emotions, especially from his dad.

KEARNS: Did the children ever have nightmares?

CLAUDIA: Yes.

KEARNS: How about Danny?

CLAUDIA: Yes.

KEARNS: Approximately when did they start?

CLAUDIA: I don't know. Probably three or four, something like that.

KEARNS: How long would this last?

CLAUDIA: I think he still has them. He would dream monsters when he was a little thing. Then he would dream about terrible things happening. About the world blowing up. This would happen pretty often. Once or twice a week.

KEARNS: Did you ever consider taking him to see a psychologist?

CLAUDIA: Everything I ever did in our marriage, I got permission, and when I would ask, James would say, "There's nothing wrong with him. He's just mean."

KEARNS: Who was responsible for taking care of the lawn?

CLAUDIA: They both were responsible along with their dad. And it was an all-day project. But the only thing they'd stop for was a drink of water.

KEARNS: What was their job?

CLAUDIA: All of it. But their biggest job was edging.

KEARNS: What would they use to edge?

CLAUDIA: A butcher knife.

KEARNS: Was there anything unusual that occurred?

CLAUDIA: Yes. They had worked all day in the yard. I had slipped them maybe a cookie and I would make Kool-Aid. All day. It was hard on a grown person, let alone on a kid. Well, he finally decided to shut it off and he picked up his tools and he started yelling. And I already had the boys in the house. I was gonna feed them. And he came stomping in wanting to know what they'd done with his pliers. "Nothing, Dad. We haven't had them." So he told me, what did I do with them? And I said, "Nothing, I haven't been out there. I haven't bothered with them." So we got flashlights and we went into the yard and we covered every inch looking for a pair of pliers. I was behind James and I saw something move in his back pocket. I said, "James." They had hung up on a heavy cord in his back pocket and were just hanging there.

KEARNS: What happened after that?

CLAUDIA: He was okay.

KEARNS: Did Danny ever have any after-school jobs?

CLAUDIA: Yes. It was at the Dairy Queen right up the street. He only had it about a week. Because his daddy made him quit.

KEARNS: Why?

CLAUDIA: When he asked to be taken for the job, I was real surprised that James told him, "Yes." He said, "The only way you're going to keep it is if you don't bring home a bad grade on your report card." So Danny kind of dropped his head, because he knew he already had a bad one. He went back to bed and I told James, "It's only just a few days to report card and he's already made a bad grade. You shouldn't hold that against him." And he said, "I said, if he made a bad grade." And sure enough he brought home a bad grade and James made him quit the job.

KEARNS: How did he make him quit the job?

CLAUDIA: He told him it was already done. You can't work anymore.

KEARNS: How did Danny react to that?

CLAUDIA: Very bad. He wanted the job so bad. And he just busted out of the house in the backyard. I think that's the way for me to remember exactly how it happened. He busted out the house and went into the backyard. James went behind him because you don't turn from James like that. You stay and you listen to whatever he has to say until he releases you—okay, I'm done. And they had a fight in the backyard.

KEARNS: What do you mean by a fight?

CLAUDIA: They had a fight. James hit him. Danny never raised his hand to his daddy in his whole life but I can't remember. He may have. I heard them in the backyard. You could hear the blows. It was James hitting Danny. And he had Danny against the utility house we had in the back-yard. And he drew back to hit Danny and Danny moved and his hand went through the plate glass. And I don't know if Danny just ran in the house or if his daddy made him come in, but he was covered in blood.

KEARNS: Who was?

CLAUDIA: Danny. He was literally. His clothes. Everything. It was in his hair. Everywhere. And I said, "My God." And he said, "It's okay, Mom." And I said, "Go in and clean up." James came in after that and he was bleeding from his hand. He had cut it pretty bad. And he said, "I'm gonna have to have stitches." Well, I kept waiting for Danny to come out of the bathroom, cause I heard the water running. And I waited a pretty good while. James had already gone to emergency to get stitches, so the best I can remember, I still heard the water running. I knocked on the door and I didn't get any answer. So I pushed on it and Danny wasn't there. The bathroom window was open and in lipstick on the mirror he had written: "I tried. I just can't make it." And there was a drive-in movie . . . oh, not too far from the house. You could walk it.

And he had taken a razor blade with him and he tried to take his life but he just couldn't do it.

KEARNS: Did he tell you this?

CLAUDIA: Uh-huh.

KEARNS: Did he ever tell of any other time when he tried to take his life when he was a child?

CLAUDIA: Yes. He was always trying to get rid of that person that his daddy made him believe he was. He had no self-esteem. No self-worth. I could say, "Danny, I love you," and he would look at me in surprise and say, "You love me, Mom?" And I would say, "Of course, I love you." "Why? What is there here for anybody to love?" And he still does that.

KEARNS: Was there hugging in your family?

CLAUDIA: Only when James was gone. When the boys got up a good size, he told me that women don't hug their children when they get up that big. And you don't kiss them or anything like that. That it looked bad. And he never liked for me to hug my dad. So he made me feel very guilty about it, so I waited until he left and then we hugged up a storm behind his back.

KEARNS: You mentioned that Danny brought home a bad grade. What was it like in the house when report cards came?

CLAUDIA: It was a day that we dreaded. Because if there was anything on that report card that was below a "C," they were going to get a whipping. And he would go over every grade. Every grade.

KEARNS: How did Danny do with his report card?

CLAUDIA: They would try to give it to me so I could sign it and get it back to school. We tried to hide it.

KEARNS: Did Danny have grades that were satisfactory to his father?

CLAUDIA: Hardly ever. Because Danny, after the third grade, Danny just kind of went down. He was really good before that. He made straight "S" which is what they used to put on report cards. But after being held back in the third grade, he just sort of gave up.

KEARNS: Are you implying that he would get a beating during report-card days?

CLAUDIA: Every report-card day. Danny always had a "D" or an "F" after the third grade. And he just sort of took it. Like, I'm gonna get it. So get it over with.

KEARNS: When he was in high school, how did he go about picking his schedule?

CLAUDIA: Well, they were never allowed to select their curriculum. They had to do it with him. And mostly he would just pick everything out for them. They rarely had an opportunity to say, "I want to take this one." The one thing I can remember Danny wanting and was able to get on his own, he wanted to be in the band. So he was allowed to do that.

Kevin did not want to be in the band. He wanted to play football. But James made him take band. But one year, I think it was their sophomore year, he completely loaded them up with every difficult subject that they just couldn't do it. I don't think a genius could have.

KEARNS: At any time when Danny was a teenager did his father put him out of the house?

CLAUDIA: Yes. We were going to church, and Danny had on blue jeans. I didn't really want him to wear blue jeans to church. "Go get your dress pants on." He really didn't want to, and I thought, "Well, I think the Lord can see him in blue jeans as well as a pair of dress pants." So I said, "Okay." When he got back, all of his clothes had been thrown into the carport by his dad. He was pushed out too. My mother and dad didn't live too far from us, so I told him, "Go there and I'll come pick you up." My sister was with me. Her daughter-in-law lived in an apartment complex. She was in pretty good with the manager there and she helped me get an apartment. And I moved out.

KEARNS: Is this another time that you separated?

CLAUDIA: Yes.

KEARNS: And how long were you gone then?

CLAUDIA: About two months, I think. Kevin was going into the navy and I was depending a whole lot on the boys to help me survive in this apartment. I worked and I made a pretty good salary but I knew I would have to get insurance and that kind of thing. Well, I couldn't tell Kevin you can't go in the navy. I just couldn't do that. So, knowing that he was going to be gone we couldn't manage, so I moved back.

KEARNS: You talked about being accused by your husband and the boys also being struck. Did your husband ever . . . threaten you with any weapons?

CLAUDIA: I didn't really take it as a threat. He did this in a joking manner. He'd take the gun and wave it. "I'm gonna getcha," he'd say. Or the knife. He had a knife that he could flick the blade out. And it wasn't one of the things with a little button, but he could just flick that knife with one hand. And he'd slide the knife down so that the tip end of it would show. And he said, "I could cut somebody open like that." *(She gave an upward motion.)* I really never took him serious. I probably should have. And he did that one time in front of a friend of mine and I just ignored it like I usually do. When he walked out the kitchen she was practically in shock. "I can't believe that you'd just sit there and let him do that." But it was part of our life, of what he was. *(She shrugged weakly.)* The way he was. Is.

KEARNS: Your husband, did he have handcuffs at any times?

CLAUDIA: Yes. There was an old man that lived down the road. He took up a lot of time with kids and he took up especially a lot of time with

Danny. One afternoon, the old man gave Danny a beer. He was fourteen or fifteen, something like that. He drank it. Made him feel like a big, grown man, I'm sure. Well, he came home and the minute he walked through the door you could smell the beer. And his daddy jumped him before he could get even through the living room and he shoved him and pushed him all the way to the bedroom. Between the bunk beds. They slept on bunk beds. They were shoving. He finally got a really good grip on Danny and pulled him all the way to the kitchen and threw him down on the kitchen chair and he handcuffed him to it. And he called the police. He put him in juvenile jail.

KEARNS: How long did he stay there?

CLAUDIA: About two or three weeks, I think.

KEARNS: Did you ever go see him?

CLAUDIA: James wouldn't let me.

KEARNS: Did anyone go see him?

CLAUDIA: Only James.

KEARNS: Did Danny ever tell you how he felt about that?

CLAUDIA: He felt betrayed. What he did certainly didn't require that kind of treatment. I told James, "If I was you, I would have made him go to bed and we'll talk about this tomorrow." I didn't feel he did anything that deserved being handcuffed and put in juvenile hall. After all, he had committed no crime. But Danny felt that I betrayed him too because I didn't go see him.

KEARNS: Did the boys drive while they were in high school?

CLAUDIA: They knew how but they had nothing to drive. They took drivers ed. But their daddy used to take them to the fairgrounds to teach them to drive. It was pre-school. Kevin was so small he had to fit in his daddy's lap in order to reach the steering wheel and look out. They hated it. Kevin would come home sometimes he'd be crying. They hated it. They were too young to expect them to go through . . . that time there was a driving course at the fairgrounds. You couldn't expect a child that age to maneuver a course like that.

CLAUDIA: [Danny] got a general discharge with honorable conditions. There was no way in the world he could handle military life. He simply didn't have the nervous system or the maturity.

KEARNS: He was nineteen when he got married.

CLAUDIA: Yes.

KEARNS: To whom?

CLAUDIA: O'Mather Halko. Then the choir director told him his music had no value. That upset him.

She told about the time when she and James were called by their daughter-in-law because Danny would not get up to go to work, and how when they went over to the house, James responded by jumping astride his nude sleeping son and putting a knife to his throat. She told of the incident with very little emotion, as though it were an ordinary occurrence. No mention was made of Danny's reaction—his embarrassment, his nudity in front of his mother. It was just one of those things. Interpretations were left to those who heard the tale.

KEARNS: Did Danny ever say anything bad about O'Mather? Even after the divorce?

CLAUDIA: Never. He always said she was a good mother and a good woman because he loves her still.

KEARNS: Did anyone ever suggest he see a psychiatrist?

CLAUDIA: A friend did take him to Shreveport Health Center, I think it's called. He did have one session with one of the ladies there. He never went back.

KEARNS: Was Danny upset at his divorce?

CLAUDIA: Very.

KEARNS: How did he show it?

CLAUDIA: That's kind of hard to say 'cause Danny had moods. He could get very quiet. He could get angry when things didn't seem to go exactly the way he wanted. He'd go off by himself. He slept a lot. An awful lot right after that time. I had forgotten about that. But it was like that was a mistake. He could be asleep and everything was okay.

KEARNS: After the marriage did he ever leave Shreveport?

CLAUDIA: Yes.

KEARNS: Do you remember how he came to leave?

CLAUDIA: Well, he had moved in with us. And like always he and his dad struck a sour note from day one. I think it just . . . he couldn't stay there anymore. So he left early one morning before I got up.

KEARNS: When was the last time you heard from him?

CLAUDIA: Next time, he was in jail, in Columbus, Georgia.

KEARNS: What was he charged with?

CLAUDIA: Armed robbery.

KEARNS: Did you ever go to see him?

CLAUDIA: Yes. He looked like somebody that had a short life. A little boy. I had gotten a letter from Danny and I don't know if James was gonna let me go see him or not. He made me wait, like a week before he said, "Let's go." But in that time I got a letter from Danny and it said, "Dear Mommy and Daddy, and there was two pages of "I love you." That's all. Just "I love you."

KEARNS: Did you actually physically see him at this time?

CLAUDIA: Yes. When we first went to the jail, the jailor made me talk to Danny through a little hole and you'd have to put your ear next to it and listen. So Danny's lawyer got a room, one of the interrogation rooms, I imagine, and he had them bring Danny in. Danny was wearing just shorts, no shoes. Nothing. He came into the room like a little kid. He went straight past me, which kind of shocked me, and he went straight to his dad and he begged him, "Say you love me. Tell me you love me. Please tell me you love me." I looked over. His lawyer had tears coming down. And his daddy was just looking at him. And he said, "Please tell me you love me." And he finally said, "I love you." It was like, I'll say it and that will shut you up. And I went around to Danny to put my arms around him to let him know someone did love him.

KEARNS: Did he ever tell you why he became involved in that robbery?

CLAUDIA: He thought that somebody would blow him away. It was another way of getting rid of that "no-account" Danny. I had money laying around the house at that time. He never took a penny. Neither one. Not Kevin either. You don't touch that. They never stole anything as far as I know. But for Danny, oh by the way, there was no bullets in the gun. He had his daddy's thirty-eight. There were no bullets in it. Of course, the person in the convenience store didn't know that. From what I understand he went outside and kind of walked. *(To get caught, she apparently meant.)*

KEARNS: Did he come home after he was released from prison?

CLAUDIA: Yes, he stayed with us. I talked to him quite a bit about getting help, but he always said, "Mom, there's nothing wrong with me." So I just let it go.

KEARNS: How was Danny's work history after he came back?

CLAUDIA: It was always broken up. He couldn't hold a job for very long. For one thing, he had no transportation.

KEARNS: How did he get from place to place?

CLAUDIA: He walked. There were two cars at our house, but he walked. There were times when James would let me take him, but very rarely.

KEARNS: Did he have to walk a long distance?

CLAUDIA: Yes. To go to any job interview you gotta walk and get out of the neighborhood.

KEARNS: Did he ever leave Shreveport again?

CLAUDIA: Yes. He went to Mississippi.

KEARNS: What happened?

CLAUDIA: The same thing. We got that call. Armed robbery.

KEARNS: Did you go to see him in Mississippi?

CLAUDIA: Yes.

KEARNS: How did he look?

CLAUDIA: He had gotten very thin and he didn't look good at all. But that was due to stress and everything he was going through then, because when Danny goes through a lot of stress, it's very hard for him to eat. But we visited him more than once. The second time he looked so much better. He'd put on weight. It seemed that he was doing really good in that area. He had learned to cope with whatever went on.

KEARNS: I believe he came [home] from Mississippi in 1988?

CLAUDIA: Something like that. He didn't have a whole lot of success finding work. He wrote a song, "I Need a Job." And he had been trying to get a job at Bush Distributing Company up the street from us as a forklift operator. He went almost every day. He got real discouraged. They would show a lot of interest, but they didn't call him in. He was sitting out in the front yard and wrote the song. I wish you could hear it. It's a darling song. "You know what I'm gonna do, Mom? I'm gonna go real early and I'm gonna walk up and down and sing my song." *(She smiled at the memory. It was the first time a smile touched her lips.)* And I said, "You do that, Danny, and maybe they'll hire you."

KEARNS: Did he seem depressed?

CLAUDIA: He was very depressed and he felt . . . well, he even told me, "I'm useless. I'm not worth anything. I can't even get a job."

KEARNS: How did he act around the house?

CLAUDIA: When it was just Danny and I, he was fine. When his dad was there, he didn't stay around long. The very last time he came home, he did get a job. My nephew had a car. He told him he could have the car for five hundred dollars. He worked at Poncho's and Western Sizzler. He saved and got the car. He worked long enough to buy the car and get insurance.

KEARNS: Do you know Bunny Mills?

CLAUDIA: She's a lady into country-western music. My husband knew her and he told Danny, "This lady might be able to help you with your music." That just floored Danny that his daddy would try to help him do anything at all in the world. But he was just elated. "I'd like to meet her too." So James invited her over for Sunday dinner and she came. She just took to Danny immediately. She listened to some of his music and said it was very good. She really was trying to promote it. She just became a really good family friend.

KEARNS: Do you know whether or not Bunny tried to take Danny to see a psychiatrist?

CLAUDIA: She's the one that took him. She tried real hard. She did take him to LSU, I think.

By this time Mrs. Rolling needed a short break and a drink of water. It was getting difficult again for her to breathe. She shifted uncomfortably in her chair and looked exhausted. Whether it was because of the underlying stress of the testimony or because of her illness was hard to determine. They resumed shortly afterward.

KEARNS: At any time, to your knowledge, did Danny's father ever threaten him with a weapon?

CLAUDIA: What I told you about the knife and he had used a gun.

KEARNS: How many times?

CLAUDIA: I have no idea. My neighbor told me one time, in particular, Danny ran into her house and she came across and talked James out of the gun.

KEARNS: Does your husband have a gun?

CLAUDIA: He still has a thirty-eight and he has a thirty-two. Is there such a thing as a thirty-two? I think that's what it is. And he has a shotgun. And I think he has another thing but I'm not sure.

KEARNS: When was the last time you saw Danny in your house?

CLAUDIA: The night of the shooting.

In her own words, Claudia Rolling told about the night in May of 1990 that Danny shot his father:

KEARNS: Why don't you explain that, okay?

CLAUDIA: Okay. *(She sighed.)* I told it so many times. *(She took a deep breath, paused, and began slowly.)* I came home from work. The work that I was doing was teaching the elderly and the handicapped how to do crafts and things like that. There were some items that I needed so I told James I was going up to Cloth World up the street, and I don't know if Danny was in the house at that time or not. He might have been in the back. But I went to Cloth World. I didn't realize it was as late as it was. There was a young black boy cleaning up and I was gonna look at patterns and he was cleaning that area. So I asked him what time it was, I think it was something like five or ten minutes to ten. So I left. When I got home, I put all my stuff on the table. I was checking it out or something. Danny came through the kitchen. We had a utility room attached to the kitchen and I had a bench there and Danny was so tall. He's six-four. He can't just stoop over like you or I can and tie his shoe. So he put his foot on the bench to tie his shoe. James came into the kitchen and started yelling, "I told you, don't put your foot on that bench!" And just before that, though, I said, "Hey, are you going out again," and he said, "Hey, are you gonna bitch at me too?" I said, "No, no." That was before the shooting thing. But I knew something really bad had gone on in that house. I could feel it. Danny's never told me what happened. Neither has James. But I could always tell. Danny put his foot on the bench and he said, "I got my foot on the bench, old man, what are y'gonna do about it?" And James said, "I'll show you what I'm gonna do about it." So he went to the back of the house. Danny just nonchalantly tied his shoes. He wasn't expecting anything. And he was going out the door. And James ran through the kitchen and he had a gun. And he ran out the door and I heard five shots. Was it five? *(She pondered, as though recounting the sounds in her head, wanting to get it right.)* Five shots. No, there was three outside and five inside. I just . . . I heard those three shots and I thought, He's dead.

KEARNS: Who did you think was dead?

CLAUDIA: Danny. He had no gun. So it had to be Danny. A neighbor saw this. James came back in the house and he said, "Call the police." And I said, "Why? If you've killed him, we'll call the police." About that time Danny busted in the back door. James had locked the door when he came in, and I thought it was strange. And Danny busted the door and he came in in a crouch, and as God is my witness, I did not see a gun in his hand. I'm not saying he didn't have one. But I didn't see it. He crouched down at the table and James was in front of our refrigerator. And he waved his gun around. And Danny said, "You wanna kill somebody, kill me, but don't hurt my mom." Because when James chased Danny out of the house and fired those three shots, I heard him say, and I'm sure Danny heard him too, he said something like, "I'll just get rid of you." That's probably not verbatim but that's as close as I can remember. So I believe that's why Danny came back. He thought James was gonna kill me. I heard . . . After Danny crouched and said that, James turned around and I covered my eyes. And I heard shots. And I thought okay, now he's dead. I heard another shot and I said, "I'd better get out of here." So I went through the living room, down the hall. Our bedroom door has a slide bolt and I bolted myself in the bedroom and I pulled a table away from the window and I unlocked the window . . . *(She was going to climb out)* but it was totally quiet. The only thing I could smell was the smoke. I couldn't hear a sound anywhere. And I said, "Okay, they're both dead. You might as well check it out." So I undid the door and I went down the hallway and I went in the kitchen and the way James was lying, I couldn't see him. So I thought they went outside again. Or something. I went around the table and that's when I found James. He was lying halfway in the kitchen and halfway in the utility room and he was conscious, [even though] he had a bullet in his head. He told me, "Call the police." So I did. There was blood on the telephone. It was kind of hard for me to figure it out. How'd the blood get on the phone. He's down there [on the floor]. But I figured it out later. Danny called work before he ever fell where he fell. I know that's what he did. And he told them that he was having problems at home and couldn't come to work. It had to be that because I hadn't touched anything. I didn't have any blood on me.

KEARNS: How was Danny acting approximately a month or two before this incident?

CLAUDIA: He was trying to get everything together to move out of the house. Kevin was going to buy a house and he was doing it strictly to get Danny out of our house. Because he thought like I did. Something terrible was going to happen. I knew it. I felt it. And James would say things like, "He's getting out of here one way or the other. I'd as soon shoot him as look at him." He had been saying things like that for two months. Not only I heard it, but Kevin heard it. And a few neighbors came over and heard it too. My sister heard him.

KEARNS: Let me go to another couple of areas now very quickly. Did Danny ever suffer any serious head injuries?

CLAUDIA: Yes. Just a few weeks before the shooting at our house, he was in a car wreck. A fatal car wreck. We had a tornado and he had been to this grill that I can never think of its name. And he was coming back down the avenue and the tornado was coming in the same direction, pretty much. Not on the ground, but it was stirring up a lot of debris. It had rained terrible. The rain was just above the curb. And then he . . . there was a young man that worked at LSU. He was a student. He said that Danny's car hydroplaned, whatever that means, and he saw it go up and hit the top of the telephone pole and he saw this white figure tumble out. It was Danny. So he stopped his car and went out and put Danny in his car and took him to LSU.

KEARNS: Danny got thrown from the vehicle?

CLAUDIA: He fell from the height of the telephone pole because he was thrown out the door.

KEARNS: And were there other instances?

CLAUDIA: When he was, oh, I don't know, four, five or six. He fell out the back doorstep and he hit his forehead and put a big dent in it. They were concrete steps. I wanted to take him to the doctor. I thought he had a concussion, 'cause his eyes rolled back. And James said, "No, he'll be okay." But if you look at Danny now, he has an eye that's dilated. He's got a pupil that's a little bit larger. It never went back to its regular size.

KEARNS: How did Danny treat you?

CLAUDIA: First and foremost, I'm his mother. In Danny's eyes, I'm the greatest lady that ever lived, with a capital "L." He always tried to protect me from anything that he thought was not for a lady's ears. He tried to protect me from hurt. 'Cause he knew I was always gonna be there for him. Kevin was the same way. Treating me the same way. They still do.

KEARNS: How do you describe Danny's level of maturity?

CLAUDIA: I don't think that Danny ever got past the level of fifteen. I know that right now he's allowed to call me. And his conversation is more mature, but every once in a while he'll go back to that little fifteen-year-old that I know so well, but I don't think he ever got much older than that.

KEARNS: In the course of your marriage, approximately how many times did you and your husband separate?

CLAUDIA: Oh, mercy. I used to have a joke about that. People would say how long have you been married, and I would say, off and on this many years. Fifteen, twenty. I don't remember. But a lot.

Once again she began to move about in the chair. Even though the chair was highbacked and softly cushioned, she could not sit in one position for very long without feeling distress. Yet she tried not to call for another break. She knew this interview was important for her son and she was going to see it through. Her answers, though, were coming more slowly and haltingly.

KEARNS: Mrs. Rolling, have you ever heard the term *multiple personality?*

CLAUDIA: Yes.

KEARNS: Did you ever suspect that Danny had some problem?

CLAUDIA: Yes, I did. We were at the kitchen table. Danny and Kevin and I. It was our life, just the three of us. This was the last time that Danny came home. We were talking. I can't remember what we were talking about. I can't remember what was said that might have triggered this, but I looked up and Danny looked totally different to me. His whole look was different. It was hard. And his voice took on a voice that I didn't recognize. It was coarse and deep, and Danny has a very . . . to be a man and to be as large as Danny is . . . his voice is very light. He has a light sound to his voice. It didn't last very long. I was kinda shocked and trying to figure this out. He just kind of flipped back and his face and his voice went back to like it should. And I said, "Danny?" And he said, "What? What happened?" He didn't know what happened. I think he surmised what happened and he told he that he had a person. He even had a name, but I can't remember the name.

KEARNS: Did he say where this person was?

CLAUDIA: It was part of him. I thought he was kidding me at first, but he said, "No, Mom, I do." And I wish I could remember the name, but I can't remember the name. It was a horrible name. Not something that I'd want to remember, I guess.

KEARNS: Did Danny have mood swings?

CLAUDIA: Yes.

KEARNS: How often did it happen?

CLAUDIA: I guess he had them all his life. They probably got more pronounced when he was fifteen or sixteen.

KEARNS: Is there a history of mental illness, mental disorder in the family?

CLAUDIA: Yes.

KEARNS: Can you please explain?

CLAUDIA: Do you want details? I'll have to go back only as far as I know. But the family never really wanted me to know anything about that kind of history. *(She cleared her throat.)* My husband's granddaddy killed his grandmother. He cut her throat from ear to ear. My husband as a little boy, he saw that. She was sitting at the table. She was soaking her feet in a big pan of water. And James remembers looking down at that water being all bloody. That was the first incident. But then they tried to say that he had been drugged. But I was told by a family member that he was not drugged, that he had always done strange things. He has an uncle that . . . his wife went to the store. He lay down on the couch, put a shotgun in his mouth and pulled the trigger and blew his head off. He had another uncle who died in a mental institute. He has a brother who lives in California who is the only one who functions and he's on medication. My husband's mother . . . we could be sitting here talking . . . and all of a sudden she'd get extremely mad about something and she'd start yelling and she'd do funny things. She'd walk up and down the porch and she'd tell people they can't park here or they can't go next door or do things like that, and I've always believed that she was schizophrenic because that's the disease I was told the family has. There's a daughter who's been alcoholic and I believe that that's the way she acts to get away from it. I'm sure there's more that I don't know about.

KEARNS: During the time you were married did you socialize with people or other couples?

CLAUDIA: We had no friends that we socialized with.

KEARNS: Did James ever bring home other police officers and their wives?

CLAUDIA: One other couple. We went to their house once and they came to our house once.

KEARNS: When was that?

CLAUDIA: Oh, years ago. Years and years ago. When Danny was just a baby.

KEARNS: Did you ever attend any social functions, picnics or dinners?

CLAUDIA: I never knew they had them. He kept me completely separate.

KEARNS: Mrs. Rolling, please describe the history of mental illness in the family. When did you find out about it?

CLAUDIA: We'd been married for years. They never discussed anything like that. They're very secretive people. We were married for a hundred years. And then one day he just told me how his granddaddy cut his grandmother's throat.

KEARNS: When did you learn that his uncle committed suicide and some of these other things?

CLAUDIA: I can't give you a date or anything, 'cause I can't remember.

KEARNS: Were the boys still at home? You knew all or most of those things before Danny left home?

CLAUDIA: Yes.

The Cross-Examination

NILON: The fight that you described between your husband and Danny, a lot of it sounds like shouting and pushing matches.

CLAUDIA: Lot of that.

NILON: Did he do the same thing to Kevin too?

CLAUDIA: Yes, but not as regular as often.

NILON: Some but not as much?

CLAUDIA: Right.

NILON: As a result of these fights or beatings, did Danny ever have broken bones?

CLAUDIA: Not from his dad.

NILON: Did he ever receive any stitches from blows he had from his dad?

CLAUDIA: No.

NILON: I think at one point you mentioned that your husband actually struck you.

CLAUDIA: Yes.

NILON: I wasn't quite sure. It sounded as though he hit you with an open hand. Is that correct?

CLAUDIA: *(She nodded.)* Right.

NILON: You stated to Mr. Kearns that you separated from your husband about fifteen or twenty times.

CLAUDIA: Yes.

NILON: Why did you keep coming back and staying with him?

CLAUDIA: You don't know how many times I've asked myself that same question.

NILON: Do you have an answer for that?

CLAUDIA: I'm not sure. I know that I do love James. I have no control over the way he is. And my feelings toward him have changed a great deal since the shooting in our house.

NILON: For the better or worse?

CLAUDIA: The worse.

NILON: Are you feelings more hostile?

CLAUDIA: No, I'm not hostile. I'd almost welcome that. It's more like . . . nothing.

NILON: So you've become what I would call ambivalent toward your husband?

CLAUDIA: A void. Empty.

NILON: You don't have the feelings that you once had?

CLAUDIA: No, I don't. I have a lot of pity for him. Because he's really suffering right now.

NILON: You had described, literally from almost day one in your marriage, numerous separations. Do you have any idea of why you kept coming back?

CLAUDIA: Well, like I say, I loved him. I had . . . I was raised to believe that you married one time. It's for life and you'd better make it good, and, too, I don't like to fail. Nobody does. I kept thinking, uh . . . the hope didn't die . . . it kept telling me it'll work out. Things would change. They would get better.

NILON: Did you think something was wrong with the marriage?

CLAUDIA: Yes.

NILON: Were you working to correct it?

CLAUDIA: I was trying real hard. I did everything I knew to do. We're still married. We're not separated. I'm still married to him.

NILON: Do you still live together?

CLAUDIA: I'm here and he's there (*pointing behind her*). That's probably the way it'll be. But I can't let him know that right now.

NILON: When did you think that the way your husband was treating Danny was inappropriate?

CLAUDIA: I always felt that.

NILON: Did there come a time when you thought the way your husband treated Kevin was inappropriate?

CLAUDIA: Yes.

NILON: Did you ever consider trying to get the boys out of that situation?

CLAUDIA: That was usually my reason for leaving. And I would get these . . . He's even been on his knees. Please come home. It won't happen anymore. There are all these good things and things will be better.

NILON: Were these the general comments he would make every time you left?

CLAUDIA: Each and every time. Makes you wonder, don't it? I don't know why I went back.

NILON: At some point going to that period of time, did you stop believing that he was sincere about that?

CLAUDIA: I think deep down I did . . . "Claudia, it's not going to work."

NILON: At some point in time in your marriage, did you feel that being married to him was detrimental to your children?

CLAUDIA: Sure, I guess. My main fear was that he would really go off the deep end and maybe hurt them that way.

NILON: Hurt them physically?

CLAUDIA: Yep, but he managed to hold himself in check to a degree.

NILON: But at some point it became pretty clear to you, from what you're saying, his way of raising the children was detrimental to them. When did you realize that?

CLAUDIA: Well, I can't tell you, like Saturday morning at ten o'clock because I don't know when. I only know I always felt that.

NILON: Even right in the beginning? Did you ever try to get the children away from that situation, away from him? Putting them with a relative or foster care?

CLAUDIA: No! You mean away from me? No, never. I could never have left my boys anyway.

NILON: So your solution would be to leave your husband?

CLAUDIA: Uh-huh, and protect them when I could.

NILON: Did you ever suggest to James that he get counseling?

CLAUDIA: Only once.

NILON: He didn't take it too well?

CLAUDIA: He didn't take it well at all.

Occasionally Claudia continued to have to take a sip of water, but mostly she held up under the interview. She spoke of the normal parts of their lives. How they studied about Jesus. Church every Sunday. Prayer meetings. Sunday school. Bible study.

CLAUDIA: They knew all about Jesus. Danny can quote almost the whole bible. It was just normal.

She claimed O'Mather saw the incident in which James held a knife at Danny's throat when he was lying naked in his own bed in the bedroom he shared with his wife. She was getting very tired now. Leaning her head back. Breathing with difficulty. Voice a little raspy.

NILON: You're currently separated from James. Living at your sister's house?

CLAUDIA: I'm separated but he doesn't really know it.

NILON: Is this separation because of your current physical condition?

CLAUDIA: It's mostly because I need care.

NILON: Who's taking care of you?

CLAUDIA: My sister. Also, too, I can't get well in my house. There's still bullet holes in the walls . . . *(She shuddered.)* And he goes over every step of the way of what he's going to do, how he's going to put everybody in jail. How he's going to kill the neighbor across the street. *(She took a deep breath.)* Nobody could get well with that going on all the time.

NILON: Has Kevin ever had any problems with the law?

CLAUDIA: No. If he did I didn't know about it.

NILON: Did Kevin always have a good report card?

CLAUDIA: His was better than Danny's. There were a couple of years there that he kinda . . . when he seemed like he didn't care anymore but he never made failing grades. They were afraid to come home on report-card day. He shook them so hard I was afraid. I read somewhere that if you shake a person too hard it could result in brain damage.

APPENDIX B

Testifying for the defense—Danny Rolling's friend, Lillian "Bunny" Mills
(Partial testimony)

KEARNS: State your occupation.

BUNNY: I'm a producer, a country-and-western singer. I'm an artist.

KEARNS: Do you know an individual by the name of Danny Harold Rolling?

BUNNY: Yes, I do.

KEARNS: Do you see him in the courtroom today?

BUNNY: Yes, I do. *(Points to Danny.)*

KEARNS: How did you come to know Mr. Rolling?

BUNNY: His daddy invited me over to dinner. He had given Danny one of the tapes. He heard it and Danny was there for dinner.

KEARNS: Had you known Mr. Rolling senior?

BUNNY: Yes.

KEARNS: What happened when you got over there?

BUNNY: They were very friendly. Danny came bouncing in the back door. This good-looking guy. "Oh my goodness, Ma," he said, "she's a beautiful woman. I'm so glad you came here." And then he said, "I think I'm gonna lose my heart." "That's okay, honey," I told him, "I'll take care of your heart." Very friendly.

After dinner she played her guitar and sang for them. "I love your guitar. Let me play," he said. As soon as he started playing some of his songs she said she recognized he had talent, that he wrote well and sang with a lot of heart. She was always looking for songs. She was interested in perhaps producing his music one day, publishing his songs and helping him in music as much as she could. She was also interested in him. She called him back that night. "I'd like to get together with you. About your music."

That was when they began dating.

KEARNS: How would he act when he came over to your house?

BUNNY: Danny was very nervous. All the time.

KEARNS: Can you describe this nervousness?

BUNNY: I would say it was acute anxiety.

KEARNS: How would he display this anxiety?

BUNNY: He would smother and he would want to go all the time. It was hard for him to catch his breath. He was nervous. That's the only way I know how to describe him.

KEARNS: Did he display this anxiety in any physical way?

BUNNY: Yes. He would go to the door and open it. Or he would raise the windows and say, "I have to have some air."

KEARNS: Was this frequent?

BUNNY: Many times.

KEARNS: Did you involve yourself in discussion about his life?

BUNNY: Many times.

KEARNS: Did he ever talk about his father?

BUNNY: All the time.

KEARNS: What would he say?

BUNNY: He would tell me that he could not get along with his father. And Danny was a very humble person. He would cry . . . He wished that he could but he couldn't. *(She cried at this point.)*

KEARNS: When you said that he would cry, was it when he spoke about his father?

BUNNY: Yes.

KEARNS: Was there ever a time when he was talking about his father when he was not crying?

BUNNY: Very seldom. Whenever he talked about his father, he usually would cry, yes.

KEARNS: When he was crying, could you describe what he would be doing?

BUNNY: He would tell me how his heart would hurt. It was almost like you could crawl inside of him yourself and feel the pain that he was feeling.

KEARNS: About how old was Danny at this time?

BUNNY: Thirty-five, thirty-six, thirty-seven.

KEARNS: Did he describe any incident that he particularly remembered was difficult between him and his father?

BUNNY: Yes, he did . . . He told me that one time when he was about sixteen, seventeen, he and his girlfriend at school had had a fight and he came home. He didn't know his father was going to be there. And his father threw him on the floor and put him in some kind of retention center. His father had called someone else to come and get him. More police. He handcuffed him. Danny said that was the most devastating point of his life. It seemed like the whole world just turned around. He couldn't seem to keep his feet on the ground anymore.

KEARNS: How long did he stay in the detention center?

BUNNY: About two weeks. He was devastated because his mother nor dad didn't come to see him.

KEARNS: Did Danny drive?

BUNNY: Yes.

KEARNS: Did he ever tell you how he learned how to drive?

BUNNY: His daddy . . . but he couldn't please his dad, his dad would always fuss at him. At one time he was so scared of his father that he wet his pants.

BUNNY: Danny was so disturbed . . . When he would come to my house he would sometimes get on his knees like a little child and tell me things were so bad at home that he couldn't live there. And I'd say, but, Danny, you can't break your parole, you have to live there. If you go see a psychiatrist maybe this will end some of your anxiety or whatever this thing is with you. You'll get well.

KEARNS: Did you make any attempts to get him to see a psychiatrist?

BUNNY: Yes, I did. I begged Danny to go. I don't remember who made the appointment, myself or Claudia.

KEARNS: Did you eventually get Mr. Rolling into the Shreveport Mental Institute?

BUNNY: Yes, I did. I went with him. He saw this lady. I don't know what her name was. I believe they talked for about an hour or so. Somehow or other, the appointments got messed up. Danny was supposed to call her, or she was supposed to call him, and after that Danny said, "I'm not going to this woman." "Danny, if she's not suitable for you they can find you another. You don't have to stick with the one assigned." Another time I took him to LSU Hospital. I don't like to use the word charity but I guess that's what it is. That's where people go when they don't have money.

KEARNS: How soon after the first time did you take him to the charity hospital?

BUNNY: It wasn't a long time after that.

KEARNS: What happened?

BUNNY: When you go there and sign in at eight o'clock in the morning you have to sit there and wait your turn and that's forever. And, of course, Danny was taking on these smothering spells, and he's walking the floor and pacing the floor and I was thinking, how in the world am I gonna keep him here long enough for this appointment. We went across the street to eat and he said, "There's no need for me to stay here. Because when I talk to these people and my dad finds out, he's gonna kill me." "Your dad's not gonna kill you just because you saw the doctor." I did persuade him to stay. Finally, when he got in, he said, "They said they can't do anything for me. I have to go back to the mental health place."

KEARNS: How long did you stay at the charity hospital?

BUNNY: About five, six, seven hours. It was most of the day.

The Cross-Examination

NILON: Did you not have a sexual relationship with Rolling during these times?

BUNNY: I feel that's my personal relationship.

JUDGE: Miss Mills, the jury has the right to know your relationship with the defendant.

BUNNY: Yes!

NILON: You also became close with Claudia Rolling. Do you consider her to be a friend?

BUNNY: I assume she's my friend.

NILON: During the time you were having a relationship with Danny, didn't she call you and advise you when she thought Danny needed some support?

BUNNY: Many times.

NILON: And wasn't it as a result of Claudia calling you about problems at home that there was discussion about going to counseling? And the whole family had agreed that they would go to counseling about the problem of adjustment?

BUNNY: All but Kevin.

APPENDIX C

Witness for the prosecution—Rolling's ex-wife, O'Mather Halko Rolling
Lummis
(Partial testimony)

SMITH: Where are you from?

O'MATHER: Alexandria, Louisiana.

SMITH: How long have you lived there?

O'MATHER: Two years.

SMITH: How long have you been married to Mr. Lummis?

O'MATHER: A little over twelve years.

SMITH: Was there a time in your life when you were married to someone else?

O'MATHER: Yes. To Danny Rolling.

SMITH: When were you married to Danny Rolling?

O'MATHER: September sixth, nineteen seventy-four.

SMITH: And how long were you married to him?

O'MATHER: 'Till nineteen seventy-seven.

SMITH: Did you know Danny Rolling when you starting attending the United Pentecostal Church?

O'MATHER: Not at first.

SMITH: When did you meet him?

O'MATHER: Sometime during church.

SMITH: Did you begin dating him?

O'MATHER: Yes. After we met.

SMITH: And your relationship became such that you planned to get married?

O'MATHER: Yes, sir.

SMITH: During the time that you were planning on getting married, from the time you met him until the time you got married, approximately how long had you known him?

O'MATHER: Approximately six months.

440

SMITH: And were you in school at that time?

O'MATHER: At that time I was working . . . I was living with a girlfriend.

SMITH: During the time you were seeing Mr. Rolling, did you have an opportunity to meet his family?

O'MATHER: I did.

SMITH: Did you know Kevin at the time?

O'MATHER: No . . . he was in the navy.

SMITH: Did you ever go to his home while you were dating?

O'MATHER: Yes, I did.

SMITH: Did you have the opportunity to observe James Harold Rolling with Danny Rolling?

O'MATHER: Yes, I did.

SMITH: How would you describe how they appeared to get along?

O'MATHER: They acted normal.

SMITH: Did you ever observe them have any strong disagreement or arguments?

O'MATHER: I never did.

SMITH: During the time, did Danny ever tell you of any concerns over his father?

O'MATHER: He never discussed that with me.

SMITH: Before you got married, did you ever spend any time with Mr. James Rolling alone?

O'MATHER: Yes, I did. The day we were supposed to get married. Mr. Rolling and my dad and myself, we spent most of the day together.

SMITH: How did Mr. Rolling behave towards you?

O'MATHER: Very well.

SMITH: Is there anything you can remember about that day that stands out in your mind?

O'MATHER: Yes, one thing. He asked me if this was . . . was I sure that this was what I wanted to do. And I told him that it was.

SMITH: Did you think there was anything unusual about being asked?

O'MATHER: Not at the time.

SMITH: Just to put this in perspective, how old were you on the day you got married?

O'MATHER: *(She thought a long time before she answered.)* Nineteen.

SMITH: How old was Danny Rolling?

O'MATHER: *(Again she thought a long time.)* I believe he was nineteen at that time. *(She seemed very uncertain.)*

SMITH: Did you have a wedding in Shreveport?

O'MATHER: Yes, we did . . . at UPC.

SMITH: Did the Rolling family attend the wedding?

O'MATHER: Yes. Both sides.

SMITH: After you married, did James Harold Rolling give support to your family?

O'MATHER: Yes, he did.

SMITH: Would you tell this court in what way he helped the marriage?

O'MATHER: They bought our bedroom suit [sic], a dining room table.

SMITH: After that did James continue to assist?

O'MATHER: There were several times he brought groceries.

SMITH: Did he ever buy things for Danny?

O'MATHER: I know there were several times that he bought Danny some clothes and he also helped him in getting a vehicle.

SMITH: How about jobs?

O'MATHER: Yes.

SMITH: What role did James Harold play in that?

O'MATHER: There were several times that Mr. Rolling would call up and tell Danny of several opportunities that were available and he would tell him that he needed to go and talk to this person and he would get an application. That sort of thing. Put in a good word for him.

SMITH: Did James Harold ever use his personal references or his position with the city to try to help him get a job?

O'MATHER: He certainly did.

SMITH: Do you know of one particular job?

O'MATHER: On the fire department.

SMITH: Did Danny get that job?

O'MATHER: No, sir.

SMITH: Did . . . was there any kind of regular scheduled time that you would be in the James Harold and Claudia home with Danny?

O'MATHER: There were lots of times. After church we would go there for Sunday dinner.

SMITH: Is that what you usually did?

O'MATHER: Lots of times.

SMITH: Were there other times?

O'MATHER: Sometimes in the evening time.

SMITH: Did you ever see father and son interact, talking with one another?

O'MATHER: Yes, I did.

SMITH: And how was that?

O'MATHER: Normal.

SMITH: Did you ever see them have fights?

O'MATHER: I never did.

SMITH: Did you ever see them have arguments?

O'MATHER: No, sir, I didn't.

SMITH: Did you ever see James Harold berate or speaking badly about Danny?

O'MATHER: Not in my presence.

SMITH: During these Sunday dinners that you would have at the house, how did everybody get along? Did you eat together?

O'MATHER: We got along just fine. We did eat together.

SMITH: At any time, while you were married, did Danny ever complain to you about how his father treated him when he was growing up?

O'MATHER: No, sir, he never did.

SMITH: Did he ever tell you that he had been mistreated by his father?

O'MATHER: He never said that to me.

SMITH: Did you ever see anything that would indicate that they had strained relationships?

O'MATHER: No, I didn't.

SMITH: Was there anything about . . . did Danny's father . . . you said Danny's father tried to assist him in getting jobs. Did he ever try to assist Danny in keeping jobs?

O'MATHER: Yes, he did.

SMITH: Tell the jury what he would do to try to help Danny keep a job.

O'MATHER: Well, several times he would talk to him, you know, about consistent. There were several times he did check on him.

SMITH: During these times when he was concerned about his keeping a job, did you ever hear him fuss at him or scream at him or anything like that?

O'MATHER: Not in my presence.

SMITH: Did you ever know of, or hear of an incident when James Harold put a knife at his throat?

O'MATHER: I did not see anything like that. I'm sure I would remember if I had.

SMITH: Did Danny ever tell you something like that happened?

O'MATHER: Never.

SMITH: Did you ever hear James Harold raise his voice?

O'MATHER: He never raised his voice to me.

SMITH: Did you ever see him raise his voice to his wife in your presence?

O'MATHER: No, I didn't.

SMITH: Did she ever complain to you about the way he treated her?

O'MATHER: No, she did not.

SMITH: You became pregnant.

O'MATHER: Yes, sir, I did.

SMITH: Approximately when did you get pregnant?

O'MATHER: The summer of nineteen seventy-five.

SMITH: During your pregnancy was there an incident when you changed about the way you felt about the marriage, or gave you concern about how you felt about the marriage?

O'MATHER: Yes.

SMITH: And what was that?

O'MATHER: I remember Danny coming back to the apartment late in the evening, and he mentioned something about . . . that he went to a neighbor's house . . . no, not a neighbor's house, someone he worked with . . . He knocked on the door and he claimed the wife came to the door with just a shirt on. That was something he had mentioned. And then, later on that evening, there was a knock on the door, and Danny was not there at the time, and there was two police officers at the door looking for him.

SMITH: Did they say why they were looking for him?

O'MATHER: Yes, they did.

SMITH: What did they say?

O'MATHER: They said that Danny had been seen peeping in windows.

SMITH: How did that affect you?

O'MATHER: Naturally, it upset me very much. It was embarrassing and humiliating. It didn't set very well with me. I admit it.

SMITH: Did you ever confront Danny about this?

O'MATHER: I remember talking to him about it, but to elaborate on what . . . his response is . . . I can vaguely remember, but I felt that I had to try to understand and, you know, work it out . . . you know, but I don't really remember anything else . . . too much about it.

SMITH: Speaking of understanding, was there ever any discussion about counseling in your household?

O'MATHER: Yes, sir, there was.

SMITH: Would you tell the jury how it came about if you recall?

O'MATHER: Basically, Mr. Rolling, Danny's father suggested it. And he suggested that, you know, it might be a good thing that we would do that, or all four of us.

SMITH: All four of you. Meaning who?

O'MATHER: Meaning his father, his mother, Danny and myself. And that he would offer to pay for the services.

SMITH: Who would pay?

O'MATHER: James Harold.

SMITH: Did that ever happen?

O'MATHER: No. Oh, I think that we went to wherever it was going to be, once, and there was never a follow-up on it.

SMITH: Was it your impression that James Rolling was supportive?

O'MATHER: Yes, sir.

SMITH: Okay. We spoke of the incident while you were pregnant about the peeking. Did Danny Rolling begin to become more absent from the marriage at night?

O'MATHER: Yeah, there were times late in the evening, and at night.

SMITH: Did you know what he was doing?

O'MATHER: No, I really don't. I never questioned him about that sort of thing.

SMITH: Did you have occasion to have a disagreement with your husband that resulted in a fight between you and him?

O'MATHER: Well, there was one incident, when he smacked me, when he hit me and I ended up with a black eye.

SMITH: Could you tell the jury what caused that incident?

O'MATHER: Well, I said something to him about his behavior, and his inconsistency at work, just . . . how disappointed I was and the way things were that shouldn't be that way. I just told him everything.

SMITH: Did you also find out that he was using at that time?

O'MATHER: Yes, sir, he was using marijuana.

SMITH: Did you reproach him?

O'MATHER: I couldn't accept it.

SMITH: How was your financial situation at the time?

O'MATHER: A lot of times we didn't have groceries that we needed.

SMITH: And when that would happen, who was the person who would help you?

O'MATHER: James Harold.

SMITH: If I may digress for just a moment. How did James Harold react to having a grandchild?

O'MATHER: I didn't . . . he acted normal to me. He treated me good, I mean.

SMITH: How about . . . did he come to the hospital?

O'MATHER: I don't recall that. After I had the baby Claudia came to the hospital and handed me some money and said it was from James, you know. She stated that he didn't send flowers. He didn't do that type of thing.

SMITH: Was the counseling . . . was this marriage counseling for you all?

O'MATHER: No, sir, not really. I'm really not sure about that. I'm really not. I'm not sure about that.

SMITH: During this first part of your marriage, did you ever hear anyone in his family talk about demons or being visited by demons or anything like that?

O'MATHER: I never did.

SMITH: Did you ever hear about Gemini or anything like that?

O'MATHER: No, I didn't.

SMITH: Did his mother ever tell you of any of Danny's problems at the time?

O'MATHER: No, sir, she never did.

SMITH: Did Danny ever have a problem with nightmares or anything like that?

O'MATHER: Not that I was aware of.

SMITH: You remained living with Danny Rolling until when?

O'MATHER: *(A long pause)* You want a specific date or time. The reason I left . . . or decided to leave was that he threatened my life with a shotgun.

SMITH: Now, when he threatened your life with a shotgun, did he point it at you?

O'MATHER: Yes, he did.

SMITH: Did he threaten to kill himself by pointing it at himself if you left?

KEARNS: Objection. Not relevant.

JUDGE: Overruled.

SMITH: Did he ever do anything like that?

O'MATHER: Not in my presence.

SMITH: The incident with the weapon, the shotgun, was that the last time you lived with Danny Rolling?

O'MATHER: *(Long pause)* I'm trying to remember. I left. And there was one other time when I did go back to him for the sake of our child. And he encouraged me that things were better, that he had money saved up. But it was a lie.

SMITH: And did he ever abandon you?

O'MATHER: There was a time that he left and he stayed gone for approximately seven to ten days. And I had no idea where he was.

SMITH: Did you have any money?

O'MATHER: No.

SMITH: Did you have any transportation?

O'MATHER: No.

SMITH: Did you file formal separation papers?

O'MATHER: Yes . . . I had a place of my own and I was living away from him.

SMITH: You actually filed separation papers and then the divorce came sometime later.

O'MATHER: Right.

SMITH: At any time before you filed separation papers, did you ever see another man during the course of your marriage?

O'MATHER: Well . . . yeah . . . some, I . . . my present husband.

SMITH: Did you date him?

O'MATHER: Well, not at first. We had been friends for years.

SMITH: When you say you saw him, did you date him before you left Danny?

O'MATHER: No. *(She laughed lightly.)*

SMITH: After you separated and moved away, you were not yet divorced, you did begin to see your present husband?

O'MATHER: Right. Correct.

SMITH: You had known him before?

O'MATHER: Yes.

SMITH: From the time you were married to the time you were separated, did you ever have an affair with Mr. Lummis?

O'MATHER: Nosir, I did not.

SMITH: Did Danny Rolling ever come in and find you with Mr. Lummis or anything like that?

O'MATHER: No, he didn't.

SMITH: Did you ever observe Mr. Rolling and Mr. Lummis ever in fact having an incident at all?

O'MATHER: One time.

SMITH: And when was that?

O'MATHER: Um . . .

SMITH: I don't care if you know the exact date. Was it after you'd been separated from Danny?

O'MATHER: Yes.

SMITH: Was it in your house?

O'MATHER: No, it was outside.

SMITH: What happened?

O'MATHER: Before my husband that I have now got out of his vehicle, Danny . . . uh . . . attacked him.

SMITH: Did Danny administer some sort of whipping?

O'MATHER: He hit him. That was about the extent of it, and afterward he left.

SMITH: And this was after you'd been away from Danny Rolling for about how long?

O'MATHER: Uh . . . maybe three months . . . more . . . I'm not certain.

SMITH: Now . . . after you left, did you ever receive any money to help raise the child?

O'MATHER: Yes.

SMITH: Who was the person who gave you money?

O'MATHER: I'm gonna say it was James Harold who gave me money.

SMITH: Did you continue to have a relationship with Claudia and James?

O'MATHER: There were several times that they came to visit. There was a time they came to get my daughter. But after that, that was about the extent of it.

SMITH: Mrs. Lummis, have you any bitterness towards Danny?

O'MATHER: Nosir, I do not.

SMITH: At the time you broke up, to your knowledge, Danny did not have criminal problems in terms of going to jail or anything like that?

O'MATHER: None whatsoever.

SMITH: At that point in time, before Danny was in any trouble, if I asked you to characterize the relationship between Danny and his father, from your observation, how would you characterize that relationship?

O'MATHER: Normal.

During O'Mather's testimony for the prosecution, Rolling sat next to Rick Parker, apparently upset and sniffling a good deal.

The Cross-Examination

KEARNS: I'm getting the impression that there is not a whole lot of information about the family background that was provided to you?

O'MATHER: That's right.

KEARNS: They didn't seem to talk much about the problems, did they?

O'MATHER: No, they didn't.

KEARNS: When you were dating, you said that you would, on occasion, go over to the Rollings?

O'MATHER: That's correct.

KEARNS: Once every two weeks?

O'MATHER: Um . . . when we were dating we didn't go a lot.

KEARNS: And I believe most of the time Mr. Rolling wouldn't be there.

O'MATHER: That's correct.

KEARNS: And I take it that most of the time you interacted with Mrs. Rolling?

O'MATHER: Yes.

KEARNS: Mrs. Rolling didn't sit much at the table did she [during Sunday dinners]?

O'MATHER: No.

KEARNS: There were only three seats at the table?

O'MATHER: Yes.

KEARNS: Mrs. Rolling would be standing?

O'MATHER: That's right.

KEARNS: That seemed to be her role? To serve at the table?

O'MATHER: Correct.

KEARNS: She never sat at the table?

O'MATHER: That's true.

KEARNS: And during the time you were dating, he was kind and considerate?

O'MATHER: Yes, he was.

The defense continued to attempt to establish during the cross-examination that O'Mather was unaware of anything that happened in the Rolling home prior to their marriage and that Danny never discussed the problems of his childhood with her. It was as though she was either completely protected from knowledge or very unaware of what was going on around her.

KEARNS: Do you recall an incident after your daughter was born that you went over to the Rolling home, and Danny went into the back room and just sits down and cries and cries and cries? Remember that?

O'MATHER: I seen him crying.

KEARNS: Do you remember that specific incident?

O'MATHER: I remember seeing him cry in the back room, yessir, I do, but how long or how much I could not tell you.

KEARNS: He never told you why?

O'MATHER: No. I just assumed it was because he was emotional about the child.

KEARNS: But he never told you what type of emotion?

O'MATHER: No, he never did.

KEARNS: Mr. Smith asked you on direct a question about whether you recalled the incident when Mr. [James] Rolling came over to the house because he didn't get up [to go to work in the morning].

O'MATHER: Yes.

KEARNS: And you have no memory of that at all?

O'MATHER: I remember Mr. Rolling coming over.

KEARNS: You do remember?

O'MATHER: Yes.

KEARNS: You don't remember where you were when that incident happened or what happened?

O'MATHER: I was in the apartment, but what happened between the both of them, I wasn't aware of it.

KEARNS: So you did not go into the bedroom?

O'MATHER: Nosir, I did not.

KEARNS: You stayed out, he went in, you don't know what happened.

O'MATHER: No.

KEARNS: His mother was there too, was she not?

O'MATHER: I don't recall his mother being there.

KEARNS: Could she have been there and you just don't remember?

O'MATHER: I feel I would remember very well if she was there. There may have been some things that I've blocked out about this whole situation, but I'm very aware of the things that happen. There are some things that I do remember very well.

KEARNS: But some things you don't remember very well.

O'MATHER: There are some things that I do not know that would go on.

Re the question of counseling:

O'MATHER: I know James Harold suggested it. He talked to all of us about it.

KEARNS: Do you remember in a deposition on October 16, 1993, in Louisiana, Mr. Nilon, Miss Singer was there and Jennifer Zidalis—you don't remember giving a statement?

O'MATHER: Yes, I do.

KEARNS: In the course of that statement, under oath, do you remember . . . the answer that was given: "Yeah, I was going to mention that to her, I can't remember what the reason was for. It didn't have anything to do with Danny and my relationship. I think it stemmed from a job situation and, you know, Danny's dad. I'm not even sure whose idea it was." Do you remember making that statement?

O'MATHER: Yessir, I do.

KEARNS: "It wasn't mine. It was either Mr. or Mrs. Rolling. We were all going to go into family group." Do you remember?

O'MATHER: Yes.

KEARNS: You weren't certain whose idea it was for the counseling?

O'MATHER: I just assumed it was James Harold's idea at one point because he offered to pay for the services. What the reasons were must have been discussed before I was even included on it.

KEARNS: This would be another family matter that you were unaware of?

O'MATHER: That's right.

KEARNS: In fact, I think that you didn't really think you should be a part of it, right?

O'MATHER: I just couldn't understand what the reason for it was. The reason I said that was because . . . uh . . . I just couldn't understand what the reason for it was.

KEARNS: Apparently there was some problem that no one told you.

O'MATHER: That's right.

KEARNS: Do you remember where you went?

O'MATHER: No.

KEARNS: Do you remember who you saw?

O'MATHER: No.

KEARNS: So you don't remember what it was for, where you went, or who you saw?

O'MATHER: No, I don't remember.

KEARNS: During the later parts of your marriage to Danny Rolling, you characterized him as being inconsistent.

O'MATHER: I'm having trouble understanding you. Could you stand closer to the mike?

KEARNS: Did you say he was inconsistent?

O'MATHER: I did say that, yes, I did.

KEARNS: And I don't believe when you were having these problems . . . you did not go over and talk to the Rollings about them?

O'MATHER: No, I didn't.

KEARNS: Mrs. Lummis, I'm going to show you a letter written by Mr. James Rolling to the prison facility. When Danny was in prison . . . The man that you claimed was so helpful sent a letter in which he blamed all of Danny's problems on his wife, O'Mather.

She said she had not known about the letter.

Bibliography

Books Cited or Consulted

Fox, James A. and Levin, Jack. *Mass Murder—America's Growing Menace.* New York: Plenum Press, 1985.

Guttmacher, Manfred S., M.D. *The Mind of the Murderer.* New York: Farrar, Straus and Cudahy, 1960.

Leyton, Elliott. *Compulsive Killers—The Story of Modern Multiple Murder.* New York: New York University Press, 1986.

Lunde, Donald T. *Murder and Madness.* San Francisco: San Francisco Book Co., 1976.

Lyght, Charles E., M.D., ed., *The Merck Manual. 11th Edition.* New York: Merck & Co., 1966.

Magee, Doug. *What Murder Leaves Behind—The Victim's Family.* New York: Dodd, Mead & Co., 1983.

Norris, Joel. *Serial Killers—The Growing Menace.* New York: Doubleday,

Redmond, Lula M., R.N., M.S. *Surviving—When Someone You Love Was Murdered.* Clearwater Fla.: Psychological Consultation and Education Services, Inc., 1990.

Ressler, Robert K., Burgess, Ann W., Douglas, John E. *Patterns and Motives.* New York: D.C. Heath & Co., 1988.

Wilson, Peter J. *Oscar: An Inquiry into the Nature of Sanity.* New York: Random House, 1974.

Newspapers, Magazines and Articles Cited or Consulted

Research material from the FBI:

Mallow, Michael. "The Lady Killers," *Savvy,* 3/82

Ressler, Robert K., M.S., Burgess, Ann Wolbert, D.N.Sc., Douglas, John E., M.S. "Rape and Rape-Murder: One Offender and Twelve Victims," *American Psychiatric Association,* 1/83

Porter, Bruce. "Mind Hunters—Tracking down killers with the FBI's psychological profiling team," *Psychology Today,* 4/83

Morgan, Guy D., "Mass/Multiple Murder Fact or Fiction," *The Fairfax Sentinel,* Fall 1992

Douglas, John. "Profiles in Criminal Personalities," *Insight,* 8/28/89

Kessler, Ronald. "Profiles of the Rapists," the Washington *Post National Weekly Edition,* 9/24/84

FBI Law Enforcement Bulletin 8/85—FBI Staff—"The Men Who Murdered," "The Split Reality of Murder," "Classifying Sexual Homicide Crime Scenes," "Crime Scene and Profile Characteristics of Organized and Disorganized Murderers," "Interviewing Techniques for Sexual Homicide Investigation," "Wanted by the FBI."

FBI Law Enforcement Bulletin 12/86—"An American Response to an Era of Violence," "NCAVC's Research and Development Program," "Criminal Profiling," "VICAP: A Progress Report," "The NCAVC Training Program," "VICAP Alert."

Sessions, Patrick. "Violent Criminal Apprehension Program: Essential Link to Joint Investigations."

Hazelwood, Robert, M.S. "An Introduction to the Serial Rapist—Research by the FBI," FBI Law Enforcement Bulletin, 9/87 "His Characteristics and Victims," *FBI Law Enforcement Bulletin, Part I,* 1/89

———. "The Serial Rapist—His Characteristics and Victims, Conclusion," *FBI Law Enforcement Bulletin, Part I,* 2/89

———. "Rape—The Criminal Behavior of the Serial Rapist," *FBI Law Enforcement Bulletin,* 2/90

Part I-Section 252. National Center for the analysis of violent crime (NCAVC), 3/24/87

Hazelwood, Robert R., and Douglas, John, Special Agents, Behavioral Science Unit, FBI Academy, Quantico, Va.

Ressler, Robert, Burgess, Ann, D'Agostino, Ralph, Douglas, John, "Serial Murder: A New Phenomenon of Homicide, Presented at the 10th Triennial Meeting of the International Assoc. of Forensic Sciences, Oxford, England, 9/84

Berne, M. D., "Cultural Aspects of Multiple Murder."

The Alligator, Gainesville, Florida

Abdo, Jaime. "Police focused on Humphrey," 11/19/92

Clark, Elizabeth. "Evidence shows possible suspect, victim connection," 11/29/92

———. "Rolling's writings reflect life in jail, public opinion," 1/20/94

Humphrey, George. "Is Ed Humphrey the overlooked victim of the slayings," 3/5/91

Schoffel, Ira. "Reports detail Rolling's travels," 11/19/92

The Daily Record, Morristown, New Jersey

"3 female students slain," August 28, 1990

Anderson, Kurt. "Student-slaying suspect narrowed to 4," 9/3/90

"Fla. students told killer still at large," 9/4/90

"Fla. crime scenes are 'most difficult,' " 9/6/90

"Fla. suspect's bond kept at $1 million," 9/7/90

"Police find promising evidence in Florida slayings," 9/8/90

"Gainesville police focus on 1 suspect," 1/24/91

The Gainesville Sun, Gainesville, Florida

Barnett, Cynthia. "Judge: Humphrey needs treatment"

————. "Humphrey's remarks made him a suspect," 11/19/92

————. "Humphrey's odyssey, from an Eagle Scout to a symbol of terror," 8/27/91

————. "Judge won't lower $1 million bond," 9/7/90

————. "Students just trying to cope," 8/30/90

————. "Melrose stunned by deaths," 8/31/90

————. "Humphrey acted obsessed with women, violence," 9/3/90

————. "Attorney to seek reduction in bond for Humphrey," 9/4/90

————. "Actions may taint evidence in court," 9/8/90

————. "Suspect's attorney: Release is near," 9/15/90

————. "Agents tell of bloody gloves," 9/16/90

————. "Grandmother slams investigation," 9/17/90

————. "Judge keeps lid on murder-probe document," 10/4/90

————. "Humphrey goes to trial in beating," 10/8/90

————. "Humphrey jury saw news accounts," 10/9/90

————. "Judge keeps data from jury," 10/10/90

————. "Humphrey found guilty of battery," 10/11/90

————. "Prison mental ward to house Humphrey," 11/16/90

————. "Accusations haunting Humphrey," 10/28/92

Cunningham, Ron. "Remembering a season of fear," 2/15/94

Currie, Danya. "Journalists question Alligator's methods," 12/29/93

————. "A brother's grief," 2/16/94

————. "Day filled with tears for families," 2/16/94

————. "Killer of 5 students left a gruesome message," 3/8/94

————. "Families ask for remembrance," March 25, 1994

————. "Rolling nearly killed others, inmate says," March 15, 1994

Danko, Jim. "Brother: Suspect innocent," 9/3/90

Dewey, Susan Lewis. "Victims friends since high school," 6/8/91

————. "Humphrey was 'hurt' to find he was a suspect," 8/27/91

Dillon, Karen, "Humphrey arrested in Colorado for violence," September 8, 1990

Dillon, Karen; Lewis, Susan. "Montana aunt: Humphrey's violent visit scared us," 9/9/90

Donnelly, John. "The murderer's horrifying path," The Miami Herald, 2/16/94

Dupont, Ronald, Jr. "Police leave murder sites; fear stays," 9/10/90

———. "Two UF students found brutally slain," 8/27/90

———. "Handgun rookies cause headaches," September 1, 1990

———. "Business as usual? No say managers," September 8, 1990

———. "UF, SFCC students return with reduced fears," September 4, 1990

English, Antonya. " 'Good majority' return to SFCC," September 5, 1990

———. "We hope case now solved, UF students say."

———. "Christa's smile just "glowed'," August 28, 1990

———. "Christa Hoyt's funeral Friday in Newberry," August 30, 1990

Greenberg, David. "Campuses keep security tight," September 3, 1990

———. "Long Range Effects Continue," January 21, 1993

Hellegaard, James. "Rolling's plea finally clears Humphrey," February 15, 1994

———. "Humphrey expresses relief," February 16, 1994

Hiaasen, Rob. "Writers rush to cash in on Gainesville murders," September 13, 1990

Hoover, Aaron. "Community still feels pain, but a sense of relief," February 15, 1994

———. "Community breathes easier after plea," February 16, 1994

———. "Rolling talked of hiding knife," February 10, 1993

Kirby, Paul. "Media, police collide," September 1, 1990

———. "Killings prompt students to take more precautions," August 28, 1990

———. "Complex managers defend security," August 28, 1990

Kirkland, Gary. "What price safety?" September 23, 1990

Kirkland, Gary; Kirby, Paul, "Business picks up pace after shock of murders," September 5, 1990

———. "Businesses affected by scare," August 30, 1990

Leithauser, Tom, "Donahue toughs it out, Turnout high despite vandal, critics," September 8, 1990

———. "Teen revealed violent streak, neighbors say," September 1, 1990

———. "Despite hitches, today's Donahue broadcast still on," September 1, 1990

Lewis, Susan, "Ohio suspect described as slick, angry," September 1, 1990

———. "More patrols puzzle residents, managers," September 22, 1990

———. "Public-information officers weather U.S. media storm," September 6, 1990

———. "Enduring summer's tragic end," September 8, 1990

———. "Trees, ribbons to honor slain college students," September 13, 1990

———. "Priorities not yet set for use of federal aid," September 14, 1990

———. "Families of slain students remember, grieve," September 16, 1990

———. "Firearms bought after killings worry police," September 17, 1990

———. "Street cops keep wary eye on city," September 24, 1990

———. "Women use slain sutdent's check," November 15, 1990

Lewis, Susan; Dupont, Ronald, Jr. "Searchers seek clues in slayings," September 14, 1990

Leithauser, Tom. "Repairman may have just missed killer," November 19, 1992

Lion, John R., "Serial Killers fascinate, repulse public at same time," September 23, 1990

Liston, Broward. "One suspect in the murders tells his story," October 28, 1992

Loughlin, Sean. "Campus crime bill goes to Bush," October 25, 1990

Lyons, Tom. "Third victim discovered; all 3 students mutilated," August 28, 1990

———. "Evidence exists for capture, chief says," August 30, 1990

———. "Investigators now headed to other states," September 2, 1990

———. "Combined forces equal to the task," September 2, 1990

———. "Police get Humphrey mental records," September 3, 1990

———. "Hearing on bond for Humphrey set," September 5, 1990

———. "Motel room checked for clues," September 6, 1990

———. "Expert: Serial killer left no trace of himself," September 7, 1990

———. "Two new assault charges are filed," September 7, 1990

———. "Search warrants in slayings case made public," September 13, 1990

———. "Task force works to plug leaks to media," September 14, 1990

———. "Gainesville's night patrols will continue, officials say," September 18, 1990

———. "Retention ponds yield little," September 20, 1990

———. "Task force adopts news 'blackout'," September 23, 1990

———. "Lab results fail to tie Humphrey to murders," September 26, 1990

———. "Register disputes claim," October 5, 1990

———. "Murder-suicide not linked to case," October 6, 1990

———. "Police plan search in slayings," October 12, 1990

———. "40 search woods for clues," October 17, 1990

————. "Woman has no ties to Rolling," August 27, 1991

————. "Stolen auto provides link," January 26, 1991

————. "Detectives see no connection to '90 slayings," June 8, 1991

Lyons, Tom; Stacy, Mitch. "Clues search leads to ponds," September 19, 1990

Lyons, Tom; Lewis, Susan. "Police increase patrols in southwest Gainesville," September 21, 1990

Lyons, Tom; Lewis, Susan. "SW area will get extra troopers," September 21, 1994

Lyons, Tom; Dewey, Susan Lewis. "Humphrey slated for release," June 6, 1991

Magrin, Jud. "Official questions suspect's relatives," September 14, 1990

————. "Suspect in slayings seeks gag on media," September 27, 1990

————. "Second suspect fighting subpoena," September 15, 1990

————. "Hoyt's unheard messages," November 19, 1992

Magrin, Jud; Liston, Broward. "Home search finds knife," September 9, 1990

Magrin, Jud; Lyons, Tom. "Police worry about ruined investigation," September 13, 1990

Magrin, Jud; Lyons, Tom; Stacy, Mitch. "Suspect tracked to Brevard; second suspect seen locally?" August 31, 1990

————. "Police say killer 'set up a play for us'," September 4, 1990

Magrin, Jud; Wheat, Jack. "Students leave campus in wake of brutal killings," August 30, 1990

Shedden, Mary. "Rolling to make first appearance on murder charges," June 9, 1992

————. "Families angry about Rollings trial delays," August 12, 1992

————. "Battle to open remaining files continues," October 28, 1992

————. "Files show probe's enormous scope," October 28, 1992

————. "Search for knife continues," February 12, 1993

————. "Authorities search for student-murder weapon," 2/13/93

————. "Inmate says Rolling confessed," February 19, 1993

————. "Inmate: Rolling said abuse, rage led to killings," February 19, 1993

————. "Danny Rolling to receive psychological evaluations," March 2, 1993

————. "Rolling's lawyer allowed to attend interviews," March 9, 1993

————. "Attorneys try to keep profit from Rolling," March 25, 1993

————. "Police reports reveal frantic hunt for killer," May 2, 1993

————. "Dad hopes wall stays a lasting memorial," June 7, 1993

————. "Could fiancée's 'mushy' letters give us insight into Rolling?" December 29, 1993

———. "Jurors face the deluge of case information," 2/14/94

———. "Families to attend," February 14, 1994

———. "Trial opens but testimony weeks away," February 15, 1994

———. "Few people knew beforehand that Rolling planned guilty plea," February 16, 1994

———. "Rolling awaits his fate," February 16, 1994

———. "Now, it's life or death," February 16, 1994

———. "Rolling's confession gives trial new focus," 2/20/94

———. "Justice carries heavy burden," February 22, 1994

———. "State of the art justice," February 28, 1994

———. "Rolling trial will stay here, judge decides," March 1, 1994

———. "Life or Death," March 6, 1994

———. "Aggravating factors support death penalty," March 6, 1994

———. "Mental health to play key role in defense," March 6, 1994

———. "Rolling's terror spree detailed," March 8, 1994

———. "Jurors view gruesome photos," March 9, 1994

———. "Humphrey to seek civil rights," March 9, 1994

———. "Agent: Rolling spied on Paules," March 10, 1994

———. "Murders admitted last year," March 11, 1994

———. "Finding his prison cell wrecked led Rolling to confess," March 12, 1994

———. "Dad pushed Rolling to anger, family says," March 15, 1994

———. "What's inside Rolling's head?" March 18, 1994

———. "Student murders judge faces decision of his life," March 27, 1994

———. "For victims' families, it's a trying ordeal," March 13, 1994

———. "Courtroom hardly full during sentencing phase," March 13, 1994

———. "Rolling's disorders severe," March 16, 1994

———. "Film may have created Rolling's 'Gemini'," March 17, 1994

———. "Rolling's fame has victims' families irate," March 19, 1994

———. "Rolling's ex-wife testifies for state," March 19, 1994

———. "Rolling's fate may take time to determine," March 20, 1994

———. "Rolling's fate goes to jury today," March 23, 1994

———. "News show turns spotlight on victims," March 23, 1994

———. "Jurors still out," March 24, 1994

———. "Rolling must die, jury says," March 25, 1994

———. "Mental-health experts say Rolling aware of his crimes," March 26, 1994

———. "Rolling admitted Louisiana murders," March 30, 1994

———. "Some trial money will return to state," March 31, 1994

———. "Rolling sang on tape before killing students," March 11, 1994

———. "Some call Rolling jury too close to the case," April 4, 1994

Shedden, Mary; Currie, Donya. "Task force pieces together Rolling's long, strange trip," May 30, 1994

Sidden, Andy. "Gag order is denied for slayings suspect," September 29, 1990

Silva, Tana. "UF officials welcome sense of closure to case," 2/16/94

Slobogin, Chris. "Clues emerge on what Rolling defense, prosecution won't do," 2/15/94

———. "Main question now is when execution will be," March 25, 1994

Stacy, Mitch. "Slayings overshadow fall semester's first day," August 28, 1990

———. "Slaying attract notice of media across nation," August 30, 1990

———. "Pool of suspects still growing," September 1, 1990

———. "Register: Case tears emotions," September 7, 1990

———. "Finding fair jurors will be tough, lawyer says," September 8, 1990

———. "Gainesville police to maintain night patrol," September 18, 1990

———. "Gainesville police to drain pond for clues," September 19, 1990

———. "Register: It's a massive whodunit," October 3, 1990

———. "Rolling's life has two sides," January 26, 1991

———. "Neighbor: 'I knew he was strange'," January 26, 1991

———. "Attorney requests imposing gag order," June 22, 1991

———. "The Suspect, Danny Rolling: an evil genius or just a loser," August 27, 1991

———. "Rolling's mental state? The doctors disagree," August 27, 1991

———. "Experts say Rolling only loosely fits the mold of a serial killer," August 27, 1991

———. "Gainesville suspect lived tortured life," August 27, 1991

———. "Rolling robbery trial goes to jury today," August 29, 1991

———. "Rolling convicted of Tampa robbery," August 30, 1991

———. "Grand jury to hear slayings case today," November 5, 1991

———. "Jurors hear evidence in UF slayings," November 6, 1991

———. "Rolling indicted in student killings," November 16, 1991

———. "Rolling to appear on more charges," March 14, 1992

———. "Prosecutor details Rolling's activities at robbery trial," March 18, 1992

———. "Coed's body found in shallow grave," March 27, 1992

———. "Sightings, psychic pointed to Rolling as killings suspect," November 19, 1992

———. "Writer says Rolling has not confessed," February 10, 1993

———. "Writer says she's in love with Rolling," February 10, 1993

———. "Rolling Pleads Guilty," February 15, 1994

————. "Register to provide commentary on TV," February 15, 1994

————. "The facets of Rolling: murder and regret," February 16, 1994

Stokes, Kay. "Probe takes financial toll," September 10, 1990

Stokes, Kay; English, Antonya. "Services held for Hoyt, Powell," September 1, 1990

Wheat, Jack. "Student leader asks peers to band together," August 28, 1990

————. "UF urges all to play it safer," August 28, 1990

————. "Activity dwindles," August 31, 1990

————. "Campus begins return to normal," September 5, 1990

————. "Briefly, grief replaces fear," September 6, 1990

————. "Top UF officials warn students to stay safe," September 28, 1990

————. "UF reinstitutes safety measures," June 8, 1991

————. "Chiles assures students, says don't overreact," June 8, 1991

"A chronology of the horror," 2/2/90

"Rumors fly about murders," 8/30/90

"Fla. killer methodical, experts say," 8/31/90

"Violence shatters quiet place," 8/31/90

"Report: Humphrey named Killer," 9/2/90

"The crisis team," 9/7/90

"Donahue show offered honest forum for residents," 9/13/90

"State gets funds to find murderer," 9/13/90

"Search turns up noose, satanic writings, pornography," 9/15/90

"I'm innocent, suspect writes," 9/23/90

"Facts are few but theories plentiful in slayings' wake," 9/24/90

"Police seek acquaintance," 10/1/90

"Evidence search scheduled today," 10/16/90

"Case may link to student slayings," 11/9/90

"Patrick Sessions arrives, says don't forget Tiffany," 6/8/91

"Hair, blood link Rolling in La.," 8/27/91

"The Leading Players," 2/14/94

"How Rolling will be sentenced," 2/15/94

"Rolling's plea agreement," 2/15/94

Sun Staff Report, "Feeling one of relief," 2/15/94

"How Rolling will be sentenced," 2/15/94

"Prosecution's statement about facts of the case," 2/16/94

"Shreveport hopes Rolling talks more," 2/16/94

"Mississippi cut sentence," 2/16/94

"Prosecution's statement about facts of the case," 2/16/94

Editorial page "A sense of closure," 2/16/94

The Ocala Star-Banner

Barnett, Cynthia. "Humphrey could be freed soon: Attorney," September 15, 1990

———. "Police took bloodied gloves in search," September 16, 1990

———. "Suspect is confused: Hlavaty," September 17, 1990

———. "Humphrey battery trial opens," October 8, 1990

———. "Press spotlight won't affect Humphrey's trial, jurors say," October 9, 1990

———. "Judge rules out hearsay in Humphrey case," October 10, 1990

———. "Humphrey found guilty," October 11, 1990

———. "Judge agrees prison too much for Humphrey," November 9, 1990

———. "UF slayings task force frustrated by secrecy," February 3, 1991

———. "Humphrey's trouble puzzles investigators," August 27, 1991

———. " 'John' put Humphrey into focus as a suspect," May 20, 1993

Bartels, Charles. "Rolling's attorney calls recent slayings 'interesting'," June 8, 1991

———. "More sanity tests ordered for Rolling," June 22, 1991

———. "UF slaying suspect returns to Marion," July 26, 1991

———. "Cashier traumatized by store's robbery," August 28, 1991

Crownover, Cathy. "Prosecutor says 'wimp' is slaying suspect," January 26, 1991

———. "Attorney objects to mental evaluation," March 12, 1991

———. "Attorney can attend Rolling's hearing," March 15, 1991

———. "Rolling gets new judge, prosecutor," May 7, 1991

———. "Rolling's competency debated," May 31, 1991

———. "In Rolling case, judges balance justice and finance debated," June 28, 1991

———. "Rolling to stand trial in Tampa," July 3, 1991

Dewey, Susan Lewis. "Slain students were friends from high school,"

———. "Rolling doesn't fit serial murder profile: Experts," February 11, 1991

———. "Community waits for justice in slayings," February 25, 1991

———. "Investigator removed from slayings case," May 10, 1991

———. "Evidence links Humphrey to scenes: Source," June 13, 1991

———. "Hair links Rolling to Hoyt: Expert," March 20, 1992

———. "Rolling convicted in robbery case," March 24, 1992

Dewey, Susan Lewis; Stacy, Mitch. "Shreveport police seek suspect's body fluids,"

Dillon, Karen; Lewis, Susan. "Relatives describe Humphrey as increasingly violent," September 9, 1990

Dupont, Ronald Jr. "Landlords clean up as police pull out," September 10, 1990

———. "National Guard, police begin search of Gainesville woods," September 14, 1990

English, Antonya. "Rolling case costs strain Alachua County," July 28, 1992

Firrone, Rima L. "Mace: Weapon or trouble-maker?" June 11, 1991

———. "Ex-cellmate says Rolling practiced acting crazy," June 12, 1991

———. "Tuneful Rolling gets life for heist," May 22, 1992

Getter, Lisa. "Slayings in Gainesville, Louisiana, similar."

Greenberg, David. "Rolling report too hasty, police say," February 14, 1993

Hoover, Aaron. "Report says convicted killer Lewis gave clues to murder weapon," February 10, 1993

Jones, Richard. "Fears mars first day for many on UF campus," August 29, 1990

———. "Investigators using DNA fingerprinting to crack slayings," May 6, 1991

Kauffmann, Laura. "Rolling to be sentenced in robbery," September 18, 1991

———. "Rolling appeals robbery conviction," March 19, 1992

———. "Rolling gets life sentence—again," September 28, 1993

Lewis, Susan. "Community joins to find an answer," September 8, 1990

———. "Residents remain on guard as police continue patrols," September 22, 1990

———. "Gainesville cops remain confident they'll catch killer," October 20, 1990

———. "Costs climb in search for killer," November 24, 1990

———. "Slaying investigation tops $1 million," December 5, 1990

———. "In Gainesville, seaarch is on for money," January 7, 1991

Long, Phil. "Suspect lived near victims," January 29, 1991

———. "Blood, hair samples taken from Rolling," February 13, 1991

———. "How slasher search narrowed to Rolling," June 8, 1991

———. "Rolling attempts suicide," June 12, 1992

———. "Jail talk reports discounted," September 17, 1991

Long, Phil; Donnelly, John. "Slayings case faces test," November 3, 1991

Louka, Loukia. "Ohio man no longer a suspect," September 15, 1990

———. "Lawmen praise the Guard," September 20, 1990

———. "Police eye string of San Diego stabbings," September 25, 1990

Lyons, Tom. "Gainesville slayings have students, parents on edge," August 28, 1990

———. "Two more slain near UF," August 29, 1990

————. "Blood, tissue testing goes on in slaying of 5," September 11, 1990

————. "Details of search warrants in Humphrey case leaked," September 13, 1990

————. "Probe of ponds turns up nothing," September 20, 1990

————. "Current lab results don't link Humphrey to killings," September 26, 1990

————. "Gainesville police officials confident of filing charges," November 1, 1990

————. " 'Visitors' get coed seeing red," December 15, 1990

————. "UF killings task force buoyed by DNA tests," January 24, 1991

————. "UF slayings suspect in Ocala jail," January 25, 1991

————. "Task force puts slayings suspect in lineup," March 21, 1991

————. "Evidence ready to indict Rolling," April 11, 1991

————. "Police debate need to conceal Rolling photo," April 12, 1991

————. "Jail pal says Rolling told of mutilation," April 19, 1991

————. "Worried boyfriend discovered body," April 20, 1991

————. "Two-killer theory unveiled," June 5, 1991

————. "Rolling agreed to blood sampling," June 8, 1991

————. "Carpet cleaner admits coed killings," June 9, 1991

————. "Carpet cleaner's story doesn't add up: Police," June 11, 1991

————. "Davis tells police tale of advance," June 12, 1991

————. "Tests keep Humphrey a suspect in slayings," July 5, 1991

————. "Woman retracts story about Rolling," August 28, 1991

————. "Humphrey to tell his side," September 14, 1991

Lyons, Tom; Turner, Kelly. "Full-time prosecutor to begin work on slayings case," April 19, 1991

Magrin, Jud. "Humphrey's kin subpoenaed," September 14, 1990

Magrin, Jud; Liston, Broward. "Teen's tip turns up knife," September 13, 1990

Magrin, Jud; Lyons, Tom. "Possible problems in handling of Humphrey," September 13, 1990

Martinez, James. "Rolling pleads innocent," July 25, 1991

————. "Evidence links Rolling, murders in Louisiana," August 27, 1991

————. "Rolling's defense: Mistaken identity," August 28, 1991

————. "Rolling faces trial in Tampa burglaries," September 24, 1991

————. "Rolling convicted in Tampa burglary," September 26, 1991

Schreuder, Cindy. "DNA tests powerful, but not perfect, scientists say," January 27, 1991

Sidden, Andy. "Judge denies gag order in slaying suspect case," September, 29, 1991

————. "Lakeland murder adds twist to Rolling case," March 1, 1191

————. "Attorney files for case info," March 14, 1991

Stacy, Mitch; Lyons, Tom. "Murder suspect says Mace led to killing," June 10, 1991

Stacy, Mitch; Stokes, Kay. "Familiar fears resurface with latest tragedy," June 8, 1991

Stokes, Kay. "Rolling's court case will be costly," January 7, 1992

————. "Davis wanted fresh start for family, neighbors say," June 11, 1991

Turner, Kelly. "Attorney recalls strange behavior," January 26, 1991

————. "Suspect leaves lasting impression on clerks," January 27, 1991

————. "Suspect crime pattern matches some of slayer's," January 31, 1991

————. "Slayings suspect called schizophrenic," February 1, 1991

Voyles, Karen. "Gatorwood urged more caution by its residents," August 29, 1990

Word, Ron. "Humphrey sentenced in beating," November 16, 1990

————. "Gainesville cops must hunt money in addition to killer," December 24, 1990

————. "Suspect blames multiple personality: Report," September 8, 1990

————. "Judge to decide if profits go to Rolling," May 1, 1993

————. "Judge sets Rolling trial for January," May 15, 1993

"Gag order sought in Gainesville slayings," September 27, 1990

"Bates no longer suspect: Newspaper," October 5, 1990

"Knife found during search in Gainesville, October 18, 1990

"Lawyers press Humphrey case," October 22, 1990

"Gainesville FHP team pulling out," October 25, 1990

"Two detained over forged check," November 15, 1990

"Police say killer will be caught," November 26, 1990

"Anti-rape groups accuse UF leadership," November 27, 1990

"Humphrey will worsen among hard-core killers: Family," December 3, 1990

"Humphrey's brother says media misled," December 7, 1990

"FPRA speakers to cover Gainesville crisis, media," December 18, 1990

"Parents of slaying victim sue landlord," December 22, 1990

"Gainesville police plan to step up patrol," December 29, 1990

"Sources point to arrest in Gainesville slayings," January 23, 1991

"Media conduct debated at slayings conference," February 23, 1991

"Accused serial killer enters innocent plea," March 6, 1991

"Lawyer's request refused in Gainesville slayings probe," March 20, 1991

"Prosecutor links tests to Rolling," April 20, 1991

"Student slayings case to go to grand jury," May 18, 1991

"Rolling now suspect in Louisiana killings," May 23, 1991

"Judge Sayawa to hear reports on Rolling's mind," May 29, 1991

"Humphrey's family angered by renewed allegations," June 7, 1991

"Grand jury indicts UF slayings suspect," June 27,1991

"Grand jury will hear case against Davis," June 27, 1991

"Woman: Rolling read up on murders," August 26, 1991

"Humphrey still a suspect in slayings, attorney says," November 30, 1991

"Lawyer seeks to tape Rollings ill mother," April 23, 1992

"Rolling to be charged today with murders of 5 students," June 9, 1992

"Rolling, other inmates moved to Lake Butler," July 8, 1992

"Rolling on TV, but no confession," February 16, 1993

"Family, classmates mourn students," February 16, 1993

"Writer, Rolling plan wedding," February 25, 1993

"Rolling's marriage may wait," February 27, 1993

"Rolling hearing scheduled for May 11," April 15, 1993

The Orlando Sentinel, Orlando, Florida

Dezern, Craig. "My Brother's Keeper," February 17, 1991

Kennedy, John. "Humphrey seeks return of his civil rights," March 10, 1994

Leusner, Jim. "Jurors hear grisly details of sex, death," March 8, 1994

———. "More details on Rolling rampage emerge," March 10, 1994

———. "On tape, Rolling pours out his tale of torment," March 11, 1994

———. "Rolling: 8 deaths for 8-year stint," March 12, 1994

———. "Lawyers build Rolling's defense on a childhood filled with abuse," 3/15/94

———. "Mother tells of change in Rolling," March 16, 1994

———. "Prosecutor: 'Exorcist' gave Rolling ideas to fool pyschologist," March 17, 1994

Sellers, Laurin; Leusner, Jim. "Police question Humphrey's kin," September 13, 1990

"A City United—Gainesville responds to a community crisis," October 19, 1990

St. Petersburg Times, St. Petersburg, Florida

Barstow, David; Griffin, Laura. "He's Guilty," February 16, 1994

———. "Cold, grisly details unfold in penalty phase," March 8, 1994

———. "Jurors shown pictures of horror," March 9, 1994

———. "Jurors spared the gory details," March 10, 1994

———. "Two audio tapes show Rolling's uneasy mind," March 11, 1994

———. "Rolling wanted to invoke horror," March 12, 1994

———. "Prosecution chips away at Rolling's case for mercy," March 16, 1994

———. "Lawyers diverge greatly on what drives Rolling," March 18, 1994

———. "Ex-wife weakens abuse defense," March 19, 1994

———. "Rolling tells judge: 'I'm sorry your honor,' " March 30, 1994

Barstow, David; Griffin, Laura. "He's Guilty," February 16, 1994

Caldwell, Alicia. "Humphrey wants to be forgotten," February 16, 1994

———. "Families of victims urge death penalty," February 16, 1994

Chachere, Vickie. "Humphrey wants his civil rights restored," March 10, 1994

Griffin, Laura. "Mom seeks sympathy for Rolling," March 15, 1994

Murphy, Chuck. "Probe made police more high-tech," February 16, 1994

Murphy, Chuck; Griffin, Laura; Ross, Jim. "Police reports detail crimes of the man called Psycho," 3/8/94

Ross, Jim. "For UF, plea brings some sense of closure," February 16, 1994

———. "Rolling deliberations continue," March 24, 1994

Ross, Jim; Barstow, David. "Rolling trial begins penalty phase," February 17, 1994

Word, Ron. "With Guilty plea come details of Gainesville deaths," February 20, 1994

———. "Killer's conscience is 'Swiss cheese,' " March 22, 1994

"Day 4 of Rolling jury selection," February 22, 1994

"Rolling attorney wants trial moved," February 26, 1994

"Jury is picked to decide fate of students' killer," March 3, 1994

The Tampa Tribune, Tampa, Florida

Bartlett, Ron. "Is he the one?" September 30, 1990

———. "Humphrey knows another suspect," September 30, 1990

———. "Humphrey's trial on assault charge set to begin today," October 8, 1990

Bartlett, Ron; L.A. Maxwell. "1 suspect ruled out as Gainesville killer," October 4, 1990

Bartlett, Ron; Thompson, Stephen. "Interviews with suspect may have been improper," September 11, 1990

Berger, Daniel. "Humphrey is finally in the clear," February 16, 1994

———. "Snitches," March 8, 1994

Cummins, Cathy. "Gainesville relieved to be spared pain," February 16, 1994

Fitzgerald, Barbara. "Brutalized city wants more than simple guilty plea," February 16, 1994

Fitzgerald, Barbara; Stidham, Jeff. "Guilty," February 16, 1994

Harger, Cindy. "University awaits Rolling sentence," Thursday, February 17, 1994

——. "Shreveport tries to distance itself from killer's fame," March 16, 1994

——. "Triple slaying case not closed in Louisiana," March 16, 1994

Loft, Kurt. "Genetic test fingers suspects," February 16, 1994

Porter, Lynn. "Woods near Gainesville to be combed by police," October 13, 1990

Thompson, Stephen. "Lawyer questions meeting," September 19, 1990

——. "Search parties scour Brevard areas looking for UF slaying clues," September 21, 1990

——. "Searchers scour woods for clues in slayings," September 21, 1990

——. "Police mum on report tests don't link any suspects to slayings of 5 students," 9/27/90

——. "Families treasure memories," September 28, 1990

——. "Brother defends Humphrey," October 2, 1990

——. "Jury picked in Humphrey trial despite widespread publicity," October 9, 1990

——. "Doctor testifies grandmother was injured during a beating," October 10, 1990

——. "Jury convicts slaying suspect in beating of his grandmother," October 11, 1990

——. "Large knife found in woods by Gainesville search party," October 18, 1990

——. "Humphrey could face charge of showing knife," October 23, 1990

Thompson, Stephen; Henry, Tom. "Girl saw big change in suspect," September 17, 1990

Willon, Phil. "Rolling jury selection moving quickly," February 17, 1994

——. "Jurors shaken by victim's photos," March 9, 1994

——. "Jury hears Rolling's confession," March 11, 1994

——. "Father blamed for Rolling's behavior," March 15, 1994

——. "State blasts Rolling's demonic defense," March 17, 1994

Willon, Phil; Harger, Cindy. "Guilty," February 16, 1994

"Relatives say Humphrey ill but innocent," September 10, 1990

"Investigators still seeking slaying clues in Gainesville ponds," September 20, 1990

"Tests fail to link man to slayings," September 26, 1990

"Troopers to end their patrol of college town haunted by killer," October 25, 1990

"Now justice awaits Danny Rolling," February 16, 1994

"Shreveport police lack evidence," February 16, 1994

"Now justice awaits Danny Rolling," February 16, 1994

"Rolling lawyers seek to move case," February 26, 1994

OTHERS

"Humphrey out, Rolling in for life," the Florida *Times Union,* September 19, 1990

Donnelly, John. "The murderer's horrifying path," the Miami *Herald,* February 16, 1994

"Suspect Offers Guilty Plea in Florida Student Killings," the New York *Times,* February 16, 1994

Rohter, Larry. "Suspect Offers Guilty Plea in Florida Student Killings," the New York *Times,* 2/16/94

Smothers, Ronald. "Left Behind in Murder Inquiry but Still Behind Bars," the New York *Times,* February 3, 1991

"Guilty Plea in Florida Murders," *Newsday,* February 16, 1994

"Life or Death Decision," *Newsday,* New York, February 17, 1994

"Jury Urges Chair for Killer," *Newsday,* March 25, 1994

Gross, Ken; Grant, Meg. "A Killer On The Campus," People, September 17, 1990

Parker, Pat. "I Don't Want To Be Here," *Police,* December 1990

"Drifter pleads guilty to 1990 murders of 5 college students in Gainesville," the *Star-Ledger,* 2/16/94

Investigative Reports Cited or Consulted

The following is just a portion of the 7,000+ Investigative Reports that were based upon leads and interviews conducted by special agents and detectives of the Multi-Agency Task Force:

Lead #5558
SA Randy Barnes, SA Singer, Richard Raymond Smith

Lead #5390
SA Dennis L. Fischer James Aubert Smith, Jr.

Lead #104009
SA Gary Akins, SAS Dennis Norred, UFP Inv Don Rogers, Carol Ann Sherrill, Lavelle Farmer McReynolds

Lead #103370
Danny Rolling, Harold L.

Humphrey, Karen Greenberg, Sondra Dennis

Lead #633
SA Gary Akins, ASAS Dennis Norred, Honolulu PD Det. Vernon Santos Lisa Au

Lead # 6009
Gary Johnson

Lead #2611
Ed Humphrey, Danny Rolling, Larry Knight

Lead #143
SA Akins Det. King, Det. Mark Corso, Warren (Eddie) Baker

Lead # 4275
SA Rick Singer, Marvin Steele

Lead #96
SA Gary Akins, ASAS Dennis Norred, Judy Clark

Lead 103705
SA Wayne Porter, Rolling photo, Mary Jess, Humphrey

Lead #202566
SA Wayne Porter
Humphrey, Rolling photo,
Eric Martin, Karen Mofet

Lead #2070
John Phelan

Lead #3158
SA Wayne Porter, Rolling
photo, Kathy Phillips,
Diana Scoville

Lead #2995
SA F. Troy, Thomas
Virgil Feist, Kirsten Feist

Lead #105714
Charles Rolling, Betty
Rolling, Larry Rolling

Lead #103494
SA W. Porter, Pamela
Biddlecomb, Ed
Humphrey, Rolling
photo-pak

Lead #6026
SA Thomas A. Yowell
Craig Harrell, Manuel
Taboada, Michael
Dockray

Lead #102431
SA Wyne Porter
Humphrey, Rolling photo,
Lisa Brockman, Jill
Sipowski

Lead #2177
Edward Humphrey,
Danny Rolling, John
Garrigues, Steven
Langston

Lead #1284
SA K Williams, CIA Jack
Dennard, CIA Elaine
Clevenger, Chris Boulis,
Henry R. Hewitt, Mike
Webb

Lead #5991
Det. Steven Dean, Danny
Rolling photo, Toren
Anderson, Eric Jones,
Sean Stanton, Tony
Schwartz, Scott Schopke,
Darryl Askeland, Connie
Kruis, Paula Tucker,
Windy Rosche, Jennifer
Ankrim, Kenneth Deane,
Nancy Webber, Austin
Frenkel, Kevin Cloud,
Larry Jordan, Donna
Aguereo, Charles
Wooten, Betty Crawford,
Nester Aguereo, Donna
Ronan, Laura Joan
Varcia, Haim Cy Rizam,
Edwina Kessler, Sheri
Boschouwitz, Mark
Arnold, Andrew Ziffer,
Daniel Pohyba, Steve
Barnhouse, Ron Dupont,
Eric Bauer

Lead #5871
SA Rick Singer
Humphrey/Bates photo,
Mike Burnett, John
Huffman, John Erikson,
Sarah Elliston, Kim
Morgan, Kevin Bushee

Lead #1046
Det. L. W. Hewitt, J. W.
McIntire

Lead #5663
Theodore Anthony
Dozios

Lead #2353
SA Randall L. Barnes, SA
Rick Singer, Kimberly
Ann McGeehan, Shelley
N. Rigaud, Frederick
Jordan Woods III,
Edward Lewis Humphrey,
Danny Rolling

Lead #1284
Chris Boulis, Henry

Robert Lewitt, Mike
Webb, John N. Brown

Lead #4390
Keith Bailey

Lead #2812
Det. Steven Dean, Det.
Alan Coleman, Sean
Joseph Prindeville, James
Harvey Applewhite, Julie
Bell

Lead #5301, 5302, 5303
& 5304
Danny H. Rolling, Karen
Beebe, Ailda I. Cosme,
Elizabeth L. Oare, Stacey
Ackerman, Trooper Futch

Lead #1736
Kevin McClure

Lead #6023
Manny Taboada, Linda
Thomas

Lead #1366
SA Don Maines, Sheila
Markley, Holly O'Donnell

Lead #5771
SA Kenneth Williams,
Det. Mary Levick
Tomothy Gatchell, Amy
Blount

Lead # 5972
Danny Harold Rolling

Lead #4536
SA V. Cassidy, Jessica
Neville, Robert Karp

Lead #1553
Det. L. W. Hewitt,
Edward King Loeffler

Lead #3824
Det. Steven Dean, Danny
Rolling, Ed Humphrey,
Jay John

Lead #1590
Christa Hoyt, Dianna Londrie, Max Schachter

Lead #2431
SA Cynthia J. Barnard Loren Brown, Edward Humphrey, Richard Bruno Scalise, Beth Michele Crisafulli, Krista Isabel Honeyman, Kati (LNU), Roger Warren Drost, Michelle Drost, Justin Martin Bowlus, Alex Alfonse, Brian Christopher Tribe, Lynn Renee Singleton, Ilene Stacey Cummings Johnson, Keith Emerson Saunders, Jean Cummings, Kevin (LNU), Tracy Paules, Paul (LNU)

Lead #2427
SA Randall L. Barnes Steven Richard Downey, Edward Humphrey, Charles Price, Rachel Olivier, Manny Taboada, Tracy Paules, Danny Rolling

Lead #2427
SA Randy Barnes, SA Rick Singer, Mark Douglas Tillman, Rachel Olivier, Manny Taboada, Tracy Paules, Ed Humphrey, Plinty (LNU)

Lead #5919
Det. Steven Dean, Det. John Westphalen, John English

Lead #4775
Mr. Patel

Lead #4780
Nolan Ard Feintuch

Lead #4972
SA V. Cassidy, FLPD

Lead #?
SAS James Myers, Wanda Klopf, Dr. R. Van Mitchell

Lead #5982
Ann Garren, Christa Hoyt

Lead #6042
Det. Steven Dean, Lt. S. J. Darnell

Lead #5250
Willie Wright, Joel Dick, Aaron Summers, Jason Dietrale, Justin (LNU), Joel (LNU)

Lead #?
Peter Rangel, Laura Danison Rangel, Carl Danison, Cindy Arnold, Elise Bril, Kathleen Rangel, Linda S. Guardo

Lead #5648
Robert E. Peeples, Connie Amidei

Lead #5908
Lake Worth PD, West Palm Beach PD, Palm Beach PD, Palm Beach Sheriffs Office, Robert Burack, Eugenio Gonzalez, Richard Wallings. Alan Pilcher, James Janota, SAS L. Newman

Lead #2877
Det. L. W. Hewitt, Christa Hoyt, Kirsten A. Hoffman, Janet D. Mowery, Robert F. Brinson, Idania M. Alvarez, Rachel M. Trollinger, Margaret H. Toombs

Lead #104688
Det. L. W. Hewitt

Barbara Thomson, Martha Gaines, Humphrey

Lead #102994
Inv. Don Rogers, Matt Adams

Lead #3191
SA Jeff Fortier, FDLE Danny Rolling, Edward Humphrey, Trinity Wood, Kevin Mitchell

Lead #5894
Danny Rolling, Ronny S. Cooper

Lead #103377
Inv. Don Rogers, UFPD Brook Clarkson, Danny Rolling

Lead #5827
SA Linda S. Dees, Manuel Taboada, Henry Bollo

Lead #4215
SA Don Maines, Richard Taylor, Larry Lowman

Lead #3821
SA Linda S. Dees, Sonja Larson, Ada Larson

Lead #202723
Caroline Ashley Maher, Alycia Jimison

Lead #5714
SA F. Troy, Sgt. Jim Eckert, ACSO, SA Tom Turk Rolling, Michael J. Kennedy, Jane A. Kelly

Lead #2723
SA Randall L. Barnes Nancy Dietrich, Danny Rolling

Lead #103771, 102711
Inv. Don Rogers, UPD

Johnnie Allen Carter, Jr.,
Shirley Moore, Johnnie
A. Carter, Sr.

Lead #2427
SA Randall L. Barnes, SA
Rick Singer, Thomas
Lubbe, Rachel Olivier,
Manny Taboada, Tracy
Paules, Kenny Vogel,
Mike Todd, Charles Price,
Mark Tillman, Chad
Shoemaker, Ronald
Browning, Humphrey,
Christy Chancy, Steve
Downey

Lead #1542
Det. L. W. Hewitt,
Patrick A. Bosfield, Jr.,
Margaret Holt

Lead #914
Det. L. W. Hewitt, SA
Dennis Fischer, Michael
Harper, Daniel Shafer

Lead #153
SA Gary Akins, ASAS
Dennis Norred, Stephen
Sherman

Lead #3802
SA Linda S. Dees, Flo
Young, Hamed
Rodriguez, Manuel
Taboada

Lead #4891, 838
SA Ken Williams, Sgt. S.
Hamel, ACSO, Michael
Cheshire

Lead #1320
Dt. L. W. Hewitt, Scott
Strickland, Katie Pratt,
Barbara Woodsmall,
Debbie Flynn, Jackie
Kerr

Lead #1420
SA Don H. Maines
Kenneth Pinsonneault,

Bert Williams of the
Florida Highway Patrol,
Scot Rosenboom, Judy
Tenzza

Lead #5016
SA Linda S. Dees, Det.
LeGran Hewitt, Christa
Hoyt, Bridgette Toombs

Lead #4562
William L. Forrest, Jr.

Lead #5894
Danny Rolling, Ronny S.
Cooper, Herbert Ellis

Lead #5994
Inv. Chris Johnson, Sgt.
William Bryan, Jack
Dennard, Danny Rolling,
Southern Bell Telephone
Company

Lead #3449
SA Lawrence Bieltz,
Officer James W. Allen,
Groveland Fla. PD,
Rolling/Humphrey, Tina
Dempsey

Lead #202993
SA Lawrence Bieltz, SAS
McMillion, Edward
Humphrey, Mr. Howard
Leonard

Lead #5747
SA Jeff Fortier, FDLE,
Lt. Sadie Darnell, GPD
Ron Wickham, Herbert
Thomas Cooper

Lead #5692
SA Rick Singer, Michael
Anton Wilson, John
Mainieri

Lead #124
SA Gary Akins, ASAS
Dennis Norred, Det. Don
Rogers, UPD, Cecil

Atkins Sams, Mary Ellen
Johnston, David Nelson

Lead #5775
SA Rick Singer, Det. Ed
Steadman, NYPD, John
Edward Brydon, Edward
Gary Brydon, Edna
Brydon, Dr. Verzi

Lead #5992
SA Jeff Fortier FDLE/
Orlando, Sgt. Dan
Snyder, Romulus, MIPD,
Karen Olivia

Lead #5667
SA Don Maines, Linda
McIntyre, Matthew Willis
Perryman

Lead #5943
SA Tom Yowell, CIA Jack
Dennard II, Homer
Rolling

Lead #2485
Laura Vogel

Lead #103691
Inv. Don Rogers, UPD,
SA Gary Akins, FDLE,
Wendy Anne Gabrielson,
Michele Cabic, Jennifer
Wilson

Lead #6037
SA Rick Singer, Chief
Jim Cooper, Deputy of
Gilchrist County Sheriff's
Dept., SA Randy Barnes,
Lt. Clayton, Sgt. Jim
Kitchen, Galveston, TX
PD, Sgt. Jim Thompson,
Inv. Felix Manas,
Kenneth Patrick Platt,
Richard Dexter Cannon,
Thomas Michael Gump

Lead #103158
SA Lawrence Bieltz,
Tonya Cook, Jeff Noss,

Tammy Johnson of the Human Resources Dept.

Lead #6063
SA Don H. Maines, Agent Davenport, Vivian Rawles

Lead #5894
Ronny Scott Cooper, Danny H. Rolling

Lead #6035
SA Rick Singer, Tony Bulatewicz, Chris Bulatewicz, Brett Williams, Tony Bulatewicz, Jr., Doug Preston, Stephen Cline

Lead #102834
Inv. Don Rogers, UPD, Doug Guy

Lead #102957, 103298
Inv. Don Rogers, UPD, Dr. Rochelle K. Ayala, Sharon Young, RN, Shirley Hill, RN, Carol Ann Houser, RN

Lead #6068
SA Don H. Maines, Danny Rolling, Corey Minard, Vicky Minard, Jesse R. Morton, Jr.

Lead #3847
Det. L. W. Hewitt, Deborah A. Carroll

Lead #6035
SA Rick Singer, Forouzandeh Forghani, Pamela Ventimiglia

Lead #6076
LuAnn, Pete, Michele, Christa Hoyt's answering machine, SA Lee Strope

Lead #62
ASAS Dennis Norred, SA

Gary Akins, Lane Thomas Kelley

Lead #3816
SA Linda S. Dees

Lead #2485
SA Randall L. Barnes, Laura Vogel

Lead #5918
SA Rick Singer, Sgt. R. S. McCleod, Jacksonville SO, James Floyd Benham, Linda Benham, Francesca Benham

Lead #6018
SA Linda S. Dees, State Attorney, Inv. Chris Johnson, Manny Taboada bank records

Lead #3055
SA Randall Barnes, Caroline Taylor, Christine Zoellner

Lead #2344
Inv. Don Rogers, Lecy Blaisdell, Mancel Eugene Jacobs

Lead #5837
SA Dennis Fischer, Michele Reducha

Lead #5894
SA Dennis Fischer, Det. LeGran Hewitt, Ronny Scott Cooper

Lead #5770
SA Jeff Fortier, FDLE, Sgt. Gerard, GPD, Det. Fred Scott, Charlotte County SO, Sharon Marie Gill

Lead #6076
SA Linda Dees, ASO Det. LeGran Hewitt, Det. Greg Weeks, Telephone

& address directory of Christa Hoyt: Kristina Arendall, Brad Glass, Marja Dela Rosa, Julie Culissa, Manny (LNU), B.K. (illegible), Kristy Breezina, Matt Bomberger, T.J. Bolton, Shane Barger, Laura Brown, Jeff Banish, Ronny Brame, John Day, Susan Cunningham, Sherri Drain, Teri Choate, Jason Davis, Hilary Croly, Ricky Cox, Jennifer Dawson, Mark Dincan, Margie Eno, Erin Herbert, Susan Gascon, Jewell Hoyt, Kevin Hegwood, Karen Harris, Sarah Hole, R.G. Hoyt (Daddy, Gary), Issac Green, Erin Gallaway, Rachel Garze, Amy Hanley, Chris Huber, Sarah Hoyt, Katie Humphrey, Nina Giesing, Alan Harris, Sarah Hole, Joyce Hesters, Zan Hutson, Nelly Grandez, Kat Jensen, Joan Livingston, Marta Konik, KISS 105, Andy Levy, Jennifer Lucas, Terry Lee, Robert Lyden, Michelle Novack, Sandy Montoto, David McDowell, Tim Miller, Lodn. NGuyen, Mylinh NGuyen, Jon T. Martin, Michele Pothier, Heather Pinner, David Pactor, Rebecca Orf, Shellie Parker, Jorge Palaw, Wayne Runnels, Jenny Russin, Stephen Ryder, Avivit Shek, Cheri Schimel

Lead #2654
SA Frank Troy, Det. Mike Chambers, AZ PD, Greg Ballar, Phoenix PD, Sgt. Jim Eckert, ASO Sarah

Louise Clark, Lon Gustav Eckert, Dean Thomas DeMartino, John Joseph Panleuer

Lead #5926
SA Wayne Porter, Steve Platt, Lab Coordinator, Carolyn Crisp, Clearwater PD, Attorney Joe Donahey, Janet Staschak

Lead #3734
SA Patricia Rodgers, Teresa Harrell, Bob Coleman, News Director, Channel 20, President of Univ. Mr. Lombarty

Lead #2594
SA Edward Dix, SA Woermer, Ralph Eugene Maples, Willie Woody, Nikki Holly, Janika Hayes, Mary Anthony

Lead #5837
SA Randy Barnes, SA Rick Singer, Eddie Clark, Lindsey Fritzel, Lanya Griggs, Tod Malone, Pat Knowles, Laura Griffen

Lead #2688
Inv. W. Benck, Dale Rey Watson

Lead #5881
Det. L. W. Hewitt, Kathleen Cantee

Lead #5928
SA Wayne Porter, SA Lee Strope, FDLE, Det. John Monroe, Jacksonville SO, Eric Witzig

Lead #5924
SA Randall L. Barnes, Lt. Chris Hord, Putnam County SO, Jesse David Baker

Lead #1753
Det. D. J. Brinsko, Gina Scaccia

Lead #2797
SA Robert A. O'Connor, Deputy B. L. Robinson, GPD Inv. Halvosa, Jackie Transue, Mike Von Konrad, Brent Baber

Lead #5905
SA Wayne Porter, Donald Lloyd Spivey

Lead #111
SA Patricia Rodgers, Ronald Raymond

Lead #3805
SA Tom Yowell, William Richard Clipson, Mr. Shawn Kelly

Lead #5865
SA Randall L. Barnes, Sgt. James Mayo, Mobile AL PD

Lead #687
SA Patricia Rodgers, Officer Deramo, NYPD, George Elliott Jarmar

Lead #?
SA Joel Norred FDLE, Inv. Don Rodgers, UPD Alexander L. Graber

Lead #5440
SA Rick Singer, Jenny Lyhne-Nelson

Lead #5809
Inv. Don Rogers, UPD, Lt. Sadie Darnell, Pete Zeller, Inv. for Medical Exam. office

Lead #5103
Det. L. W. Hewitt, Ft. Walton PD

Lead #256
SA Wayne Poret, SA Larry Ruby, Christopher Hays

Lead #0429 & 0274
SA Wayne Porter, SA Patricia Rodgers, Cpl. Gary Manning, Sr., GPD, Nancy Eckerd, Technician Ani Zobel, Steve Platt of FDLE, Jacksonville, Bureau Chief, David Howard Lamb, Pam Rogers, Pat Wilson, Martha, Helen, Sally Ann Martin, Karen, Mr. & Mrs. Walter Melvin McCormick

Lead #5566
Inv. Steven Dean, Eric Grig, Charles Fain King

Lead #5426
SA Rick Singer, SA Randy Barnes, Carey Seaton Nelms, Ron Wheadon, Chris Briary, Rob Alerts

Lead #5837
SA Randall L. Barnes, SA Rick Singer, Jimmy Andrews, Damig Jiang, Nguu Ha, Ly Trann

Lead #5837
SA Rick Singer, SA Tom Yowell, Larry Akins, Wendy Rosche, Antonia Tartaglione, Jennifer Springer, Timothy Harris, Paul Saladin, Phillipe Broccard, James Carmichael, Earnest Carasco, Sandra Duyck, Deborah Hughes, Chris Graham, Susan Healey, Leroux, Denise Seel, Stephen Longyear, Keirney Ciotti, Timothy Loog, Gerri Atalig,

Sharon Lott, Tabatha Colella, James Lynch, Joseph Kasper, Kim Mandel, Marc Perryman, Serena Newvine, Laura Song, Steve Prince, Sherri Talkington, Amy Skandera, Marlene Cosma, Jennifer Weaver, Vicki Escobio, Amanda Buren, Dorian Greene, Kevin Myers, Adam Deal, John Conrad, Rebecca Kurdupski, Tina

Lead #5220
SA Rick Singer, Mark Allen Unruh

Lead #3149
SA F. Troy, Keith G. Smith

Lead #4796
Det. L. W. Hewitt, Adam Zimmerman

Lead #679
SA Patricia Rodgers, Pam Duvall

Lead #5563
SA Rick Singer, Joel Lance Tanner, Joseph O'Nolan

Lead #5925
Inv. Don Rogers, Julie Branch

Lead #5570
SA Rick Singer, David Anthony Klaes, Linda Klaes

Lead #3151
SA F. Troy, Gary Lynn Pickerell

Lead #5486
Det. L. W. Hewitt, SA Cassidy, Shiel Bruce, Eric L. Ballon

Lead #5958
SA Wayne Porter, Stephen Bates, Linda Coban, Teresa Welch, Trish Blanten, Tommy Smith, Linda Lillard

Lead #5564
SA Rick Singer, Joseph Dennis O'Nolan, Joel Tanner

Lead #4055
SA L. W. Hewitt, Buster Lipham, Bill Pinner

Lead #5837
SA Jeff Fortier, FDLE, Flannan McGrath, Andrea Mack, Ed Latour, Christine Goukler, Carolyn Hendricks, Chuck Gragosian, Archie Wilkinson, Cindy Robinson, Charlotte Wigglesworth, Karen Connor, Mark Marino, Pat Pagano, Melissa Pfau, Scott McCarthy, Robert Cox, Harry King

Lead #5871
SAs Barnes, Singer, Wilma Clibrey, Jana Alsip, Leo Davis, Ollie Gregory

Lead #3773
SA Miles Cooper, Bryan Oulton, Scott Henratty, Miguel Ocasio

Lead #1015
Det. LeGran Hewitt, Det. Greg Weeks, Telephone & address book of Christina Hoyt in possession

Lead #3814
SA Robert S. Kinsey, Toni Stevens

Lead #4424
SA Robert Kinsey, Kip Stephen Malcolm, Ada Helen Malcolm

Lead #4461
SA John P. King, Pat Sherfield, Marjorie Weiner, Censari Abare

Lead #2418
Det. L. W. Hewitt, Sidney McGrath, Mark Goddard

Lead #5871
SA Rick Singer, SA Randy Barnes, Bai Chen, Joseph Guenther, Duc Diep, Brandon Selle, Li Shiang Chen

Lead #5871
SAs Singer, Linda Dees, SA Mike Mann, Bill Johns, Rolando Molina, Melanie Joseph, Ronald Riggins, Jean Jordan Paradise, Douglas Neira, Andre Burgess, Adrienne Bonelli, Guido Franco, Kelly Henn, Chrissy Franco, Sean Lambert, Kirsten Neely, Chris Herndon, Patty Stoner, Lori Willett, Jeff Carey, Lyse Sweet, Toni Lamerson, Steve Ryan, Elizabeth

Lead #0708
SA Robert S. Kinsey, Paul Daniel Schwartz, Richard & Alice Schwartz, Russell Schwartz, Michele Pothier, Richard Pollard, Mark Pothier, Bridgette, Todd (LNU)

Lead #4727
SA Cynthia Barnard, Theresa Ann Garren, Ralph Hoyt, Diana Hoyt,

Bridgette Toombs, Scott Knowles, Chris Keefer, Rick Miller, Geoff Mossberg, Chris Hayes, Terry Lee, Chris Keefer, Kim Whaley, Michaela Lemen, Nicole Hollingsworth, Jennifer Mulhearn, Shawn Gardner, Jennie Fox

Lead #3962
SA Randall L. Barnes, Wayne Larson

Lead #5871
SA Rick Singer, SA Randy Barnes, Yu Kong Ting, Haz-Chywon Shyu, Steve Tung, Yu-Koung Ting, Chin-Jung Kao, Ae Martin Soon, Sue Brown, Chung-Fu Tsai

Lead #0115
SA Patricia Rodgers, MaryAnn Holzschuhern

Lead #3338
SA Wayne Porter, SA Bob O'Connor, SA Linda Dees, Lynda Agnew

Lead #4397
SA L. W. Hewitt, Sgt. A. Baxter, Deputy, K. O'Hara, Christa Hoyt's residence

Lead #4933
SA F. Troy, Harvey Pleimar

Lead #4727
SA Cynthia Barnard, Cpl. James Ward, Theresa Ann Garren

Lead #002408
SA Tommy Ray, Pat Siracusa, Ilene Sharp, Scott Greint

Lead #?
Inv. Don Rogers, UPD, Davis Sean Humphreys

Lead #?
SA M. A. Cervellera, Ed Humphrey

Lead #003013
SA M. Cervellera, Southern Bell

Lead #3534
Sgt. Jim Eckert, James Doud

Lead #2988
Inv. Don Rogers, UPD, SA Don King, Raymond Sumpter, Steve Records

Lead #2351
SA Randall L. Barnes, SA Rick Singer, Jeanette Camacho

Lead #5927
SA Tom Yowell, Sgt. Robert L. Garrett, Columbus PD, D.A. Doug Pullen, James Harold Rolling

Lead #2478
SA John Burton, FDLE, Marion County Sheriff Lt. Larry Gerald, Judy Ditty

Lead #002431
SA Gary Nehrbass, Lisa Brockman, Jill Sipowski

Lead #2705
SA Edward Dix, Michael Dykslag, Dirk Smith, Emma Mayfield

Lead #003011
SA M. Cervellera, Southern Bell, Ed Humphrey

Lead #?
SA M. Cervellera, 1st Union Bank, Ed Humphrey bank records

Lead #841
Inv. Don Rogers, Dr. Lester Goldman

Lead #2836
SA Vinny Cassidy, Corrine Davis

Lead #3428
SA V. Cassidy, Ronnie R. Norris, Allan Robbins, Eric Jensen

Lead #?
CIA Janice Vores, SA A. L. Strope, Ed Humphrey

lead #?
Inv. Don Rogers, UPD, Bill Pinner

Lead #3004
SA John Halliday, Steve Davenport, Scott Sellers, Kimberly Krogwlski, Bruce Bergdoll, Mike Bramley, Ellen Vanwert, David Fulwood

Lead #003010
SA M. Cervellera, Southern Bell, Christina Powell, Ed Humphrey

Lead #3543
SA Wayne Porter, Jim Litchford, Analyst Elaine Clevenger

Lead #5874
SA V. Cassidy, Buford Turlington

Lead #5974
SA Patricia Rodgers, SA J. O. Jackson, J.M. Kelly, Regional Postal Inspector

Lead #3889
SA F. Troy, Roger G. Manning

Lead #5927
SA Tom Yowell, Sgt. Robert L. Garrett, Columbus PD, District Attorney Doug Pullen, Det. J. Ross, Columbus PD, Major Miles, Muscogee County SO, James Harold Rolling, Claudia H. Rolling, Kevin James Rolling, (following are inmates) Lester Adams, Wm. C. Anderson, Jeffery Emmons, Clyde Evans, Terry Flowers, Claude M. Hamilton, Robert Lamb, Bobby L. Morgan, Henry V. Morgan, Bryan Potter, Bryan Schmalbofer, Arthur Sears, Rof Uwe Vilicic, Stephen J. Vinson, Huey E. Weatherhead, Micky G. Woods, Charles L.

Lead #5927
SA Tom Yowell, Jeanette Caughey

Lead #4222
SA F. Troy, Mr. Pierre Jerome LaLonde, Paula Gransdeu, Ms. Joyce Vande Carr, Travis J. Marchand

Lead #5878
SA Cynthia J. Barnard, Det. B.D. Vickers, Det. Diamond of Tampa PD, Circuit Judge Behnke, SA Steve Davenport, William Tucker, Steven Stark, SA Thomas Turk, Terry Payne of Tampa PD, Reynaldo & Patricia Rio, Robert B. Teem

Lead #5879
SA Cynthia Barnard, Det. Ryan Garrett, Christopher Osborne, Joe Brennan

Lead #5927
SA Tom Yowell, Jeanette Caughey, Homer Rolling, Harold Rolling, Doris & James Griffin, Cavis Rolling

Lead #5714
SA Jeff Fortier, Gainesville Plasma Ctr.

Lead #5774
SA Cynthia J. Barnard, Det. D.M. Osada, Officer J.L. Power, Peter Scott Winters, Ronald Forstrom, Anil Arvindam, Nitin Nigam

Lead #5889
SA Cynthia Barnard, Sgt. Gerry Lacertosa of the Sarasota PD, Sgt. Bill Sullivan, Det. Russell Marquis and Cecil Elkins, Michael J. Kennedy

Lead #5922
SA Wayne Porter, Donald David Rolling, Mira (Donald's mother), (Mira Rolling), Joe Donald Rolling, Kevin Rolling, Det. Barnes, Ventura SO

Lead #5878
SA Cynthia J. Barnard, Lawrence Dale Lawrence and Holli Jo Paula, Officer Farnell, SA Steve Davenport, Crime lab analyst William Tucker, SA Thomas Turk, Herman Tim

Lead #5775
SA Cynthia Barnard, Det.

Ryan Garrett of Hillsborough County SO, Christopher Osborne

Lead #5886
SA Cynthia Barnard, SA Steve Davenport, Ida Rotunda, William L. Rotunda, Miriam Beasley, Robert Darfus, Linda Darfus, Gary Pearsell

Lead #5892
SA Cindy Barnard, SA Steve Davenport, James Robert Ford

Lead #5871
SA Rick Singer, SA Randy Barnes, Kimberly Ann Barnard, Juan Cordova, Stephanie Stevens

Lead #5941, 5923, p263
SA Patricia Rodgers, State Attorney Inv. Chris Johnson, Lillian Magdeline Mills, Mrs. R. Seelan

Lead #5939, 5923, p269
Patricia Rodgers, Chris Johnson, Lillian Magdeline Mills, Mrs. Ogden

Lead #?
Inv. William Halvosa, Randy Sermons

Lead #5892
SA Cynthia J. Barnard, SA Steve Davenport, SA James Hanley, FBI James Robert Ford, Derek Kabobel

Lead #5871
SA Rick Singer, SA Randy Barnes, Dan Fellows, Alice Stogner, Ruth Wilson, Donna

Martin, Donna Dow, Kim
Ottenschot, Stephanie
Lee, Courtney Meyer,
Steve Douglas

Lead #3187
Det. L. W. Hewitt, SA
Leslie Ave, SA John
Burton, Tony Danzy,
Mary Collier, Chris
Marmo, SA D. Maines,
Inv. M. Snook and Al
Weikel, FBI

Lead #5923, 5953 p265
SA Patricia Rodgers,
Chris Johnson, Lillian
Magdeline Mills, Debbie
Stipick

Lead # 5714
SA Patricia Rodgers,
Chad Ducharme

Lead #?
Inv. William T, Halvosa,
Dan Warnock, Matt
Kulmacz

Lead #5887
SA Cynthia Barnard, SA
Steve Davenport, Maryon
Decker

Lead #5837
SA Jeff Fortier, James
Chapman

Lead #135
SA Patricia Rodgers,
Lydia Huber

Lead #5714
SA Patricia Rodgers, Cpl.
Danny Fogger SPD,
Truman Cooley

Lead #5837
SA V. Cassidy, Det. Dan
Brinsko, Richard Munn,
Joe Thomas

Lead #1519
SA D. Maines, Sharon
Carroll, Kenneth L.
Rollins

Lead #5714
Danny Fogger SPD, Det.
Danny Foster SPD, SA
Patricia Rodgers,
O'Mather Halko

Lead #5141
SA Kenneth Williams, SA
James Lockley,
Christopher Joseph
Smith, Carol Hyde, Allen
Tripp, Anne Haisley, Erin
Strachan Watson, Jill
Slappery, Tommy Carroll

Lead #5990 p296
SA Cindy Barnard, Steve
Smith, Teresa Cousins,
Lola Seaman

Lead #6015
SA Jeff Fortier, FDLE,
Det. Frank Denning of
Johnson County, KS, SO,
Larry Pirner, Mr. Feliz
Brown, Eloise Madison,
Arthur Lee Morton, Lillie
Harris, Tamela Martinez,
Rosa Lee Thomas, Rose
Frank, John Tejada,
JoAnn Robinson

Lead #4222
SA F. Troy, Pierre
Jerome Lalonde, Joyce
Vande Carr, Paula
Gransdew

Lead #5922
SA Wayne Porter, Det.
Barnes, Ventura, SO,
Donald David Rolling,
Mira Rolling, Joe Donald,
Kevin Rolling

Lead #6009
Det. Steven Dean, Det.
Gary Dahmer, Johnson

County, KS, SO, Alan
Weist, Richard Conkling,
Desi Sanders, Geno
Green, Lavena Brown,
Kim Enyart, Gary
Johnson, Lillian Collier

Lead #5983
CIA Jack L. Dennard, SA
Jeff Fortier, Mr. Andrew
J. Casey, Mr. Alan B.
Tietsen

Lead #5837
SA Jeff Fortier, Rick
Brenner, Theresa Ann
Garren, Dorothy Downs,
Sam Cox

Lead #5417
SA Dennis L. Fischer,
Corrections officer
Sharon Roberts, Marion
County Jail, Danny
Rolling

Lead #5837
SA Leslie Ave, Joy
Willingham, Ann Garrin,
Jennifer (LNU), Edward
Phitzenmeir

Lead #5892 p293
SA Barnard, SA
Davenport, LolaLee
Seaman, Steve (LNU)

Lead #5990 p300
SA Cynthia J. Barnard,
SA Steve Davenport,
Theresa Lynn Cousins,
Steve (LNU), Donna
Robinett, Joann
Parkinson, Carlos Malave,
Sarah Jeane

Lead #5023
SA A. L. Strope, Bureau
Chief Robert Smith, Asst.
Bureau Chief Jack Wise,
SAS J. O. Jackson, SA
John Burton, Christina L.
Hoyt

Lead #?
Ron Ward, AP Writer,
Stephen J. Weinbaum,
Jacksonville defense
attorney, Marion County,
Sgt. Donna Borgioni,
Theresa Ann Garren,
Rick Brenner

Lead #?
Sarah Louise Clark

Lead #5926
Joe Donahey, Attorney at
Law, Janet Staschak

Lead #687
George Elliott Jamar

Lead #5837
Eddie Clark, Lindsey
Fritzel, Lanya Griggs, Tod
Malone, Pat Knowles,
Laura Griffen

Lead #2688
Dale Rey Watson

Lead # 5881
Cathleen Canty

Lead #0429 & 0274
David Howard Lamb,
Pam Rogers, Pat Wilson,
Martha Wilson, Helen
Wilson, Walt Lamb, Sally
Ann Martin

Lead #3149
Keith G. Smith

Lead #5486
Eric Lewis Ballon

Lead #5958
Linda Coban, Teresa
Welch, Trish Blanten,
Tommy Smith, Linda
Lillard

Lead #5928
Dina Faye Kichler

Lead #5924
Jessie David Baker

Lead #2792
Jacqueline Michelle
Transue, Mike Von
Konrad, Brent Baber,
Jackie Smith, Alachua
County SO Deputy, B. L.
Robinson, Alachua
County SO Deputy

Lead #5905
Donald Lloyd Spivey

Lead #111
Ronald Raymond

Lead #?
William Richard Clipson

Lead #5220
Mark Allen Unruh

Lead #3151
Gary Lynn Pickerell

Lead #5566
Eric Grig, Charles Fain
King

Lead #5426
Carey Seaton Nelms, Rob
Alerts, Ron Wheadon,
Chris Briary

Lead #5865
Sgt. James Mayo, Mobile
PD

Lead #3734
Teresa Harrell

Lead #5440
Jenny Lyhne-Nelson,
Jeffrey Eric Malinsky

Lead #5809
Peter Zeller, Medical
Examiner

Lead #5103
Sgt. Bruhn, Ft. Walton
PD

Lead #256
Christopher Hays

Lead #5570
David Anthony Klaes,
Linda Klaes

Lead #4796
Adam Zimmerman

Lead #679
Pam Duvall, George
(LNU)

Lead #5563
Joel Lance Tanner,
Joseph Dennis O'Nolan

Lead #1590
SA Cynthia J. Barnard,
Max Schachter, Diana
Londrie

Lead # 5648
Inv. Don Rogers, UPD,
Tom Innskeep, Robert
Ernest Peeples, Connie
Amidei

Lead 5982
CIA J. Dennard, SA Jeff
Fortier, Ann Garren

Lead #5894
SA Dennis L. Fischer,
Ronny S. Cooper,
Richard Taylor

Lead #202723
SA Randall L. Barnes, SA
Bruce Woerner of Ft.
Myers field office, Alycia
Jimison, Caroline Maher

Lead #4780
SA Cynthia J. Barnard,
Sgt. Johnson, Austin PD,
Nolan Ard Feintuch

Lead #?
SA Frank Troy, CIA
Martha Whitaker

Lead #4775
Det. L. W. Hewitt, Mr.
Patel

Lead #4562
SA Randall Barnes, Det.
Matt Barr, Alachua
County SO, Mr. William
L. Forrest

Lead #5894
SA Dennis Fischer,
Herbert Ellis, Asst. Public
Defender, Columbia
County, Ronny Scott
Cooper, SA J. O.
Jackson, Chris Johnson

Lead #6038
SA Cynthia Barnard, Det.
Diane Creston of Palm
Beach SO. Carl Danison,
Peter Rangel, Laura
Danison Rangel, Cindy
Arnold, Kathleen Rangel,
PBSO Analyst Tammy
Gempel, Linda S. Guardo

Lead #5250
SA Chuck Riley, SAS
Bruce McMann, Brevard
County Attorney Joel
Dick, Asst. State Attny.
Ben Garagozlo, Willie
Wright, Justin, Joel, Jason
Dietrale, Aaron Summers

Lead #5837
Jimmy Andrews, Damig
Jiang, Nguu Ha, Tran Ly

Lead #5837
Larry Aikens, Tabatha
Lott, John Carmichael,
Joseph Lynch, Antonia
Tartaglione, Sherri Prince,
Timothy Harris, Marlene
Skandera, Phillipe
Broccard, Vicki Weaver,

James Carmichael,
Dorian Buren, Denise
Healey, Adam Myers,
Keirney Longyear,
Jennifer Springer, Gerri
Loog, Paul Saladin,
Robbie Hemmes, Jennifer
Cosma, Ernest Carasco,
Amanda Escobia, Stephen
Seel, Kevin Greene,
Timothy Ciotti, Rebecca
Conrad, Sharon Atalig,
Wendy Rosche, Kim
Kasper, Sandra Duyck,
Tina Kurdupski, Chris
Graham, Amy Talkington,
Deborah Hughes, Susan
Leroux, Marc Mondell,
Laura Newvine, James
Colella, John Deal,
Serena Perryman, Steve
Song, Stacey Ruben,
Travis Knight, Harold
Augenstein, Keith
Chastain, Jamie Robert,
Charles Weeks, Patricia
O'Gorman, Lisa Vigurs,
Edward Heidtman, Patty
Cowing, Craig Kobrin,
Theodore Heinemann,
Vargas Marco, Richard
Lennon, Chip Orr,
Forrest Dodd, Andrew
Stone, Colin Johnson,
Scott Harkneff, Cedric
Wynn, Tom Trowbridge,
Jill Blystone, Karsten
Johnson, Kathylene Bisela

Lead #5925
Julie Kay Branch

Lead #5837
Nial McLoughlin, Joyce
Mazourek, Matt Watford,
Lorane Hoover, Marnie
Benson, Randi Stockdill,
Michelle Neuman, Amy
Rott, Carolyn Pugh,
Michelle Dunn, Jody
Pampel, Julie Barnhardt,
Judy Clark, Allison
Gardner, Kim Lyons,

Alexandra Mejia, Rene
Otto, Linda Markley,
Trina Fosness, Catherine
Hughes, Greg Schultz,
Robert Snyder, Jeff
Spires, Phillip Roth,
Leigh Phi, Candice
Krepp, Karen Allen,
Kimberly Krepp, Tina
Torning, Candace
Vassillion, Kathryn Bibb,
Cheryl Halpern, Tammy
Goodwin, Erin Malloy,
Larry Caruso, Scott
Quisling, Paublo Elizalde,
Shera Oppenheimer, Tera
Goldstein, Wendy
Coufino, Desiree
Gabrera, Amy Gergick,
Renee Treanor

Lead #2418
Sidney McGrath, Mary
Goddard

Lead #5871
Bai Chen, Joseph
Guenther, Duc Diep,
Brandon Selle, Li Shiang
Chen, Yu Kong Ting,
Haz-Chywon, Steve Tung,
Yu-Koung Ting, Chin-
Jung Kao, Ae Martin
Soon, Sue Brown, Chung-
Fu Tsai, Wilma Clibrey,
Jana Alsip, Leo Davis,
Ollie Gregory, Kirsten
Lambert, Bill Johns, Patty
Herndon, Melanie
Joseph, Jean Paradise,
Toni Sweet, Andre Neira,
Elizabeth Ryan, Guido
Bonelli, Rolando Molina,
Chrissy Henn, Ronald
Riggins, Douglas Jordan,
Lori Stoner, Adrienne
Burgess, Carey Lyse,
Kelly Franco, Steve
Lamerson, Sean Franco,
Chris Neely

Lead #0115
Mary Ann Holzschuhern

Lead #4055
Buster Lipham, Bill Pinner

Lead # 3962
Wayne Larson

Lead #?
Bryan Oulton, Terry Otto, Miguel Ocasio, Scott Henratty, Dawn Otto

Lead #3338
Lynda Agnew

Lead #4397
Keith O'Hara, Alachua Co. SO, Alan Baxter, Alachua Co. SO

Lead #?
Harvey Pleimar

Lead #2478
Judy Ditty

Lead #?
David Sean Humphreys

Lead #841
Dr. Lester Goldman

Lead #2836
Corrine Davis

Lead #3889
Roger Manning

Lead #4222
Pierre Jerome Lalonde, Joyce Vande Carr, Paula Gransdew

Lead #5878
Larry Mawrence, Holli Jo Paula

Lead #3814
Toni Stevens

Lead #4424
Kip Stephen Malcolm, Ada Helen Malcolm

Lead #4461
Pat Sherfield, Marjorie Weiner

Lead #?
Pat Siracusa, Ilene Sharp, Scott Greint

Lead #?
Michael Dykslag, Emma Mayfield, Dirk Smith

Lead #5874
Buford Turlington

Lead #2351
Jeanette M. Camacho

Lead #5927
Lester Adams, Wm. C. Anderson, Jeffrey Emmons, Clyde Evans, Terry Flowers, Claude M. Hamilton, Robert Lamb, Bobby L. Morgan, Henry V. Morgan, Bryan Potter, Arthur Schmalbofer, Rof Uwe Sears, Stephen J. Vilicic, Huey E. Vinson, Micky G. Weatherhead, Charles L. Woods, Danny Rolling, James Harold Rolling, Claudia H. Rolling, Kevin James Rolling

Lead #5878
Reynaldo Rio, Patricia Rio, Anthony Rio, Robert Benjamin Teem

Lead #0708
Paul Daniel Schwartz, Richard Schwartz, Alice Schwartz, Russell Schwartz, Michelle Pothier, Richard Pollard, Mark Pothier

Lead #4727
Theresa Ann Garren

Lead #?
Lisa Brockman, Jill Sipowski

Lead #3534
James Doud

Lead #2988
William S. Records

Lead #3428
Ronnie R. Norris, Allan Robbins, Eric Jensen

Lead #5774
Officer M. D. Mazza, Officer L. Johnson, Officer R. P. Medkiff, Tampa PD, Tiffany Salagaras, Lori Cayasso, Donald Jenkins

Lead #5774
Peter Scott Winters, Ronald Forstrom, Anil Arvindam, Nitin Nigam, Tiffany Salagaras, Lori Cayasso, Donald Jenkins, Christopher Osborne

Lead #5879
Rodney R. Burgamy

Lead #5887
Maryon Decker

Lead #5871
Courtney Meyer, Dan Fellows, Alice M. Stogner, Ruth Wilson, Donna L. Martin, Donna L. Dow, Kim L. Ottenschot, Stephanie E. Lee

Lead #5941, 5923
Lillian M. Mills, Mrs. R. Seelan

Lead #5714
Chad Ducharme, Rhonda Terrell

Lead #?
Dan Warnock, Matt Kulmacz, Ben Boukani, Norma Boulain

Lead #5837
Joy Willingham, Edward Phitzenmier, Jennifer (LNU), Ann Hoyt Garren

Lead #3847
Deborah Anne Carroll

Lead #5889
Michael J. Kennedy, Michael Joseph Kennedy

Lead #5892
James Robert Ford

Lead #5837
James Chapman

Lead #3187
Tony Danzy, Chris Marmo, Mary Collier, Joanna Senft

Lead #5923, 5953
Lillian M. Mills, Debbie Stipick

Lead #5837
Richard Munn

Lead #?
SA Patricia Rodgers, O'Mather Lymas

Lead #6015
Patricia Farnan, Rita Cane, Donald Johnson

Lead #62
Lane Thomas Kelley

Lead #5886
Mike Kennedy, Ida Rotunda, William L. Rotunda, Miriam Beasley, Robert Darfus, Linda Darfus, Gary Pearsell

Lead #5871
Kimberly Ann Barnard, Juan Cordova, Stephanie Stevens

Lead #5939, 5923
Lillian M. Mills, Mrs. Odgen

Lead #?
Randy Sermons, Tampa Tribune

Lead #?
Kevin Rolling, Mira Rolling

Lead #?
Rick Brenner, Theresa Ann Garren

Lead #5837
Michelle Reducha

Lead #6076
Analyst Elaine Clevenger, Christa Hoyt notebook, Elizabeth Spongler, Tommy Samples, Suzi Schwartz, Kim Sumner, Tammy Underwood, Jennifer Worley, James G. Willingham (papa), Cathy Warren, Willingham, Randy Wynne, James Wurston, Kristina Arendall & Brad Glass, Marja Dela Rosa, Julie Culissa, Manny, B. K., Kristy Breezina, Matt Bomberger, T. J. Bolton, Shane Barger, Laura Brown, Jeff Banish, Ronny Brame, John Day, Susan Cunningham, Sherri Drain, Teri Choate, Jason Davis, Hilany Croly, Ricky Cox, Jennifer Dawson, Mark Duncan, Margie Eno, Erin Hebert, Susan Gascon, Jewell Hoyt, Kevin Hegwood, Karen

Harris, Sarah Hole, R. G. Hoyt, Issac Green, Erin Gallaway, Rachel Garze, Amy Hanley, Chris Huber, Sarah Hoyt, Katie Humphrey, Nina Giesing, Alan Harris, Sarah Hole, Joyce Hesters, Zan Hutson, Nelly Grandez, Kat Jensen, Joan Livingston, Marta Konik, Andy Levy, Jennifer Lucas, Terry Lee, Robert Lyden, Michelle Novack, Sandy Montoto, David McDowell, Tim Miller, Lodn NGuyen, Mylinh NGuyen, Jon T. Martin, Michele Pothier, Heather Pinner, David Pactor, Rebecca Orf, Shellie Parker, Jorge Palaw, Whyne Punnels, Jenny Russin, Stephen Ryder, Avivit Shek, Cheri Schimel, Elizabeth Spongler, Tommy Samples, Suzi Schwartz, Kim Sumner, Tammy Underwood, Jennifer Worley, Randy Wynne, Jason Wurston

Lead #137
SA Gary Akins, ASAS Dennis Norred, Inv. Don Rogers, UPD, Alanna Cohen

Lead #5768
SA Jeff Fortier, Lt. Lewis Fannin of Troy AL PD, Tommy Wayne Plunkett, Kevin Sam Cox

Lead #6020
Inv. Don Rogers, UPD, Shand's Hospital

Lead #6021
Inv. Don Rogers, UPD VA Hospital police

Lead #303994
Inv. Don Rogers, Susan
White, Fouad Cobty

Lead #3055
Caroline Taylor, Christine
Zoellner

Lead #4008
SA Don H. Maines, Det.
Leunenberger of the
Edgewater PD, James R.
Mitchell

Lead #6022
Inv. Don Rogers, UPD,
Univ. Police Dept.
officers

Lead #202988
Inv. Don Rogers,
Raymond Sumpter

Lead #2344
Mancel E. Jacobs, Lecy
Blaisdell

Lead #4236
SA Don H. Maines, Sgt.
Russell of Peabody, Mass.
PD, Eugene Raasch

Lead #6035
David Herring, Joan
Forster, Mauricio
Malagon, Renee Judge,
Stein Berger, Terri Dunn,
Chris Cairns, Hank Jacob,
Terry Polk, Greg Figler,
Thomas Hubbard, Jason
Kodish, Dan Bigalow,
Christian Eiler,
Forouzandeh Forghani,
Pamela Ventimiglia

Lead #6073
Kenneth W. Overstreet

Lead #103365
Inv. Don Rogers, Mrs.
Vaugh Hinkel, George C.
Panagos

Lead #3004
SA W. Porter, SA
Fischer, Ron Adams,
Roger Fedora, Ray
Gormally, Jr.

Lead #5912
SA F. Troy, Mr. James
Ebeling, Robert Jeffery
Barrus

Lead #5636
SA Jeff Fortier, Deputy
Sheriff Rodney Benthall,
ACSO Frank Joseph
Lukoski

Lead #3859
SA Wayne Porter, James
Waugh, Randy Hamilton

Lead #6012
Kenneth Biros

Lead #754
Det. Steven Dean, James
Ruane

Lead #4320
LuAnn Martin

Lead #6025
SA Tom Yowell, Michael
Dockray, Jerry Mauldin

Lead #2427
SA Randall L. Barnes, SA
Rick Singer, Rachel
Olivier, Pliny Joseph
Olivier, James David
Philips, Kenneth George
Holder, Brent Greer

INDEX